Venture Capital
Volume I

Wherever possible, the articles in these volumes have been reproduced as originally published using facsimile reproduction, inclusive of footnotes and pagination to facilitate ease of reference.

For a list of all Edward Elgar published titles visit our site on the World Wide Web at
www.e-elgar.com

Venture Capital
Volume I

Edited by

Mike Wright

*Professor of Financial Studies and Director of the Centre for Management
Buy-out Research
Nottingham University Business School, UK*

Harry J. Sapienza

*Carlson Chair in Entrepreneurship
University of Minnesota, USA*

and

Lowell W. Busenitz

*Associate Professor of Management and John and Mary Nichols Faculty Fellow
University of Oklahoma, USA*

An Elgar Reference Collection
Cheltenham, UK • Northampton, MA, USA

Published by
Edward Elgar Publishing Limited
Glensanda House
Montpellier Parade
Cheltenham
Glos GL50 1UA
UK

Edward Elgar Publishing, Inc.
136 West Street
Suite 202
Northampton
Massachusetts 01060
USA

A catalogue record for this book is available from the British Library.

Library of Congress Cataloguing in Publication Data

Venture capital / edited by Mike Wright, Harry J. Sapienza, and Lowell W. Busenitz.
     p. cm. — (Elgar mini series) (Elgar reference collection)
  Includes bibliographical references and indexes.
  1. Venture capital. I. Wright, Mike, 1952– II. Sapienza, Harry J., 1949– III. Busenitz, Lowell W., 1952– IV. Series. V. Series: Elgar reference collection

  HG4751.V458 2003
  332'.0415—dc22

2003047250

ISBN   1 84376 247 1 (3 volume set)

Printed and bound in Great Britain by MPG Books Ltd, Bodmin, Cornwall

Contents

Acknowledgements

The editors and publishers wish to thank the authors and the following publishers who have kindly given permission for the use of copyright material.

Baylor University for article: Ken Robbie, Mike Wright and Brian Chiplin (1997), 'The Monitoring of Venture Capital Firms', *Entrepreneurship Theory and Practice*, **21** (4), Summer, 9–28.

Blackwell Publishing for article: Gordon C. Murray (1995), 'Evolution and Change: An Analysis of the First Decade of the UK Venture Capital Industry', *Journal of Business Finance and Accounting*, **22** (8), December, 1077–106.

Elsevier Science for articles: Jeffry A. Timmons and William D. Bygrave (1986), 'Venture Capital's Role in Financing Innovation for Economic Growth', *Journal of Business Venturing*, **1**, 161–76; Michael Gorman and William A. Sahlman (1989), 'What Do Venture Capitalists Do?', *Journal of Business Venturing*, **4**, 231–48; Juan B. Roure and Robert H. Keeley (1990), 'Predictors of Success in New Technology Based Ventures', *Journal of Business Venturing*, **5** (4), 201–20; William A. Sahlman (1990), 'The Structure and Governance of Venture-Capital Organizations', *Journal of Financial Economics*, **27**, 473–521; Edgar Norton and Bernard H. Tenenbaum (1993), 'Specialization versus Diversification as a Venture Capital Investment Strategy', *Journal of Business Venturing*, **8**, 431–42; Sophie Manigart (1994), 'The Founding Rate of Venture Capital Firms in Three European Countries (1970–1990)', *Journal of Business Venturing*, **9**, 525–41; Bernard S. Black and Ronald J. Gilson (1998), 'Venture Capital and the Structure of Capital Markets: Banks Versus Stock Markets', *Journal of Financial Economics*, **47** (3), March, 243–77; Raphael Amit, James Brander and Christoph Zott (1998), 'Why Do Venture Capital Firms Exist? Theory and Canadian Evidence', *Journal of Business Venturing*, **13**, 441–66; Leslie A. Jeng and Philippe C. Wells (2000), 'The Determinants of Venture Capital Funding: Evidence Across Countries', *Journal of Corporate Finance*, **6** (3), September, 241–89; Urs von Burg and Martin Kenney (2000), 'Venture Capital and the Birth of the Local Area Networking Industry', *Research Policy*, **29** (9), 1135–55.

Institute for Operations Research and the Management Sciences (INFORMS) for article: Tyzoon T. Tyebjee and Albert V. Bruno (1984), 'A Model of Venture Capitalist Investment Activity', *Management Science*, **30** (9), September, 1051–66.

Journal of Law and Economics and University of Chicago for article: Paul Gompers and Josh Lerner (1996), 'The Use of Covenants: An Empirical Analysis of Venture Partnership Agreements', *Journal of Law and Economics*, **XXXIX** (2), October, 463–98.

RAND Journal of Economics for article: Samuel Kortum and Josh Lerner (2000), 'Assessing the Contribution of Venture Capital to Innovation', *RAND Journal of Economics*, **31** (4), Winter, 674–92.

Taylor and Francis Ltd (http://www.tandf.co.uk/journals) for articles: Kevin N. McNally (1994), 'Sources of Finance for UK Venture Capital Funds: The Role of Corporate Investors', *Entrepreneurship and Regional Development*, **6** (3), July–September, 275–97; Gordon C. Murray (1998), 'A Policy Response to Regional Disparities in the Supply of Risk Capital to New Technology-based Firms in the European Union: The European Seed Capital Fund Scheme', *Regional Studies*, **32** (5), 405–19.

Every effort has been made to trace all the copyright holders but if any have been inadvertently overlooked the publishers will be pleased to make the necessary arrangement at the first opportunity.

In addition the publishers wish to thank the Library of the University of Warwick and the Library of Indiana University at Bloomington, USA for their assistance in obtaining these articles.

Introduction

Mike Wright, Harry Sapienza and Lowell W. Busenitz[1]

Recent years have witnessed massive development in both the venture capital market and in academic research relating to this market. The size of funds committed to venture capital investments has increased substantially in existing developed markets such as the US and UK, while the phenomenon has taken hold in countries in Europe and Asia in particular where until recently activity has been extremely limited.

Commensurate with these market developments, academic research on venture capital, which emerged in the early 1980s principally in entrepreneurship journals, has become recognized in mainstream finance, economics and management journals.

In the light of these developments it seemed to us timely to draw together the diverse range of contributions to the venture capital literature. Our aims in putting together this collection are threefold. First, we sought to identify leading contributions to this developing area from the past two decades. Second, we wanted to reflect the growing multidisciplinarity of research on venture capital. Third, we attempted to highlight the need to recognize international differences in venture capital markets.

In structuring the presentation of articles we reflect both the environment in which venture capital markets operate and the behavior of venture capital firms. The first volume comprises articles that deal with the role of venture capital and the operation of venture capital markets, including policy issues and sources of funds for venture capital investment. In addressing the behavior of venture capital firms, Volumes II and III essentially adopt a venture capital life-cycle approach. The articles in Volume II cover the earlier stages in the process, notably deal generation and screening, valuation and structuring, financial contracting, the strategies adopted by venture capitalists (VCs) and the factors that contribute to achieving investment success. In Volume III we bring together articles that examine issues concerned with monitoring and protecting value in venture capital investments, the mechanisms by which venture capitalists add value to their investees, how VCs deal with problem investments, the nature of inter-relationships between VCs, and the harvesting of gains from investments.

This Introduction summarizes the main contribution of each of the articles in the collection, situates them in the context of the development of the field and suggests areas for further research. Each chapter is summarized in Table 1 in terms of the conceptual framework adopted, the data used and the key findings. It is not our intention in this Introduction to provide a comprehensive review of the venture capital literature. Interested readers are referred to Wright and Robbie (1998) and Gompers and Lerner (1999) for overviews.

Table 1. Summary of Articles

Chapter/article	Issues/research questions	Theoretical perspective	Data	Key conclusions and contribution
Volume I				
1 Tyebjee & Bruno (1984)	1. Phases of the venture capital process 2. Criteria for evaluating expected returns and risks of investment opportunities	Primarily descriptive, with financial theory notion of risk-return trade-off	1. Primary survey data (both telephone and mailed questionnaires) from 41 venture capitalists about 90 deals 2. Structured interviews with venture capitalists to help interpret data	1. Identify five phases as deal origination, screening, evaluation, deal structuring and post-investment involvement 2. Criteria for assessing expected returns cluster into market attractiveness, product differentiation, managerial capability, environmental threat resistance, and cash-out potential 3. Expected returns appear to be a function of market attractiveness and product differentiation; risk appears a function of managerial capability and environmental threat; cash-out potential is not related to either risk or return expectations 4. Interviews lead them to conclude that the model under-represents the importance of quality of management
2 Timmons & Bygrave (1986)	1. The role venture capital plays in financing technological innovation 2. The differences between investors in the most innovative technology-based ventures and the least innovative ones 3. Trends in venture capital, 1967–1982	Primarily descriptive with some references to resource dependence	1. Venture Economics secondary database 2. Field interviews	1. Investment in highly innovative technology ventures (HITVs) was steadily increasing over the observation period 2. 1st round investing in HITVs is a highly specialized management, not capital-intensive activity 3. Convertible preferred shares are increasingly used to allow venture capitalists replacement of management and control without majority ownership
3 Gorman & Sahlman (1989)	1. How much time do VCs spend with their portfolio companies? 2. What roles do VCs play in their portfolio companies?	Descriptive	Survey data based on 49 responses from VCs	1. That VCs spend approximately half of their time monitoring their investments 2. VCs spend about 80 hours a year if they serve on the board and they usually make relatively brief visits 3. When firms fail, they attribute the problem to managerial causes
4 Manigart (1994)	1. Why are new organizations created? 2. It is hypothesized that the population density has an inverted U-shaped effect on the founding rate of venture capital organizations	Population ecology	Secondary data sources such as *European Guide to Venture Capital*, UK, French and European trade directories, membership list of the European Venture Capital Association	1. Consistent with population ecology theory, the density of the industry influences the overall founding rate. When density is low, adding a new organization to the industry raises the probability of a subsequent founding. The opposite is true when the density is high 2. Cross-border populations also have an impact. When populations in border countries emerge before the local population, legitimation for the emergence of the local population is increased

x

	Purpose/Objectives	Theory/Framework	Data/Method	Findings
5 Murray (1995)	1. Environmental factors driving growth of UK venture capital 2. Influence of above factors on future performance of VC industry	Porter Competitive Forces Model	1. Secondary VC industry association data 2. Semi-structured interviews with 22 leading CEOs of VC firms and intermediaries in 1990	1. Industry reached maturity in terms of Porter's five forces 2. Future likely to involve increased rivalry and concentration, need to demonstrate enhanced performance or exit, more specialist VCs and entry to overseas markets
6 Amit, Brander & Zott (1998)	Explaining why VC firms exist. Their central hypothesis is that VCs emerge because they develop specialized abilities in selecting and monitoring entrepreneurial projects	Agency theory	1. Survey data of over 100 Canadian VCs 2. Survey of the economic impact of 387 firms receiving VC funding	1. VCs exist because they are better at identifying moral hazard and adverse selection in entrepreneurial ventures 2. VCs prefer investment in firms with a track record over pure start-ups to minimize information asymmetries and moral hazard 3. A negative relationship is found between the extent of VC ownership and firm performance
7 Black & Gilson (1998)	Develop theory: 1. Analysing link between bank and stock market-based systems and the venture capital market 2. Explaining importance of exit and form of exit in US venture capital market	Capital market theory; contracting theory; comparative corporate governance	Secondary industry data and data on exits	1. Potential for exit through initial public offering (IPO) in stock market-centered capital markets allows VC and entrepreneur to contract implicitly over control; this is not duplicable in bank-centered systems 2. Economies of scope among contributions by VC providers and VC investors' need for quantitative measure of VC funds' skills explain importance of exit strategy 3. Best strategy for bank-centered systems to overcome path-dependent barriers to VC market development is to piggyback on institutional infrastructure of stock market-centered systems
8 Jeng & Wells (2000)	Determinants of size of venture capital markets in 21 countries	Various	Secondary data from IMF, VC industry associations, Venture Economics, international stock exchanges, existing literature, etc.	1. For 1986–1995, IPOs strongest driver of venture capital investing together with government policies and, over time, private pension fund levels. GDP and market capitalization growth not significant 2. Early stage financing affected by labor market rigidities; later stage affected by IPOs
9 Roure & Keeley (1990)	1. Effects of management, venture strategy, and environment on success of technology-based new ventures 2. Responses to time pressure and uncertainty	Organization behavior, industrial organization, and strategic management frameworks	Data on 36 portfolio companies of one venture capital firm. Ratings made by the researchers from original business plans. Rates of return calculated as amount of funds invested in venture over IPO price or price per share paid at last investment round	Independent variables at original business plan, subsequent financial returns as dependent variable. (1) Completeness of the founding team and technical product superiority are positively related to success; (2) expected time for product development and buyer concentration are related to success in inverted U

Table 1 continued

Chapter/article	Issues/research questions	Theoretical perspective	Data	Key conclusions and contribution
10 Murray (1998)	Analysis of the progress and effectiveness of a policy response to regional disparities in the supply of risk capital to new technology	Primarily descriptive but implicit market failure theory	Personal interviews with senior investment managers from 21 out of 22 funds in ten countries	1. Scheme achieved goals of encouraging private investment into innovative technology-based young firms 2. Scale-related problems question the economic viability of the scheme in terms of meeting long-term commercial and regional development objectives
11 Von Burg & Kenney (2000)	An analysis of the role of VCs in creating local area network (LAN) industry	Synthesis of dominant design and social construction theories of technological development	Reviews of industry journals, consultants' reports and other materials, 46 telephone interviews with VCs, entrepreneurs and senior corporate officials 1995–1999	1. Construction of LAN firms was emergent rather than orderly 2. Absence of a dominant design created problems for VCs has made it difficult to envisage firms dedicated to producing LANs 3. The VC investment decision is better understood as an attempt to construct an entity and space
12 Kortum & Lerner (2000)	Influence of venture capital on patented inventions in the US	Production function theory	Annual data for 20 manufacturing industries for 1965–1992. Industry R&D expenditures from US National Science Foundation. Venture Funding data from Venture Economics	1. Increases in venture capital activity in an industry associated significantly higher patenting rates 2. Ratio of VC to R&D averaged less than 3 per cent during 1983–1992 yet VC accounted for 8 per cent of industry innovations in this period
13 Sahlman (1990)	1. Description and analysis of structure of VC organizations 2. Analysis of relationships between funds providers, VC firms and investees	Agency theory	1. Secondary data provided by Venture Economics 2. Informal interview and archival survey of 25 VC firm management teams, 150 venture capitalists and 50 VC-backed entrepreneurial management teams over 8-year period to 1990	1. Industry developed standard operating procedures and contracts to deal with information asymmetries between principals and agents 2. Important insight that VC organizational form may have wider implications for role of active investors in corporate governance in general
14 McNally (1994)	Analyses significance of corporate sources of finance for VCs, their characteristics and their advantages and disadvantages	Corporate venturing; portfolio diversification?	1. Secondary industry data 2. Primary face-to-face and telephone survey data	1. Corporate VC remains undeveloped in the UK because of unwillingness of corporations to invest and reluctance of VCs to seek these funds because of adverse prior experience 2. A large majority of VCs support its encouragement
15 Gompers & Lerner (1996)	Explore the use of covenants and restrictions in long-term contracts governing investments in VC-backed ventures	Agency theory and long-term contracts	1. 140 US-based independent private partnerships primarily engaged in VC investments 2. Examined the contracts in the files of two gatekeepers and one limited partner	1. Factors examined: (1) proxies for supply and demand conditions for VC services and (2) probability of opportunistic behavior both have a significant effect on the number of covenants that are used. 2. These results probability of supply and demand and the probability of opportunistic behavior covary and should be examined simultaneously

Author	Focus	Theory	Method	Findings
16 Robbie, Wright & Chiplin (1997)	Nature of monitoring of venture capital firms by their funds providers	Agency theory	1. Secondary industry data 2. Primary face-to-face interviews and survey data	1. Statistically significant differences between monitoring requirements for independent and captive VCs 2. Most VCs reported that funds providers had a passive approach to monitoring, but this was expected to become more active 3. Some expectation of a shift toward return targets set on basis of Internal Rate of Return (IRR) in relation to asset classes and combination of IRR and cash generated
17 Norton & Tenenbaum (1993)	How do VCs control risk? The portfolio diversification versus the investment in specialization and specific information are pitted against one another	Managing risk through portfolio theory or through information and specialization	Survey responses from 98 members (32.7 per cent response rate) of the National Venture Capital Association	1. One way to diversify risk is to use the portfolio method. Unsystematic risk can be reduced by investing in a diversified set of firms for industries. However little support was found for this approach 2. VCs can control their risk by specializing in technical and product expertise as well as through gaining specialized information. The evidence in this study consistently supported this view by suggesting that VCs tend to specialize rather than diversify across industries and various stages of funding
Volume II				
1 MacMillan, Siegel & Subba Narasimha (1985)	1. Most important criteria used to make new venture funding decisions 2. Weighting of criteria or their relative importance 3. Criteria related to proposal rejection	Replication and extension of Tyebjee & Bruno (1984); largely descriptive	1. Interview of 14 VCs to identify key criteria 2. Questionnaire received from 102 venture capitalists on the criteria	1. Quality of the entrepreneur ultimately determines decision: five of top ten criteria involve entrepreneur experience (track record industry experience, leadership experience) or personality (capable of sustained effort, able to evaluate and react well to risk). Other key criteria are required rate of return and market growth rate 2. 'Critically flawed' ventures are those that have a significant flaw in entrepreneur 3. Six types of risks are assessed by VCs: risk of total loss, exit risk, implementation risk, competitive risk, risk of management failure, risk of leadership failure 4. Investors seem to be one of three types: those who carefully assess risks; those who seek to exit quickly; those who like to keep options open
2 Amit, Glosten & Muller (1990)	This study focuses on the decision entrepreneurs make whether to develop their ventures independently or with the assistance of VCs	Agency theory	Theoretical model	1. If the skill level of entrepreneurs is common knowledge, all will choose to involve VCs 2. The less able entrepreneurs will choose to involve VCs 3. Given that information asymmetries often exist, entrepreneurs can invest in information that will reveal their skill level
3 Harvey & Lusch (1995)	Traditional approaches to the due-diligence process are reviewed and then expanded to include intangible assets, auditing procedures, and the composition of the due-diligence team	Due diligence review and extension	Non-empirical	1. The due-diligence process should move beyond just the verification of the legal, accounting and tax matters 2. The expanded function of due diligence should include the macro environment, production, management, marketing and information system audits 3. The due-diligence team should be multidisciplinary in nature and be led by a 'champion'

Table 1 continued

Chapter/article	Issues/research questions	Theoretical perspective	Data	Key conclusions and contribution
4 Fiet (1995)	How do VCs use informants to help manage market risk and agency risk in their investments. Trust of informants is also considered	Transaction cost economics and social embeddedness	Survey data involving 141 responses from venture capital investors and 81 business angels	1. The more either type of investor is concerned with market or agency risk, the less likely they are to use informal network informants 2. VC investors consult their formal network sources more frequently than do business angels 3. Business angels seem to distinguish between informants who are close associates and those who are mere acquaintances. The close associates were consistently used as informants
5 Muzyka, Birley & Leleux (1996)	1. How do European VCs make trade-offs among investment selection criteria? 2. Are there any effects of stage, industry preference, required returns that cause these to vary?	Industrial organization and strategy roots, but largely embedded in existing descriptive work	1. Conducted seven in-depth interviews and scanned existing literature to construct criteria 2. Questionnaires from 73 VCs scattered across ten European countries; evaluated 53 pairs of trade-offs on 36 criteria using conjoint analysis	1. Confirmed that European selection is much like that found in US: management team leadership and capabilities dominate over market and deal characteristics 2. Little or no variation is found by stage, industry, geographic preference or by country 3. Product-market criteria appear only moderately important
6 Smart (1999)	The methods used by venture capitalists to assess: 1. the human capital of prospective management teams 2. the accuracy of various measures 3. the assumptions VCs appear to make about the accuracy of these methods	Psychological assessment theory	1. Questionnaires from 51 venture capitalists on 86 deals 2. Validating interviews by a second source to assess the reliability and validity of the the primary questionnaire	1. Work sample is most used technique 2. Past-oriented interview is accurate for both early and late stage ventures; work samples is a good predictor in early stage ventures but negatively related in late stage ventures 3. Styles of assessment and assumptions of accuracy vary widely
7 Shepherd (1999)	1. Extent of match between VCs' assessment of new venture potential for survival and strategy theory 2. Relative importance of market, competition, and management factors in assessment of survival probability	Industrial organization and population ecology views	Mailed and interview-collected surveys of 66 Australian VCs	1. VCs use market, competition and management attributes in manner consistent with theory 2. Consistent with past studies on venture success criteria, managerial factors play a larger role in the assessment than market or competition factors

	Research questions	Theory/background	Data/Methodology	Findings
8 Zacharakis & Shepherd (2001)	1. Are VCs overconfident? 2. Does overconfidence influence decision accuracy? 3. Under what conditions are VCs likely to exhibit higher levels of overconfidence?	Behavioral decision theory	Primary – policy capturing experiment involving 51 VCs making 50 investment decisions	1. Results indicate that VCs are indeed overconfident and that overconfidence negatively affects VC decision accuracy 2. The level of overconfidence depends on the amount of information, the type of information, and whether the VC strongly believes the venture will succeed or fail
9 Bygrave (1988)	1. Differences in investment networks of low innovative venture capital firms (LIVCs) and high innovative venture capital firms (HIVCs) 2. The structure and frequency of networking in LIVCs and HIVCs	Resource exchange theory	Venture Economics database; randomly drawing 1/3 of 464 VCFs; investigated in more depth were the 61 'top' VCFs who had invested in the most portfolio companies; from this set of 61 the top 21 who invested mainly in high innovative technology were compared with the top 21 who invested mainly in low innovative technology	1. The most important resources flow through the networks are access to deal flow, the spreading of financial risk and knowledge 2. The sharing of resources cannot be explained solely by the need to spread financial risk 3. Consistent with resource exchange theory, the amount of co-investing depends upon the uncertainty faced by VCFs; specifically, HIVCs were involved in significantly more co-investing than LIVCs
10 Steier & Greenwood (1995)	1. Role of business plans and existing relationships in penetrating venture capital networks 2. Effects of staged financing and multiple-partner arrangements on the progress of VC-backed ventures	Grounded theory approach	Interviews, site visits, and archival data (including due-diligence reports, investment proposals, planning and legal documents, press clippings, etc.) used in a case-study approach. Collected 1990–1993 about one venture	1. Attracting the first investor is a major hurdle; the presence of one led to the interest of many. Investors who had previously rejected the business plan joined once other investors known to them were present. This occurred even if the rejected business plan remained unchanged 2. After initial investment, the subsequent financing process itself was frustrating and problematic for management because of the time needed to collect information, to have investors assess it, and to negotiate new agreements 3. Investor-generated delays occur between reaching agreed milestones and the provision of money needed to move forward; no mechanisms appeared to exist to coordinate investor decision 4. Decisions on venture funding were affected by the timing of other projects of the investors, regardless of the merits of the funding request 5. Investors devote more attention to establishing collaborative activity than to managing collaborative relationships 6. Business plans themselves are less central than previously thought, though still of importance
11 Manigart, DeWaele, Wright, Robbie, Desbrières, Sapienza & Beekman (2000)	1. Differences in valuation methods used by VCs in the US, the UK, Belgium, the Netherlands and France 2. Differences in importance of VCs accord to different sources of information in these same five countries	Finance and institutional theory as background to largely descriptive study	Mailed questionnaires – 72 in US, 66 in UK, 14 in Belgium, 32 in France, 24 in the Netherlands	1. The four highest rated valuation methods were EBIT multiples, discounted future cash flows, price/earnings multiples, and recent transactions in the venture's sector; the method rankings were different in each country, but all seemed to rely on one method, method, using the others as checks 2. Own due-diligence report was the no. 1 source of information for valuation in all countries but France, where it was no. 2; the overall coherence of the business plan and the profit and loss part of the plan was also uniformly ranked high; interviews with the entrepreneurs was ranked very high everywhere but the UK, where it was ranked no. 12

Table 1 continued

Chapter/article	Issues/research questions	Theoretical perspective	Data	Key conclusions and contribution
12 Admati & Pfleiderer (1994)	Resolution of agency problems arising in multi-stage VC financial contracting	Agency theory; contracting theory	No data – conceptual article	1. The first round VC as inside investor always makes optimal investment decisions if and only if it holds a fixed-fraction contract, where it always receives a fixed fraction of the pay-offs and finances that same fraction of future investment 2. This contract eliminates incentives for VC to misprice securities in later financing rounds
13 Hellmann (1998)	Why and under what circumstances entrepreneurs voluntarily relinquish control to VCs	Incomplete contracting theory	No data – conceptual article	1. Control may be necessary for VCs to have incentives to add value to the company 2. Entrepreneurs may cede control and risk being replaced if loss of private benefits under replacement outweighs the monetary benefit to the company
14 Kirilenko (2001)	Attempt to reconcile theoretically the disproportionate distribution of control rights in VC deals resulting from adverse selection	Incomplete contracting theory; game theory	No data – conceptual article	1. Higher degree of adverse selection associated with more control rights allocated to the VC 2. Entrepreneur compensated for a greater loss of control through better terms of financing, ability to extract higher rents from asymmetric information and better risk sharing
15 Gupta & Sapienza (1992)	Factors influencing VCFs' preferences for industry diversity and geographic scope of investment portfolio	Portfolio diversification theory and business risk theory	Secondary data on 169 VCFs from *Pratt's Guide to Venture Capital Sources*	1. VCFs specializing in early stage ventures prefer less industry diversity and narrower geographic scope; the same is true for smaller VCFs (i.e., those with less capital under management) 2. Corporate VCFs prefer less industry diversity but broader geographic scope 3. Results suggest that some VCFs do not attempt to spread risk by diversity but to manage it by building up expertise
16 Carter & Van Auken (1994)	How do VCs differ in their preferences for investments based on stages of development?	Financial and risk perspective	Survey responses from 69 US VCs	1. VCs do have differences in preferences for investment projects based on stages of development 2. Early stage VC investors are apparently less interested in the management of risks but are more willing to exercise control over the project by spending more time with the venture in the early stages 3. Early stage investors favour the IPO as the means of exiting the project
17 Fiet (1995)	Do VCs have different risk avoidance strategies than business angels? Assumes that information to reduce a risk can be acquired but at a cost	Risk and information economics	Survey data from 141 VCs and 83 business angels	1. Five types of agency risk were viewed by business angels to be more important than market risk information 2. VCs seem to specialize in market risk and to a greater degree than do business angels. Perhaps VCs have learned to protect themselves contractually from agency risk issues with contractual arrangements

# Authors	Focus	Theory	Data/Source	Observations/Inferences
18 De Clercq, Goulet, Kumpulainen & Mäkelä (2001)	Specialization versus diversification strategies in an emerging venture capital market (i.e., Finland); specifically, industry, stage, and geographic scope issues	Agency and business risk theories	Data from secondary source: Finnish Venture Capital Association (data on 483 portfolio firms of 28 venture capital firms; level of analysis is venture capital firm level)	1. Over time, Finnish VCFs tended to specialize by industry while expanding the scope of investing by stage and location 2. Less experienced VCFs followed a similar pattern but more slowly adapted these practices 3. In general, evidence of response to the trade-offs between returns and both agency and business risk are evident
19 Sahlman & Stevenson (1985)	1. The phenomenon of 'capital market myopia' wherein individual participants in capital markets ignore the collective implications of their individual decisions 2. The chains of events that signal and, if not heeded, lead to capital market myopia	Largely a description of events, with reference to the 'greater fool' theory	Extensive use of secondary data compiled from the likes of Venture Economics, the Securities Data Company, the *Venture Capital Journal*, and *DISK/TREND Report*	Observations: 1. Taking a broad view of industry events is necessary to avoid myopia. This could have and should have been done 2. A critical mass of technological 'bets' and investment 'bets' spurred, enabled, and ultimately defeated one another Inferences: 1. Early entry does not guarantee success; late entry almost always leads to failure 2. High growth opportunity, a fundamental criterion for venture capital investing, does not always lead to high returns
20 Brophy & Gunther (1988)	Risk/return characteristics of publicly traded VC funds	Portfolio diversification theory	Weekly total returns data over 5 years 1981–1985 for 12 listed VC funds compared with 12 randomly selected open mutual funds with objective of maximizing capital gain	1. Portfolios show systematic risk below S&P 500 and sample of mutual funds and higher returns than both benchmarks 2. Support for fund of funds portfolio strategy of institutional investors as correlation between VC fund returns is low suggesting firm-specific risk characteristics may be reduced by diversification
21 Gompers & Lerner (2000)	Analysis of the impact of inflows of capital into VC funds on the valuation of the funds new investments	DCF valuation theory; exogenous shifts in funds supply in a market segmented from other financial sectors	1. 4069 venture investments from 1987 to 1995 from VentureOne database 2. Various industry directories and electronic databases 3. Information on capital inflows to VC funds	1. Inflows of capital into VC funds increases the value of new investments controlling for firm characteristics and public market valuations 2. Changes in valuation not related to ultimate success of firms 3. Competition for a limited number of attractive investments responsible for rising prices
22 Hellmann & Puri (2000)	Relationship between market strategy and investor type. Does choice of investor impact outcomes in product market?	Product market strategy theory	149 venture and non-venture backed firms in Silicon Valley selected on basis of stratified random sample 1994–97 Interviews and archival data from Rich's Everyday Sales Prospecting Guide, Technology Resource Guide to Greater Silicon Valley, Venture Economics, VentureOne	1. Innovators are more likely to be financed by VCs than are imitators 2. Innovators faster in obtaining VC financing 3. Presence of a VC is associated with faster time to market, especially for innovators

Table 1 continued

Chapter/article	Issues/research questions	Theoretical perspective	Data	Key conclusions and contribution
Volume III				
1 Rosenstein (1988)	How do the boards of VC-backed technology firms differ from typical corporations and conventional small businesses?	Primarily descriptive with some governance background	Interviews with six venture capital partners in the Dallas Texas area	1. High technology VC-backed firms have boards with high power relative to management 2. Boards of VC-backed firms are typically small with outsiders rather than management in control. Board meetings are frequent and they frequently address progress that is being made with firm strategies 3. Outside board members typically view their involvement as being value added
2 MacMillan, Kulow & Khoylian (1989)	To examine how VC involvement correlates with venture performance	Descriptive	Survey data with responses from 62 VCs	1. VCs were most involved in the financial aspects of the venture 2. Three levels of involvement: *laissez-faire*, moderate and close tracker 3. No difference in venture performance was found based on the level of VC involvement
3 Rosenstein, Bruno, Bygrave & Taylor (1993)	1. Extent and usefulness of venture capitalists' involvement as board members of ventures 2. Differences in boards and value-adding when a 'top-20' VCF holds a seat on the board	Descriptive (TMT issues)	Questionnaire data from 162 high-tech ventures in phase 1. A follow-up telephone interview of 98 of the 162. The analyses of 'top-20' versus non-top-20 differences were based on this latter group of 98 interview-based survey responses	1. Generally, advice from venture capitalists is rated equally valuable to that of other board members; boards that had a VC from 'top-20' VCF as lead investor rated advice from venture capitalists as significantly higher than other board members, but the difference was not great 2. Greatest help from VCs came as sounding boards, monitors of performance, CEO recruitment/replacement, and crisis management 3. Getting venture capital only to gain advice is a questionable strategy for entrepreneurs
4 Sapienza & Gupta (1994)	Antecedents of venture capitalists' involvement in their portfolio companies	Information processing theory and agency theory	1. Questionnaire data from the CEOs of 51 ventures and the lead investor in these 51 ventures 2. Secondary data from *Pratt's Guide to Venture Capital Sources* 3. Semi-structured interviews with 30+ VCs and ten entrepreneurial CEOs	1. High levels of goal congruence between CEOs and VCs are associated with less interaction in VC–CEO pairs 2. Further, less VC experience, earlier stage of ventures, and greater geographic proximity are associated with less VC involvement; however VCs' level of ownership is not related to interaction 3. Agency and information processing explanations provide some explanatory power to involvement, a practice previously assumed to be driven by individual style only
5 Lerner (1995)	Examines the role of VCs as monitors of private firms using evidence from board of directors	Governance issues/ some agency theory assumptions	Venture Economics database – 653 rounds of financing of 271 biotechnology firms between 1978 and 1989	1. VCs within 5 miles of the firm's headquarters are twice as likely to be on the board as a VC 500 miles away 2. Board composition changes when there is a CEO turnover between rounds of funding. The number of VCs on the board goes up significantly at the time when there is CEO turnover. There were no significant changes in other board representation groups

	Purpose	Theory	Method/Data	Findings
6 Sweeting & Wong (1997)	Post-investment relationships where the VC has a policy of 'hands-off' monitoring	Agency theory; learning over VC life cycle	Single VC case study. Multiple interviews with VC investment controllers (5) and investees (7)	1. Stages of VC investment process matched to targeting, selecting and structuring deals compatible with VC firm's hands-off style 2. Relationship between VC and investees conforms more to a Joint Venture if investees performing well
7 Gomez-Mejia, Balkin & Welbourne (1990)	Investigates the role of VCs in the management of high-tech firms	Institutional power and organizational dependence	A qualitative field study involving interviews with ten VCs and ten entrepreneurs	1. Entrepreneurs and VCs view VC influence as positive when it involves financial concerns and boundary spanning activities 2. Entrepreneurs and VCs hold opposite views about the contributions that VCs make to the internal management of the firm 3. VC involvement in internal management issues is generally seen as negative
8 Ehrlich, De Noble, Moore & Weaver (1994)	To determine how initial relationships are established and maintained between entrepreneurs and VCs		Survey data from 47, mostly high-tech, entrepreneurs receiving funding from VCs and private investors	1. The type of investor that entrepreneurs get their money from is just as important as the amount of capital raised 2. Entrepreneurs receiving funding from private investors desired more investor involvement 3. VCs provided more help in selecting the venture's management team while private investors tend to give entrepreneurs more reporting and operational flexibility
9 Sapienza, Manigart & Vermeir (1996)	1. Antecedents of venture capitalists' assistance and monitoring via face-to-face interaction. 2. Antecedents of value added	Agency theory, business risk, and information processing theory	1. Survey and interview data collected in the US in 1988 2. Survey data in the UK, France and the Netherlands in 1992, replication of earlier survey	1. VCs in the US and the UK appear to expend more effort in value-adding activities than those in France and the Netherlands; interaction does not appear systematically related to venture performance; however, later stage ventures attract less attention than early stage ventures 2. VC venture capital industry experience is negatively related to interaction, but their experience specific to the venture's industry is positively related; a similar pattern appears for value added 3. The importance accorded to the various VC roles were consistent in all three countries: strategic roles were deemed most value-adding, interpersonal roles were next, followed by networking roles
10 Gifford (1997)	1. VCs incentives to allocate time so as to maximize profits of entrepreneurs and of limited partners 2. Preferences of VC and entrepreneur for timing of IPO 3. Preferences of VC and limited partner for maturity ventures selected	Agency theory	None. Mathematical modeling	VCs' incentives are such that they allocate attention among ventures and venture funds less frequently than required to maximize the entrepreneurs' and limited partners' profits; however, the VC does efficiently allocate time so as to maximize the total profits of all ventures

Table 1 continued

Chapter/article	Issues/research questions	Theoretical perspective	Data	Key conclusions and contribution
11 Ruhnka, Feldman & Dean (1992)	Investigation of living dead investments (investments not meeting target returns but not failing)	Descriptive	1. Interviews with managing partners of six VC firms 2. Survey responses from 80 VC firms	1. Living dead conditions arise from deficiencies in management and markets, missed opportunities and unexpected competition 2. Living dead investments generally occur during stage of pushing for rapid growth and market share 3. VCs predict that 20.6 per cent of investments will end as living dead, but that successful turnaround or exit is achieved in 55.9 per cent of cases; VCs aim to sell the company but only after at least one attempt at turnaround 4. Successful turnaround associated with factors that caused the problem that can be controlled by the VC
12 Fiet, Busenitz, Moesel & Barney (1997)	Antecedents of VC initiatives to dismiss members of the entrepreneurial team	Agency theory, power, and procedural justice	Primary survey data based on 121 responses from entrepreneurs receiving at least first round funding from VCs	1. VC initiated dismissals that occurred in about 35 per cent of the cases 2. At least partial support was found for agency theory. Power theory, and procedural justice theory in explaining antecedents of VC dismissals of entrepreneurial team members
13 Bruton, Fried & Hisrich (1997)	1. Impact of strategic versus operational roles of CEOs on their dismissal by VCs 2. Impact of CEO replacement on performance 3. Impact of outside versus inside replacement	Upper echelon and strategic management theory	Primary survey of 68 responses from US VC firms	1. Strategic failings (making strategic decisions, working with the board, allocating resources, motivating employees) more likely to lead to CEO dismissal than operational ones 2. Venture performance improves following dismissal 3. No difference in performance between inside and outside replacements with industry experience; but outsiders without industry experience led to higher performance 4. This is one of very few articles to focus on the causes and outcomes of CEO dismissal
14 Zacharakis, Meyer & DeCastro (1999)	1. Causes of own new venture failure as seen by VCs 2. Causes of own new venture failure as seen by entrepreneurs 3. Attributions of both as to causes of failure for others' ventures	Attribution theory	Structured interviews with eight entrepreneurs of 'failed or failing' and with VCs in five of these ventures. Content analysis of interviews to draw conclusions	1. Entrepreneurs attribute their own failure to both internal and external causes, with slightly greater mentioning of internal causes 2. Opposite of all prior research, VCs more frequently cited external causes 3. Both entrepreneurs and VCs attribute the failure of other similar ventures to internal causes
15 Sapienza & Korsgaard (1996)	How entrepreneurs' provision of information affects VCs' trust in them, commitment to their decisions, frequency of monitoring, and intention to reinvest	Procedural justice theory	Composed of two studies: 1. In Study 1, the data are derived from an experiment involving 44 business students 2. In Study 2, most of the data are received from a mail survey of 118 venture capitalists; secondary data from *Pratt's Guide to Venture Capital Sources* is also used	1. The frequency and timeliness of feedback from entrepreneurs significantly influences how VCs perceive and support them. Specifically: timely feedback increases VCs' trust and their commitment to entrepreneurs' decisions; it decreases monitoring; evidence regarding a positive effect on intention to re-invest is partial 2. The amount of influence VCs have on entrepreneurs also increases trust and commitment

				Findings
16 Cable & Shane (1997)	1. Factors influencing VC–entrepreneur cooperation versus defection (opportunism) 2. Differences in the strength of the influences on the two parties	Prisoner's dilemma framework	No data – conceptual article	1. Lack of an efficient replacement market makes cooperation critical to success 2. Framework relaxes the assumption of a hierarchical VC–entrepreneur relationship that is a part of agency theory 3. Opportunity costs and asymmetric information influence decision to cooperate. Specifically, time pressure, pay-off to cooperation, information available, personal similarity and transaction procedures
17 Busenitz, Moesel, Fiet & Barney (1997)	Examines how various conditions in place at the time of first-round funding impact the entrepreneurs' perceptions of fairness in their treat from VCs. The VC–entrepreneur relationship is assumed to be two-way	Procedural justice	Survey data from 116 firms receiving at least first round funding	1. The number of VCs on the board and constraining covenants did not significantly impact perceptions of fairness but earn-out arrangements had a negative effect 2. Industry experience along with time as a team in the venture were both found to be negatively related to perceptions of fairness. However, if the venture team had worked together before, the effect was positive
18 Megginson & Weiss (1991)	In firms that go public, does the presence of VCs certify that the offering price of the issue reflects all available and relevant inside information?	Information asymmetries	Matched-pair sample of 320 VC-backed firms with 320 non-VC-backed firms that went public in the 1983–1987 timeframe. Archival data	1. The presence of VCs in the offering firm certifies the quality of the issue through their investment in financial and reputational capital 2. VC-backed firms are able to attract higher quality underwriters and auditors as well as a larger institutional following than non-VC-backed IPOs
19 Cyr, Johnson & Welbourne (2000)	1. Examine the effect of VC backing on the likelihood of a firm having a dedicated human resource (HR) person 2. Examine the combined effect of VC backing and the presence of a VP of HR	Mid-range theory involving human resource leadership	Secondary data from IPO prospectuses: 242 non-VC-backed firms and 160 VC-backed firms	1. VC-backed firms are more likely to have VPs of HR than non-VC-backed firms 2. The presence of a VP of HR had no direct effect on stock price three years after the IPO. The interaction between the presence of a VP of HR with VC backing was also non-significant
20 Brav & Gompers (1997)	Long-run underperformance of venture and non-venture backed IPOs	Asymmetric information theory; rational asset pricing models; behavioral finance theory	1. 934 VC-backed IPOs 1972–1992 and 3407 non-VC-backed IPOs 1975–1992 2. CRSP share price data and Compustat data	1. VC-backed IPOs outperform non-VC-backed IPOs using equal weighted returns but underperformance of latter less using value weighting 2. VC-backed firms do not significantly underperform using factor asset pricing models but non-VC-backed do 3. Non-VC-backed IPOs' underperformance more likely to be affected by investor sentiment

Table 1 continued

Chapter/article	Issues/research questions	Theoretical perspective	Data	Key conclusions and contribution
21 Lerner (1994)	Timing of initial public offerings by venture capital firms	IPO timing theory	Sample of 350 privately held venture-backed biotechnology firms 1978–1992 from: 1. IPO prospectuses and S-1 registration documents 2. Secondary data provided by Venture Economics and Recombinant Capital 3. Contacts with companies and VCs, *Pratt's Guide to Venture Capital Sources*	1. Biotechnology firms go public when equity valuations are high and employ private financings where values are lower 2. Seasoned venture capitalists proficient at taking companies public near market peaks
22 Gompers (1996)	Do young VC firms take companies public earlier than older VCs in order to establish a reputation and raise new funds?	Reputation and signaling theory; grandstanding theory	433 venture-backed IPOs 1978–1987 and first IPOs by 62 VC funds	1. Companies backed by young VC firms are younger and more underpriced at IPO than those backed by established VCs 2. Young VCs have been on the board for less time, hold smaller equity stakes and time the IPO to coincide with raising money for follow-on funds
23 Wright et al. (1993)	Influences on buy-out longevity in four European countries and control devices used by financiers to ensure exit	Contingency theory; life-cycle theory	1. Primary population data based on archival and survey information 2. Primary face-to-face interview data	1. Considerable differences between countries in nature, timing and extent of exit 2. Formal processes to control exit can be problematical, resulting in flexibility 3. Management key role in influencing exit
24 Wright, Robbie, Thompson & Starkey (1994)	1. Influences on longevity of management buy-outs 2. Development of theory of buy-out longevity	Agency theory; life-cycle theory	1. Primary population data based on archival and survey information 2. Primary interview and archival data based on case studies	1. Significant differences in longevity of small and large buy-outs and of buy-outs from different sources 2. Ownership, financial and market environment influence heterogeneity of buy-out longevity
25 Petty, Bygrave & Shulman (1994)	Analysis of the five most common ways of realizing investments in entrepreneurial ventures	Net present value; agency theory	1. Review of evidence 2. Secondary deal data 3. Face-to-face interviews	1. Choice of harvest method depends on investment opportunities facing firm, strength of management team and stability of cash flows 2. Decision about whether, how and when to exit not independent of entrepreneur's personal goals 3. Failure to plan for inevitable harvest will have negative consequences for value realized by entrepreneur and VC
26 Wright, Robbie & Ennew (1997)	Relative attractiveness to VCs of serial entrepreneurs compared with novice entrepreneurs	Assets and liabilities of entrepreneurial experience; adverse selection and VC contracting	Two primary surveys of venture capital firms	1. Previous entrepreneurial experience only one among several investment criteria considered by VCs for serial entrepreneurs 2. Assets of previous experience generally exceed liabilities for serial entrepreneurs 3. VC-backed serial entrepreneurs do not perform better than novice venture-backed entrepreneurs

Volume I, Part I   Systemic Issues: Early Views

Pioneering work in the practices of VCs relied heavily on primary field research complemented with secondary data from Venture Economics. This early work helped to shape later views of the venture capital process, the role of venture capital in financing and creating the emergence of new technology-driven industries, and the practices and concerns of venture capitalists themselves. In many ways, a research agenda that is still being articulated and pursued was laid out in these key early works.

Chapter 1 by Tyebjee and Bruno forms the basis of much subsequent work on the venture capital 'cycle' or process. Their grounded approach allowed them to articulate in detail key phases in the operations of venture capital firms. Later works (e.g., Gompers and Lerner, 2000; and Sahlman, Volume I, Chapter 13) elaborated on the ideas and insights of this early work. This study also formed a starting place for the examination of the criteria used by VCs to assess deals. Deal selection criteria and deal selection processes were probably the most studied areas in venture capital in the early 1990s. Later, examinations of the relationship between criteria and portfolio success and of the consistency of VCs' application of their decision criteria continued this robust stream of research. This latter point on the consistent application of criteria may be seen as a forerunner to the work on cognitive biases in VC decision making (see, for example, in Volume II, Shepherd, Chapter 7; Zacharakis and Shepherd, Chapter 8). Whereas the statistical relationships in Tybejee and Bruno's data in Chapter 1 pointed to the significance of market attractiveness and product differentiation for forming expectations regarding expected returns, interview data led Tyebjee and Bruno to speculate that the model under-represented the importance of management quality to the assessment and to the process. Subsequent research has corroborated this adjusted view. This work is also noteworthy for its effective use of multiple methods, of multivariate analyses, and its practical, interpretive approach.

The Timmons and Bygrave study (Chapter 2) is one of the first pieces explicitly to recognize the policy implications of venture capital for the encouragement of high-technology new ventures. Like the Tyebjee and Bruno chapter, their study is largely descriptive but provides important detail not available elsewhere and provides careful observation of the emerging phenomenon of venture capital as the engine of high-technology innovation in the US. They noted that the incidence of funding highly innovative technology ventures was steadily increasing over the 15-year period between 1967 and 1982. Furthermore, they highlighted an interesting aspect of the venture capital process: it is a highly specialized *management* activity, rather than being primarily a capital-intensive activity. They articulated how the emergence of convertible preferred shares was used as a management tool to give VCs adequate control without the limiting requirement of majority ownership.

Gorman and Sahlman's study (Chapter 3) is a commonly cited article that describes how VCs spend their time. Gorman and Sahlman focus on the specific activities of VCs and their allocation of time across phases of the venture capital process and across ventures. They draw attention to the impact on time allocation of VCs' taking lead versus non-lead roles, of stage of venture development, of position of the VC within the Venture Capital Firm (VCF) (i.e., general partner versus staff), and of the distance between the VCF and the venture. Their assessment that VCs spend just over half their time in post-investment activities helped to spark another major stream of research on venture capital: post-investment activities and roles of VCs. Further, Gorman and Sahlman's article highlights VCs' roles in the boards of new ventures and their use of boards to monitor and control decisions. In short, the primary legacy of this work is the literature that examines post-investment activities (see, for example, Volume III, Parts I, II, and III), work on boards and CEO dismissal (e.g., Bruton *et al.*, Volume III, Chapter 13; Rosenstein *et al.*, Volume III, Chapter 3), and also Gifford's (Volume III, Chapter 10) work on the time allocation problem of VCs and its agency implications. Also worth noting in this work is Gorman and Sahlman's finding that VCs overwhelmingly attribute venture failures to managerial shortcomings rather than market forces or bad luck. The irony here is that VCs play a central role in selecting the very managers with whom they find fault and claim to play some part in their development as well.

Part I of our first volume introduces three classic works that continue to exert some influence on research on the management side of venture capital studies. Some reflection on what these works observe in the mid-1980s indicates that, despite the vicissitudes of wildly volatile markets, much of the landscape is still today as it was then: VCs still engage in fund raising, deal origination, screening, evaluation, deal structuring, and post-investment monitoring and exit. Venture capital still tends to focus upon and play an important role in funding and developing high-technology opportunities. Interestingly, anecdotal evidence suggests that (1) the market boom of the late 1990s drove VCs toward spending more time on fund raising and deal building activities and less on post-investment activities than reported in Gorman and Sahlman, but (2) the crash of the early days of the new millennium has driven VCs back to spending time and effort on developing winners among the portfolio companies by renewed interest in post-investment assistance.

Volume I, Part II   Systemic Issues: Macro-Perspectives of the 1990s

The question of why VC markets develop at different times and at different rates between countries is an important one. The later macro-perspective articles presented in this section are marked by their adoption of theoretical perspectives largely absent from the earlier studies. The articles use different conceptual perspectives to analyse the development of venture capital markets.

Manigart (Chapter 4) finds strong support for the population ecology perspective and that density of VC firms in the industry has a strong effect on the founding of new VC firms. This study also examined the population of VC firms in bordering countries. She found that the populations in neighboring countries have a positive effect on each other. Legitimating effects do not stop at the geographic borders. Yet, the competition for resources (capital, people, deals) among geographically different populations is limited in this industry.

Murray's (Chapter 5) study applied Porter's analytical framework to understanding the development of a venture capital industry, with particular application to the UK industry during its initial mature phase. The study sought to examine how the environmental influences on the industry were likely to affect the future size and structure, conduct and performance of the industry. This chapter also addresses the factors influencing the provision of investment capital to venture capital firms. Murray emphasizes the importance at this stage of the development of the market for firms to demonstrate terminal performance of their funds in order to be able to raise further funds.

Building from the assumption that information asymmetries are central to entrepreneurial financing, Amit *et al.*'s (Chapter 6) main point is that VCs exist precisely because they develop special expertise in reducing information-based market failures through careful selection, monitoring, and other means.

The important article by Black and Gilson (Chapter 7) takes a systemic view of the factors influencing the development of VC markets by comparing bank versus stock market-based systems. Black and Gilson explain the presence of much stronger VC industries in stock market-centered systems by arguing that a well-developed stock market permits VCs to exit through an initial public offering (IPO) and that the ability to realize gains in this way is critical to the existence of a vibrant VC market. They also suggest that VCs' combination of financial and non-financial services loses its efficiency advantages as the portfolio company matures. Hence, recycling VC investors' capital through exit and re-investment is efficient for both the VC investee firm and the VC. They are sceptical about arguments that bank-based systems have functionally equivalent mechanisms for funding start-ups, suggesting that different activities are allocated to different countries on the basis of specialization, so that more developed VC markets experience more high-technology investments. These arguments are consistent with suggestions that the Japanese market, for example, is characterized more by imitative innovation rather than radical innovation, and that this is associated with the conservatism of the banks. Black and Gilson argue that these institutional factors are more important than cultural differences in the willingness of individuals to take risks. They also point out that other path-dependent factors, such as secondary institutions that more severely penalize failure make it difficult for bank-centered systems to establish appropriate institutional infrastructures from scratch.

The interesting study by Jeng and Wells (Chapter 8) is one of the first to analyse differences in the factors influencing the development of VC markets in different countries. Jeng and Wells find that IPOs are the strongest driver of venture capital investing, which lends support to the Black and Gilson argument regarding the importance of stock markets. However, Jeng and Wells also note that, surprisingly, market capitalization growth is not a significant determinant of venture capital while government policies can have a strong impact through setting the regulatory framework. They also make an important distinction between the factors affecting the development of early stage and later stage venture capital activity, notably that IPOs are a significant determinant only of later stage venture capital investing across countries.

Although these recent studies have begun to shed light on differences in the rate of development and nature of venture capital markets between countries, two particular emerging international aspects have yet to be examined.

First, trends suggest that previously underdeveloped venture capital and private equity markets are now showing signs of growth; in some cases, this growth is significant (Lockett and Wright, 2002). There is a need for analysis of the dynamic aspects of institutional, market and other factors that may be contributing to these changes. Different economic and fiscal environments can lead to very different patterns of venture capital fund raising and investment in developing compared with US/Western European markets. Nye and Wasserman (1999) compare the evolution and current status of venture capital in Israel and India. They show that while both countries are rich in brainpower, differing levels of political support, physical infrastructure, cultural learning, and other factors have contributed to radically different outcomes in their growing VC markets. There is also the need to understand the heterogeneity within apparently similar regions. Asia, for example, contains both developed and emerging countries as well as countries with English-, Germanic- and French-based systems of corporate law (La Porta *et al.*, 1998). These factors can have different impacts on the development of venture capital markets which are as yet not well understood (Lockett and Wright, 2002). Bruton, Ahlstrom and Singh (2002) argue that, while venture capital in most of Asia focuses on funding mature firms in slow growth sectors of the economy rather than start-ups, the venture capital industry in Singapore tends to fund high technology start-ups. They attribute this difference to the institutional environment, particularly the regulatory environment created by the government and its agencies. Adaptation by venture capitalists to Singapore's institutional environment has resulted in greater support for high technology start-ups. Cognitive (cultural) institutions that play a role in how venture capitalists manage their investments in the region also impact how venture capital firms operate in Singapore, particularly causing foreign venture capitalists to adapt their methods.

Differences between legal frameworks as well as motivations for investing in venture capital can also lead to variations in the form of venture capital firm to be found in different countries, notably in terms of the ability to structure limited partnerships, and the relative importance of captive, corporate and public sector venture capital firms in different parts of the region. These differences may also impact the nature of the approach of venture capital firms to the various stages in the venture capital process.

Second, there is a growing trend in the internationalization of the activities of venture capital firms. There is a need to understand the rationale for these strategies, the factors involved in the selection of which international markets to enter, the entry modes and processes, and the extent to which firms adapt their behavior from their domestic markets. Interestingly, in Chapter 8 Jeng and Wells express surprise that venture capitalists in countries with underdeveloped IPO markets do not appear to avail themselves of the more developed IPO markets in other countries. Black and Gilson see piggybacking of this kind as a means by which countries lacking the institutions to develop a venture capital market can avoid the problem of creating the necessary multiple new institutions and can help overcome the path dependency of the existing system. The extent to which VC-backed firms seek IPOs in foreign markets is as yet an under-researched area. Further research might usefully examine the links between the presence of a foreign VC on the board of a company and the eventual IPO in that foreign country as well as the influence of the extent to which a firm's market is sufficiently global to be attractive to international investors.

Cultural differences may be important in explaining cross-country differences in venture capital firm behavior as well as the behavior of domestic and foreign venture capital firms within the same market. Various studies have compared the behavior of venture capital firms in different markets but there has been little work that directly addresses the internationalization of venture capital firms. This general point may have particular resonance concerning the internationalization of US and European firms into Asia and the Pacific Rim. Wright, Lockett and Pruthi (2002) examine internationalization issues in the Indian venture capital market with respect to information and valuation. Hurry, Miller and Bowman (1992) examine the monitoring behavior of Japanese venture capital firms in the US. They show that US venture capital firms are more likely to have greater incentives and ability to monitor investees than Japanese venture capital firms as they tend to make fewer investments and take larger equity stakes. These differences they suggest were largely attributable to the different rationales for venture capital investment by the firms from the two countries; the former seeing investments in terms of projects that will earn returns while the latter view investments as options to be taken up when the investor is ready.

Volume I, Part III   Policy Issues and Technology-Based Ventures

The role of venture capital firms in the promotion of technology-based ventures has received considerable policy attention. Bank debt is unlikely to be an appropriate source of external finance for these firms which often are started and developed with very limited collateral and which need to retain funds within the firm to finance further innovations rather than it being paid out as bank interest (Berger and Udell, 1998). Several studies have associated the US's superior commercialization of new technologies with the existence of a vibrant venture capital market (Florida and Kenney, 1988; Kenney and von Burg, 1999).

Although there have been various policy initiatives to stimulate venture capital involvement in technology-based ventures in a number of countries, there is relatively little systematic research on the effectiveness of government policy toward the promotion of venture capital. Lerner (1999) examines the impact of the US Small Business Innovation Research Program which has provided financial support for small high-technology firms since 1983 in terms of employment and sales growth. Lerner shows that firms receiving awards from the program grew significantly faster than other matched firms over a decade and were more likely to attract venture financing. Interestingly, superior performance of awardees was focused on firms in regions with substantial venture capital and was most pronounced in high-technology industries. Lerner suggests that receipt of an award serves an important certification function but that distortions in the award process may have adversely affected the program's effectiveness, notably among firms receiving large subsidies (which did not perform better than those receiving smaller subsidies) and in those regions with fewer high technology firms.

Chapter 10 by Murray presents an interesting attempt to evaluate the effectiveness of a scheme designed to increase the supply of risk capital to seed stage investments, an aspect of VC funding that in Europe has been problematical. The chapter examines various aspects of the approach of the funds based on a venture capital life-cycle structure. Although the chapter identifies a relative high failure rate of investees, it does suggest that jobs were created at a relatively low cost.

In the tradition of Sandberg and Hofer (1987), Roure and Keeley (Chapter 9) take an essentially strategic management perspective on the initial conditions that may lead to long-term success for technology-based new ventures. By using in-depth analyses of business plans provided by a single venture capital firm they are able to construct profiles of the initial strategies, founding teams, and environmental conditions facing 36 ventures. Their market-based measure of success looks at IPO price or most recent valuation over the sum of investments put into the focal venture. Though results are weak (as they were also for Sandberg and Hofer) they do appear to support a multidimensional model of venture success. This study also provides a slight twist on the prior investigations of the selection criteria (see Volume II, Part I), but the twist is significant. Rather than using investors' judgments of what factors may be significant, they examine how entrepreneurs' own articulation of their resources (in technical and business plans) is related to later success. This approach foreshadows the later re-examination of investor criteria conducted by Zacharakis, Shepherd and colleagues (e.g., Zacharakis and Shepherd, Volume II, Chapter 8).

Von Burg and Kenney (Chapter 11) provide an analysis of how VCs deal with assessing investees in cases where a completely new market is created in which there is little hard evidence on which to base decisions. This particular case is important as it demonstrates situations where entrepreneurs backed by VCs can outmanoeuvre established large firms. The VCs were actively involved in creating new firms in conjunction with the entrepreneurs. Investment decisions were contingent and often hinged on quite idiosyncratic criteria.

A more rigorous quantitative analysis is provided by Kortum and Lerner (Chapter 12) who use production function analysis to consider the contribution of VCs to innovation. The chapter pays particular attention to causality issues. There is a danger that without such adjustments the role of VCs may be overstated since the arrival of technological opportunities may impact the apparent level of patenting. The authors exploit the legal changes during the period that led to an exogenous increase in venture capital as one means of addressing this issue. They also use research and development (R&D) expenditures to control for the arrival of opportunities. They introduce dummy variables for years to control for the effect of legal changes regarding the filing of patents. The study also controls for the danger that VC-backed firms simply patent more inventions, in order to impress funders, rather than actually increasing innovative activity.

Volume I, Part IV   Fund Providers

Discussions about venture capitalists are usually implicitly linked to the funding that they provide to entrepreneurial firms. However, venture capitalists are also usually engaged in raising monies from investors such as corporations, institutional investors, insurance companies and individual investors. The research articles in this section begin to address these issues. The realization that VCs have to raise funds and are accountable to other stakeholders raises two critical issues. First, how is the relationship between VCs and their investors managed? Second, do different types of investors influence the way the VC firm functions in terms of the type of investments they make and the way they relate to the funded entrepreneurs? We now discuss these two issues that future research might consider addressing.

Investor–VC Relationships

The seminal article by Sahlman (Chapter 13) was the first to analyse the structure of VC organizations. It was one of the early articles to suggest that an agency theory perspective might be quite useful in understanding VC relationships. This article provides analysis of both the relationship between (1) VC firms and their funds providers and (2) VC firms and their investees, that is the ventures in which they invest, as well as the contractual arrangements that govern these relationships. While most research has traditionally focused on the relationship between VCs and those receiving VC funding, that is a focus on the VC–investee relationships, a few articles have addressed fund providers' relationships with VCs. In this vein, McNally (Chapter 14) examined the indirect investments by corporations into VC funds. While there is a professed willingness of corporations to be involved in VC funding, this study, conducted in the UK, draws attention to the mismatches of expectations and behaviors that have contributed to the difficulties in this type of relationship. The Robbie, Wright and Chiplin (Chapter 16) article is also devoted to the relationship between VCs and their fund providers. They note the need for VCs to develop a relationship with fund providers through more frequent personal communication and information on VC investments.

The relationship between venture capitalists and the entrepreneurs they fund has emerged as an important dyad (Sapienza and Gupta, Volume III, Chapter 4). This initial group of articles on fund providers and their relationship with VCs suggests that great potential is certainly there for researchers to see the dyad involving fund providers and VCs as a further important avenue of inquiry. The principal–agent relationship as suggested by Sahlman (Chapter 13) certainly has provided a rich theoretical foundation for examining the VC–entrepreneur relationship. However, given the constantly changing dynamics of the VC industry, additional research probing other approaches involving risk considerations and trust as well as trust and fairness issues are likely to be constructive areas for future inquiry (Volume III, Part IV).

The Type of Investor in VC Firms

Some research has started to examine the effect that different types of VC firms may have on the ventures in which they invest. For example, VC firms that are headed by former entrepreneurs may attain higher returns in their funds compared to the returns in those funds operated by a government entity. In going back one step further, it appears as though different types of investors in VC funds may affect the type of investments that a VC firm is likely to make and that the relationship will carry forward with their funded entrepreneurs.

While agency theory generally assumes that capital owners are basically homogeneous, an emerging assumption is that different types of owners are likely to have different preferences in the types of ventures that are funded by VCs (Hoskisson *et al.*, 2002). In the VC domain, it would be interesting to examine if different types of investors in VC funds such as non-financial corporations versus financial institutions versus government entities exert different types of influence. For example, the types of ventures that are funded, the governance arrangements that VCs utilize with their funded entrepreneurs, the level of innovation that the funded ventures are likely to pursue, or the type of exit strategies that VC firms carry out may differ based on the type of investors that dominate the VC fund.

In sum, the type and impact of investors in VC funds has only begun to be explored. Sahlman (Chapter 13) laid an important foundation by outlining the middle ground that VCs often play. The Norton and Tenenbaum (Chapter 17) work shows that VCs do differ in the type of investments that they pursue. However, we know very little about the source of these different preferences. In short, much interesting work lies ahead in discovering with looking at the types of investors that are putting money into VC funds and the impact that they may be having on VC firms.

Volume II, Part I   Deal Generation, Screening and Assessment

It is widely recognized that venture capitalists invest in only a very small fraction of the business ventures that they examine. The ultimate investment decision to invest in only a small handful of business ventures by venture capitalists has intrigued many researchers. The seminal work by MacMillan, Siegel and Subba Narasimha (Chapter 1) provided strong evidence that VCs see entrepreneurial experience and personality as very central to the decision of whether or not to invest. The common nomenclature heuristic here is that VCs can invest in 'B' level ideas as long as they have an 'A' level entrepreneur or entrepreneurial team. The apparent importance of management or team quality to the VC investment decision was again supported by Muzyka, Birley and Leleux (Chapter 5).

These research findings raise some important issues. One of these is, if the entrepreneur or the entrepreneurial team is so important, then why do industry experts tend to put so much emphasis on the business plan? One explanation explored by Muzyka and colleagues was that perhaps VCs say or believe one thing about the centrality of the entrepreneur in the decision process but in actual practice they look at a variety of other factors that actually become quite important. Perhaps there is a timing issue as well. The importance of the entrepreneur may be critical in the very early stages of the evaluation process but the importance of the business plan may emerge as negotiations continue and move towards the due diligence phase. Another approach that further research is starting to consider is the weighting of alternative criteria. Could it be that issues like potential agency problems, industry attractiveness, the stage of technological development or the size of the investment affect decision weightings? We suspect that future inquiry could shed important light on some of these issues.

Another important issue to emerge from this stream of research is how VCs actually evaluate entrepreneurial talent. To say that entrepreneurial talent is important is one thing, but actually to evaluate entrepreneurial talent may be quite another. Chapter 6 by Smart, using self-rated measures, starts to get at this issue by examining how VCs evaluate management in the pre-investment phase, but this study relies on self-rated measures. Several studies have attempted to use conjoint analysis to evaluate the decision processes of venture capitalists. One of the strengths of this analytical approach is that it gets at 'theories in use' as opposed to 'espoused theories'. A potential shortcoming of this technique is whether the decision scenarios used really reflect the decisions of VCs in practice. Further challenging work remains in this key area of research.

Related to the importance of the management team in the pre-funding era is the potential agency problem. Questions have been raised about the importance of agency problems as they relate to the VC–entrepreneur relationship. Could it be that as long as VCs perceive that a potential agency problem may exist with the entrepreneurial team, nothing matters more than the 'quality' of the management team? Perhaps, once potential agency concerns largely subside, the importance of the entrepreneurial team gives way to other issues such as the business plan, technological considerations and the like.

Most of the discussions about VC screening and assessment have centered somewhat introspectively on VCs and their specific decision processes. Fiet (Chapter 4) draws attention to the importance of informants for VCs in the decision process, and identifies specifically differences between VCs and business angels in their decision processes. VCs often use informants that are part of their formal and informal networks to gather additional information surrounding a potential venture. In the overall scheme of VC decision making regarding whether or not to make a specific investment, the source of information about the management team, the technology and industry involved may very well help us more clearly understand some of the current gaps in VC screening and assessment of VC decision making.

Volume II, Part II   Valuation and Structuring

Issues beyond venture-specific criteria play a role in eventually making the investment decision and structuring a deal. The three works collected in this part of Volume II examine how other factors play a role in structuring and evaluating the deal. Bygrave's work (Chapter 9) is primarily interested in how and why the set of investors in a particular deal is constructed as it is. Steier and Greenwood (Chapter 10) focus especially on the entrepreneur's task of attracting the first investor and how the accomplishment of that task affects the attraction of additional investors; however, this study also delves into the post-investment phase to consider how the 'success' in attracting multiple investors affects the later development of the venture. Manigart *et al.* (Chapter 11) take a multi-country view of valuation methods and due-diligence information sources. Together, the three works imply that the social and institutional framework of venture capital investing within a given country help shape who is involved in particular deals and how they assess the deals themselves. Let us now consider each work in turn.

Bygrave's (1988) seminal work (Chapter 9), abstracted from his extensive dissertation, introduces resource exchange theory to explain the structure of venture capital co-investment networks. Bygrave's key insight is the importance of information sharing to the deal valuation and co-investing structure of venture capital deals. Contrary to the view of venture capital co-investing as being solely or primarily an effort to spread financial risk, Bygrave makes a powerful case for viewing venture capital networks as resource-sharing arrangements. He argues that the most important resources to flow through networks are access to deal flow, knowledge, and the spreading of financial risk. Further, consistent with resource exchange theory, Bygrave argues that the amount of co-investing depends most importantly upon the level of uncertainty faced by investors: the greater the uncertainty, the more co-investing. Bygrave implies that this co-investing with respected partners serves to address some of the 'psychological risk' of investing in highly uncertain contexts.

The publication of Bygrave's work was followed by relative neglect of the syndication of venture capital investments for over a decade. Notable exceptions during this period were the studies by Lerner (Volume III, Chapter 21), Steier and Greenwood (Volume II, Chapter 10) and Chiplin *et al.* (1997). Steier and Greenwood (Chapter 10) approach the valuation and deal structuring issue from the perspective of the entrepreneur and posit that VCs and entrepreneurs use totally different frameworks in making decisions. Similar to Sapienza (1989; 1992), Steier and Greenwood note that entrepreneurs rely on support and reassurance from venture capitalists. In a somewhat odd parallel to Bygrave's observation in Chapter 9 of the importance of the syndicate in deal flow and deal co-investing, Steier and Greenwood find that attracting the first investor is a major hurdle; once the first one commits, others follow – even those who may have previously rejected the deal. Indeed, they conclude that the business plan itself may be much less important to the process than previously thought. The latter part of this work assesses the longer-term effects on the entrepreneur of being the 'beneficiary' of funding from multiple investors. In short, Steier and Greenwood provide an interesting unfolding of some of the dysfunctions of syndicated investing from the perspective of the entrepreneur. Their central thesis is that the presence of multiple investors causes delays because of disagreements and timing differences among investors. Thus, they posit, if multiple investors are going to be involved, VCs must make arrangements to ensure that this inevitably complex decision-making structure does not damage the chances of the venture developing as it should. This position resonates somewhat Gifford's (Volume III, Chapter 10) later examination of the agency problems VCs pose for entrepreneurs and limited partners.

More recently, interest in syndication has revived with quite a spate of studies. These recent studies have explored further the motives for syndication. Lockett and Wright (2001) have shown that the dominant motive for VC firms in the UK to syndicate their deals is spreading financial risk through risk sharing. Manigart *et al.* (2002) conduct a pan-European study and find that the risk-spreading motive is common across all countries. Cumming (2002) has empirically shown that the number of portfolio companies in Canadian VC funds increases when they actively syndicate, everything else equal, while Zacharakis (2002) has shown that there is less syndication in riskier US early stage deals than in less risky but larger expansion stage deals.

The reputation of the parties involved in the syndicate has been identified as important in the process (Sorenson and Stuart, 2001; Wright and Lockett, 2002). Better-established firms with a track record of success will have a more valuable reputation and will become a more attractive partner for others. Lerner's study (Volume III, Chapter 21) of the biotechnology industry that found evidence that in first round investments established VC firms syndicate with one another, and in later rounds they syndicate with less-established organizations.

Syndication may also enable VC firms to increase the portfolio they can optimally manage through resource sharing. Jääskeläinen *et al.* (2002) show that the number of IPOs of portfolio companies of US VC managers increases when they manage more companies, up to a certain optimum. This optimum can be increased through syndication. Manigart *et al.* (2002) show that European VC executives syndicate less, either as lead or as non-lead investor, when they manage more portfolio companies, in contrast with North American practices (Jääskeläinen *et al.*, 2002; Cumming, 2002).

Brander *et al.* (2002) argue that the need to access specific resources for the ex-post management of investments, rather than for the selection of investments, is a more important driver for syndication, based on their empirical finding that Canadian syndicated VC deals have higher rates of return than stand-alone projects. Sorenson and Stuart (2001) have shown that the probability that a VC firm will invest in a distant company increases if there is a syndicate partner with whom they have previously co-invested, and if that syndicate partner is located near the target company. This effect is stronger the more repeated syndicate partners a VC firm has.

One theme to emerge from these recent studies is that there appears to be different behavior between North American and European markets. It seems either that European VC firms adopt a suboptimal investment strategy, or that performance dynamics in the European VC industry are different from those in North America. This may partly reflect differences in the emphasis in two regions on early versus late stage investments. Further research is needed to explore the institutional influences on these apparent differences in behavior.

Manigart *et al.* (Chapter 11) take an entirely different approach to the structuring and valuation issue. Rather than examining how VCs are linked to one another or use personal references as a heuristic to judge business plans, they examine the various valuation methods and sources of information that VCs use to make valuations and investment decisions. They look at the valuation methods and information sources used by venture capitalists in the US, the UK, Belgium, France and the Netherlands. It is interesting that they find that in all countries VCs appear to use multiple methods of valuation but prefer to rely on one primarily; VCs' central preference varies by country and is not easily explained by financial or organization (e.g., institutional) theory. Nonetheless, it is fair to say that highly uncertain environments do not lend themselves to conventional financial valuation methods. Manigart *et al.* speculate that some differences may reflect differences in the nature of the markets (e.g., earlier stage investing in the US), differences in the stage of the country's evolution in the industry, or differences in governance and legal structures of the industries. Again, no single answer appears to explain all patterns satisfactorily. These issues appear ripe for future study.

A key similarity across the three works reproduced here is their suggestion of the importance of the way the VC industry itself is ordered within country boundaries. The inter-relationships among investment firms and among investors appears to affect strongly what investments get funded and in what ways. Yet the dynamics of these phenomena are still relatively under-researched and not well understood.

Volume II, Part III   Financial Contracting

The finance-related literature has paid considerable attention to the role of financial contracting in venture capital. Sahlman (Volume I, Chapter 13) drew attention to the nature of the financial contracts used to govern the relationships both between venture capital firms and their funds providers and between venture capital firms and their investees. Early theoretical work by Cooper and Carleton (1979) and Chan *et al.* (1990) examined the role of contracts in multi-stage venture capital projects. In Chapter 12, Admati and Pfleiderer present an important advance in the theorizing of venture capital contracts relating to multi-stage VC investments by considering the possibility of asymmetric information, reflecting the problem that early stage VCs become inside investors with greater information than subsequent investors.

Hellmann (Chapter 13) provides an interesting and important theoretical explanation of why entrepreneurs may be prepared to provide VCs with extensive control rights. This chapter introduces the notion of renegotiation of control rights at the time an entrepreneur is replaced. Hellmann shows theoretically that investor control is more likely when entrepreneurs are more constrained and less experienced and skilful. The model provides a conceptual basis for the later Hellmann and Puri article (Part V, Chapter 22; see below) by suggesting that entrepreneurs may self-select those kinds of investors (i.e., VCs) that have specialist monitoring and added value skills.

Kirilenko (Chapter 14) provides a further development of earlier theories of the distribution of control rights in VCs by relaxing the assumption that control is a binary variable. Kirilenko assumes that control is a continuous variable and that control rights are not proportionate to the number of shares held by VCs or entrepreneurs.

Recent empirical work by Kaplan and Strömberg (2001) examines the extent to which VC contracts in practice reflect theoretical expectations. They find that the contracts adopted by VCs allow them to allocate separately cash-flow rights, voting rights, board rights and other control rights. These rights are frequently found to be contingent on observable measures of financial and non-financial performance, especially for early stage investments. Voting and control rights tend to be allocated such that if an investee performs poorly the VC obtains full control. If an investee's performance improves, the entrepreneur is likely to obtain increased control, while if the investee does very well the VC is likely to get cash-flow rights but reduced control rights. VCs tend to have greater control in early stage investments where the business has yet to generate revenues. Importantly, cash-flow incentives and control rights mechanisms were used as complements not as substitutes. Kaplan and Strömberg (2001) suggest that the allocation of control rights between the venture capitalist and the entrepreneur are central to financial contracts and note that despite the prevalence of contingent contracting, contracts are inherently incomplete.

Volume II, Part IV   Strategies of Venture Capital Firms

Strategizing on the part of venture capital firms is implicit in the prior sections of this volume. We have seen that venture capital firms use various heuristic criteria and methods for screening and selecting individual ventures, for valuing and structuring individual deals, and for contracting with particular entrepreneurs. In an early study, Robinson (1987) examined the strategic configurations that venture capital firms assume in terms of sources of funding, use of staff resources, stage preference, and use of financial resources. In contrast, Volume II, Part IV examines the strategies used by venture capital firms to mitigate the agency and business risks inherent in a portfolio of investments.

Gupta and Sapienza's work (Chapter 15) is one of the first to recognize explicitly the strategy of specialization as an answer to the issues of uncertainty facing VCs. Two alternative strategies for reducing risk in a portfolio are diversification and specialization. Diversification (or, conversely, specialization) can be achieved along the dimensions of venture stage, industry, or geographic scope; further, these dimensions may interact. Indeed, Gupta and Sapienza point out that VCs specializing in early stage investments tend to specialize also along industry and geographic scope. These investors appear to seek to gain a foothold by building expertise in a narrower set of ventures in order to 'manage' business risk rather than diversify away systematic risk. Gupta and Sapienza also point out that the propensity to diversify varies by type of venture capital firm as well. They found that corporate venture capital firms tend to be more industry-focused but less geographically focused than private venture capital firms.

Consistent with Gupta and Sapienza, Carter and Van Auken (Chapter 16) find that some VCs are more interested in early stage investments while others prefer later stages. However, whereas Gupta and Sapienza speculated that early stage investors are able to 'manage' the greater risks of their early stage investing because of the deeper knowledge that accrues to specialized investing, Carter and Van Auken argue that early stage investors are less concerned with the management of risks but are willing to exercise control. Specifically, they suggest that early stage investors exercise more control over entrepreneurs by spending more time in the initial analysis and by replacing management should the need arise. It could be added that their 'control' hypothesis is also evident in post-investment activities as well: VCs have been found to spend more time overseeing early stage than late stage ventures (Gorman and Sahlman, Volume I, Chapter 3; Sapienza, 1992).

Fiet (Chapter 17) considers not early versus late stage investors but risk avoidance strategies employed by business angels versus those employed by venture capital firm investors. Fiet uses an information economics perspective which assumes that information can be used to reduce the riskiness of a deal in areas related to that information. Fiet argues that VCs have learned to protect themselves contractually from agency risk using boilerplate contractual terms and conditions; they are therefore less concerned with agency problems surrounding new deals but focus more on market risks. Conversely, angels who have less experience in contracting and personal due diligence and perhaps greater market experience are concerned more with agency risks.

De Clercq *et al.* (Chapter 18) take a step beyond the earlier Gupta and Sapienza (Chapter 15) article by examining the patterns in realized rather than intended portfolio strategy. While the sample necessarily involves a small number of firms, it includes most of the participants in the industry. Furthermore, the study is an examination of a newly developing venture capital market (Finland) over critical early years. The strategic view (i.e., dominance of firm choice) developed here provides an interesting contrast to the population ecology view (i.e., dominance of industry forces) developed by Manigart (Volume I, Chapter 4). Consistent with the earlier Gupta and Sapienza study, De Clercq *et al.* find evidence of greater specialization in the face of uncertainty. At the same time, they found that less experienced venture capital firms tended to be less specialized in general than more experienced Finnish firms. On an industry level, it was found that specialization of firms was increasing over time. If we assume that firms individually and collectively 'learn' over time, these two findings together suggest that greater specialization may be a superior strategy, at least in Finland.

Volume II, Part V   Success Factors, Returns and Performance

Sahlman and Stevenson's (Chapter 19) stunning critique of the venture capital industry was the lead article in the first edition of the *Journal of Business Venturing*, the primary academic outlet for work taking a managerial view of venture capital. It could be viewed as a lone voice, at that time, questioning the almost legendary 'wisdom' and acuity of venture capitalists. Sahlman and Stevenson compile an impressive array of secondary information to support their case that venture capitalists (and others) could have and should have avoided the investment disaster of the Winchester Disk Drive industry. From the practice side, it is difficult to say whether the central cautionary tale has been heeded by market participants: we have witnessed at least three severe up-and-down rides industry-wide since that time. From a research perspective, the intellectual cousins of this work are in the stream of literature that examines and questions the omniscience, consistency and rationality of individual venture capitalists. This later work (embodied in articles by Zacharakis, Shepherd and others), however, are perhaps more forgiving in that individuals' failings may be seen to some degree in terms of bounded rationality. Sahlman and Stevenson see no such excuse for the investors in the Winchester Disk Drive industry; they opine that all the information was readily available to the participants and attribute failings as herding behavior at best and tunnel vision at worst.

Brophy and Gunther's study (Chapter 20) aims to overcome the problems of previous studies of distinguishing between firm-specific and market-related risk in VC funds' returns. This is a rare study of VC fund performance and the first to look at the potential benefits from pursuing a fund of funds strategy which is now an important issue for institutional investors seeking to enter the venture capital market. Given the problems in identifying performance data for VC funds, most of which are privately held, this study was particularly interesting, although data on returns on privately held funds is now more available, especially from national venture capital associations.

Valuation of VC investments poses major problems because of private information, uncertainty, and so on. Gompers and Lerner (Chapter 21) present an important analysis of the determinants of valuations of VC investments that shows that valuations of VC investments is not so much determined by changes in an investment's prospects as determined in discounted cash flow (DCF) calculations but by changes in the capital inflows. This analysis raises important implications concerning the impact of shifts in capital flows on the pace and direction of technological innovation as changes in capital inflows may raise or lower VCs' thresholds regarding standards for funding firms.

Hellmann and Puri (Chapter 22) construct a very interesting dataset that importantly uses archival and survey data of both VC- and non-VC-backed firms. The study is the first to examine the inter-relationship between type of investor and aspect of market behavior of start-ups. The study has important implications because its findings indicate that appropriateness of choosing an involved investor depends on product market strategy and that VCs play different roles in different companies. VCs are found to have an impact on the development path of a start-up firm. A firm's choice of financier can secure first mover advantages.

Volume III, Part I   Post-Investment Involvement: Monitoring and Protecting Value

Once VCs have carefully analysed a venture, performed their due diligence and made their financial investments, they typically concern themselves with monitoring and protection issues. To fulfil their monitoring and protection concerns, VCs can pursue a variety of channels. The articles included in this section suggest that the most common methods for protecting their interests include contractual arrangements, the gathering of on-going information, and formal and informal involvement with the funded ventures. The MacMillan, Kulow and Khoylian article (Chapter 2) is the seminal work in this group. They established that VCs primarily involve themselves in the categories of financial, strategic and operational areas with VCs tending to be involved with the financial aspects of the venture. The MacMillan *et al.* article also established that the level of VC involvement varies substantially from *laissez-faire* to moderate and close tracker. However, this study found no significant differences in venture performance based on the level of VC involvement.

The Rosenstein (Chapter 1) and Rosenstein *et al.* (Chapter 3) articles draw important attention to the role that VCs often play on the board of directors of the firms in which they invest. Rosenstein (Chapter 1) found that the boards of high-technology VC-backed firms typically had substantial power and that the outsiders were generally in control rather than management. He also found that boards regularly grapple with firm strategies. Rosenstein *et al.* (Chapter 3) address whether and how VC firms add value to their portfolio companies by asking chief executive officers (CEOs) to evaluate the contributions of VCs on the board versus non-VC outsiders on the board. In their final analysis, they found that those ventures with lead investors from a top VC firm were perceived as adding more value. Assuming that perceptions are reasonable, the issue still remains of whether the other members on the board are independent of the presence of VCs.

Chapter 4 by Sapienza and Gupta is one of the earlier theory-driven works to use information processing theory and agency theory. More specifically, this work addresses why there are large variations in VC involvement, a gap left by the MacMillan *et al.* research in Chapter 2.

They found that high goal congruence between the CEO and VCs are associated with less interaction in the VC–CEO dyads. They also found that less VC experience, earlier stage ventures, and greater geographic distance are associated with less VC involvement; however VCs' level of ownership is not related to the amount of interaction.

In sum, this work indicates that VC involvement has more to do with decision-making requirements based on levels of uncertainty as well as agency-driven concerns. Lerner (Chapter 5) also found support for the geographical proximity idea with VCs twice as likely to serve on the board if they are within five miles of the venture. Lerner also found that the number of VCs on the board goes up significantly at the time when there is CEO turnover. Combining the findings of the Lerner (Chapter 5) and Rosenstein (Chapter 1) studies, the occasional dismissal of the venture managers is solid evidence of the ongoing activity of VCs in monitoring and protecting their investments after initial funding has been made.

Mitchell, Reid and Terry (1995) and Sweeting and Wong (Chapter 6) push the common boundaries of VC involvement. In again taking an agency perspective, Mitchell and colleagues provide an interesting study that examines in detail the accounting information and systems adopted by VCs in monitoring investees. In essence, they find that the information needs of VCs extend well beyond those generated by conventional accounting statements. Despite more detailed access, they find that information asymmetries still exist. In the case analysis conducted by Sweeting and Wong, they find that VCs sometimes take a 'hands-off' approach to overseeing their investments and structure their deals in a way that is compatible with this approach.

VC Firm Competencies

As noted above, Rosenstein *et al.* (Chapter 3) draw attention to the top 20 VC firms. Some VC firms appear to be better at monitoring and interacting with their funded ventures than others. While little or no theory has been introduced to explain why this might be the case, it would appear that resource-based theory could better guide further inquiry here. Resource-based theory focuses on a firm's idiosyncratic, costly to copy knowledge, or competence, whose exploitation may give it a competitive advantage (Barney, 1991; Wernerfelt, 1984). The developing consensus is that resources that are unique to a firm can lead to a competitive advantage for the firm that possesses such resources. Instead of debating whether VCs add value to their funded firms with their non-financial contributions, resource-based logic would suggest that the unique resources that make up the individual VC firm represent the potential means for adding value to the ventures in which they invest. That is, extending their competencies would be most highly valuable for adding value to the entrepreneurial ventures in which they invest. After assessing its stock of knowledge, venture capital firm partners could evaluate their existing industry and utilize their competencies and leverage them by specializing in certain types of deals. If an enterprise is selected for funding by a VC firm with both industry and deal competencies, the judgment investment decision is probably based on the possession of a firm's unique knowledge – knowledge that on average has been shown to be positively related to the eventual success of its investments.

Volume III, Part II   Post-Investment Involvement: Adding Value

The concept of venture capitalist value-added is a common one in the literature yet there is not a clear, universal definition. In the broadest terms, some use it to mean any value brought by venture capital firms beyond the value of the funds invested; such value might include greater visibility and legitimation of the venture as well as all the direct assistance, advice and expertise provided by the venture capital firm. However, most intend just the latter part of the foregoing definition: value created through the assistance, expertise, and advice offered by the venture capital firm during the post-investment phase of the relationship. Following in the tradition of MacMillan *et al.* in Chapter 2 and Sapienza and Timmons (1989), managerial literature has focused on the activities and roles through which venture capitalists add value to their portfolio companies during the period in which they hold equity in the ventures.

Gomez-Mejia, Balkin and Welbourne (Chapter 7) show that VCs are deeply involved in establishing policies and monitoring managerial activities in high-technology firms. The extent of their influence is moderated by such factors as stage in the organizational life cycle, size of the capital firm, whether or not the VC is the lead investor, perceived venture performance, and background of the entrepreneur. These results are highly consistent with other work on venture capitalist involvement. Gomez-Mejia *et al.* also found that CEOs view the VC's influence as positive in terms of financial concerns and boundary spanning activities. However, they found that VCs' involvement in internal management issues is generally seen as negative. They conclude that CEOs and VCs appear to hold opposite views about VCs' contributions to the internal management of the firm.

Ehrlich *et al.* (Chapter 8), also studying primarily high-technology investments, compared how initial relationships are established and maintained for venture capitalists versus private investors. They concluded that the type of investor is as important, if not more important, than the amount of money received in determining the nature of the assistance provided. In comparison to those that received venture capital, those who had private investors desired more involvement on the part of the investor. For example, venture capitalists provided more help in selecting the venture's management team. However, entrepreneurs acknowledged that private investors tended to provide greater reporting and operational flexibility. These reflections are consistent with the Gomez-Mejia *et al.* chapter, and they foreshadow the later work of Busenitz *et al.* (Part IV, Chapter 17, see below) who sought to understand factors relating to entrepreneurs' receptivity to investors' advice.

Chapter 9 by Sapienza, Manigart and Vermeir extends Sapienza's earlier (1989; 1992) work on venture capitalist involvement and value-added in post-investment activities. Beyond the direct findings, perhaps what is most interesting about this work is what it reveals about the US venture capitalist practices in comparison to those in the European market. First, the greater tendency for earlier stage investing in the US is noteworthy because of the significant differences in demands this choice puts on VCs. Clearly, greater uncertainty, risk, and potential return accompany this choice. VCs in the UK put in effort at a rate more similar to US VCs than to their European counterparts; this is interesting, given that later stage investing in the UK is comparable to elsewhere in Europe. Despite the differences in amount of time and face-to-face interaction across these countries, the relative importance of VCs' roles follow the same pattern in all four markets: strategic roles (including sounding board, strategic and financial advice) are most important; interpersonal roles (coaching and being a friend or confidant) are next; and networking roles (recruiting managers and supplying contacts with customers, suppliers, and the like) are third in importance. In the Netherlands and France the interpersonal roles are seen as just slightly more important than the networking roles; in the US and the UK, the interpersonal roles approach the strategic roles in perceived importance. These results, later replicated in Asia, support Sapienza's (1992) contention that the social aspect of VC work had previously been undervalued.

Gifford's theoretical article (Chapter 10) elegantly models much of what has been empirically recognized in the literature, and also introduces an interesting twist to the agency view of the venture capital process. Specifically, the increasing drift of the venture capital industry toward larger and later stage funds is viewed as the product of the dual agency role of the venture capitalist as general partner. In Chapter 10, venture capitalists are assumed to add value to funded ventures by allocating time and attention to them; similarly, they are assumed to make better investments for limited partners by devoting more time to searching and evaluating opportunities. These conditions lead to an inevitable trade-off in attention. Venture capitalists cannot maximize both, but by appropriately suboptimizing in each they can maximize the total profits of all ventures. This analysis also shows why venture capitalists may prefer to exit ventures before maximizing the value of those individual ventures but to the benefit of the overall portfolio and why venture capitalists are likely to prefer more mature investments than would the limited partners. An interesting point that Gifford makes is that her VC-as-agent model supports identical outcomes to the more popular VC-as-principal models. The work contributes to the value-added literature not by arguing for or demonstrating the value-added of venture capital but by showing the implications of value-added created through effort: effort must be allocated appropriately between venture assistance and new opportunity search to maximize the overall value of the portfolio.

Volume III, Part III   Post-Investment Involvement: Intervention and Problem Cases

Surprisingly few studies have been conducted about failed or failing venture capital investments. Most of those that study difficulties within failing ventures, like the studies in this section of our anthology, focus on antecedents, consequences, and roles of venture capitalists in managerial venture team dismissal. VCs tend to attribute venture failure to managerial problems, and their most powerful remedy is dismissal. The works in other parts of this anthology that focus on selection criteria, selection processes, and cognitive biases and limitations of venture capitalists look at the other side of the coin, that is, how may venture capitalists pick better managers? A follow-on to that question is implicitly a topic of several sections of this volume: once selected, how may VCs better develop their managers during the post-investment period? Three of the four studies below focus on dismissal; only the first study below looks at alternative routes to dealing with venture problems.

Ruhnka, Feldman and Dean (Chapter 11) conducted a novel study that, unlike most others, focuses on the large body of VC investments that are not failing but do not meet target returns. Such firms are colorfully known in the industry as 'the living dead' and comprise a larger proportion of all portfolio companies than any other. Estimates vary, but most estimates tend to hover around a two-six-two rule. That is, out of every ten investments, two will succeed in a big way, six will survive but fall well short of targets (these are the living dead), and two will fail outright. The Ruhnka *et al.* study set out to provide some insight into this important group of investments and into how VCs can deal with them. Their research shows that VCs attribute their problems to deficiencies in management, in markets slow to develop, in missed opportunities, and in unexpected competition. These views echo some of those observed in Gorman and Sahlman (Volume I, Chapter 3) on outright failures, especially if managers should be held accountable for missed opportunities and misjudged competition. The onset of disappointing performance appears to occur during the stage of rapid push for growth and market share. Interestingly, if industry statistics are correct, VCs in this study appeared to be perhaps over-optimistic about the prospects for salvaging value out of their living dead. Most sought to sell off these investments, usually after attempting a turnaround. Given the proportion of venture capital investments represented by 'the living dead', this would appear to be a particularly fruitful area for further study.

Fiet *et al.* (Chapter 12) examine the antecedents of VC initiatives to dismiss members of the entrepreneurial team. Gorman and Sahlman (Volume I, Chapter 3) and Ruhnka *et al.* (Chapter 11) show that it is likely that VCs may be quite often tempted to resort to this rather drastic means of dealing with disappointing performance. Fiet *et al.* indicate that at least one member of the entrepreneurial management team was replaced in 35 per cent of the ventures they studied. In order to minimize such disruption, VCs can include contractual covenants that attempt to align interests or minimize the likelihood of dismissal. They found that provisions limiting salaries paid to managers were related to fewer dismissals. This suggests that the use of contractual covenants can effectively align a new venture top management team's financial incentives with those of the VC and the board of directors. However, actual dismissal covenants were found to be an ineffective means of preventing dismissal. The overall size of the board was also negatively related to the probability of entrepreneur dismissal; the number of VC board members is associated with the greater probability of dismissal.

Bruton, Fried and Hisrich (Chapter 13) fill a much-needed gap by examining what specific failings appear most related to dismissal. It has been a long-acknowledged fact that VCs place great stock in the importance of the quality of the venture's entrepreneurial leadership (e.g., Tyebjee and Bruno, Volume I, Chapter 1; MacMillan *et al.*, Volume II, Chapter 1; Muzyka *et al.*, Volume II, Chapter 5). Gorman and Sahlman (Volume I, Chapter 3) also noted that VCs overwhelmingly attribute venture failure to managerial incompetence. Yet few studies have connected the dots to examine exactly what types of failings most lead VCs to push for new leadership in their investments. Bruton *et al.* address this issue by examining the determinants of VCs' decisions to seek dismissal. However, they go a step further to examine whether VCs believe that such replacements make a significant and positive difference in the fate of the venture. Bruton *et al.* find that VCs see the strategic activities as most crucial in dismissal decisions, whereas more operational types of failings are more easily overlooked. Further, they show that VCs believe that the replacements have a significant net positive effect on performance. The absence of objective performance data and the impossibility of examining this question in a controlled experimental manner make it difficult to assess whether VCs' perceptions are accurate. Nonetheless, the fact that VCs strongly believe that dismissal can have a strong positive influence has significant practical implications for entrepreneurs.

Zacharakis, Meyer and DeCastro (Chapter 14) used three unique approaches to examining investors' attributions of venture failure. First, Zacharakis *et al.* employed in depth interviews rather than questionnaires to collect attributions of failure. Second, they collected the impressions of both entrepreneurs and VCs; for five of the eight entrepreneurs interviewed, the VCs also were interviewed. Third, they collected attributions of entrepreneurs and VCs not only about their own failed ventures but also on *other similar failed ventures*. Contrary to all prior research, the four VCs in their sample (one responded on two ventures) attributed a greater proportion of the blame for their failed investments to market conditions rather than to management failings. Perhaps contributing to the unexpected external attributions of VCs may be the fact that the failures occurred during the very difficult market conditions of the early 1990s. However, the small and narrow sample (eight computer firms funded in Colorado) makes generalization difficult. Entrepreneurs, contrary to the authors' expectations, more frequently mentioned their own internal failings than external conditions as causes for poor performance; however, entrepreneurs blamed management inadequacy for other similar ventures' failures to an even greater extent than they did their own. An important issue raised by Zacharakis *et al.* is that the external attributions made by VCs in this study may indicate a recognition of the responsibility that VCs have in selecting, shaping and aiding the managers of their investments.

Volume III, Part IV   Investor–Entrepreneur Interactions: Relational Perspectives

The personal interaction between VCs and the entrepreneurs that they fund is no doubt an important relationship. Some of the early research efforts by Gorman and Sahlman (Volume I, Chapter 3) established that VCs spend approximately half of their time with the entrepreneurs that they fund. While the level of involvement obviously differs from VC to VC (MacMillan *et al.*, Volume III, Chapter 2), the interest around the interaction between the VC and those that they fund continues to grow. Gorman and Sahlman refer to this relationship as a partnership and Sapienza (1992) and Bygrave and Timmons (1992) talk about VCs being a sounding board for the entrepreneurs they fund to discuss the various strategic issues facing the venture.

Since some of the early findings about the involvement of VCs with the entrepreneurs that they fund, several important attempts have been made to develop more systematic theory about this important relationship. Sapienza and Korsgaard (Chapter 15) introduced the social exchange framework into the literature to explain the behavior and decision-making preferences of VCs. This article is the first explicitly to theorize and model the impact of the non-economic considerations on investment decisions and progress of ventures. From a procedural justice perspective, they found that the frequency and timeliness of feedback from entrepreneurs significantly influences how VCs perceive and support them. Specifically, timely feedback increases VCs' trust and their commitment to entrepreneurs. This feedback also decreases monitoring; and may have a partial evidence for a positive affect on re-investment decisions. The amount of influence VCs have on entrepreneurs also increases trust and commitment.

In assuming that social context influences economic exchanges, Cable and Shane (Chapter 16) introduce a prisoner's dilemma logic to the VC–entrepreneur decision to cooperate. Going beyond the unitary perspective of agency theory, they view VCs as occupying both principal and agent roles. Consistent with economic perspectives, the general motivations of the two parties are assumed to be identically self-interested. However, one of the key contributions of this work is to highlight which factors are expected to be more salient to the entrepreneur and when certain factors will have their greatest influence on VC and entrepreneur decisions to cooperate with each other or defect.

Adding to the work by Sapienza and Korsgaard (Chapter 15), that procedural justice arguments may have important implications for the VC–entrepreneurship relationship, Busenitz *et al.* (Chapter 17) examined contractual factors (among other things) that may impact perceptions of fairness in the VC–entrepreneur relationship. If the VC–entrepreneur relationship is so critical to a venture and if the dynamics of social exchange have an important effect on the success of a venture, then perceptions of fairness within the VC–entrepreneur relationship may be critical. If entrepreneurs judge their VCs to be unfair, collaborative discussions between them are much less likely to occur. Findings from this study suggest that some governance mechanisms put in place at the time of funding and the background of the new venture team do frame the perceived sense of fairness in the VC–entrepreneur relationship.

In an overall sense, initial indications are that social exchange dynamics have important implications for economic exchange. An early indication from this research is that the VC–entrepreneur relationship is a very rich context in which to examine such phenomena further. If process issues are a non-trivial element within the VC–entrepreneur relationship (and as well as other intraorganizational relationships), then they deserve closer examination. Stated differently, a 'hands-on' approach by VCs will not in and of itself lead to superior returns. How that involvement is conducted and the development of that relationship is highly likely to be critical. The potential benefits of cooperative relationships are frequently being discussed as critical and strategic for today's business environment. However, numerous difficulties arise in managing both the complexities involved and the need to bring together the varied cultures of two or more organizations.

The VC literature frequently alludes to the need for a quality management team with the implications that the quality of the entrepreneurial team is the most important element of venture success. If a given VC is consistently able to fund 'A'-level management teams with solid cognitive capabilities and diversity, then perhaps VCs need to be particularly careful with their interactions with entrepreneurs. Over-involvement by VCs is likely to be perceived as meddling by the entrepreneurs and perhaps interpreted as VCs attempting to rule with a heavy hand. However, asking questions and playing the devil's advocate while simultaneously maintaining respect for the quality of the entrepreneurial team is likely to have positive results. A challenge for VCs may be to continue to express confidence in the entrepreneurial team, assuming that it is of high quality, after the initial honeymoon is over. If VCs fund an 'A'-level entrepreneurial team, they should continue to be treated with great fairness and respect.

Volume III, Part V   Harvesting and Exits

Venture capital firms can realize their gains from investments in several ways. IPOs are typically viewed as the most attractive exit route and have received the greatest amount of research attention. There is evidence that unseasoned IPOs generally result in significant underpricing. Several arguments have been used to explain underpricing, although the principal rationale is signaling theory. In order to address the asymmetric information problems associated with firms coming to market where issuers know more about the firm than do investors, there is a need to send signals to potential investors concerning the future prospects of these firms. Studies have examined various measures of signals, including the amount of retained equity by entrepreneurs, the prestige of underwriters, the reputation of auditors, the number of risk factors identified in the prospectus, the age and size of the firm, the uses to which proceeds will be put, the amount of proceeds raised, the offer price, and the presence of a venture capital investor. The presence of a venture capital investor may help to reduce uncertainty for potential investors by signaling that the IPO firm has good performance prospects.

Megginson and Weiss (Chapter 18) show that VC backing reduces the mean and median degree of IPO underpricing and that such backing significantly reduces the underwriting spread charged by the investment banker handling the issue. They also found that VC-backed issuers are able to attract more prestigious auditors and underwriters than non-VC-backed issuers. VC-backed firms elicit greater interest from institutional investors during the IPO and are able to go public at a younger age than other firms.

Lerner (Chapter 21) shows that seasoned venture capital firms appear to be particularly good at taking companies public near market peaks but rely on private financings when valuations are lower. Venture capital firms can influence the timing of the IPO decision by virtue of their board seats as well as their more informal role as advisors to management. Lerner builds on the notion that venture capital firms provide funds in stages to firms in the biotechnology sector and that each funding round presents an explicit choice to go public or remain private.

Gompers' highly interesting article (Chapter 22) provides a novel analysis of the different behavior of experienced and less experienced VC firms. This chapter provides an alternative perspective on Lerner's arguments. The article develops a model of VC grandstanding which demonstrates that new VC firms are willing to incur costs by taking companies public earlier than would maximize returns on those individual companies and earlier than would established VC firms. This behavior acts as a signal to the market that the VC has the necessary skills to select investments that have a high probability of going public and hence of generating greater returns. This action is crucial as only good performers will be able to raise new funds. Older VC firms with established reputations do not need to signal as investors have already evaluated their performance.

Brav and Gompers (Chapter 20) is a major study that first identifies the sources of the general long-run underperformance of IPOs documented in earlier studies. They find that VC-backed IPOs outperform non-VC-backed IPOs using equal weighted returns and that VC-backed firms do not significantly underperform benchmark market returns using factor asset pricing models but non-VC-backed IPOs do. Ritter and Welch (2002) caution, however, that long-run studies of the extent of underpricing in particular are highly sensitive to the methodology and the time period selected.

Cyr *et al.* (Chapter 19) provide an explanation for the returns accruing to IPO firms based on the key premise that VCs prefer complete well-balanced founding teams and that superior performance of IPO firms is likely to accrue to such top management teams. Their findings suggest that VC-backed firms are more likely to have human resource (HR) vice presidents (VP) than non-VC-backed firms. Also risk does appear to moderate the likelihood of having a VP of finance – firms with higher levels of risk were more likely to have a VP of HR. They did not find any evidence that the combination of VC backing and the presence of a VP of HR leads to higher performance. Both the direct and interaction effects were non-significant.

A meta-analysis of short-run IPO underpricing that aggregates the findings from a number of studies finds that, in contrast to expectations, venture-backed IPOs were positively associated with underpricing (Daily *et al.*, 2002). However, there is also evidence that the interaction of top venture capital firms and top underwriters has a stronger impact on IPO firm market capitalization than the impact of venture capital backing in isolation (Lange *et al.*, 2001).

Bradley *et al.* (2001) examine the effect on underperformance of IPOs after the end of the lock-up period following flotation and find that the negative effect is more pronounced for venture-backed IPOs. They attribute this effect to VCs distributing shares to their limited partners on expiry of the lock-up and limited partners immediately selling the shares. There is also evidence that general partners (i.e., VCs and leveraged buy-out financiers) relinquish control through open market sales rather than selling a strategic block, suggesting that corporate control considerations related to blockholders may not be of primary importance for these companies (Ritter and Welch, 2002).

Few studies have examined the operating performance of VC-backed firms but Jain and Kini (1995) show that VC-backed IPOs have superior post-issue operating performance compared to non-VC-backed IPOs over a three-year post-issue period. They also show that the extent of superior performance is positively associated with the quality of venture capitalists' monitoring. Further research might usefully examine the post-IPO influence of VCs up to and after the end of the lock-up period. Although not a rigorous empirical study, Chapter 25 by Petty *et al.* is one of the first to draw attention to a range of exit options that are generally more common than IPOs for harvesting venture capital investments. Importantly, they also emphasize the importance of the role of the entrepreneur in the timing and nature of the harvesting decisions, not just financial investors.

In the US, the leveraged and management buy-out market has traditionally been viewed as quite separate from the venture capital market. In Europe, management buy-outs (MBOs) are a major part of the venture capital market. Management buy-outs are now becoming a worldwide phenomenon with private equity firms, some of which may also invest in traditional early stage equity financing, playing a key role in their investment. Wright *et al.* (Chapter 23) provide a comparative study of the factors influencing the longevity of venture-backed MBOs in four European countries, showing how differences between markets contribute to different patterns and rates of exit. The chapter develops a contingency model concerning the factors influencing buy-out longevity. In a companion article, Wright *et al.* (Chapter 24) provide an important extension of the debate about the longevity of VC investments and MBOs in particular by examining the whole spectrum of buy-outs rather than just a partial view focused on large transactions and examine the factors that contribute to longevity.

Wright, Robbie and Ennew (Chapter 26) provide insights into what happens after venture capital firms exit from an investment. Their novel study for the first time explicitly examines the links between venture capital firms and entrepreneurs with whom they recontract and hence introduces a dynamic aspect to the relationship between venture capital firms and entrepreneurs. This research keys into the growing interest regarding habitual entrepreneurs (Westhead and Wright, 1998) and addresses important issues concerning whether it is beneficial for venture capital firms to continue to invest in entrepreneurs with whom they have had successful relationships in the past rather than starting again with an unknown entrepreneur. This study also raises interesting questions regarding the impact of learning on the part of the entrepreneur regarding the contracting process that may have implications for the timing and nature of returns to venture capital investors.

Note

1. The editors contributed equally to this Introduction and their names are listed in reverse alphabetical order.

References

Barney, J.B. (1991), 'Firm resources and sustained competitive advantage', *Journal of Management*, **17**, 99–120.

Berger, A.N. and Udell, G.F. (1998), 'The economics of small business finance: the roles of private equity and debt markets in the financial growth cycle', *Journal of Banking and Finance*, **22**, 613–73.

Bradley, D., Jordan, B., Roten, I. and Yi, H.-C. (2001), 'Venture capital and IPO lock-up expirations: an empirical analysis', *Journal of Financial Research*, **42**, 465–92.

Brander, J.A., Amit, R. and Antweiler, W. (2002), 'Venture capital syndication: improved venture selection versus the value-added hypothesis', *Journal of Economics and Management Strategy*, **11** (3), 423–52.

Bruton, G., Ahlstrom, D. and Singh, K. (2002), 'The impact of the institutional environment on the venture capital industry in Singapore', *Venture Capital*, **4** (3), 197–218.

Bygrave, W. and Timmons, J. (1992), *Venture Capital at the Crossroads*, Boston: Harvard Business School Press.

Chan, Y., Siegel, D. and Thakor, A. (1990), 'Learning, corporate control and performance requirements in venture capital contracts', *Journal of Finance*, **38** (5), 1543–68.

Chiplin, B., Robbie, K. and Wright, M. (1997), 'The syndication of venture capital deals: buy-outs and buy-ins'. In Reynolds, P., Bygrave, W. *et al.* (eds), *Frontiers of Entrepreneurship Research*, Wellesley, MA: Babson College.

Cooper, I. and Carleton, C. (1979), 'Dynamics of borrower–lender interaction: partitioning final payoff in venture capital finance', *Journal of Finance*, **34** (2), 517–29.

Cumming, D.J. (2002), The Determinants of Venture Capital Portfolio Size: Empirical Evidence. Working paper, University of Alberta School of Business.

Daily, C., Certo, S., Dalton, D. and Roengpitya, R. (2002), IPO Underpricing: A Meta-Analysis and Research Synthesis. Paper presented at the Strategic Management Society Annual Conference, Paris.

Florida, R. and Kenney, M. (1988), 'Venture capital and high technology entrepreneurship', *Journal of Business Venturing*, **3** (4), 301–19.

Fried, V.H. and Hisrich, R.D. (1995), 'The venture capitalist: a relationship investor', *California Management Review*, **37**, 101–13.

Gompers, P. and Lerner, J. (1999), *The Venture Capital Cycle*, Cambridge, MA: MIT Press.

Hall, J. and Hofer, C.W. (1993), 'Venture capitalists' decision criteria in new venture evaluation', *Journal of Business Venturing*, **8**, 25–42.

Hoskisson, R.E., Hitt, M.A., Johnson, R.A. and Grossman, W. (2002), 'Conflicting voices: the effects of institutional ownership heterogeneity and internal governance on corporate innovation strategies', *Academy of Management Journal*, **45**, 697–716.

Hurry, D., Miller, A. and Bowman, E. (1992), 'Calls on high-technology: Japanese exploration of venture capital investments in the US', *Strategic Management Journal*, **13**, 85–101.

Jääskeläinen, M., Maula, M. and Seppä, T. (2002), The Optimal Portfolio of Start-Up Firms in Venture Capital Finance: The Moderating Effect of Syndication and an Empirical Test. Paper presented at the Babson Kaufmann Entrepreneurship Conference 2002, Boulder.

Jain, B. and Kini, O. (1995), 'Venture capitalist participation and the post-issue operating performance of IPO firms', *Managerial and Decision Economics*, **16** (6), 593–606.

Kaplan, S. and Strömberg, P. (2001), 'Venture capitalists as principals: contracting, screening and monitoring', *American Economic Review*, **91** (2), 426–30.

Kenney, M. and von Burg, U. (1999), 'Technology, entrepreneurship, and path dependency: industrial clustering in silicon valley and route 128', *Industrial and Corporate Change*, **8** (1), 67–103.

Lange, J., Bygrave, W., Nishimoto, S., Roedel, J. and Stock, W. (2001), 'Smart money? The impact of having top venture capital investors and underwriters backing a venture', *Venture Capital*, **3**, 309–26.

La Porta, R., Lopez-De-Silanes, F., Shleifer, A. and Vishny, R. (1998), 'Law and finance', *Journal of Political Economy*, **106**, 1113–55.

Lerner, J. (1999), 'The Government as venture capitalist: the long-run impact of the SBIR Program', *Journal of Business*, **72** (3), 285–318.

Lockett, A. and Wright, M. (2001), 'The syndication of venture capital investments', *OMEGA: The International Journal of Management Science*, **29**, 375–90.

Lockett, A. and Wright, M. (2002), 'Venture capital in Asia and the Pacific Rim', *Venture Capital*, **4** (3), 183–96.

Lockett, A., Murray, G. and Wright, M. (2002), 'Do UK venture capitalists still have a bias against investment in new technology firms?', *Research Policy*, **31**, 1009–30.

Manigart, S., Lockett, A., Mueleman, M., Wright, M., Landstrom, H., Bruining, H., Desbrières, P. and Hommel, U. (2002), Why do European Venture Capital Companies Syndicate? Paper presented at Babson-Kaufmann Entrepreneurship Conference, Boulder.

Mitchell, F., Reid, G. and Terry, N. (1995), 'Post investment demand for accounting information by venture capitalists', *Accounting and Business Research*, **25**, 186–96.

Nye, D. and Wasserman, N. (1999), 'Patterns of VC evolution: comparing the Israeli and Indian venture capital industries', *Journal of Private Equity*, **3** (1), 26–48.

Ritter, J. and Welch, I. (2002), 'A review of IPO activity, pricing and allocations', *Journal of Finance*, **57** (4), 1795–828.

Robinson, R.B., Jr. (1987), 'Emerging strategies in the venture capital industry', *Journal of Business Venturing*, **2**, 53–77.

Sandberg, W.A. and Hofer, C.W. (1987), 'Improving new venture performance: the role of strategy, industry structure and the entrepreneur', *Journal of Business Venturing*, **2** (3), 215–29.

Sapienza, H.J. (1989), Variations in Venture Capitalist–Entrepreneur Interactions: Antecedents and Consequences. Unpublished Doctoral Dissertation, University of Maryland.

Sapienza, H.J. (1992), 'When do venture capitalists add value?', *Journal of Business Venturing*, **7**, 9–27.

Sapienza, H.J. and Timmons, J.A. (1989), 'The roles of venture capitalists in new ventures: what determines their importance?', *Best Paper Proceedings, Academy of Management*, 74–8.

Seppä, T. and Jääskeläinen, M. (2002), How the Rich Become Richer in Venture Capital: Firm Performance and Positions in Syndication Networks. Paper presented at the Babson Kaufmann Entrepreneurship Conference 2002, Boulder.

Sorenson, O. and Stuart, T. (2001), 'Syndication networks and the spatial distribution of venture capital investments', *American Journal of Sociology*, **106**, 1546–88.

Wernerfelt, B.A (1984), 'Resource-based view of the firm', *Strategic Management Journal*, **5**, 171–80.

Westhead, P. and Wright, M. (1998), 'Novice, portfolio and serial founders: are they different?', *Journal of Business Venturing*, **13** (3), 173–204.

Wright, M. and Robbie, K. (1998), 'Venture capital and private equity: A review and synthesis', *Journal of Business, Finance and Accounting*, **25** (5–6), 521–70.

Wright, M. and Lockett, A. (2004), 'The structure and management of alliances: syndication in venture capital investments', *Journal of Management Studies*, forthcoming.

Wright, M., Lockett, A. and Pruthi, S. (2002), 'Internationalization of western venture capitalists into emerging markets: risk assessment and information in India', *Small Business Economics*, **19** (1), 13–29.

Zacharakis, A. (2002), Business Risk, Investment Risk, and Syndication of Venture Capital Deals. Paper presented at the August 2002 Academy of Management Meeting, Denver.

Part I
Systemic Issues: Early Views

[1]

MANAGEMENT SCIENCE
Vol. 30, No. 9, September 1984

A MODEL OF VENTURE CAPITALIST
INVESTMENT ACTIVITY*

TYZOON T. TYEBJEE AND ALBERT V. BRUNO

School of Business, University of Santa Clara, Santa Clara, California 95053

The paper describes the activities of venture capitalists as an orderly process involving five sequential steps. These are (1) Deal Origination: The processes by which deals enter into consideration as investment prospects, (2) Deal Screening: A delineation of key policy variables which delimit investment prospects to a manageable few for in-depth evaluation, (3) Deal Evaluation: The assessment of perceived risk and expected return on the basis of a weighting of several characteristics of the prospective venture and the decision whether or not to invest as determined by the relative levels of perceived risk and expected return, (4) Deal Structuring: The negotiation of the price of the deal, namely the equity relinquished to the investor, and the covenants which limit the risk of the investor, (5) Post-Investment Activities: The assistance to the venture in the areas of recruiting key executives, strategic planning, locating expansion financing, and orchestrating a merger, acquisition or public offering. 41 venture capitalists provided data on a total of 90 deals which had received serious consideration in their firms. The questionnaire measured the mechanism of initial contact between venture capitalist and entrepreneur, the venture's industry, the stage of financing and product development, ratings of the venture on 23 characteristics, an assessment of the potential return and perceived risk, and the decision vis-à-vis whether to invest. The modal venture represented in the database was a start-up in the electronics industry with a production capability in place and seeking $1 million (median) in outside financing. There is a high degree of cross-referrals between venture capitalists, particularly for the purposes of locating co-investors. Factor analysis reduced the 23 characteristics of the deal to five underlying dimensions namely (1) Market Attractiveness (size, growth, and access to customers), (2) Product Differentiation (uniqueness, patents, technical edge, profit margin), (3) Managerial Capabilities (skills in marketing, management, finance and the references of the entrepreneur), (4) Environmental Threat Resistance (technology life cycle, barriers to competitive entry, insensitivity to business cycles and down-side risk protection), (5) Cash-Out Potential (future opportunities to realize capital gains by merger, acquisition or public offering). The results of regression analyses showed expected return to be determined by Market Attractiveness and Product Differentiation ($R2 = 0.22$). Perceived risk is determined by Managerial Capabilities and Environmental Threat Resistance ($R2 = 0.33$). Finally, a discriminant analysis correctly predicted, in 89.4% of the cases, whether or not a venture capitalist was willing to commit funds to the deal on the basis of the expected return and perceived risk. The reactions of seven venture capitalists who reviewed the model's specification were used to test its validity.
(FINANCE—INVESTMENT CRITERIA; FINANCIAL INSTITUTIONS—INVESTMENT; RESEARCH AND DEVELOPMENT—PROJECT SELECTION; STATISTICS—REGRESSION—VENTURE CAPITAL)

Introduction

Venture capital has become an increasingly important source of financing for new companies, particularly when such companies are operating on the frontier of emerging technologies and markets. It plays an essential role in the entrepreneurial process. The purpose of this paper is to model the deal flow in a venture capital firm, namely the stages in the consideration, scrutiny and disposition of venture investment deals. The theory of equity markets is well developed in finance; it will not be reviewed here. These theories are typically oriented toward equity financing in publicly traded companies. Venture capital investments, however, differ in several important aspects (Poindexter 1976). First, venture capital is usually invested in new firms which have very little performance history. As a result, the investor cannot rely on historical performance data, as in the case of the stock market. Second, the investment is typically in small firms and the nature of the investor and investee relationship involves a higher degree of direct involvement as

*Accepted by Burton V. Dean; received June 13, 1983. This paper has been with the authors 1 month for 1 revision.

0025-1909/84/3009/1051$01.25

compared to the relatively inactive role of investors in publicly traded companies. Third, venture capital investments are illiquid in the short term because of the lack of efficient capital markets for equity shares of privately held companies. Long horizons of product and market development make valuation difficult. Moreover, the legal restrictions that apply to the resale of such investments lock the investor in for a certain period. Fourth, when a venture capitalist invests in a new startup, it is usually with the implicit realization that future rounds of capital infusion may have to be financed before the initial investment can bear fruit (Cooper and Carleton 1979).

The lack of capital markets for the financial instruments of small, new companies introduces considerable problems in studying venture capital investments within the paradigm of the capital asset pricing model. The absence of a clearing price determined by the market makes the valuation of an investment vulnerable to the subjective assessment procedures of the analyst. One study of 29 SBIC funds found that venture capital funds enjoy a rate of return 63% higher than Standard & Poor's market index returns. This premium, however, is offset by a higher risk; the variability of the firm's returns were higher than that of the market index return (Poindexter 1976). Poindexter concludes that venture capital markets are efficient since higher returns are offset by higher risk. Using a considerably different methodology, Charles River Associates (1976) reached the same conclusion.

The efficiency of venture capital markets is a central public policy concern because of the latter's goal of stimulating the flow of funds to new, small companies. However, the efficiency proposition provides little insight into the decision process of venture capitalists, other than the implication that they select investments with potential returns high enough to offset the higher risk. In the next section we develop a descriptive model of the activities or processes involved in managing a venture capital fund. Portions of the model are empirically tested on the basis of interviews with venture capitalists, and analyses of the characteristics and disposition of deals which they had recently considered. This methodology is not without its problems. In the experience of the authors, venture capitalists are reluctant to violate the confidentiality of their investees. Also they are not receptive to highly structured measurement instruments, which are perceived to be time consuming to complete. They view every deal and every venture capital fund to be peculiar to itself, and resist the generalizations which behavioral scientists wish to impose upon them. For this reason, research methodology which relies on the cooperation of venture capitalists in divulging data on their activities is likely to suffer from a high nonresponse bias and criticisms regarding the generalizability of small sample research. It is with this backdrop that we seek to model the activities of venture capitalists.

Model of the Venture Capitalist's Investment Activity

The investment activity of a venture capitalist is modeled as a sequential process involving five steps (see Figure 1). The first step is one of *deal origination* which describes how venture capitalists become cognizant of potential investment activities. The second step is a *screening* process by which venture capitalists seek to concentrate only on a manageable set of potential deals. The *evaluation* step involves an assessment of the potential return and risk of a particular deal. If the outcome of the evaluation process is a favorable one, the venture capitalist enters into a negotiating process with the potential investee so as to *structure the deal* in terms of the amount, form and price of the investment. Once a deal is consummated, the venture capitalist typically has close contact with the venture. These *post-investment activities* include setting up controls to protect the investment, providing consultation to the fledgling management of the venture, and, finally, helping orchestrate the merger, acquisition, or public offering which would create a public market for the investment.

On the basis of several previous studies (Dorsey 1977; Hoffman 1972; Poindexter 1976; Timmons and Gumpert 1982; Wells 1974) we can describe the salient features of each of these steps as follows:

Step 1—Deal Origination. The venture capitalist faces a very poorly defined environment within which to find prospective deals. The typical investment prospect is too small a company to be readily identifiable as a potential candidate. For this reason, we could expect that various intermediaries play an important role in matching venture capital investors with fledgling ventures with cash needs.

Step 2—Screening. Venture capital firms typically have small staffs. As a result, these firms must screen the relatively large number of potential deals available and consequently invest in only a fraction of the deals which come to their attention. Their screening criteria reflect a tendency to limit investments to areas with which the

VENTURE CAPITALIST INVESTMENT ACTIVITY 1053

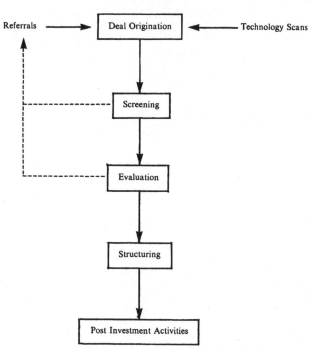

FIGURE 1. Decision Process Model of Venture Capitalist Investment Activity.

venture capitalist is familiar, particularly in terms of the technology, product and market scope of the venture.

Step 3—Evaluation. As noted before, most ventures in search of capital have very little, if any, operating history. The venture capitalist has to rely on a subjective assessment procedure based upon the business plan presented by the venture's management. Venture capitalists do weigh risk and return in their decision whether or not to invest in a particular deal, but few formalize this assessment into a computation of an expected rate of return or determine its sensitivity to future uncertainties. Instead, the evaluation procedure seeks to subjectively assess the venture on a multidimensional set of characteristics. Table 1 shows the characteristics found to be important in previous studies. Not surprisingly, these criteria are similar to those found in several new product evaluation models (Montgomery and Urban 1969; O'Meara 1961; Pessemier 1982). It is interesting to note, however, that none of these criteria reflects how a prospective deal may correlate with one already in the venture capitalist's investment portfolio.

Step 4—Deal Structuring. Once the venture capitalist has decided that a deal is acceptable, the deal will be consummated only if the venture capitalist and the entrepreneur are able to structure a mutually acceptable venture capital investment agreement. From the perspective of the venture capitalist, the agreement serves several purposes. First, it establishes the price of the deal, that is the equity share the entrepreneur will give up in exchange for the venture capital (Golden 1981). Second, it establishes protective covenants which limit capital expenditures and management

1054   TYZOON T. TYEBJEE AND ALBERT V. BRUNO

TABLE 1

Venture Evaluation Criteria

WELLS (1974) Sample: Eight Venture Capital Firms (Personally interviewed)		POINDEXTER(1976) Sample: 97 Venture Capital Firms (Mailed questionnaires)	TYEBJEE & BRUNO (Study I) Sample: 46 Venture Capitalists (Telephone survey, open-ended questions)	
Factor	Average Weight	Investment Criteria by Rank Order Of Importance	Factor	% of Respondents Mentioning
Management Commitment	10.0	1. Quality of Management	1. Management Skills & History	89
Product	8.8	2. Expected Rate of Return	2. Market Size/Growth	50
Market	8.3	3. Expected Risk	3. Rate of Return	46
Marketing Skill	8.2	4. Percentage Equity Share of Venture	4. Market Niche/Position	20
Engineering Skill	7.4	5. Management Stake in Firm	5. Financial History	11
Marketing Plan	7.2	6. Financial Provisions for Investor Rights	6. Venture Location	11
Financial Skill	6.4	7. Venture Development Stage	7. Growth Potential	11
Manufacturing Skill	6.2	8. Restrictive Covenants	8. Barriers to Entry	11
References	5.9	9. Interest or Dividend Rate	9. Size of Investment	9
Other Participants in Deal	5.0	10. Present Capitalization	10. Market/Industry Expertise	7
Industry/Technology	4.2	11. Investor Control	11. Venture Stage	4
Cash-Out Method	2.3	12. Tax Shelter Consideration	12. Stake of Entrepreneur	4

salaries. Covenants also establish the basis under which the venture capitalist can take control of the board, force a change in management or liquidate the investment by forcing a buy-back, a merger, acquisition or public offering even though the venture capitalist holds a minority position. The covenants may also restrict the power of the venture management to dilute the equity of the original investors by raising additional capital elsewhere (Cooper and Carleton 1979; Glassmeyer 1981). Third, through a mechanism known as the earn-out arrangement, where the entrepreneur's equity share is determined by meeting agreed upon performance objectives, the venture capitalist is able to assess the entrepreneur's expectations for the venture (Leland and Pyle 1977; Ross 1977).

Step 5—Post-Investment Activities. Once the deal has been consummated, the role of the venture capitalist expands from investor to collaborator. This new role may be via a formal representation on the board of directors or via informal influence in market, supplier and creditor networks. The intensity of involvement in the venture's operations differs from one venture capitalist to another. However, most of those interviewed agree that it is undesirable for a venture capital company to exert control over the day-to-day operations of the venture. If a financial or managerial crisis occurs, the venture capitalist may intervene and even install a new management team.

Finally, venture capitalists typically want to cash-out their gains five to ten years after initial investments. To this end, they play an active role in directing the company towards merger, acquisition or a public offering. Bruno and Cooper (1982) followed up on 250 startups of the sixties. They found that over half of these had either gone public, or had been merged or acquired.

The post-investment activities of venture capitalists vis-à-vis their portfolio companies have been ignored by the bulk of research on venture capital. In particular, the venture capitalist's decision-making process for second and subsequent rounds of financing for ventures already in his portfolio remains a fertile area of research.

Method

The results of two databases, referred to as Study I and Study II, are presented in the next section. These databases are described briefly below.

Study I

A telephone survey of 46 venture capitalists in California, Massachusetts and Texas. Of these, half were SBIC's. The telephone survey used a structured questionnaire which asked about how ventures are evaluated. The responses were open-ended and their analysis is based upon a post-hoc categorization of responses.

Study II

Venture capital firms listed in Pratt's directory (1981) of venture capital were contacted by mail to solicit their participation in a study of investment decision criteria. The mailing was restricted to the 156 venture capital firms in the states of California, Massachusetts, and Texas as these states account for a major portion of the venture capital industry, particularly as it applies to high technology startups. Forty-one venture capital firms agreed to participate in the study. For nonparticipants, the dominant reason for refusing to participate was the sensitivity of the information we requested. A second reason was the busy schedule of the venture capitalists. Finally, several firms disqualified themselves as participants in the survey as they were either inactive in new investments or only invested in deals put together by others. The 41 cooperating venture capital firms were mailed a structured questionnaire on which to evaluate deals under consideration. We asked that they indicate their decision vis-à-vis investing in that deal. Ninety completed evaluations were returned by the 41 participants, an average of 2.2 deals per participating venture capitalist. The industries represented in the 90 deals in our sample were computers, semiconductors and telecommunications (59.6%), energy (13.5%), consumer goods (10.1%) and miscellaneous industries including transportation, construction and biomedical (16.8%).

A major problem with the methodology used in this study for describing the evaluation step is that it may be biased in favor of the results obtained. In particular, the statistical relationships between subjectively assessed characteristics of deals and the venture capitalist's decision regarding them may reflect a post-hoc rationalization of the decision. To mitigate this problem, the methodology includes a validation component in which the key results described in the next section were presented to 7 venture capitalists and their reactions recorded. The validation component was administered by mail and its outcome is discussed following the next section.

Results

In this section, the results from Studies I and II are discussed within the context of the five-step model developed earlier. While the data and results are largely focused on the deal evaluation step of the model, results for the first two steps are also presented. The last two steps, namely deal structuring and post-investment activities, are not considered in this section, but will be discussed in the validation section which follows.

Step 1—Deal Origination

Potential deals are brought to the attention of venture capitalists from three sources. In Study II, 25.6% of the 90 deals in the sample originated as unsolicited cold calls from entrepreneurs. The typical response of the venture capitalist is to request the inquirer to send in a business plan. The second source is through a referral process. Sixty-five percent of the deals were referred to the venture capitalist. A third of the referrals came from within the venture capital community, 40% were referred by prior investees and personal acquaintances, 10% were referred by banks and the remainder involved an investment broker.

Of those deals referred by other venture capitalists, a substantial number represent the case of the referring venture capitalist acting as a lead investor and seeking the participation of other venture capital funds. This practice, known as a syndication, is becoming more prevalent as venture capital firms seek to diversify their portfolios over a larger number of deals. Syndication offers the capability of adding investments to the portfolio without adding to the administrative burden, the bulk of which is borne by the lead investor.

The third mechanism of deal origination is the active search for deals by the venture capitalist. The venture capitalist sometimes played an active role in pursuing companies at the startup stage or those at the critical point of needing expansion financing. The venture capitalist monitors the environment for such potential candidates through an informal network and attendance at conventions, trade shows and special conferences by groups such as the American Electronics Association. An extreme variant of this active role occurs when the venture capitalist first decides which technology markets he would like to add to his portfolio and uses executive search agencies to locate the management team for the venture. In such cases, the roles of venture capitalist and entrepreneur overlap considerably.

Step 2—Screening

The venture capital firm receives a large number of proposals; far more than they can possibly fund with the size of the staff and portfolio of the typical venture fund. Wells (1974) reports that in seven venture capital funds, the annual number of proposals received ranged between 120 and 1,000, with an average of about 450 per year. Broad screening criteria are used to reduce this set to a more manageable number for more indepth evaluation. The initial screening is based upon four criteria:

(1) *The size of the investment and the investment policy of the venture fund.* The lower limit of this policy is determined by the fact that a venture capital company is run with a lean staff and it cannot afford to spread its portfolio over too many small deals because the subsequent control and consultation demands placed on the venture capitalists are essentially the same regardless of the size of the investment. Brophy (1981) reports that of 73 venture capitalists surveyed in 1979 the average number of deals invested in was 5.6 and the average portfolio size was ten ventures. The upper boundary of the investment policy is determined by the capitalization of the portfolio and the desire to maintain an investment base which is diversified across several ventures. However, the upper limit to the investment policy is relatively flexible because a venture capitalist may consider larger deals with the intent of soliciting the participation of other venture capital funds. In fact, in our research we found that the venture capital community is highly inbred with a substantial amount of participation across funds, leading many entrepreneurs to conclude that the venture capital market involves substantially less competition between suppliers than is indicated by the mere count of number of funds in existence. Brophy (1981) estimates that approximately 80% of the venture capital deals struck in 1980 involved the participation of more than one venture capital fund and about a third of the deals involved five or more participants. Fifty-six percent of the deals analyzed in Study II involved the participation of more than one venture capital fund. In the case of two-thirds of the deals which were given a positive evaluation, the venture capitalist was himself willing to commit less than 75% of the amount requested, with the balance to be raised by inviting the participation of other venture capital funds.

The investment policy, in terms of the maximum and minimum amounts which will be considered, is quite heterogeneous across venture capital firms (Timmons and Gumpert 1982). The dollar amount requested in the 90 deals examined in Study II reflects this diversity. The amounts range from $30,000 to $7,500,000, with the median amount being $1,000,000. About a third of the deals were for less than $500,000 and another third were for amounts in excess of $1,500,000.

(2) *The technology and market sector of the venture.* Of 46 venture capitalists interviewed in Study I, 29 used this screening criterion. The venture capitalist is investing in more than a company. Implicitly, he/she is investing in the future of a particular technology or market. For this reason, the venture capitalist must have some familiarity with the technology or the market of the proposed venture. This leads to an implicit specialization in a few technology markets because of the inability of the venture capital fund's manager to be well-versed across a large number of technologies or markets. Also, venture capitalists tend to favor nascent technology industries over mature technologies, the industrial market over the consumer market, and products over services.

The 90 deals in Study II, which presumably had passed initial screening, demonstrated these preferences. More than three out of four were in technology-intensive industries, only a tenth were in the consumer goods sector, and over 90% were manufacturing companies. Sixty-four percent of the deals were described by the venture capitalist as involving either a new technology or a new application of an existing technology, 18% were described as improvements on current products, and the remaining 18% were described as me-too products.

(3) *Geographic location of the venture.* Of 46 venture capitalists interviewed in Study I, 9 used this screening criterion. When a venture capitalist invests in a company, he expects to meet regularly with the management of the new venture. To maintain travel time and expense at manageable levels, some venture capitalists limit their investment activity to major metropolitan areas with easy access. Sometimes, this screening criterion will be ignored if the venture capitalist can involve the participation of another venture capital fund which is close to the venture's location and which can oversee the venture with greater ease. Though most venture capital companies do not actively pursue a policy of restricting their investment activity to a specific geographic boundary, their portfolios often exhibit this specialization because of a tendency of entrepreneurs to search for capital close to their venture's home where their banking, legal and accountancy contacts are strongest.

(4) *Stage of financing.* Of 46 venture capitalists interviewed in Study I, 22 used this screening criterion. Venture capital infusions into a company occur at several points in the life cycle of the venture. Seed capital refers to funds invested before the venture exists as a formal entity. Venture capitalists rarely invest seed capital and entrepreneurs typically turn to informal sources for this money (Wetzel 1981). Startup capital refers to financing for establishing the operation; subsequent rounds of financing are used for expanding operations. Brophy (1981) reports that of 196 venture investments in 1978, 34.2% were for startups, 40.3% were for first round expansion and 19.4% were for second round expansion (6.1% were unclassified).

In Study II, the 90 deals showed a very similar profile to Brophy's data: 45.6% were startups, 22.2% were first round expansion deals and 21.1% were second round expansion deals. Described in another manner, in the case of 23% of the deals the product was still at the design stage, in the case of another 23% a working prototype had been developed and in the case of the remaining 54% the product was already in production.

These aggregate statistics, however, hide the fact that the risk preferences of venture capital funds differ. As a result, some funds will commit capital to later stage rounds only. Others will not commit to later stage rounds unless they have already invested in the venture in the prior rounds.

Step 3—Evaluation

We asked cooperating venture capitalists to rate several deals which had passed their initial screen and were under serious consideration. The deals were rated on 23 criteria

1058   TYZOON T. TYEBJEE AND ALBERT V. BRUNO

TABLE 2

Factor Structure of Evaluation Criteria

Evaluation Criteria	Factor 1	Factor 2	Factor 3	Factor 4	Factor 5
Management Skills (6.6%)*	0.15	− 0.07	0.85	0.16	0.10
Marketing Skills (8.9%)	0.31	− 0.06	0.80	− 0.07	− 0.03
Financial Skills (6.6%)	− 0.23	− 0.01	0.74	0.16	0.12
References of Entrepreneur (16.7%)	0.24	0.09	0.48	0.16	0.33
Technical Skills (7.8%)	0.11	0.72	0.01	− 0.12	0.27
Profit Margins (13.4%)	0.19	0.62	0.25	− 0.02	− 0.04
Uniqueness of Product (11.1%)	0.14	0.87	− 0.02	0.03	0.06
Patentability of Product (30.0%)	− 0.02	0.67	− 0.31	0.27	0.01
Raw Material Availability (31.1%)	0.12	0.18	− 0.07	0.05	− 0.07
Production Capabilities (30.0%)	0.11	0.11	0.06	0.04	− 0.03
Access to Market (12.3%)	0.66	0.07	0.14	0.13	0.24
Market Need for Product (12.2%)	0.79	0.07	0.00	0.12	0.04
Size of Market (10.0%)	0.84	0.03	0.00	0.10	0.07
Growth Potential of Market (13.3%)	0.66	0.35	0.06	− 0.20	0.20
Freedom from Regulation (16.7%)	0.09	− 0.09	− 0.20	0.07	0.41
Protection from Competitive Entry (12.3%)	− 0.01	0.36	− 0.12	0.77	0.24
Resistance to Economic Cycles (12.2%)	0.28	0.32	0.27	0.59	− 0.38
Protection from Obsolescence (17.8%)	0.10	− 0.19	0.12	0.75	0.17
Protection against Down-side Risk (13.4%)	0.02	− 0.13	0.09	0.70	0.18
Opportunities for Exit (15.6%)	0.28	0.15	0.12	0.24	0.76
Merger/Acquisition Potential (17.8%)	0.12	0.20	0.25	0.12	0.80
Hedge Against Current Investments (53.3%)	—	—	—	—	—
Tax Benefits (34.4%)	—	—	—	—	—
% Variance Explained	22.5	12.9	9.6	8.2	7.2

*Percentage of deals for which evaluation was not reported.

(see Table 2) using a four-point rating scale (Poor = 1, Adequate = 2, Good = 3, Excellent = 4). In addition to rating the venture on the 23 criteria, the participant also rated the venture on overall expected return and risk, respectively. A straightforward measure of expected return proved intractable because in 42% of the cases the venture capitalist was unable to assign a numerical estimate of the expected rate of return. For this reason, expected return was measured on a four-point scale (Low = 1, Moderate = 2, High = 3, Very High = 4). The perceived riskiness of the deal was measured by asking the venture capitalist to assign a subjective probability to the venture being a commercial failure. Finally, the venture capitalists indicated their decision regarding the deal. Of the 90 deals in the sample, 25 were rejected, 43 were found to be acceptable and thus fundable, 18 were pending further investigation, and in the case of 4 deals, the decision was not specified.

Table 2 lists the 23 items which served as the basis for evaluating deals under consideration. The number in parentheses next to each item reports the frequency with which deals received no evaluation at all on each of these criteria. A deal would not be evaluated on a particular criterion if it did not enter the decision-making process. The frequency of missing responses was particularly high in the case of five of the evaluation criteria. The patentability of the product was not evaluated in 30% of the cases. Manufacturing aspects such as raw material availability and production capabilities were not evaluated in almost one-third of the cases. The tax benefits of the investment were not evaluated in 34.4% of the deals. Finally, the extent to which the investment offset or hedged the risk of the existing portfolio was not evaluated in 53.3% of the cases.

Why do these five items sustain such a high nonresponse rate? Though the data themselves do not answer these questions, it is possible to speculate why this occurs. There is a disillusionment with the patent process and many entrepreneurs and venture capitalists feel that the public disclosure of the product design in the patent application leads to more competitive entry rather than less. Venture capitalists generally do not worry about raw material and production capabilities as these are technical problems easily solved if the product and its marketing are viable. Tax benefits are not relevant in evaluating many deals because venture capitalists see their mission as reaping capital gains rather than providing tax shelters for the investors in their fund. Finally, the fact that a deal's relationship to the existing portfolio is not evaluated in more than half the cases is consistent with the results of Study I. Of the 46 venture capitalists interviewed, 28 claimed that they evaluated each deal on its own individual merit. Only one of the interviewees claimed that impact on portfolio risk was formally analyzed.

All the scales, with the exception of the two which had the highest rate of missing data, namely the tax benefits and hedge against current portfolio, were factor analyzed.

The varimax factor loadings are given in Table 2. A five-factor solution explains 60.4% of the variation in the 21 rating items. Adding a sixth factor would have added an incremental 6.3% of the variance explained; however the interpretability of this sixth factor was poor (each factor was interpreted on the basis of the items which load most heavily on it).

Based upon the factor structure in Table 2, we conclude that venture capitalists evaluate potential deals in terms of five basic characteristics. The first characteristic which we labeled *Market Attractiveness* depends upon the size, growth and accessibility of the market and on the existence of a market need. The second characteristic reflects *Product Differentiation* which is determined by the ability of the entrepreneur to apply his technical skills in creating a product which is unique can deter competition through patents and enjoy a high profit margin. The third characteristic reflects the *Managerial Capabilities* of the venture's founders. This capability results from skills in managing several business functional areas and is associated with favorable references given to the entrepreneurs. The fourth factor represents the extent to which the venture is resistant to uncontrollable pressures from the environment. These pressures may result from obsolescence due to changing technology, from sensitivity to economic conditions or from low barriers to entry by competition. This factor was labeled *Environmental Threat Resistance*. The final factor represents the extent to which the venture capitalist feels that the investment can be liquidated or "cashed out" at the appropriate time. This is labeled as *Cash-Out Potential*.

The next step was to profile each deal in terms of the five dimensions. A score was computed for each deal on each factor as an average of the ratings of the items which loaded heavily on the factor.[1] For each factor, a Cronbach alpha was computed as an indication of the reliability of that factor. The Cronbach alpha values are reported on the diagonal of the matrix in Table 3. These range from 0.71 to 0.79. Table 3 also reports the intercorrelation of the factors.

A linear regression model was used to relate each deal's scores on the five dimensions to subjective estimates of its level of expected return and perceived risk, respectively. The expected return was estimated on a four-point scale. Risk was

---

[1]The items used in computing each factor score are those blocked in Table 1, with the exception of "Reference of Entrepreneur" and "Patentability of Product" which were excluded as they lowered the Cronbach alpha reliability.

TABLE 3

Cronbach Reliability and Intercorrelation of Evaluation Factors[1]

	Market Attractiveness	Product Differentiation	Managerial Capabilities	Environmental Threat Resistance	Cash-Out Potential
Market Attractiveness	0.79*	0.35*	0.20*	0.48*	0.39*
Product Differentiation		0.76	0.12	0.33*	0.25*
Managerial Capabilities			0.77	0.18	0.18
Environmental Threat Resistance				0.71	0.26
Cash-Out Potential					0.77[2]

[1] Cronbach alpha reliability is reported on the diagonal. The off-diagonal elements are Pearson correlation coefficients between the factors.

[2] The Cronbach alpha when only two items are used in constructing a scale is equivalent to the Pearson correlation between the two items.

* $p < 0.05$.

estimated in terms of the probability of commercial failure: the higher the probability of failure, the greater the riskiness of the venture.[2] Table 4 reports the results of the two regressions.

The evaluation scores are able to explain 33% of the variance in perceived risk and 22% of the variance in estimated rate of return. The R^2 values associated with the two regressions are significant at the 0.01 level.

Two aspects of the deal's evaluation have a significant impact on the risk associated with the deal. A lack of managerial capabilities significantly increases the perceived risk ($p < 0.05$).The relative magnitudes of the beta coefficients show that managerial capabilities have the strongest effect on reducing the riskiness of the deal and resistance to environmental threats has the next highest effect. Other characteristics of the deal do not influence the perceived risk at a significant level.

Two different aspects of the deal's evaluation influence the expected rate of return. Attractive market conditions have the strongest effect ($p < 0.01$) and a highly differentiated product has the next highest effect ($p < 0.05$). Other characteristics of the deal do not significantly influence the expected return.

Interestingly, the cash-out potential of a venture does not seem to influence either perceived risk or return. This is particularly surprising because without a merger, acquisition or public offering, the investor is severely constrained in realizing any gains.

TABLE 4

Determinants of Risk and Return Assessment

Dependent Variable	Market Attractiveness	Product Differentiation	Managerial Capabilities	Environmental Threat Resistance	Cashout Potential	Adjusted R^2
Risk	− 0.05	− 0.12	− 0.46[a]	− 0.23[b]	0.01	0.33[a]
Return	0.40[a]	0.26[b]	0.03	0.02	− 0.13	0.22[a]

[a] Significant at the 0.01 level.
[b] Significant at the 0.05 level.

[2] The correlation between expected risk and return was −0.13. This relationship is not statistically significant.

In our sample of 90 deals, 43 were endorsed as acceptable investments, 25 were denied funds and the balance were either pending a decision or no decision was specified. Discriminant analysis was used to examine the ability of the perceived risk and return to distinguish between rejected and accepted deals. For this purpose, we analyzed only the 68 deals for which a definite decision was made.

The standardized discrimination function coefficients of the two predictor variables, expected return and perceived risk, are 0.52 and -0.87, respectively. The signs are as expected; namely, a high expected return increases the likelihood that the deal is accepted and a high perceived risk increases its likelihood of being rejected. The fact that the signs of the discriminant coefficients are different, i.e., one is positive whereas the other negative, indicates a trade-off relationship between risk and return, a lower expected return is acceptable if offset by a lower risk.

The predictive ability of the discriminant function can be evaluated in terms of the accuracy with which it can classify deals as accepted or rejected. 68.4% of the deals actually rejected were classified as such and 95.2% of the deals actually accepted were classified as such. Together, this represents 86.9% of the deals being correctly classified. The predictive ability of a discriminant function can be evaluated by comparing the percentage of cases correctly classified against two criteria (Morrison 1969).

Proportional Chance Criterion: $C_{pro} = \alpha^2 + (1 - \alpha)^2$,

Maximum Chance Criterion: $C_{max} = \max(\alpha, 1 - \alpha)$,

where α and $1 - \alpha$ are the proportions in each group.

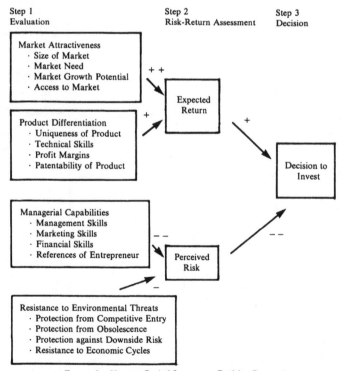

FIGURE 2. Venture Capital Investment Decision Process.*

*The $++$, $+$, $-$, $--$ symbols indicate the direction and magnitude of the parameters describing the relationships of variables.

TABLE 5
Validation of the Model

	Venture Capitalist No. 1	Venture Capitalist No. 2	Venture Capitalist No. 3
DEAL ORIGINATION Most deals are referred to the venture capitalist rather than being cold contacts.	Agrees, but do get many cold contact deals. They tend to be considerably lower quality on average than "referred" deals.	Agrees.	Agrees.
A little less than half of the deals referred to the venture capitalist are referred by a former investee or a personal acquaintance; about a third are referred by other venture capitalists.	Agrees.	Agrees. In this case, "personal acquaintance" includes lawyers, auditors, and investment bankers that are well known to the venture capitalist.	Substantially true. A large number of deals come from personal or professional acquaintances. Number from other venture capitalists seems to be for early stage deals.
Referrals by other venture capitalists are often in the form of an invitation to participate in a deal.	Agrees.	Agrees.	Not true in our experience. Often other venture capitalists invite us to examine a deal in conjunction with themselves. Their hope is to leverage our expertise and perspective in analyzing the deal. Quite often this may lead to a negative investment decision.
Sometimes a venture capitalist may select an industry of interest and set up a venture by searching out a management team. Such cases are rare. The more typical approach is when the venture capitalist lets the deal come to him.	Agrees.	Agrees.	Substantially true. Just as often as selecting an industry, however, we have more typically selected a management team and built a company around them.
DEAL SCREENING The most commonly used screening criteria are the size of investment, the technology and/or market, the stage of financing, and the geographic proximity.	Interesting management team may be most important screening criterion.	Size of investment is not critical in the investment decision. Experience level of management group is the most important criterion.	The size of investment is often used as an excuse for turning a deal down but rarely would stand in the way of our participation if everything else seemed good. Technology and/or market are of interest but more particularly relate to barriers of entry achievable or ultimate size of the company achievable. Stage of financing has been a criteria for us in the past, i.e., we focus on first or second round deals. Geographic location has not been a concern. However, it is often used as an excuse to turn a deal down.
DEAL EVALUATION The decision to invest is based upon the expected return relative to the risk level. The best indicators of return prospect are (a) Market Attractiveness (size & growth potential, market used and ability of the venture to access the market).	Agrees.	The capabilities of the management team is a better indication of expected return than risk level.	Overall, I believe your conclusions are correct. Factored into this, however, are issues such as portfolio diversification, other investors and the size of capitalization required. Ability to develop a particular technology and bring it to market at a particular time represents a substantial risk in many deals. Overall, it is very difficult to be comprehensive and succinct at the same time in stating all of the factors entering into a deal evaluation.
(b) Product Differentiation (uniqueness of product, technical skills, profit margins/value added, patents). The best indicators of the risk level are: (a) Managerial Capabilities (management, marketing, financial skills, entrepreneur's background).	Agrees. Agrees.		
(b) Protection from Uncontrollables (competition, obsolescence, economic cycles).	Agrees.		
DEAL STRUCTURING Convertible preferred stock is the typical form of financing. Equity share required is determined by pay-out expectations relative to rate of return objectives.		Agrees.	With rare exceptions, all of our financing involve convertible preferred stock. Debt is used only in very rare instances for our partnership. A distinction should be made here between SBIC style financings versus more traditional mainstream venture capital financing; SBIC's are more prone to finance with debt instruments.
The entrepreneur's equity is determined by earn-out conditions.	In our experience, earn-out agreements are quite rare and counter productive for both the management team and venture capitalists.		Price is determined largely by the quality of the opportunity as well as comparable opportunities which have recently been financed. In general we receive liquidity either through merger or public stock offering.
The negotiations regarding the earn-out agreement give insight into the entrepreneur's expectations for the venture.			
POST INVESTMENT ACTIVITIES The venture capitalist provides the venture with management guidance and business contacts. A representative of the venture capital firm generally sits on the board. The venture capitalist plays a significant role in orchestrating a merger, acquisition on public offering.	"Management guidance" can cover a lot of sins. Critical input most often comes in the areas of: (1) Recruiting key executive or managers to fill out the team. (2) Acting as a sounding board to CEO on self-evaluation and evaluation of other top management (3) Strategy development.	Agrees.	Management guidance and business contacts vary widely depending on the particular investment and our level of involvement. This level of involvement is tied directly to our participation on the board. However, we sit on the board in less than one-third of our portfolio companies, and typically only those deals in which we are lead investors. I would view our role in orchestrating a merger acquisition or public offering as relatively minor compared to our role as a management sounding board.

TABLE 5
(*continued*)

Venture Capitalist No. 4	Venture Capitalist No. 5	Venture Capitalist No. 6	Venture Capitalist No. 7
Agrees.	Founders have become very sophisticated. They develop relationship with lawyer and apprise bank contact of their intentions to start company.	Agrees.	Agrees.
Agrees.	They also use their network, especially banks, lawyers and former associates who have started companies. This helps the targeting of vc potentials as well as providing introductions.	More than 1/2, 1/2 by other v.c.'s. Also past 6 present investees, corporate contacts 6 personal accounts	Agrees.
Agrees			Agrees.
Agrees.			Agrees.
For us, I would rank in priority: (1) Management team (2) Technology/market (3) Stage of financing (4) Size (5) Location (only re being lead investor).	Missing is the most important... the people! I check the founders out before I will have first meeting.	We use potential return on capital as an early screening criterion.	Agrees.
Agrees. Agrees.	We don't actually use separate determinants of risk & return. Rather we use 3 evaluation criteria, weighted as follows: 40% – management quality/experience 40% – market (big wave can carry many surf boards) 20% – product niche, i.e., segmentation (performance/competition and many other implications)	Quality of management reflects return potential rather than the risk.	Managerial capabilities are an indicator of return prospects relative to the risk level.
Convertible preferred stock is typical for us: note that we discourage dividends.	One way to handle the question of performance is through a buy-back provision where the stock position of the entrepreneur is vested over a period of time. This allows for the replacement of poor/marginal performers and the ability to use repurchased (non-vested) stock to attract replacement in the management team. Past experience in the realized valuation of comparable ventures which we have backed help determine the equity split between entrepreneur & us in future deals. For example, if we expect a company to have an upside potential of $10 million, we might put in $4 million and expect 40% equity in the venture.	Equity share is determined by the total equity valuation process; earn-out conditions are not used by our firm.	Converts were used more in the mid-seventies. They're still used by SBIC's but typically not by conventional VC partnerships. There hasn't been a convert in our last 40–50 investments. Equity share is determined by pay-out required expectations <u>and</u> by an assessment of the value currently represented by the business. Most VC's I know won't get involved in an earn-out. I haven't done one in 14 years in the business. You strike a deal with the management at the outset. Hopefully more equity is provided over time to successful management, but there's no way to take it away from them unless they leave or are fired. If you replace "earn-out" with "equity split," the statement would more accurately describe our reality.
For us, board seats for at least some venture investors. At least some of the venture capital investors, & especially the lead investor. should have representation on the board.	We agree. We especially contribute as follows: Help in recruiting key people Serve as sounding board to first time CEO Security check on strategy (OEM or direct sales, etc.)	We always serve on the board of our portfolio companies. We provide our portfolio companies with assistance in such areas as identifying legal counsel, performing compensation audits, focusing the product or service, recruiting management, locating additional capital and guiding acquisition/merger decisions	Agree, but only one VC may be on the board even if there are 2–3 VC's in the deal, i.e., all of the investors don't go on the Board.

In our study, 43 of 68 deals were accepted ($\alpha = 0.63$) and 25 of 68 deals were rejected ($1 - \alpha = 0.37$). Thus $C_{pro} = 0.53$ and $C_{max} = 0.63$. Since the discriminant function classified 86.9% of the cases correctly, it performs considerably better than both the proportional chance criterion and the maximum chance criterion.

Figure 2 is a schematic representation of how evaluation criteria have an impact on the venture capitalist's decision to invest, as inferred by Study II. In summary, the attractiveness of the market and the product's differentiation are related to the expected return. A capable management team and resistance to environmental threats indicate a lower risk of commercial failure. Finally, the decision to invest is determined by the risk vs. return expectations vis-à-vis a venture. As expected, venture capitalists are risk-averse and profit-oriented in their decision and, moreover, they are willing to invest in risky deals if offset by the profit potential.

Neither Study I nor II collected any data relevant to the deal structuring (Step 4) or post-investment activities (Step 5) aspects of the model in Figure 1. These were addressed in a more general fashion in the validation component described in the next section.

Validation of the Model

Seven cooperating venture capitalists agreed to participate in a follow-up study to validate the model. The participants were selected to provide representation from the viewpoint of the various types of venture capital investors. Included in the set of cooperating venture capitalists were: a large venture capital firm which also participates in underwriting new equity issues; a small venture capital partnership composed of successful entrepreneurs who have sold their companies; a venture capital partnership with several generations of funds ranked in the top five in terms of number of deals made and dollars invested for 1982; a well-known venture capital firm which specializes in a narrow high technology industry segment; an SBIC; an individual venture capitalist investor; and a venture capital partnership substantially owned by a major banking institution. Each of the participating venture capitalists was asked to review the specification of the components of our model. These are summarized in the left-hand column of Table 5. Also the venture capitalists were asked to elaborate upon their reaction to the validity of the model. These responses are also shown in Table 5.

In general, there is agreement with the model's specification. Some of the comments elaborate upon the model specifications; others take exception with selected components of the model. The major departures from the model's specification are as follows:

(1) The model may have under-represented the extent to which venture capitalist's stress the quality of the management team as an early screening criterion. Also, the size of investment is not a screening criterion for several respondents.

(2) There was considerable disagreement with our statistical result that the quality of the management team influences risk but not expected return. Three of the seven respondents feel that management capabilities are an indicator of potential return rather than risk. A more fundamental issue is raised by VC5. This respondent does not formally distinguish between risk and return, as was implicitly assumed in our formulation.

(3) Earn-out arrangements are not extensively used in structuring deals. VC5 offers insight into a different type of deal structure which tries to achieve the same objective as an earn-out. In an earn-out arrangement, the share of the entrepreneur is determined by the venture's performance, thereby giving the investor control if the performance is poor. Instead, VC5 achieves much the same effect by the use of a "vesting" arrangement. Since the share of the entrepreneur vests over time, this gives the investor control in the early development of the venture even though his ultimate share may be a minority position.

Though the responses in Table 5 are in general agreement with our model's specification, there is a disturbing lack of common structure to the way the 7 venture capitalists reacted to the model. The diversity of the responses, both in content and style, demonstrates the heterogeneity in the practices of different venture capital firms. This heterogeneity cautions against too rigid a specification in any model describing venture capital management.

Conclusions

The purpose of this paper is two-fold. The first is to stimulate an interest in modeling the management of venture capital funds. The second is to provide entrepreneurs with insights which can help in their dealings with venture capitalists.

With respect to the first objective, the value of the study may perhaps be as much in what it did not achieve as in what it did achieve. A five-step model of the activities of venture capitalists has been developed. The model, however, is highly descriptive and lacks a theoretical basis. Moreover, the model is admittedly simplistic. A more rigorously specified model, however, could not capture the heterogeneity of practices across the many venture capital firms. Wells (1974) achieved a higher level of specificity in his modeling of venture capital fund management, but only at the expense of a unique model for each of the firms in his relatively small sample. Finally, the empirical portion of this paper has focused on the first three steps, and especially the third step, of the model. Most of the previous research on this topic share the same focus. In contrast, the fourth and fifth steps, namely deal structuring and post-investment activities, have not received much attention. In particular, the pricing of venture capital investments, in terms of the equity relinquished has not been modeled. Also, since most ventures involve several rounds of financing, the implications of future capital needs on investment decisions in earlier rounds of financing need to be explored. These limitations of the model presented in this paper are, hopefully, the stimuli for a continued interest in modeling venture capital investments.

The second objective of this paper is to provide potential entrepreneurs with insight into the way venture capitalists manage their funds. These insights are also valuable to managers in large companies who wish to improve their allocation of resources to internal ventures competing for new business development funds. First, professional relationships with CPAs, lawyers, bankers and successful entrepreneurs who have a high degree of credibility with the venture capital community is a help in locating capital. Second, the venture capital community is often smaller than it seems due to the high incidence of syndication whereby several venture capitalists co-invest in a venture. Third, venture capitalists differ in the screening criteria used to guide their investments. Most deals would have to match the investor's industry and geographic preferences, risk preferences for different financing stages, and investment policy in terms of the amount they will invest in a single deal. Finally, four aspects of the business plan are used to evaluate the riskiness and potential profit associated with a particular deal. These are (1) the marketing factors and the venture's ability to manage them effectively, (2) product's competitive advantages and uniqueness, (3) quality of the management team, particularly in its balance of skills, (4) exposure to risk factors beyond the venture's control, e.g., technological obsolescence, competitive entry, cyclical sales fluctuations. In presenting a deal to a venture capitalist, these four aspects should be used to favorably position the venture.[3]

[3] This research was funded by a National Science Foundation Grant NSF PRA-8006620-A01.

References

BROPHY, D. J., "Flow of Venture Capital 1977-1980," in *Frontiers of Entrepreneurship Research*, K. H. Vesper (Ed.), Babson College, Wellesley, Mass., 1981, 246–280.

BRUNO, A. V. AND A. C. COOPER, "Patterns of Development and Acquisitions for Silicon Valley Startups," *Technovation*, Elsevier Scientific Publishing Company, Amsterdam, Netherlands, 1982, 275–290.

CHARLES RIVER ASSOCIATES, "An Analysis of Venture Capital Market Imperfections," NTIS Report PB-254996, National Bureau of Standards, Washington D.C., 1976.

COOPER, I. A. AND W. T. CARLETON, "Dynamics of Borrower-Lender Interaction: Partitioning Final Payoff in Venture Capital Finance," *J. Finance*, 34 (1979), 517–529.

DORSEY, T. K., "The Measurement and Assessment of Capital Requirements, Investment Liquidity and Risk for the Management of Venture Capital Funds," unpublished doctoral dissertation, University of Texas, Austin, 1977.

GLASSMEYER, E. F., "Venture Financing Techniques," in S. E. Pratt (Ed.), *Guide to Venture Capital Sources*, Capital Publishing Corp., Wellesley, Mass., 1981, 64–66.

GOLDEN, S. C., "Structuring and Pricing the Financing," in S. E. Pratt (Ed.), *Guide to Venture Capital Sources*, Capital Publishing Corp., Wellesley, Mass., 1981, 67–76.

HOFFMAN, C. A., "The Venture Capital Investment Process: A Particular Aspect of Regional Economic Development," unpublished doctoral dissertation, University of Texas, Austin, 1972.

LELAND, H. E. AND D. H. PYLE, "Informational Asymmetries, Financial Structure, and Financial Intermediation," *J. Finance*, 32 (1977).

MONTGOMERY, D. B. AND G. L. URBAN, *Management Science in Marketing*, Prentice-Hall, Englewood Cliffs, N.J., 1969, 303–312.

MORRISON, D. G., "On the Interpretation of Discriminant Analysis," *J. Marketing Res.*, 6 (May 1969), 156–163.

O'MEARA, J. O., "Selecting Profitable Products," *Harvard Business Rev.*, 39 (1961), 84–85.

PESSEMIER, E. A., *Product Management: Strategy and Organization*, John Wiley, New York, 1982, 347–351.

POINDEXTER, J. B., "The Efficiency of Financial Markets: The Venture Capital Case," unpublished doctoral dissertation, New York University, New York, 1976.

PRATT, S. E. (Ed.), *Guide to Venture Capital Sources*, Capital Publishing Corp., Wellesley, Mass., 1981.

ROSS, S. A., "The Determination of Financial Structure: The Incentive Signalling Approach," *Bell J. Econom.*, 8 (1977), 23–40.

TIMMONS, J. AND D. GUMPERT, "Discard Many Old Rules About Getting Venture Capital," *Harvard Business Rev.*, 60 (1) (1982).

TYEBJEE, T. T. AND A. V. BRUNO, "Venture Capital Decision Making" in *Frontiers of Entrepreneurship Research*, K. H. Vesper (Ed.), Babson College, Wellesley, Mass., 1981, 281–320.

WELLS, W. A., "Venture Capital Decision Making," unpublished doctoral dissertation, Carnegie-Mellon University, 1974.

WETZEL, W. E., JR, "Informal Risk Capital in New England," in *Frontiers of Entrepreneurship Research*, K. H. Vesper (Ed.), Babson College, Wellesley, Mass., 1981, 217–245.

[2]

VENTURE CAPITAL'S ROLE

IN FINANCING INNOVATION

FOR ECONOMIC GROWTH

JEFFRY A. TIMMONS and
WILLIAM D. BYGRAVE
Babson College

EXECUTIVE SUMMARY

*Previously, there has been little empirical evidence about the role of venture capital in fostering technological innovation. Recent research, sponsored by the National Science Foundation and Babson College and completed with our colleagues Stanley E. Pratt and Norman Fast (**Venture Economics** and **Venture Capital Journal**) shed some new light on the flow of venture capital to highly innovative technological ventures from 1967–1982.*
The evidence suggests that venture capital not only plays a significant role, but that it is a unique kind of investing in terms of when, where, and how it is done. Ironically, this research indicates that the "capital" in venture capital is the least important ingredient in fostering technological innovation. Rather, it is management intensive, requiring very early involvement by venture capitalists in nurturing budding innovators and technology, and thereby bird-dogging and accelerating the emergence of highly innovative technologies. Further, the post-1979 reduction of the capital-gains tax has led to unprecedented growth and development in the venture-capital industry. One result has been that a new industry structure is emerging, and along with it some new danger signals for the future flow and commercialization of technological innovation. Several lessons emerge from our findings that hold implications for venture capital investors and entrepreneurs alike.
Successful venture-capital investing in technologically innovative firms requires more than just risk money. Savvy entrepreneurs seek out venture capitalists with noteworthy reputations for their nonmonetary, high value-added contributions to fledgling firms. Venture capitalists who can play a highly constructive role in emerging firms can attract higher-quality ventures. Qualities commonly cited by entrepreneurs are: helping to find the select key management-team members; providing credibility with suppliers and customers; and helping to shape strategy when the daily pressures postpone this vital task. As one put it, "It is far more important whom you obtain funding from than how much and at what price."
Investing in technologically innovative ventures is a more specialized business than suggested

Address correspondence to Jeffry A. Timmons, Babson College, Babson Park, Massachusetts 02157.

Journal of Business Venturing 1, 161–176 (1986)
© 1986 Elsevier Science Publishing Co., Inc., 52 Vanderbilt Ave., New York, NY 10017

0883-9026/86/$03.50

162   J.A. TIMMONS AND W.D. BYGRAVE

by the common stereotype of homogeneity among venture capitalists. Fewer than 5% of the 464 venture-capital firms in our study accounted for nearly 25% of all the investments in highly innovative technological ventures. Investors possess specialized know-how, including a web of contacts and networks, a great degree of syndication of deals, and a great intensity of involvement. The message for technology entrepreneurs is clear: focus on venture-capital firms with reputations for proven performance in your technology and market, especially with your targeted customers.

Contrary to the notion that venture-capital investors sit and wait for business plans and innovative ideas to come to them and then simply write checks, many of the most active firms do just the opposite: they engage in active "outreach" and "bird-dogging" efforts to identify exceptional innovators with the relevant technical expertise and commitment to bring about the commercialization of promising technologies. They also team with innovators and entrepreneurs to create an "acceleration effect" by actually compressing the time span and increasing the velocity at which new technologies are brought to commercial maturity and societal utility. Founders and investors alike have related numerous examples of highly innovative technological ventures that became realities in what they believed to be one-fourth to one-half the time that would have been required within a large, established firm.

Looking ahead, the new venture-capital climate of the mid-1980s offers both bane and blessing.

As the pool of capital has exploded, the industry has become more diverse and specialized than ever before. Sharp differences are visible in terms of investing objectives, criteria, and strategy, focusing on particular stages, size, and a technology-market niche. Megafunds of $100 + million have been raised, and as funds get larger the minimum investment escalates, typically $1 million or more now. Entrepreneurs in search of venture capital need to be more knowledgeable and focused than ever before.

Significant portfolio problems continue to surface as the would-be "pearls" of 1982–1984 become "lemons" in 1985–1986. One result of this is the drying up of funds for seed and start-up investments. Many venture capitalists are simply overburdened by cleaning up problems in their own portfolios and in replacing management. Fortunately, some innovative venture capitalists have seen opportunity in this adversity, and a handful of specialized seed and first-stage funds have been launched.

Ironically, many of the trends and pressures in the venture-capital industry in the mid-1980s may inadvertently shift investing attention away from more innovative technological ventures. The implications of these changes are painful for entrepreneurs, investors, and the nation. How can technological innovation and international competitiveness be achieved if the venture-capital community is unable—or unwilling—to contribute as greatly to the funding of new innovations as it has in the past? Where will technology entrepreneurs find the risk capital and "value-added involvement" so vital to commercial success? And how can venture-capital pools provide the handsome yields on invested capital of the past if they shift their investing to later-stage ventures?

On the brighter side, we are still in an era of unprecedented opportunity for entrepreneurs and investors alike. Even with the sharp drop in new funds available in venture-capital pools to an estimated $2.5 billion in 1985, this is still 25 to 50 times greater than the annual flow of new venture capital during the dismal 1970s. The recent industry shake-up, coupled with a continuance of the favorable capital-gains tax, should foster a healthier, if not wiser and more disciplined, venture-capital industry during the remainder of the decade.

VENTURE CAPITAL AND INNOVATION

The contribution of small, high-technology companies to technological innovation and economic development has become a topic of interest to both public- and private-sector policy makers. Research highlighting the magnitude of that contribution has demonstrated that smaller high-technology companies and the process by which they develop are important phenomena. If current research findings hold true, this class of small businesses is the source of a majority of "radical" technological innovations and a disproportionately large share of employment growth (Aggarwal 1973; Bearse and Konopki 1979; Faucett 1971; Shapero 1969; Timmons et al. 1983–84; Tyebjee and Bruno 1984; U.S. Congress, House 1979).

As a critical element in the establishment and growth of many of these small, high-technology companies, venture capitalists provide financing as well as management services (Brophy 1981; Timmons et al. 1985; Timmons 1981). Although less visible than the high-technology companies themselves, the venture-capital industry also plays a role in techno-logical and economic development through its direct involvement in the development of small, high-technology companies. This role, however, is not well understood. The venture-capital industry is generally perceived as an agglomeration of homogeneous firms, whereas, in fact, they are quite heterogeneous. Differing objectives, strategies, resources, locations, associations, and organizational forms result in a great deal of variety within the venture-capital industry. This diversity needs to be understood and incorporated into well-focused research designs if studies of the venture-capital industry are to be most productive.

Relevant Literature

Previous research dealing with the venture-capital industry has generally focused on three subjects: 1) the decision criteria used in making successful venture-capital investments and the characteristics of those investments; 2) the performance of venture-capital portfolios and individual investments; and 3) the availability and costs of venture capital.

Decision-Making Criteria and Investment Characteristics

Many of the studies on decision-making criteria and characteristics of successful investments are unpublished, as noted by Tyebjee and Bruno (1981; 1984) in a preliminary report of their results. Furthermore, they tend to point out the considerable difficulty in conducting any research in their field. The investing and screening process has been examined by Briskman (1968), Aggarwal (1973), and Wells (1974). The characteristics of successful ventures have been examined by Von Hippel (1973), Hoban (1976), Wells (1974), and Poindexter (1976). Most of these studies confirm the general belief that the quality of the founding team and marketability of the idea are central to success.

Performance of Venture-Capital Portfolios and Individual Investments

In 1977 several studies on performance from the early 1970s were summarized by Timmons and his colleagues, who showed that new ventures supported by venture-capital companies had a significantly lower failure rate—roughly 20% to 30%—than the 80% to 90% failure rate for new firms in the economy at large. DeHudy, Fast, and Pratt (1981) analyzed the portfolios of five prominent venture-capital firms (218 investments) and reported a rate of complete failure of 14.7%, with 3.2% of the investments responsible for 31% of the total return. Huntsman and Hoban (1980) reported a 17% failure rate for portfolio investments and an average annual return of 18.9% for three leading venture-capital firms. Rubel (1972) examined 378 new venture investments and found a loss rate of only 15%, postulating the superior performance of venture capital–backed companies versus new businesses in general. Osborn (1975) examined the performance of the SBIC program from its 1958 origin to 1970. He concluded that the balance of debt versus equity financing and the asset base of the venture depends on the size of the SBIC.

Of special significance are studies that showed that high-technology ventures funded by venture-capital investors achieved higher rates of survival and success. For example, Roberts (1970) found a 20% failure rate; Taylor (1969) reported a 35% failure rate for 279 high-technology companies; and Faucett (1971) found that among start-up investments by 14 venture-capital companies, only 18% lost money.

Other studies have looked at the role and performance of corporate venture capital and venture groups (Tektronix 1978; Dunn 1975; Fast 1978; 1981). These and similar studies generally show an uneven record of poor performance due to such factors as slow corporate decision making, lack of top management commitment, and unfocused or dispersed business technology or acquisition objectives.

Availability and Costs of Venture Capital

Bean, Schiffel, and Mongee (1975) concluded that little is really known about potential market imperfections involving the availability of venture capital, whereas research by Charles River Associates (1976) showed that small, technology-based firms paid higher interest rates and yielded a higher rate of return than did other small ventures. Shapero (1969) found that loan officers who were familiar with high-technology firms were willing to make loans more frequently without full equity collateral and, in addition, helped guide the operations of the borrowing firm to increase its likelihood of success. The Diebold Group (1974) studied 231 ventures and recommended government guarantees for one-half of the investments in new, technology-based firms, so as to increase availability of venture capital. Earlier studies by Dominquez (1971) and Ofer (1975) reported on the distribution, availability, and allocation of venture capital.

Innovation, Technology Transfer, and Entrepreneurship

More recently, Abetti and Stuart (1985) have documented an extensive review of the state-of-the-art knowledge of the interrelationships of innovation, technology transfer, and entrepreneurship. This literature concludes that invention alone is not enough. Innovation—the critical next step—is the offspring of invention combined with technology transfer and entrepreneurship. There is growing evidence that specialized venture-capital investing know-how can play a vital role in this process.

Highly Innovative Technological Ventures: What Is Different?

Focused Inquiry

From 1982 to 1984, a National Science Foundation (NSF)–sponsored research project[1] was undertaken to develop a greater understanding of the process by which new companies are developed through the interaction of technologically innovative entrepreneurs and venture capitalists. The objectives of the study included: 1) determining the characteristics of these technology-oriented venture capitalists and entrepreneurs; 2) examining the factors that influence the supply of venture capital to developing small, high-technology companies; and 3) determining whether or not public-policy instruments may be used effectively in this process.

[1]This study was conducted by Dr. Jeffry A. Timmons, Professor of Entrepreneurial Studies at Babson College, Wellesley, Massachusetts; Mr. Stanley E. Pratt, Dr. Norman D. Fast, and Ms. Roubina Khoylian of Venture Economics, Wellesley Hills, Massachusetts; and Dr. William D. Bygrave of Bryant College, Smithfield, Rhode Island. It was sponsored by the National Science Foundation under IS182-13157, with support from Babson College. Any opinions, findings, conclusions, or recommendations expressed in this study are those of the authors and do not necessarily reflect the views of the National Science Foundation or our colleagues.

Three fundamental hypotheses were explored in our research:

1. A certain segment of the venture-capital industry is responsible for the creation, financing, and development of a surprisingly large share of small, high-technology companies. Although a large portion of the venture-capital industry participates in such financings, *a smaller subset of venture-capital firms actively generate such investment opportunities and play the critical role in their development*. Therefore, generalizations that are drawn from analyses and studies of the operations of the venture-capital industry as a whole may not provide accurate insights into that segment of the industry that is most responsible for the creation and development of innovative, high-technology companies.

2. A certain type (or types) of entrepreneur is involved in organizing and operating these new, high-technology companies. These entrepreneurs possess certain common characteristics such as educational background, career paths, and professional associations that make them effective in their role and particularly attractive to venture capitalists as new venture managers. Therefore, accepted generalizations regarding entrepreneurs as a population may not be relevant for this subgroup.

3. These subgroups of venture capitalists and entrepreneurs are responsible for the establishment of small, high-technology companies. It is also hypothesized that: 1) many of the successful new technology-based ventures involve management teams rather than a single entrepreneur; 2) in many cases, venture capitalists play a key role in the formation of these teams; and 3) in some cases entrepreneurs who have successfully developed a prior venture move on to create other new ventures (often financed by the same venture capitalists), thus recycling their entrepreneurial skills.

Research Questions

This study sought answers to a number of questions:

- Are there differences between "highly innovative" technological ventures (HITVs) and "least-innovative" technological ventures (LITVs)?
- What factors and characteristics distinguish the HITVs and LITVs, as well as the venture-capital firms that emphasize these types of investments?
- What trends characterize the flow of venture capital from 1967 through 1982?
- What policy implications and recommendations emerge from the findings and interviews with entrepreneurs and investors?

Methodology

The study was carried out in 3 parts. First, 1501 of the first-round portfolio investments made from 1967 through 1982 and recorded on the *Venture Economics* database were categorized as to their technological innovativeness. The flow of venture capital to these 1501 firms was examined and HITV investments were compared to LITV investments.

Second, 464 venture-capital firms (with one or more investments in those 1501 companies) were categorized as to their involvement with and emphasis on HITVs and LITVs.

Finally, selected field interviews focused on the dynamics of innovative-technology entrepreneurs working with venture capitalists to spawn, finance, and develop tomorrow's technology-based industries.

This study could potentially have direct application to both NSF's operating programs and to other federal, state, and local-government programs and policies. For example, the Small Business Innovation Research program currently operated by NSF should benefit from an intensive analysis of the elements and processes involved in developing innovative, high-technology companies. In addition, local economic-development organizations are likely to find a delineation of the process by which new, high-technology companies are formed to be valuable to the design of their own program strategies (current interest in the growth of new, high-technology companies as an instrument for economic development is rapidly increasing in the economic-development community) (Bean et al. 1975; DeHudy et al. 1981a).

The *Venture Economics* database of about 4000 venture capital–backed portfolio companies was randomly accessed to create a new database of 1501 investments during the period 1967 to 1982, sorted by four-year periods beginning in 1967, inclusive. All financial flows were normalized to 1981 dollars to capture the real dollar investments, because the post-1967 period has been so inflationary. These investment dollars are for the first round of venture capital in that particular venture. Samples were rated independently by three researchers to distinguish the extent of technological innovativeness of each of these firms, based upon the company and product descriptions in the database, at the time of that initial round of financing. Initially, several criteria, such as technology, product, application, marketing, process, and systems, were evaluated by applying to each a scale of 1 to 7. Tests of inter-rater reliability using the BMDP statistical package resulted in the use of *Technological Application* ($r = .89$) and *Overall Technological Innovativeness* ($r = .93$) as the best differentiators of innovativeness.

Cluster analyses were used on a sample of 185 rated firms to determine whether or not subgroups could be identified by innovativeness and to develop hypotheses without contaminating the database. Distinct subgroups emerged for the *Highly Innovative, Least Innovative,* and *The Rest* (using the Hotellings test of two random subsamples resulted in p values of .0000). Analyses and comparisons against the variables in the database were then performed on the two subgroups.

The same procedure was used to identify and compare the 464 venture-capital firms in terms of the extent of their involvement in *Highly* or *Least* innovative technological ventures.

Several cautions should be noted in considering the findings. Although the database is the most elegant of its kind available anywhere, it is less than perfect. Some missing values for certain variables were encountered and are inevitable in such research. Because the majority of the firms in the database are privately held, intimate details of product, technology, and performance are less than ideal. Finally, if any biases are built into the database, they would be skewed toward the most recent period 1979 to 1982, because the data in this period tends to be more complete and considerably more venture-capital investing activity has occurred. However, this also quite fairly represents the emerging nature of this relatively new industry.

SUMMARY OF PRINCIPAL FINDINGS

A significant increase in overall venture-capital investment activity began in 1979 (in 1981 dollars), as did a surge in initial financings of highly innovative technological ventures compared to the least innovative.

- The total pool of venture capital has grown from approximately $2.5 to $3.0 billion from 1969 through 1977 ($6.2 to 4.5 billion in real 1981 dollars) to $7.6 billion by the end of 1982 ($7.1 billion in 1981 dollars). The amount of new capital being added annually to the total pool increased from a low of 10 million ($17 million in 1981 dollars) in 1975 to $1.7 billion in 1982 ($1.589 billion in 1981 dollars). Epilogue: in 1983 $4.5 billion was committed, whereas 1984 saw a decline to $3.1 billion (Timmons et al. 1983–84). By early 1985 the total pool was about $16.5 billion.

• As the pool of venture capital has grown, the volume of new (first-round) venture-capital investments has also risen over the last few years. Annual disbursements, which were only $250 million in 1975 ($423 million in 1981 dollars), had increased to $1.8 billion by 1982 ($1.7 billion in 1981 dollars).

• In the sample of 1501 first-round investments during 1967–1982, the flow of venture capital going to HITVs during the 1979–1982 period grew to $586.4 million, exceeding the amount invested in LITVs for the first time since 1967–1970 and greatly exceeding the $102.6 million invested during 1975–1978. Investments in HITVs as a percentage of all the 1501 investments increased from a low of 18.8% from 1971–1974 to 47.2% during 1979–1982. In 1982, HITV investments outnumbered LITVs by nearly 2.5 to 1.

Changes in the federal capital-gains tax in 1969 and 1978 were followed swiftly by dramatic changes in the flow of new funds into venture capital firms.

• The increase in the maximum capital-gains tax rate from 25% to 48.2% in 1969 was followed by an immediate decrease in new capital committed to venture-capital funds. The inflow of new capital dropped from $171 million in 1969 to $97 million in 1970 (from $424 million to $227 million in 1981 dollars) and continued to decrease. With the reduction of the maximum tax rate in 1978 to 28%, new capital commitments surged to $570 million for 1978 from only $39 million in 1977 (from $59 milion to $795 million in 1981 dollars.)

There has been significant growth in the number of first-round investments in start-up HITVs during 1979–1982.

• Overall, the number of first-round start-up investments increased from 72 in 1967–1970 to 774 in 1979–1982. In 1979–1982 compared to 1967–1970 there were nearly six times as many HITV start-up investments. The latest four years accounted for 158 of the 221 HITV start-up investments since 1967, or 71.5%. In contrast, there were just 43 LITV start ups during 1979–1982.

• There was an increase in the number of investments in start ups compared with later stages. During the 1967–1982 period the number of start-up investments in HITVs (221) was two and one-half times greater than first-round investments in start-up LITVs (89), and accounted for 71.3% of all start ups.

• Although the number of HITV start ups has increased, the proportion of HITV start ups has decreased from a high of 75% during 1971–1974 to 49.7% during the 1979–1982 period. In contrast, expansion financings accounted for only 6% of HITV investments during 1967–1970 but had increased to 26.8% in 1979–1982.

HITV investing actually requires less capital than do initial investments in the least-innovative ventures.

• First-round investing in highly innovative technological ventures is a quite specialized, management—not capital—intensive activity.

168   J.A. TIMMONS AND W.D. BYGRAVE

- Compared to the *Least-Innovative* firms, HITV investing does not require more capital. First-round investments in HITVs during 1979–1982 were only 74% of the average investment in LITVs ($1.535 vs. $2.066 million in 1981 dollars—significant at $p < .0178$[2]). This was also true by stage: seed-stage HITVs received on the average just over one-half the amount of money that went to LITVs, and start-up stage HITVs averaged $1.6 million vs. $3 million for LITVs. This pattern was true for later-stage investments as well.

- The larger, capital-intensive venture-capital firms are no more involved in investing in HITVs than are the smaller firms. The amount of capital under management was not significantly different between those venture-capital firms emphasizing either HITVs or LITVs.

There is a core group of highly skilled and experienced venture-capital firms accounting for a disproportionate share of HITV investing.

- The 21 venture-capital firms that were most active in HITV investing represent less than 5% of the 464 firms in our database, yet they were involved in nearly 25% of all the investments in HITVs.

- This specialized know-how includes a wide web of contacts and networks among the HITV community, a greater degree of syndication, and a greater intensity of involvement in these fledgling firms. The heavy involvement with the portfolio companies usually occurs through the originators or lead investors, who often serve as members of the boards of directors.

Venture capitalists' investments in highly innovative technological ventures are made at a significantly earlier stage of the venture than are investments in the least innovative firms.

- Nearly two-thirds of the first-round investments in HITVs occurred at the seed and start-up stages (249) rather than at later stages (125).

- During the 1967–1982 period the number of start-up investments in HITVs (221) was two and one-half times greater than was the number of start-up investments in LITVs (89). HITVs accounted for 71.3% of these combined start ups. Seed-stage investing in HITVs was three times greater than in LITVs (28 vs. 9) and accounted for 75.7% of all seed-stage investments in HITVs and LITVs.

In 1981 and 1982, a significant increase has occurred in the proportion of initial investments in seed-stage[3] HITVs compared to all other stages of investments during 1967–1980.

- The recent increase in all seed investments is surprisingly large. In 1981 and 1982 there was a total of 29 investments. This is a notable increase compared to 16 for the prior 14 years (1967–1980).

---

[2]The significance or p level refers to the probability that the differences in these means have occurred by chance. The .0178 indicates that there is a very low probability—178 out of 10,000—that these numbers occurred by utter coincidence. A p level of .05 or smaller is considered statistically meaningful.

[3]A seed financing involves a venture at the proof-of-concept stage. It may involve product development but rarely involves initial marketing. Start-up financing is provided to companies for use in product development and initial marketing: companies may be in the process of getting organized or have been in business a short time but have not sold their product commercially.

- During the years 1981 and 1982, the portion of HITV seed investments to all other stages of HITV investments was 10.3% (18:174). Earlier (1967–1980), these seed investments (10:207) were less than one-half that portion 4.8% ($p = .057$).

- In the last two years, HITV seed investment outpaced all previous HITV seed investments by nearly 2:1 ($p = 0.57$).

- Overall, 28 out of a total of 796 (3.5%) first-round investments in HITVs between 1967 and 1982 went to seed-stage firms. During the most recent period, 1979–1982, seed-stage first-round investments in HITVs accounted for 7.2% of all HITV investments during the four years. This is more than in the 1971–1974 (4.4%) and 1975–1979 (5%) periods, but less than in the 1967–1970 (9.4%) period.

Venture-capital firms active in HITVs create substantial value-added contributions to their portfolio companies as a result of their intense, early involvement.

- Founders of HITVs reported that they actively seek out those venture capitalists with noteworthy reputations for their nonmonetary, high value-added contributions to fledgling firms. This highly active role includes finding and selecting key management team members, making customer and supplier introductions, providing credibility to these customer and suppliers as well as with bankers, and emphasizing and accelerating a thoughtful focus on strategy and future plans when overwhelming current pressures might postpone such planning.

- Founders of HITVs uniformly reported that, "It is more important whom they obtain funding from than how much and at what price."

- Venture capitalists who emphasize HITV investing perform a highly catalytic role in finding and blending the necessary combination of people, technology, and opportunities to bring unproven ideas to commercial reality.

There are definite geographical oases wherein founders, technologists, and venture capitalists cluster to account for the bulk of HITV investing.

- Confirming the well-known industry pattern, some areas of the country are more fertile than others for growing new companies with a technological bent and high ambitions. Venture-capital firms with main offices in California (42.9%), New York (23.8%), and Massachusetts (9.5%) accounted for over three-fourths of all HITV investing. Less than one-half of the investment in LITVs was accounted for by firms in those three states.

- Independent, private, venture-capital firms accounted for 85.7% of all HITV investing and are even more concentrated, by main office, in these three states. Less than 5% of the 464 venture-capital firms analyzed accounted for 25% of all HITV investments.

There is a bird dog phenomenon characteristic of those venture-capital firms focusing on highly innovative technological ventures in the form of "outreach" to identify promising opportunities.

- Contrary to the notion that venture-capital investors sit and wait for business plans and ideas to come to them, many of these firms engage in active outreach and bird-dogging efforts to identify exceptional innovators with the relevant technical expertise and commitment to bring out the commercialization of promising technologies. With their business-seeding and building know-how, they play a unique bridging and coalition-building role in bringing together values and talents of the academic and scientific cultures that spawn highly innovative technologies.

There is an "acceleration effect" resulting from the venture capitalists' intense involvement in the creation of highly innovative technological ventures.

- Innovators, entrepreneurs, and investors working together accelerate the velocity and compress the time span of bringing new technologies to commercial maturity and societal utility. Founders and investors alike gave numerous, detailed examples of HITVs that became realities in what they believed to be one-fourth to one-half the time probably required within large, established organizations.

POLICY IDEAS AND RECOMMENDATIONS

There was a near consensus that one of the most vital roles the federal government can play is to increase support for basic research in the sciences.

- There was a shared view among participants in the study that the roots of new technological opportunities depend upon a continuing flow of knowledge from basic research.

- University and technical centers suffer from insufficient federal support for the basic research needed to foster quality education for training and developing the human capital necessary to support the subsequent flow of new technology.

A general hands-off view was voiced when it came to federal, regional, and state involvement in the process.

- There was a shared fear that more active government involvement might well do more harm than good. From the venture capitalists in particular came a consensus that the existing market mechanism was working precisely as it should.

- Considerable concern was expressed by entrepreneurs and investors alike that the federal government and congress may overestimate the potential contributions of high-technology firms as "economic saviors" of the United States. No one we talked with suggested that even the glimpse of a panacea is locked inside all the high-technology hype and publicity. Although most wished that broad-based economic renewal were that simple, the realities are that it is not. There is a noticeable difference between being an important contributor to such renewal and being a cure-all.

Support was voiced for specific action in the tax and regulatory areas.

- There was broad-based agreement that the reduction of the effective capital-gains tax rate from 48.5% to 28%, and subsequently to 20%, was the single most important factor in fostering the rebirth of venture-capital investing that began in 1979. Surprisingly, few argued that a further reduction, although always helpful, would make a vital difference in HITV investing activity.

- Potentially more venture-capital activity could be drawn by HITVs if they became more attractive investment opportunities. By eliminating all capital-gains taxes on investments held for at least four or five years, the potential return on HITV investments would be raised. Such a proposal would tend to favor the patient investor rather than encourage the early-in, early-out investor.

- The proposed Department of Labor ERISA ruling on "plan-asset" legislation would require fiduciary responsibility by the pension-fund manager for each individual portfolio investment in the venture-capital fund in which the pension fund has an investment as a limited partner. Such a regulation is a potentially enormous barrier to all venture-capital investing, but especially for HITVs, because they are more elusive and difficult to evaluate and to defend than are LITVs once such an investment goes sour.

- Tax policies to improve the cash flow of HITVs would significantly enhance their attractiveness for entrepreneurs and investors alike. Accelerated depreciation schedules and targeted write-offs for very early R&D intensive expenditures were frequently mentioned.

- A careful examination and possible amendment of the antitrust laws as they may inhibit joint research and development efforts is needed.

- No mention was made of the need for action in the area of patent legislation or rulings affecting hard technology. Most felt this was a relatively unimportant area. The exception, of course, concerns the protection of intellectual property in the rapidly exploding computer-software technology and applications areas.

MID-1980s NEW VENTURE-CAPITAL CLIMATE AND INNOVATION: BANE OR BLESSING?

The dramatic dollar increases alone in the pool of venture capital do not reveal the underlying changes occurring in an industry that was dormant—some say nearly extinct—throughout the 1970s. For one thing, there has been a surge of new firms formed, and many new professionals have entered business. By early 1985, for example, among the 600-plus firms, over half the venture capitalists were believed to have fewer than four years experience in the business. For another, the typical size of the new funds were considerably larger, and for the first time in the industry's history $100 + million megafunds were raised, such as the $178 million fund completed in early 1985 by Welsh, Carson, Anderson, and Stowe. Along with the larger fund size and the scarcity of experienced venture capitalists to invest all the new funds, the minimum first-round investment tended to gravitate upward, exceeding $1 million, and in some instances even more. During 1982–1983, for example, some microcomputer software start ups attracted $5 to $8 milion, spent primarily to gain a distribution toehold.

The industry's growth has not been the domain of the United States alone. For instance, as recently as 1979 there was no organized, active venture-capital investment in the United Kingdom, where today over 160 firms exist. Similarly, no firms existed in 1979 in Sweden and over 150 firms are now active; in Australia, where over a dozen new firms have emerged; and in Japan, where several exist. New firms have surfaced in such countries as Italy, Belgium, Holland, the Philippines, Spain, Kenya, South Korea, and Brazil. Typically, they have sought to establish close linkages to U.S. funds with an international bent.

Recent Trends and Directions

Funds Are More Specialized, Less Homogeneous

Even today there exists a stereotype of venture capital investing. To most entrepreneurs and outsiders, the industry appears to be uniform in practice and homogeneous in objective.

After all, who has not heard the epitaph "vulture capitalists" or the invective "They follow each other like sheep?" Yet, just the opposite is true when you take a closer look at the industry. This and other research on venture-capital investing paint a picture different from the common stereotype. In short, the industry has become more diverse, specialized, and less uniform than is generally thought. Sharp differences are visible in terms of investing objectives and criteria, strategy, and focusing on particular stages, sizes, and market-technology niches.

Emergence of Feeder Funds

Accompanying this specialization is a new farm-team system that has surfaced. New regional centers of venture-capital investing exist today that were nonexistent in the 1970s: in Atlanta, Denver/Boulder, Washington/Baltimore, Texas, and the Southwest. Large, established venture-capital firms have crafted both formal and informal relationships with new funds in these areas. Often, one general partner of the established fund will provide time and know-how to the new fund. They may share deal flow and co-invest in a syndicated deal.

More often than not, these new funds focus on seed-stage or start-up deals that can feed later deals to the more conventional, mainstream venture capital firm with which they are associated. Take, for instance, Zero Stage Capital, a $5 million Boston fund specializing in seed-stage investments. As only a handful of other funds have done, they plan to raise a "first-stage fund" of around $25 million to make follow-on investments in those seed ventures that are succeeding. They can thereby avoid turning to others to fund their expansion needs.

Similarly, a relationship exists between Atlanta Technology Development Fund (ATDC) and Welsh, Carson, Anderson & Stowe (WCAS), the large and well-known New York City fund. One of the WCAS general partners provides active advice and know-how to ATDC. ATDC, a $12+ million fund, seeks out smaller-seed and start-up investments in new technology-based firms. Should a portfolio firm reach the explosive-growth stage, the venture is then an attractive prospect for the much deeper pockets of WCAS.

With all the hoopla surrounding high-technology firms in recent years, numerous opportunities in low-, moderate-, and nontechnological areas have been overlooked by most. This opportunity-driven venture-capital investing process is responding just as one would hope. Specialized funds are also emerging to capture these overlooked niches. For example, historically, very few deals were done in nontechnology consumer-product companies. Today, as an example, one new fund specializes in leveraged buy-outs in consumer retail products and merchandizing companies. The general partners have lengthy operating experience in the industry.

Smaller-Seed and Start-Up Investments Drying Up

One result of these trends is an apparent evaporation of funds for smaller-seed and start-up stage investments in the latter half of 1984, which is continuing into 1985. According to *Venture Capital Journal*, about 43% of all venture-capital investments in 1983 went to start-ups. In 1984 this number had dropped sharply. The high valuations of 1983's raging-bull market for IPOs were followed by sharp drops in 1984 and a shortfall of funds to fuel rapid growth through public issues. To illustrate, the *Venture Capital* 100 index of publicly traded firms backed by venture capital (tracked by the *Venture Capital Journal*) fell for the first time since its inception from a 1983 high of 1100 to 550 by early 1985.

Start-up and first-stage investments in the $200-to-$600-thousand range have been especially hard hit. Why is this so? Beyond the industry trends noted above are other factors contributing to this. Many venture-capital firms have numerous troubled ventures in their portfolios. As a result, the premium time of those general partners often most experienced and skillful at finding, nurturing, and growing innovative technological ventures is being allocated to salvaging or turning around problem ventures, such as disk drives, some microcomputer-hardware firms like Gavilan Computers, and software ventures.

For another thing, because start-up and first-stage investing demands the greatest intensity of involvement by venture-capital investors, this type of venture has felt the greatest effects. Many investors are heavily occupied in cleaning up their portfolios and leveraging their limited time by seeking numerous bargains in the greatly devalued OTC market, as well. Still other venture-capital funds, lacking seasoned partners who know how and are willing to work with start-ups and first-stage ventures, are avoiding such ventures entirely. Consequently, the level of start-up and first-stage activity is down sharply from 1983.

New Legal Environment

One side effect of the heated competition in venture capital in recent years is a more sophisticated, legal, and contractual environment. When compared to the previous ten years, notable shifts and innovations can be discerned in the governing legal process and documents that accompany venture-capital deals. It also appears that the frequency and extent of litigation are growing; for the first time, suits have been brought by limited partners, entrepreneurs, and, surprisingly, even their own general partners against venture-capital firms.

The final document governing the investor-entrepreneur relationship—called the investment agreement—can be a few inches thick and can comprise two volumes. In it are very specific terms and conditions that define the rights and obligations of the founders and investors. Although such agreements have been a part of the process since its inception, new areas are addressed in a detail not common previously. These include the ownership of patents, trade secrets, and proprietary product rights. Also covered in unusually great detail is the impact on key employees of employment agreements, ownership, compensation, vesting provisions, and specific restrictions on the so-called "lettered stock" issued to investors and founders. Finally, the prevalent use of convertible preferred shares to make equity investments has been accompanied by the creation of specific rights of investors to actually replace management and control the company under certain circumstances, even though the investors may hold initially less than a majority of the common stock.

THE FUTURE: DANGER SIGNALS AHEAD FOR TECHNOLOGICAL INNOVATION

What effect might the new venture-capital climate—and the possible impediments it might induce—have on the rate and intensity of commercialization of technological innovation?

One implication suggested is that a shortfall may be emerging in the United States for venture capital to fuel seed, start-up, and first-stage ventures. Ironically, this seems to be occurring at a time when there has never been a larger total pool of venture capital available. A specific gap appears to be emerging for seed, start-up, and early-stage ventures needing $50 to $600 thousand of venture capital. Current trends and pressures are combining to create a gap, because investors are increasingly averse to making start-up and first-stage investments of this size.

174 J.A. TIMMONS AND W.D. BYGRAVE

Ironically, many of the trends and pressures in the venture-capital industry in the mid-1980s—larger funds looking for larger minimum investments, with an aversion to start ups and a more stringent legal structure of deals—may inadvertently shift investing attention away from more innovative technological ventures. Especially for those concerned with fostering technological innovation, the implications are painful. How can technological innovation be encouraged if the venture-capital community is unable or unwilling to contribute so disproportionately to the funding of new innovations as it has in the past? If innovations fail to attract sources of seed and start-up capital, won't they become stillborn? What alternative sources of funding may be encouraged to fill such a void?

To make matters worse, the current slowdown and aversion to such investments by the mainstream venture-capital community may be exacerbated by recent federal tax proposals that could raise the capital-gains tax. Nothing will more decisively slow the flow of venture capital—particularly to high technology ventures—and thus the pace of technological innovation, than the proposed increase of the current capital-gains tax to 35% or more.

On the brighter side, researchers and policy makers should consider this an era "rich in opportunities" for conducting research in these relatively uncharted waters. The issues raised by our findings and the implications emerging from the current climate far outweigh the available empirical knowledge and any theory construction of the relationships among technological innovation, technology transfer, venture-capital financing, and entrepreneurship.

REFERENCES

Abetti, Pier A., and Stuart, Robert W. Feb. 1985. Entrepreneurship and technology transfer: Key factors in the innovation process. IC^2 Conference, Austin, Texas.

Aggarwal, V. 1973. The selection criteria and evaluation techniques used by venture capitalists. MBA thesis, Graduate School of Business Administration, University of California, Berkeley.

Bean, A.S., Schiffel, D.D., and Mongee, M.E. 1975. The venture capital market and technological innovation. *Research Policy* 4:380–408.

Bearse, P., and Konopki, D. Spring 1979. A comparative analysis of state programs to promote new technology based enterprises. *The New England Journal of Business and Economics*.

Birch, D.L., 1979. The job generation process. MIT Program on Neighborhood and Regional Change. Cambridge, Mass.

Brophy, D.J. 1981. The flow of venture capital, 1977–1980. In *Frontiers of Entrepreneurship Research*, pp. 246–280.

Briskman, F. 1968. Venture capital: The decision to finance technically-based enterprises. 1976. thesis, MIT, Cambridge, Mass.

Charles River Associates. 1976. An analysis of venture capital market imperfections. NTIS Report PB-254996. Washington, D.C.: National Bureau of Standards.

Charpie, Robert A. (ed.). 1967. Technological innovation: Its environment and management. U.S. Department of Commerce Panel on Invention and Innovation. Washington, D.C.: U.S. Government Printing Office.

Daugherty, W.K. Apr. 1980. The limited partnership: A financing vehicle. *Journal of Small Business Management* 18 (2):55–60.

DeHudy, T.D., Fast, N.D., and Pratt, S.E., 1981a. *The Venture Capital Industry: Opportunities and Considerations for Investors*. Capital Publishing Corporation.

DeHudy, T.D., Fast, N.D., and Tarpley, F., 1981b. Economic growth through new business development. *Economic Development Commentary*, submitted for publication, Fall 1981.

Diebold Group, Inc. 1974. Venture capital investment guarantee study. NTIS Report PB-252867. Washington D.C.: National Science Foundation.

Dominquez, J. 1971. *Venture Capital.* D.C. Heath.

Dunn, D.T. 1975. New ventures departments at consumer package-goods firms. PhD dissertation, School of Business, University of Virginia, Charlottesville, Va.

Fast, N.D. 1978. The rise and fall of corporate new venture divisions. PhD dissertation, Harvard Business School, Cambridge, Mass.

Fast, N.D. March 1979. A visit to the new venture graveyard. *Research Management.*

Fast, N.D. March 1981. Pitfalls of corporate venturing. *Research Management* 24(2).

Faucett, R.B. 1971. The management of venture capital investment companies. MS thesis, Sloan School, MIT, Cambridge, Mass.

Hill, Christopher, and Utterback, James M. 1979. *Technological Innovation for a Dynamic Economy.* Elmsford, N.Y.: Pergamon.

Hoban, James P., Jr. 1976. Characteristics of venture capital investments. PhD dissertation, University of Utah, Provo.

Huntsman, B., and Hoban, J.P., Jr. Summer 1980. Investment in new enterprise: Some empirical observations on risk, return and market structure. *Financial Management* 44–51.

Ofer, A. 1975. *Survey of Venture Capital Industry.* National Venture Capital Association.

Osborn, R. Spring 1975. Providing risk capital for small business: Experience of the SBICs. *Quarterly Review of Economics and Business.*

Poindexter, John B. 1976. The efficiency of financial markets: The venture capital case. PhD dissertation, New York University, New York.

Pratt, Stanley E. (ed). 1983. *Guide to Venture Capital Sources,* 7th ed. Wellesley Hills, Mass.: Capital Publishing Company.

Pratt, Stanley E. July 1981. Capital transfusion 1981. *Venture Capital Journal.*

Roberts, E.B. Dec. 1970. How to succeed in a new technology enterprise. *Technology Review.*

Shapero, A. May 1969. The role of the financial community in the formation, growth, and effectiveness of technical companies: The attitude of commercial loan officers. Final Report to the Ozarks Regional Commission.

Smollen, L.E., and Levin, M.A. 1979. The role of small business in research, development, technological change and innovation in New England. In *A Region's Struggling Savior.* Waltham, Mass.: Small Business Foundation of America, pp. 69–126.

Taylor, C. 1969. *Starting Up in the High Technology Industries in California.* Wells Fargo Investment Co.

Tektronix 1978. *Venture Capital: A New Ventures Technique for Industrial Firms.*

Timmons, J.A., Smollen, L.E., and Dingee, A.L.M. 1985. *New Venture Creation,* 2nd ed. Homewood, Ill.

Timmons, J.A., 1985. Venture capital: More than money? In *Pratt's Guide to Venture Capital Sources,* 9th ed., Stanley E. Pratt, ed. Wellesley, Mass.: Venture Economics.

Timmons, J.A., 1981. Venture capital investors in the U.S.: A survey of the most active investors. *Frontiers of Entrepreneurship Research 1981.* Wellesley, Mass.: Babson College, pp. 199–216.

Timmons, J.A., 1982. Venture capital in Sweden. *Frontier of Entrepreneurship Research 1982,* Wellesley, Mass.: Babson College, pp. 294–321.

Timmons, J.A., and Gumpert, D.E. Jan.-Feb. 1982. Discard many old rules for raising venture capital. *Harvard Business Review.*

Timmons, J.A., Bygrave, W.D., and Fast, N.D. 1983. The flow of venture capital to high technology ventures 1967–1982. In *Frontiers of Entrepreneurship Research 1983.* Wellesley, Mass.: Babson College.

Tyebjee, T.T., and Bruno, A.V. 1984. *Venture Capital Allocation Decisions and Their Performance.* Santa Clara, Cal.: National Science Foundation.

Tyebjee, T.T., and Bruno, A.V. 1981. Venture capital decisions making: Preliminary results of three empirical studies. In *Frontier of Entrepreneurship Research 1981.* Wellesley, Mass.: Babson College.

176 J.A. TIMMONS AND W.D. BYGRAVE

U. S. Congress, House. *Small, High Technology Firms and Innovation Report Prepared by Subcommittee on Investigations and Oversight of the Committee on Science and Technology.* 96th Congress, 2nd session, 1979.

U. S. Congress, Senate. 1979. Innovation—startup, growth and survival of small, new technology firms. Joint hearing before the House Committees on Science and Technology and Small Business and the Senate Select Committee on Small Business. 96th Congress, 2nd session.

Venture Economics. 1981. *Venture Capital Investment—1980.*

Venture Economics. June 1, 1981. Venture capital investment in national needs areas. Report submitted to the U.S. Small Business Administration.

Von Hippel, E. 1973. An exploratory study of "corporate venturing"—A new product innovation strategy. PhD dissertation, Carnegie-Mellon University, Pittsburgh.

Wells, W. 1974. Venture capital decision-making. PhD dissertation, Carnegie-Mellon University, Pittsburgh.

[3]

WHAT DO

VENTURE

CAPITALISTS

DO?

MICHAEL GORMAN
McKinsey & Company

WILLIAM A. SAHLMAN
Harvard Business School

EXECUTIVE SUMMARY

This paper presents the results derived from 49 responses to a questionnaire mailed to 100 venture capitalists in late 1984. The purpose of the survey was to shed light on the relationship between venture capitalists and their portfolio companies. The survey revealed that the venture capitalists who responded spend about half their time monitoring nine portfolio investments; of these, five are companies on whose boards they sit. For the latter group, a venture capitalist typically devotes 80 hours of on-site time and 30 hours of phone time per year in direct contact with each company. The most frequently performed service for portfolio companies is to help raise additional funds, with strategic analysis and management recruiting also mentioned as important roles. Finally, the venture capitalists in the survey had replaced an average of three CEOs during their careers; weak senior management was considered to be the dominant cause of venture failure.

INTRODUCTION

Over the past five years, there has been an explosion in the level of activity in the venture capital market. In 1984, in excess of $4.5 billion of new capital was committed to the industry, an amount over six times greater than the amount committed in 1980. Over the same period, approximately 148 new venture capital partnerships were formed, while 303 new funds were created by existing venture capital firms. The perceived importance of venture capital in economic growth has grown at a rate at least as high (if not higher) than

Address correspondence to Dr. William A. Sahlman, Harvard University, Graduate School of Business Administration, Baker 436, Soldier's Field, Boston, MA 02163.

This article has benefited from the comments of two anonymous referees.

Journal of Business Venturing 4, 231–248
© 1989 Elsevier Science Publishing Co., Inc., 655 Avenue of the Americas, New York, NY 10010

0883-9026/89/$3.50

232 M. GORMAN AND W.A. SAHLMAN

the rate of growth of invested capital. The role of venture capital in the formation and nurturing of companies like Genentech, Apple Computer, Tandem, Lotus Development, Federal Express, and People Express has attracted the attention of academics, investors, and public policymakers.

In this context, it seems particularly important to try to understand the process of venture capital investing. Phrased more directly, What do venture capitalists do?[1] To begin to answer this question, we developed a questionnaire that was distributed to a group of venture capitalists in December of 1984. A primary goal of the questionnaire was to shed light on the relationship between the venture capitalists and their portfolio companies. Among the general areas covered by the questionnaire were:

- How much time do venture capitalists spend with their portfolio companies, and how is that time distributed?

- What roles do venture capitalists play in their portfolio companies?

- What happens to the relationship between venture capitalist and portfolio company during periods of adversity?

This paper is divided into five sections. In the first section (The Survey), the methodology is presented and the characteristics of the survey sample are summarized. The second section (The Venture Capital Investment Process) explores the survey results as related to achieving a general understanding of the venture capital business. The third section (The Venture Capitalist/Portfolio Company Relationship) addresses the principal questions motivating this study. The composition of venture capital portfolios, the allocation of each venture capitalist's time across all activities and among portfolio companies, and the nature of their contributions are each considered in turn. In the fourth section (Coping with Troubled Investments), we examine the role of venture capitalists during periods when the companies in which they invest fall on hard times. The paper concludes with a summary.

THE SURVEY

During the first week of December 1984, a three-page survey was distributed to approximately 100 venture capitalists. A statistical summary of the survey questions and responses can be found in Appendix 1. Mr. Nissan Boury of E.M. Warburg, Pincus & Co., Inc., a venture capital firm in New York City, was extremely helpful during the preparation of the survey, as were Messrs. Chris Brody, Andy Gaspar, and Jeffrey Harris, also of Warburg, Pincus, as well as Ms. Denise O'Leary of Menlo Ventures.

We received 49 responses to the survey. The respondents represented firms that manage in aggregate $5.6 billion of venture capital or roughly 40% of the estimated industry resources.[2] In an industry in which there are many relatively new entrants, respondents were drawn principally from firms that are well established. The mean age of the firms in the sample was 12 years, with the oldest firm claiming 38 years of operation and only three firms less than three years old. Among the respondents themselves, the typical individual had seven years of venture capital experience, with a high of 22 years. Few individuals

---

[1]There are a number of useful references on venture capitalists and their role in venture firms. Particularly relevant are Kozmetsky and Smilor (1985), Pratt (1987), Silver (1985), Robinson (1987), Sahlman and Soussou (1985), Sahlman (1986), and Wilson (1985).

[2]Virtually all of the aggregate data on the venture capital industry are drawn from various publications of Venture Economics in Wellesley Hills, Massachusetts. Some of the data are summarized in Appendix 2.

TABLE 1

	Mean	Median	Std. Dev.	High	Low
Firm capital under management ($ millions)	$147.5	125.0	$112.5	$600.0	$5.0
Age of firm (years)	13.9	13.0	11.6	38.0	1.5
Respondent's experience (years)	7.4	5.0	5.4	22.0	1.0

from firms with less than $60 million under management were surveyed, even though firms of this size represent a significant share of all venture firms. Only eight of the responding firms were founded in the past four years, a time when venture fund formation was occurring at an unprecedented rate. The sample statistics are summarized in Table 1.

Although the respondents worked with generally well-established venture capital firms, many of the respondents had more limited experience than the age of their associated firms might lead one to expect. The majority of those responding, 31 individuals, claimed less than six years of venture capital investing experience. This proportion is approximately the same as that for the overall industry. Indeed, the proportion of individual respondents with more than nine years of experience (18 of 49) is probably higher than the industry norm. Also, venture capital is for the most part a nonhierarchically organized profession: most of the respondents with less than six years' experience nonetheless entered the business as partners or at most served brief apprenticeships.

It is important to note, however, that many of the respondents have been industry participants only during relatively good times for the industry. Moreover, as will be stressed later, the responses to any survey reflect the environment at the time of the survey; 1984 was a year of considerable pressure in the industry, given the collapse in high technology stock prices and the decline in new capital being committed to the industry.

THE VENTURE CAPITAL INVESTMENT PROCESS

The survey yielded interesting information about the investment behavior of venture capitalists and venture capital firms. For instance, almost all venture capitalists reported an investment horizon fixed at between five and seven years. One venture capitalist claimed a ten year expected term of investment, several cited four years, and the remainder fell in the five- to seven-year category.

By contrast, wide variations appeared in the reported rate of new investment. New investments per year per firm ranged from a high of 30 to a low of 4, with a mean of 11.2 new investments per year (standard deviation, 5.6). Furthermore, the rate of new investments was not strongly correlated with firm size. The survey indicates that small venture firms, despite their size, often make substantial numbers of new investments per year relative to medium-size firms, whereas many large firms make surprisingly few investments.

The survey calls into question an allegation against venture capitalists commonly found in the press that they farm out their work to junior associates. When asked to specify the "number [and function] of individuals currently responsible for monitoring portfolio investments," 20% reported that none of their "associate-level" individuals were acting in this capacity. The remainder commonly reported that one or two of the firm's associates dis-

TABLE 2

	Mean	Median	Std. Dev.	High	Low
Number of active partners per firm	4.7	4.0	2.5	15.0	1.0
Number of investments managed per partner	8.0	8.0	3.5	20.0	4.0
Number of seats on boards per partner	5.1	5.0	2.0	8.5	0.0

charged this responsibility, but for significantly fewer investments than would a partner. Specifically, whereas the mean firm had 4.7 partners monitoring investments, the mean number of associates in this role was 2.6. The number of investments monitored per partner was 8.8 as compared with only 3.6 for the associates who were playing this role. Finally, while each partner was on five boards, associates were only on one board.

Summary data concerning the activities of partner-level venture capitalists are presented in Table 2.

THE VENTURE CAPITALIST/PORTFOLIO COMPANY RELATIONSHIP

In this section, we will divide our exploration of the venture capitalist/portfolio company relationship into three parts. We first examine data on the composition of respondents' portfolios. Sample patterns in the allocation of venture capitalists' time are then explored. Finally, venture capitalists' characterizations of their contributions to their companies are considered.

Portfolio Composition

Respondents were asked to list the number of companies for which they were personally responsible and to classify these companies into one of the following categories:

1. They serve as lead investor, having invested at the seed or start-up phase (lead).
2. They invested at the seed or start-up stage, but are not the lead investor (nonlead).
3. They are a later-stage, nonlead investor (late stage).

Note that these categories indicate at what stage in the life of the company the respondent first invested, not the stage at which the company currently finds itself. The typical respondent monitored 4.5 companies as the lead investor, 2.5 as a nonlead, early-stage investor, and 3.8 as a late-stage investor. The variation is summarized in Table 3.

Looking at averages alone, one might be tempted to say that the typical venture capitalist is relatively evenly diversified across these three distinct categories of investment behavior. The averages mask considerable variations in portfolio composition.

Without further data, definitive statements are not possible. However, it seems likely that venture capitalists (and their firms) tend to specialize in terms of the stage at which they invest and the role they take. The time demands and skill demands on the investor are likely to result in such focused strategies.

We know from the preceding discussion that the respondents maintain portfolios ranging in size from as few as 4 to as many as 35 investments, with a mean of 11. How much

TABLE 3

	Mean	Median	Std. Dev.	High	Low
Number of companies in which the respondent serves as:					
Lead investor	4.1	4.0	1.9	8.0	0.0
Nonlead early-stage investor	2.5	2.0	2.3	10.0	0.0
Late-stage investor	3.8	3.9	3.9	20.0	0.0
All categories	10.3	8.0	4.9	25.0	4.0

time do venture capitalists allocate to companies in their portfolio, as opposed to other activities? How do they distribute their time among investments that fall into each of the three categories described above?

Allocation of Time

The survey results indicate that venture capitalists spend the majority of their time managing their portfolios. Although the survey results are likely influenced by the time of its administration (December 1984), when many venture capitalists faced problems with portfolio companies, the information portrayed in Figure 1 is nonetheless impressive.

Most venture capitalists spend more than half their time with their portfolio companies. The median respondent spends 60% of his or her time on portfolio management.

How is this time allocated? As a proxy for time devoted to portfolio management, we asked respondents to report on the time they typically spend in *direct* contact with their investments. This measure, of course, excludes any work they do for companies that does not involve direct contact (e.g., reviewing written reports or contacting others on the company's behalf). Respondents were asked to report how much time they typically spend in direct contact with their companies by estimating their number of visits, typical length of visits, number of phone calls, and typical call length.

Not unexpectedly, we found that when venture capitalists play a lead investor role, they devote much more time than do nonlead or late-stage investors. In fact, a venture capitalist acting as lead investor will invest ten times the direct hours he or she would in a late-stage investment (for summary statistics see Appendix 1).

Notwithstanding this large discrepancy in relative commitment between the lead and nonlead investor roles, the absolute amount of time devoted to companies by active investors would not support a view of venture capitalists as individuals deeply involved on a day-to-day basis in the management activities of their portfolio investments. A typical early-stage investment gets a little more than two hours of direct attention per week from its lead venture capitalist. Nonlead venture capitalists contribute another three-quarters of an hour per week.

The venture capitalist tends to spend time with companies in small increments. Typically, lead-investing venture capitalist shows up frequently, 1.5 times a month, but stays only five hours each time. Nonlead venture investors, who were nonetheless there from the beginning, come half as often and and, when they do, stay two-thirds as long. Late-stage investors come to one four-hour meeting each quarter. Together, these statistics might imply that venture capital involvement is principally crisis or project oriented, like the efforts of

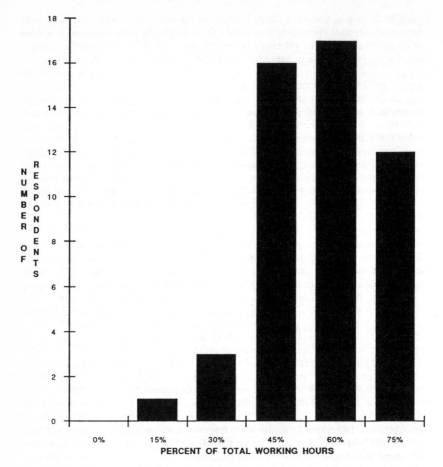

FIGURE 1   Percent of hours spent monitoring or assisting portfolio companies.

attorneys, consultants, and similar service providers. Alternately, the data would be consistent with a description of the venture capitalist's role as primarily a monitoring function,
not unlike the role of a senior manager in a large company overseeing many business units.

Respondents were fairly consistent across the sample in the amount of time reported
in contact with portfolio companies. For example, whereas the mean time spent on-site per
year by a venture capitalist who served as lead investor in a company was 80 hours (standard
deviation of 44 hours), only one individual claimed he typically spend more than 200 hours
per year with companies as a lead investor.

What do venture capitalists do during their time with a portfolio company?

Contributions of the Venture Capitalist

We asked venture capitalists to indicate whether they performed each of several services for
their companies; if so, to state how often; and, finally, to rank the services they provide in

TABLE 4

Form of Assistance	Rank	Frequency
Help obtaining additional financing	1.9	75.0
Strategic planning	2.4	67.5
Management recruitment	2.6	62.5
Operational planning	4.1	55.0
Introductions to potential customers and suppliers	4.6	52.5
Resolve compensation issues	5.6	55.0

order of importance. In Table 4, the services that venture capitalists provide are listed in the order in which venture capitalists tended to rank them. To the right of each service category are two scores. The first indicates the mean rank venture capitalists assigned this service, when they mentioned it. For example, a score of 2.0 would mean that venture capitalists, on average, ranked this service second in importance among the services they provide. The second score indicates the frequency with which portfolio companies receive this service from the venture capitalist. To illustrate, a score of 75.0 would indicate that, on average, 75% of the companies in which venture capitalists are actively involved receive this service from their venture capitalist.

Write-in candidates, each offered by a single respondent, that might well have received additional votes had they been listed included (7) serving as the entrepreneur's confidant, (8) introductions to service providers such as lawyers and public relations firms, (9) managing the investor group, (10) recruitment of board members, and, for venture capital subsidiaries of major corporations, (11) access to the resources of the parent company. Each write-in category was generally suggested only once or twice and was usually ranked third or fourth by the respondent submitting it.

From these results, it seems that venture capitalists provide three critical services in addition to providing money: 1) building the investor group (32 of 44 respondents who indicated they help raise more money ranked this service first or second in importance), 2) reviewing and helping to formulate business strategy, and 3) filling in the management team. These services require that one venture capitalist remain in frequent but by no means constant contact with portfolio companies. Company performance is monitored regularly, and when more funds are needed or when there is a gap in the management team, the venture capitalist's involvement escalates.

COPING WITH TROUBLED INVESTMENTS

The field upon which venture capitalists play is littered with the remains of failed companies. A few, such as Osborne Computer, Ovation Technologies, or Gavilan Computer, have failed spectacularly enough as to invite the brief attention of the business community at large. But these meteoric conclusions are hardly typical of a venture capitalist's experience, no more typical, perhaps, than the phenomenal, industry-founding successes that have earned the venture business its present reputation. Much more common is the phenomenon know euphemistically among venture capitalists as "the living dead," a phrase that refers to venture-backed companies that have failed to meet expectations but that nonetheless squeeze out a stable, independent existence. When aggregated with the outright failures discovered along the way, the "living dead" probably make up the majority of most mature venture capital portfolios.

Why is the failure rate (when compared with initial expectations) so high?

There are a few obvious answers. For one thing, most venture businesses are launched despite numerous and often consequential uncertainties that can be resolved only by going foreword. Furthermore, venture-backed companies have extremely limited resources, so unexpected snags can quickly exhaust available reserves of cash and people.

Venture-backed companies are thinly staffed and thinly capitalized by design. Venture capitalists, for their part, generally seek to provide their entrepreneurs with only the minimum of cash required. They tend to dole out financing in discrete amounts closely matched to the attainment of clear milestones, enabling them to limit damage by refusing additional financing if the company appears unsuccessful in the early stages. Meanwhile, entrepreneurs, because they are motivated to retain for themselves as much as they can of their business's value, are loath to incur any up-front expenditure that might conceivably be avoided. Selling too much of the company at the earliest stages amounts to an expensive mortgage on the future wealth against which the entrepreneur has wagered his or her career. Thus both venture capitalists and entrepreneurs willingly conspire to impose stringent limits on the resiliency of their enterprises.

Failure may also occur if the management of the company or the quality of its product is not up to the demands placed upon it by the marketplace or if competitors capture its target customers.[3] Even the venture capital industry itself may contribute to business failure. In a recent paper, William Sahlman and Howard Stevenson (1985) document the six-year-long parade of venture capital investors into an emerging segment of the computer data storage industry. In all, 43 start-ups were funded in an industry segment that could be expected in the long run to support perhaps four.

Thus, "failure" is at the very least endemic to the venture capital process, an expected, commonplace event; in some cases, the process itself may even promote failure. How do venture capitalists respond to this hazard of their profession? What do venture capitalists see as the most common causes of failure? Do their perceptions of the causes of failure influence the actions they take when their investments appear threatened? What are the implications of high failure rates of the relationship between venture capitalists and their portfolio companies?

The results of our survey indicate that venture capitalists, as a whole, have straight-forward answers to the questions posed above. In an industry where failure is frequent, where both venture capitalists and entrepreneurs take actions at the outset of launching businesses that make failure, in a statistical sense, likely to occur, venture capitalists almost uniformly attribute failures they have observed to shortcomings in senior management.

We asked venture capitalists the following question: "Consider companies with which you have been associated that have fallen seriously short of their objectives, so far short as to endanger the company's continued independent existence. For a maximum of three such companies, identify which of the following eleven factors were major contributors to their difficulties and then rank the contributing factors in order of importance."

It is a difficult question to answer. Fortunately, most respondents took the time to respond, enabling us to construct a sample of 96 troubled companies. In 91 of 96 cases, venture capitalists cited senior management as a "contributing factor." In 62 of those cases,

---

[3]See also Vesper (1980) and Bruno, Lendecker and Harder (1986) for more insights on the failure of ventures.

TABLE 5

	Frequency (%)	Rank	Std. Dev.
Management problems			
(1) Ineffective senior management (SMAN)	95	1.6	1.0
(2) Ineffective functional management (FMAN) (i.e., finance, marketing, etc.)	50	2.5	1.1
Market problems			
(3) End user market failed to develop as expected (MKT)	43	2.7	1.9
Company failed to capture share due to:			
(4) Poor channel selection/channel resistance (DIST)	35	3.3	1.5
(5) Competition (COMP)	34	3.0	1.3
(6) Poor product/market fit (FIT)	28	3.5	1.7
Product problems			
(7) Development delayed or unsuccessful (DEVT)	51	2.4	1.4
(8) Manufacturing failure (MFG)	11	2.9	1.4
(9) Poor product performance (PROD)	18	4.2	1.4
(10) Inadequate quality control (QUAL)	13	4.7	2.4

The abbreviated codes are used in Figure 2.

or roughly 65% of the entire sample, venture capitalists cited senior management as *the most important contributing factor*.

Interestingly, only seven companies, drawn from the experience of three respondents, were judged to have failed *solely* due to senior management. To what causes other than senior management do venture capitalists assign responsibility for business failure?

The responses of venture capitalists are shown in tabular form in Table 5 and graphically in Figure 2. The three columns to the right of each factor in Table 5 refer to 1) the frequency, expressed as a percentage, with which venture capitalists cited this factor as one contributing to business failure, 2) what mean rank of importance they tended to assign it when it was mentioned, and 3) how widely respondents' rankings varied (number shown equals the standard deviation).

Figure 2 highlights several interesting facts. First of all, in general, the more frequently a factor was mentioned, the more important the role it was deemed to play. The only exceptions to this general trend are manufacturing problems that occur infrequently, but, when they do occur, cause grave problems. ("Other" problems, cited infrequently, included "overhead ahead of market," "delay/lack of financing," "price competition," "cost control," "lack of effective marketing strategy"; most of these seem to fall into one of the categories listed.)

"Development delayed or unsuccessful" emerges as the culprit in over 50% of the cases, and its high ranking indicates that delay in product development was the major cause of venture failure cited by respondents excluding those causes related to management. Problems of functional management are cited as the third most critical cause of failure. Taken as a group, marketing problems of one sort or another hold down a consistent fourth place, with a pair of product problems bringing up the rear.

Venture capitalists recognized the existence of other major contributing factors, but almost in unison they assigned to those factors lesser significance than to the actions of

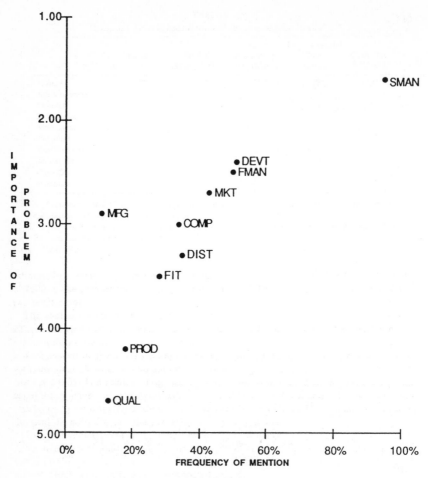

FIGURE 2   Failure causes.

senior management. The message of their responses is clear: Senior management is the critical ingredient that makes or breaks venture-backed businesses.

What are we to make of this? Certainly, the presence of competent senior management is an important ingredient in the success of an entrepreneurial venture. And, of course, no senior management is ever as good as it might have been, and so in every case senior management can be said to have contributed to their company's failure by virtue of their inadequacies. Before the discussion is ended, however, it should be noted that survey respondents' unequivocal belief that senior management represents the principal cause of entrepreneurial failure is not inconsistent with several plausible alternative explanations.

For one thing, the nature of the venture capitalist's role in portfolio companies may contribute to a tendency among venture capitalists to equate venture failure with senior management ineffectiveness. From the survey, we know that venture capitalists who act as lead investors visit their companies about once every three weeks. Typically, they stay for a morning or an afternoon. We know, too, that their principal concerns are with upcoming financings, hiring and firing of managers at the highest level, and setting strategy. Given these facts about the substantive nature of their interaction with portfolio companies, one can reasonably infer that when venture capitalists visit, they typically meet with senior management. With whom do they spend 30 hours a year on the phone?—senior management. To whom did they commit the funds at the start-up stage, when employees were few, if any?—senior management. And when things get tough, it is senior management who delivers bad news. It may not be far from the truth to say that, to the venture capitalist, the entrepreneur *is* the company. Given these facts of venture capitalist behavior documented by the survey, it is not surpising that any failure of the company is by definition viewed as a personal failure.

Venture capitalists and entrepreneurs alike think of accepting venture capital as equivalent to entering into a partnership. Ideally, they structure a relationship where their two interests are brought into alignment, where the economics of their agreement lead each party, simply by following his or her self-interest, to advance the other's interest as well. When things are proceeding reasonably well in the underlying business, venture capitalist/entrepreneur arrangements in fact function this way. But our conversations with entrepreneurs and venture capitalists alike indicate that when things go badly, the interests of the two parties diverge. The entrepreneur, motivated by a dream of building a company, is intent that the company survive, that the dream be kept alive. The venture capitalist, by contrast, is intent on preserving the value of his or her capital investment and maximizing the return on his or her scarce resource, time. These two viewpoints may lead to conflict in various forms: Should "excessive" costs be cut by firing employees or eliminating expenditures? Should additional cash be advanced even though milestones have not yet been met? Should the business be sold to a corporate suitor? Other manifestations of the conflict might easily be imagined. In such circumstances, one might expect that the entrepreneur, whose actions are founded on interests suddenly different from those of the venture capitalist, would be perceived by the investing group as, at best, an annoyance, and at worst as a selfish and destructive force at the head of "their" company.

The venture capitalist, acting through the board of directors, typically gains the power to fire senior management in the initial negotiation. We asked venture capitalists how often they resorted to this final privilege. The answer is, "Frequently." The mean (in the statistical sense) venture capitalist has initiated the firing of three CEO/Presidents, or one CEO/President per 2.4 years of venture investing experience. Given that a venture capitalist typically monitors only nine companies at a time, and expects to hold each investment five to seven years, this represents a noticeably high incidence of what is for all parties a traumatic experience. It seems clear that one of the most significant, not to mention dramatic, things that venture capitalists do is to evaluate management and, when they feel it to be necessary, to dismiss a company's leadership.

CONCLUSIONS

What do venture capitalists do?

Venture capitalists find new investment opportunities and appear to add them at the rate of two per person per year.

They spend better than half of their time monitoring approximately nine investments

242   M. GORMAN AND W.A. SAHLMAN

for which they are personally responsible. Of these, five were companies they helped found and on whose board of directors they serve.

They visit their companies relatively frequently, though for reasonably short periods each time. All told, a venture capitalist will spend 80 hours a year on-site with a company on whose board he or she serves. Frequent telephone conversations fill the gaps between visits and amount to an additional 30 hours per year. In addition, the venture capitalist works on the company's behalf by attracting new investors, evaluating strategy against new conditions, and interviewing/recruiting new management candidates.

When venture-backed companies fail, the venture capitalist sometimes is led to dismiss current management and seek new leadership. Venture capitalists find overwhelmingly that the cause of venture failure, when it occurs, lies with senior management; among nonmanagerial causes, they cite product development failures in half the cases.

APPENDIX 1   Survey of Venture Capitalists Concerning Their Relationship
with Portfolio Companies

SECTION I

1. Please fill in the table below. Use judgement and approximations where precise data would be difficult to assemble.

Category	Response
Firmwide	
a) Capital under management	_____
b) Number of years in venture capital business	_____
c) Number of individuals currently responsible for monitoring portfolio investments	
Partner level	_____
Nonpartner level	_____
d) Number of portfolio investments for which typical individual is currently responsible	
Partner level	_____
Nonpartner level	_____
e) Number of Boards of directors on which typical individual serves	
Partner level	_____
Nonpartner level	_____
f) Number of new investments per year (assume steady inflow of new capital at current rate; exclude follow-on investments)	_____
g) Period (years) you would expect to hold typical investment	_____
h) Number of years in venture capital business	_____
Respondent Only	
i) Number of portfolio investments for which you are personally responsible by role played:	
Lead investor	_____
Piggyback investor (early stage)	_____
Late-stage investor	_____
j) Number of boards of directors on which you serve	_____

2. Roughly speaking, what percentage of your working hours over the course of a year do you devote to monitoring and assisting portfolio companies? (Check one.)

_____0% _____ 15% _____ 30% _____45% _____ 60% _____ 75% _____ 90%

SECTION II

1. For approximately what percentage of your portfolio companies would you describe your role as essentially passive?

_____0% _____ 15% _____ 30% _____45% _____ 60% _____ 75% _____ 90%

2. For companies in which you play an active role, please answer the following question: In addition to contributing capital, what are the forms of assistance you offer to portfolio companies, and for approximately what proportion of your portfolio companies do you in fact provide each form of assistance? Please rank these services in order of their importance. (If you perform a service listed below, check the appropriate box, i.e., "I perform this service for between __ % and __ % of my portfolio companies." If you do not perform the service, leave the boxes blank.)

		Frequency			
Rank	Form of Assistance	0–25%	25–50%	50–75%	75–100%
_____	Introductions to potential customers and suppliers	_____	_____	_____	_____
_____	Management recruitment	_____	_____	_____	_____
_____	Help obtaining additional financing	_____	_____	_____	_____
_____	Strategic planning	_____	_____	_____	_____
_____	Operational planning	_____	_____	_____	_____
_____	Resolve compensation issues	_____	_____	_____	_____
	Other (please list)				
_____		_____	_____	_____	_____
_____		_____	_____	_____	_____

3. Please use your experience and judgement to provide esimates for the table below. Respond with reference to the portfolio companies for which you are personally responsible.

	Portfolio company for which you were a seed or start-up investor		
	Lead	Nonlead	Late-stage investor
Visits per year	_____	_____	_____
Length of typical visit (hours)	_____	_____	_____
Phone conversations per month	_____	_____	_____
Length of typical conversation (min.)	_____	_____	_____

SECTION III

1. Consider companies with which you have been associated that have fallen seriously short of their objectives, so far short as to endanger the company's continued independent existence. For a maximum of three such companies, identify which of the following factors were major contributors to their difficulties and then rank the contributing factors in order of importance.

		Company		
Rank	Contributing Factor	No. 1	No. 2	No. 3
	Management Problems:			
_____	Ineffective senior management	_____	_____	_____
_____	Ineffective functional management (i.e. finance, marketing, etc.)	_____	_____	_____
	Market problems:			
_____	End user market failed to develop as expected	_____	_____	_____
	Company failed to capture share due to:			
_____	Poor channel selection/channel resistance	_____	_____	_____
_____	Competition	_____	_____	_____
_____	Poor product/market fit	_____	_____	_____
	Product problems:			
_____	Development delayed or unsuccessful	_____	_____	_____
_____	Manufacturing failure	_____	_____	_____
_____	Poor product performance	_____	_____	_____
_____	Inadequate quality control	_____	_____	_____
	Other (please list)			
_____		_____	_____	_____

2. Have you ever initiated the removal of company managers? If yes, how many times and which managers?

	Number of Times I	
	Initiated Removal	Agreed to Removal
CEO	_____	_____
President	_____	_____
Functional Managers (e.g., Marketing)	_____	_____

3. Have you ever assumed a management role in a portfolio company? What role or roles have you assumed? How long did you remain in the role(s)?

Summary Response Data

Variable	Mean	Std. Dev.	High	Low	Number of Responses
SECTION I					
1. a) Capital under management (millions of dollars)	$147.5	$112.5	$600.0	$5.0	49
b) Firm years in business	11.6	7.3	38.0	1.5	49
c) Number responsible for portfolio management					
Partner level	4.7	2.5	25.0	1.0	49
Nonpartner level*	2.6	1.8	8.0	1.0	36
d) Investments per person					
Partner level	8.8	3.5	20.0	4.0	49
Nonpartner level*	3.6	3.0	11.0	0.0	35

Summary Response Data (*Continued*)

Variable	Mean	Std. Dev.	High	Low	Number of Responses
SECTION I					
e) Boards per person					
Partner level	5.0	3.0	21.0	0.0	49
Nonpartner level*	1.0	1.2	4.0	0.0	36
f) Annual rate of new					
investment	11.2	5.6	30.0	4.0	49
g) Years investments are held	5.8	1.1	10.0	4.0	49
h) Respondent years in business	7.4	5.4	22.0	1.0	49
i) Number of investments					
respondent manages					
Lead investor	4.5	3.5	25.0	0.0	49
Piggyback investor					
(early stage)	2.5	2.3	10.0	0.0	48
Late-stage investor	3.8	3.9	20.0	0.0	48
j) Respondent board seats	4.9	2.9	12.0	0.0	49
2. Hours spent monitoring and					
assisting portfolio (percent of					
total hours)	55.9%	14.6%	75.0%	15.0%	49
3. For the following types of investments,					
estimate the extent of your direct contact.					
Lead investor					
Visits per year	18.7	12.9	80.0	0.0	47
Visit duration (hours)	4.9	2.7	15.0	0.0	47
Annual hours on-site	80.5	44.0	262.5	0.0	47
Phone conversations					
(per month)	7.5	5.0	25.0	0.0	47
Conversation length (min.)	21.9	15.4	90.0	0.0	46
Annual telephone hours	34.5	37.9	225.0	0.0	46
Nonlead piggyback					
Visits per year	9.1	5.1	25.0	1.0	44
Visit duration (hours)	3.4	1.7	9.0	0.5	44
Annual hours on-site	30.8	23.5	99.0	3.0	44
Phone conversations					
(per month)	2.8	2.7	12.0	0.0	43
Conversation length (min.)	14.4	6.9	30.0	0.0	43
Annual telephone hours	8.0	8.6	48.0	0.0	43
Late-stage investor					
Visits per Year	4.7	2.8	15.0	1.0	43
Visit Duration (Hours)	2.9	1.7	10.0	0.5	42
Annual Hours On-Site	12.9	10.3	40.0	3.0	42
Phone Conversations					
(per month)	1.3	1.4	6.0	0.0	41
Conversation Length (min.)	13.2	10.3	45.0	0.0	41
Annual Telephone Hours	3.9	5.3	24.0	0.0	41

SECTION II

1. Indicate how frequently you perform each of the following services for your portfolio's companies.

246   M. GORMAN AND W.A. SAHLMAN

Note: The four choices included 0–25%, 25–50%, 50–75%, and 75–100%. We have used the medians
        12.5%, 37.5%, 62.5%, and 87.5% to compute the statistics shown.

Variable	Mean (%)	Std. Dev. (%)	High (%)	Low (%)	Number of Responses
Introductions to customers, suppliers, etc.	52.5	27.5	87.5	87.5	47
Management recruitment	62.5	25.0	87.5	12.5	48
Seeking additional financing	75.0	10.0	87.5	12.5	48
Strategic planning	67.5	22.5	87.5	12.5	49
Operational planning	55.0	27.5	87.5	12.5	47
Resolution of compensation issues	55.0	27.5	87.5	12.5	45
Other					
Entrepreneur's confidant	75.0	12.5	87.5	62.5	2
Introductions to service providers	75.0	12.5	87.5	62.5	2
Manage investor group	75.0	12.5	87.5	62.5	2
Evaluate management	62.5	25.0	87.5	37.5	2
Help form and manage board	12.5	0.0	12.5	12.5	1
Evaluate acquisitions	62.5	0.0	62.5	62.5	1
Access to resources of a large company	87.5	0.0	87.5	87.5	1

2. Rank the following ways you might assist your portfolio companies in order of their importance.

Note: "Mean" here indicates the average rank this form of assistance received when it was mentioned.
        "Number" indicates how often it was mentioned.

Variable	Mean	Std. Dev.	High	Low	Number of Responses
Introductions to customers, suppliers, etc.	4.6	1.5	8.0	2.0	43
Management recruitment	2.6	1.4	6.0	1.0	44
Seeking additional financing	1.9	0.9	4.5	1.0	44
Strategic planning	2.4	1.1	5.0	1.0	45
Operational planning	4.1	1.4	7.0	1.0	44
Resolution of compensation issues	5.6	0.8	7.0	3.0	41
Other					
Entrepreneur's confidant	4.0	0.0	4.0	4.0	2
Introductions to service providers	5.0	0.0	5.0	5.0	1
Manage investor group	1.5	0.0	1.5	1.5	1

SECTION III

1. Identify which of the following factors were major contributors to the difficulties of a troubled company with
   which you have been associated and rank them in order of importance

	Mean	Std. Dev.	High	Low	Number of Responses
Management problems					
Ineffective sr. management	1.6	1.0	5.0	1.0	91
Ineffective functional management	2.5	1.1	6.0	1.0	48

SECTION III

	Mean	Std. Dev.	High	Low	Number of Responses
Market problems					
End user market failed to develop	2.7	1.9	10.0	1.0	41
Channel problems	3.3	1.5	8.0	1.0	34
Competition	3.0	1.3	6.0	1.0	33
Product/market fit	3.5	1.7	7.0	1.0	27
Product problems					
Development delayed	2.4	1.4	6.0	1.0	49
Manufacturing failure	2.9	1.4	6.0	1.0	11
Poor product performance	4.2	1.4	8.0	3.0	17
Inadequate quality control	4.7	2.4	10.0	2.0	12
Other	2.7	0.9	5.0	2.0	

2. How many times have you initiated the removal of a company's CEO/President?

	3.0	2.1	8.0	0.0	

*For sample *with* associates.

APPENDIX 2 Summary Data on the Economy and Venture Capital Markets

Row	1978	1979	1980	1981	1982	1983	1984
Macroeconomic data							
1 Nominal gross national product	2,164	2,418	2,633	2,938	3,058	3,310	3,662
2 Percent change in GNP deflator	7.4	8.6	9.3	9.4	6.0	4.2	3.8
3 Percent change in real GNP	5.0	2.8	−0.3	2.6	−1.9	3.3	6.7
4 Consumer price inflation	9.0	13.3	12.4	8.9	3.9	3.8	4.2
5 Unemployment rate	6.1	5.8	7.1	7.6	9.7	9.5	7.5
6 Industrial product index (mfg)	146.8	153.6	146.7	150.4	137.6	147.7	163.2
7 Net business formation index	128.2	128.3	122.4	118.6	113.2	115.0	117.1
8 Business failure rate (per 10,000)	23.9	27.8	42.1	61.3	89.0	109.7	79.7
Financial market data							
9 3-Month U.S. treasury bills	7.2	10.0	11.5	14.1	10.7	8.6	9.6
10 Corporate Aaa bonds	8.7	9.6	11.9	14.2	13.8	12.0	12.7
11 Prime interest rate	9.1	12.7	15.3	18.9	14.9	10.8	12.0
12 Standard & Poor's 500 index (EOY)	96.1	107.9	135.8	122.6	140.6	164.9	167.2
13 NASDAQ composite index (EOY)	139.3	152.3	208.2	223.5	340.7	328.9	258.9
14 Venture 100 index [EOY]	261.5	369.7	655.7	569.8	715.7	842.6	536.3
Venture capital and IPO activity							
15 Net new commitments to the venture capital industry ($mil)	600	300	700	1,300	1,800	4,500	4,200
16 Total venture capital pool ($mil)	3,500	3,800	4,500	5,800	7,600	12,100	16,300
17 Estimated disbursements to portfolio companies ($mil)	550	1,000	1,100	1,400	1,800	2,800	3,000
18 Median size of public venture funds ($mil)	15.0	24.5	20.0	19.6	22.0	25.2	30.0
Total new partnership formation							
19 Number	13	14	22	37	54	89	101
20 Amount ($mil)	216	170	661	866	1,423	3,460	3,300
Public underwritings of companies with net worth							

248   M. GORMAN AND W.A. SAHLMAN

APPENDIX 2   *(Continued)*

Row	1978	1979	1980	1981	1982	1983	1984
21 Less than $5MM (no.)	21	46	135	306	113	477	224
22 Amount Raised ($mil)	129	183	822	1,760	619	3,671	1,190
All initial public offerings							
23 Number of offerings	45	81	237	448	222	884	548
24 Amount raised ($mil)	249	506	1,397	3,215	1,446	12,619	3,832

Most of the data in rows 1 though 11 represents averages for the relevant time period. EOY, end of year (or period) data.
Source: Economic Report of the President, various issues; Venture Economics, Wellesley, Massachusetts (row 15–22); *Going Public: The IPO Reporter,* Howard & Company, Philadelphia, PA (rows 23 and 24); Casewriter Estimates.

REFERENCES

Bruno, A.V., Lendecker, J.K., and Harder, J.W. 1986. Patterns of failure among Silicon Valley high technology firms. In J.A. Hornaday, R. Peterson, R. Ronstadt, and K.H. Vesper, eds., *Frontiers of Entrepreneurship Research 1986.* Babson College, Wellesley, MA: Center for Entrepreneurial Studies.

Kozmetsky, G.G., and Smilor, R.W. 1985. *Financing and Managing Fast-Growth Companies: The Venture Capital Process.* New York: Lexington Books.

Macmillan, I.C., Siegel, R., Narashima, P.N. and Sabbe. 1985. Criteria used by venture capitalists to evaluate new venture proposals. *Journal of Business Venturing* 1(1):119–128.

Robinson, R.D., Jr. 1987. Emerging strategies in The venture capital industry. *Journal of Business Venturing* 2(1):53–77.

Sahlman, W.A., and Soussou, H. 1985. Note on the Venture Capital Industry (1981). Case #9-285-096. Boston: Harvard Business School.

Sahlman, W.A. 1986. Note on the Venture Capital Industry—Update (1985). Case #9-286-060. Boston: Harvard Business School.

Silver, D.A. 1985. *Venture Capital: The Complete Guide for Investors.* New York: John Wiley & Sons.

Vesper, K.H. 1980. *New Venture Strategies.* Englewood Cliffs, NJ: Prentice Hall.

Wilson, J.W. 1985. *The New Venturers: Inside the High Stakes World of Venture Capital.* Reading, MA: Addison-Wesley.

Part II
Systemic Issues: Macro-Perspectives of the 1990s

[4]

THE FOUNDING RATE

OF VENTURE CAPITAL FIRMS

IN THREE EUROPEAN

COUNTRIES (1970–1990)

SOPHIE MANIGART

University of Ghent, Belgium

EXECUTIVE SUMMARY

In this article, the sectorial and environmental forces that facilitate or inhibit the creation of venture capital companies are studied in the three European countries where the industry is most developed: the United Kingdom, France, and the Netherlands. The focus is on the start-up phase of the industry, the period from 1970–1990. The founding of firms can be studied on four different levels: entrepreneurial, organizational, population, and macroeconomic. In this study, a population approach is taken; this implies that we do not attempt to explain any single founding, but rather the aggregate number of foundings that occur in an industry in a certain period in a certain country.

According to the organizational ecology theory, the population density (i.e., the total number of organizations in a population) is the major environmental factor that affects the founding rate through two processes. Initially, when the density is low, each founding eases new foundings, because the simple prevalence of a form tends to give it legitimacy (thereby spurring imitations), the training ground for qualified personnel grows and the supporting networks are widened and strengthened. The legitimation process does not grow forever: once enough organizations of a certain kind exist, legitimation attains a ceiling. As the number of organizations increases, the second process becomes dominant: the competition for resources (raw material, personnel, customers, capital) grows, leading to a negative relationship between the density and the founding rate, everything else being equal. Thus, the founding rate declines as the number of organizations increases, once a threshold is reached. The major hypothesis that is tested here is that the population density has an inverted U-shaped effect on the founding rate of venture capital organizations.

In addition, the effect that the venture capital firms of the three countries have on each other is studied. Two populations are said to interact when the populations affect each other's growth rate,

Address correspondence to Sophie Manigart, Faculty of Economic and Applied Economic Sciences, De Vlerick School voor Management, University of Ghent, Hoveniersberg 4, B - 9000 Ghent, Belgium.

This study was financed by the Interuniversitary College for Doctoral Studies in Management, Brussels; it was part of the doctoral dissertation. An earlier version was first presented at the 1993 Babson Entrepreneurship Research Conference. The author thanks the members of the dissertation committee, especially Hubert Ooghe and William Bygrave, and two anonymous reviewers for their helpful comments.

Journal of Business Venturing **9**, 525–541

© 1994 Elsevier Science Inc., 655 Avenue of the Americas, New York, NY 10010

0883-9026/94/$7.00

526 S. MANIGART

but the interaction need not be symmetrical. The second hypothesis, tested in this study, is that populations in different countries have a positive effect on each other and not a competitive effect because the legitimating effect does not halt at geographical borders. Yet, the competition for resources (capital, people, deals) among geographically different populations is limited in this industry.

This study is valuable because until now, the existing ecological studies focus on long-established industries. Testing. the theory in a young industry that emerged only in the seventies (in Europe) has merits in its own right, because the technological progress after the Second World War has altered the organizational environment tremendously. The communication and transportation revolutions may have especially influenced the way in which organizations interact with each other and with the environment. The venture capital firms are furthermore special in the way they are organized with the dual structure of management company and investment fund(s). If the theory holds in this young industry, important additional evidence will be given that the theory is truly applicable to "populations of all types, in any time period, and in any society" (Carroll 1988, p. 18). Finally, this study extends the theory by giving evidence on how industries in different countries may interact upon each other.

We show empirically that the major factor that influences the overall founding rate in each of the three countries is the density of the industry, i.e., the number of organizations that already exist in the industry; this confirms the population ecology theory. When the density is low, adding a new organization to the industry raises the probability of a subsequent founding; when the density is high, the contrary is true. The institutional changes considered here, such as the establishment of tax transparent legal entities or state guarantees against losses (in the Netherlands) and the establishment of secondary stock markets, do not significantly influence the founding rate in any of the three countries. Moreover, the Dutch foundings are positively influenced by the British density and the French foundings by the Dutch density; the British foundings are, on the contrary, negatively influenced by the Dutch density. The competitive effects between the Netherlands and the U.K. are thus more important than initially thought.

The relationship between the density and the founding rate is the strongest, most consistent, and most significant relationship found in this study. Thus, the number of organizations that already exist in an industry is very important in explaining the founding of organizations, apart from, for example, the personality of the entrepreneur or from the networks in which he or she is involved. This indicates that, when trying to explain the founding of organizations, the industry structure, and more specifically the number of organizations that exist at the moment of the founding, cannot be ignored.

INTRODUCTION

One of the most fundamental questions in entrepreneurial research is "Why are new organizations created?" This question can be studied on four different levels: entrepreneurial, organizational, population, and macroeconomic (Van de Ven et al. 1984). The entrepreneur is considered to be the driving force for the initiation and the start-up of new businesses in the *entrepreneurial approach*. Various studies take this approach, where the economists emphasize the entrepreneur as agent of change or profit maximizer (e.g. Schumpeter 1934), whereas the psychologists take a personality trait perspective (e.g. McClelland 1961). The *organizational approach* takes the organization and the overall network of people involved in its creation as the focus of the analysis. This view led to studies on the social networks that support the entrepreneur (Aldrich and Zimmer 1986) and on the social and environmental structures surrounding the founding of an organization (e.g. Stinchcombe 1965; Van de Ven 1980). In the *macroeconomic* approach, all firms created during a certain period of time in a certain region are the unit of analysis, regardless of to which industry they belong. Regional differences in founding rates are explained by cultural and economical characteristics, such as the unemployment rate (e.g. Westhead and Moyes 1991).

In an intermediate level of analysis, the *population ecology approach* takes a whole industry or the "population of organizations" as the unit of analysis. Ecology can be defined in a zoological or botanical context as "the study of the way in which organisms live in their environments." Translated to the study of organizations, the ecological approach is not concerned with how to start a specific firm, but with how structural, political, and environmental economic conditions affect the creation and dissolution of firms in an industry (Van de Ven 1980). The organizational ecology theory views the emergence, growth, and decline of a population of organizations as a result of the driving forces of the environment (Winter 1990; Bygrave 1993).

As the present study will mainly rely on population ecology arguments, these will be explicated later. This approach implies that we do not attempt to explain any single organizational founding, but rather the aggregate number of foundings that occur in a certain period in a certain country. The basic ecological hypothesis with respect to organizational foundings is that the founding rate rises when the number of organizations that already exist in a certain population is low but increases. Once a certain threshold is reached, however, every increase in the number of organizations decreases the probability of a subsequent founding (e.g. Hannan and Freeman 1977, 1989).

This hypothesis has already been confirmed in a variety of industries (Hannan and Carroll 1992). Why, then, is an additional study appropriate? A first reason is that each study provides a case study of a particular industry in a certain country or region; finding the same hypothesized relationships in another industry strengthens the validity of the theory. A second reason is that, until now, the existing ecological studies have focused on long-established industries, such as the beer brewing industry, the newspaper industry, the insurance industry, etc. However, it is likely that the early phase of development of an industry may well have changed dramatically after the Second World War, due to the tremendous technological progress that has been made since then (Boone and van Witteloostuijn 1994). The communication and transportation revolutions may have especially influenced the way in which organizations interact with each other and with the environment. For example, as the news spread faster and information was more readily available, the legitimation process may have been dramatically shortened. Therefore, testing the theory in a young industry that emerged only in the seventies (in Europe) has merits in its own right. If the theory is confirmed in this young industry, important additional evidence will be given that the theory is truly applicable to "populations of all types, in any time period, and in any society" (Carroll 1988, p. 18).

The venture capital firms are furthermore special in the way they are organized: they often have the dual structure of an independent management company and fund(s) under management, in contrast to the more "traditional" organizations that have been studied until now. If the theory holds for this industry, the first part of Carroll's quotation is strengthened. Finally, this study extends the theory by giving evidence on how industries in different countries may interact with each other.

CREATION OF ORGANIZATIONS IN A POPULATION ECOLOGY PERSPECTIVE

The population ecology approach focuses on the effects of environmental constraints and competition within and between populations to explain the processes of expansion and decline of populations of organizations (Aldrich, McKelvey, and Ulrich 1984, p. 68). Organizations are viewed as "open systems," acknowledging the role of the environment in shaping organizational structures, apart from the role of management.

528   S. MANIGART

According to organizational ecology theory, the major environmental factor that affects the founding rate (through two processes) is the population density, i.e. the total number of organizations in a population.[1] Initially, when the density is low, each founding eases new foundings (Hannan 1986; Hannan and Freeman 1989; Hannan and Carroll 1992), because the training ground for qualified personnel grows and the supporting networks are widened and strengthened. Moreover, the simple prevalence of a form tends to give it legitimacy, as posited in the institutional theory of organizations (Zucker 1983), where legitimation is defined as the process whereby an organization justifies to a peer or superordinate system its right to exist, that is, to continue to import, transform, and export energy, material, or information. However, the legitimation process does not grow forever. Once enough organizations of a certain kind exist, legitimation attains a ceiling and does not increase any more (Hannan and Freeman 1989, p. 133). In this approach, the population density is a proxy variable for the legitimation, which is not directly observable.

As the number of organizations grows, the second process becomes dominant: the competition for resources increases, inducing a negative relationship between density and founding rates, everything else being equal (Hannan and Carroll 1992, p. 95). Given a set of environmental conditions that sets a carrying capacity, i.e., the maximum number of organizations in a certain population that can thrive on the available limited resources (Hannan and Freeman 1989, pp. 123–129), then the more abundant the number of competitors, the fiercer the competition will be, and the fewer incentives there will be for the founding of new organizations. Moreover, new entrants compete with established firms who have survived selectionist pressures and who are likely to fit well with the environment (Hannan and Freeman 1977). Thus, the founding rate declines as the number of organizations increases. Both processes lead to the relationship between population density and the founding rate, depicted in Figure 1. The first hypothesis that will be tested here is that the population density has an inverted U-shaped effect on the founding rate of venture capital organizations.

Apart from the relationship between the founding rate and the density, Delacroix and Carroll (1983, p. 275) hypothesize that there is a relationship between the founding rate and prior foundings. At first, prior foundings encourage potential entrepreneurs to create a new organization by signaling a fertile niche. When the number of foundings increases, however, the competition for resources becomes so fierce that foundings will be discouraged. These combined effects lead to an inverted U-shaped relationship between prior foundings and current foundings.

In addition, the effect that the venture capital firms of the three countries have on each other is studied. Two populations are said to interact when the populations affect each other's growth rate, but the interaction need not be symmetrical (Barnett and Carroll 1987). In order to model the interacting effects of different geographical populations, the concept of "local" and "non-local" density (Barnett and Carroll 1987) is used, where local density refers to the density in the geographical population of interest and non-local density refers to the total density in the other countries. The second hypothesis tested in this study is that venture capital populations in different countries have a commensalistic or symbiotic effect on each other and

---

[1] It may be useful to measure the size of a population of organizations in terms of the aggregate *size* of the organizations (instead of counting numbers). Hannan and Freeman (1989, pp. 130–131) argue, however (when talking about labor unions): "We think that the *number* of unions in a society is an interesting sociological variable in its own right. A society in which, say, all union members belong to a single union has a quite different structure from one in which the same number of members are organized into a thousand unions . . . . A society with one huge organization of a certain type has a quite different structure from that of a society with many smaller organizations of the same type even though the aggregate size, in terms of members or resources, may be the same . . . . We focus on rates of founding . . . because these rates control fluctuations in numbers of organizations and organizational forms. So it makes sense to ask how these rates depend on the numbers themselves."

FOUNDING RATE OF VENTURE CAPITAL FIRMS **529**

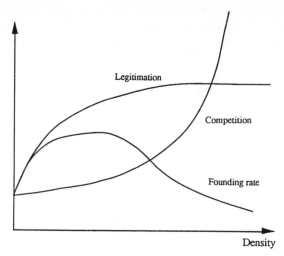

FIGURE 1 The relationship between the population density and the founding rate.
Source: Adapted from Hannan and Carroll (1992, p. 95).

not a competitive effect, but non-local population effects are weaker than local population effects.

Indeed, increasing density in one country increases the legitimacy of the form in all countries, as we assume that this effect is not limited by geographical boundaries. It is indeed plausible to assume that a growing venture capital industry in one country serves as an example for potential investors and venture capital managers in a different country. The American venture capital industry, for example, served as an example for the European one. The former emerged after the Second World War, and the early European funds were set up with experienced American venture capital managers and investors in funds or even subsidiaries of American funds. In this way, the American industry legitimized the European one, by signaling that venture capital is an appropriate financial intermediary and by actively supporting the industry. Because the degree of legitimation of the form is not equal in every geographical population at the same moment in time, the effect will not be symmetrical, leading to commensalism or symbiosis.

The competition for resources (capital, people, deals) among geographically different populations, on the other hand, is limited in the populations of interest (Ooghe et al. 1991, pp. 392–393; EVCA 1990): there are very few funds raised outside the home country or invested abroad in the period of the study.[2] This shows that the resources in one country are not lowered when new venture capital companies are founded in another country, thus limiting the competition.

A major assumption in population bio-ecology is that each member of a population exerts roughly the same demand on the resource environment. A simple count of the number of members in the population is therefore the normal way to proceed to assess the density. Although populations of organizations exhibit considerable diversity in size among members,

---

[2] The European venture capital industry has become slightly more international since 1990.

530   S. MANIGART

the same members counting approach is taken to define density in organizational ecology. Hannan and Freeman (1989, p. 131) argue that, although the study of some aggregate measure of density (e.g. based on size) may be interesting, the number of individual organizations in a population is an interesting variable in its own right.

THE VENTURE CAPITAL INDUSTRY IN THE NETHERLANDS, FRANCE, AND THE U.K.

The foregoing theory will be tested in the European venture capital industry. Bygrave and Timmons (1992, pp. 72–73) warn that there is no accepted definition of venture capital; what is understood by venture capital differs from country to country. The definition of the European Venture Capital Association (EVCA) is most suited for the European approach of venture capital taken in this study. With slight omissions, it goes as follows (EVCA 1990, p. 11):

> A venture capitalist is an operational unit or person:
>
> - who can prove substantial activity in the management of equity or quasi-equity financing for the start-up and/or development of small- and medium-sized unquoted enterprises . . .
> - whose main objective is long-term capital gains to remunerate risks . . .
> - who can provide active management support to investees.

The European venture capital industry differs from the American one in that it is much younger: Whereas the industry emerged after World War II in the United States, the first real signs of formal venture capital in Europe were encountered in the United Kingdom in the seventies; this financing means spread over the Continent in the early eighties (Ooghe et al. 1991).[3] Taking the American industry as a model, the industry in Europe shows many similarities with the older counterpart, but it is still smaller in size both in absolute terms as well as in relation to the size of the economy (Tyebjee and Vickery 1988; Ooghe et al. 1991). However, Roure et al. (1990) report that in 1988 "European venture capitalists invested more than their U.S. counterparts for the first time—more in absolute amount and as a fraction of gross domestic product." Ooghe et al. (1991, p. 401) warn that the European venture capital industry cannot be approached as a single, undifferentiated industry. Each country has its own structures, institutions, and policies, thus the venture capital industries in the different countries have unique characteristics.

The focus of this study is on the founding of venture capital firms in only three European countries—the United Kingdom, the Netherlands, and France—because the venture capital industry has the longest history and is most developed in these three countries (Ooghe et al. 1991). The venture capital industry emerged only in the early or late 1980's in most of the other European countries. As the scope of the present study is longitudinal, the history of the industry has to be long enough to yield meaningful results, thus excluding all the countries in which the venture capital industry emerged in the last decade.

---

[3] There were some companies that provided equity capital for unquoted companies much earlier, e.g. 3i in the United Kingdom and Investco in Belgium. These were, however, isolated initiatives. This does not imply that these companies are not important; on the contrary, 3i is still today by far the most important provider of equity capital in the U.K.

A second reason for choosing these three countries is a consequence of the fact that they have the most developed venture capital industry: the data that are available for these countries are more complete and better documented than the data on other countries. The time span of the study is limited from 1970 to 1990 for statistical reasons. Although some venture capital organizations existed before 1970, their founding was not studied, because there were too few foundings before 1970.

Why, then, was the venture capital industry chosen? It is an industry that emerged only two decades ago, which makes it particularly suitable to test organizational ecology arguments in the early phase of the emergence of an industry. Second, this industry has until now always been studied as a facilitator for the founding of other firms. It has a multiplier effect on the founding of other firms and even on whole industries (Bygrave and Timmons 1992, chap. 9). Here, we look at how they influence the founding of their own competitors. Third, the organizational form of a venture capital firm is very specific (most individual firms have a dual structure with a management company on the one hand and one or more funds on the other hand); this makes the venture capital industry interesting for the testing of business theory. Finally, Murray (1991) reports that British industry participants perceive the increase in the number of new entrants in the industry as one of the two greatest changes in the 1980s.

THE MODEL

Hannan (1986) developed a simple model to express the relationships between the population density and the founding rate. An indirect approach is taken to analyze legitimation and competition, because these processes cannot be observed directly (Hannan and Carroll 1992). First, assume that legitimacy (L) and competition (C) are the only processes that matter, i.e. the changing environmental and institutional conditions that could affect the carrying capacity are controlled for. Then, the founding rate at time t, $\lambda(t)$, which is the variable of interest, can be written as[4] $\lambda(t) = a(t)\, L_t/C_t$
with

L_t = legitimacy = $f_1(Dens_t)$
C_t = competition = $f_2(Dens_t)$
$Dens_t$ = population density

where the subscript t denotes the coefficient taken at time t. The following function allows for the relationship between the density and the founding rate, given in the first hypothesis, and includes the proposed relationship with the previous foundings, Fprev (Hannan and Carroll 1992, p. 62):

$$\lambda(t) = g(t)\, \exp(\alpha_1\, Dens_t - \alpha_2\, Dens_t^2 + \gamma_1\, Fprev_t - \gamma_2\, Fprev_t^2)$$

with α_1, α_2, γ_1, and $\gamma_2 > 0$; $|\alpha_1| > |\alpha_2|$ and $|\gamma_1| > |\gamma_2|$. If indeed a maximum founding rate is observed and if the founding rate drops thereafter, the process implies the existence of a carrying capacity for the population.

There are two important classes of environmental effects[5] that have to be controlled for: first, the changes that affect the carrying capacity of the population, i.e., the changes that affect the main resources, and second, the effects that influence the legitimation process. When resources are more abundant, the carrying capacity rises, implying that the number of

---

[4] a(t) is a function of time, that will be explicated later.
[5] The operationalization of the variables is given in the DATA section.

532   S. MANIGART

venture capital organizations that can thrive in any country increases. Roure et al. (1990, p. 247) found that the European venture capital industry is resource-driven: venture capitalists "place the burden for regulating the flow of funds totally on the prospective investors in venture capital." This implies that an increased carrying capacity will have a positive effect on the founding rate.

Previous studies found three effects that are likely to affect the capital available for the venture capital industry in the U.S. (Bygrave and Shulman 1988; Bygrave and Timmons 1992, chap. 11). These are the risk-free interest rate, the level of the stock market activity, and the creation and activity of a secondary stock market. An increasing *risk-free interest rate* (ILT for the long-term interest rate and IST for the short-term interest rate) will decrease the capital available for venture capital investments, because this raises the required return on the venture capital investment. The creation of a *secondary stock market* (2MARKET),[6] on the other hand, creates an interesting exit route for venture capital investments, effectively raising the expected return on investment (Roure et al. 1990). An increasing level of stock market activity increases the expected venture capital returns. Although the introduction of a typical venture capital investment is only considered 5 to 10 years after the investment is made, Bygrave and Timmons (1992, p. 265) assume "that the public perception may be biased by existing market conditions." More capital is thus attracted to the industry when the stock markets are healthy, and this in turn positively affects the founding rate. It is furthermore likely that investment opportunities are more abundant when the global economic environment, measured by gross national product (GNP), is high. Thus a rising GNP increases the founding rate of venture capital organizations. The growth of the GNP (GNPGR) may be perceived as a signal of healthy economic outlooks, and a positive growth is also expected to increase the founding rate.

Furthermore, the institutional changes that increase the legitimacy of the form are expected to increase the founding rate (Singh et al. 1991). The legal establishment of a specific organizational form, especially set up for venture capital investments and often allowing for a favorable tax treatment, enhances the legitimacy of the form on the one hand and the expected return on the other hand. This is expected to have a positive effect on the founding rate of venture capital organizations in that specific country. The status of "Business Expansion Scheme" funds in the U.K. and of "Fonds Commun de Placement à Risque" in France were established in March 1983, whereas the French "Société de Capital Risque" was created in July 1985. No new legal organizational forms were created in the Netherlands, but the "Particuliere Participatie Maatschappij"-rule, which provides a partial insurance against losses and was established in April 1984, is believed to have had an important effect. A comparable initiative in France is the creation of Sofaris in December 1982, which acts as a reinsurer for the venture capital industry.

Finally, it is widely believed that changes in the *capital gains tax rate*, relatively to the income tax rate, heavily influence the flow of funds (e.g. Tyebjee and Vickery 1988). However, Bygrave and Shulman (1988) extensively show that, when including the other explanatory variables, the change in capital gains tax does not influence the flow of capital into the industry in the United States. This is due to the clientele effect: there are institutional investors for whom the capital gains tax rate is of no concern.

---

[6]In the U.K., there was also a Third Market during a part of the period considered. The effect of the establishment of this market was analyzed in the same way as that of the Second Market, but it proved to be very small and insignificant and is therefore not considered further in this study. These additional analyses may be obtained from the author.

The effect of the covariates (given in $\underline{x}$, the vector of covariates) are modeled as log-linear relationships, as this assures the non-negativity of the founding rate. The complete model is then:

$$\lambda(t) = \exp(\alpha_1 \, \text{Dens}_t - \alpha_2 \, \text{Dens}_t^2 + \gamma_1 \, \text{Fprev}_t - \gamma_2 \, \text{Fprev}_t^2 \exp(\underline{\beta}\underline{x}_t)$$

with

α_i = the effects of the density, to be estimated;

γ_i = the effects of the previous foundings, to be estimated;

$\underline{x}_t$ = the vector of all covariates;

$\underline{\beta}$ = the vector of parameters, to be estimated.

METHOD OF ANALYSIS

The models are estimated with event history and event count analyses. Because the focus of the study is longitudinal and dynamic, static methods of analysis are not appropriate since they assume that the object of study is in equilibrium, whereas the interest here is in the very process of change. Furthermore, the dependent variables are not normally distributed. Finally, the number of events occurring to the population, the central variable in the analyses, is not a continuous variable, but rather discrete and non-negative. The methods of analysis must take this into account: predicting fractions of foundings or negative foundings is meaningless.

When using event history analysis (Kalbfleish and Prentice 1980), the observation period is broken up into the intervals between the events, the founding of a venture capital firm. Each interval is then treated as a separate observation (Kalbfleish and Prentice 1980, p. 185) and the estimation methods estimate the time between two events in *continuous* time. A second method is to break up the observation period into disjointed time intervals occurring in a series and to count the number of events that occur in every period; this method is discrete in nature. It is called "*event count* analysis," "*discrete time* analysis," or "Poisson regression analysis" (to contrast with the previous continuous time method of analysis).

When the exact founding times are known, the continuous time analysis has to be preferred, because it uses more information than the discrete time analysis. In this study, the data of the French and the British population are not accurate enough to use event history analysis. Time series are therefore constructed with the counts of the number of foundings in specified periods of time. Three-month periods are used in this study, giving $21 \times 4 = 84$ data points.

The models are estimated with maximum likelihood (ML) techniques (Kalbfleish and Prentice 1980, p. 119). It was felt that not all covariates helped in explaining the founding rates because the macroeconomic variables are multicollinear, and so finding which ones fit best to the data will improve the significance of the other parameters. Therefore, we tried to find the smallest subset of variables that was the most effective. In order to achieve this, a one-way backwards procedure was used (Elandt-Johnson and Johnson 1980, p. 368). The base model includes the density (squared), the previous foundings (squared), and all macroeconomic covariates estimated (nine variables). The discrimination among the models to find the best models was done with a chi-square statistical test (the level of significance to discriminate between two models is always the .05 level, two-sided test).

DATA

A secondary data sources approach was taken to gather the data on the venture capital firms, because all data needed are objective data and historical events have to be covered. Directories

534   S. MANIGART

on the venture capital industry are the main secondary data sources: Venture Economics'
European Guide to Venture Capital (1985 and 1988), British, French, and European trade
directories and journals (from 1983 until 1992) and the membership lists of the European
Venture Capital Association and of the national venture capital associations. These sources
are complemented with trade journals and newspaper articles.[7]

Three types of firms exist[8] (Murray 1991, p. 86):

- independent venture capital organizations, which raise all their capital in the market;
- captive venture capital organizations, which get all their capital from the parent
  company or from the government;
- semi-captive venture capital organizations, which not only get capital from the parent
  company, but also raise part of it in the market (Murray calls this group "affiliates").

The founding of a (semi-)captive organization does not always lead to the creation of a new
company, but rather to the entry of an existing company into a new industry. Hannan and
Freeman (1989, p. 224) posit that, although the specific process of creation may differ, the
basic population arguments still hold. This argument is consistent with the findings of Van de
Ven et al. (1989), where in-depth case studies showed that the core processes for the founding
of a new firm and the establishment of a new division of an existing firm are the same.
Therefore, the three types of firms are taken together. The founding day of an independent or
semi-captive firm is taken as the day of its legal establishment. The founding day of captive
firms is often difficult to judge, as they often begin their operations as a venture capitalist
while still a part of the parent company. In this case, the day of their first investment is taken
as the founding date.

Two dependent variables are important in this study: the time interval between two
foundings of venture capital firms (measured in days) for the continuous time analyses and the
quarterly number of foundings for the discrete time analyses. Both variables are derived from
the exact founding dates of the venture capital firms. When the exact founding date (year,
month, and day) is unknown, a random founding day and/or month (drawn from a uniform
distribution to assure that every day has an equal chance of being chosen) is assigned to
complete the founding dates.[9]   For the 5% of the foundings for which the year of founding
is unknown, the first year in which some data source mentions the existence of the
organization is taken as the year of founding. Similarly, for the organizations that
disappeared, but for which the exact year of disbanding is unknown, the last year in which
their existence is reported is taken as the last year of their organizational lives.[11]

Figure 2 gives the yearly number of foundings of venture capital firms in the three
countries. In the Netherlands, 104 venture capital firms were founded between 1970 and
1990. The exact legal founding date (year, month, and day) is known for 75 of the 104 firms.

---

[7] The database, primarily established from secondary data sources, was discussed with industry watchers in
order to complete it; additional information was gathered directly from the firms when needed.

[8] Only the founding of venture capital firms (or management companies) is relevant here, and not the founding
of additional investment funds managed by an existing management company.

[9] Another approach would be to work with missing values. The estimation techniques do not handle missing
values in the dependent variables, however. It is therefore necessary that every event gets assigned a founding date.

[10] Sensitivity analyses are done by constructing three data sets with different random days. The results are very
robust for all the analyses: the same variables are significant and the significant coefficients all point in the same
direction. Detailed results may be obtained from the author.

[11] It is necessary to know the exact day of disbanding in order to construct the independent density variable.

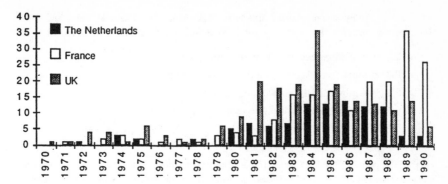

FIGURE 2   Yearly number of foundings in the three countries.

This high level of precision allows us to perform analyses in continuous time. In France, 192 venture capital firms were founded between 1970 and 1990; the exact founding date is known for 17 of the 192 organizations, and the year and month of founding are known for 107 firms. In the U.K., 208 venture capital firms were founded; the exact founding date is known for only seven of them, and the month and year of founding are known for 91 of the foundings. The level of precision with which the founding dates are known is thus slightly lower than for the French data set and much lower than for the Dutch data set. Discrete time analyses are required for the French and British data.

It can be seen from Figure 2 that there were only a few foundings recorded in the first decade of the study in each of the three countries. The growth of the industry took off in the beginning of the 1980's and reached a peak in the years 1984–1985 in the U.K. and the Netherlands. The growth occurred later in France, but the number of foundings remained high until 1990. The figure confirms that the industry emerged first in the U.K., then spread to the Netherlands and thereafter to France.

Three types of independent variables are used in this study: population level, macroeconomic, and institutional covariates. There is an important difference in the precision with which the covariates are measured. The population level and institutional covariates are computed at the date of every founding and thus differ for each founding (continuous time analysis) or at the beginning of each quarter (discrete time analysis), whereas the macroeconomic covariates are measured at the end of the year.

The population-level covariates are as follows:

- Dens: the density, measured *just before* the event took place, computed as $Dens_t = Dens_{t-1} + N_{t-1,t} - E_{t-1,t}$ with $N_{t-1,t}$ = number of foundings and $E_{t-1,t}$ = number of disbandings in the time interval (t–1, t);

- $Dens^2 = Dens \times Dens/1000$;

- Fprev = the number of foundings that occurred in the *year before* the founding;

- $Fprev^2 = Fprev \times Fprev/100$.

These measures are derived from the data set. Because it is recommended that the variables have roughly the same order of magnitude when estimating the models, $Dens^2$ is always divided by 1000 and $Fprev^2$ by 100. The population level variables are computed at the start of each quarter for the discrete time analysis.

536   S. MANIGART

Data on the environmental conditions are taken from the Statistical Yearbooks of the European Commission. The macroeconomic covariates, different for the three countries, are

- ILT: the inflation-corrected, long-term interest rate, in %;
- IST: the inflation-corrected, short-term interest rate, in %;
- SMI: the growth of the stock market index, in %;[12]
- GNP: the inflation corrected gross national product $\times 10^{-9}$ (expressed in local currency);
- GNPGR: the growth of the inflation-corrected GNP, in %.

Finally, the period covariates (modeled as dummy variables) differ for each country. They include important changes in the legal environment, the founding of the national venture capital association, and the founding of a secondary stock market. The exact date on which a new law became operative or on which the venture capital association was founded is known in the three countries; this allows the exact splitting up of the time period before and after the institutional change occurred.

FINDINGS

Table 1 gives the estimates of the best fitting, sparsest models for the founding rates of venture capital firms in the three countries of interest. The variables that appear in every model are the density and the density squared. The signs of the coefficients are in the hypothesized direction and the coefficients are significantly different from zero. This supports the first hypothesis that the variable that has the highest influence on the founding rate of venture capital firms is the number of firms that already exist in the industry. When the number of firms is low, adding a new firm raises the founding rate, but after a certain point, every new firm decreases the probability of a new founding. The turning point is reached for a density of 71 firms in the Netherlands, 125 firms in France, and 98 firms in the U.K. When more than that specific number of firms exists in the industry, the competitive effect becomes dominant.

The effect of the previous foundings is less pronounced. The variable does not appear in every model and the estimates of the coefficients are not statistically significant.[13] The previous foundings do not influence the founding rate of Dutch firms, but they slightly increase the founding rate of French firms and have an inverted U-shaped effect on the founding rate of British firms. This part of the theory is only weakly supported in the U.K., but not in the other countries.

It is remarkable to see that, whereas the effect of the density on the founding rate is significant and similar in the three countries, the effects of the other macroeconomic

---

[12] Most venture capital–backed IPOs are introduced on a secondary stock market, which implies that the secondary stock market index is in fact a measure of the expected returns. However, the primary stock market index is used in this study, because there were no secondary stock markets in the 1970's and the early 1980's, and thus no secondary stock market indices then. In order to be consistent throughout the whole period of study, the stock market index of the primary market in each of the three countries is taken.

[13] Although the coefficients are not significant, their mere presence shows that including these variables improves the fit of the models significantly (.05 level) in France and in the U.K. This implies that this variable does significantly influence the founding rate. Moreover, as the object of the analysis is a whole population and not a sample, the significance is less an issue here than in other studies.

TABLE 1 Estimation of the Founding Rates

	The Netherlands[a]	France[b]	U.K.[b]
Constant	−5.008[d]	−4.684[d]	−4.141[d]
Density	0.323[d]	0.033[d]	1.336[d]
Density^2	−2.285[d]	−0.131[d]	−0.070[d]
Previous foundings		0.008	0.026
Previous foundings^2			−0.111
ILT	0.083	−0.020	
IST		0.110	
GNP	−0.143[d]		
GNPGR	−0.294[c]		0.000
2MARKET	−1.868[c]		
Maximum for density	71	125	98

[a] Continuous time estimation.
[b] Discrete time estimation.
Significance levels: [c] .01; [d] .005 (one-sided tests).

covariates, which are widely believed to influence the growth of the industry, are much smaller, less significant, less homogeneous, and often contrary to what is expected. The long-term interest rate has a positive effect on the founding rate in the Netherlands and a negative effect in France, but no effect in the U.K. The effects of GNP and its growth are significantly negative in the Netherlands, (not significantly) positive in the U.K. and do not appear in the French models. The creation of a secondary stock market has a negative effect on the founding rate of Dutch venture capital firms, contrary to the expectations, and no effect on the founding rate of the French and British firms. The creation of a special legal entity for venture capital investments or the establishment of state guarantees does not appear in any of the models. This indicates that the population density is the strongest effect influencing the founding of venture capital firms in the three countries. This is particularly strong evidence in favor of the population ecology theory.

Does this imply that the venture capital industry would have grown as much without the institutional and environmental changes? Not at all. Changes in the environment are important, because they alter the carrying capacity of the industry. A higher carrying capacity implies that the population has additional resources to expand or vice versa. It is through this relationship that environmental changes influence the density and thus the founding rates. In young populations, however, the carrying capacity is not yet attained; therefore, the populations are able to grow *independently* from the environmental changes (Pianka 1978). In order to clarify this point, we will take as an example an environmental change that increases the carrying capacity. In a mature population, where the carrying capacity is reached, this change will have a positive effect on the founding rate and/or a negative effect on the mortality rate, thus leading to a higher density. When the carrying capacity is not yet reached, then the resources are so abundant for the newcomers that an increase in the carrying capacity will have no effect on the founding rate. This explains why there were so few environmental effects in this study.

Table 2 gives the estimates of the models, including the influence of non-local density. We see that non-local density does indeed influence the local founding rate in all models. The base relationship between the local density and the founding rate does not change when adding the effect of the non-local density, although the significance is lowered in some models.

The density in the U.K. influences the founding rate in the Netherlands, the density in the Netherlands influences the founding rate in France, and the Dutch and French densities

TABLE 2 Estimation of the Influence of Non-local Density

	The Netherlands[a]	France[b]	U.K.[b]
Constant	−7.183[c]	−0.973[d]	−0.879[c]
ILT	−0.116	−0.080	
IST		0.081	
GNP	−0.005		
GNPGR	−0.029		−0.000
2MARKET	−1.450		
DensL	0.309[c]	0.119[d]	0.130[c]
DensL^2/1000	−1.859[c]	−0.360[c]	−0.453[c]
FprevL		−0.052[d]	−0.133
FprevL^2/100			11.965
DensN		0.048	−0.195[d]
DensN^2/1000		−0.214[c]	1.388[d]
DensU	0.013		
DensU^2/1000	−0.206		
Maximum for DensL	83	165	143
Extremum for DensNL	31	112	70

Abbreviations: L, local population; NL, non-local population; N, Dutch population; U, British population.
[a] Continuous time estimation
[b] Discrete time estimation
Significance levels: [c] 0.05; [d] 0.01; [e] 0.005 (one-sided tests)

influence the founding rate in the U.K. Non-local density influences the founding rate in some geographical populations, but not in all of them and the effect of non-local density is lower than the effect of local density, as expected. The signs of the effect of the non-local density, however, are not as expected from hypothesis 2, as it is not solely legitimizing. The effect of the British density on the Dutch founding rate and that of the Dutch density on the French founding rate has an inverted U-shape; the maximum is found for a density well within the observed density range. The effect of the Dutch and the French density on the British founding rate is U-shaped, but the main effect of the non-local density is negative and thus competitive, contrary to hypothesis 2.

The results show that the British venture capital industry had a positive effect on the founding of Dutch venture capital firms and the Dutch venture capital community on the founding of French ones in the early phase of the industry. The positive effect, however, does not last forever. Once the populations in the respective countries grow, the competitive effect takes the lead, and more organizations in a non-local population depresses the founding of local organizations. This implies that there is more intercountry competition for resources than hypothesized, but the non-local competition is lower than the local competition. This intercountry competition for scarce resources is likely to be caused by the competition for capital in the first place (if there is not enough capital, the creation of the venture capital firm is inhibited) and competition for interesting deals in the second place.

The picture is different for the British venture capital industry. The strongest effect experienced by the British founding rate comes from the Dutch industry. The main effect is negative: the higher the Dutch density, the more the founding of a British venture capital organization is inhibited. This indicates that the Dutch industry does not legitimize the venture capital population in the U.K. This is not surprising, as it is only a formal recognition of the fact that the British industry came into existence before the Continental industries. The hypothesis on the effect of non-local density thus has to take into account potential time lags between the originating of different geographical populations. When population X emerges before population Y, then population Y cannot legitimize the form in population X, but it can compete with population X when it becomes sufficiently large. This seems to be the effect that the Dutch population has had on the British population.

The main result of these findings is that the competition among the three countries is stronger than expected from the cross-border investment and capital raising activity. This leads to the following refined hypothesis:

> Increasing non-local density increases the legitimation and thus the founding rate, when the non-local population emerges before the local population. When the local population emerges before the non-local population, then the non-local population does not legitimize the local population and may even compete with the local population.

CONCLUSION

The relationship between the density and the founding rate is the strongest, most consistent, and most significant relationship found in this study that supports the population ecology theory. Failing to include this variable in subsequent studies on organizational foundings will lead to a misspecified model. Thus, the number of organizations that already exist in an industry is very important in explaining the founding of organizations, apart from (for example) the personality of the entrepreneur or from the networks in which he or she is embedded. This indicates that when explaining the founding of organizations, it is very important to look at the industry structure, and more specifically at the number of organizations that exist at the moment of the founding.

A further fruitful stream of research would be to investigate the relationship between the population density on the one hand and the legitimation and competition processes on the other hand. A weakness of the theory is that it assumes that the population density is a proxy variable for the legitimation and competition processes, as these cannot be measured directly. This weakness allows for alternative explanations for the density dependence of the founding rate. Apart from legitimation and competition, a higher density might for example result in increased learning or spur imitation effects. The positive relationship between the density and the founding rate might also be the result of a diffusion process. Clarifying this point would be an interesting study.

This study brings further insight into the possible interactive effects of different geographical populations in their early history. It is shown that the interactive effects are not solely positive, and thus the models have to allow for competitive effects. The influence of populations that emerge in a different time period is acknowledged in the refined hypotheses and is particularly important in the early life of a population.

Important questions remain unanswered, such as "Why does one geographical population emerge before another one?" More precisely for this study "Why did the British population emerge before the Dutch population and the Dutch one before the French one ?" Answering this question requires, among other things, the study of speciation, i.e. the close scrutiny of the founding of the first organization in a certain industry in a particular country. It is furthermore not clear where the turning point in the density dependence model lies. Being able to predict this point would enhance the practical implications of the theory.

A further interesting route for research is to test population ecology hypotheses on the survival of the venture capital organizations. This has not been done in this study, because of the specific nature of venture capital companies in usually getting enough financial resources

540   S. MANIGART

at the start-up to survive for a decade, unlike most other organizations. This characteristic will make it worthwhile to study what drives the survival of venture capital companies.

REFERENCES

Aldrich, H.E., McKelvey, B., and Ulrich, D. 1984. Design strategy from the population perspective. *Journal of Management* 10(1):68–86.

Aldrich, H., and Zimmer, C. 1986. Entrepreneurship through social networks. In D.L. Sexton and R.W. Smilor, eds., *The Art and Science of Entrepreneurship*. Cambridge, MA: Ballinger, pp. 3–23.

Amit, R., Glosten, L., and Muller, E. 1993. Challenges to theory development in entrepreneurship research. *Journal of Management Studies* 30(5):815–834.

Barnett, W.P., and Carroll, G.R. 1987. Competition and mutualism among early telephone companies. *Administrative Science Quarterly* 32(2):400–421.

Boone, C., and van Witteloostuijn, A. 1994. Industrial organization and organizational ecology: the potentials for cross-fertilization. *Organization Studies* (forthcoming).

Bygrave, W.D. 1993. Theory building in the entrepreneurship paradigm. *Journal of Business Venturing* 8(4):255–280.

Bygrave, W.D., and Shulman, J.M. 1988. Capital gains tax: bane or boon for venture capital? *Frontiers of Entrepreneurship Research*. Wellesley, MA: Babson College.

Bygrave, W.D., and Timmons, J.A. 1992. *Venture Capital at the Crossroads*. Boston, MA: Harvard Business School Press.

Carroll, G. 1988. *Ecological Models of Organizations*. Cambridge, MA: Ballinger

Delacroix, J., and Carroll, G.R. 1983. Organizational foundings: an ecological study of the newspaper industry of Argentina and Ireland. *Administrative Science Quarterly* 28(2):274–291.

Elandt-Johnson, R.C., and Johnson, N.L. 1980. *Survival Models and Data Analysis*. New York: John Wiley and Sons.

European Venture Capital Association. 1990. *Venture Capital in Europe in 1990*. London: EVCA/Peat Marwick McLintock.

Hannan, M.T. 1986. *A Model of Competitive and Institutional Processes in Organizational Ecology*. Technical Report 86-13. Ithaca, NY: Department of Sociology, Cornell University.

Hannan, M.T., and Carroll, G.R. 1992. *Dynamics of Organizational Populations: Density, Legitimation and Competition*. Oxford: Oxford University Press.

Hannan, M.T., and Freeman, J. 1977. The population ecology of organizations. *American Journal of Sociology* 82(5):929–964.

Hannan, M.T., and Freeman, J. 1989. *Organizational Ecology*. Cambridge, MA: Harvard University Press.

Kalbfleish, J.D., and Prentice, R.L. 1980. *The Statistical Analysis of Failure Time Data*. New York: J. Wiley and Sons.

McClelland, D.C. 1961. *The Achieving Society*. New York: Free Press.

Murray, G.C. 1991. The Changing Nature of Competition in the UK Venture Capital Industry. *National Westminster Bank Quarterly Review* November 1991:65–80.

Ooghe, H., Manigart, S., and Fassin, Y. 1991. Growth Patterns of the European Venture Capital Industry. *Journal of Business Venturing* 6(6):381–404.

Pianka, E.R. 1978. *Evolutionary Ecology*. New York: Harper and Row.

Roure, J.B., Keeley, R.H., and Van Der Heyden, T. 1990. European venture capital: strategies and challenges in the 90's. *European Management Journal* 8(2):243–252.

Schumpeter, J.A. 1934. *The Theory of Economic Development*. Cambridge, MA: Harvard University Press.

Singh, J., Tucker, D., and Meinhard, A. 1991. Institutional change and ecological dynamics. In Walter W. Powell and Paul J. DiMaggio, eds., *The New Institutionalism in Organizational Analysis*. Chicago: University of Chicago Press.

FOUNDING RATE OF VENTURE CAPITAL FIRMS 541

Stinchcombe, A.L. 1965. Social structure and organizations. In James G. March, ed., *Handbook of Organizations.* Chicago: Rand McNally, pp. 142–193.

Tyebjee, T.T., and Vickery, L. 1988. Venture Capital in Western Europe. *Journal of Business Venturing* 3(3):123–136.

Van de Ven, A.H. 1980. Early planning, implementation and performance of new organizations. In J.R. Kimberly, R.H. Miles, and Associates, eds., *The Organizational Life Cycle: Issues in the Creation, Transformation and Decline of Organizations.* San Francisco: Jossey-Bass, pp. 83–133.

Van de Ven, A.H., Hudson, R., and Schroeder, D.M. 1984. Designing new business startups: entrepreneurial, organizational, and ecological considerations. *Journal of Management* 10(1):87–107.

Van de Ven, Andrew H., Venkataraman, S., Polley, Douglas, and Garud, Raghu. 1989. Processes of new business creation in different organizational settings. In Andrew H. Van de Ven, Harold L. Angle, and Marshall Scott Poole, eds., *Research on the Management of Innovation.* New York: Harper and Row, pp. 221–297.

Westhead, P., and Moyes, T. 1991. *Reflections on Thatcher's Britain: Evidence from New Production Firm Registrations 1980–88.* Paper presented at RENT V: Research in Entrepreneurship Theory. Växjö University, Sweden, November 28–29.

Zucker, L.G. 1983. Organizations as institutions. In S.B. Bacharach, ed., *Research in the Sociology of Organizations.* Greenwich, CT: JAI Press, vol. 2, pp. 1–47.

[5]

Journal of Business Finance & Accounting, 22(8), December 1995, 0306-686X

EVOLUTION AND CHANGE: AN ANALYSIS OF THE FIRST DECADE OF THE UK VENTURE CAPITAL INDUSTRY

GORDON C. MURRAY*

INTRODUCTION

After almost ten years of uninterrupted growth, the UK venture capital industry has entered its second decade of activity in a more competitive and hostile environment than most of its participants can remember. Venture capital, a part of the burgeoning financial services sector, was one of the most vigorous growth areas of the British economy in the 1980s. In 1981, some thirty venture capital organisations committed £66 million of investments to 163 investee companies (Lorenz, 1989). Eleven years later, in 1992, the UK industry invested a total of £1,326 million in 1,297 enterprises world wide, primarily small and medium sized, unquoted companies (British Venture Capital Association 1993). This represented, in real terms, an annualised growth rate over the period of 27%. The number of venture capitalist companies peaked in 1989 at 124 full members of the British Venture Capital Association (BVCA).[1] The industry, between 1985 and 1992, had invested a cumulative £8.8 billion in approximately ten thousand companies.

The UK has become, after the United States and Japan (Bannock, 1991), the largest venture capital centre in the world. While venture capital has grown significantly in continental Europe since the mid 1980s (Tyebjee and Lister, 1988), the UK industry continues to dominate European activity taking 39% of the total of Ecu 4,701 million in new European investment in 1992 (European Venture Capital Association, 1993[2]). The UK is an active exporter of venture capital investment and expertise to other European Community countries as well as being a significant importer and exporter of venture finance from/to the US.

Since 1989, the year in which new funds into the industry and venture capital investments peaked, confidence in UK venture capital has been tested by a number of very public casualties, particularly among some of the largest management buy-outs and buy-ins (MBOs/MBIs). The MBO of Lowndes

*The author is from the University of Warwick. (Paper received February 1994, revised and accepted June 1994)

Address for correspondence: Gordon C. Murray, Warwick Business School, University of Warwick, Coventry CV4 7AL, UK.

1078   MURRAY

Queensway (£460 million) was subsequently put into liquidation and, also in
the recession-hit, domestic furnishing retail market, the MBOs of MFI/Hygena
(£718 million) and Magnet (£667 million) each needed substantial refinancing
in 1990. In 1993, the troubled MBI of Isosceles/Gateway (£2,375 million) was
still subject to the repeated renegotiation of finance with its bankers four years
after its genesis.[3] This loss of confidence, reflecting wider concerns as the UK
economy slid into recession, was also corroborated in reports from several
independent venture capitalists noting the increasing difficulties of raising
substantial new funds from 1989 onwards.

This paper seeks to examine the nature of the environmental factors which
have driven the growth of UK venture capital activity, and to determine how
these factors are likely to influence both the future size and the structure, conduct
and performance of the industry. The factors which have influenced the
provision of investment capital to venture capital firms are particularly explored,
including the implications on the industry's future of a dearth of new finance.

Given the industry's role in financing both the genesis of what Story et al.
(1989) term 'fast track' firms (via seed and start-up capital) and the restructuring
of existing, established firms (via management buy-out/buy-in, expansion, and
secondary purchase investments), it is suggested that the industry's future size
and activity have an important bearing on issues of both small firm financing
and the market for corporate control in the UK. It is further argued that a
financial service sector which has developed and changed so rapidly within its
relatively short life span is a subject worthy of greater academic attention.
However, with few notable exceptions (Pratt, 1990; Dixon, 1991; Sweeting,
1991; and Wright et al., 1994), the interest among UK finance and accountancy
researchers remains remarkably muted. This is in stark contrast to the
established corpus of research on the US venture capital industry by American
academics.

Despite the British Government's support in the November 1993 Budget
for third party equity financing of unquoted businesses, there remains little
empirical evidence on the performance of UK venture capital funds or the
nature of risk/reward trade-offs between different types of venture capital activity
including issues of fund specialisation or diversification. The absence of rigorous
cross country comparisons in Europe and between Europe and the US is a
particular omission. The apparent inability for venture capitalists to create
successful funds for early stage and/or technology based businesses is of special
concern for policy makers (Murray, 1993). As Dixon (1991) has observed, the
venture capital industry appears to embrace few of the portfolio management
instruments widely available to other financial service sectors. (This is a view
supported by Tyebjee and Bruno, 1984; and Ruhnka and Young, 1991, in
their US studies.) It is thus argued that the established UK industry represents
a fruitful, but as yet poorly exploited, source of enquiry for finance-based
academics.

METHODOLOGY

The data presented in this paper on the nature of change within the UK (and its comparison to the US) venture capital industry are primarily derived from industry statistics published by the two national associations: the British Venture Capital Association (BVCA) and the National Venture Capital Association (NVCA), respectively. Findings are further supported with reference to the increasing body of empirical research conducted in the UK and USA. (Where BVCA data are used, UK trend figures can only be given up to and including 1991, with the exception of 1992 UK investment value. In 1992, the BVCA materially changed the basis on which statistics from members were collected. For the first time both secured and unsecured debt has been aggregated with equity investment. As the BVCA notes in its Report on Investment Activity 1992, direct comparisons cannot be made between figures in 1992 and prior years).

The paper also uses extensively, analyses based on the findings of a survey of the UK venture capital industry undertaken in 1990 by the author at the request of the BVCA (Murray, 1991). Commitment to this study was assisted by a widespread concern among the BVCA's members that the industry was not likely to sustain the remarkable growth rate of the previous decade. This data is employed to fit secondary sources of industry statistics into an analytical framework of structural and operational change over the period.

The 1990 BVCA Survey

In order to investigate the contemporary process of change in the UK industry, the CEOs of twenty venture capital organisations were approached with the active co-operation of the British Venture Capital Association (BVCA). In addition, two further participants, deemed by the BVCA to have expert knowledge of the UK industry, were also interviewed. The respondents were questioned on their opinions as to:

(i)   the key successes and failures of the industry's performance over the decade 1980–90,
(ii) the genesis, nature and effect of major changes in the competitive environment impacting on the industry over this period,
(iii) the major competitive changes, including both opportunities and threats, likely to face the industry over the next five years 1991–95,
(iv) those factors which would be material to the future success of the industry, and to individual venture capital firms.

The process of the twenty-two interviews was based on an extended, semi-structured discussion with the CEO respondents. In seeking their views, the respondents were not prompted with pre-defined lists. Other than setting the

1080   MURRAY

subject areas for the interview, the respondents were encouraged to articulate their own perceptions of the key factors influencing present and future changes within the UK venture capital industry.

Sample Selection

All twenty venture capital organisations contacted agreed to participate in the survey. The sampling procedure was not random. The criteria used to select the research respondents were that they were:

(i)   seen by their peers as leading participants in the UK venture capital industry,

(ii) controlled large and successful[4] venture capital organisations,

(iii) had been active participants in the industry throughout the majority of the 1980s.

The purpose of the survey was to ascertain the opinions of a sample of venture capitalists reckoned by their peers to be *leaders* in their industry in both the quality of their experience and the size of funds under their control. Given that the sample concentrated on a number of the largest and, arguably, most influential firms in the industry, the research method was not designed to obtain a statistically representative view of *all* sectors of the UK venture capital community.

The average size of the funds managed by the 19 venture capital firms (i.e. excluding 3i plc) was £223.5 million with a standard deviation of £201.4 million (primarily because one small fund specialising in high technology start-ups with funds under management of £9 million was included in the sample). Only two other venture capital firms in the sample had funds under management of less than £100 million. The sample included 3i plc, the largest venture capital firm in the world with funds under management of over £2.5 billion. In total, the sample represented 65% of the 29 UK venture capital firms with funds under management of over £100 million in 1990.

INDUSTRY TRENDS IN THE 1980s

The UK venture capital industry, as it is presently recognised, had its genesis in the late 1970s/early 1980s. While equity investments in unquoted companies were regularly undertaken by a number of banks and finance houses before the last decade, they were generally seen as a specialist and largely peripheral element of a wider corporate finance activity (Hannah, 1992). With the notable exception of 3i plc (formerly ICFC), there were few organisations of any significant size with a predominant interest in small unquoted investments. This situation was to change markedly in the 1980s with the renaissance of governmental and corporate financiers' interest in entrepreneurial and small firm activity.

CHANGE AND THE UK VENTURE CAPITAL INDUSTRY   1081

Decline in Rate of Industry Growth: Funds Invested

Actual and potential industry growth may be measured, respectively, in terms of the annual total investment committed by venture capitalists to investee companies and by reference to the amounts of external finance raised for future investment activity by the industry. In 1992, the UK venture capital industry invested £1,326 million of equity in 1,297 companies world wide (BVCA, 1993). In 1991, the last year of comparable UK trend information published by the BVCA, £989 m. was invested in 1,196 UK companies. Investment activity had declined by 30% in nominal terms for two successive years against the peak year of 1989 when £1,647 m. was invested world-wide and £1,420 m. in the UK.

Some six months before the 1990 annual UK statistics were released, only two of the twenty-two BVCA survey respondents believed that investments would continue to grow for the next three years, including 1990/91. Seventeen respondents (77%) estimated that the growth of new funds invested would decline, in nominal terms, for the next three years from the peak of the 1989 figure by an average of 26%. In reality, the decline in the total value of nominal investment between 1989–92 was 19.5%.

The period, 1980–91, saw the UK economy move from one recession through a period of significant economic growth and into the start of a second recession. In order to show the real underlying growth in UK venture capital activity, the annual investment data, i.e. domestic investments made by UK venture capitalists, were deflated to real (1985 = 100) figures, using an 'investment goods' deflator, and then adjusted for economic cyclicality using an index of GDP at constant factor cost (see Figure 1). The trend in UK venture capital

Figure 1

Annual UK Investment by BVCA Members 1981–91

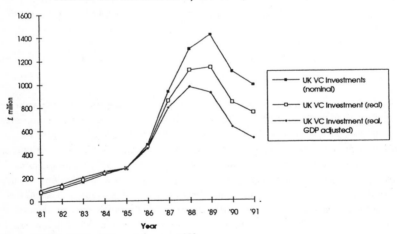

Source: BVCA, 1984–1993; and Lorenz, 1989.

1082 MURRAY

Figure 2

UK Venture Capital Activity and FTA Index 1981−91

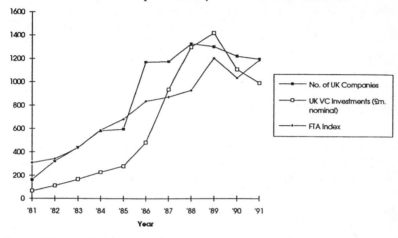

Source: BVCA, 1984−1993; and Lorenz, 1989.

activity over time shows a pronounced sigmoid curve reflecting a distinct period of growth followed by a marked decline in investment activity.[5] It is to be expected that an industry based on future growth expectations of investee companies is highly sensitive to underlying change in the macro-economy. However, this paper argues that the influence of the wider economic environment has also served to engender a process of major changes to the structure, conduct and performance of the industry, which will continue irrespective of the UK economy's move out of recession.

The US venture capital industry has shown a marked pattern of cyclicality, since its inception in the early post Second World War period, in both the level of annual funds raised and the profitability of subsequent investments (Bygrave et al., 1989). Similar extensive time series data is not available for the younger UK industry. However, as Figure 2 shows, the growth of UK venture capital industry activity appears to be closely associated with traded stock movements over time.[6] Given long run, cyclical trends in the price movement of stocks, it is plausible that the decline from 1989 to 1991 in UK venture capital activity was the result of adverse economic and stock market conditions on investors' short run confidence.

However, the sensitivity of venture capital activity to the movement in UK stock prices does not confound the assertion of industry maturity. It is feasible that the consequences of lower stock prices on the potential profitability of venture capital firms' portfolios became a catalyst for the necessary restructuring of a young and unstable industry where the number of investing firms and

CHANGE AND THE UK VENTURE CAPITAL INDUSTRY   1083

the supply of funds to invest had grown too large to support the present and likely future deal flow. The nature of the industry which responds to contemporary incentives post the 1989–1992 recession will be markedly different from the industry in the mid to late 1980s. It is likely to be characterised by a smaller number of larger, and more product/market focused, surviving firms (Murray, 1992). All BVCA survey respondents believed that the number of venture capitalist firms in the UK industry would decline over the next five years.

Funds Raised by the Venture Capital Industry

The likelihood of a decline in the future rate of venture capital investments is also supported by the annual figures for the value of new, institutional funds raised by independent UK venture capital firms.[7] However, it should be noted that the investment into independent funds is only one part of the industry's total resources. Captives organisations, which are owned by a financial services parent including banks, insurance companies and pension funds, undertook 25% of the value of total equity investment in 1991. On the revised BVCA reporting basis of 1992, captives and semi-captive organisations (i.e. a captive organisation also managing an independent fund) invested 50% of the equity and debt provided by the industry.

The funding of independent venture capital organisations grew rapidly through the 1980s, peaking in 1989 at £1,684 million. The level of funding, post 1989, has reflected the anxieties felt by many institutional investors as to the potential for attrative future returns from UK venture capital activity (see *Financial Times* Annual Venture Capital Surveys 1990–1992). The nominal figure for 1992, at £347 million, was 79% lower than the 1989 funds raised. In real terms, 1992 represented the lowest sum raised by the UK industry since 1984. There is a two or three year lag between creating a new fund and making substantial new investments in a portfolio of client companies. Unless there

Table 1

Capital Commitments to UK Independent Funds, Nominal and Real
(1985 values)

	1983	1984	1985	1986	1987	1988
Nominal £m	112	195	278	239	684	612
Real £m	123	206	278	229	626	528

	1989	1990	1991	1992	1993	
Nominal £m	1684	830	368	347	479	
Real £m	1354	630	279	272	375	

Source: Venture Economics Ltd., 1992, and BVCA, 1992–1994.

1084   MURRAY

is a sustained reversal in the downward trend in new inward investment in independent venture capital firms, it is likely that this will be reflected directly in the reduced value of annual investments from 1993/94 onwards once the UK industry's estimated £1 billion of uninvested funds (BVCA, 1993) is used up.

Increase in Market Information

In 1993, there were 119 'full' (i.e. investor) members of the BVCA. Including non BVCA members, there are likely to be less than 150 UK organisations with a primarily economic purpose of venture capital investment. This statistic excludes 'informal investors' (aka 'business angels') which invest in unquoted companies from their own personal resources (Harrison and Mason, 1992). Thus, the UK venture capital industry is small when measured by the number of firms within the industry. The firms themselves may also be characterised as 'small firms' if defined by the number of executive staff. The median size of the UK venture capital firm in 1991 was 7 investment professionals (Venture Economics, 1992). This small scale, with most firms spatially concentrated in a few major cities (Mason and Harrison, 1991), facilitates the level of inter-firm communication. Several BVCA survey respondents referred to the industry as a 'club' in which everyone knows everyone else.

The incidence of deal sharing ('syndication') between venture capitalists; communications via the BVCA; the regular reporting of deals through the statistics of Venture Economics and the trade press; and the physical concentration of many of the larger organisations within the City of London has meant that the level of inter-firm communication is high. However, for both the institutional providers of venture capital funds and the potential, investee firm clients, access to information has been more problematic. Both parties incur significant monitoring or search costs, respectively. BVCA survey respondents noted that, in the present competitive climate, venture capitalists would have to put materially more resources into both marketing to institutions and subsequently keeping them better informed on the state of investments undertaken in the funds to which they have subscribed, if they are to retain investors' confidence. A recent survey of institutional investors cited small firms' stock performance and venture capital as UK fund managers' two greatest concerns in late 1991 (Alexander, 1991).

Arguably, the most critical need to facilitate an efficient market for venture capital is for reliable figures on the performance of the funds of individual venture capital organisations to become widely available to institutions wishing to choose between competing new funds. The relatively early stage of the development of the UK venture capital industry and the fact that most funds have been raised since 1987 as 'closed end' funds for ten year periods has meant that, with few exceptions, detailed, terminal performance information does not yet exist. The 1992 Chairman of the BVCA announced that the provision of comparative performance data would be a major responsibility of his year's tenure. This announcement reflected the BVCA's concern at the growing unease felt by many institutional investors in venture capital as to the likely net terminal performance of their investments (Brakell, 1988).

Institutional investors' fears have been exacerbated by the highly ambivalent performance data of the US venture capital industry where fund returns post the vintage 1982/83 year have been disappointing (Bygrave et al., 1989). This has been directly reflected in a decline of 59% in nominal, new capital commitments to independent, private US venture capital firms from 1983 to 1991 (NVCA, 1993). The paucity of information available to institutional investors in venture capital is not purely due to issues of timing. In the US, Bygrave (op cit., p. 93) noted that 'published information on rates of return was skimpy and not very reliable', despite the organised venture capital industry in the US being over 40 years old. Chiampou and Kallett (1989, p. 2) also similarly observed in their American study of the risk/return profile of venture capital that 'the lack of even working studies on this topic is remarkable'.

For the potential investee recipient of venture capital funds, the accountant is the primary and most important source of information and access to venture capitalists (Llanwarne, 1990; Murray et al., 1995; see also Hustedd and Pulver, 1992). As an intermediary between the potential client and venture capitalist investor, the accountancy firms perform an important market allocation role. The power of major accountancy firms as a conduit for future deal flow reached its apogee with the practice of 'beauty parades' whereby accountants and their investee firm clients required a shortlist of several interested venture capitalists to make competitive presentations from which a subsequent investor was selected.

This practice has subsequently moderated, post 1990, as venture capitalists reacted strongly against a practice which they viewed as giving excessive power to the accountant at the cost of the venture capital firm. The BVCA survey respondents acknowledged that the more professional management teams, particularly those from the larger MBOs, were increasingly well informed of the competitive offerings from individual venture capitalists and had increased their relative negotiating power. However, 58% of respondents still believed that potential clients did not have an accurate understanding of the uses of venture capital. The inability of the majority of financial intermediaries to redress this information asymmetry was supported by a 1991 study of accountants and bank managers which identified their limited understanding of venture capital; 85% of accountants and 92% of bank managers surveyed 'never or rarely' had experienced any personal contact with venture capitalists (Hovgaard, 1991).

Contemporary research on the UK MBO/MBI market by Murray et al. (1995) supports Hovgaard's findings as to the variable role of financial advisers in the investee applicants' search for venture capital finance. A 1993 survey of seventy CEOs having undertaken a UK management buy-out or buy-in of

1086   MURRAY

between £2−10 million deal value in the last three years indicated that only 25% of the respondents rated their financial advisers as 'highly influential' in the *identification* of appropriate sources of venture capital. Only 9% of managers similarly rated their advisers as highly influential in the final venture capital *selection* decision. Forty percent of the managers interviewed had chosen a venture capitalist *before* commissioning a financial adviser to assist the management team in the deal process.

Increase in Buyer Power

Porter's (1979) popular 'competitive forces model', which is based on managerial economics antecedents, seeks to determine the ability of a firm or industry to sustain long term, supra-normal profits by reference to the degree of existing inter-firm rivalry and to the power balance between four interest sets — customers, suppliers, new entrants, and providers of substitute products/services. In using this model, it is therefore of fundamental importance both to define who are buyers from and who are suppliers to the venture capital industry. Sahlman (1989) in the US and Lloyd (1989) in the UK have each used this model to analyse the changing competitive environment facing venture capital firms. Using Porter's terminology, these authors see institutional providers of capital as the *suppliers* and investee companies as the *customers* for the venture capital firms.

It is argued that this analysis is incorrect (Murray, 1991b). Rather, it is suggested that the providers of finance, be they external sources for independent firms or internal sources for captive organisations, are the 'primary customer'[8] of the venture capitalist. It is to these providers that the venture capitalists have to justify the performance of their investment activities, and ultimately to reward by the provision of rates of return commensurate with the peculiar risks and illiquidity of investment in venture capital funds. When venture capital firms seek contributions for the financing of a new fund, it is the institutions which control the purchase decision, and select the recipient of their funds between an increasing number of venture capital firms competitively seeking new capital. The power of the institutional funders is also evidenced by their ability to set increasingly tight constraints on the rewards of the venture capital fund's general partners (Gregory, 1991).

The investee company clients should more properly be seen as the 'raw material' or 'firm stock' from which the investors' value added and capital gain is derived. In Porter's terms, the applicant firms seeking venture capital finance are suppliers. Their limited bargaining power, which is in part a function of their inexperience of the finance raising process, is reflected in the stark statistic that approximately 95% of applicants for finance are rejected by the venture capitalists (Bannock, 1991; and Dixon, 1991).

This changing balance of power is also a consequence of the supply and demand conditions pertaining at the time of the transaction. The reduction in new capital available from institutions, post 1989, has occurred at a time when several independent venture capitalists firms have fully invested their earlier funds. The recent recession exacerbated funding issues by increasing the finances required to support vulnerable investee companies within the venture capitalists' existing portfolios. The husbanding of power by institutional investors may also be a consequence of the excessive investment expectations created by the venture capital industry. A remarkable 74% of the BVCA survey respondents agreed with the statement that 'UK venture capitalists had oversold the potential returns of their industry to institutional funders'.

One prescriptive response by major UK institutional investors to imperfect information has been the creation of an informal 'Venture Investors' Circle' at which issues of common interest are discussed. This forum, which embraces some twenty major investors, thus provides funders with the opportunity to discuss the nature of the relationship between the institutions and venture capitalists. It is unlikely that the existence of a better informed and powerful caucus of institutional investors will do other than increase the bargaining power of the investors *vis à vis* the venture capital supplicants for their funds during a period of capital scarcity. The extent of their potential power can be evidenced by Initiative Europe's (1994) estimate that independent venture capital firms are currently attempting to raise £1.25 billion of new funds. This figure is approximately four times the size of funds raised in either 1992 or 1993.

Increase in Inward International Competition

Financial services are becoming increasingly global in scope (Bryan, 1993). As a market grows, it can become attractive to international companies provided the revenue and cost structures of product and service provision enable profitable market entry and development (Kay, 1990). With the exception of approximately ten (primarily American) organisations, the UK venture capital industry has remained determinedly domestic in ownership. International investors have largely preferred to enter the UK market by participating in a UK originated fund managed by a British venture capital firm. In the peak year of 1989, new capital commitments by overseas investors to independently managed funds grew nearly five fold to represent 42.3% of the total funds raised that year. Foreign investment was to decline by over half (53%) in 1990, and by 1992 represented 36% of the £347 million of new funds raised (Venture Economics Ltd., 1991/92).

The twenty-two BVCA survey respondents were asked their views on the likelihood of foreign companies either creating new venture capital firms in the UK or, conversely, acquiring existing UK firms. While it was agreed that an increased foreign presence in the UK could occur, 86% of respondents did not see it as a significant future trend. When asked to estimate the number of such transactions over the next five years (1991—95) the median category was 6—10 deals. Firms from the United States were seen as the most likely acquirers (12 respondents) followed by continental Europe (8) and Japan (7). Survey respondents were also asked to estimate the number of total new entrants into the UK venture capital industry over the period 1991–95. An average response of sixteen firms was given. When asked to describe the types of new entrants only three respondents (13.6%) mentioned overseas companies.

The reason cited for this lack of international threat was the high level of development of the mature and competitive UK market in comparison to other European markets. This maturity, and the consequent limitation on supernormal profits, was seen as the most significant barrier to entry. Respondents believed that mainland Europe presented more attractive opportunities for non-UK venture capitalists. They also noted that contemporary problems (in 1990) of loan defaults and capital adequacy in US and Japanese banking would reduce the likelihood of new entrants from either country becoming a serious threat in the UK in the short term. These opinions appear to have been correct. No major (i.e. >£100 million fund) foreign-owned venture capital operation has been established in the UK since 1990.

Decline in Industry Profitability

For the management company of an independent venture capital fund, the sources of income are primarily two-fold. An annual management fee is paid by the institutional investors as a proportion of the total funds invested. At the end of the investment period, the general partners in the venture capital company normally participates in any capital gain of the fund, i.e. the 'carried interest', subject to a prior agreed 'hurdle rate' which is designed to ensure a minimum real return to investors before the management company is rewarded. As Sahlman (1991, p. 11) has noted, if the fund is successful, the capital gain accruing to the partners is likely to be significantly greater than their combined base salaries and bonuses. The managers of captive funds, who are essentially employees of the parent company, do not have the opportunity of a carry on internally raised funds but are usually rewarded by bonus schemes.[9]

It was noted by all BVCA survey respondents that the incomes paid to venture capitalists as management fees by the limited partner investors in their funds were coming under increased pressure as bargaining power moved to the advantage of the institutional customers. Gregory (1991) also notes the increasing conditions put on the release ('draw down') of funds and the repatriation of capital gains to investors. The industry standard is for the venture capitalist to be paid a fee of between two and two and a half percent per annum in order to cover the costs associated with managing the fund and the ensuing portfolio of investments. These percentage costs are largely consistent with US funds (Sahlman, 1991; and Bygrave and Timmons, 1992). Respondents observed that, in a period of capital scarcity, venture capitalists were under increasing pressures to accept lower incomes. One-off commissioning fees

CHANGE AND THE UK VENTURE CAPITAL INDUSTRY   1089

Figure 3

Comparison of Private and Quoted UK Company Price-Earnings Ratios
1987–93

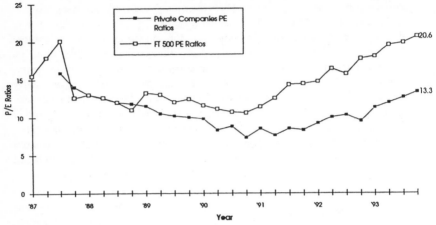

Source: Stoy Hayward/Acquisitions Monthly 1994.

charged by the venture capitalist when raising a new fund, which were common
in the early and mid 1980s, have disappeared. However, there have not been
similar pressures to reduce the venture capitalist's carried interest. Investors
appear to wish to maintain a key management incentive for fund performance.
The recent innovation in the UK since the late 1980s of a US practice whereby
consultants, termed 'gatekeepers', act on behalf of the funding institutions in
their identification and selection of high performing venture capitalist firms
is a possible further means by which pressures to reduce operating costs will
be applied to the industry.

   As noted, the primary means by which a venture capital firm accrues capital
gain, as opposed to operating income, is through its share of the aggregate,
appreciation in value of its successful investments when they are sold. The selling
price at which an investment exits from the venture capitalist's portfolio and
the timing of the exit are the two most important external determinants on
fund profitability (Bygrave et al., 1989). From 1980 to 1987, the market value
of firms, as measured by the price-earning ratio of the *Financial Times 500 Index*,
rose from six to twenty. It has taken the six succeeding years for this ratio to
return to 1987 levels. Over the same period, post black Monday in October
1987, the price earnings ratios of UK private companies have performed
relatively less well. At the end of 1992, the Private Company Index stood at
a 43% discount to the price earnings ratios of the FT 500 companies — the
widest gap for several years (*Financial Times*, 25 January, 1993, p. 16). Twelve
months later, in December 1993, private company price earnings ratios, at
13.3, were still only 84% of their 1987 high point.

1090 MURRAY

From 1989 until the latter half of 1992, the use of public stock markets as an exit channel through which venture capital portfolio companies could be sold had become extremely difficult. Exceptionally, no private companies raised funds by joining the Unlisted Securities Market in the first quarter of 1991.[9] Only two MBOs exited by stock market flotation in the whole of 1991 compared to 132 in the period 1985−1988 (Centre for Management Buy-Out Research, 1992). Trade sales, which represent the dominant exit route, were similarly depressed reflecting cash flow and profitability constraints facing would-be acquiring firms in an international recession. However, the substantial increase in the value of UK equities in 1992/93 was also mirrored in a spate of Initial Public Offerings (IPOs) of venture backed companies in the four quarters July 1992 to June 1993. Excluding non-commercial, company stock market listings (mainly investment trusts) venture backed company flotations represented 48 % of the total of the 75 IPOs floated during these four quarters. MBOs represented 50 % of the 36 venture-backed flotations (BVCA, 1993b). This fickle interest by the London Stock Market in venture backed issues appears to parallel the similarly erratic pattern seen towards the attraction of IPOs to US investors over recent years (Bygrave and Timmons, 1992).

Thus, firms which invested substantial portfolio funds in the high price period from 1985 to 1987 have found subsequently their ability to realise investments (typically, over an approximate five year cycle, Bannock, 1991) at an attractive capital gain difficult for other than their most attractive investee companies. In effect, they have bought high and have had to sell low in a period of depressed firm prices as measured by stock market indicators or trade sale statistics. While the upward trend of small firm stock prices might appear to give some cause for optimism, it is necesary to remember that venture backed flotations barely reach double figures each year. UK venture capital firms have regularly invested in over 1,000 investee companies annually since 1987. Given the difficulties of obtaining attractive exit values during the recent recession, the stock of investee firms in the collective portfolio of the UK venture capital industry, which investors would wish to exit via an IPO, is likely to be very substantially greater than the praticable opportunity this channel represents. It is salutary to observe that, for MBOs, which remain the most popular investment activity of the UK venture capital industry, the CMBOR only recorded 12 flotations for the three years 1990−92, compared to 34 in both 1987 and 1988 (CMBOR, 1993).

All twenty-two BVCA survey respondents agreed that the difficulties of realising attractive exit prices would produce casualties in the UK venture capital industry as well as making institutional investors increasingly nervous of making unquoted investments in smaller companies via venture capital funds. Smaller, independent venture capital firms, i.e. with < £50 million of funds under management, were seen as particularly vulnerable. However, respondents believed that the dearth of new funds would extend to all firms which cannot demonstrate an attractive investment performance to potential funders.

CHANGE AND THE UK VENTURE CAPITAL INDUSTRY 1091

The computed return to the venture capitalist's investment, the annualised Internal Rate of Return (IRR), at which the deal is struck can be used as a surrogate for the price of its finance (Dixon, 1991). While individual firm data were not requested, several BVCA survey respondents noted that the IRRs at which deals were concluded had diminished over the 1980s. In 1991, an attractive MBO deal was likely to be accepted with a projected IRR in the low thirties (Murray and Lott, 1995). The same deal in 1985 would have been negotiated at an IRR around ten percentage points higher. Given the systematic risk associated with start-ups or early stage deals and their relative unpopularity to the majority of venture capital firms (Lorenz, 1989; and Bannock, 1991), price pressures have here remained less in evidence. Respondents stated that they would still expect IRRs of at least sixty percent per annum for such deals to be considered seriously.

Increase in Industry Leavers

Until 1989, the barriers to entry were low and approximately one hundred new venture capital firms entered the UK industry over the decade. This growth phase ended in 1989 and the industry was subsequently characterised by leavers rather than new firm entrants. However, a number of primarily regional funds have recently been created which confound, in the short term, forecasts of a shake-out. That the industry has not contracted more rapidly (see Figure 4) is a function of the high barriers to exit. Once a venture capital firm has raised a fund and is fully invested in a number of client companies, it is committed to running the fund for its allotted period. In the event of making unattractive investments, the fund still has to nurture its remaining investee companies until an exit can be arranged. The alternatives are allocating shares of the unquoted portfolio company to the private investors or organising a 'fire sale' in an attempt to regain some liquidity. Both alternatives are likely to be commercially unattractive to the institutional investors. This combination of low entry and high exit barriers is likely to increase competition between industry incumbents for both deal flow and new capital funding.

Over half the BVCA survey respondents shared a common belief that a number of existing venture capitalists with indifferent investment records would face the prospect of a 'funds famine' in the coming five years, 1991–95. This was seen as the single biggest threat to the future of the industry and was mentioned, unprompted, by 59% of the sample. If additional funds are not forthcoming, these organisations, on winding down and realising the 'rump' of their portfolios, will be obliged to exit from the industry. Seventy seven percent of respondents saw this as the most common reason for a firm leaving the venture capital industry. They suggested that only a minority of these firms will be attractive as merger of acquisition targets to either financial institutions or other, more successful, venture capital firms. However, present uncertainties do present the potential for arbitrage activity and structural changes might encourage 'portfolio brokers' (or, more accurately, 'breakers'). While there

1092 MURRAY

Figure 4

Actual and Projected Growth of BVCA Full Membership 1983−95

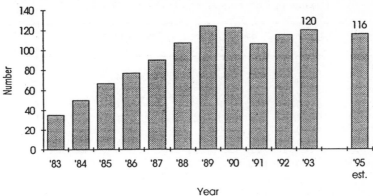

Source: BVCA, 1993.

is some evidence of limited activity, Initiative Europe (1994) only identified five transactions by 1993 in which UK funds have been terminated through acquisition by larger or more successful organisations.

In 1990, the BVCA survey respondents forecast that, on average, 24 firms would exit from the UK industry in the next five years. With an average of 16 new entrants also forecast, the stock of firms in 1994 was projected to decline marginally to around 116 i.e. very nearly the number of BVCA full members in 1993.[11] Since 1991, eleven new firms have entered the industry. The majority of these are smaller regional based funds or captives. Similarly, seven firms have unequivocally left the industry rather than remaining dormant, i.e. not investing or unable to invest. Six of the seven exiting companies were captives with only a peripheral interest in venture capital finance.

Thus, it would be more correct to describe this restructuring as a 'fade-out' rather than a precipitant process of 'shake-out'. In practice, the change in BVCA membership has been occasioned almost entirely by a smaller number of industry leavers than the greater flows forecast. This is likely to reflect the noted high exit costs. Performance pressures were seen as becoming particularly acute for poorly performing independents (noted by 59% of respondents) without the support of a powerful parent organisation, and small venture capital firms not enjoying a strong 'niche' position nor significant scale or scope economies (noted by 45% of respondents).

Concentration of Market Share

The number of firms in a market takes no cognisance of the market power

Table 2

Annual Funds Raised by Independent UK Venture Capital Firms
(excluding BES Funds) for the Period 1985 to 1991[13]

Year	Top Four Funds £m	Average Top Four Funds £m	Total Funds Raised £m	Top Four Funds % Total Raised
1985	83.3	20.8	133.3	62.4
1986	93.5	23.4	212.9	43.9
1987	353.0	88.3	685.1	51.5
1988	356.6	89.2	667.5	53.4
1989	1084.0	273.5	1695.9	64.5
1990	427.0	106.8	852.1	50.1
1991	151.5	37.9	275.9	54.9

Source: Venture Economics Ltd., 1993.

of individual organisations. The importance of industry structure was explicitly recognised by several BVCA survey respondents who commented that there were only about twenty to thirty 'real' players in the UK venture capital market. From the period 1986 to 1989 inclusive, the four largest fund raisers have represented an increasing proportion of the total funds raised each year. With the exception of 1986, in the period 1985—91, the top four fund raisers, which are not the same firms every year, have accounted for over 50% of the total value of institutional investment raised.

This process of concentration is corroborated by reference to the Venture Economics Ltd.'s Special Reports 'Resources of the UK Venture Capital Industry', published for the years 1987—91. (The figures for 3i plc have been excluded from these survey results.) In 1987, in a sample of 107 firms, 27 venture capitalists had funds under management exceeding £50 million. By 1991, the number of firms with funds above £50 million had increased to 41 (44%) of the sample of 93 venture capital firms. At the lower end of the scale, the number of firms with funds under £5 million had dropped from 22 in 1987 to 13 in 1991.

Figure 5 shows graphically the degree of concentration existing in the UK industry by 1992. If 3i plc is excluded, twenty-eight firms each managed funds in excess of £100 million. Collectively, their resources represented 77% of the total funds controlled by the full membership of the BVCA. The driving forces towards concentration in the industry are three-fold. As institutional funders, with the assistance of gatekeepers, become more able to discriminate between successful and unsuccessful firms, the market moves to reward disproportionately the successful firms with additional capital. Similarly, firms with poorer performances experience a dearth of new funds. Secondly, there are, as Sahlman (op. cit.) notes, economies of both scale and scope operating to the advantage of a management company or partnership which operates simultaneously more than one fund. Larger funds with a commensurately larger

1094 MURRAY

Figure 5

Concentration of UK Investments by Fund Size, 1991/92

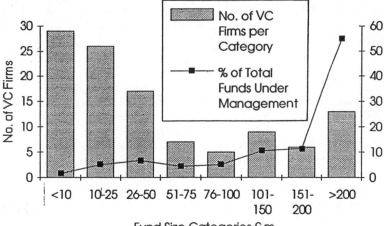

Source: derived from BVCA Directory 1992/3.

deal flow may also have the benefit of 'learning curve effects' if the cost of the investment process declines over time with accumulated volume.

The third factor encouraging the growth in fund size is the compensation benefits captured by the managers of a large fund. The percentage fee charged by the venture capital company to manage the fund on behalf of the limited partners, at 2–2.5%, does not appear to decline with the size of fund. This 'stickiness' of the management fee has appeared to operate both in the UK and the US. Thus, managers have a direct incentive to increase the size of the funds under their management, irrespective of the performance implications on portfolio management, given that a number of the operating costs do not rise proportionately to the additional funds managed. The issue of divergent interests, or 'agency costs' (Jensen and Meckling, 1976), between the managing and private partners of a fund has come to the fore as institutions have downgraded their expectations on net returns from a number of their investments. Initiative Europe (1994), reflecting on the substantial fee-based remuneration of the management in a number of poorly performing funds, suggested contentiously that on occasions the institutions have been 'mugged'. The economic attraction of managing a large level of aggregate funds is supported in a survey conducted by Hays Management Consultants (1988) on US venture capitalists' remuneration. The total compensation of a managing partner of a venture capital firm controlling funds of over $200 million was, at $581,000 per annum, over three times the size of his/her opposite number managing a fund of $25 million.

CHANGE AND THE UK VENTURE CAPITAL INDUSTRY   1095

The outcome of these factors was that, throughout the 1980s, the UK industry had become increasingly polarised into a small number of large, and increasingly international, venture capital firms with combined funds in excess of £100 million. By 1991, there were 29 such funds. The remainder of the industry included a large concentration (55 firms) of small players each controlling funds of less than £25 million.

The Importance of Management Buy-Outs

The single biggest product for the UK venture capital industry throughout the 1980s and early 1990s has been the Management Buy-Out (MBO). The need to restructure over-diversified, multi-enterprise businesses in an increasingly competitive environment resulted in a substantial supply of new businesses which required external equity to complement the management team's limited personal resources. The substantial growth of acquisition activity in the mid 1980s also increased the supply of MBOs as the acquiring companies resold parts of the purchased company not required in the enlarged business.[12]

In 1992 MBOs/MBIs accounted for 35% and 57% of the number and value, respectively, of the combined activity of the UK market for corporate control. Over the period 1979—92, 3,952 MBOs with an aggregate value of £21.7 billion were financed. Over the same period, there were a further 829 Management Buy-Ins (MBIs) created with an aggregate value of £7.9 billion. Although 1990

Figure 6

Growth of Management Buy-Outs and Buy-Ins 1980—92

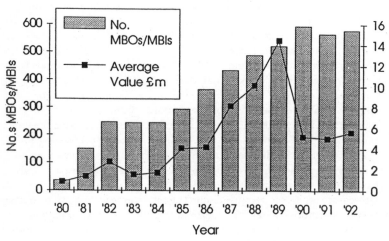

Source: CMBOR 1993.

was a record year for the number of total transactions, with 484 new MBOs recorded (a growth in number of 29.8% over 1989), the average value of individual deals dropped sharply to £5.1 million from the exceptional figure of £10.4 million in 1989 (CMBOR, 1994). MBO/MBI activity was broadly sustained in 1992 with 445 MBOs and 134 MBIs representing aggregate investment of £3.26 million, the highest annual value of total deals since the record year of 1989 when transactions worth £7.5 billion were completed.

The importance of MBOs/MBIs can be evidenced if their value is removed from UK annual investment statistics. When excluded, venture capital investment has declined in nominal value terms over the last four years from £565 million in 1988 to £445 million in 1991. In the latter year, MBOs/MBIs represented 55% of total UK investment by the industry.

The BVCA survey respondents estimated that MBOs would continue to be the single most important product in the UK venture capital industry, still representing 51% of the value of annual transactions in 1995. Respondents also believed that a greater proportion of annual investment (1995 estimate 36%, 1991 actual 34%) would be applied to later stage financing including development capital, secondary finance and, reflecting the problems of recession, rescue-type, refinancing deals. The ability to provide capital for firms that remain basically sound but are financially constrained as traditional sources of borrowing and new equity become less available during a recession was seen as the single biggest contemporary opportunity in late 1990, being mentioned by 59% of respondents. In this context, UK venture capitalists have become increasingly interested in the novel activity of investing in smaller, quoted companies (see *UK Venture Capital Journal*, March/April 1991).

The Role of Debt in Venture Capital Financing

The industry has been characterised by the flexibility and creativity with which deals can be initiated and financed. Notable in the latter part of the 1980s was the growth in sophisticated quasi debt/quasi equity instruments, most importantly 'mezzanine' finance. At its zenith in 1989, mezzanine financing at £933.3 million represented 16% of total deal value in MBOs/MBIs. One year later, the value of mezzanine finance had plummeted six fold to £155.5 million (CMBOR, 1992) as the risk to subordinated, quasi-debt in over-geared, larger (i.e. >£10 million) MBO deals became apparent. The growth in these instruments had allowed increasingly larger deals to be financed with a corresponding increase in the indebtedness of the deal. The well publicised problems of corporations which have funded expansion and acquisition with a heavy reliance on debt, both within and outside the venture capital arena, have had the consequence of encouraging a significant trend away from highly indebted deals. KPMG (Oct.–Dec. 1992) noted that the gearing (i.e. debt + mezzanine divided by equity) on larger MBOs had dropped from a ratio of 5.9:1 in the last six months of 1989 to a more conservative ratio of 1.7:1 two years later.

Twenty-one of the twenty-two BVCA survey respondents believed that there would be a significant and conservative move to a greater proportion of equity in the financing of future venture capital deals. This trend was also a recognition (noted by 10 respondents) that the clearing banks were increasingly refusing to provide senior debt financing without investors providing significantly higher contributions of equity to around 40—50% of deal value. There was a greater divorce of opinions about the future use of mezzanine funding. Nine respondents (41%) believed that it would increase in importance over the next five years. Five of these respondents also saw venture capitalist firms becoming a more important source of mezzanine finance as specialist providers withdrew from this activity, at least in the shorter term. Recent statistics support the trend to more conservative financing of larger (>£10 million) MBOs/MBIs. The role of mezzanine has continued to reduce, declining from 15% of total funding in 1990 to 7% in 1991. This shortfall has been made up by equity providers who in 1991 provided 34% of total funding of £2,620 million with the remaining 57% being supplied by debt providers (KPMG, 1991).

The latter half of the 1980s saw an increase in the size of venture capital backed deals culminating in the Reedpack MBO in 1988 of £805 million and the Gateway/Isosceles MBI in 1989 of £2,375 million. While the average value for an MBO over the 1980s was £5.9 million, between 1987—92 inclusive there were 14 MBO/MBIs of over £250 million and 290 MBO/MBIs of between £10—250 million (KPMG, April/June 1993). Venture capital over the decade grew from a useful form of specialist finance for start-ups and refinancing non-core enterprises out of the corporate parent to a major financial instrument within the wider market for corporate control. The attraction of MBOs was such that a number of funds were created in the late 1980s specifically for the financing of large MBOs (and to a lesser extent MBIs) of deal sizes of £50 million and above. Current analyses from CMBOR and KPMG suggest that, while the economic attraction of size remains, a more cautious approach by investors to larger deals is likely to exist for the foreseeable future or, at least, until a sustained upturn in economic activity in the UK is unequivocally demonstrated.

Search for New Markets/Internationalisation

The UK industry has placed increased emphasis in establishing continental European operations, either as wholly owned subsidiaries or as alliances and joint ventures with domestic partners in the new country markets (CMBOR, 1991). With few exceptions, the only other market of interest to UK venture capitalists outside continental Europe has been the United States.

The substantial 1990 increase in investments by UK venture capitalists into continental Europe from £47 million in 1988 indicated the relative attraction of these emerging markets, despite the considerable legal and fiscal barriers to unquoted equity investments in several European countries (CMBOR, 1991). KPMG estimated that the annual value of continental European MBOs had by the end of 1990 reached parity with the value of UK MBOs at £2.8 billion

Table 3

National and International Investment by UK Venture Capitalists
1989—91

	Number of Financings			Amount Invested £ million		
	1989	*1990*	*1991*	*1989*	*1990*	*1991*
UK	1,302	1,221	1,196	1,420	1,106	989
US	156	178	92	127	62	70
Contin. Europe	94	150	94	97	223	92
Overseas	17	10	4	3	3	2
Total	1,569	1,559	1,386	1,647	1,394	1,153

Source: BVCA 1992.

each. They forecast that continental activity would, in 1991, exceed for the first time UK values (KPMG, January 1991). However, EVCA figures for 1992 indicate that the UK has re-established its dominance representing 61% of European MBO/MBI activity by value (EVCA, 1993).

As the deadline for full harmonisation of the EC by the end of 1992 approached, Europe has replaced the US as the second most important investment focus of UK venture capitalists. This geographic expansion of the contemporary venture capital model from its US origins to the UK, subsequently to Western Europe and, more recently, to the Pacific Rim and Eastern Europe is an apposite illustration of the 'international product life-cycle' (Murray, 1990).

The BVCA survey respondents were asked if they saw continental Europe as a major opportunity for the UK venture capital industry. Seventeen respondents (77%) agreed that it was. However, five respondents challenged this view arguing that the opportunities had either been over estimated or that, while opportunities did exist, they would only be available to a limited number of well resourced organisations that had effectively nurtured cross-border linkages. In terms of the most likely areas of attractive deal flow, the growing European MBO market was seen as the area of highest potential, (45% of respondents) followed by the opportunities from arranging the succession in family firms (41% of respondents). Figures from CMBOR show a total of 1,548 MBOs/MBIs valued at $25.07 billion were undertaken in 14 continental European countries over the period 1989—92 inclusive (CMBOR, 1993). These figures give the UK a four year average, total European market share by value of 53%, albeit almost entirely derived from domestic investment in UK firms.

Rationalisation of Existing Products and Services

A frequent criticism repeatedly made of the UK venture capital industry is the modest amounts of money which it allocates both to start-up/early stage

CHANGE AND THE UK VENTURE CAPITAL INDUSTRY   1099

Table 4

Start-Up and Early Stage UK Venture Capital Investments 1987—91

	1987	1988	1989	1990	1991
Start-Ups:					
Number	191	202	177	199	158
Value (£m)	75	70	86	76	35
% Total Invested	8	5	6	7	4
Early Stage:					
Number	133	182	344	141	115
Value (£m)	45	60	129	52	23
% Total Invested	5	5	9	5	2

Source: BVCA, 1992.

companies and to high technology related investments (for example, see Confederation of British Industry criticisms reported in the *Financial Times*, 6th May, 1993).

Seventy seven percent of the BVCS survey respondents observed that this paucity of what Bygrave and Timmons term as 'classic venture capital' represented the single most important failing of the industry to date. Over the decade of the 1980s, the UK industry had become increasingly focused on large MBO deals, particularly in the retail sector. In 1991, 158 start-up and 115 other early stage financings were allocated 4% and 2%, respectively, of the total funds invested by BVCA members that year compared to £544 million (55% of annual investment) on 288 MBOs and MBIs.

BVCA survey respondents estimated that start-ups and early stage deals would take on average 14% of total investments in 1995. There is little evidence to support the size of this estimate as, with the exception of 1989, the value of investment into early stage deals has declined since 1985. The availability of pre-start up funds, i.e. 'seed capital', is even more difficult with the UK figure for 1991 being estimated at less than 0.035% of total funds invested (EVCA, 1992; Murray and Francis, 1993; and Murray, 1995).

The BVCA survey respondents gave no optimism for expecting an increase in new technology investments (i.e. computer related, electronics, medical and biological, and communications). By 1995, 40% of the respondents believed this area of investment would be a lower proportion of total investment than the 1989 figure of 12%. One third of respondents (35%) believed that technology investment would increase as a proportion of the total while 25% of respondents thought that it would remain at the 1989 level. The recently released figures of the BVCA (1993) support the pessimists with technology investment declining to 9% of total UK investment value (including debt provided by venture capitalists) in 1992.

A 1991 survey of 40 UK venture capitalists, which were prepared to consider

Table 5

Technology Related Investments as a Percentage of the Value of Total
UK Venture Capital Investments 1987–91

	1987	*1988*	*1989*	*1990*	*1991*
% Technology	15.9	8.5	12.0	14.0	13.0

Source: BVCA, 1992.

technology-related investment, indicated that venture capitalists imposed higher
rates of return in the evaluation process when compared to non technology
proposals. Technology related proposals also had to be more international in
market scope in order to gain funding (Murray and Lott, 1994). Table 5 shows
clearly the increasing disillusionment with technology projects from 1987 which
was occasioned by the commercial difficulties of a number of funds which had
specialised in technology investments. These figures contrast dramatically with
the US where 80% of the annual investment of $1,358 million by NVCA
members was directed to technology-related enterprises in 1991. Software
investment alone took 25% of all disbursements (Venture Economics Inc.,
1992). Even after removing the influence of MBOs/MBIs and Leverage Buy-
Outs on UK and US investment figures respectively, the US invests *pro rata*
nearly three times (29% *v* 83%) as much of its annual venture capital
disbursements in technology-related investments in 1991 (Murray, 1993).

It is a reflection of the UK reality that, until recently, 'replacement equity'
in later stage deals, primarily buy-outs, have produced better risk/return yields
than the more speculative areas of true venturing or 'new equity' within the
UK market. Classic venture capital activity, both in start-up and early stage
deals, needs specialist skills from the venture capital provider (Roberts, 1991a;
and Sweeting, 1991). The costs associated with selecting and subsequently
supporting such activities allow few economies of scale or scope and have
increasingly become the focus of smaller, more specialist venture capital firms.
However, a small number of larger, portfolio based, UK firms still undertake
both types of deal albeit as a minority activity.

Increased Emphasis on Costs and Services

The largest operational cost for venture capital firms is their specialist workforce.
There are no public data on whether or not the increased competitive climate
has produced a decline in management incomes and only anecdotal evidence
which suggests that the industry is starting to slim down its labour force.[13] The
unpopularity of start-up/early stage deal, as indicated above, is in part due
to the staff cost implications of monitoring and supporting a large number of

CHANGE AND THE UK VENTURE CAPITAL INDUSTRY   1101

small entrepreneurial investments (Murray, 1991a; and Bannock, 1991).

Ironically, cost pressures generated from the institutions' greater negotiating power over fee incomes and the carry (Gregory, 1991) have grown at a time when investee companies may well expect a greater level of service and support from their investors. The effects of recession have increased the need to support existing portfolio companies. A 1990 press article on the industry suggested that up to one third of portfolio companies 'were now on the sick list' (Gant, 1990).

Twenty (91%) of the BVCA survey respondents believed that investee companies would in future want a closer relationship with their venture capitalist or would expect greater involvement from them. However, only 62% of the sample believed that the industry would actually become more 'hands on'. The support available to the client may become a more important selling point in differentiating a firm from its competitors in seeking new dealflow. The efficacy of closer venture capital involvement on the performance of the investee company has been questioned by some authors (Macmillan et al., 1989; and Fredriksen et al., 1990) although seen as more positive by others (Sweeting, 1991). For several of the smaller but non-specialist venture capitalists with scarce executive resources and limited funds to contract in specialist skills, such a trend could be problematic. The disproportionate cost of client support was cited as one of the major problems associated with making small, seed capital funds commercially viable (Murray and Francis, 1992).

UNITED STATES' PARALLELS AND EUROPEAN IMPLICATIONS

The BVCA survey was completed in the last months of 1990 and concentrated exclusively on the experiences of UK venture capital firms. However, parallels since the early 1980s between the UK venture capital industry and its more established American counterpart are impressive. The increasing difficulties in the investment climate for venture capital noted in the annual reports of the National Venture Capital Association from 1989 onwards and Swartz's (1991) contemporary evaluation of short term problems (i.e. poor returns; unrealistic investor expectations; decline in venture capital firm numbers; excessive numbers of undifferentiated late entrants; and concentration in fund suppliers) could as easily have been written about the UK industry post 1988.

The UK experience is starting to mirror the cyclicality evidenced in the US industry with the latter's current decline from the historically high activity levels of 1986/7 after a sustained period of growth since 1980. The US industry experienced an erratic fall in the number of venture-backed 'Initial Public Offerings' (IPOs) from the 1983 peak (121 at $3031 million) to the 1988 nadir (36 at $789 million). 1992 saw a strong recovery in this market with a record 151 companies generating a total amount offered of $4,420 million (NVCA,

1102   MURRAY

1992) mirroring the recent activity in the UK IPO market in 1992/93. The annual level of investment has also seen an upturn in the US. In 1991, $1,358 million was invested — the lowest annual figure since 1981. One year later, this figure had doubled to $2,543 million, although, excluding years 1990 and 1991, this was still the lowest level of nominal investment activity since 1982.

The confidence of institutional investors in private venture capital firms has also appeared to have increased. After a ten year low point in 1988 ($1,388 million), new capital commitments in 1992 grew 84% to $2,550 million. Irrespective of the 9% (i.e. 53 firms) of industry leavers over the period 1989–92, the industry has continued to concentrate. By 1992, seventy firms, representing 11% of the NVCA membership, controlled $17.84 billion of managed funds, or 57% of the total pool of funds committed to the US industry.

This paper's primary concentration on the UK venture capital industry is purposive. The UK in 1992 accounts for nearly two-fifths (39%) of total European annual investment (EVCA, 1993). The UK experience continues to cast a long shadow over the rest of Europe just as the US experience has influenced UK venture capital firms. Through the integrating work of the EVCA and the increasing number of international alliances between UK and other European venture capital firms, the lessons of the UK industry have been rapidly absorbed and adapted on the mainland of Europe.

Continental European countries have not invested heavily in technology based, new investments which overall took only 12% of total annual disbursements in 1992. Similarly, unlike the UK in the early 1980s, continental European venture capital firms did not start by investing significantly in start-up activity before developing into secondary financing activities. With the exception of Finland (39%), Spain (23%), and to a lesser extent Portugal (14%) and Italy (11%), the majority of European countries invest under 10% of annual funds at the seed capital or start-up stages. The continental industry has, *ab initio*, developed largely as a source of expansion and replacement capital. In 1992, these two categories took 46% and 9%, respectively, of total investment. MBOs/MBIs accounted for a further 40% of annual investment (EVCA, 1993).

Just as the continental European industries have developed rapidly to assume a similar investment pattern to the UK, they will more quickly have to face the strategic issues currently concerning the UK industry. As Europe becomes more integrated, the dominance of country based, venture capital markets will be challenged. For the larger deals, syndication may become more transnational in scope. Over time, investors, including banks and insurance companies, will wish to see acceptable, risk adjusted returns on this novel asset class from their venture capital intermediaries or specialist, equity providing subsidiaries. Changing market and environmental parameters will require individual firms to make decisions regarding their product/market choices. Like their UK counterparts, strategic competence will become a necessary precursor of success. In making these decisions, the recent history of the UK venture capital industry may offer informative parallels.

Table 6

Porter's Model of Industry Maturity

Environmental Changes:	Occurrence in UK VC Industry by 1993
Decline in Rate of Industry Growth	yes
Increase in Market Information	yes
Increase in Buyer/Supplier Power	yes
Increase in International Competition	no
Consequences and/or Firm Responses:	
Decline in Industry Profitability	yes
Increase in Industry Leavers	yes (but limited)
Concentration of Market Share	yes
Search for New Products and Services	yes
Search for New Markets/Internationalisation	yes
Rationalisation of Existing Products and Services	yes
Increase in Emphasis on Costs and Services	yes

Source: Porter, 1980.

CONCLUSIONS

The responses from the BVCA survey respondents, supported by industry statistics, suggest that the present dynamics of the UK venture capital industry closely fit Porter's (1980) model of industry maturity. Since 1989, there have occurred clear signs of the onset of maturity after allowing for the influence of external economic trends. The recent recessionary climate has negatively affected the value of current investments in client firms while making the institutional funders, or primary customers, more circumspect about the long term performance of venture capital investment. Their caution is seen in the contemporary difficulties experienced by UK venture capitalists in raising new funds.

Changing UK demand/supply conditions for venture capital in the last decade of the 20th Century is likely to result in a significant increase in inter-firm rivalry which will similarly encourage the trend for greater concentration in the industry. The ability to market effectively their financial products and services to prospective investee clients will become a key element of future success for UK venture capitalists. Similarly, the need to demonstrate performance in terms of risk adjusted, return on capital to institutional or parent funders will become imperative. Over the current decade, funders will increasingly be able to see the terminal performance details of existing venture capital, fixed term funds. The poor performance of some funds will oblige unsuccessful venture capitalists to leave the industry as their ability to attract future funds disappears.

Increased competitive pressure on the domestic market will likely produce

1104 MURRAY

more specialist product offerings (e.g. greater client advice/support or sector specialisms) by individual firms. The industry is, at present, remarkable for the near absence of product/service differentiation between the majority of competing firms. The maturity of the UK market has also prompted several larger UK venture capital firms to set up new offices in continental Europe. However, given the relative ease of the international transferability of specialist skills in financial services, the continued specificity of country markets and the dominance of local providers, particularly banks, the opportunity for UK firms to profit from the internationalisation of their markets remains, as yet, unproven. None the less, the opportunity for continental venture capital firms to profit from UK and US experiences in crafting their own strategic responses does exist.

NOTES

1 While the BVCA does not represent all UK venture capital firms within its membership, the larger firms are almost universally full members.
2 EVCA annual statistics in 1993 covered 18 European countries.
3 In July 1992, the 70 + institutions involved in financing Isosceles were involved in urgent refinancing of the MBI. The £400 million equity contribution in the original deal structure was likely to be rendered worthless (*Financial Times*, 9th July, 1991 p. 24). MFI was subsequently floated on the UK main market in 1993.
4 This was a subjective assessment made by the Council of the BVCA.
5 A liner regression of annual, nominal investment values between 1981 and 1991 against an average GDP index, as the independent variable, indicates a high level of association (correlation coefficient = 0.96, F ratio = 114).
6 A regression of annual, nominal investment activity against the *Financial Times All Shares Index*, 1981–91 as the independent variable, also shows a strong association (correlation coefficient = 0.908, F ratio = 42).
7 These figures do not include the funds raised internally by captive organisations such as bank owned venture capitalists. The finances raised by 3i are also excluded.
8 Edwin Goodman, President of Hambro America Inc., also suggests that US venture capitalists have ignored their real 'customers' (*Pension World*, July 1989, pp. 35–36).
9 This may help to explain the increase, post 1987, in semi-captive organisations establishing independent funds in tandem with existing, parental funding.
10 Given the continuing decline in the number and value of companies quoted on the USM, the planned closing of the USM in 1996 has been widely reported (*Financial Times*, 30 November, 1992, p. 16).
11 Contemporary industry opinion in 1993 was that the number of leavers will be substantially higher in the medium term than that forecast in 1990. However, a number of smaller venture capital firms have recently joined the BVCA taking its current full membership at the start of 1994 to 120.
12 If the annual value of MBOs/MBIs is regressed against the annual value of UK M&A activity from 1979–92, a correlation coefficient of 0.898 is obtained (F value 50.2).
13 Since 1990, 3i plc has undertaken a major cost reduction programme involving the closure of five UK regional offices in addition to a number of overseas offices, and a significant reduction in professional staff numbers.

REFERENCES

Anon. (1991), *Pension Fund Investment Survey — the Performance Challenge* (Alexander Consulting Group).
Bannock, G. (1991), *Venture Capital and the Equity Gap* (National Westminster Bank).
Brakell, J.R. (1988), 'Institutional Investor Expectations from Investment in Venture Captial', *1988 Guide to European Venture Capital Sources* (Venture Economics Ltd).

CHANGE AND THE UK VENTURE CAPITAL INDUSTRY   1105

British Venture Capital Association (1992/93), *Report on Investment Activity 1991/2* (BVCA).
_____ (1993a), *Directory 1993/4* (BVCA)
_____ (1993b), *High Proportion of New Flotations are Venture Backed*, Press Release: 19th Occtober (BVCA).
Bryan, L.L., M. Muth, P.S. Wufflie and D. Hunt (1993), 'The New World of Financial Services' *The McKinsey Quarterly*, Vol. 2, pp. 59–106.
Bygrave, W., N. Fast, R. Kholyian, L. Vincent and W. Yue (1989), 'Early Rates of Return of 131 Venture Capital Funds Started 1978–1984', *Journal of Business Venturing*, Vol. 4, pp. 93–105.
_____ and J. Timmons (1992), *Venture Capital at the Crossroads* (Harvard Business School Press).
Centre for Management Buy-Out Research (eds.) (1991), *The Economist's Guide to European Buy-Outs* (Economist Publications).
_____ (1992), *Management Buy-Outs of Companies From Receivership* (University of Nottingham).
_____ (1993), *UK Management Buy-Outs 1992/3* (University of Nottingham).
Dixon, R. (1991), 'Venture Capital and the Appraisal of Investments', *Omega*, Vol. 4, NO. 19, pp. 333–44.
European Venture Capital Association (1993), *1992 EVCA Yearbook* (KPMG).
Fredriksen, O., C. Olofsson and C. Wahlbin (1990), 'The Role of Venture Capital in the Development of Portfolio Companies', Paper for the Strategic Management Society's Strategic Bridging Conference, Stockholm (September).
Gant, J. (1990), 'Portfolios, Provisions, and Above All, Pragmatism', *Acquisitions Monthly* (November), pp. 4–8.
Gorman, M. and W.A. Sahlman (1989), 'What Do Venture Capitalists Do?', *Journal of Business Venturing*, Vol. 4, No. 4, pp. 231–248.
Gregory, R. (1991), *An Examination of the Fund Raising Environment for UK Venture Capitalists 1989–91*, unpublished MBA dissertation (Warwick Business School, University of Warwick).
Hannah, L. (1992), *The Financing of Innovation 1880–1980* (Economic & Social Research Council).
Harrison, R.T. and C.M. Mason (1992), 'International Perspectives on the Supply of Informal Venture Capital', *Journal of Business Venturing*, Vol. 7, pp. 459–475.
Hovgaard, S. (1991), *London Business School/British Venture Capital Association Survey on Venture Capital in the UK* (BVCA).
Hustedd, R. and G. Pulver (1992), 'Factors Affecting Equity Capital Acquisition: the Demand Side', *Journal of Business Venturing*, Vol. 7, No. 4, pp. 363–374.
Jensen, M. and W. Meckling (1976), 'Theory of the Firm: Managerial Behaviour, Agency Costs and Ownership Structure', *Journal of Financial Economics*, Vol. 3, pp. 305–360.
Kay, J.A. (1990), 'Identifying the Strategic Market', *Business Strategy Review* (Spring), pp. 2–24.
KPMG Peat Marwick McLintock (1991–1993), *Management Buy-Out Statistics* (KPMG).
Llanwarne, P.A. (1990), *Survey of the Attitudes of Small, High Growth Companies Towards Venture Capital*, unpublished BMA Dissertation (Warwick Business School, University of Warwick).
Lloyd, S. (1989), 'Special Report: An Industry on the Brink of the 1990s', *UK Venture Capital Journal* (November), pp. 10–15.
Lorenz, T. (1989), *Venture Capital Today*, 2nd Edn (Woodhead Faulkner).
Macmillan, I.C., D.M. Kulow and R. Khoylain (1989), 'Venture Capitalists' Involvement in Their Investments: Extent and Performance', *Journal of Business Venturing*. Vol. 4, No. 1, pp. 27–47.
Mason, C.M. and R.T. Harrison (1991), 'Venture Capital, the Equity Gap and the "North-South Divide" in the United Kingdom', in M.B. Green (ed.) *Venture Capital International Comparisons* (Routledge), pp. 202–247.
Murray, G.C. (1989), 'The Birth of a Pan-European Industry', *The European Buy-Out Directory 1990–91* (Venture Corp/Pitman), pp. 13–29.
_____ (1991a), *Change and Maturity in the UK Venture Capital Industry 1991–95* (BVCA).
_____ (1991b), 'The Changing Nature of Competition in the UK Venture Capital Industry', *National Westminster Bank Quarterly Review* (November), pp. 65–80.
_____ (1992), 'A Challenging Market Place for Venture Capital', *Long Range Planning*, Vol. 25, No. 6, pp. 79–86.
_____ (1993), *Third Party Equity Support for New Technology Based Firms in the UK and Continental Europe*, Paper presented at the Six Countries Programme workshop, Montreal.
_____ (1995), 'An Assessment of the First Three Years of the European Seed Capital Fund Scheme', *European Planning Studies*, Vol. 2, No. 4, pp. 435–461..

1106   MURRAY

Murray, G.C. and D. Francis (1992), *The European Seed Capital Fund Scheme: A Review of the First Three Years* (Commission of the European Communities, DGXXIII).
_____ and J. Lott (1995), 'Have Venture Capital Firms a Bias Against Investment in High Technology Companies?', *Research Policy*, Vol. 24, pp. 283–299.
_____, B. Nixon, P. Pounsford and M. Wright (1995), 'The Role and Effectiveness of UK Professional Intermediaries in the Selection of a Venture Capital Partner', *International Journal of Bank Marketing* (forthcoming).
Porter, M.E. (1979), 'How Competitive Forces Shape Strategy', *Harvard Business Review* (March/April), pp. 137–145.
_____ (1980), *The Competitive Strategy: Techniques for Analysing Industries and Competitors* (The Free Press, Macmillan Inc.).
Pratt, G. (1990), 'Venture Capital in the United Kingdom', *Bank of England Quarterly Bulletin* (February).
Roberts, E.B. (1991a), 'High Stakes of High Tech Entrepreneurs: Understanding Venture Capital Decision Making', *Sloan Management Review* (Winter), pp. 9–20.
_____ (1991b), *Entrepreneurs in High Technology* (Oxford University Press).
Robinson, R.R. (1987), 'Emerging Strategies in the Venture Capital Industry', *Journal of Business Venturing*, Vol. 2, No. 1, pp. 53–77.
Ruhnka, J. and J. Young (1991), 'Some Hypotheses About Risk in Venture Capital Investing', *Journal of Business Venturing*, Vol. 6, pp. 115–133.
Sahlman, W.A. (1989), *The Changing Structure of the American Venture Capital Industry* (National Venture Capital Association Annual Conference).
_____ (1991), 'Insights from the American Venture Capital Organisation', Working Paper (Harvard Business School, Division of Research).
Storey, D., R. Watson and P. Wynarczyk (1989), *Fast Growth Businesses Case Studies of 40 Small Firms in the North East of England*, Paper No. 67 (Department of Employment).
Swartz, J. (1991), 'The Future of the Venture Capital Industry', *Journal of Business Venturing*, Vol. 6, pp. 89–92.
Sweeting, R.C. (1991), 'Early Stage New Technology Based Businesses: Interactions with Venture Capitalists and the Development of Accounting Techniques and Procedures', *The British Accounting Review*, Vol. 23, No. 1, pp. 3–21.
Thornton, S. (1994), *UK Venture Industry Review* (Initiative Europe).
Tyebjee, T. and A. Bruno (1984), 'A Model of Venture Capital Activity', *Management Science*, Vol. 30, No. 9, pp. 1051–1066.
_____ and L. Vickery (1988), 'Venture Capital in Western Europe', *Journal of Business Venturing*, Vol. 3, pp. 123–136.
Venture Economics Inc. (1990–1993), *National Venture Capital Association 1989–92 Annual Reports* (NVCA).
_____ (1990), *Current State of US Venture Capital*.
Venture Economics Ltd. (1988), 'Special Report: Resources in the Venture Capital Industry', *UK Venture Capital Journal* (July/August), pp. 8–14.
_____ (1989), 'Focus on Fund Raising in 1989', *European Venture Capital Journal* (May/June), pp. 6–12.
_____ (1990), 'Special Report: Resources of the UK Venture Capital Industry', *UK Venture Capital Journal* (July/August), pp. 8–14.
_____ (1991a), 'Special Report: Capital Commitments to UK Funds in 1990', *UK Venture Capital Journal* (January/February), pp. 12–20.
_____ (1991b), 'Special Report: Venture Capital Investment in Quoted Companies', *UK Venture Capital Journal* (March/April), pp. 8–13.
Wright, M., K. Robbie, S. Thompson and K. Starkey (1994), 'Longevity and the Life-Cycle of Management Buy-Outs', *Strategic Management Journal*, Vol. 15, pp. 215–227.

[6]

ELSEVIER

WHY DO VENTURE

CAPITAL FIRMS EXIST?

THEORY AND CANADIAN

EVIDENCE

RAPHAEL AMIT, JAMES BRANDER,
AND CHRISTOPH ZOTT
*University of British Columbia, Vancouver,
British Columbia, Canada*

**EXECUTIVE
SUMMARY**

This paper investigates the role of venture capitalists. We view their "raison d'être" as their ability to reduce the cost of informational asymmetries. Our theoretical framework focuses on two major forms of asymmetric information: "hidden information" (leading to adverse selection) and "hidden action" (leading to moral hazard). Our theoretical analysis suggests four empirical predictions.

1. *Venture capitalists operate in environments where their relative efficiency in selecting and monitoring investments gives them a comparative advantage over other investors. This suggests strong industry effects in venture capital investments. Venture capitalists should be prominent in industries where informational concerns are important, such as biotechnology, computer software, etc., rather than in "routine" start-ups such as restaurants, retail outlets, etc. The latter are risky, in that returns show high variance, but they are relatively easy to monitor by conventional financial intermediaries.*
2. *Within the class of projects where venture capitalists have an advantage, they will still prefer projects where monitoring and selection costs are relatively low or where the costs of informational asymmetry are less severe. Thus, within a given industry where venture capitalists would be expected to focus, we would also expect venture capitalists to favor firms with some track records over pure start-ups.*

Address correspondence to Professor Raphael Amit, Faculty of Commerce, 2053 Main Mall, University of British Columbia, Vancouver, BC V6T 1Z2, Canada (e-mail: <amit@commerce.ubc.ca>; phone: (604) 822-8481).

We thank two anonymous referees and the editor for very helpful comments. We also thank Paul Gompers, who served as the discussant on the paper at the Economic Foundations of Venture Capital Conference held at Stanford University in March 1997. In addition, we owe a substantial debt to Mary Macdonald and Ted Liu of Macdonald & Associates Ltd. for providing access to the data. (Individual data records were provided on an anonymous basis.) We gratefully acknowledge financial support from Social Sciences and Humanities Research Council of Canada (SSHRC) grant no. 412-93-0005, and from Industry Canada. C. Zott also acknowledges financial support from Doktorandenstipendium aus Mitteln des zweiten Hochschulsonderprogramms (DAAD). The authors are associated with the W. Maurice Young Enterpreneurship and Venture Capital (EVC) Research Centre at UBC. The EVC web page is located at http://pacific.commerce.ubc.ca/evc/

Journal of Business Venturing **13**, 441–466
0883-9026/98/$19.00
PII S0883-9026(97)00061-X

To clarify the distinction between point 1 and point 2, note that point 1 states that if we look across investors, we will see that venture capitalists will be more concentrated in areas characterized by significant informational asymmetry. Point 2 says that if we look across investment opportunities, venture capitalists will still favor those situations which provide better information (as will all other investors). Thus venture capitalists perceive informational asymmetries as costly, but they perceive them as less costly than do other investors.

3. *If informational asymmetries are important, then the ability of the venture capitalist to "exit" may be significantly affected. Ideally, venture capitalists will sell off their share in the venture after it "goes public" on a stock exchange. If, however, venture investments are made in situations where informational asymmetries are important, it may be difficult to sell shares in a public market where most investors are relatively uninformed. This concern invokes two natural reactions. One is that many "exits" would take place through sales to informed investors, such as to other firms in the same industry or to the venture's own management or owners. A second reaction is that venture capitalists might try to acquire reputations for presenting good quality ventures in public offerings. Therefore, we might expect that the exits that occur in initial public offerings would be drawn from the better-performing ventures.*

4. *Finally, informational asymmetries suggest that owner-managers will perform best when they have a large stake in the venture. Therefore, we can expect entrepreneurial firms in which venture capitalists own a large share to perform less well than other ventures. This is moral hazard problem, as higher values of a venture capitalist's share reduce the incentives of the entrepreneur to provide effort. Nevertheless, it might still be best in a given situation for the venture capitalist to take on a high ownership share, since this might be the only way of getting sufficient financial capital into the firm. However, we would still expect a negative correlation between the venture capital ownership share and firm performance.*

Our empirical examination of Canadian venture capital shows that these predictions are consistent with the data. In particular, there are significant industry effects in the data, with venture capitalists having disproportionate representation in industries that are thought to have high levels of informational asymmetry. Secondly, venture capitalists favor later stage investment to start-up investment. Third, most exit is through "insider" sales, particularly management buyouts, acquisitions by third parties, rather than IPOs. However, IPOs have higher returns than other forms of exit. In addition, the data exhibit the negative relationship between the extent of venture capital ownership and firm performance predicted by our analysis. © *1998 Elsevier Science Inc.*

INTRODUCTION

In both Canada and the United States, venture capital finance is a significant form of financial intermediation. There is no strict regulatory definition of the venture capital industry, unlike commercial banking or insurance but, generally speaking, venture capital firms provide privately held "entrepreneurial" firms with equity, debt, or hybrid forms of financing, often in conjunction with managerial expertise. In Canada these firms are playing an increasingly important role. As reported in Macdonald & Associates (1996), between the end of 1991 and the end of 1995, the amount of capital under management by Canadian venture capital firms grew from C$3.2 billion (or about $3.8 billion in 1995 dollars) to C$6 billion, implying an annualized real growth rate of about 12% per year. The rate of new investment by venture capital firms grew even more rapidly, rising from C$290 million in 1991 (or C$306 million 1995 dollars) to C$669 million in 1995, which corresponds to real growth of more than 20% per year.

Despite its growing importance, the venture capital industry has received much less academic scrutiny than other parts of the financial sector.[1] This applies both to the-

---

[1] The venture capital industry is more difficult to study than other financial industries such as banking, insurance, stock markets, etc. Little of the relevant information is in the public domain, since the firms financed by venture capitalists are privately held and therefore do not have the same public reporting requirements as publicly traded

ory and to empirical investigation. At the theoretical level, perhaps the most fundamental question to ask about the venture capital industry is why it exists at all. Why have a set of specialized firms that focus on financing the entrepreneurial sector? Even if there were no dedicated venture capital firms, a combination of commercial banks, investment banks, private investors, and stock exchanges providing the necessary intermediation could still be imagined. In fact, among entrepreneurial firms, most finance is provided by banks and private investors (including family members), and many young entrepreneurial firms "go public" on stock exchanges without first seeking venture capital finance. In seeking to understand venture capital finance, it therefore seems important to ask what exactly is the niche filled by venture capital firms.

The primary objective of this paper is to present a theory explaining the existence of the venture capital industry and investigate the consistency of this theory with empirical observations. Our basic hypothesis is that informational asymmetries are the key to understanding the venture capital industry. Previous papers have focused on the importance of asymmetric information in venture capital markets, and several authors have suggested that a central distinction between venture capitalists and other financial intermediaries is that venture capitalists operate in situations where asymmetric information is particularly significant. In this paper we provide a simple formal model that distinguishes venture capitalists from other potential investors on the basis of their ability to deal with informational asymmetries. This model is also used to draw inferences about how venture capital financing would be expected to work. These predictions are then compared with the actual pattern of venture capital investment in Canada. This link between theory and empirical evidence is the main contribution of the paper.

There are two major forms of informational asymmetry. One type, sometimes referred to as "hidden information," occurs when one party to a transaction knows relevant information that is not known to the other party. For example, an entrepreneur developing a new product may have a much better idea about whether the product will actually work than does the venture capitalist who may finance the venture. The problem arises because the informed party typically has an incentive to misrepresent the information. The entrepreneur, for example, may have an incentive to overstate the likelihood of successful product development. Furthermore, the market may become crowded with "low-quality" projects, precisely because it is hard for investors to distinguish between good-quality and poor-quality projects. This phenomenon is called adverse selection. Potential investors understand that adverse selection exists and may therefore be wary of funding such entrepreneurial endeavours.[2]

The other type of informational asymmetry is often described as "hidden action." In this situation one party to a transaction cannot observe relevant actions taken by the other party (or at last cannot legally verify these actions). For example, an investor in an entrepreneurial firm might not be able to observe whether the entrepreneur is working hard and making sensible decisions, or whether the entrepreneur is planning to "take the money and run." This problem leads to what is called "moral hazard." The

---

firms. Also, regulatory scrutiny of the industry is modest compared to other financial services, therefore relatively little information arises from regulatory activities. Finally, as there are no organized exchanges for venture capital investments, no information derives from that source.

[2] A local financial advisor summed up a typical reaction: "You can meet ten enterpreneurs at a party and each one will tell such a good story that you will want to invest your life savings. Remember, however, that you will lose money on at least 7 out of the 10. My policy is never to invest in entrepreneurial ventures."

informed party then has an incentive to act out of self interest, even if such actions impose high costs on the other party.

Both adverse selection and moral hazard may arise in any investment environment, but they seem particularly acute in entrepreneurial finance. With large established firms, investments are made safer by the use of existing assets as collateral, and the development of reputation. Collateral and reputation effects can mitigate the negative effects of both adverse selection and moral hazard. Because entrepreneurial firms lack assets to provide as collateral, and because they lack the "track record" necessary to establish their reputation, the effects of informational market failures are more severe in entrepreneurial finance than in financing established firms.

Our central hypothesis is that venture capitalists emerge because they develop specialized abilities in selecting and monitoring entrepreneurial projects. In other words, venture capitalists are financial intermediaries with a comparative advantage in working in environments where informational asymmetries are important. This is their niche.[3]

The next section of our paper provides a brief review of relevant literature, followed by a section that sets out a formal model of venture capital finance with associated empirical predictions. The fourth section describes the data set obtained from Macdonald & Associates, and the fifth section compares the theoretical predictions with the data. The final section contains concluding remarks.

LITERATURE REVIEW

Akerlof (1970) is normally taken as the starting point of the formal analysis of informational asymmetry. Akerlof describes a situation where sellers of used cars have private information about the quality of their cars, but buyers cannot discern quality differences before purchase. In this setting, low-quality cars or "lemons" dominate the market, thus the market "selects" adversely. Akerlof showed that this adverse selection is inefficient in that potentially efficient (i.e., Pareto-improving) trades will not take place.

Adverse selection problems can arise in many circumstances. For example, in insurance markets, buyers may know their true risk better than insurance companies (as in Pauly (1974)), and in labor markets, workers may be more aware of their abilities than potential employers are (as in Spence (1973)). Spence points out that one natural market response to adverse selection is "signalling," where an informed party (usually the seller of the high-quality item) provides some signal of high quality. Thus, for example, product warranties may be signals of high quality. Rothschild and Stiglitz (1976) emphasize the rolle of screening, under which the uninformed party offers a contract or set of contracts that cause informed parties to self-select into different groups.

Hidden action (and moral hazard) was first discussed in insurance markets, where insured parties can take actions that either decrease or increase the risk of hazard. For example, after purchasing auto insurance, the insured party can either drive safely or dangerously. Early influential work on moral hazard includes Arrow (1973) and Pauly (1974), who showed that moral hazard causes market failure. Moral hazard problems are particularly important in many situations where one party acts as an agent for another party, such as when a client hires a lawyer, or the seller of a house hires a sales agent. In these situations, the "principal" cannot perfectly observe the effort (or other actions) of the agent. Jensen and Meckling (1976) argue that agency relationships are

---

[3] This analysis focuses on the venture capitalist's role as a buyer of entrepreneurial assets. Venture capitalists must also be good at selling these assets. That is, they must also exit effectively from their investments.

the key to understanding the modern firm. Thus, for example, the managers of the firm can be viewed as the agents of the owners, who might in turn be viewed as the agents of other investors in the firm.

Adverse selection and moral hazard are often viewed as crucial determinants of venture capital financing. Sahlman (1990), for example, postulates that contracting practices in the venture capital industry reflect informational asymmetries between venture capitalists and entrepreneurs, and argues that the lack of operational history aggravates the adverse selection problem. MacIntosh (1994) also asserts the basic idea that informational asymmetries are fundamental in the venture capital sector, and this point is also emphasized in Amit, Glosten, and Muller (1993). Various other papers implicitly recognize the importance of informational issues. For example, MacMillan, Zemann, and Narashima (1987) provide a valuable discussion of how venture capitalists screen new projects.

Chan (1983) highlights the role of venture capitalists in reducing the adverse selection problem in the market for entrepreneurial capital. He shows that an adverse selection result derives from the absence of any informed venture capitalists in the sense that only inferior projects are offered to investors. However, the introduction of informed investors may overcome this problem, leading to a Pareto-preferred solution. Amit, Glosten, and Muller (1990) present an agency model in which investors are uncertain about the entrepreneur's type when submitting investment bids. The authors relate the venture capital financing decision to the entrepreneur's skill level and predict which entrepreneurs will decide to enter into an agreement with venture capitalists.

Sahlman (1990) notes that staged investment, which creates an option to abandon the project, is an important means for venture capitalists to minimize agency costs.[4] The role of staged investment as a monitoring device is also examined by Gompers (1995). In addition, the active involvement of venture capitalists in the operation of their investee companies might mitigate the moral hazard problem. The empirical significance of the role of venture capitalists as monitors is supported by Barry et al. (1990) and by Lerner (1995). In addition, Lerner (1994) suggests the use of syndication (i.e., coordinated investment by two or more venture capitalists) as a method of reducing problems caused by informational asymmetries. Two other useful papers that describe actions that venture capitalists can take to reduce problems arising from informational asymmetries include Tyebjee and Bruno (1984) and Fried and Hisrich (1994).

Chan, Siegel, and Thakor (1990) seek to explain various "rules of thumb" in venture capital contracting practices as a response to informational asymmetries and, in a related paper, Hirao (1993) assumes that the entrepreneur's unobservable actions affect the venture capitalist's learning process, and uses this context to study the effects of different contracts. A more general overview of research challenges in the venture capital area is given by Low and MacMillan (1988).

Despite a number of empirical and descriptive studies on venture capital practices and activities, including some of those already mentioned and also MacMillan, Siegel, and Narashima (1985), Bygrave and Timmons (1992), and Gompers and Lerner (1994), among others, empirical work on venture capital finance is still relatively modest in scope compared to the analysis of other financial intermediaries. Our paper seeks to add to this literature. Specifically, we provide a formal model that uses asymmetric information to explain the existence of venture capitalists, then compare the predictions of this theoretical structure with evidence on venture capital finance in Canada.

---

[4] Admati and Pfleiderer (1994) and Hellmann (1994) provide formal models of staged finance in the venture capital context.

A THEORY OF VENTURE CAPITAL FINANCE

An entrepreneur has a potential project and seeks potential investors. To keep the analysis simple we assume that the project requires fixed financial input I from an investor. The expected cash flow from the project, net of production costs, is denoted R (for "net operating revenue"). This expected net operating revenue depends in part on the effort, e, provided by the entrepreneur and it depends in part on the underlying project quality, q. In addition, the outcome depends on a random variable, u, with expected value 0. The realized net cash flow is therefore

$$R(e,q) + u \tag{1}$$

where the expected operating revenue is $R(e,q)$. We assume that entrepreneurs and investors are risk-neutral expected value maximizers. We, therefore, ignore u and work with R. Variable u plays one important role, however. Given unobservable random uncertainty, as represented by u, it is not possible for an investor who knows project quality q to infer effort e from the cash flow realization.

If e cannot be observed by the investor, then it is a hidden action and gives rise to a moral hazard (or "agency") problem. If q is known to the entrepreneur, but not to the investor, then it is hidden or private information and gives rise to potential adverse selection. The presence of exogenous uncertainty, as represented by random variable u, does not in itself cause market failure. R is taken to be increasing in e and q. We also assume that there are decreasing marginal returns to effort. The effort effects can be written formally as

$$R_e > 0, \qquad R_{ee} < 0 \tag{2}$$

where subscripts denote (partial) derivatives.

Let the share of the proceeds that go to the investor (possibly a venture capital firm) be denoted α^s. The expected return V to the investor is

$$V = \alpha R(e,q) - I \tag{3}$$

The expected return to the entrepreneurial firm, denoted π (for "profit"), is its share of the proceeds, net of the costs of effort e.

$$\pi = (1 - \alpha)R(e.q) - e \tag{4}$$

Variable e is normalized so that providing e units of effort imposes cost e on the entrepreneurial firm.

Moral Hazard

To demonsrate the moral hazard problem, assume initially that q is known to both parties. A profit maximizing entrepreneur will maximize (4) with respect to e, leading to the following first order condition:

$$\pi_e = (1 - \alpha)R_e - 1 = 0 \text{ or } R_e = 1/(1 - \alpha) \tag{5}$$

---

[s] The implied contract has a linear structure. The results in this section are therefore predicated on the assumption of linear contracts. Non-linearities, such as buyback options for entrepreneurs, are not considered here, but might be useful in mitigating some of the addressed informational problems. We thank seminar participants at MIT for pointing this out.

The second order condition for a maximum is $(1 - \alpha)R_{ee} < 0$. Noting that the factor $(1 - \alpha)$ is presumed to be strictly positive and using (2), this second order condition must hold.

The efficient or "first-best" level of effort e* is determined by maximizing the sum of (3) and (4) with respect to e. This sum, denoted S, is

$$S = R(e,q) - I - e. \tag{6}$$

Maximizing (6) with respect to e yields the following first order condition

$$R_e = 1 \tag{7}$$

It follows form (5), (7), and (2) that the entrepreneur will choose less than the efficient level of effort as long as α is strictly positive. This is the moral hazard problem. It is illustrated in Figure A1 in Appendix 1. It follows from the corresponding algebra and Figure A1 that effort is declining in α.

$$de/d\alpha < 0 \tag{8}$$

It is possible that the moral hazard problem might render the project infeasible. The inveestment is attractive to the investor only if the return equals or exceeds the alternative value that can be obtained by investing I elsewhere. Let this required return or opportunity cost be denoted r. Then feasibility requires

$$(1 + r)I \leq \alpha R(e(\alpha),q) \tag{9}$$

The problem is that there may be no value of α that allows (9) to be satisfied. If the expected return to the investor is too low, this suggests raising α, but then e will fall (from (8)), reflecting the idea that the entrepreneur will provide less effort as his stake in the firm falls.

Feasibility for the entrepreneur requires that the expected profit given by (4) exceed the return from the entrepreneur's best alternative, which can be normalized to equal 0. It is possible that effort level e* would in principle allow feasibility for both investor and entrepreneur, but that the actual effort relationship, $e(\alpha)$ would not allow the project to be financed. Thus the moral hazard problem may cause the market to fail.

We now introduce the idea that investors can monitor the entrepreneur and, at some cost, induce the entrepreneur to provide additional effort. Denote the monitoring cost m. The expected return to the investor is therefore

$$V = \alpha R(e(\alpha,m),q) - I - m \tag{10}$$

If the responsiveness of e to m is low, then the investor will not bother to monitor, as the cost will exceed the benefit. Some investments may be worthwhile, without monitoring, in spite of the moral hazard problem, but many projects will be abandoned. If e is highly responsive to monitoring, then the investor will undertake monitoring and will elicit an effort level closer to "first-best" level e*. Projects that are not financed by other investors will be feasible for investors who are good at monitoring (i.e., those for whom the responsiveness of e to m is high).

It is also possible that the investor provides valuable services, s, to investee companies. These services (e.g., providing strategic and operational advice, aid in fundraising, adding reputation, etc.) are observable by the entrepreneur. Ignoring monitoring for the moment and normalizing the cost of providing s to 1 per unit, the expected return to the investor is now

448 R. AMIT ET AL.

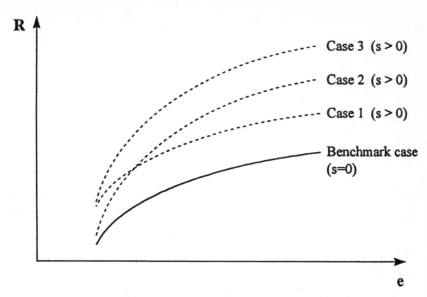

FIGURE 1 Effects of services on expected net revenues.

$$V = \alpha R(e(\alpha), q, s) - I - s \qquad (11)$$

We can think of the effect of $s > 0$ on the operating revenues R in the following way. Services s can produce a direct (positive) effect on R through $R_s > 0$ (case 1), or can have an indirect (positive) effect on R through enhancing the marginal productivity of the entrepreneur's effort, or $R_{es} > 0$ (case 2). When both effects are present, $R_s > 0$ and $R_{es} > 0$, we have case 3. Figure 1 illustrates these different cases and compares them with the benchmark case where $s = 0$.

Case 1 is defined as the case in which the investor's provision of s does not affect the entrepreneur's productivity of effort, R_e, but raises revenues directly. Let us assume that this effect is additive. For each effort level e expanded by the entrepreneur, the provision of $s > 0$ by the investor will increase the venture's revenues by ΔR. This is expressed in Figure 1 as a parallel upward shift of the graph of R(e) from the benchmark case to case 1. With respect to the moral hazard problem this means that, relative to the benchmark case, R_e and thus the entrepreneur's incentive constraint (5) remain unchanged in case 1. Therefore our basic analysis for $s = 0$ still holds (see equations (1)–(9) and Appendix 1). In other words, the moral hazard problems in the benchmark case and case 1 are identical.

In cases 2 and 3, however, the provision of s improves the productivity of e, and R_e is consequently shifted upward. This results in steeper curves for cases 2 and 3 in Figure 1. The entrepreneur's incentive constraint (5) is affected by this change, and therefore a new analysis of the moral hazard problem is required. Let us denote the case where $s = 0$ with superscript 0 and cases 2 or 3 where $s = k > 0$ with superscript s. "First-best" effort levels are denoted e*, "second-best" effort levels e'. The new situation is depicted in Figure 2.

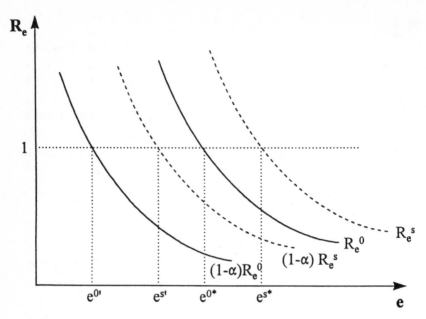

FIGURE 2   First- and second-best effort levels in base case ($s = 0$) and under $R_{es} > 0$.

Figure 2 is based on the different possibilities of how s can affect R; it also draws on the previous discussion of the standard moral hazard problem (without monitoring or services rendered). It allows us to conclude that the moral hazard problem persists for $s > 0$ even if $R_{es} > 0$. In this case, the "second-best" effort level $e^{s'}$ is still smaller than the "first-best" effort e^{s*}. However, relative to the base case scenario, the entrepreneur is now willing to put forth more effort ($e^{s'} > e^{0'}$).

Thus, the provision of s might contribute to the realization of projects which otherwise would have been abandoned, as they did not fulfill the investor's original feasibility constraint (9). Considering s, the investor's feasibility constraint now becomes

$$(1 + r)\,I + s \le \alpha R(e(\alpha), q, s) \tag{12}$$

If s is not prohibitively high, then it might relax this constraint through its direct and indirect positive effect on R. Thus, investors who are skilled at providing value-creating services to their portfolio companies will undertake certain projects which other, less skilled investors will shun.

There is ample evidence that venture capitalists provide valuable services to their portfolio companies. Gorman and Sahlman (1989) compiled a list of such services from a survey of venture capital investors. The five highest ranked and most frequently used activities can either be interpreted as directly enhancing investee revenues (e.g., introduction to potential customers and suppliers, assistance in obtaining additional financing) or as enhancing the entrepreneur's productivity of effort and thus indirectly boosting investee revenues (e.g., strategic planning, management recruitment, operational planning).

We now turn to the case in which both monitoring and services are considered.

The effects of s on R might be important enough to render projects feasible which were infeasible even with optimal monitoring. In fact, it seems natural to assume that a combination of monitoring and the provision of services constitutes a powerful tool in the hands of specialized investors to reduce moral hazard problems. Note, for example, that the entrepreneur's "second-best" effort provided in the case where $s > 0$ and $m > 0$ might be higher than the "first-best" effort in the benchmark case where $s = 0$ and $m = 0$. (Refer to Figure 2 and recall that if e is sufficiently responsive to m, $e^{s'}$ might get fairly cose to $e^{s'}$ under an optimal monitoring regime.)

Another point worth emphasizing is that providing services to entrepreneurs might make it easier and thus cheaper for investors to monitor them. Denoting $M(m|s)$ as the monitoring costs at a given level of s, it is very likely, for example, that $M(m|s > 0) < M(m|s = 0) = m$. Thus, the return to the investor given monitoring and services is

$$V = \alpha R(e(\alpha,m),q,s) - I - s - M(m|s) \qquad (13)$$

We note that investors who are good at monitoring and providing valuable services to their portfolio companies are likely to invest in firms with more severe moral hazard problems, as their feasibility constraint is more likely to be fulfilled.

Adverse Selection

A similar pattern emerges when adverse selection is considered. Assume that the venture capitalist chooses the optimal amount of services rendered and the optimal amount of monitoring effort, giving rise to associated values of e and s for any given α. Quality level q is now unobservable to the investor. Suppose that the range of q is such that the average quality project does not yield enough expected returns (for any value of α) to allow both (13) and (4) to be positive. Thus, the average project is *not* worth funding. Formally, we can write the investor's expected return as

$$EV = \int_q [\alpha R(e(\alpha,m(\alpha)),q,s(\alpha)) - I - s(\alpha) - M(m(\alpha)|s(\alpha))]f(q)dq < 0 \qquad (14)$$

where $f(q)$ is the probability density function for project quality. To simplify this expression, we subsume the terms that do not bear directly on the analysis of the hidden information problem into investor's costs C. With

$$C = I + s(\alpha) + M(m(\alpha)|s(\alpha)) \qquad (15)$$

inequality (14) reduces to

$$EV = \int_q [\alpha R(q) - C]f(q)dq < 0 \qquad (16)$$

Inequality (16) says that the expected value across all projects is negative. However, some of the individual projects (those in the upper end of the quality distribution) may be very valuable. Suppose, for example, that the top 40% of projects could generate a positive net profit. Unfortunately, the entire market will normally fail in this situation, as it will typically not be worthwhile for investors to provide financing, even though many individual projects are worthwhile.

Now suppose that an investor can acquire information about the quality of an individual project by spending d before making the actual investment I. Parameter d can be interpreted as the cost of "due diligence." This cost determines the probability, $p(d)$, with which an investor can establish whether the quality of a certain project exceeds a

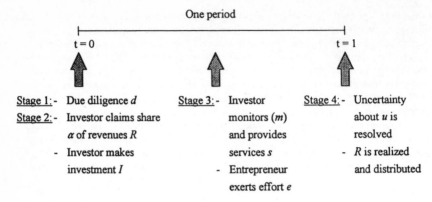

FIGURE 3   Venture capital investment process.

threshold level of quality. We denote this threshold level of quality as q^0. Let us implicitly define q^0 as follows:

$$
\begin{aligned}
V = \alpha R(q) - C = 0 && \text{for } q = q^0 \\
V > 0 && \text{for } q > q^0 \\
V < 0 && \text{for } q < q^0
\end{aligned}
\tag{17}
$$

The "detection function" $p(d)$ is assumed to have the following properties:

$$
p(d = 0) = 0,\; p(d = \infty) = 1,
\tag{18}
$$
$$
p'(d) > 0 \text{ and } p''(d) < 0
$$

Let us restate the assumptions concerning the sequence of events in the above model. Investment in an entrepreneurial firm is a one period, multi-stage process as illustrated in Figure 3. In the first stage, the investor incurs an up-front cost of d in order to assess the quality of a potential investment. With probability $p(d)$ the investor will become informed about q and will, therefore, find out whether $q \geq q^0$ or $q < q^0$. Only in the former case an investment will be made. With probability $(1 - p(d))$, however, the investor will remain uninformed about q and, due to (16), refrain from investing. Stage 3, in which the entrepreneur displays effort and is monitored and supported by the investor, and stage 4, in which the benefits from the investment are reaped and distributed, occur only if in stage 1 q is found to be greater than q^0.

The expected net return to the investor can therefore be expressed as

$$
EV = p(d) \Big|_{q > q^0} (\alpha R(q) - C)f(q)dq - d
\tag{19}
$$

Feasibility now requires that

$$
r(I + d) \leq EV
\tag{20}
$$

It follows immediately from (17), (18), and (20) that investors who are good at doing due diligence in the sense that low values of d yield a given value of p are likely to engage in due diligence, select high quality projects (i.e., projects with positive expected return), and make investments.[6] These are the investors that become venture capitalists. (For further formal analysis of the advise selection case, see Appendix 2).

We should emphasize that we assume that the efforts undertaken by the venture capitalist are not subject to free riding. That is, another investor cannot simply observe the venture capitalist who has undertaken diligence and then underbid him. Typically venture capitalists are able to keep the results of diligence and monitoring confidential until after financial contracts have been signed. Free riding does occur but, given the informational asymmetries in the venture capital sector, it seems plausible to abstract from free riding here.

Implications

The above formulation provides the simplest configuration that reflects the idea that venture capitalists are those investors who become skilled at selecting good projects in environments with hidden information and are good at monitoring and advising entrepreneurs who might otherwise be vulnerable to moral hazard problems. The implications of this modeling framework are outlined below.

1. Venture capitalists will operate in environments where their relative efficiency in selecting and monitoring investments and providing value-enhancing services gives them a comparative advantage over other investors. For example, as we have seen in the "hidden action" case, it may take effective monitoring m and specific services s to make a project attractive for an investor. In the "hidden information" case, on the other hand, market failure can be avoided if the probability of detecting whether a project is worth supporting is high enough for sufficiently low due diligence costs. This suggests strong industry effects in venture capital investments. We would expect venture capitalists to be prominent in industries where informational concerns are important, such as biotechnology, computer software, etc., rather than in "routine" start-ups such as restaurants, retail outlets, etc. The latter are risky, in the sense that random variable u has high variance, but they are situations that are relatively easy to monitor by conventional financial intermediaries, whereas the former draw much of their value from idiosyncratic knowledge that is much harder to assess. In principle, in-depth knowledge of traditional industries, such as retailing, is not less advantageous than in-depth knowledge of high-tech industries, but there is some evidence that such wisdom is harder to obtain for knowledge-based industries where informational asymmetries are, therefore, likely to be higher. (See Industry Canada (1994) on the particular difficulties and challenges that investors and lenders face with regard to the assessment of knowledge-based small- and medium-sized enterprises.)
2. Within the class of projects where venture capitalists have an advantage, venture capitalists will still prefer projects where selection, monitoring, and service costs are relatively low or, in other words, where the costs of informational asymmetry are less severe. In the presence of moral hazard, investors would prefer projects for which e is more responsive to m, and/or for which R and/or R_e are more responsive to s.

---

[6] We acknowledge that the structure of the venture capital investment process as depicted in Figure 3 is a simplification. Venture capitalists make investments even if they are not completely certain that $q > q^0$ and therefore they may earn negative returns on individual investments. However, taking this fact into account does not change the analysis except to add some additional algebra. (Note that in our model expected returns to venture capital investments are positive, but actual returns can be negative if $u < 0$.)

In the presence of adverse selection, projects with a highly responsive p(d) would be favored over those where the detection of quality is more difficult and thus more costly. Thus, within a given industry where venture capitalists would be expected to focus, we would expect venture capitalists to favor firms with some track record over pure start-ups. To clarify the distinction between point 1 and point 2, note that point 1 states that if we look across investors, we will see that venture capitalists will be more concentrated in areas characterized by significant informational asymmetry. Point 2 says that if we look across investment opportunities, venture capitalists will still favor those situations that provide better information (as will all other investors). Thus venture capitalists perceive informational asymmetries as costly, but they perceive them as less costly to deal with than do other investors.

3. If informational asymmetries are important, then the ability of the venture capitalist to "exit" may be significantly affected. Ideally, the venture capitalists might wish to sell off their share in the venture after it "goes public" on a stock exchange. If, however, these investments are made in situations where informational asymmetries are important, it may be difficult to sell shares in a public market where most investors are relatively uninformed. Public investors probably have a less responsive function p(d) and therefore (19) could be negative for them. This concern invokes two natural reactions: One is that many "exits" would take place through sales to informed investors, such as other firms in the same industry as the venture or to the venture's own management or owners. These informed investors probably have similar, if not better detection functions p(d) than the venture capitalist. A second reaction is that venture capitalists might try to acquire reputations for only presenting good quality ventures in public offerings. (However, this is an argument drawing on a multiperiod scenario and would therefore require an extension of our model). Therefore, we might expect that the exits that occur in initial public offerings would be drawn from the better-performing ventures.[7]

4. The model implies that dR/de ($= R_e$) > 0 and $de/d\alpha < 0$. Together these two properties imply $dR/d\alpha < 0$. Other things equal, we can expect entrepreneurial firms in which venture capitalists own a large share to generate lower net returns. This would be due to the moral hazard problem. Higher values of α reduce the incentives of the entrepreneur to provide effort. Nonetheless, it still might be optimal in a given situation for the venture capitalist to take on a high ownership share, as this might be the only way of getting sufficient financial capital into the firm. However, we would still expect a negative correlation between the venture capital ownership share and firm performance.

We note, however, that the model also suggests a negative relationship between R and α for another reason. Specifically, the selection constraint for investors is that $\alpha R \geq (1 + r)I$ or $R \geq (1 + r)I/\alpha$. If the venture capital market were very competitive so that investors earned no rents, then this selection constraint would hold with equality, and there would be an exact negative relationship between expected net operating revenues and α, whether or not moral hazard was present. Even if venture capitalists earn some expected rents, this selection constraint will still rule out combinations of low α and low R, which will tend to induce a negative correlation between R and α. The basic

---

[7] Empirical work by Megginson and Weiss (1991) and Gompers (1996) is consistent with the idea that the reputation of venture capitalists is very important at the IPO stage.

logic is that, for a given investment I, investors will need to be compensated by a large ownership share α if the expected net operating revenues are relatively low.

THE DATA SET

The data used for this study were collected by Macdonald & Associates Ltd. and made available to us on a confidential and anonymous basis. In addition, no individual firm-specific information is reported or discussed in our analysis. The data are derived from two surveys. The first survey, referred to as the "investment survey," began as an annual survey in 1991 and became quarterly in 1994. It asks just over 100 Canadian venture capital firms to identify their investees and provide some information about each investment and divestiture. Investees are recorded in the database and follow-up information is requested in subsequent surveys. The investment survey asks about the amount and stage of each investment and also seeks information about the venture capitalist's ultimate divestiture of its holdings in each investee.[8]

This survey, which covers the period from 1991 through the first quarter of 1996, seeks to obtain comprehensive information from all Canadian venture capital providers. In an effort to get full information about the investee firms, the survey is sent to venture capital companies (as just noted) and other investors who have investments in the venture-backed investees. However, some relevant venture capital providers may have been overlooked in the survey, and some surveyed venture capitalists may not report all of their investments. Nonetheless, Macdonald & Associates Ltd. estimate that the investment survey identifies 90–95% of the underlying population of Canadian firms supported by Canadian venture capitalists.

The second survey, referred to as the "economic impact" survey, began in 1993 and is conducted annually. It seeks additional information about the investees identified in the investment survey. Thus, economic impact information is sought about each investee that received an investment in or after 1991. Retrospective information is also requested. Suppose, for example, that an investee received an investment in 1991. The venture capitalist making the investment would have received a 1993 economic impact questionnaire asking for information about this investee going back as far as 1987. In many cases not much retrospective information can be provided, but the database contains economic information on a reasonable number of investees going back as far as 1987. The date of the investee's original startup (which in some cases is well before 1987) is also reported.

The response rate for the economic impact survey over its three year life has varied between 56% and 74% (i.e., information has been received on 56% to 74% of the targeted investee firms). If the investment survey identifies 90–95% of the relevant underlying population, then the effective sample coverage is between 50% (.9 times 56%) and 70% of the underlying population. The economic impact survey collects balance sheet and income statement information on the investees (including revenues and taxes paid). It also collects information on the structure and amount of their employment, and the nature of their industry.

A typical investee enters the data set when it receives its first investment from a

---

[8] This "exit" information, which is obtained on a regular basis from the investment survey, was complemented in November 1995 by an additional survey addressed to venture capital providers who had previously reported on divestitures.

venture capitalist. It may receive investments from additional venture capitalists as well. Subsequent rounds of investment may also occur. Eventually, an investee leaves the sample. This occurs when all venture capitalists have either written off (in the case of failure) or "cash in" their holdings in the investee. Thus, the data set contains a series of "life histories" for venture capital-backed firms.

A "record" refers to information for one particular investee firm for one particular year. There are 387 investee firms in the data availabale from the economic impact survey, but information on about 18 of these firms is significantly incomplete. The remaining 369 firms provide 1,298 reasonably complete records, and, therefore, have an average of about 3.5 records each. The investment survey data includes information on 1,086 Canadian investees. For some purposes, complete matched records are necessary,[9] but much interesting and relevant information is available from just the economic impact data (1,298 records on 369 companies) or just the investment data (2,017 records on 1,086 companies).

These data sets target Canadian investees supported by the Canadian venture capital industry. A Canadian entrepreneurial company that received support exclusively from venture capitalists based in the United States or Asia and had no support from Canadian venture capitalists would not be in our data set. This set of firms is probably fairly small, but there is no data available on its magnitude. It seems unlikely that this omission introduces much systematic bias over most subjects of interest in the data. Despite some possible selection bias in the economic impact data, the data set as a whole remains an important and unique data source.

INVESTMENT PRACTICES OF CANADIAN VENTURE CAPITALISTS

We now present some empirical evidence that addresses the predictions of the theoretical framework outlined in section 3. Some of this data, together with other empirical information on the Canadian venture capital industry is provided by Amit, Brander, and Zott (1997). Before considering the implications of informational asymmetries, we provide a general characterization of important financial variables in the data, as shown in Table 1. All relevant table entries are in thousands of 1995 Canadian dollars. As this table implies, the size of investee companies varies substantially, with a few large firms that make the average values much larger than the median values. The median investee has about 50 Canadian employees and annual revenues of C$6 million. A typical ownership share for the venture capitalist is approximately 30%.

The data in Table 1 also imply that firms in the data set spend, on average, about 3.5% of their revenues on R&D. This is about the same as the overall ratio of R&D spending to revenues for the Canadian economy as a whole. We should note, however, that these rather moderate R&D expenses may be due to different accounting standards that prevail in small and relatively young companies in contrast to large and established firms. Revenues per Canadian employee are $148,800, and the average long term debt to equity ratio is a conservative 0.77. (The long term debt to equity ratios derived from Canadian COMPUSTAT data is estimated to be 1.75 for companies of all sizes, and

---

[9] Matching the two data bases, we obtain 408 complete records on 302 investee companies. These numbers are low primarily because there are only 339 investee companies with records in both databases and because, for each investee, matches occur only in years when investments were undertaken.

456 R. AMIT ET AL.

TABLE 1 Summary Financial Data: 1987–94 (in Real $1995)

	Mean ($000s)	Median ($000s)	Standard deviation	No. of records
Total assets	22,928	5,540	70,707	1,277
Total equity	8,777	1,893	25,254	1,274
VC-share of equity (%)	34	30	30	1,218
Retained earnings	848	154	10,098	1,127
Total fixed assets	10,745	1,996	52,353	1,257
Long-term debt	6,729	1,056	28,122	1,157
Revenue	23,657	6,177	56,077	1,290
Investments in property, plant and equipment	1,954	222	8,180	1,161
R&D expenditures	837	79	2,098	1,067
Taxes paid	461	25	1,315	1,027
# of Canadian employees	159	50	301	1,293

Source: Macdonald & Associates Ltd. Economic Impact Database.

0.90 for companies with annual sales less than $100 million.) The low debt-equity ratio may reflect the limited borrowing capacity of entrepreneurial firms. We note also that the average investee is profitable enough to pay nontrivial amounts of tax.

We now consider the implications of the information-based model described in Section 3. One of the implications was that venture capital would be focused on industries where the importance of monitoring and due diligence expertise is particularly great. Table 2 presents information about the industry breakdown of the investee companies, and compares these investment shares with the shares of these industries in total output (as measured by Canadian gross domestic product (GDP)).

TABLE 2 Industry Classification

	Early stage investment* (no. of investees)	Total investment* (no. of investees)	% of early investment	% of total investment	% of total output
Biotechnology	95.4 (43)	121.5 (51)	17	6	0
Communications	83.7 (32)	225.1 (63)	15	10	5
Manufacturing and industrial equipment	78.7 (82)	461.6 (261)	13	21	24
Computer (hardware and software)	70.0 (100)	314.4 (182)	12	14	3
Miscellaneous	67.1 (58)	314.7 (178)	12	15	34
Medical/health	58.4 (34)	176.1 (59)	10	8	3
Energy/environmental technology	57.4 (33)	134.6 (68)	10	6	4
Consumer related	31.7 (27)	296.3 (109)	6	14	26
Electrical components and instruments	25.0 (42)	125 (89)	4	6	2
Total:	567.2** (451)	2169.3 (1060)	99**	100	101**

* In C$ mill; ** Due to rounding. Sources: Macdonald & Associates Ltd. Investment Database. Output shares are based on estimates from Statistics Canada "Gross Domestic Product by Industry," 1996, cat. no. 15-001-XPB.

TABLE 3 Age of Venture-Backed Companies

Year founded	# of companies	% of total
1994	23	6
1993	22	6
1992	20	5
1991	28	7
1984–1990	163	42
1974–1983	85	22
Before 1974	38	12
Total	379	100

Source: Macdonald & Associates Ltd. Economic Impact Database.

As can be seen from Table 2, venture capital is much more heavily represented in biomedical areas, computers, and communications than would be implied by overall output shares of these industries in the economy as a whole. Venture capital has a slightly smaller share of manufacturing and industrial equipment than the economy as a whole, and a much lower share of "consumer related" and "miscellaneous" industries. The main components of these categories are the retail sector and various services. This picture is even more pronounced when only early stage venture capital investments are considered. It seems very plausible that the industries where venture capitalists concentrate the most are those where informational asymmetries are most severe. It is, of course, possible that venture capitalists invest relatively heavily in high-tech industries for reasons unrelated to information. For example, the high-tech sector may simply have a disproportionately large number of new investment opportunities. More specifically, it is a growth sector, and any growth sector will appear to have high levels of new investment from most financial intermediaries, including venture capitalists. Even so, venture capitalists have a heavier relative investment in high-tech industries than other financial intermediaries, and informational reasons offer a plausible explanation for this. Thus, Table 2 is consistent with our theoretical expectations.

The second major implication of the information-based theory developed in Section 3 is that within the sectors where venture capitalists operate, they still prefer to invest in firms where the adverse selection and moral hazard problems are least severe. The following information is consistent with this expectation. First, Table 3 shows the age structure of the investee firms.

As shown on Table 3, quite a few investee companies are surprisingly old. Fully 12% of the 379 companies for whom information on age is available were founded prior to 1974. Since the data set is limited to firms that received at least one infusion of venture capital in 1991 or later, some firms obtain venture capital financing long after being founded. (We note, however, that these firms might have obtained earlier venture capital infusions. Our data suggests that many recorded investments are indeed follow-up investments.)

Furthermore, this information suggests that it takes longer than commonly perceived, and perhaps more venture capital than originally anticipated, to bring some investee firms to the stage at which exit is feasible. A company may be founded well before it obtains its first venture capital investment. These data raise the possibility that venture capital focuses on expansion of existing small companies rather than on the start-up phase. Tables 4 and 5 provide more information on this point.

Table 4 shows how many investments correspond to each stage in the entrepreneurial firm's life. It is based on investment records of investee companies that are in the

458   R. AMIT ET AL.

TABLE 4   Number of Investments by Stage and Year

	Early stages			Later stages					
	SE	ST	ES	EX	AC	TU	WC	OT	Count
1991	3	100	—	85	12	22	—	36	258
1992	15	111	—	65	23	41	2	50	307
1993	5	116	—	125	18	23	25	37	349
1994	3	128	11	206	12	23	—	15	398
1995	8	130	112	241	11	21	2	44	569
1996(Q1)	5	42	12	54	3	11	—	9	136
Total	39	627	135	776	79	141	29	191	2017

Key: SE = seed; ST = start-up; ES = other early stage investments; EX = expansion; AC = acquisition; TU = turnaround; WC = working capital; and OT = other. Source: Macdonald & Associates Ltd. Investment Database.

Investment Database and includes investments made betwen 1991 and the first quarter of 1996. A given investee may obtain financing from multiple venture capitalists, and may also receive multiple rounds of investment from a given venture capitalist. Each investment, which may include debt, equity, or both, is recorded separately. We observe that a full 60% of the investments made over the period covered by our sample are late stage investments. As early stage investments are both smaller (from Table 5) and less numerous (Table 4) than late stage investments, we can infer that the venture capital industry seems to focus more on growth and development of firms than on start-up activity. Tables 3 to 5 show that venture capitalists focus on firms with a long enough track record to provide significant information about the underlying quality of the venture. Pure start-up activity, where adverse selection and moral hazard problems are most severe, is less significant than later stage investment.

Figure 4 depicts the relative importance of debt and equity in an average or representative investment by stage. There are, for example, 39 seed investments in total. The total equity in these 39 investments is $21.89 million, giving an average of $561,000, while the total debt is $2.34 million, resulting in an average of only $60,000 (note that most seed investments have no debt). Figure 4 shows that equity is relatively more important at the early stages, and debt becomes more significant later, although equity remains more important in abolute terms for every stage except working capital.

The third major implication of our information-based approach is that we might expect exit to be dominated by "insider" activity rather than by public offerings. Figure 5 shows the pattern of exits in the data and indicates that only about 16% of exits occur after initial public offerings (IPOs). About 10% are third party acquisitions, often by

TABLE 5   Average Size of Investments by Stage and Year (in C$000's)

	Early stages			Later stages					
	SE	ST	ES	EX	AC	TU	WC	OT	Total
1991	489	678	—	1165	2003	1424	—	1374	1058
1992	900	617	—	1104	1283	628	480	1480	925
1993	836	1101	—	1714	1665	1620	362	1662	1394
1994	425	677	854	1227	2338	1521	—	2391	1128
1995	414	688	1005	1300	2341	436	1378	1564	1098
1996(Q1)	101	1034	847	1297	2260	1601	—	890	1151
1991–96	621	771	997	1316	1824	1107	378	1559	1127

Source: Macdonald & Associates Ltd. Investment Database.

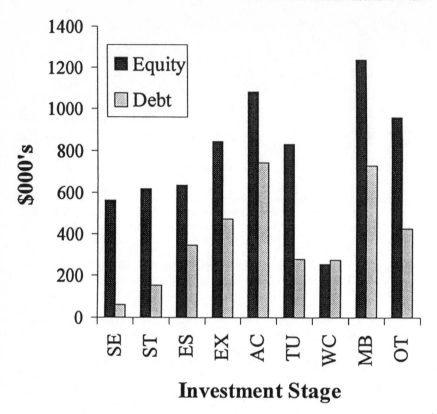

FIGURE 4   Average debt and equity by investment stage 1991–1996(Q1).

a firm in the same industry as the venture. The largest category of exit is company buy-outs, in which the venture capitalist's holding is sold to officers or managers of the in-vestee. Fully 37% of exits are in this category. Secondary purchases are purchases of the venture capitalist's holding by a third party in a private transaction that is not an overall acquisition. The "other" category consists of exits for which the exit mode was not identified, but we believe that most of these are company buyouts. Approximately 17% of exits were in the "write-off" category. If informational asymmetries are impor-tant, it is not surprising that IPOs account for only a small share of exits while company buyouts are much more important. We wish to note, however, that the small share of IPOs may also partly reflect a minimum scale necessary to sustain a public market in a stock.

Our theoretical framework also suggests that returns would differ by exit vehicle and that, in particular, IPOs would have high returns precisely because venture capital-ists seek to reduce the adverse selection problem confronted by buyers of IPOs by only "going public" with relatively strong investee firms. These returns shown in Table 6 are consistent with our expectations. Write-offs, of course, represent a 100% loss over the holding period. Among the other forms of exit, IPOs are relatively profitable. Secondary

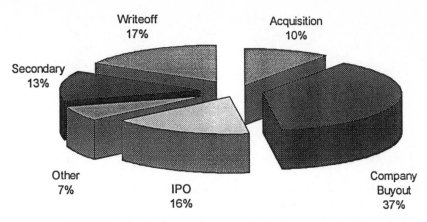

FIGURE 5   Distribution of venture capital exits (percentage of exits).

purchases (i.e., secondary sales from the exiting venture capitalist's point of view) are similarly profitable in aggregate, although with only 11 observations, it is difficult to regard the return to secondary purchases as highly meaningful. In any case, the high return to IPOs is consistent with our expectations.

The final prediction of our model is that the venture capitalist's ownership share should be negatively associated with the firm's performance. This derives both from moral hazard and the venture capitalist's participation constraint that expected returns should at least equal the return from alternative investments. In addition, it is possible that a negative correlation between a venture capitalist's ownership share α and a measure of firm performance could arise from dilution in a multi-period process (i.e., the possibility that low performance leads to high α). Unfortunately, we do not have adequate data, such as data on a venture capitalist's ownership share in the start-up phase, to correct for dilution.

It is difficult to measure firm performance directly, but revenues per unit asset and taxes paid should both be good measures of performance. Table 7 reports the results

TABLE 6   Estimated Real Annual Returns by Exit Type

	Mean of individual real annual returns*	Standard deviation of individual returns	No. of observations	Real annual return of sum of investments**
IPO	43%	62%	26	26%
Acquisition	36%	61%	16	9
Secondary purchase	23%	41%	11	29%
Company buyout	2%	15%	37	0%
Writeoff	100% loss over holding period	—	24	100% loss over holding period
Other	2%	18%	7	13%

* Individual annual returns are calculated as: [(Proceeds from investment − cost of investment) $^\wedge$ (1/holding period) − 1]. ** This number is calculated as: [(Sum of proceeds from investment − sum of costs of investment) $^\wedge$ (1/average holding period) − 1]. Source: Macdonald & Associates Ltd. Investment Database.

TABLE 7   Effect of Venture Capital Share on Performance (Tobit Regressions)

Dependent vbl.	Expl. variable	Coefficient	Std. error	T-stat	P-value
TaxesPaid	VCshare	−10.59	1.95	−5.44	.000
	log(Age)	454	61	7.44	.000
	Const.	−696	155	−4.50	.000
TaxesPaid/Assets	VCshare	−28.27	5.94	−4.76	.000
(×10000)	log(Age)	488	187	2.61	.009
	Const.	−578	474	−1.22	.223
Revenues/Assets	VCshare	−46	20	−2.30	.021
(×1000)	log(Age)	−386	649	−0.60	.55
	Const.	8958	1604	5.59	.000

Source: Macdonald & Associates Ltd. Economic Impact Database.

arising from regressing these measures of firm performance on the venture capital ownership share, correcting for age of the firm.

As can be seen from these regressions, there is a statistically strong negative relationship between the venture capitalist's ownership share and these measures of firm performance. Ideally, we would like to use profit as a measure of success, but profit is not available in the data. However, profit is closely related to taxes paid, so taxes should normally be a good proxy for profit. We acknowledge, however, that for emerging growth companies, taxes paid may be a poor preditor of their value creation potential. Note that taxes are truncated from below at 0. (Firms do not pay negative taxes no matter how poor their performance.) Accordingly the estimation is done using Tobit estimation rather than ordinary least squares. The basic finding is that there is a strong negative relationship between whatever measure of performance we use and the share of the venture owned by the venture capitalist. This could be the result of either the moral hazard or the venture capitalist's self-selection constraint. It is also possible that ventures for which α is high pay out more earnings to the venture capitalist, and, therefore, have lower future earnings. However, normalizing for asset size should mitigate this concern.

We emphasize that the amount of variation explained by the venture capital share is low. Thus, while the coefficient on the venture capital share is significant, variations in this share are, at most, a minor determinant of performance. It is also important that these results not be interpreted as suggesting that venture capital investment should be viewed as a negative influence, or that other sources of finance are better than venture capital. Venture capital investments could be an imortant positive influence on every firm in the data set, and could be the best source of financial capital available, and we would still expect to observe a negative correlation between venture capital ownership and performance. What the negative correlation tells us is that the best performing companies tend to be those in which the venture capital ownership share is not too high. However, if financial requirements are high and the owner's sources are meagre, then a substantial venture capital share might be the best option, even if there is an associated moral hazard problem, as the alternative might be outright failure of the company.

CONCLUDING REMARKS

The theoretical framework we offer focuses on informational issues. Specifically, we view asymmetric information as the central feature of venture capital investment. Both

462   R. AMIT ET AL.

major forms of asymmetric information, "hidden information" (leading to adverse selection) and "hidden action" (leading to moral hazard) are included in our analysis. While the model abstracts from some important elements of the venture investment process (such as bargaining, syndication, etc.), we believe that the informational issues are perhaps the most central issues to focus on at this stage.

We have shown that this information-based approach is consistent with the data on Canadian venture capital investments. Moral hazard and adverse selection create a market failure in entrepreneurial financing, which might lead many worthwhile projects to be unfunded or underfunded. The more skilled the venture capitalist is in reducing these sources of market failure, the more effectively this sector will function. Venture capitalists exist because they are better at this function than unspecialized investors. However, venture capitalists cannot eliminate adverse selection and moral hazard. Furthermore, these problems are more acute for younger firms, and most acute for start-ups. This explains why venture capitalists focus on later stage entrepreneurial firms. Later stage firms have a track record that provides information to the entrepreneur, and they have enough assets to reduce the problem associated with limited collateral under limited liability. By virtue of their expertise, venture capitalists are better at dealing with informational problems than are other investors (on average), but this advantage shows up most in later stage entrepreneurial firms rather than at the start-up stage.

This theoretical structure is also consistent with the pattern of exit. If asymmetric information is important, and remains important even at the exit stage, then outside public investors will not be in the best position to evaluate the assets of the entrepreneurial firm, and insiders will be in a better situation to buy out the venture capitalist's position. These insiders might be management or officers of the investee, or they might be other firms in a related business. Thus, it is not surprising that IPOs account for only a modest fraction of exit. In addition, our model predicts a negative relationship between the extent of venture capital ownership and firm performance. This relationship is found in the data.

There are several natural extensions to the line of reasoning presented in the paper. One complicating factor is the possibility that a venture capitalist's cost of monitoring an entrepreneur might vary with the venture capitalist's ownership share. It is sometimes suggested that it is easier for the venture capital firm to monitor if it has a larger ownership share. In our model, this would suggest that m would exogenously depend on α. Furthermore, we recognize that many aspects of venture capital activity have not been captured in our analysis. In particular, we abstract from staged investment, which is a common feature in venture capital finance and can serve to ameliorate problems caused by asymmetric information. It would be interesting to extend our model to a multi-period analysis.

The challenge we and other researchers face is to develop theoretical structures that can be subject to empirical investigation. Ideally such theories should also provide normative implications for practice. Our paper is a small but hopefully useful step in this direction.

REFERENCES

Admati, A., and Pfleiderer, S. 1994. Robust financial contracting and the role of venture capitalists. *Journal of Finance* 49(2):371–402.

Akerlof, G. 1970. The market for lemons: Quality uncertainty and the market mechanism. *Quarterly Journal of Economics* 84(3):488–500.

Amit, R., Brander, J., and Zott, C. 1997. Venture capital financing of entrepreneurship in Canada. In Paul Halpern, ed., *Capital Market Issues in Canada*. Industry Canada, Ottawa.

Amit, R., Glosten, L., and Muller, E. 1990. Entrepreneurial ability, venture investments, and risk sharing. *Management Science* 36(10):1232–1245.

Amit, R., Glosten L., and Muller, E. 1993. Challenges to theory development in entrepreneurship research. *Journal of Management Studies* 30(5):815–834.

Arrow, K. 1973. *The Limits of Organization*. New York: Norton.

Barry, C., Muscarella, C., Peavy, J., and Vetsuypens, M. 1990. Venture capital in the creation of public companies: evidence from the going-public process. *Journal of Financial Economics* 27(2): 447–71.

Business Development Bank of Canada (Annual, 1993–95), *Economic Impact of Venture Capital* (Montreal).

Bygrave, W., and Timmons, J. 1992. *Venture Capital at the Crossroads*. Boston, MA: Harvard Business School Press.

Chan, Y. 1983. On the positive role of financial intermediation in allocations of venture capital in a market with imperfect information. *Journal of Finance* 38(5):1543–1561.

Chan, Y., Siegel, D., and Thakor, A. 1990. Learning, corporate control and performance requirements in venture capital contracts. *International Economic Review* 31(2):365–381.

Fried, V., and Hisrich, R. 1994. Toward a model of venture capital investment decision making. *Financial Management* 23(3):28–37.

Gompers, P. 1995. Optional investment, monitoring and the staging of venture capital. *Journal of Finance* 50(5):1461–1489.

Gompers, P. 1996. Grandstanding in the venture capital industry. *Journal of Financial Economics* 42(1):133–156.

Gompers, P., and Lerner, J. 1994. A note on the venture capital industry. *Harvard Business School Note* N9-295-065.

Gorman, M., and Sahlman, W.A. 1989. What do venture capitalists do? *Journal of Business Venturing* 4(4):231–248.

Hellmann, T. 1994. Financial structure and control in venture capital. Stanford University Working Paper.

Hirao, Y. 1993. Learning and incentive problems in repeated partnerships. *International Economic Review* 34(1):101–119.

Industry Canada, June 1994. Financing the new economy: towards a positive conspiracy. *Project Report.*

Jensen, M., and Meckling, W. 1976. Theory of the firm: managerial behavior, agency costs, and ownership structure. *Journal of Financial Economics* 3(4):305–360.

Lerner, J. 1994. The syndication of venture capital investment. *Financial Management* 23(3):16–27.

Lerner, J. 1995. Venture capitalists and oversight of private firms. *Journal of Finance* 50(5):301–318.

Low, M., and MacMillan, I. 1988. Entrepreneurship: past research and future challenges. *Journal of Management* 14(2):139–161.

Macdonald & Associates Ltd. (annual) *Venture Capital in Canada: Annual Statistical Review and Directory*, (Association of Canadian Venture Capital Companies: Toronto).

MacIntosh, Jeffrey G. 1994. Legal and Institutional Barriers to Financing Innovative Enterprise in Canada, Discussion Paper 94–10, School of Policy Studies, Queen's University, Kingston.

MacMillan, I., Siegel, R., and Narashima, P. 1985. Criteria used by venture capitalists to evaluate new venture proposals. *Journal of Business Venturing* 1(1):119–128.

MacMillan, I., Zemann, L., and Narashima, P. 1987. Criteria distinguishing successful from unsuccessful ventures in the venture screening process. *Journal of Business Venturing* 2(2):123–137.

Megginson, W., and Weiss, K. 1991. Venture capitalist certification in initial public offerings. *Journal of Finance* 46(3):879–903.

464   R. AMIT ET AL.

Pauly, M. 1974. Overinsurance and public provision of insurance: the roles of moral hazard and adverse selection. *Quarterly Journal of Economics* 88:(1):44–54.

Rothschild, M., and Stiglitz, J. 1976. Equilibrium in competitive Insurance Markets: an essay on the economics of imperefect information. *Quarterly Journal of Economics* 90(9):629–649.

Sahlman, W. 1990. The structure and governance of venture-capital organizations. *Journal of Financial Economics* 27(2):473–521.

Spence, M. 1973. Job market signalling. *Quarterly Journal of Economics* 87(3):355–374.

Tyebjee, T., and Bruno, A. 1984. A model of venture capital investment activity. *Management Science* 30(9):1051–1066.

APPENDIX 1

Illustration of the Basic Moral Hazard Problem

Figure A1 shows the marginal cost of effort (a horizontal line) and the marginal expected benefit of effort (given by R_e). The efficient amount of effort occurs where marginal benefit equals marginal cost, and is denoted e* in the diagram. The marginal benefit perceived by the entrepreneur is only $(1 - \alpha)R_e$, which is strictly below R_e. It follows that the amount of effort actually chosen, denoted e', is less than the efficient amount. The basic problem is that the entrepreneur cannot precommit to provide effort level e*. Once financing is obtained and share α of the firm has been sold to the investor, the entrepreneur will only provide effort level e'. If the investor and the entrepreneur could contract over e, then they could agree that e* would be provided, but this is impossible under the assumption that e cannot be observed (or at least legally verified) by the investor.

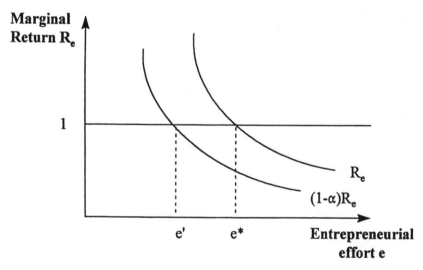

FIGURE A1   Moral hazard.

APPENDIX 2

Formal Analysis of the Adverse Selection Problem

From (18) we derive the first-order condition

$$EV_d = p'(d) \int_{q^0}^{\infty} (\alpha R(q) - C)f(q)dq - 1 = 0 \tag{A2.1}$$

where F is the cumulative distribution of q. Let

$$K = \int_{q^0}^{\infty} (\alpha R(q) - C)f(q)dq \tag{A2.2}$$

Then (A2.1) simplifies to

$$p'(d) = \frac{1}{K} \tag{A2.3}$$

To derive the second-order condition, EV_d is differentiated with respect to d, yielding

$$EV_{dd} = p''(d) \int_{q^0}^{\infty} (\alpha R(q) - C)f(q)dq$$
$$= p''(d) \, K \tag{A2.4}$$

It follows from (17) and (18) that (A2.4) is strictly negative, which is the precondition for (A2.3) to yield a maximum.

(A2.3) has interesting implications. Suppose that R(q) is such that there are many worthwhile projects and a few projects that have very low negative expected returns. q^0 is therefore low. Specifically, assume that K is relatively large, resulting in a rather low value of p'(d), which in term implies a relatively large optimal value of d (if a solution to (A2.3) exists at all). Thus, with such a constellation of parameters, it pays to invest high d in due diligence. On the other hand, if R(q) is such that K is relatively small (which may happen if there are only few attractive projects and many 'lemons,' i.e., if q^0 is high), this will result in a relatively small optimal value of d (depending, of course, on the shape of p(d)).

In order to illustrate the point that an investor with a highly responsive detection function p(d) (say, investor h with a detection function $p(d^h)$) is more likely to invest in projects with high asymmetry of information than an investor with a less responsive p(d) (say, investor l with a detection function $p(d^l)$), let us consider the following case. Assume that q^0 is high and K is small, resulting, according to (A2.3), in a large p''(d). This is fairly realistic, as the pattern of returns of venture capitalists is usually skewed with most investments generating either disappointing or negative returns and only a few becoming 'stars'.

It may happen that investor h finds it worthwhile to spend $d^{h*} > 0$ (which is the value of d^h that satisfies A2.3) and go ahead with project $q \geq q^0$, while investor l finds that the optimal value of d^l is $d^{l*} = 0$ and thus refrains from investing. (Of course, even if $d^{h*} > 0$, the investor's feasibility constraint (20) has to hold before investment l is made.) These points are illustrated in Figure A2.

Note that for some values of K, both d^{l*} and d^{h*} can be positive in our example. Then it pays even for investor l to do due diligence. Again, it also depends on constraint (20) whether either investor l or h or both find the investment attractive.

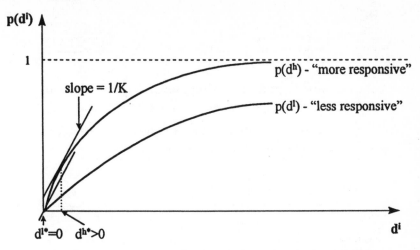

FIGURE A2 Optimal due diligence for different detection functions p(d).

[7]

ELSEVIER   Journal of Financial Economics 47 (1998) 243–277

Venture capital and the structure of capital markets: banks versus stock markets[1]

Bernard S. Black[a],*, Ronald J. Gilson[a,b]

[a] Columbia University School of Law, New York, NY 10027, USA
[b] Stanford University School of Law, Stanford, California 94305, USA

Received 18 July 1996; accepted 29 August 1997

Abstract

The United States has many banks that are small relative to large corporations and play a limited role in corporate governance, and a well developed stock market with an associated market for corporate control. In contrast, Japanese and German banks are fewer in number but larger in relative size and are said to play a central governance role. Neither country has an active market for corporate control. We extend the debate on the relative efficiency of bank- and stock market-centered capital markets by developing a further systematic difference between the two systems: the greater vitality of venture capital in stock market-centered systems. Understanding the link between the stock market and the venture capital market requires understanding the contractual arrangements between entrepreneurs and venture capital providers; especially, the importance of the opportunity to enter into an implicit contract over control, which gives a successful entrepreneur the option to reacquire control from the venture capitalist by using an initial public offering as the means by which the venture capitalist exits from a portfolio investment. We also extend the literature on venture capital contracting by offering an explanation for two central characteristics of the U.S. venture capital market: relatively rapid exit by venture capital providers from investments in portfolio companies; and the

* Corresponding author. Tel.: 212/854-8079; fax:212/854-7946; e-mail: bblack@law.columbia.edu.

[1] The authors are grateful for helpful suggestions from the editor and an anonymous referee, and from Anant Admati, Erik Berglof, Stephen Choi, Kevin Davis, Uri Geiger, Victor Goldberg, Paul Gompers, Joseph Grundfest, Ehud Kamar, Michael Klausner, Joshua Lerner, Ronald Mann, Paul Pfleiderer. Mark Ramsayer, Charles Sabel, Allen Schwartz, and Omri Yadlin, and from participants in workshops at Columbia Law School, Harvard Law School, Stanford Law School, the Max Planck Institute (Hamburg, Germany), and the American Law and Economics Association. Research support was provided by Columbia Law School and the Roberts Program in Law and Business, Stanford Law School. We thank Laura Menninger, Nishani Naidoo, Annette Schuller, and Ram Vasudevan for research assistance.

244   *B.S. Black, R.J. Gilson/Journal of Financial Economics 47 (1998) 243–277*

JEL classification: G23; G32

Keywords: Venture Capital; Exit Strategy; IPO; Comparative corporate governance

1. Introduction

Contrasting capital markets in the United States with those of Japan and Germany has become a commonplace activity. The United States has a large number of comparatively small banks that play a limited role in the governance of large corporations, and a well developed stock market with an associated market for corporate control that figures prominently in corporate governance. In contrast, Japanese main banks and German universal banks are few in number but larger in size, relative to Japanese and German firms, and are said to play a central corporate governance role in monitoring management (e.g., Aoki, 1994; Roe, 1994). Neither country has an active market for corporate control.

Advocates of bank-centered capital markets claim that this structure fosters patient capital markets and long-term planning, while a stock market-centered capital market is said to encourage short-term expectations by investors and responsive short-term strategies by managers (e.g., Edwards and Fischer, 1994; Porter, 1992). Advocates of stock market-centered systems (e.g., Gilson, 1996) stress the adaptive features of a market for corporate control which are lacking in bank-centered systems, and the lack of empirical evidence of short-termism.

Paralleling the assessment of the comparative merits of stock market and bank-centered capital markets, scholars have also sought to explain how the United States, Germany, and Japan developed such different capital markets. Recent work has stressed that the characteristics of the three capital markets do not reflect simply the efficient outcome of competition between institutions, in which the most efficient institutions survive. The nature of the American capital market – a strong stock market, weak financial intermediaries, and the absence of the close links between banks and nonfinancial firms said to characterize the Japanese and German capital markets – reflects, at least in part, politics, history and path-dependent evolution, rather than economic inevitability (e.g., Black, 1990; Gilson, 1996; Roe, 1994). Much the same seems to be true of Germany and Japan (Hoshi, 1993; Roe, 1994). To be sure, competitively driven evolution hones efficiency, but institutions that emerge are shaped at critical stages by the random hand of events and the instrumental hand of politics.

In this article, we seek to contribute to two literatures. First, we extend the debate about the relative efficiency of bank- and stock market-centered capital markets by documenting and explaining a second systematic difference between

B.S. Black, R.J. Gilson/Journal of Financial Economics 47 (1998) 243–277   245

the two systems: the existence of a much stronger venture capital industry in stock market-centered systems.

We define 'venture capital', consistent with American understanding, as investment by specialized venture capital organizations (which we call 'venture capital funds') in high-growth, high-risk, often high-technology firms that need capital to finance product development or growth and must, by the nature of their business, obtain this capital largely in the form of equity rather than debt. We exclude 'buyout' financing that enables a mature firm's managers to acquire the firm from its current owners, even though in Europe, so-called 'venture capital' firms often provide such financing – more often, in many cases, than the financing that we call venture capital.

Other countries have openly envied the U.S. venture capital market and have actively, but unsuccessfully, sought to replicate it. We offer an explanation for this failure: We argue that a well developed stock market that permits venture capitalists to exit through an initial public offering (IPO) is critical to the existence of a vibrant venture capital market.

Understanding this critical link between the stock market and the venture capital market requires that we understand the implicit and explicit contractual arrangements between venture capital funds and their investors, and between venture capital funds and entrepreneurs. This brings us to our second contribution: We extend the literature on venture capital contracting by offering an explanation for two characteristics of the United States venture capital market. First, we explain the importance of exit – why venture capital providers seek to liquidate their portfolio company investments in the near to moderate term, rather than investing for the long-term like Japanese or German banks. Second, we explain the importance of the form of exit: why the potential for the venture capital provider to exit from a successful start-up *through an IPO*, available only through a stock market, allows venture capital providers to enter into implicit contracts with entrepreneurs concerning future control of startup firms, in a way not available in a bank-centered capital market. Thus, we make explicit a functional link between private and public equity markets: The implicit contract over future control that is permitted by the availability of exit through an IPO helps to explain the greater success of venture capital as an organizational form in stock market-centered systems.

Section 2 of this article motivates the theoretical analysis by contrasting the venture capital markets in the United States and Germany. Section 3 develops the importance of exit from venture capital investments to the viability and structure of the venture capital industry. Exit serves two key functions. First, venture capital investors specialize in providing portfolio companies with a combination of financial capital, monitoring and advisory services, and reputational capital. The combination of financial and nonfinancial services loses its efficiency advantages as the portfolio company matures. Thus, recycling venture capital investors' capital through exit and reinvestment is jointly efficient for the provider and the portfolio company. Second, exit facilitates contracting between venture capital managers (persons with expertise in identifying and developing promising new businesses) and providers of capital to venture capital managers. The exit price gives capital providers a reliable measure of the venture capital manager's skill. The exit and reinvestment cycle also lets capital providers withdraw capital from less skilled venture capital managers or managers whose industry-specific expertise no longer matches the nature of promising start-up firms. It supports an implicit contract under which capital providers reinvest in the future limited partnerships of successful venture capital managers.

Section 4 focuses on the implicit contract over control between the entrepreneur and the venture capital fund. The potential to exit through an IPO allows the entrepreneur and the venture capital fund to enter into a self-enforcing implicit contract over control, in which the venture capital fund agrees to return control to a successful entrepreneur by exiting through an IPO. This implicit contract cannot readily be duplicated in a bank-centered capital market. Section 5 compares the predictions from our informal model to evidence about the success of venture capital in other countries, including Canada, Great Britain, Israel, and Japan. Section 6 considers alternative explanations for the observed international patterns of venture capital development, especially differences in legal rules. Some of these reasons may have predictive power, but none has enough power to displace our theory as an explanation for a substantial portion of the observed intercountry variation. Section 7 considers the implications of the symbiosis between stock markets and venture capital markets for efforts by other countries to expand their venture capital markets. Section 8 concludes.

2. The venture capital industry in the United States and Germany

In this section, we compare the venture capital industries in the United States and Germany in order to motivate the theory developed in Sections 3 and 4, in which a stock market-centered capital market (present in the United States but absent in Germany) is a precondition to a substantial venture capital industry.

The United States has a much more fully developed venture capital market than Germany. The differences are of both size and substance. The United States has a larger number of funds and the funds themselves are larger relative to each country's economy. Substantively, United States funds are more heavily invested in early-stage ventures and high-technology industries, while German venture capital provides primarily later-stage financing in lower-technology industries.

The United States venture capital market is quite large. As of the end of 1994, 591 U.S. venture capital funds had total investments (from which the fund had not yet exited or written off) of around $34 billion (Venture Capital Yearbook, 1995). New investment in venture capital funds in 1996 was $6.5 billion (Fig. 1). In recent years, venture capital-backed firms have raised several billion dollars

B.S. Black, R.J. Gilson/Journal of Financial Economics 47 (1998) 243–277   247

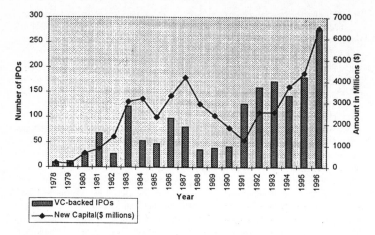

Fig. 1. Venture capital-backed IPOs and new venture capital commitments. Number of initial public offerings of venture-capital-backed companies (left-hand scale), and amount of new capital commitments to venture capital funds (right-hand scale), between 1978 and 1996. Source: Venture Capital Journal and Venture Capital Yearbook (various dates); Economist, Mar. 29, 1997 (survey of Silicon Valley)

annually through IPOs, including a 1996 total of $12 billion; they form a significant portion of the total IPO market (Venture Capital Yearbook, various years through 1997; Brav and Gompers, 1997).[2] Between 1991 and 1996, there were 1059 venture capital-backed IPOs, an average of over 175 per year (see Table 1), as well as 466 exits through acquisition of the venture-capital-backed firm.

Fig. 1 shows the annual variation in the number of venture-capital-backed IPOs, as well as the amount of new capital committed to venture capital funds. Inspection of Fig. 1 suggests a correlation between the availability of exit through IPO (proxied by the number of venture-capital-backed IPOs) and investor willingness to invest in venture capital funds (measured by new capital commitments), with perhaps a one-year lag between a change in the number of IPOs and a resulting change in the amount of capital committed. This correlation is consistent with the theory developed below on the link between the stock market and the venture capital market.

---

[2] An alternate way to measure the importance of venture-capital-backed IPOs is to measure the firms' market capitalization rather than the amount of funds raised in the IPO. The 276 venture-capital-backed firms taken public in 1996 had a mean market capitalization of $209 million and total market capitalization of $58 billion (Venture Capital Journal, April, 1997).

248 *B.S. Black, R.J. Gilson / Journal of Financial Economics 47 (1998) 243–277*

Table 1
VC-backed IPOs, public acquisitions, and private acquisitions

Number of initial public offerings of venture-capital-backed companies and number of sales of venture-capital-backed companies, between 1984 and 1996.

Year	VC-backed IPOs	Exits via acquisitions		
		Of private companies	Of already public companies	Total
1984	53	59	27	86
1985	47	83	18	101
1986	98	90	30	120
1987	81	113	27	140
1988	36	106	29	135
1989	39	101	45	146
1990	42	76	33	109
1991	127	65	19	84
1992	160	90	4	94
1993	172	78	14	92
1994	143	99	no data	no data
1995	183	98	no data	no data
1996	276	94	no data	no data

Source: Venture Capital Journal (various dates) (data for acquisitions of already public companies was available only through 1993)

The visual impression of a correlation between venture-capital-backed IPOs and new capital commitments to venture capital funds is confirmed by a simple regression of capital contributions in year $X + 1$ (as a dependent variable) against number of venture-capital-backed IPOs in year X (Table 2). Regression 1 below shows that the number of IPOs in year X correlates strongly with new capital contributions in year $X + 1$. Regression 2 adds year as an additional possible explanatory variable. The correlation between number of IPOs in year X and new capital commitments in the following year remains statistically significant as a predictor of new capital commitments in the following year. These regressions are not intended to fully capture the factors that affect capital commitments to venture capital funds, but do confirm the visual correlation evident from Fig. 1.

United States venture capital funds obtain capital from a range of sources, but pension funds are the largest contributor. Pension funds have provided roughly 40% of the capital raised by venture capital funds over the last 10 years or so (Table 3). In Germany, on the other hand, banks supply the majority of venture capital commitments.

Seed, startup and other early stage investments that take a company through development of a prototype and initial product shipments to customers

B.S. Black, R.J. Gilson/Journal of Financial Economics 47 (1998) 243–277   249

Table 2
Correlation between venture capital backed IPOs and new capital commitments to venture capital funds

Least-squares regression of capital contributed to venture capital funds ($ millions) in year $X + 1$ against number of initial public offerings of venture-capital backed companies in year X. Based on data from 1978–1996 as shown in Fig. 1. t-statistics in parentheses. *** (**) (*) = significant at 0.001 (0.01) (0.05) level.

Dependent variable	Independent variable(s)			R^2	Number of observations
	Intercept	VC-backed IPOs in year X	Year		
1 Capital contribution in year $X + 1$	1015 ($t = 2.35$)*	20.2 ($t = 4.54$)***		0.56	18
2 Capital contribution in year $X + 1$	− 137846 ($t = − 0.93$)	15.1 ($t = 2.17$)*	70.1 ($t = 0.94$)	0.59	18

Table 3
United States and Germany capital raised by venture capital funds by type of investor

Percentage of capital raised by venture capital funds in the United States and Germany, by type of investor, for 1992–1995.

	1992	1993	1994	1995
United States				
Corporations	3%	8%	9%	2%
Private individuals & families	11	8	9	17
Government agencies	—	—	—	—
Pension funds	42	59	46	38
Banks and insurance companies	15	11	9	18
Endowments and foundations	18	11	21	22
Other	11	4	2	3
Total	100%	100%	100%	100%
Germany				
Corporations	7%	9%	8%	10%
Private individuals & families	6	7	8	5
Government agencies	4	6	7	8
Pension funds				9
Banks	53	52	55	59
Insurance companies	10	12	12	6
Endowments and foundations	–		—	—
Other	17	14	10	2
Total	100%	100%	100%	100%

Sources: European Venture Capital Association Yearbook (1995); Bundesverband Deutsche Kapitalbeteiligungsgesellschaften Jahrbuch [German Venture Capital Association Yearbook] (various years through 1996); Venture Capital Yearbook (various years through 1997).

250   *B.S. Black, R.J. Gilson/Journal of Financial Economics 47 (1998) 243–277*

Table 4
United States and Germany venture capital disbursements by stage of financing

Percentage of capital disbursed by venture capital funds in the United States and Germany, by nature of investment, for 1992–1995.

	1992	1993	1994	1995
United States				
Seed	3%	7%	4%	
Startup	8	7	15	
Other early stage	13	10	18	
Expansion	55	54	45	
LBO Acquisition	7	6	6	
Other	14	16	12	
Total	100%	100%	100%	
Germany				
Seed	1%	1%	2%	2%
Startup	6	7	8	6
Expansion	45	66	54	65
LBO Acquisition	24	25	36	18
Other	25	—	—	8
Total	100%	100%	100%	100%

Sources: European Venture Capital Association Yearbook (1995); Bundesverband Deutsche Kapitalbeteiligungsgesellschaften (BVK) Jahrbuch [German Venture Capital Association Yearbook] (various years through 1996); Venture Capital Yearbook (various years through 1997).

accounted for about 37% of new capital invested by venture capital funds in 1994 (Table 4). Later-stage expansion financing represented another 45% of 1994 investments. Because venture capitalists usually stage their investments (Sahlman, 1990; Gompers, 1995), most expansion financing goes to companies that received early-stage financing. Thus, the bulk of venture capital investments go to firms that receive venture capital financing very early in their life. Moreover, most investments go to technology-based companies; in 1994, 68% of new investments went to these companies (Venture Economics, 1995).

Lest venture capital be dismissed as trivial in amount, and therefore not an important factor in comparing corporate governance systems, we note that mature firms which began with venture capital backing assume macroeconomic significance in the U.S. economy. They play a major, often dominant role in several important and rapidly growing sectors where the United States is recognized as a world leader, including biotechnology (for example, Genentech and Biogen); personal computers and workstations (for example, Apple, Compaq, and Sun Microsystems); many personal computer components and related devices such as hard drives and routers (for example, Seagate Technologies, Connor Peripherals, and Cisco Systems); personal computer software (for example, Lotus Development and Harvard Graphics); and semiconductors (for example, Intel and Advanced Micro Devices).

B.S. Black, R.J. Gilson / Journal of Financial Economics 47 (1998) 243–277   251

The German venture capital industry is a fraction of the size of the United States industry. Only 85 venture capital organizations existed at the end of 1994, with DM 8.3 billion ($5.5 billion) in cumulative capital commitments (European Venture Capital Yearbook, 1995) and annual investments of under $400 million. Venture capital investments were 0.01% of German GDP in 1994; only one-sixth of the U.S. level. This comparison understates the difference in venture capital activity between the two countries because the European definition of venture capital is broader than the American definition. These organizations received the majority of their capital from banks (55%) and insurance companies (12%). Pension funds are not a factor in the German market because German corporate and government pension obligations are largely unfunded.

The German venture capital industry also differs from the United States in its aversion both to early-stage investment (Table 4) and to investment in high-technology industries (Harrison, 1990). In 1994, only 8% of the venture capital invested went to startup companies, and only 2% to seed financing. Technology-related investments comprised only 11% of all new investments.

In Germany, as in the United States, exit by the venture capital fund is the norm, but the form of exit differs. Exit through the stock market is largely unavailable, although a handful of German venture capital-backed firms have gone public on Britain's AIM (Alternative Investment Market). The venture capital fund's exit therefore comes principally through the company's repurchase of the venture fund's stake (a strategy not available to the rapidly growing firms that are the predominant recipients of venture capital financing in the United States), or through selling the company. Table 5 shows the exit strategies employed by German venture capital funds for 1995. Of the 12 exits through IPO, only one was in Germany; the rest were on foreign markets.

This section has only sketched the United States and German venture capital markets. But it demonstrates the pattern we seek to explain: the existence in the

Table 5
Exits by German venture capital funds, 1995

Type of exit from portfolio companies by German venture capital funds for 1995.

Exit type	Number of firms
Buyback by portfolio company	166
Sale of portfolio company	74
Block sale of venture capital fund's stake	8
Initial Public Offering	12
(IPOs on foreign stock markets)	(11)
Other	4
Total	264

Source: Bundesverband Deutsche Kapitalbeteiligungsgesellschaften Jahrbuch [German Venture Capital Association Yearbook] (1996)

United States of a dynamic venture capital industry centered on early stage investments in high-technology companies and the absence of a comparable industry in Germany.

3. The importance of exit by the venture capital fund

The first step in understanding the link between the stock market and the venture capital market involves the importance of exit by the venture capital fund from its investments. We develop below an informal theory for why exit by venture capital providers from their successful investments is critical to the operation of the venture capital market, both for the relationship between a venture capital fund and its portfolio companies, and for the relationship between the fund and its capital providers. Florida and Kenney (1990) argue that U.S. venture investors' refusal to act as long-term investors in portfolio companies weakens United States competitiveness. Our analysis provides an efficiency justification for exit.

The need for an exit strategy does not itself explain the distinctive properties of exit through an IPO and, therefore, the special role of an active IPO market. We develop that relationship in Section 4.

3.1. Exit from the venture capital fund – portfolio company relationship

Venture capitalists provide more than just money to their portfolio companies. Three additional contributions loom large (Bygrave and Timmons, 1992; Barry, 1994; Lerner, 1995; Gorman and Sahlman, 1989): management assistance to the portfolio company, analogous to that provided by a management consulting firm; intensive monitoring of performance, reflecting the incentives to monitor arising from equity ownership and the power to act using the venture capitalist's levers of control; and reputational capital, that is, the venture capitalist's ability to give the portfolio company credibility with third parties, similar to the role played by other reputational intermediaries such as investment bankers.

3.1.1. Management assistance

The typical venture capital fund is a limited partnership run by general partners who are experienced at moving companies up the development path from the startup stage and market knowledge based on other investments in the portfolio company's industry and related industries (Sahlman, 1990; Gompers and Lerner, 1996). With this experience, the venture capitalist can assist a management-thin early-stage company in locating and recruiting the management and technical personnel it needs as its business grows, and can help the company through the predictable problems that high-technology firms face in moving

B.S. Black, R.J. Gilson/Journal of Financial Economics 47 (1998) 243–277   253

from prototype development to production, marketing, and distribution. The venture capital fund's industry knowledge and experience with prior startup firms helps it locate managers for new startups (Carvalho, 1996).

3.1.2. Intensive monitoring and control

Venture capital funds have both strong incentives to monitor entrepreneurs' performance, deriving from equity ownership. They also receive strong control levers, disproportionate to the size of their equity investment. One control lever results from the staged timing of venture capital investment. The initial investment is typically insufficient to allow the portfolio company to carry out its business plan (Gompers, 1995; Sahlman, 1990). The venture capitalist will decide later whether to provide the additional funding that the portfolio company needs. The company's need for additional funds gives its management a performance incentive in the form of a hard constraint, analogous to the use of debt in leveraged buyouts.[3]

The typical contractual arrangements between a venture capital fund and a portfolio company provide other control levers. The venture capitalist typically receives convertible debt or convertible preferred stock that carries the same voting rights as if it had already been converted into common stock (Benton and Gunderson, 1993; Gompers, 1997).[4] The venture capital fund commonly receives greater board representation – often an absolute majority of the board – than it could elect if board representation were proportional to overall voting power. Board control lets the venture capital provider replace the entrepreneur as chief executive officer if performance lags.[5] Even where the venture capitalist lacks board control, the investor rights agreement gives the venture capital provider veto power over significant operating decisions by the portfolio company.

---

[3] Gompers (1995) explains the extra control rights given to the venture capital fund as a response to adverse selection problems in early-stage financing, where information asymmetries between the entrepreneur and the venture capital fund are greatest.

[4] The standard contractual package for an early-stage venture capital investment consists of a convertible preferred stock purchase agreement; the portfolio company's certificate of incorporation; and an investor rights agreement. The purchase agreement, through detailed representations and warranties, documents the portfolio company's condition at the time of the venture capital investment. The certificate of incorporation sets out the voting and other rights of the venture capital fund's convertible debt or preferred stock. The investor rights agreement contains the portfolio company's ongoing obligations to the venture capital fund, including detailed negative covenants and such things as registration rights.

[5] Hellman (1995a) explains why an entrepreneur would give the venture capitalist this right: to reduce the cost of capital, thereby increasing the share of the equity the entrepreneur retains. We discuss the reputation market necessary to prevent the venture capitalist from misusing this power in Section 4.

3.1.3. Reputational capital

Much like an investment bank underwriting an initial public offering (Gilson and Kraakman, 1984; Booth and Smith, 1986), the venture capital fund acts as a reputational intermediary. Venture capital financing enhances the portfolio company's credibility with third parties whose contributions will be crucial to the company's success. Talented managers are more likely to invest their human capital in a company financed by a respected venture capital fund, because the venture capitalist's participation provides a credible signal about the company's likelihood of success. Suppliers will be more willing to risk committing capacity and extending trade credit to a company with respected venture capital backers. Customers will take more seriously the company's promise of future product delivery if a venture capitalist both vouches for and monitors its management and technical progress. Moukheiber (1996) provides an account of the reputational power of Kleiner, Perkins, Caufield and Byers, a leading venture capital fund. Later on, the venture capitalist's reputation helps to attract a high quality underwriter for an initial public offering of the portfolio company's stock (Lerner, 1994a; Megginson and Weiss, 1991).

The venture capital fund's proffer of its reputation to third parties who have dealings with a portfolio company is credible because the fund is a repeat player, and has put its money where its mouth is by investing in the portfolio company. The fund's reputation is crucial for its own dealings with investors in its existing and future limited partnerships, with other venture capitalists in syndicating investments in portfolio companies and in negotiating with entrepreneurs concerning new portfolio investments (Sahlman, 1990; Lerner, 1994b). Consistent with a reputational analysis, Brav and Gompers (1997) report that venture-capital-backed IPOs do not suffer the long-run underperformance reported for IPOs in general.

Like a venture capitalist's provision of financial capital, its non-financial contributions are also staged, albeit informally. A venture capitalist can choose not to make or return telephone calls to or from a portfolio company or its suppliers, customers, or prospective employees. The fund's power to withhold its management assistance and reputational capital reinforces its incentive and power to monitor.

The management assistance, monitoring, and service as a reputational intermediary that a venture capitalist provides share a significant economy of scope with its provision of capital. This scope economy arises from a number of sources. The portfolio company must evaluate the quality of the venture capital fund's proffered management assistance and monitoring. Similarly, potential employees, suppliers, and customers must evaluate the credibility of the fund's explicit and implicit representations concerning the portfolio company's future. Combining financial and nonfinancial contributions both enhances the credibility of the information that the venture capitalist provides to third parties and bonds the venture capitalist's promise to the portfolio company to provide

B.S. Black, R.J. Gilson / Journal of Financial Economics 47 (1998) 243–277   255

nonfinancial assistance. The venture capitalist will suffer financial loss if it reneges on its promise of nonfinancial support. Combining financial and non-financial contributions also lets investors in venture capital funds evaluate a fund's nonfinancial contributions by measuring its return on investment. Lin and Smith (1995) also link the venture capitalist's financial and nonfinancial investments. Finally, there is the customary role of monitoring in ensuring that the portfolio company's managers do not divert to themselves some of the company's income stream.

The non-capital inputs supplied by venture capital providers have special value to early-stage companies. As the portfolio company's management gains its own experience, proves its skill, and establishes its own reputation, the relative value of the venture capital provider's management experience, monitoring, and service as a reputational intermediary declines.[6] Thus, by the time the portfolio company succeeds, the venture capital provider's nonfinancial contributions can be more profitably invested in a new round of early-stage companies. But because the economies of scope discussed above link financial and nonfinancial contributions, recycling the venture capitalist's nonfinancial contributions also requires the venture capitalist to exit – to recycle its financial contribution from successful companies to early-stage companies.

3.2. The exit and reinvestment cycle for venture capital funds and capital providers

The efficiency of exit for the venture capitalist-portfolio company relationship complements a similar efficiency arising from the relationship between the venture capitalist and the investors in its limited partnerships. The cycle of financial commitment to early-stage firms, followed by exit from these investments, responds to three contracting problems in the venture capitalist – capital provider relationship. First, capital providers need a way to evaluate venture capitalists' skill, in order to decide to which managers to commit new funds. Second, capital providers need to evaluate the risks and returns on venture capital investments relative to other investments, in order to decide whether to invest in venture capital, and how much to invest. Third, capital providers need to be able to withdraw funds from less successful managers, or from managers whose industry-specific expertise no longer matches current investment opportunities. Yet the very specialization that explains why capital providers hire venture capitalists rather than invest directly ensures that capital providers

---

[6] Compare Rajan's (1992) analysis of the trade-off between a bank-like lender who has the ability to monitor the borrower's on-going performance and public investors who cannot monitor. As the borrower's quality improves, the returns to monitoring decrease, and the most efficient capital provider shifts from a monitoring bank-like lender to a non-monitoring investor. Diamond (1991) discusses a similar generational theory in which optimal investor type depends on a firm's stage in its life-cycle.

cannot easily assess whether a venture capital fund's ongoing investments are or are likely to become successful, or how successful they are likely to be.

Exit by the venture capital manager from specific portfolio investments provides a benchmark that lets capital providers evaluate both the relative skill of venture capital managers and the profitability of venture capital relative to other investments (Gompers, 1996). At the same time, payment of the exit proceeds to capital providers lets the capital providers recycle funds from less successful to more successful venture capital managers.

Conventional limited partnership agreements between venture capital funds and capital providers reflect the efficiency of exit for this relationship. The limited partnership agreement typically sets a maximum term for the partnership of 7–10 years, after which the partnership must be liquidated and the proceeds distributed to the limited partners (Sahlman, 1990). During the term of the limited partnership agreement, the proceeds from investments in particular firms are distributed to limited partners as realized. Moreover, venture capital funds have strong incentives to exit from their investments, when feasible, well before the end of the partnership period. A fund's performance record, based on completed investments, is the fund's principal tool for soliciting capital providers to invest additional funds in new limited partnerships.

The explicit contract between capital providers and the venture capitalist, requiring liquidation of each limited partnership, is complemented by an implicit contract in which capital providers are expected to reinvest in future limited partnerships sponsored by successful venture capital funds. The expectation of reinvestment makes it feasible for venture capital funds to invest in developing infrastructure and expertise that will outlive the term of any one limited partnership, and could not be justified by the returns on the modest amount of capital that a venture capitalist without a track record can expect to raise. Fig. 2

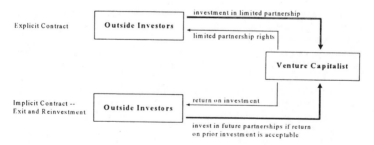

Fig. 2. Implicit and explicit contracts between venture capitalists and outside investors.

B.S. Black, R.J. Gilson/Journal of Financial Economics 47 (1998) 243–277   257

illustrates the explicit and implicit contracts between venture capitalists and their investors.

In sum, exit is central to the venture capital manager's accountability to capital providers. The efficiency of exit for the venture capital fund – capital provider relationship complements its efficiency properties for the portfolio firm – venture capital fund relationship. Taken together, they provide a strong rationale for exit from individual portfolio investments as a critical component of a viable venture capital industry.

4. The availability of exit by IPO: Implicit contracting over future control

The analysis in part 3 establishes the importance of an exit strategy to the venture capital market. But it does not differentiate between stock market-centered and bank-centered capital markets. A stock market makes available one special type of exit – an initial public offering. But another exit strategy is available to venture capital funds in both bank-centered and stock-market centered capital markets: the fund can cause the portfolio company to be sold to a larger company. Indeed, even in the United States, venture capitalists frequently exit through sale of the portfolio company rather than through an IPO (Table 1). A third exit option – leveraging the portfolio company so it can repurchase the venture capitalist's stake – is generally not feasible for the fast-growing, capital-consuming companies that are the typical focus for venture capital investing in the U.S.

Exit through sale of the portfolio company is likely to be the most efficient form of exit in some cases. For example, innovation may be better accomplished in small firms while production and marketing may be better accomplished in large firms. In this circumstance, selling a startup company to another firm with manufacturing or marketing expertise can produce synergy gains. These gains can be partly captured by the startup firm through a higher exit price (Bygrave and Timmons, 1992).

In other cases, an IPO may be the most efficient form of exit. The potential for an IPO to provide a higher-valued exit than sale of the company must be considered plausible, given the frequency with which this exit option is used in the United States. Viewed ex ante, venture capital financing of firms for which exit through IPO will (or might turn out to) maximize exit price could be a positive net present investment in a stock-market-centered capital market, but not in a bank-centered capital market. But this difference should affect investment decisions only at the margin. Thus, it cannot easily explain the dramatic differences between the venture capital industries in the United States and Germany, both in size and in type of investment.

Thus, we are only part of the way towards a theory that explains the observed link between venture capital markets and stock markets. We have shown why venture capital providers need an exit strategy. What remains to be shown is that the potential for exit through IPO, *even if exit often occurs through the portfolio company's sale*, is critical to the development of an active venture capital market. This part shows that the potential for exit through IPO allows the venture capital provider and the entrepreneur to enter into an implicit contract over future control of the portfolio company in a manner that is not readily duplicable in a bank-centered system.

4.1. The contracting framework

In a contracting framework, the relevant time to assess the influence of an IPO's availability (and therefore the importance of a stock market) on the operation of the venture capital market is when the entrepreneur and venture capital provider contract over the initial investment, not when exit actually occurs. A number of authors have modeled aspects of this contract, including the staging of the venture capitalist's funding, which vests in the venture capital provider the decision whether to continue the portfolio company's projects (Admati and Pfleiderer, 1994; Gompers, 1995), and the venture capital fund's purchase of a convertible security both to mitigate distributional conflicts between the entrepreneur and the venture capitalist associated with a future sale of the firm (Bergloff, 1994), and to solve an adverse selection problem among prospective entrepreneurs (Marx, 1994; Gompers, 1997). Our informal model seeks to explain three additional characteristics of venture capital contracting: (1) the parties' ex ante joint preference that the venture capital fund exit through an IPO; (2) how the entrepreneur's preference that the fund use this exit strategy if it becomes available ex post is expressed through a self-enforcing implicit contract over future control; and (3) how this implicit contract provides the entrepreneur with incentives that are not easily duplicated if sale of the portfolio company is the only exit option. Because the incentive properties of this contract go to the heart of the entrepreneurial process, its availability in a stock-market-centered capital market links the venture capital market and the stock market and can explain the absence of vigorous venture capital in countries with bank-centered capital markets.

Our IPO exit model requires three noncontroversial assumptions: (i) the entrepreneur places substantial private value on control over the company she starts; (ii) it is not feasible for an untested entrepreneur to retain control at the time of the initial venture capital financing; and (iii) it is feasible for a successful entrepreneur to reacquire control from the venture capitalist when the venture capitalist exits. We discuss each assumption below.

A private value for control is a standard feature in venture capital models and, more generally, in models that seek to explain the incentive properties of capital structure (Holmstrom and Tirole, 1989; Grossman and Hart, 1988; Harris and Raviv, 1988). Moreover, for entrepreneurs, the assumption appears to be

B.S. Black, R.J. Gilson/Journal of Financial Economics 47 (1998) 243–277   259

descriptively accurate. The failure rate for startup companies is high enough[7] so that, without a large private value for control, many potential entrepreneurs would decide not to leave a secure job to start a new company. It is also apparent that ceding to the venture capital provider the power, frequently exercised, to remove the entrepreneur from management is a significant cost to the entrepreneur (Hellman, 1995a).

Even if entrepreneurs value control highly, they cannot demand its retention at the time that they are seeking venture financing. The typical entrepreneur has not previously run a startup company. Venture capitalists rationally insist on retaining control to protect themselves against the risk that the entrepreneur would not run the firm successfully or will extract private benefits from the firm instead of maximizing its value to all investors.

The situation changes once a startup firm has succeeded. The entrepreneur has proved her management skill and provided some evidence that she can be trusted with other peoples' money. Returning control to the entrepreneur could now maximize firm value. Even if not, the value lost may be less than the entrepreneur's private value of control. The opportunity to regain control also provides an incentive, beyond mere wealth, for the entrepreneur to devote the effort needed for success. This possibility squarely raises the contracting problem that we address below: How can the venture capitalist commit, ex ante, to transfer control back to the entrepreneur, contingent on a concept as nebulous as 'success'?

4.2. The entrepreneur's incentive contract

When the entrepreneur sells an interest in her company to a venture capital fund, the venture capitalist receives both a residual interest in the firm's value, typically in the form of convertible preferred stock or debt and significant control rights, both explicit (for example, the right to remove the chief executive officer) and implicit (for example, the right to decide whether the firm can continue in business through staged funding). In return, the company and the entrepreneur get three things. The portfolio company receives capital plus nonfinancial contributions including information, monitoring, and enhanced credibility with third parties. This explicit contract is illustrated in Fig. 3. In addition, the entrepreneur receives an implicit incentive contract denominated in control. The structure of this incentive contract depends on the availability of an IPO exit strategy.

---

[7] See Gompers (1995) (16% of portfolio companies are liquidated or go bankrupt), Barry (1994) (one-third of venture capital investments result in losses). Sahlman (1990) (one-third of venture capital investments result in losses). Additionally, a significant percentage of would be entrepreneurs never secure venture funding at all.

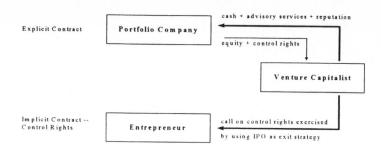

Fig. 3. Implicit and explicit contracts between venture capitalist and entrepreneur.

To begin with, an IPO is available to the portfolio company only when the company is successful. Indeed, the frequency with which a venture capital fund's portfolio companies go public is a central measure of the venture capitalist's success in the eyes of investors in venture capital funds (Gompers, 1996). When an IPO occurs, the entrepreneur receives two things. Like the venture capital provider, the entrepreneur gets cash to the extent that she sells some of her shares in the offering, plus increased value and liquidity for unsold shares. In addition, the entrepreneur reassumes much of the control originally ceded to the venture capitalist. The venture capitalist's percentage stake is reduced by its direct sale of shares,[8] by the venture capitalist's in-kind distribution of shares to its investors (Gompers and Lerner, 1997), and by the company's sale of new shares in the IPO to dispersed shareholders. The now-public firm also no longer depends on the venture capitalist for continuation decisions through staged funding; the public equity market is available. The greater liquidity of the venture capitalist's remaining investment after the IPO also reduces the venture capitalists' incentive to monitor (Coffee, 1991 discusses the tradeoff between monitoring and liquidity).[9] The venture capitalist's need to monitor the portfolio company intensively is further reduced because some of the monitoring task will now be undertaken by stock market analysts. On average, venture

---

[8] Over the years 1979–1990, lead venture capitalists sold shares in some 27% of IPOs of venture capital backed companies. The incidence of venture capitalist sales increased to 37% in the last three years of that period. (Lin and Smith, 1995).

[9] The increased liquidity and the venture capitalist's ability to sell off its investment gradually after the initial public offering is critical because the underwriter will typically limit the amount that the venture capitalist can sell in the IPO and over the following six months lest the market draw an unfavorable inference about the portfolio company's future value from the venture capitalist's sales (Benton and Gunderson 1993).

B.S. Black, R.J. Gilson/Journal of Financial Economics 47 (1998) 243–277   261

capital funds reduce their holdings of a portfolio company's shares by 28% within one year after an IPO (Barry et al., 1990). Three years after the IPO, only 12% of lead venture capitalists retain 5% or more of the portfolio company's shares (Lin and Smith, 1995).

Finally, and most significantly, the explicit contract between the venture capital fund and the portfolio company ensures that important control rights that were initially given to the fund, including guaranteed board membership and veto power over business decisions, disappear on an initial public offering whether or not the fund sells any shares at all in the IPO. Typically, the terms of the convertible securities held by the venture capital fund require conversion into common stock at the time of the IPO (Gompers, 1997); the negative covenants contained in the investor rights agreement also terminate on an IPO (Benton and Gunderson, 1993). In short, the venture capital fund's special control rights end at the time of an IPO, leaving the fund with only the weaker control rights attendant to substantial stock ownership. Even this control will diminish over time as the venture capital fund reduces its remaining stock position. Control becomes vested in the entrepreneur, who often retains a controlling stock interest and, even if not, retains the usual broad discretion enjoyed by chief executives of companies without a controlling shareholder.

The opportunity to acquire control through an IPO exit if the company is successful gives the entrepreneur a powerful incentive beyond the purely financial gains from the increased value of her shares in the firm. In effect, the prospect of an IPO exit gives the entrepreneur something of a call option on control, contingent on the firm's success.

Contrast this outcome with what the entrepreneur receives when the venture capital provider exits through sale of the portfolio company to an established company. As in an IPO, the entrepreneur receives cash or the more liquid securities of a publicly traded acquirer. Control, however, passes to the acquirer, even if the entrepreneur remains in charge of day-to-day management. Thus, if an IPO exit is not available, the entrepreneur cannot be given the incentive of a call option on control exercisable in the event of success. Exit through an IPO is possible only in the presence of a stock market; its role in the contract between the venture capitalist and the entrepreneur links the venture capital market and the stock market.

4.3. Feasibility of the implicit contract over control

It remains to demonstrate the feasibility of the implicit incentive contract over control and its superiority to an explicit contract. We undertake these tasks in this and the next subsection. The difficulty of defining success and the potential advantages of an implicit contract are suggested by the parties' use of an implicit contract involving staged funding to handle the pre-IPO decision as to whether and on what terms the venture capitalist will provide additional financing.

The feasibility problem is to specify a self-enforcing implicit contract: (i) whose terms are clear; (ii) whose satisfaction by the entrepreneur is observable; and (iii) whose breach by the venture capital provider would be observable and punished by the market. Consider the following stylized implicit contract: The entrepreneur will be deemed sufficiently successful to exercise her call option on control and the venture capital provider will exit through an IPO, so long as a reputable investment banker will underwrite a firm commitment offering. The need to clearly specify the conditions under which the entrepreneur can exercise the call option on control is met, not by defining numerical performance standards that the portfolio company must meet, but by delegating the performance assessment to a third party. Investment bankers have an incentive to seek out (or respond to inquiries from) portfolio companies whose performance has been strong enough to allow a successful public offering. A central feature of the investment banker's role in a public offering is as an information intermediary who proffers its reputation on behalf of the portfolio company much as the venture capitalist provides credibility to the portfolio company at an earlier stage in its development. The investment banker's internal standards for companies it is willing to take public, made credible by its willingness to commit its own capital and reputation to the offering, provide a self-enforcing statement of the conditions for exercise of the entrepreneur's call option.

The second requirement, that the entrepreneur's satisfaction of the exercise conditions be observable, is met in the same way. The investment banker's offer to take the portfolio company public is directly observable by the venture capital provider and the entrepreneur and is credible because the investment banker has the right incentives to honestly evaluate a portfolio company's performance.

The final requirement, that the venture capitalist's breach of the implicit contract be observable and punishable by the market, is also met. Observability results from the character of the venture capital market. The universe of portfolio companies sufficiently successful to merit a public offering is limited, as is the number of venture capital providers. Both sides of the market are relatively concentrated, with a significant number of portfolio companies geographically concentrated and the offices of a significant percentage of U.S. venture capital providers found along a short strip of Sand Hill Road in Silicon Valley (Saxanian, 1994). Moreover, venture capital funds typically specialize in portfolio companies geographically proximate to the fund's office.[10] While

---

[10] Lerner (1994a) reports that venture capital providers located within five miles of a portfolio company are twice as likely to have a board representative than providers located more than 500 miles distant. The fact that in 1996, 40% of total venture capital disbursements were to portfolio companies in California (Venture Capital Yearbook, 1997) provides further evidence of venture capital provider concentration sufficient to support a reputation market.

B.S. Black, R.J. Gilson/Journal of Financial Economics 47 (1998) 243–277   263

proximity facilitates monitoring, it also facilitates the emergence and maintenance of a reputation market. A claim by an entrepreneur that a venture capital
provider declined to allow a portfolio company to go public when a reputable
investment banker was available would quickly circulate through the community. Finally, venture capital providers are repeat players, who typically seek at
regular intervals to raise funds for new limited partnerships, which must then
invest in new portfolio companies, before prior limited partnerships are completed (Sahlman, 1990). In the competition to be lead venture investor in the
most attractive companies, a reputation for breaching the implicit contract for
control is hardly an advantage.

The viability of reputation market constraints on venture capitalist behavior
is confirmed by another aspect of the overall venture capitalist-entrepreneur
relationship. The venture capitalist's staged capital commitment gives the venture capitalist the option to abandon short of providing the portfolio company
sufficient funds to complete its business plan. This gives the entrepreneur
incentive to perform, gives the venture capitalist incentives to monitor, and
reduces agency costs by shifting the continuation decision from the entrepreneur
to the venture capitalist. However, this pattern, coupled with the right of first
refusal with respect to future financing typically given to the venture capitalist
(Sahlman, 1990), also permits the venture capitalist to act opportunistically.
What can the entrepreneur do if the venture capitalist opportunistically offers to
provide the second-stage financing necessary for the entrepreneur to continue at
an unfair price? The entrepreneur could seek financing from other sources, but
the original venture capitalist's right of first refusal presents a serious barrier:
who would incur the costs of making a bid when potential bidders know that
a bid will succeed only when a better informed party – the original investor
– believes the price is too high? A reputation market can police this potential for
opportunism.[11]

4.4. Superiority of the implicit contract over control

An explicit contract that specifies the operating performance necessary to
entitle the entrepreneur to reacquire control is a difficult undertaking. Creating
a state-contingent contract that specifies the control consequences of the full
range of possible states of the world over the four- to ten-year average term of
a venture investment, without creating perverse incentives, is a severe challenge
both to the parties' predictive powers and their drafting capabilities. It is in
precisely these circumstances that an implicit contract is likely to have a comparative advantage over an explicit contract.

---

[11] Admati and Pfleiderer (1994), who model the shift of the continuation decision to the venture
capitalist, do not address this problem.

Moreover, the venture capitalist will be willing to cede control only at the time of exit, not before. Yet a mechanical formula cannot ensure that a reputable underwriter will be willing to take the portfolio company public. In addition, the venture capitalist must actively cooperate for an IPO to succeed. At the same time, the venture capitalist cannot unduly 'puff' the portfolio company's prospects, because the capital markets will punish this behavior through reduced marketability of IPOs of other portfolio companies. Thus, a supposedly explicit contract, defining when the entrepreneur and the venture capital fund have the right to take the portfolio company public, cannot easily be enforced. Such a contract would be substantially implicit in fact, even if explicit in form. Thus, it is not surprising that entrepreneurs and venture capitalists, for the most part, do not seek to contract explicitly over control.

Finally, the implicit/explicit dichotomy presented above oversimplifies the real world. In fact, some elements of the contract over control are explicit, while others are left implicit. For example, cessation of the venture capital fund's special control rights at the time of an IPO is explicitly required, while the timing of the triggering event – the IPO – is left implicit. Conversion of the venture capitalist's convertible securities into common stock special rights is sometimes explicitly required if the portfolio company achieves defined financial milestones, even without an IPO (Benton and Gunderson, 1993; Gompers, 1997). Also, consistent with the greater importance of control earlier in a firm's life, the venture capitalist's explicit control rights are generally stronger, the earlier the stage of the investment (Gompers, 1997).

4.5. Consistency with empirical evidence

In our model, successful entrepreneurs often prefer exit by IPO, and have the implicit contractual right to demand this form of exit not only when it maximizes firm value compared to the alternative of sale of the firm, but also when the entrepreneur's private value of control outweighs the entrepreneur's loss in share value. Our model predicts that the venture capitalist's successful exits will take place disproportionately through IPO. If so, IPO exits will be more profitable than exits through sale of the portfolio company, by more than can plausibly be explained by the different values available through these different forms of exit.

This prediction is confirmed. Gompers (1995) reports that venture capital funds earn an average 60% annual return on investment in IPO exits, compared to 15% in acquisition exits; see also Petty et al. (1994); Sagari and Guidotti (1993). MacIntosh (1996) reports that IPO exits are more profitable in Canada as well. It is not plausible that these large differences could arise if the venture capitalist chose in each case the exit that maximized return on investment.

B.S. Black, R.J. Gilson/Journal of Financial Economics 47 (1998) 243–277   265

5. Evidence from other countries

We have developed an informal theory in which the success of early stage venture capital financing of high-growth, often high-technology firms, is linked to the availability of exit through an initial public offering. The weak form of the theory is that IPO exit is preferred by entrepreneurs. This preference leads to an implicit contract over control between the entrepreneur and the venture capitalist, in which the entrepreneur's success is rewarded by giving the entrepreneur the option to reacquire control through an IPO exit. This theory is consistent with the evidence discussed in part 2 of a correlation between frequency of IPO exit and amount of new capital contributed to venture capital funds, and the evidence in Section 4.5 that successful exits occur disproportionately through IPO.

The strong form of our theory is that the entrepreneur's preference for control is strong enough to significantly impair the development of a venture capital market in countries where exit by acquisition is the only viable option. This section offers an informal test of the strong form of our theory: Does the theory predict the observed success of venture capital in different countries with different types of capital markets? We provide data on Germany and the United States in part 2; we survey several other countries below.

5.1. Japan

We have only limited quantitative data on the size of the venture capital industry in Japan. However, the quantitative and qualitative data that we have (primarily from Milhaupt, 1997) is consistent with our theory: Japan, with its bank-centered capital market, has relatively little venture capital. In 1995, there were only 121 venture capital funds, of which more than half were affiliated with banks and run by the parent bank's employees. The employees of bank-affiliated funds commonly rotate through jobs in the bank's venture capital affiliate and then return to the parent bank. Thus, they are unlikely to develop the special skills needed to evaluate high-technology investments. Another 25 Japanese venture capital funds were run by securities firms or insurance companies.

Unlike American venture capital funds, which primarily provide equity financing, Japanese funds, perhaps reflecting their parentage, provide funds mostly through loans. Where American venture capital funds concentrate on high-tech businesses, and are the principal capital source for many startup high-tech firms, Japanese venture capital firms rarely invest in high-technology firms. Instead, they concentrate on manufacturing and services, including such mundane investments as small shops and restaurants. As of 1995, Japanese venture capital funds owned more than 10% of the stock of only one biotechnology company, two new materials firms, and 12 electronics firms.

5.2. Great Britain and Other European Countries

The similarity between Germany and Japan in the weakness of their venture capital industries strengthens the empirical support for the claim that bank-centered capital markets do not develop a strong venture capital industry. The converse claim is that stock-market centered capital markets can develop a strong venture capital industry. In particular, our theory predicts that Great Britain, with its active stock market, should have comparatively strong venture capital industries. This prediction is also supported by the evidence. British GDP is only about two-thirds of Germany's, yet its venture capital industry is almost five times larger, measured by cumulative capital committed (Economist, 1996); new capital commitments are comparable to the United States as a per-centage of GDP. Ireland, with its easy access to the London stock market, also has relatively high venture capital as a percentage of GDP. Britain and Ireland are the clear European leaders in venture capital, with everyone else far behind.

Table 6 shows new funds raised by venture capital funds in 1993 and 1994 as a percentage of GDP. Great Britain's lead over everyone else would be greater still if the data were classified by the venture capital fund's home country,

Table 6
New capital committed to venture capital funds, 1993–1994 (percent of GDP)

New capital commitments to venture capital funds, as percent of national GNP, for various countries between 1993 and 1994.

Country	Year		Average: 1993–1994
	1993	1994	
United States	0.03%	0.06%	0.05%
Great Britain	0.09	0.27	0.18
France	0.06	0.07	0.06
Italy	0.02	0.02	0.02
Germany	0.01	0.01	0.01
Netherlands	0.04	0.07	0.05
Spain	0.03	0.01	0.02
Sweden	0.06	0.06	0.06
Ireland	0.04	0.25	0.15
Portugal	0.06	0.07	0.06
Belgium	0.04	0.03	0.04
Denmark	0.01	0.08	0.04
Switzerland	0.03	0.02	0.03
Norway	0.05	0.03	0.04
Finland	0.01	0.04	0.02
Iceland	0.06	0	0.03
Austria	0	0	0

Source: European Venture Capital Association, 1995.

B.S. Black, R.J. Gilson/Journal of Financial Economics 47 (1998) 243–277   267

because British-based venture capital funds invest substantial amounts through affiliates in other European countries.

These data understate the relative size of the U.S. venture capital industry. European venture capital firms are less specialized than their American counterparts and are often affiliated with commercial banks. The European Venture Capital Association defines 'venture capital' to include leveraged buyouts and buyins, and replacement of a firm's existing financing. In contrast, leveraged buyout firms in the United States are a distinct industry from venture capital firms; venture capital is also distinct from non-venture private equity financing. Non-venture uses of funds by European 'venture capital' firms are substantial. For example, in Great Britain, 47% of capital commitments in 1994 went to buyins and buyouts, and only 8% to early stage financing. In France, 40% of venture capital comes from banks, and in 1994, 51% of funds committed went to buyouts, buyins, and replacement financing, while only 9% went to early stage financing.

5.3. Canada

Our evidence on Canada is drawn primarily from the recent survey by MacIntosh (1996). Canada has a relatively open IPO market – both domestic IPOs and access to the U.S. IPO market. Thus, our theory predicts that Canada should have a relatively active venture capital industry. The Canadian data are difficult to interpret because of heavy government intervention in the venture capital industry. Labor Sponsored Venture Capital Corporations (LSVCCs), which must be formed by a labor union, receive substantial tax benefits. As a result, they dominate the Canadian venture capital industry. These funds tend to invest more conservatively than other venture capital funds. The largest single LSVCC fund, the Solidarite fund, is owned by the government of Quebec.

Still, there is substantial evidence that Canadian venture capital funds, especially private funds, play a large role in early-stage financing of high-technology Canadian firms. In 1994, private independent funds had C$1.8 billion under management, and all Canadian venture capital firms had C$4.5 billion under management. The latter figure is comparable to the United States after adjusting for the size of the economy. Moreover, 25% of new capital went to early-stage financing – a figure similar to that for the United States, and much higher than for European and Japanese venture capital firms. The percentage of early-stage investments is likely higher than this for non-LSVCC funds. In Canada, as in the United States, IPO exit is common and the highest-return exits are through IPOs.

5.4. Israel

Israel offers an interesting case study of how an existing venture capital industry can adapt when the option of a domestic IPO is taken away through

268   B.S. Black, R.J. Gilson/Journal of Financial Economics 47 (1998) 243–277

regulation. The Israeli economy has grown rapidly during the 1990s, partly in response to deregulation of a formerly heavily government-controlled economy. High-technology startups, often financed by venture capital funds, have been an important element in this growth (Gourlay, 1996). Multiple elements have contributed to the Israeli high-technology and venture capital industries, including government guarantees against large losses by publicly traded venture capital funds in the form of a put option on the fund's shares, government creation of incubator facilities for startup firms, and a substantial influx in the early 1990s of immigrant scientists from Russia.

In the early 1990s, Israeli high-technology firms often went public on the Tel Aviv Stock Exchange at a very early stage. After a stock price crash in early 1994, the Tel Aviv Stock Exchange adopted listing rules that limited IPOs by early-stage companies. Israeli venture capital funds have nonetheless continued to flourish by shifting their IPOs from the Tel Aviv Stock Exchange to the NASDAQ market. Giza Group (1996) reports the results of 16 IPOs of venture capital-backed Israeli companies from 1993 through early 1996, of which 14 were on NASDAQ, one on the British 'AIM' small-firm market, and one on the Tel Aviv Stock Exchange. As of March 31, 1997, 62 Israeli companies had listed securities on NASDAQ, including 22 in 1996 alone; most were high-tech companies. The cumulative total exceeds any other country's except Canada's, and far exceeds any other country's relative to GDP.

6. Alternative explanations for intercountry variations in venture capital

We have developed in this paper an informal theory, based on the stock market's role in providing contracting options not available in a bank-centered capital market, that may partially explain cross-country variations in venture capital. In this section, we evaluate briefly several alternative explanations for the different levels of venture capital financing in stock market-centered and bank-centered capital markets. We first consider a claim of functional irrelevance: institutional differences between stock market-centered and bank-centered systems do not affect economic outcomes because bank-centered systems have developed functionally equivalent means for financing early-stage entrepreneurial activities. We then turn to explanations that acknowledge differences between countries in their ability to provide financing for high-technology ventures, but assign causation differently than we do.

While our analysis here is only suggestive, differential performance between the United States and Germany in industries where venture capital plays a significant role in the U.S. suggests that Germany has not yet developed a functional substitute for venture capital. Alternative explanations may account for some of this functional difference, but none appears able to fully displace the account of cross-national differences offered here.

B.S. Black, R.J. Gilson/Journal of Financial Economics 47 (1998) 243–277   269

6.1. Institutional but not functional differences

Different methods of organizing capital markets do not necessarily dictate corresponding functional or performance differences. For example, empirical research by Kaplan (1994a,b) and Kaplan and Minton (1994) suggests that Japanese and German companies change top management in response to poor earnings and stock price performance about as often and as quickly as United States companies, despite the three countries' quite different corporate governance institutions. The similar outcomes could reflect the impact of selection on path-dependent corporate governance systems. That three leading industrial economies change senior management under roughly the same circumstances may reflect a selection bias. By limiting the sample to these successful systems, we observe only systems that, within the constraints established by their particular institutions, have solved reasonably well the central corporate governance problem of replacing poorly performing managers (Gilson, 1996; Kaplan and Ramseyer, 1996).

The same functional equivalence argument can be made with respect to differences in how successful economies finance entrepreneurial activities. If other financing methods, such as bank financing of startup companies or internalization of the entrepreneurial process by large companies, yields the same performance as the United States' venture capital market, then the institutional differences are historically interesting but not functionally significant.

The empirical evidence needed to assess the functional equivalence argument for venture-capital financed industries is not available, but anecdotal evidence makes us skeptical about functional equivalence. The United States has become a world leader in precisely those industries, notably biotechnology and computer-related high technology, in which the venture capital market figures centrally (Powell, 1996). Moreover, in both Europe and the United States, large pharmaceutical companies are responding to biotechnology entrepreneurship not by funding the entrepreneurs directly, but instead by providing later-stage financing and partnering arrangements to entrepreneurial companies, mostly U.S.-based and originally financed through U.S. venture capital (Powell, 1996; Hellman, 1995b; Lerner and Merges, 1997). The result is not functional equivalence but specialization: Different activities are allocated to different countries on the basis of differences in their venture capital markets.

6.2. The role of pension fund financing of venture capital

In both Japan and Germany, pension funds do not invest in venture capital. In Germany, corporate pension obligations are typically unfunded, so large private pension plans do not exist. Japan has moderate sized corporate pension plans, but these plans are barred by law from investing in venture capital (Milhaupt, 1997). In the United States, in contrast, the Department of Labor in

270   *B.S. Black, R.J. Gilson / Journal of Financial Economics 47 (1998) 243–277*

1979 explicitly sanctioned pension fund investment in venture capital. As shown in Table 3, pension plans now provide over 40% of total investment in U.S. venture capital funds.

Differences in pension fund size and regulation can explain part, but in our judgment only part, of the cross-national differences in the size of the venture capital industry. Funded pension obligations, as in the United States, as opposed to unfunded pension obligations in Germany, dictate only who makes employee pension investments, not the investments themselves. A company with an unfunded pension plan, in effect, incurs an unsecured debt – its promise to pay pensions when workers retire. The company can invest the funds thus made available in any way it chooses, including in venture capital. German firms could also voluntarily fund their pension obligations, as many American firms did even before ERISA established minimum funding requirements in 1973. The pension plan could then invest in venture capital, if it so chose.

In the U.S., the unclear legality of pension fund investments in venture capital between 1973 and 1979 sterilized this pool of investable funds. Not surprisingly, the 1979 regulatory change resulted in a flow of funds into the previously restricted area. German firms have never been subject to an investment restriction similar to 1973–1979 U.S. regulation.

More generally, money is the ultimate fungible commodity, and venture capital commitments are a tiny fraction of total business investment – in the U.S., around $5 billion annually compared to gross investment of over $1 trillion. If there were attractive profits to be made from venture capital investing, it seems likely that funds would be available from other sources, even if not from pension plans. After all, the Germans and the Japanese save more than Americans as a percentage of GDP, merely in different forms.

6.3. Differences in labor market regulation

Germany and a number of other Western European countries impose substantial restrictions on layoffs, especially severance payment obligations. These rules impose costs on startup businesses and thus could discourage their formation. Variations in labor market restrictions correlate with observed national variations in venture capital. Germany has strong layoff protections and little venture capital. Japan has few formal restrictions on layoffs, but the common practice by large companies of hiring only recent college graduates and promising them lifetime employment reduces labor market mobility (Gilson and Roe, 1997). In contrast, the United States and Britain have more flexible labor markets and more active venture capital markets.

Labor market regulation and practices could well affect the vitality of venture capital. For example, Gilson (1997) argues that weak enforcement of covenants not to compete is a factor in the strength of venture capital in California; Hyde (1997) argues that the concentration of venture-capital-backed firms in Silicon

B.S. Black, R.J. Gilson/Journal of Financial Economics 47 (1998) 243–277   271

Valley both supports and depends on what he calls 'high velocity' labor markets. But labor market regulation, as a partial explanation for the vitality of venture capital markets, seems unlikely to fully displace our explanation, based on differences in capital markets.

Consider Germany as an example. Severance obligations build over time; they are much less burdensome for a startup firm that fails after a few years of operation than for a mature firm that closes a plant that has operated for decades. Moreover, unpaid severance obligations are of little significance if a firm goes bankrupt – they merely expand the pool of unsecured claims on the firm's assets.

Moreover, labor market restrictions do not map perfectly onto national patterns in venture capital activity. Canada has moderately strong labor market restrictions; Ireland and Israel have strong restrictions comparable to West Germany's. Yet these countries also have strong venture capital. This pattern is consistent with their access to stock markets: the London market for Ireland; the U.S. market for Israel; and U.S. and domestic stock markets for Canada.

6.4. Cultural differences in entrepreneurship

A final explanation is cultural. Germans and Japanese could be less entrepreneurial and less willing to risk failure than Americans, leading to lesser demand for venture capital services (Milhaupt, 1997, discusses Japanese culture). Cultural explanations for different patterns of economic activity are hard to evaluate. They can be partly tautological. In economically successful countries like Germany and Japan, the forces of economic selection will cause culture and economic institutions to become mutually supportive. Because both are endogenously determined, observing that cultural institutions support existing economic patterns tells us nothing about causation. For present purposes, the more interesting issue is not a static inquiry into the current equilibrium of culture and economic institutions, but a dynamic one: how can culture and institutions change in response to exogenous changes in the economic environment (North, 1990, 1994). We briefly consider this issue from an instrumental perspective in Section 7.

However, there is some reason for skepticism about claims of large cultural differences in willingness to take risks. People in all countries found large numbers of businesses, most of which fail. The empirical regularity to be explained is *not* why the Germans and Japanese do not start risky new businesses, but why they do not start many *high-technology* businesses, with few tangible assets on which a bank can rely for partial return of its investment. The success of immigrant entrepreneurs in countries with strong venture capital (for example, Russian immigrants in Israel and Asian immigrants in the United States) suggests that entrepreneurs will emerge if the institutional infrastructure needed to support them is available. After all, Russia and India are also not

272   *B.S. Black, R.J. Gilson Journal of Financial Economics 47 (1998) 243–277*

known for their cultural support of entrepreneurship. Moreover, efforts to find large cross-cultural differences in entrepreneurship between the U.S. and Russia at the close of the Communist period have failed, even though these two countries ought to exhibit much larger differences than the United States, Germany, and Japan (Shiller et al., 1991, 1992).

7. Implications for venture capital in bank-centered capital markets

Exploring the implications of the link between venture capital markets and stock markets is more complicated than the simple admonition that bank-centered capital markets should create a stock market. That straightforward approach has been tried before and failed. For example, France and Germany created special stock exchange segments for newer, smaller companies during the 1980s that, by the mid-1990s, had been shuttered or marginalized (Rasch, 1994). Nonetheless, the financial press still stresses the absence of a venture capital market as being at the root of the European high technology sector's poor performance, particularly with respect to Germany (e.g., Fisher, 1996a,b), and three efforts are underway to try again to create stock markets that cater to small high-technology companies. The Alternative Investment Market of the London Stock Exchange began trading in June 1995 and now lists over 200 firms (Price, 1996). Euro NM, a consortium of the French Le Nouveau Marche', which began trading in February, 1996, the German Neur Market, and the Belgian New Market, is scheduled to begin full operation in 1997. Finally, EASDAQ, an exchange explicitly patterned after the U.S. NASDAQ and of which the NASD is a part owner, opened on September 30, 1996 (Pickles, 1996). This flurry of stock market creation, taken with the explicit goal of enhancing the European venture capital market, suggests that there may be value in exploring the normative implications of the stock market-venture capital market link.

We begin our analysis of this link by stressing the path dependency of national capital markets. It is not merely a stock market that is missing in bank-centered systems. The secondary institutions that have developed in bank-centered systems, including the banks' conservative approach to lending and investing, and social and financial incentives that less richly reward entrepreneurial zeal and more severely penalize failure (See Harrison, 1990 (Germany); Milhaupt, 1997 (Japan)), are less conducive to entrepreneurial activity than the secondary institutions of stock market-centered capital markets. More critically, experienced venture capitalists, able to assess the prospects of new venture and to provide the nonfinancial contributions that venture capitalists supply in the United States are absent, as are investment bankers experienced in taking early-stage companies public. Neither institution will develop quickly. A strong venture capital market thus reflects an equilibrium of a

B.S. Black, R.J. Gilson/Journal of Financial Economics 47 (1998) 243–277   273

number of interdependent factors, only one of which is the presence of a stock market.

For example, Germany today faces a chicken and egg problem: a venture capital market requires a stock market, but a stock market requires a supply of entrepreneurs and deals which, in turn, require a venture capital market. In addition, German entrepreneurs who care about future control of their company must trust venture capitalists to return control to them some years hence and must further trust that the stock market window will be open when they are ready to go public. The institutional design issue is how to simultaneously create both a set of mutually dependent institutions and the trust that these institutions will work as expected when called upon.

In such a path-dependent equilibrium, the cost of change is the guard rail that keeps us on the path. We remain in an equilibrium less efficient than would be possible without the transaction costs of creating the institutions needed to support alternatives (Kohn, 1995). While we do not aspire to offer a solution here, our analysis suggests an approach to creating the conditions conducive to a vigorous venture capital market: avoid the problem of creating multiple new institutions by piggybacking on another country's institutions. If this is successful, a profit opportunity and corresponding potential for the development of local institutions will be created.

Most obviously, in the increasingly global capital market, the German venture capital market could follow Israel's lead in relying on the United States stock market and its supporting infrastructure. A German company that maintains accounting records in a fashion consistent with U.S. standards – arguably much less of a burden when done from the beginning than if implemented by a conversion, as when Daimler-Benz listed its shares on the New York Stock Exchange – confronts no regulatory barrier to listing on NASDAQ, the exchange most suitable to venture-capital-backed IPOs. At present, over 100 European companies, including one German company, list their shares on NASDAQ. Many of these listings represent the initial public offering of the company's stock. With NASDAQ comes its institutional infrastructure. For example, both Hambrecht and Quist and Robertson, Stephens and Co., leading investment bankers for venture-capital-backed IPOs in the United States, are opening European offices and holding conferences to introduce American venture capital funds to European entrepreneurs (Lavin, 1996). Silicon Valley law firms are also actively recruiting European IPO candidates.

The availability of this institutional infrastructure, without the costs of establishing it from scratch, can shorten the shadow of the past and, in the medium term, induce the development of competing local institutions. For example, in the near term, foreign venture capitalists will likely find it profitable to hire and train locals to help them find profitable investment opportunities. In the medium term, some of these people, once trained, will form their own firms and compete with their former employers.

274   *B.S. Black, R.J. Gilson/Journal of Financial Economics 47 (1998) 243–277*

8. Conclusion

In this paper. we have examined one of the path-dependent consequences of the difference between stock market-centered and bank-centered capital markets: the link between an active stock market and a strong venture capital market. We have shown that economies of scope among financial and nonfinancial contributions by venture capital providers, plus venture capital investors' need for a quantitative measure of venture capital funds' skill, can explain the importance of an exit strategy. Moreover, the potential for exit through an IPO, possible in a stock-market-centered capital market, allows the venture capitalist and the entrepreneur to contract implicitly over control, in a manner that is not easily duplicable in a bank-centered capital market. Finally, we have suggested that the best strategy for overcoming path dependent barriers to a venture capital market in bank-centered systems is to piggyback on the institutional infrastructure of stock-market-centered systems.

Our model seeks to explain the importance of a possible IPO exit for a high-growth firm financed by a venture capital fund, for which exit by the fund is desirable at a stage in the firm's life when it is still consuming rather than generating capital. For a mature, cash-generating firm, another exit strategy that preserves the entrepreneur's control is possible: the firm itself can buy back the venture capital fund's stake, perhaps by borrowing the needed funds. This strategy permits a somewhat different implicit contract over control between the fund and an entrepreneur: if the firm is successful enough to buy out the fund, the fund will acquiesce in this strategy even if this form of exit does not maximize the fund's return on an individual investment. In the United States, this form of exit is associated not with venture capital funds but with 'leveraged buyout' funds. In Europe, which has a less clear distinction between venture capital and leveraged buyouts, this form of exit is common when venture capital funds invest in management buyouts of mature firms. We plan to explore in future work the possible extension of our model to the leveraged buyout industry.

References

Admati, A., Pfleiderer, P., 1994. Robust financial contracting and the role of venture capitalists. Journal of Finance 49, 371–402.

Aoki, M., 1994. Monitoring characteristics of the main bank system: an analytical and developmental view. In: Aoki, M., Patrick, H. (Eds.), The Japanese Main Bank System: Its Relevance for Developing and Transforming Economies. Oxford University Press, Oxford.

Barry, C., 1994. New directions in venture capital research. Journal of Financial Management 23, 3–15.

Barry, C., Muscarella, C., Peavy J., III, Vetsuypens, M., 1990. The role of venture capitalists in the creation of a public company. Journal of Financial Economics 27, 447–471.

B.S. Black, R.J. Gilson/Journal of Financial Economics 47 (1998) 243–277   275

Benton, L., Gunderson, R.,Jr., 1993. Portfolio company investments: hi-tech corporation, venture capital and public offering negotiation. In: Halloran, M., Benton, L., Gunderson, R., Jr., Kearney, K., del Calvo, J. (Eds.), Law and Business, Inc. Harcourt Brace Jovanovich, New York.

Bergloff, E., 1994. A control theory of venture capital finance. Journal of Law, Economics and Organization 10, 247–267.

Black, B., 1990. Shareholder passivity reexamined. Michigan Law Review 89, 520–608.

Booth, J., Smith, R., 1986. Capital raising, underwriting and the certification hypothesis. Journal of Financial Economics 15, 261–281.

Brav, A., Gompers, P., 1997. Myth or reality? The long-run underperformance of initial public offerings: evidence from venture and nonventure capital-backed companies. Journal of Finance, forthcoming.

Bundesverband Deutsche Kapitalbeteiligungsgesellschaften (BVK) Jahrbuch [German Venture Capital Association Yearbook], various years through 1996 (BVK, Berlin, Germany).

Bygrave, W., Timmons, J., 1992. Venture capital at the crossroads. Harvard Business School Press. Cambridge, MA.

Carvalho, A., 1996. Venture capital as a network for human resources allocation. Unpublished working paper. University of Illinois.

Coffee, J., 1991. Liquidity versus control: The institutional investor as corporate monitor. Columbia Law Review 91, 1277–1368.

Diamond, D., 1991. Monitoring and reputation: the choice between bank loans and directly placed debt. Journal of Political Economy 99, 689–721.

Economist, 1996. Going for the golden egg. Sept. 28, 1996, at 89.

Edwards, J., Fischer, K., 1994. Banks, finance and investment in Germany. Cambridge University Press, Cambridge.

European Venture Capital Association, 1995. EVCA Yearbook 1995. Ernst and Young, London, England.

Fisher, A., 1996a. A venture across the pond. Financial Times, July 24, 1996, 12.

Fisher, A., 1996b. Germans urged to take a risk for jobs. Financial Times, July 16, 1996, 2.

Florida, R., Martin, K., 1990. The Breakthrough Illusion: Corporate America's Failure to Move from Innovation to Mass Production. BasicBooks, New York.

Gilson, R., Kraakman, R., 1984. The mechanisms of market efficiency. Virginia Law Review 70, 549–644.

Gilson, R., Roe, M., 1997. Lifetime employment: Labor peace and the evolution of Japanese corporate governance. Unpublished working paper. Columbia Law School.

Gilson, R., 1996. Corporate governance and economic efficiency. Washington University Law Quarterly 74, 327–345.

Gilson, R., 1997. The legal infrastructure of high-technology industrial districts: Silicon Valley and covenants not to compete. Unpublished working paper. Stanford Law School.

Giza Group, 1996. Survey of venture capital and investment funds in Israel: August 1996 Update. Giza Group, Tel Aviv, Israel.

Gompers, P., 1997. An examination of convertible securities in venture capital. Journal of Law and Economics, forthcoming.

Gompers, P., 1996. Grandstanding in the venture capital industry. Journal of Financial Economics 42, 133–156.

Gompers, P., 1995. Optimal investment, monitoring, and the staging of venture capital. Journal of Financial Economics 50, 1461–1489.

Gompers, P., Lerner, J., 1996. The use of covenants: an empirical analysis of venture partnership agreements. Journal of Law and Economics 39, 463–498.

Gompers, P., Lerner, J., 1997. Venture capital distributions: short-run and long-run reactions. Unpublished working paper. Harvard Business School.

276   B.S. Black, R.J. Gilson/Journal of Financial Economics 47 (1998) 243–277

Gorman, M., Sahlman, W., 1989. What do venture capitalists do? Journal of Business Venturing 4, 231–248.

Gourlay, R., 1996. The development of a venture capital industry lies behind the economic success of a new breed of high-tech Israeli company. Financial Times, April 30, 1996, 14.

Grossman, S., Hart, O., 1988. One share-one vote and the market for corporate control. Journal of Financial Economics 20, 175–202.

Harris, M., Raviv, A., 1988. Corporate governance: voting rights and majority rules. Journal of Financial Economics 20, 203–235.

Harrison, E., 1990. The West German venture capital market. Peter Lang, Frankfurt am Main, Frankfurt, Germany.

Hellman, T., 1995a. The allocation of control rights in venture capital contracts. Research Paper No. 1362. Stanford Business School, Stanford.

Hellman, T., 1995b. Competition and cooperation between entrepreneurial an established companies: the viability of corporate venture investments. Unpublished working paper. Stanford Business School, Stanford.

Hyde, A., 1997. High-velocity labor markets. Unpublished working paper. Rutgers Law School.

Hoshi, T., 1993. Evolution of the main bank system in Japan. Unpublished working paper. University of California at San Diego.

Kaplan, S., 1994a. Top executive rewards and firm performance: a comparison of Japan and the United States. Journal of Political Economy 102, 510–546.

Kaplan, S., 1994b. Top executives, turnover, and firm performance in Germany. Journal of Law, Economics and Organization 10, 142–159.

Kaplan, S., Minton, B., 1994. Appointments of outsiders to Japanese boards: determinants and implications for managers. Journal of Financial Economics 36, 225–258.

Kaplan, S., Ramseyer, J., 1996. Those Japanese firms with their disdain for shareholders: another fable for the academy. Washington University Law Quarterly 74, 403–418.

Kohn, M., 1995. Economics as a theory of exchange. Unpublished working paper. Dartmouth College Department of Economics, Dartmouth, NH.

Lavin, D., 1996. The sky's the limit. Convergence 2, 8.

Lerner, J., 1995. Venture capitalists and the oversight of private firms. Journal of Finance 50, 301–318.

Lerner, J., 1994a. The syndication of venture capital investments. Financial Management 23, 16–27.

Lerner, J., 1994b. Venture capitalists and the decision to go public. Journal of Financial Economics 35, 293–316.

Lerner, J., Merges, R., 1997. The control of strategic alliance: an empirical analysis of biotechnology collaborations. Working paper No. 6014. National Bureau of Economic Research.

Lin, T., Smith, R., 1995. Insider reputation and selling decisions: the unwinding of venture capital investments during equity IPOs. Unpublished working paper. Claremont Graduate School.

MacIntosh, J., 1996. Venture capital exits in Canada and the U.S. Unpublished working paper. University of Toronto Faculty of Law.

Marx, L., 1994. Negotiation of venture capital contracts. Unpublished working paper. University of Rochester.

Megginson, W., Weiss, K., 1991. Venture capital certification in initial public offerings. Journal of Finance 46, 879–903.

Milhaupt, C., 1997. The market for innovation in the United States and Japan: Venture capital and the comparative corporate governance debate. Northwestern University Law Review 91, 865–898.

Moukheiber, Z., March 25, 1996, Kleiner's web. Forbes, 40–42.

North, D., 1994. Economic performance through time. American Economic Review 84, 359–368.

North, D., 1990. Institutions, institutional change, and economic performance. Cambridge University Press, Cambridge, England.

Petty, W., Bygrave, W. Shulman, J., 1994. Harvesting the entrepreneurial venture: a time for creating value. Journal of Applied Corporate Finance. Spring, 48–58.

Pickles, C., 1996. One answer to Europe's capital needs. Wall Street Journal, Europe, October 23, 1996.

Porter, M., 1992. Capital disadvantages: America's failing investment system. Harvard Business Review, Sept.–Oct, 65–82.

Powell, W., 1996. Inter-organizational collaboration in the biotechnology industry. Journal of Institutional and Theoretical Economics 152, 197–215.

Price, C., 1996. EASDAQ pins hopes on NASDAQ. Financial Times, Sept. 30, 1996, 23.

Rajan, R., 1992. Insiders and outsiders: the choice between informed and arm's length debt. Journal of Finance 47, 1367–1400.

Rasch, S., 1994. Special stock market segments for small company shares in Europe – what went wrong? Discussion Paper No. 93-13. Center for European Economic Research.

Roe, M., 1994. Strong managers, weak owners: the political roots of American corporate finance. Princeton University Press, Princeton.

Sahlman, W., 1990. The structure and governance of venture capital organizations. Journal of Financial Economics 27, 473–522.

Sagari, S., Guidotti, G., 1993. Venture capital: the lessons from the developing world for the developing world. Financial Markets. Instruments and Investments 1, 31–42.

Saxanian, A., 1994. Regional Advantage: Culture and Competition in Silicon Valley and Route 128. Harvard University Press, Cambridge, MA.

Shiller, R., Boycko, M., Korobov, V., 1991. Popular attitudes toward free markets: the Soviet Union and the United States compared. American Economic Review 81, 385–400.

Shiller, R., Boycko, M., Korobov, V., 1992. Hunting for homo sovieticus: situational versus attitudinal factors in economic behavior. Brookings Papers on Economic Activity, 127–181.

Venture Capital Yearbook, various years through 1997. Venture Economics Publishing, New York.

[8]

ELSEVIER

Journal of Corporate Finance 6 (2000) 241–289

Journal of
CORPORATE
FINANCE

www.elsevier.com/locate/econbase

The determinants of venture capital funding: evidence across countries

Leslie A. Jeng [a,*], Philippe C. Wells [b]

[a] *Boston University School of Management, Boston, MA, USA*
[b] *Bain Capital, USA*

Abstract

This paper analyses the determinants of venture capital for a sample of 21 countries. In particular, we consider the importance of initial public offerings (IPOs), gross domestic product (GDP) and market capitalization growth, labor market rigidities, accounting standards, private pension funds, and government programs. We find that IPOs are the strongest driver of venture capital investing. Private pension fund levels are a significant determinant over time but not across countries. Surprisingly, GDP and market capitalization growth are not significant. Government policies can have a strong impact, both by setting the regulatory stage, and by galvanizing investment during downturns. Finally, we also show that different types of venture capital financing are affected differently by these factors. In particular, early stage venture capital investing is negatively impacted by labor market rigidities, while later stage is not. IPOs have no effect on early stage venture capital investing across countries, but are a significant determinant of later stage venture capital investing across countries. Finally, government funded venture capital has different sensitivities to the determinants of venture capital than non-government funded venture capital. Our insights emphasize the need for a more differentiated approach to venture capital, both from a research as well as from a policy perspective. We feel that while later stage venture capital investing is well understood, early stage and government funded investments still require more extensive research. © 2000 Elsevier Science B.V. All rights reserved.

JEL classification: G3
Keywords: Venture capital; Initial public offerings; Gross domestic product

---

* Corresponding author. 595 Commonwealth Avenue, Boston, MA 02215, USA. Tel.: +1-617-353-2353; fax: +1-617-353-6667.

E-mail address: ljeng@bu.edu (L.A. Jeng).

242   *L.A. Jeng, P.C. Wells / Journal of Corporate Finance 6 (2000) 241–289*

1. Introduction

Venture capital has been the driving force behind some of the most vibrant sectors of the US economy over the past two decades. Venture capitalists were instrumental in fostering the tremendous growth of firms such as Microsoft, Compaq, Oracle, and Sun Microsystems, which were all founded less than 20 years ago, but have rapidly become dominant players in the high technology arena. While the contributions venture capital makes to the economy overall are underexplored, there exists a widespread belief that venture capital is instrumental in bringing innovations to market at a rapid pace, thereby creating economic growth, jobs, and opportunities for further technological innovation. The 1997 National Venture Capital Association annual study on the impact of venture capital sheds light on some of the job-creating abilities of the sector. The study reveals that between 1991 and 1995, venture-backed companies increased their staffs on average 34% per year. Over the same time period, Fortune 500 companies decreased staffing levels 4% per year.[1]

The growth rate of venture capital funding has been high in many countries, but funding levels still vary significantly (see Table 1). In this paper, our goal is to understand the determinants of growth in the venture capital industry. Our work builds on that of Black and Gilson (1998), who examine the importance of well-developed stock markets and initial public offerings (IPOs) for venture capital financing. Black and Gilson's empirical work tests only the significance of IPOs over time in the US. We test a number of other factors in addition to IPOs, and use panel data for 10 years and 15 countries. The factors we test are the ones enumerated in the literature on venture capital: IPOs, gross domestic product (GDP) and market capitalization growth, labor market rigidities, financial reporting standards, private pension funds, and government programs.

Our results indicate that IPOs are the most important determinant of venture capital investing. Private pension fund levels impact venture capital over time, but not across countries. Our analysis demonstrates the necessity of separating venture capital into early (seed and startup) and later (expansion) stage investing, both for the purposes of analysis and for policy considerations. In particular, we show that different types of venture capital are differently affected by the determinants of venture capital. Thus, labor market rigidities negatively affect early stage venture capital investments, but have no impact on later stage venture capital investments. IPOs have no impact on early stage investments across countries, but are a significant determinant for later stage venture capital investments. Government funded venture capital is not as strongly determined by IPOs as non-government funded venture capital. Finally, our qualitative analysis of government programs

---

[1] *Seventh Annual Economic Impact of Venture Capital Study* (1997), National Venture Capital Association, Venture One, Coopers & Lybrand L.L.P.

L.A. Jeng, P.C. Wells / Journal of Corporate Finance 6 (2000) 241–289 243

gives further insight into the role government funds can play as a catalyst for private sector funding.

This paper is organized as follows: Section 2 discusses the role of small firms in the economy and the link between these firms and venture capital from the perspectives of financial intermediation, corporate governance, and entrepreneurship. Section 3 explains how venture capital firms are organized and how they work. Section 4 surveys the theories that explain what factors affect venture capital investments. Section 5 discusses the data, while Section 6 covers the regression methodology. Section 7 presents our empirical results. Section 8 discusses the role of government programs and includes case studies of the venture capital experience of Israel and Germany. Section 9 concludes.

2. The role of venture capital in the economy

Before we discuss venture capital in more detail, we first need to clarify our use of the term, since it is defined differently in the US and Europe. Venture capital, as we use the term, refers to one type of private equity investing. Private equity investments are investments by institutions or wealthy individuals in both publicly quoted and privately held companies. Private equity investors are more actively involved in managing their portfolio companies than regular, passive retail investors. The main types of financing included in private equity investing are venture capital and management and leveraged buyouts. Outside of the US, the term venture capital is frequently used to describe what we have just referred to as private equity.

The definition of venture capital, as it is used in the US, and as we use it in our paper, comprises three types of investing — seed, startup, and expansion investment — and excludes buyouts. These types represent three stages of investing which are defined with reference to the stage of development of the company receiving the investment.

Seed capital is the very first type of financing a newly founded company might want to secure. These funds are typically used to fund initial product research and development and to assess the commercial potential of ideas. Startup investments, on the other hand, are targeted at companies that have moved past the idea stage and are gearing up to produce, market, and sell their products. Companies at this stage still use more cash than they generate. Investments in either seed or startup stage are also referred to simply as early stage investments.

After a company has passed through the early stage, it becomes a potential candidate for expansion stage investing. In the expansion stage, a company that has already established its product in the marketplace often needs additional capital to fund the growth of its manufacturing and distribution capacity, as well as to fund further R&D.

244   *L.A. Jeng, P.C. Wells / Journal of Corporate Finance 6 (2000) 241–289*

Table 1
Country comparison

Countries	Venture capital (US$ in millions)			Early stage (US$ in millions)			Private equity new funds (US$ in millions)		
	1986[a]	1995[b]	CAGR%	1986[a]	1995[b]	CAGR%	1986[c]	1995[d]	CAGR%
Australia	417	888	45.9	17	54	76.5	239	249	0.8
Austria	1.9	1.4	-3.8	2	0.4	-16.5	1	2	1.6
Belgium	195	139	-3.7	67	8.4	-20.7	344	210	-5.4
Canada	152	412	15.4	65	182	15.7	230	1,133	19.4
Denmark	22	19	-1.6	4.6	4.5	-0.2	32	37	1.7
Finland	9.7	38	21.7	1.5	1.0	32.4	54	69	3.4
France	195	444	9.6	32	35	1.2	168	1055	22.6
Germany	43	694	36.4	9	116	32.8	50	274	20.9
Ireland	17	25	4.7	8	1	-18.9	34	16	-7.9
Israel	NA	NA	NA	NA	NA	NA	60	139	18.0
Italy	21	246	31.5	11	60	20.9	203	354	6.4
Japan	2351	2524	7.4	18	11	-38.3	258	604	23.7
Netherlands	128	471	15.6	31	100	14.0	260	337	2.9
New Zealand	0.7	3.8	461.9	NA	0.9	NM	14	33	135
Norway	14	154	40.9	1.2	7	28.6	14	60	22.8
Portugal	0.3	57	101.1	0.3	9	54.3	2	143	67.4
Spain	34	180	20.4	14	24	5.7	0	190	-2.35
Sweden	61	31	-7.1	7	9	3.0	114	614	20.5
Switzerland	13	28	9.0	10	1	-22.7	6	64	29.5
United Kingdom	65	883	3.5	158	36	-15.2	777	2363	13.2
United States	3181	3651	1.5	333	1093	14.1	8800	28,369	13.9

The other category of investments included in private equity, in addition to venture capital, is buyouts. Buyouts are usually applied to more mature companies. In a leveraged buyout, debt is used to acquire a company and reduce its equity base. Management buyouts are leveraged buyouts where current management takes control of its company.

Our primary interest is specifically in venture capital, not private equity. We believe venture capital in particular merits interest for several reasons. The past performance of venture capital-backed companies shows that venture capital has been very successful at backing companies with innovative technologies and tremendous growth potential. Companies such as Apple, Compaq, Digital Equipment, Intel, Microsoft, and Sun Microsystems were all backed by venture capital. As a measure of the success of these companies, we can consider their total market capitalization, which in July 1997 was US$369 billion.

The National Venture Capital Association 1997 report gives further evidence on the beneficial impact of venture capital. In addition to creating jobs at a much faster rate than Fortune 500 companies, venture capital-backed firms have done well even when compared to other high growth companies. 1995 revenue growth for venture capital-backed high growth companies was 36.8% compared to 23.8% for non-venture capital-backed high growth companies.

2.1. The role of venture capital in financial intermediation

Venture capital firms serve as financial intermediaries in a market where lenders and borrowers find it costly to get together. The costs are due to adverse selection and moral hazard, and the cost of administration, information gathering, and search efforts. By and large, the literature focuses on the important role banks play as financial intermediaries (Mayer, 1988; Fama, 1985; Myers and Majluf, 1984). However, for startup ventures, bank financing may not be optimal. In the US, for example, banks are prohibited from holding equity. But startups have few other tangible assets, and the prohibition makes it difficult for banks to obtain

---

Notes to Table 1:

Venture Capital includes seed, startup and expansion stage investments. Early stage includes only seed and startup investments. Private Equity New funds raised is defined as committed, but not yet paid, capital to private equity funds, i.e., includes money raised for all stages of investment. Source: European Venture Capital Journal, The Guide to Venture Capital in Asia, Venture Economics for US figures, MacDonald and Associates for Canada's figures and the Giza Group for Israel's figures.

[a]1988 figures for Canada, Finland and Norway. 1992 Estimated figures for Australia and Japan. 1993 estimated figures for New Zealand.

[b]1994 estimated figures for Australia and New Zealand. 1993 estimated figures for Japan. 1994 figures for Portugal.

[c]1989 figures for Australia and Japan. 1988 figures for Finland and Norway. 1993 figures for New Zealand 1990 figures for Israel.

[d]1994 figures for Australia, New Zealand and US and 1993 figures for Japan.

246   *L.A. Jeng, P.C. Wells / Journal of Corporate Finance 6 (2000) 241–289*

reasonable collateral on loans to startups. This severely restricts banks' willingness to take the additional risk associated with these new companies. In addition. since startups require a lot of cash in the early stages to finance their growth, debt-based finance is usually inappropriate from a cash management perspective as it strictly ties the cash flows of companies.

Even in countries such as Japan and Germany, where banks can hold equity, startup ventures are not highly funded by banks. This is to a large extent due to corporate governance issues discussed in the next section.

Given the need for financial intermediaries for startups and the unsuitability of banks to this role, the venture capital organization arose to fill this void in startup financing. American Research and Development, founded in Massachusetts in 1946, was the first modern venture capital organization. Venture capital is especially attractive because its equity finance structure gives companies the necessary leeway in their repayment schedule. In addition, by focusing on startups, venture capital firms achieve expertise and economies of scale in locating and financing potentially successful startup ventures.

Gompers (1994) examines "Angels" as an alternative source of funding for startups. "Angels" are essentially wealthy individuals who finance startups out of their own funds. While "Angels" represent an important source of financing, their scope is limited by the wealth of these individuals. "Angels" are not a viable source for large amounts of capital. Another source of startup financing is large corporations. However, Sykes (1990) finds that these programs have had limited success.

2.2. Venture capital vs. other forms of corporate governance

Startup firms present a unique set of issues for corporate governance which makes venture capital particularly suited to the sector. They operate in new markets, where information about the nature of the market is generally poor. Furthermore, they do not have an established track record which could be used as a baseline performance measure. Because so much of their value lies in their potential for future growth and so little in their current, tangible assets, startups place particular demands on monitors of financial performance. Jensen (1993) describes the type of investor needed in this environment as "active investor".

Active investors are investors who have a large financial interest in their investments, and can still provide an impartial view of the management of these firms. Some of the most common financial intermediaries, such as pension funds, insurance companies and money managers, are unable to perform the role of active investor due to legal structures and customs. Roe (1990) outlines the various restrictions on US banks, insurance companies, and mutuals, which prevent them from holding a large equity stake in any one company and from being actively involved on the boards of their investment companies.

L.A. Jeng, P.C. Wells / Journal of Corporate Finance 6 (2000) 241–289 247

Sahlman (1990) and Jensen (1993) find that venture capitalists solve the corporate governance and monitoring problem through extensive initial due diligence about startup companies' businesses. Furthermore, they maintain a close relationship by frequently visiting and talking to company management. The venture capitalists also sit on the boards of directors. In some instances, they even perform some key corporate functions for the firm, such as running the corporate finance department and working with suppliers and customers.

While countries such as Japan and Germany do not have restrictions on equity holding by banks, their banks are still not very adept at filling the necessary role as monitor for startups due to institutional design. A few banks dominate Japan's and Germany's banking industry and, often, only those companies with close relationships to these banks can obtain financing. Also, because they are large and provide a wide range of services, these banks do not have the specialization and focus required to handle small startups. Their involvement in management issues at the firms they lend to is often minimal. Edwards and Fischer (1994) document that German banks do not play an active role in management and that bank representation on boards is generally very small.

Large companies can also play an active role in the development of smaller enterprises with new ideas. However, this governance model possesses many attributes that reduce the chances of success for startups. Hardymon et al. (1983) find that legal difficulties often arise over whether the corporation has access to ventures' proprietary information. In addition, corporate venture capital groups within large organizations may not be able to operate autonomously (Siegel et al., 1988). Furthermore, Sahlman (1991) points out that the approval process within large enterprises is neither fast nor effective enough. He also notes that the entrepreneur is not sufficiently motivated, due to the absence of any equity participation and any negative repercussions of failure.

Thus, venture capitalists are the only ones who can really successfully provide the type of corporate governance that startups need.

2.3. Venture capital and entrepreneurship

While the entrepreneurship literature does not emphasize the role of venture capital, its insights suggest that venture capital can be quite important in the context of entrepreneurial challenges. The recent literature, as summarized by Holmes and Schmitz (1990), focuses on the importance of technological innovation and of matching up entrepreneurs with appropriate projects.

Opportunities for creating new products arise over time as a consequence of technological innovation and demographic change, while the ability to exploit these opportunities varies across the population. Not everyone is capable of starting a new business, and those who have started one are not necessarily capable of managing it competently. Even good business projects must be matched with an appropriate entrepreneur if they are to succeed. If the success of a project

248   *L.A. Jeng, P.C. Wells / Journal of Corporate Finance 6 (2000) 241–289*

hinges vitally on finding a suitable entrepreneur, venture capitalists can greatly aid the success of a project by providing a matching function. They can also assist the process by developing the manager's skills after she has been brought in, and by bringing in additional management talent as needed.

Furthermore, the literature on entrepreneurship finds that liquidity constraints are binding and, therefore, critical to entrepreneurs (Evans and Jovanovich, 1989). This underscores the importance of venture capital as a way to circumvent liquidity constraints.

3. Venture capital structure and functioning

Both the private equity and the venture capital sectors differ across countries. Their differences start with organizational form. In the US and UK, firms are organized as limited partnerships, while in France and Germany they have a different organizational structure with far more involvement of banks (Lerner, 1995a,b). Another difference in organizational form is the prevalence of so-called captive funds in Europe and their relative absence in the US. Funds are labeled captive if more than 80% of their financing derives from one source. In many instances, captive funds are subsidiaries of banks. In France, in 1995, captive funds accounted for 37.1% of new funds raised.

The management style of venture capitalists differs across countries as well. In Japan and Germany, venture capital firms are not as actively involved in managing their investments as in the US. Japanese and German venture capitalists have traditionally not held board representation, nor have they been involved in day-to-day management issues. Hurry et al. (1991) present evidence on the different degree of involvement of US and Japanese venture capital firms. They show that US firms tend to make fewer investments, but take larger equity stakes in each investment. This strategy confers an advantage over the Japanese one because it allows the venture capitalists to better focus on managing and understanding a few companies and gives them a greater incentive to monitor.

The composition of funding sources also differs dramatically by country. If we consider all private equity investing, the US private equity market received 38%[2] of its funds from pension funds in 1995. In Germany, by contrast, pension funds supplied only 8.6% of new funds raised and banks supplied 57.2% in that same year.[3]

Tables 2–4 indicate how levels of venture capital and private equity differ across time and across countries. In order to compare the order of magnitude of

---

[2] Represents percent of capital commited to independent private funds. Does not include SBIC, family groups or corporate affiliates. Venture Capital Yearbook, 1996.

[3] EVCA Yearbook.

L.A. Jeng, P.C. Wells / Journal of Corporate Finance 6 (2000) 241–289 249

Table 2
Venture capital investment as per mil of average GDP

Country	1986	1987	1988	1989	1990	1991	1992	1993	1994	1995	Average level (per mil)	Average growth (%)	CAGR (%)
Australia	NA	NA	NA	NA	NA	NA	0.364	0.358	1.198	1.336	0.814	82	54
Austria	0.014	0.027	0.011	0.058	0.044	0.025	0.006	0.004	0.002	0.007	0.020	60	−7
Belgium	1.207	1.056	0.282	0.444	0.370	0.612	0.737	0.414	0.327	0.628	0.608	8	−7
Canada	0.206	0.252	0.275	0.229	0.197	0.270	0.267	0.413	0.569	0.855	0.353	20	17
Denmark	0.201	0.243	0.211	0.123	0.111	0.168	0.072	0.134	0.170	0.132	0.156	5	−5
Finland	NA	NA	0.087	0.064	0.182	0.203	0.174	0.262	0.282	0.358	0.202	34	22
France	0.194	0.302	0.558	0.516	0.551	0.620	0.464	0.433	0.539	0.336	0.451	12	6
Germany	0.031	0.036	0.045	0.108	0.334	0.386	0.362	0.342	0.376	0.375	0.240	45	32
Ireland	0.425	0.876	0.655	0.416	0.795	0.892	0.584	0.377	0.629	0.557	0.620	15	3
Israel	NA	NA	NA	NA	NA	NA	NA	NA	NA	NA	NA	NA	NA
Italy	0.021	0.060	0.081	0.208	0.168	0.403	0.418	0.234	0.210	0.295	0.210	54	34
Japan	NA	NA	NA	NA	NA	NA	0.052	0.038	NA	0.216	0.102	−28	61
Netherlands	0.532	0.482	0.546	0.503	0.783	0.795	0.684	0.608	1.063	1.433	0.743	15	12
New Zealand	NA	NA	NA	NA	NA	NA	NA	0.016	0.041	0.517	0.191	658	463
Norway	NA	NA	0.126	0.011	0.520	0.465	0.242	0.420	0.689	1.337	0.476	645	40
Portugal	0.004	0.127	0.072	0.217	0.588	0.727	0.709	1.073	1.185	0.990	0.569	378	84
Spain	0.087	0.221	0.171	0.154	0.125	0.376	0.302	0.322	0.307	0.425	0.249	36	19
Sweden	0.313	0.250	0.131	0.163	0.202	0.079	0.055	0.148	0.524	0.158	0.202	27	−7
Switzerland	0.068	0.010	0.175	0.166	0.205	0.122	0.245	0.159	0.222	0.105	0.157	17	5
UK	0.793	1.057	1.080	1.224	1.076	0.883	0.816	0.726	0.100	1.033	0.969	5	3
US	0.556	0.867	0.434	0.408	0.308	0.177	0.366	0.349	0.457	0.638	0.456	12	2

Venture capital investment levels for 21 countries. Venture capital investment is defined as startup + seed + expansion investments. Data on venture capital is taken from the EVCA yearbooks, AVCA yearbooks, MacDonald and Associates, and Venture Economics. Average growth is the arithmetic annual growth rate over the time period considered. CAGR is the geometric annual growth rate over the time period considered.

Table 3
Early stage investment as per mil of average GDP

Country	1986	1987	1988	1989	1990	1991	1992	1993	1994	1995	Average level (per mil)	Average growth (%)	CAGR (%)
Australia	NA	NA	NA	NA	NA	NA	0.069	0.044	0.191	0.526	0.207	159	97
Austria	0.014	0.027	0.001	0.053	0.012	0.006	0.000	0.001	0.0001	0.002	0.012	1300	−19
Belgium	0.417	0.311	0.085	0.146	0.061	0.170	0.089	0.071	0.091	0.038	0.148	−0.4	−23
Canada	0.082	0.100	0.118	0.088	0.067	0.112	0.138	0.176	0.178	0.376	0.144	25	18
Denmark	0.041	0.037	0.050	0.089	0.057	0.051	0.009	0.033	0.036	0.031	0.043	25	−3
Finland	NA	NA	0.013	0.028	0.082	0.102	0.078	0.090	0.074	0.096	0.071	48	33
France	0.032	0.039	0.119	0.088	0.105	0.033	0.042	0.016	0.026	0.027	0.053	20	−2
Germany	0.007	0.012	0.012	0.035	0.027	0.031	0.036	0.039	0.060	0.063	0.032	39	28
Ireland	0.194	0.299	0.315	0.017	0.028	0.127	0.037	0.099	0.071	0.026	0.121	43	−20
Israel	NA	NA	NA	NA	NA	NA	NA	NA	NA	NA	NA	NA	NA
Italy	0.011	0.014	0.002	0.019	0.014	0.066	0.067	0.007	0.053	0.071	0.033	184	23
Japan	NA	NA	NA	NA	NA	NA	0.005	0.003	NA	0.047	0.018	−45	105
Netherlands	0.127	0.059	0.107	0.058	0.094	0.103	0.082	0.085	0.173	0.304	0.119	24	10
New Zealand	NA	NA	NA	NA	NA	NA	NA	0.000	0.019	0.062	0.027	237	237
Norway	NA	NA	0.011	0.006	0.067	0.027	0.023	0.000	0.153	0.061	0.055	176	28
Portugal	0.004	0.047	0.029	0.037	0.178	0.133	0.110	0.090	0.143	0.087	0.086	153	41
Spain	0.037	0.155	0.098	0.076	0.033	0.094	0.077	0.046	0.033	0.056	0.070	41	5
Sweden	0.034	0.080	0.012	0.041	0.024	0.008	0.006	0.012	0.012	0.043	0.027	57	3
Switzerland	0.050	0.036	0.040	0.073	0.072	0.014	0.002	0.018	0.035	0.004	0.034	70	−26
UK	0.194	0.191	0.254	0.218	0.160	0.086	0.070	0.066	0.082	0.042	0.136	−12	−16
US	0.058	0.055	0.068	0.070	0.045	0.021	0.074	0.062	0.102	0.191	0.075	36	14

Early stage investment levels for 21 countries. Early stage investment is defined as startup + seed investments. Data on venture capital is taken from the EVCA yearbooks, AVCA yearbooks, MacDonald and Associates, and Venture Economics. Average growth is the arithmetic annual growth rate over the time period considered. CAGR is the geometric annual growth rate over the time period considered.

L.A. Jeng, P.C. Wells / Journal of Corporate Finance 6 (2000) 241–289 251

Table 4
Private equity new funds raised as per mil of average GDP

Country	1986	1987	1988	1989	1990	1991	1992	1993	1994	1995	Average level (per mil)	Average growth (%)	CAGR (%)
Australia	NA	NA	NA	0.829	0.157	0.964	0.314	0.713	0.881	1.672	0.790	101	12
Austria	0.011	0.032	0.115	0.016	0.007	0.000	0.000	0.000	0.000	0.009	0.019	43	−2
Belgium	2.133	2.409	0.218	0.414	0.221	0.592	0.522	0.635	0.549	0.946	0.864	22	−9
Canada	0.483	0.835	0.840	0.384	0.235	0.501	0.621	1.195	1.520	2.349	0.896	32	19
Denmark	0.288	0.331	0.215	0.079	0.358	0.246	0.099	0.128	1.028	0.253	0.302	93	−1
Finland	NA	NA	0.484	0.316	0.230	0.109	0.042	0.145	0.526	0.641	0.312	50	4
France	0.168	0.758	0.697	1.754	1.079	1.273	0.907	0.855	1.077	0.799	0.937	49	19
Germany	0.036	0.238	0.114	0.178	0.543	0.642	0.636	0.152	0.215	0.148	0.290	80	17
Ireland	0.864	1.091	1.263	0.628	0.515	1.087	1.243	0.848	5.254	0.360	1.315	55	−9
Israel	NA	NA	NA	NA	NA	0.896	1.478	3.313	1.642	0.716	1.610	21	−5
Italy	0.204	0.129	0.268	0.260	0.224	0.256	0.526	0.421	0.450	0.419	0.316	17	8
Japan	NA	NA	NA	0.088	0.288	0.245	0.258	0.161	NA	0.400	0.240	45	29
Netherlands	1.080	0.412	1.063	0.721	0.380	0.475	0.395	0.551	1.063	1.025	0.717	17	−1
New Zealand	NA	NA	NA	NA	NA	NA	NA	0.340	0.694	0.231	0.422	19	−18
Norway	NA	NA	0.129	0.002	0.630	0.368	0.136	0.730	0.440	0.520	0.369	3658	22
Portugal	0.036	0.184	0.163	1.926	0.426	0.227	0.329	1.779	2.388	NA	0.924	206	54
Spain	0.000	0.489	0.239	0.175	0.409	0.374	0.470	0.575	0.187	0.450	0.337	21	−1
Sweden	0.592	0.598	0.135	0.180	0.991	0.613	1.855	0.864	1.633	3.101	1.056	78	20
Switzerland	0.033	0.451	0.109	0.198	0.566	0.119	0.258	0.371	0.284	0.240	0.263	167	25
UK	0.955	2.363	2.403	4.053	2.758	1.665	1.669	1.752	5.433	2.761	2.581	35	13
US	1.539	3.095	2.221	2.518	1.110	1.226	1.751	2.243	3.384	4.960	2.405	23	14

Private equity new funds raised for 21 countries. Private equity new funds raised includes funds raised for venture capital and buyouts. Data on venture capital is taken from the EVCA yearbooks, AVCA yearbooks, the GIZA Group, MacDonald and Associates, and Venture Economics. Average growth is the arithmetic annual growth rate over the time period considered. CAGR is the geometric annual growth rate over the time period considered.

private equity and venture capital funding across countries, we normalize our figures by average GDP for each country. Table 4 shows how, in relative terms in 1995, the US had the greatest amount of new fund flows into private equity. Averaged over the whole time period, however, the UK had slightly higher flows into private equity than the US.

The compound annual growth rate of new funds raised was also similar for both countries. This, however, masks some strong differences between the two. US private equity suffered a downswing which bottomed out in 1990, and then steadily rebounded over the next 5 years. UK private equity hit its trough only 1 year later, but then stagnated until 1994.

An even more interesting difference, from the perspective of this paper, concerns the difference in early stage investment patterns between countries. If we again look at the US and UK, we see that the UK suffered a steady, unabated decline in early stage investing that took place over the whole time period (see Table 3). As a per mil of GDP, early stage investing dropped from 0.19 to 0.04 in the UK from 1986 to 1995. In the US, by contrast, early stage investing followed closely the development of private equity, with a trough in the early 1990s and steady recovery since then.

The emphasis on early stage investing is strong and growing in some countries, such as Australia, Canada, the Netherlands, and the US. In other countries — Germany, Japan, and the UK, to name just a few — private equity is more involved in later stage financing. For example, in 1994, 36% of Germany's private equity[4] was invested in later stage investments. However, for the same time period, only 18% of US private equity[5] was similarly invested.

While we recognize that great differences exist in venture capital and private equity firms across countries, we limit our description of organizational structure to the case of the US limited partnership. Since our main interest lies with venture capital and not private equity, we find it advantageous to use the US as an example given the specialization in venture capital that prevails there.

Venture capital firms in the US are typically organized as limited partnerships with the venture capitalists serving as general partners and the investors serving as limited partners. It was not until the early 1980s that the limited partnership became the predominant form of venture capital funds in the US In 1980, only 40% of funds were limited partnerships, but by 1992, over 80% of venture capital funds were organized as such (Gompers and Lerner, 1996). The US venture capital industry exhibits a high degree of geographic concentration. Gompers and Lerner find that 25% of US venture capital firms were based in California over the 1972–1992 time period. A large portion of new capital committed comes from

---

[4] EVCA Yearbook.

[5] Includes LBOs, Acquisitions, Bridge Loans and Public Purchases. Source: Venture Capital Journal, July 1996.

L.A. Jeng, P.C. Wells / Journal of Corporate Finance 6 (2000) 241–289   253

pension funds, endowments, and insurance companies and banks. In 1995, they provided 38%, 22% and 18%, respectively, of new capital committed.

In general, a venture capital firm will manage several pools of capital. Each of these pools of capital, also referred to as funds, is structured as a separate limited partnership. Venture capital firms invest in a broad range of industries, not just high technology startups. A fund will invest in projects over the first 3 to 5 years of its existence. Investments and appreciation are paid out to the partners over the remainder of the fund's life.

We have already spoken about the importance of the monitoring that takes place between venture capitalists and entrepreneurs. The relationship between venture capitalist and entrepreneur is marked by the following monitoring and control arrangements:

- Monitoring frequency. Gompers (1995) shows how decreases in industry ratios of tangible assets to total assets, higher market to book ratios and greater R & D intensities lead to more frequent monitoring.
- Compensation schemes that are designed to provide the entrepreneur with the appropriate incentives. Equity-based compensation gives the entrepreneur the incentive to focus on growth.
- Active involvement of the venture capitalist with the company through board representation. Lerner (1995a,b) shows that venture capitalists' involvement as directors is more intense when the need for oversight is greater.
- Use of convertible securities. These give the venture capitalists the option of selling their stake back to the entrepreneur.

The need for monitoring also extends to the relationship between the investor and the venture capitalist. Just as the entrepreneur has an incentive to deviate from behavior that is optimal for the venture capitalist, the venture capitalist has an incentive to deviate from behavior that is optimal for the investor. Investors monitor venture capitalists in the following ways:

- The life of the venture capital fund is limited, which means that the venture capitalist cannot keep the money forever. The limited lifespan of venture capital funds also ensures that disagreements over when and how to distribute funds are minimized.
- Limited partners can withdraw from funding the partnership after the initial capital investment. In practice, limited partners rarely withdraw their funds from the partnership. They are more likely to withhold new funds from venture capitalists in future fundraising efforts.
- Venture capitalists are explicitly prohibited from self-dealing, i.e., receiving preferential investment terms different from those granted to the limited partner.

In the late 1980s the use of covenants became very popular. The average number of covenants used per contract grew from 4.4 to 7.9 between the two periods of 1978–1982 and 1988–1992, respectively (Gompers and Lerner, 1996). However, Gompers and Lerner (1996) find that restrictive covenants are only used in the most serious cases because they are very costly to negotiate. They also find that the use of covenants decreases during periods of high demand for venture funding, since the supply of venture capitalist services is rather limited. In this situation, the reduction of covenants is viewed as increased compensation for the venture capitalist.

4. Factors that affect venture capital

The previous section described how venture capitalists manage their investments. This section lays out the theoretical underpinnings of our empirical analysis, and explains what the driving forces are behind venture capital flows. We recognize that we have not included all factors that practitioners would deem important for venture capital. Specifically, we think that capital gains tax rates and the efficiency of bankruptcy procedures also impact venture capital. We encounter difficulties, however, in finding good measures for these variables to include in our empirical analysis. Thus, for instance, while we believe that capital gains taxes are important, using data on individual capital gains tax rates, we find no statistically significant impact on venture capital and, for this reason, we do not report the results in our regressions.

4.1. Initial public offerings

The main risk faced by investors and venture capitalists is the risk of not getting their money back. Thus, a viable exit mechanism is extremely important to the development of a venture capital industry. Furthermore, an exit mechanism is essential to the entrepreneur for two reasons. First, it provides a financial incentive for equity-compensated managers to expend effort. Second, it gives the managers a call option on control of the firm, since venture capitalists relinquish control at the time of the IPO (Black and Gilson, 1998).

We focus on IPOs as an exit mechanism for the following reasons. While there are many mechanisms to liquidate a fund, the literature shows that the most attractive option is through an IPO. A study conducted by Venture Economics (1988) finds that US$1.00 invested in a firm that eventually goes public yields a 195% average return (or an average cash return of US$1.95 over the original investment) for a 4.2-year average holding period. The same investment in an acquired firm only provides an average return of 40% (or a cash return of only 40 cents) over a 3.7-year average holding period. Also, if regaining control is important to the entrepreneur, IPOs are clearly the best choice, given that the other option, trade sales, frequently entails loss of control. Trade sales are sales of a

Table 5
Percentage of divestments that are trade sales

Country	1991 (%)	1992 (%)	1993 (%)	1994 (%)	1995 (%)	Mean (%)
Austria	22	50	100	NA	24	49
Belgium	52	NA	57	51	32	48
Denmark	24	7	70	62	85	50
Finland	67	37	0	10	48	32
France	41	56	57	33	48	47
Germany	NA	NA	NA	NA	NA	NA
Ireland	82	76	19	13	64	51
Italy	86	89	57	21	52	61
Netherlands	48	44	22	24	44	36
Norway	15	49	18	40	15	27
Portugal	NA	100	57	90	56	76
Spain	72	62	20	31	24	42
Sweden	13	40	78	43	25	40
Switzerland	40	4	24	33	47	30
UK	24	22	41	30	36	30

Trade sales and divestments are measured in local currency terms. Divestments include all private equity. The number reported represents trade sales as a percentage of divestments. The data are taken from the EVCA yearbooks.

startup company to a larger company (also referred to as a strategic buyer). Table 5 shows the importance of trade sales in Europe. The percentage of divestments

Table 6
Percentage of divestments that are public offerings

Country	1991 (%)	1992 (%)	1993 (%)	1994 (%)	1995 (%)	Mean (%)
Austria	0	0	0	NA	0	0
Belgium	2	NA	0	20	39	15
Denmark	24	55	0	0	0	16
Finland	0	0	0	0	1	0.2
France	10	2	12	21	8	11
Germany	NA	NA	NA	NA	NA	NA
Ireland	0	0	0	0	0	0
Italy	5	0	3	0	12	4
Netherlands	8	5	20	12	6	10
Norway	1	17	37	6	31	18
Portugal	0	0	0	0	NA	0
Spain	2	1	0	1	0	1
Sweden	1	0	16	0	52	14
Switzerland	0	2	8	15	0	5
UK	13	34	36	47	45	35

Public offerings and divestments are measured in local currency terms. Divestments include all private equity. The number reported represents public offerings as a percentage of divestments. The data are taken from the EVCA yearbooks.

accounted for by trade sales ranges from 30% in the UK to 76% in Portugal over the whole time period considered (Table 6).

To account for the importance of exit mechanisms, we include both current and lagged IPOs in our statistical analysis. We do not have an explicit measure of trade sales. Increased volume of IPOs should have a positive effect on both the demand and supply of venture capital funds. On the demand side, the existence of an exit mechanism gives entrepreneurs an additional incentive to start a company. On the supply side, the effect is essentially the same; large investors are more willing to supply funds to venture capital firms if they feel that they can later recoup their investment.

4.2. Labor market rigidities

Labor market rigidities present an obstacle to venture capital growth. Sahlman (1990) discusses how labor market rigidities form a large barrier to the success of venture capital investing in countries such as Germany and Japan. In Japan, for instance, leaving a company is not only considered dishonorable, but departing individuals also lose valuable benefits of seniority. Also, should the individual fail in his new venture, it would be difficult for him to find new employment, which would lead to a further loss of social standing. Labor market rigidities are frequently cited as one important reason why venture capital is not more prevalent in Europe and Asia.[6]

Labor market rigidity should impact the demand for venture capital funds negatively (i.e., the higher labor market rigidity, the less demand for venture capital funds we would expect). Strict labor laws make hiring employees difficult for companies, because they deprive the company of the flexibility to let people go later on, should this become necessary. In addition, large benefits payments, which typically accompany more rigid labor markets, make it more expensive to hire in the first place.

We use two measures of labor market rigidity. One reflects rigidity in the market for skilled labor, the other reflects rigidity in the overall labor market.

4.3. Financial reporting standards

Small startup firms are risky prospects. If the market does not have good information on these companies, investors will demand a high risk premium, resulting in more expensive funding for these companies. This cost of asymmetric information can be reduced if the country in which the company operates has strict accounting standards. With good accounting regulation, venture capitalists need to spend less time gathering information to monitor their investments.

---

[6] The Economist (1997), "Venture Capitalists: A Really Big Adventure."

L.A. Jeng, P.C. Wells / Journal of Corporate Finance 6 (2000) 241–289 257

We include an independent variable that measures the level of accounting standards in the various countries for public firms. Since we are dealing with private firms in our sample, we use this variable as a proxy for reporting standards of private firms. On the supply side, this variable should have a positive effect on the supply of venture capital funds.

4.4. Private pension funds

Raising money from pension funds provides numerous advantages to the venture capitalist. Venture capitalists can quickly raise a large amount of investment capital solely by approaching a few large pension funds. Furthermore, with only a few investors, a venture capital firm can economize on the amount of time expended on keeping its investors apprised of its activities. In addition, with changes in legislation and perceived high rates of return, many pension funds became eager to lend to venture capitalists. For all these reasons, private pension funds are an important source of venture capital funds in the US. In 1994, pension funds provided 46% of venture capital money in the United States (Black and Gilson, 1998).

On the other hand, raising money from pension funds may present a few disadvantages. For instance, in the US, there may be regulatory compliance issues with ERISA. In addition, managers of pension funds are sophisticated investors who may require additional disclosure. However, these issues do not present a huge barrier for venture capitalists to raise money, especially for venture capitalists with good reputations.

We have included private pension fund data as an independent variable in our regressions. Private pension funds should have a positive effect on the supply of new funds to venture capital firms. There is no reason to believe that private pension funds have any effect on demand for venture capital funds.

4.5. Macroeconomic variables

The state of the country's economy will also have an effect on venture capital. Acs and Audretsch (1994) suggest that macroeconomic fluctuations influence startup activity in general. Macroeconomic expansions are found to lead to an increase in the number of startups. Since an increase in startup activity increases demand for venture capital funds, we expect a positive relationship between macroeconomic expansion and venture capital investing. We use GDP growth to measure macroeconomic fluctuations in our analysis and expect this variable to be positively correlated with venture capital investment.

We also include growth in market capitalization as an explanatory factor for venture capital investing. We believe that increases in market capitalization create a more favorable environment for investors in general. Therefore, increases in market capitalization should be met by greater supply of funds to venture capital investments.

258   *L.A. Jeng, P.C. Wells / Journal of Corporate Finance 6 (2000) 241–289*

4.6. Government programs

Many governments have begun to recognize the benefits of venture capital and have made efforts to fund startup businesses. Lerner (1997) provides preliminary evidence that government funded programs can yield favorable benefits. However, O'Shea (1996) points out that there may also be disadvantages to these efforts. For instance, government spending on venture capital may hinder the development of a private venture capital sector. Furthermore, many are sceptical about the government's ability to appropriately target healthy ventures. In addition to looking at government funding in our statistical analysis, we also discuss on a more descriptive level the importance of various government programs in Section 8.1.

5. Data

This paper empirically examines 21 countries: Austria, Australia, Belgium, Canada, Denmark, Finland, France, Germany, Ireland, Israel, Italy, Japan, the Netherlands, New Zealand, Norway, Portugal, Spain, Sweden, Switzerland, the United Kingdom and the United States. These countries are selected based on availability of information.

We use panel data covering the years 1986–1995. Data on venture capital investments, early stage investments, and new funds raised are obtained from The European Venture Capital Journal, Asian Venture Capital Journal, The GIZA Group for Israel figures, Macdonald's and Associates for Canada figures and Venture Economics for US figures.

Venture capital investments refer to the total amount disbursed by venture capitalists for seed, startup and expansion stage investments. Early stage investments only include funds used for seed and startup investments. Our New Funds Raised number is dictated by data availability. Ideally, we would look at new funds raised for venture capital. However, the closest we can come to that figure is new funds raised for private equity. New Funds Raised is defined as total funds raised for all private equity investing and includes committed, but not yet paid, capital. Typically, the capital promised by investors to venture capitalists is not immediately paid to the venture capitalists. Most agreements call for a 25–33% cash commitment up-front and stipulate when addition cash is to be phased in at future dates (Sahlman, 1990). The total amount of investment promised to the venture capitalists is referred to as committed capital, even though only approximately one third is initially paid in.

Country GDP data in local currency are provided by the IMF's International Financial Statistics Yearbook. Market capitalization data (annual end of period figures) in billions of US dollars are provided by the IMF's Emerging Markets Fact Book. Total Private Pension fund figures in US Dollars are provided by

L.A. Jeng, P.C. Wells / Journal of Corporate Finance 6 (2000) 241–289   259

InterSec Research. Exchange rates (annual end of period rates) are obtained from the IMF's International Financial Statistics and are expressed as national currency unit per SDR.

IPO data are available for 1986–1995 for Canada, Japan and the US, 1989–1995 for the UK, and 1991–1995 for Australia, other European Countries and New Zealand. They are provided by the Federation Internationale des Bourses de Valeurs, Securities Data, Nomura Securities and the Toronto Stock Exchange. These figures exclude privatizations, real estate trusts, utilities and closed-end funds.

Ratings on accounting standards are measured by an index provided by International Accounting and Auditing Trends, Center for International Financial Analysis and Research. This index is created by examining and rating companies' 1990 annual reports on their inclusion or omission of 90 accounting items. A minimum of three companies in each country were studied.

We include two measures of labor market rigidity. Our first measure gauges the amount of flexibility in a country's skilled labor market, by measuring the average job tenure of individuals who have completed some or all tertiary education. This statistic best represents the class of individuals who are likely to start new enterprises. For the US, this figure is 7.4 years while for Germany and Japan it is 10.5 and 9.5 years, respectively. Our second measure refers more generally to the entire labor market. It measures the percent of the labor force that has job tenure greater than 10 years. This statistic attempts to capture the flexibility of all individuals to leave their current position to join a startup. While there exist better measures of labor turnover,[7] none offers as broad a cross-section as these two statistics. Data for these two measures are provided by the OECD's 1997 Employment Outlook, Chapter 5 (Draft) and 1994 Employment Outlook, respectively.

We also use variables from the law and finance literature (La Porta et al.) to measure the efficiency of financial markets. The categorization of legal systems as reported by La Porta et al. (1996) divides countries into four legal traditions: English, French, German, and Scandinavian. The English legal tradition is also referred to as the common law tradition, while the other legal traditions can be grouped together as the civil law traditions. The different legal traditions differ by the extent to which shareholder and creditor rights are protected in the various countries. The common law tradition provides the best legal protections, while the French tradition is the worst in this respect.

The variables Rule of Law, Anti-director Rights, and One Share One Vote all describe the amount of protection that shareholders can expect in a given country.

---

[7] The Employment Outlook, OECD publishes labor turnover rates which measure the movements of individuals into jobs (hirings) and out of jobs (separations) over a particular period. In addition, it mentions that labor tenure is correlated with labor turnover.

Table 7
Variable descriptions

Variable	Description	Sources
Early Stage Investments	Early stage investments (Seed and Startup, both government and private sector funded) divided by average GDP	European Venture Capital Journal, Asian Venture Capital Journal, Macdonald's and Associates for Canadian data and Venture Economics for US data
Early Stage Investments w/o government funds	Estimated Early Stage Investments, funded by private sector sources, divided by average GDP	European Venture Capital Journal, Asian Venture Capital Journal, Macdonald's and Associates for Canadian data and Venture Economics for US data
New Funds Raised	Annual New Funds raised (both government and private sector funded) domestically divided by average GDP. Includes committed but not yet paid capital	European Venture Capital Journal, Asian Venture Capital Journal, Macdonald's and Associates for Canadian data and Venture Economics for US data
New Funds Raised w/o government funds	Annual New Funds raised domestically divided by average GDP. Excludes Government funds. Includes committed but not yet paid capital	European Venture Capital Journal, Asian Venture Capital Journal, Macdonald's and Associates for Canadian data and Venture Economics for US data
Venture Capital Funds	Annual Expansion and Early Stage Investments (both government and private sector funded) divided by average GDP	European Venture Capital Journal, Asian Venture Capital Journal, Macdonald's and Associates for Canadian data and Venture Economics for US data
Venture Capital Funds w/o government funds	Estimated Expansion and Early Stage Investments, funded by private sector sources, divided by GDP	European Venture Capital Journal, Asian Venture Capital Journal, Macdonald's and Associates for Canadian data and Venture Economics for US data
IPOs	Total Market Value of IPOS divided by average GDP	FIBV, Nomura Securities Securities Data, Toronto Stock Exchange
Labor Market Rigidity (educated)	Average tenure of Employees with some or completed tertiary education	OECD's Draft 1996 Economic Outlook Chapter 5
Labor Market Rigidity (general)	Percent of labor force with a tenure greater than 10 years	OECD's 1993 Economic Outlook
Accounting Standards	Ratings on Accounting Standards	International Accounting and Auditing Trends, Center for International Financial Analysis and Research
Private Pension Growth	Percentage change in Private Pension Fund Levels	InterSec Research
Private Pension Levels	Private Pension Fund Levels divided by GDP	InterSec Research
Market Capitalization Growth	Percentage change in Market Capitalization	Emerging Market's Fact Book, International Monetary Fund

L.A. Jeng, P.C. Wells / Journal of Corporate Finance 6 (2000) 241–289   261

Table 7 (*continued*)

Variable	Description	Sources
GDP Growth	Percentage change in GDP	International Financial Statistics, International Monetary Fund 1995

They are taken from La Porta et al. (1996). Rule of Law reflects the law and order tradition in a country, as measured by the International Country Risk Guide. The scale ranges from 0 to 10, with lower scores for a weaker law and order tradition. Anti-director Rights is an index aggregating shareholder rights. This index is formed by adding one for each of the following conditions: (1) when the country allows shareholders to mail their proxy vote; (2) when shareholders are not required to deposit their shares prior to the General Shareholders' meeting; (3) when cumulative voting is allowed; (4) when an oppressed minorities mechanism is in place; or (5) when the minimum percentage of share capital that entitles a shareholder to call for an Extraordinary Shareholders' Meeting is less than or equal to 10%. The index ranges from 0 to 5. One Share One Vote equals one if the company law or the commercial code of the country requires that ordinary shares carry one vote per share. Otherwise it is zero.

Table 7 provides a summary of the variables used in this paper and their sources.

6. Methodology

We use a linear specification for the supply and demand schedules of venture capital funds. In our regression analysis, we estimate the coefficients of the equilibrium specification.

6.1. Supply and demand structural equations

As explained in Section 4, we believe the following factors (in addition to return percentage) influence the supply of venture capital: IPOs, accounting standards, GDP growth, and market capitalization growth. The following simple equation describes the supply of venture funds in the economy:

$$\text{Venture capital funds supplied}_{it}$$
$$= \alpha_0 + \alpha_1 \text{ Return percentage}_{it} + \alpha_2 \text{ IPOs}_{it} + \alpha_3 \text{ Accounting standards}_i$$
$$+ \alpha_4 \text{ GDP percentage growth}_{it}$$
$$+ \alpha_5 \text{Market capitalization percentage growth}_{it}$$

Section 4 also describes the variables that we believe are important for demand for venture capital: IPOs, accounting standards, labor market rigidities, GDP growth and market capitalization growth. A simple equation for the demand side of venture capital is as follows:

Venture capital funds demanded$_{it}$

$$= \beta_0 + \beta_1 \text{ Return percentage}_{it} + \beta_2 \text{ IPOs}_{it} + \beta_3 \text{ Accounting standards}_i$$

$$+ \beta_4 \text{ Labor market rigidities}_i + \beta_5 \text{ GDP percentage growth}_{it}$$

$$+ \beta_6 \text{ Market capitalization percentage growth}_{it}$$

To obtain the equilibrium, we solve the supply equation for return percentage, and substitute this expression into the demand equation. Then, taking into account the equality in equilibrium of supply and demand, we solve for the equilibrium quantity. Equilibrium Condition:

Venture capital funds$_{it}$

$$= \pi_0 + \pi_1 \text{ IPOs}_{it} + \pi_2 \text{ Accounting standards}_i$$

$$+ \pi_3 \text{ Labor market rigidities}_i + \pi_4 \text{ GDP percentage growth}_{it}$$

$$+ \pi_5 \text{ Market capitalization growth}_{it}$$

where, in equilibrium, Venture capital funds supplied$_{it}$ = Venture capital funds demanded$_{it}$ = Venture capital funds$_{it}$.

The equilibrium for new funds raised is analogous. The only difference is that the supply of new funds is also affected by private pension funds. Our regression analysis considers two different forms of the equilibrium equation: the cross-sectional form and the within form.

6.2. Between regression (cross-section regression)

The between regression captures the difference in venture capital investments between countries as a result of differences in characteristics across countries.

$$\overline{\text{Venture capital funds}_i}$$

$$= \pi_0 + \pi_1 \overline{\text{IPOs}_i} + \pi_2 \text{ Accounting standards}_i$$

$$+ \pi_3 \text{ Labor market rigidities}_i + \pi_4 \overline{\text{GDP percentage growth rate}_i}$$

$$+ \pi_5 \overline{\text{Market capitalization percentage growth rate}_i}$$

where

$$\overline{\text{Venture capital funds}_i} = \text{Average of venture capital funds over time}$$

and likewise for other variables.

L.A. Jeng, P.C. Wells / *Journal of Corporate Finance 6 (2000) 241–289* 263

Table 8
Venture capital investments, between regressions

Independent variables	Dependent variables					
	(1) Venture capital w/o gov't funds	(2) Venture capital w/o gov't funds	(3) Venture capital w/o gov't funds	(4) Venture capital	(5) Venture capital	(6) Venture capital
IPOs	0.0953 (2.934)[a]	0.0718 (2.067)[b]	0.0976 (3.986)[a]	0.0901 (2.180)[b]	0.05814 (1.382)	0.0899 (2.851)[a]
Accounting Standards	−0.00002 (−1.723)[c]	−0.000005 (−0.341)	−0.00002 (−2.514)[a]	−0.00002 (−1.482)[d]	0.000006 (0.349)	−0.00002 (−2.039)[b]
Labor Market Rigidity (educated)	−0.00003 (−0.612)		−0.00003 (−0.634)	−0.00002 (−0.270)		−0.00002 (−0.296)
Labor Market Rigidity (general)		−0.00001 (−0.969)			−0.00001 (−0.580)	
Market capitalization growth	−0.0002 (−0.294)	−0.0004 (−0.537)	−0.00018 (−0.320)	−0.00013 (−0.163)	−0.00007 (−0.081)	−0.0001 (−0.171)
GDP growth	0.0005 (0.117)	0.0007 (0.176)		−0.00005 (−0.010)	0.0019 (0.393)	
Constant	0.0014 (1.603)[c]	0.0010 (0.769)	0.0015 (1.984)[b]	0.0015 (1.297)	0.00015 (0.097)	0.0015 (1.545)[c]
R^2	0.6502	0.7119	0.6497	0.4924	0.6004	0.4923

Between regression of 15 countries. The dependent variables are venture capital (i.e., early stage and expansion) investments with and without government funds, divided by average GDP. The independent variables are: (1) IPOs divided by average GDP; (2) Accounting Standards; (3) Labor Market Rigidity (educated); (4) Labor Market Rigidity (general); (5) Percentage change in Market capitalization; (6) Percentage change in GDP. T-statistics for coefficients in parentheses.

[a] Significant at 1% level.
[b] Significant at 10% level.
[c] Significant at 15% level.
[d] Significant at 20% level.

Table 9

(A) Venture capital investments, between regressions (1993–1995)[1]

Independent variables	Dependent variables			
	(1) Venture capital w/o gov't funds 1993–1995	(2) Venture capital w/o gov't funds 1994–1995	(3) Venture capital 1993–1995	(4) Venture capital 1994–1995
IPOs	0.1043 (5.070)[a]	0.0814 (4.925)[a]	0.0929 (3.731)[a]	0.0701 (3.693)[a]
Accounting Standards	−0.00003 (−4.566)[a]	−0.00002 (−3.215)[a]	−0.00003 (−3.416)[a]	−0.00002 (−2.263)[a]
Labor Market Rigidity (educated)	−0.00005 (−1.171)	−0.00004 (−0.846)	−0.00005 (−0.916)	−0.00002 (−0.320)
Market capitalization growth	0.00134 (2.857)[a]	0.0021 (2.723)[a]	0.0015 (2.692)[a]	0.0026 (2.875)[a]
GDP Growth	−0.0071 (−1.352)	−0.0096 (−1.851)[b]	−0.0069 (−1.089)	−0.0111 (−1.858)[b]
Constant	0.0025 (3.543)[a]	0.0024 (3.161)[a]	0.0024 (2.741)[a]	0.0020 (2.322)[a]
R^2	0.8102	0.8447	0.7161	0.7885

L.A. Jeng, P.C. Wells / Journal of Corporate Finance 6 (2000) 241–289

265

(B) Venture capital investments, between regressions[2]

Independent variables	Dependent variables					
	(1) Venture capital w/o gov't funds	(2) Venture capital w/o gov't funds	(3) Venture capital w/o gov't funds	(4) Venture capital	(5) Venture capital	(6) Venture capital
GDP Growth	0.0025 (0.685)	0.0033 (0.634)	0.0030 (0.785)	0.0028 (0.700)	0.0037(0.657)	0.0030 (0.707)
Rule of Law	0.0000 (−0.106)	0.0000 (0.020)	0.0000 (−0.002)	0.0000 (0.251)	0.0000 (0.324)	0.0000 (0.277)
One Share One Vote		0.0001 (0.221)	0.0001 (0.785)		0.0001 (0.239)	0.0000(0.316)
Anti-director rights			0.0001(0.292)	0.0000 (0.018)	0.0000 (0.051)	0.0001 (0.269)
French origin	−0.0001 (−0.622)	−0.0001 (−0.558)	−0.0003 (−0.953)	−0.0004[b] (−1.895)	−0.0004[c] (−1.697)	−0.0003 (−1.044)
German origin	−0.0004[b] (−2.181)	−0.0005[b] (−1.908)	−0.0002 (−0.845)	−0.0003[d] (−1.435)	−0.0003 (−1.258)	−0.0003 (−0.859)
Scandinavian origin	−0.0004[c] (−1.762)	−0.0004[c] (−1.576)				
Constant	0.0006 (0.505)	0.0004 (0.273)	0.0001 (0.107)	0.0002 (0.138)	0.0000 (−0.025)	0.0000 (−0.020)
R^2	0.52	0.53	0.56	0.51	0.51	0.52

[a]Significant at 1% level.
[b]Significant at 10% level.
[c]Significant at 15% level.
[d]Significant at 20% level.
[1]Between regression of 15 countries for 1993 to 1995 time span. The dependent variables are venture capital (i.e., early stage and expansion) investments with and without government funds, divided by average GDP. The independent variables are: (1) IPOs divided by average GDP; (2) Accounting Standards; (3) Labor Market Rigidity (educated); (4) Percentage change in Market capitalization; (5) Percentage change in GDP. T-statistics for coefficients in parentheses.
[2]Between regression of 15 countries. The dependent variables are venture capital (i.e., early stage and expansion) investments with and without government funds, divided by average GDP. The independent variables are (1) GDP growth; (2) Rule of Law; (3) One Share One Vote; (4) Anti-director Rights; (5) French legal origin; (6) German legal origin; (7) Scandinavian legal origin. T-statistics for coefficients in parentheses.

The dependent variables used in the between regressions are: new funds committed, venture capital investment (seed, startup and expansion stage investments) and early stage investment (seed and startup investments). Each variable is normalized by average GDP. Early stage investments, venture capital investments, and new funds raised all include government funds. However, we believe that government funding is driven by considerations different from the ones driving private sector funding. Therefore, we also consider the three dependent variables without public source funds.

6.3. Within regression (fixed effects regression)

The within regression captures the difference in venture capital funds due to changes over time of the independent variables.

$$\text{Venture capital funds}_{it} - \overline{\text{Venture capital funds}_i}$$

$$= \pi_0 + \pi_1 \left(\text{IPOs}_{it} - \overline{\text{IPOs}_i} \right)$$

$$+ \pi_2 \left(\text{GDP percentage growth rate}_{it} - \overline{\text{GDP percentage growth rate}_i} \right)$$

$$+ \pi_3 \left(\text{Market capitalization percentage growth rate}_{it} \right.$$

$$\left. - \overline{\text{Market capitalization percentage growth rate}_i} \right)$$

where, $\overline{\text{Venture capital funds}_i}$ = average of Venture capital funds over time and similarly for other variables.

The dependent variables examined are the same ones that we use in the between regressions. We also consider lags of GDP and market capitalization growth. However, these independent variables are not significant and the results do not change. For this reason, we do not report these regressions.

7. Results

Tables 8–11 report the results from the between regressions. Tables 12–14 contain results from the within regressions.

7.1. Between regression results

Table 8 reports results from the between regression of venture capital investments on IPOs, accounting standards, labor market rigidities, market capitalization and GDP growth. The explanatory power of all the regressions is high, with R^2s ranging from 0.49 to 0.71. The coefficient on IPOs is positive and statistically significant for virtually all specifications. This lends support to the hypothesis advanced in Section 4 that high levels of IPOs in a country will lead to more venture capital.

L.A. Jeng, P.C. Wells / Journal of Corporate Finance 6 (2000) 241–289 267

Table 10
Early stage investments, between regressions

Independent variables	Dependent variables					
	(1) Early stage investments w/o gov't funds	(2) Early stage investments w/o gov't funds	(3) Early stage investments w/o gov't funds	(4) Early stage investments	(5) Early stage investments	(6) Early stage investments
IPOs	0.0044 (0.652)	−0.0007 (−0.117)	0.0073 (1.395)[d]	0.0024 (0.289)	−0.0040 (−0.579)	0.0049 (0.761)
Accounting Standards	−0.000001 (−0.582)	9.3×10^{-9} (−0.004)	−0.000002 (−1.421)[d]	−0.000001 (−0.409)	−0.000003 (0.985)	−0.000002 (−1.001)
Labor Market Rigidity (educated)	−0.00002 (−1.469)[d]		−0.00001 (−1.367)	−0.00001 (−0.981)		−0.00001 (−0.921)
Labor Market Rigidity (general)		−0.000006 (−2.625)[a]			−0.000006 (−2.016)[b]	
Market capitalization growth	−0.00003 (−0.233)	−0.0002 (−1.365)	−0.00004 (−0.297)	0.00002 (0.099)	−0.00007 (−0.493)	−0.00009 (0.060)
GDP growth	0.0006 (0.704)	0.00037 (0.509)		0.0005 (0.504)	0.0005 (0.681)	
Constant	0.00024 (1.269)	0.00029 (1.275)	0.0003 (1.867)[b]	0.0002 (0.939)	0.00008 (0.315)	0.0003 (1.387)[d]
R^2	0.3672	0.6760	0.3323	0.1740	0.6152	0.1507

Between regression of 15 countries. The dependent variables are early stage (i.e seed and startup) investments with and without government funds, divided by average GDP. The independent variables are (1) IPOs divided by average GDP; (2) Accounting Standards; (3) Labor Market Rigidity (educated); (4) Labor Market Rigidity (general); (5) Percentage change in Market capitalization; (6) Percentage change in GDP. T-statistics for coefficients in parentheses.

[a] Significant at 1% level.
[b] Significant at 10% level.
[d] Significant at 20% level.

Table 11

(A) Private equity new funds raised, between regressions[1]

Independent variables	Dependent variables					
	(1) Private equity new funds raised w/o gov't funds	(2) Private equity new funds raised w/o gov't funds	(3) Private equity new funds raised w/o gov't funds	(4) Private equity new funds raised	(5) Private equity new funds raised	(6) Private equity new funds raised
IPOs	0.2113 (2.125)[b]	0.2429 (2.219)[b]	0.2366 (2.856)[a]	0.1928 (1.940)[b]	0.2368 (2.237)[b]	0.2143 (2.605)[a]
Accounting Standards	0.00002 (0.558)	0.000002 (0.029)	0.00001 (0.368)	0.00003 (0.961)	0.000009 (0.121)	0.00003 (0.899)
Labor Market Rigidity (educated)	−0.00013 (−1.066)		−0.00011 (−1.024)	−0.0001 (−0.906)		−0.0001 (−0.875)
Labor Market Rigidity (general)		−0.00004 (−0.819)			−0.0004 (−0.779)	
Private Pension Fund growth	0.00075 (0.343)	−0.0003 (−0.191)	0.0003 (0.166)	0.0003 (0.131)	−0.0004 (−0.267)	−0.00008 (−0.043)
Market capitalization growth	−0.00041 (−0.346)	−0.0010 (−0.391)	−0.0005 (−0.467)	−0.0001 (−0.097)	−0.0008 (−0.336)	−0.0002 (−0.187)
GDP growth	0.0071 (0.533)	0.0056 (0.393)		0.0060 (0.455)	0.0068 (0.497)	
Constant	−0.00015 (−0.051)	0.0013 (0.196)	0.0006 (0.276)	−0.0011 (−0.376)	0.0007 (0.109)	−0.0004 (−0.175)
R^2	0.8332	0.8552	0.8253	0.8381	0.8639	0.8325

L.A. Jeng, P.C. Wells / Journal of Corporate Finance 6 (2000) 241–289 269

(B) Private equity new funds raised, between regressions[2]

Independent variables	Dependent variables			
	(1) Private equity new funds raised w/o gov't funds	(2) Private equity new funds raised w/o gov't funds	(4) Private equity new funds raised	(5) Private equity new funds raised
IPOs	0.1409 (0.570)	0.2654 (1.974)c	0.1580 (0.636)	0.2619 (2.033)c
Accounting Standards	0.00002 (0.223)	0.000002 (0.023)	0.00002 (0.263)	0.000009 (0.106)
Labor Market Rigidity (educated)	−0.0001 (−0.586)		−0.0001 (−0.598)	
Labor Market Rigidity (general)		−0.00005 (−0.838)		−0.00005 (−0.849)
Private Pension Fund growth	0.0024 (0.468)	−0.0006 (−0.327)	0.0017 (0.327)	−0.0007 (−0.419)
Private Pension Fund levels	0.0010 (0.379)	−0.0007 (−0.414)	0.0006 (0.246)	−0.0008 (−0.482)
Market capitalization growth	−0.0008 (−0.333)	−0.0010 (−0.376)	−0.0006 (−0.262)	−0.0009 (−0.335)
GDP growth	0.0132 (0.581)	0.0009 (0.044)	0.0111 (0.487)	0.0016 (0.084)
Constant	−0.0007 (−0.108)	0.0022 (0.287)	−0.0007 (−0.103)	0.0017 (0.233)
R^2	0.8365	0.8630	0.8331	0.8737

In addition to the explanation we present above, one could offer another explanation for why the coefficient on IPOs is positive. This explanation involves reverse causality: Since venture capital investments frequently end up as IPOs, a higher level of such investments will lead to a higher level of IPOs down the road. Thus, our coefficient would be positive not because more IPOs lead to more venture capital, but because higher levels of venture capital eventually show up as greater amounts of IPOs.

To test for this reverse causality story, we examine several subpanels of our original panel, where the subpanels cover shorter time periods. The time periods are chosen such that investment projects started during the period will not have had enough time to progress to the IPO stage. The time periods are 1992–1995 and 1993–1995, and the results are contained in Table 9A. The results allow us to reject the reverse causality story, as the coefficient on IPOs remains positive and significant.

Another way to test the reverse causality explanation is to look at the factors underlying IPOs, which are not dependent on venture capital. La Porta et al. (1996) analyze the legal determinants of IPO finance as part of their study into the legal determinants of external finance. They find that Rule of Law has a large positive effect on the number of IPOs. Furthermore, a higher degree of Anti-director Rights also leads to more IPOs. Even when they correct for specific differences in shareholder rights, they find that civil law countries (the German and French origin ones in particular) still have a significant negative impact on the amount of IPOs in a country.

By regressing venture capital investments on shareholder rights and legal origin dummies in Table 9B, we can show to what extent these investments are dependent on the variables underlying IPOs. Rule of Law and Anti-director Rights are not significant in this regression. The civil law variables, however, are. The

---

Notes to Table 11:

[1] Between regression of 13 countries. The dependent variables are new funds raised for private equity (i.e., venture capital and buyouts) with and without government funds, divided by average GDP. The independent variables are: (1) IPOs divided by average GDP; (2) Accounting Standard Regulation; (3) Labor Market Rigidity (educated); (4) Labor Market Rigidity (general); (5) Percentage change in Private Pension Funds; (6) Percentage change in Market capitalization; (7) Percentage change in GDP. *T*-statistics for coefficients in parentheses.

[2] Between regression of 13 countries. The dependent variable are new funds raised for private equity (i.e., venture capital and buyouts) with and without government funds divided by average GDP. The independent variables are (1) IPOs divided by average GDP; (2) Accounting Standard Regulation; (3) Labor Market Rigidity (educated); (4) Labor Market Rigidity (general); (5) Percentage change in Private Pension Funds; (6) Private Pension Fund levels, (7) Percentage change in Market capitalization;(8) Percentage change in GDP. *T*-statistics for coefficients in parentheses.

[a] Significant at 1% level.

[b] Significant at 10% level.

[c] Significant at 15% level.

L.A. Jeng, P.C. Wells / Journal of Corporate Finance 6 (2000) 241–289 271

Table 12
Venture capital investments, within regressions

Independent variables	Dependent variables			
	(1) Venture capital w/o gov't funds	(2) Venture capital w/o gov't funds	(3) Venture capital	(4) Venture capital
IPOs	0.0257 (3.094)[a]	0.0148 (2.100)[a]	0.0260 (2.882)[a]	0.0164 (2.207)[a]
Lagged IPOs	0.0076 (0.982)		0.0106 (1.269)	
Market capitalization growth	−0.00003 (−0.390)	−0.000007 (−0.097)	−0.00003 (−0.327)	0.000003 (0.037)
GDP growth	−0.0005 (−0.514)	−0.0000005 (−0.001)	0.0003(0.243)	0.00073 (0.966)
Constant	0.0003 (5.289)[a]	0.0003 (7.179)[a]	0.0003 (5.084)[a]	0.0004 (7.196)[a]
R^2	0.1632	0.0586	0.1679	0.0733

Within regression of 17 countries. The dependent variables are venture capital (i.e., early stage and expansion) investments with and without government funds, divided by average GDP. The independent variables are: (1) IPOs divided by average GDP; (2) Lagged IPOs; (3) Percentage change in Market capitalization; (4) Percentage change in GDP. *T*-statistics for coefficients in parentheses.
[a]Significant at 1% level.

272   *L.A. Jeng, P.C. Wells / Journal of Corporate Finance 6 (2000) 241–289*

Table 13
Early stage investments, within regressions

Independent variables	Dependent variables			
	(1) Early stage investments w/o gov't funds	(2) Early stage investments w/o gov't funds	(3) Early stage investments	(4) Early stage investments
IPOs	0.0051 (2.271)[a]	0.0018 (0.970)	0.0054 (2.309)[a]	0.0020 (1.026)
Lagged IPOs	0.0008 (0.406)		0.0011 (0.512)	
Market capitalization growth	0.000002 (−0.099)	0.000002 (0.093)	0.0000007 (0.031)	0.000004 (0.209)
GDP growth	0.00002 (0.062)	0.0001 (0.629)	0.00005 (0.157)	0.0002 (0.815)
Constant	0.00004 (2.598)[a]	0.00005 (3.858)[a]	0.00005(2.981)[a]	0.00006 (4.293)[a]
R^2	0.0919	0.0179	0.0970	0.0228

Within regression of 18 countries. The dependent variables are early stage (i.e., seed and startup) investments with and without government funds, divided by average GDP. The independent variables are: (1) IPOs divided by average GDP; (2) Lagged IPOs; (3) Percentage change in Market capitalization; (4) Percentage change in GDP. *T*-statistics for coefficients in parentheses.
[a] Significant at 1% level.

L.A. Jeng, P.C. Wells / Journal of Corporate Finance 6 (2000) 241–289 273

German and Scandinavian countries in particular have lower levels of venture capital investing. These results indicate that the same factors driving IPOs also drive venture capital investments. The connection between IPOs and venture capital investing appears more substantial than the reverse causality story would indicate. It appears that structural factors are driving the positive relationship between the two, and that we are not just observing the move, over time, of venture capital flows into IPO flows.

When we include government funded investments in total venture capital, the significance of IPOs drops, as measured by the *t*-statistic (Specifications 4–6). This implies that government investments are less sensitive to IPOs. From this, we infer that government funded venture capital supports investments in environments that are less favorable to venture capital (i.e., in environments where the IPO market is not strong).

The government funded projects might nevertheless be sensible from an economic perspective, and might offer adequate returns. In order to decide whether this is the case, it would be helpful to have data on rates of return. There is some US evidence that government supported venture capital can select good projects. Lerner (1999) shows that companies that receive SBIR awards experienced higher growth relative to a matched sample. However, without more comprehensive data on returns for the various funds in our sample, we are unable to say whether government funds support high-return projects in environments that otherwise would not have supported them, or whether government funds back low-return projects. Our result does, however, indicate that government involvement can generate venture capital investments where otherwise there would have been none.

The variable for accounting standards has a statistically significant negative coefficient. This result is surprising, as we expect a positive coefficient. This finding could be explained as follows: as we mentioned earlier, the accounting standards under consideration are those used by public firms. Therefore, they only provide a proxy for accounting standards at privately held firms. This proxy may not be correctly measuring the private firms' accounting standards. Furthermore, Wright and Robbie (1996) provide evidence that accounting information is only one part of the venture capitalist's assessment process. While accounting information is an important piece in the decision making process, other elements, such as discussions with personnel and access to unpublished and subjective assessments, are also widely used. This insight, however, could only explain why accounting standards do not have a positive significant coefficient. The statistically significant negative coefficient, however, can still not be entirely understood.

Table 10 contains the results from the between regression of early stage investments on IPOs, labor market rigidities, accounting standards, market capitalization and GDP growth. While labor market rigidity was not significant in the regressions on venture capital, the coefficients on labor market rigidities in this specification, with early stage venture capital, are negative and significant. The

Table 14

(A) Private equity new funds raised, within regressions[1]

Independent variables	Dependent variables			
	(1) Private equity new funds raised w/o gov't funds	(2) Private equity new funds raised w/o gov't funds	(3) Private equity new funds raised	(4) Private equity new funds raised
IPOs	0.0736 (2.188)[a]	0.0509 (2.109)[a]	0.0617 (1.819)[b]	0.0344 (1.218)
Lagged IPOs	0.0721 (2.355)[a]		0.0632 (2.043)[a]	
Private Pension Fund growth	−0.0002 (−0.388)	−0.00009 (−0.479)	−0.0002 (−0.481)	−0.00007 (−0.299)
Market capitalization growth	0.00007 (0.234)	−0.00002 (−0.092)	0.000002 (0.006)	0.00007 (0.235)
GDP growth	0.0026 (0.585)	0.0023 (1.048)	0.0003 (0.064)	0.0039 (1.181)
Constant	0.0004 (1.607)[c]	0.0006 (3.839)[a]	0.0006 (2.527)[a]	0.0007 (3.139)[a]
R^2	0.2060	0.0504	0.1448	0.0450

(B) Private equity new funds raised, within regressions[2]

Independent variables	Dependent variables	
	(1) Private equity new funds raised w/o gov't funds	(3) Private equity new funds raised
IPOs	0.0731 (1.976)[b]	0.0786 (2.110)[a]
Lagged IPOs	−0.0078 (−0.206)	−0.0083 (−0.217)
Private Pension Fund growth	−0.0004 (−0.897)	−0.0004 (−0.898)
Private Pension Fund levels	0.0036 (2.552)[a]	0.0036 (2.576)[a]
Market capitalization growth	−0.0001 (−0.275)	−0.00006 (−0.179)
GDP growth	0.0036 (0.804)	0.0031 (0.684)
Constant	−0.0002 (−0.600)	−0.0002 (−0.545)
R^2	0.3426	0.3251

L.A. Jeng, P.C. Wells / Journal of Corporate Finance 6 (2000) 241–289   275

significance for overall labor market rigidity is higher than that for rigidity of the more highly educated labor market. These results confirm the hypothesis advanced in Section 4 that labor market rigidities pose a hindrance to venture capital.

There are several reasons why labor market rigidities might affect early stage venture capital and not later stage venture capital. First, the probability of an early stage investment going bankrupt is higher, which increases the probability that the employees of the venture will have to find other jobs. All things being equal, this will be more difficult in a country with higher labor market rigidity. Also, given the liquidity constraints of an early stage venture which, in most cases, has no regular revenue stream, it is increasingly difficult to hire employees because the environment offers the employer less flexibility to let people go and imposes higher costs of benefits for unemployment insurance, etc.

It is surprising that the coefficient on IPOs in the early stage investment specification of Table 10 is not significantly different from zero. This implies that countries with higher levels of IPOs do not have significantly higher levels of early stage venture investments as well. This is particularly puzzling in light of our results later on, in Table 13, which show that early stage investments are sensitive to IPOs over time. Since IPOs are significant in the fixed effects, within regression specification of Table 13, it is likely that we have not identified all the variables which affect early stage venture capital in the between regression. Another signal that we do not have all relevant variables is that the R-squareds for early stage investments, with a range of 0.15 to 0.68 (Table 10), are much lower than the R^2s for venture capital investment, which range from 0.49 to 0.71. One variable that might account for some of the unexplained variation is the amount of trade sales that take place. Trade sales are another exit mechanism, in addition to IPOs. We do not, however, at present have a measure for the prevalence of trade sales.

When we consider new funds raised for all private equity endeavors in Table 11A and B, we find, as we found for venture capital investments, that IPOs have a positive and significant coefficient. As was the case for venture capital invest-

---

Notes to Table 14:

[a]Significant at 1% level.

[b]Significant at 10% level.

[c]Significant at 15% level.

[1]Within regression of 14 countries. The dependent variables are new funds raised for private equity (i.e., venture capital and buyouts) with and without government funds, divided by average GDP. The independent variables are: (1) IPOs divided by average GDP; (2) Lagged IPOs; (3) Percentage change in Private Pension funds; (4) Percentage change in Market capitalization; (5) Percentage change in GDP. *T*-statistics for coefficients in parentheses.

[2]Within regression of 14 countries. The dependent variables are new funds raised for private equity (venture capital plus buyouts) with and without government funds, divided by average GDP. The independent variables are: (1) IPOs divided by average GDP; (2) Lagged IPOs; (3) Percentage change in Private Pension Funds; (4) Private Pension Fund levels; (5) Percentage change in Market capitalization; (6) Percentage change in GDP. *T*-statistics for coefficients in parentheses.

ments, the explanatory power of our regressions is quite high, with R^2s ranging from 0.82 to 0.87. Since we are considering funds raised for projects that range in size and riskiness across a broad spectrum, a variable that affects smaller, riskier ventures such as labor market rigidity, does not have a significant coefficient.

The coefficients on pension fund levels and growth rates are not statistically significant. We think that this is due, in part, to the fact that pension funds are regulated differently in the sample countries. The regulations hypothesis is supported by the evidence in Table 14A and B, which shows that, once fixed effects are taken into account, pension fund levels do have a positive and significant impact on new funds raised.

In all regressions, contrary to our expectation, the coefficients on GDP and market capitalization growth are not statistically significant. The absence of significance on our macro-economic variable, GDP growth, underscores the importance of IPOs as the main explanatory factor for venture capital and private equity investments.

7.2. Within regression results

The within regressions allow us to understand how variation across time in the explanatory variables affects venture capital, early stage investments, and new fund flows. Table 12 reports the results of the within regression of venture capital investments on IPOs, lagged IPOs, market capitalization growth and GDP growth. The current level of IPOs has a positive, significant coefficient, emphasizing, once again, the importance of IPOs. The other variables are statistically insignificant.

Table 13 reports the results of the within regression for early stage investments. IPOs have a positive effect on the level of early stage investments from year to year. Thus, even though the average level of IPOs does not affect the amount of early stage investments (as we saw in Table 10), early stage investments are still affected by yearly fluctuations in the amount of IPOs.

Table 14A and B reports results on within regressions of new funds raised. IPOs are again strongly significant with a positive sign. Lagged IPOs are also positive and statistically significant in Specifications 1 and 3 of Table 14A. Table 14B shows that private pension fund levels have a positive and significant coefficient, as expected. Again, the implications of these results indicate the omission of an individual country effect in the between regressions which is being picked up in the fixed effect regression.

8. Descriptive analysis

In addition to the statistically measurable factors of the previous section, specific details of institutions, regulation, and culture also affect venture capital.

L.A. Jeng, P.C. Wells / Journal of Corporate Finance 6 (2000) 241–289   277

For this reason, we include a study of government programs for venture capital, as well as brief case studies on venture capital in Germany and Israel. In Germany, venture capital has grown a lot. However, it has still not reached the level of significance that it has in the US or the UK. Israel, by contrast, is an example of successful venture capital development outside of the US. In 1993, new funds raised (per mil of GDP) in Israel exceeded those of any other country within our sample.

8.1. The role of government programs

Government schemes for assisting private equity vary widely, from providing legal infrastructure to establishing funds that invest directly in private equity projects. We examine some of the larger government programs, and show how they influence private equity flows.

Getting the basic legal and tax structures into place appears to be an important factor in aiding the development of private equity funds. For example, the US and the UK, which have good basic regulations, have high levels of private equity and venture capital investments as a percentage of GDP. Austria, on the other hand, lies on the opposite extreme of this spectrum. With no special legal structure for private equity firms and no tax or other incentives aimed at the industry, private equity investment languishes and shows no sign of growth in the near future.

Portugal furnishes another example of the importance of providing an appropriate legal environment for private equity. In 1986, when Portugal had even lower levels of private equity investment (again measured as a proportion of GDP) than Austria, the Portuguese government created a new type of corporate structure, the venture capital corporation. These venture capital corporations were granted a number of tax benefits as follows:[8]

- Exemption from the new company incorporation tax
- Exemption from income tax and other taxes during the year of incorporation and the three following years
- After this period, deduction from tax of the profits appropriated to reserves and reinvested in venture capital projects during the following 3 years

As a consequence, private equity investments in Portugal increased dramatically (by a factor of 38) between 1986 and 1987.

In addition, growth of private equity in Portugal benefited from direct government funding. Through a variety of government agencies (the most important being the two EC supported regional development agencies NORDEPIP and

---

[8] EVCA Yearbook.

SULDEPIP), the Portuguese government contributed strongly to the growth in private equity funds in the early 1990s. In 1992, government agencies contributed Esc 460 million (US$3.1 million) to new funds raised, or 15% of the total. By 1994, this figure had grown to Esc 12.8 billion (US$80.5 million), which represented 57% of new funds raised. Thus, the large increase in government financing was met by a similarly large increase in private funds. The increase in private funding appears sustainable, independent of continued large government programs. Thus, when government funding decreased from Esc 12.8 billion (US$80.5 million) in 1994 to Esc 2 billion (US$13.4 million) in 1995, an increase in bank funding from Esc 8.9 billion (US$59.5 million) to Esc 13.7 billion (US$91.7 million) made up much of the shortfall.[9]

In Norway, government funded private equity investments appear to have been a strong factor involved in rebuilding private equity after the banking crisis of the late 1980s. In 1989, Norway's private equity market bottomed out with only NKr 8 million (US$1.2 million) in investments (less than 10% of the level of the previous year). The resurgence in the industry in 1990 (when NKr 392 million (US$66.4 million) was invested) is, according to the EVCA, in part a consequence of a NKr 800 million (US$120.9 million) program launched by the government in 1989 as a way of strengthening the Norwegian venture capital industry.[10]

In 1993, the Norwegian State Industrial and Regional Development Fund was started. This marked a transition point in the government's share of venture capital investing. From 1993 to 1995, government source investments increased from NKr 120 million (US$16 million) , which constituted approximately one third of total investments, to NKr 535 million (US$84.7 million), or 50% of private equity investments. Furthermore, the government's involvement appears to have spurred other types of investors, as total investment moved from NKr 350 million (US$46.6 million) to NKr 990 million (US$156.7 million) over the same period of time.[11]

Governments can also play a strong role in influencing the growth of other sources of funds. For example, Ireland experienced a large surge in new funds raised as a consequence of a government-recommended increase in private equity investments by pension funds. A commitment of IR £50 million (US$70.5 million) boosted new funds raised considerably, from IR £23 million (US$32.4 million) in 1993 to IR £150 million (US$232.1 million) in 1994.[12]

Similarly, in the US around 1980, a large flow of new funds in venture capital was unleashed with changes in the Employment Retirement Income Securities

---

[9] ibid.
[10] ibid.
[11] ibid.
[12] ibid.

L.A. Jeng, P.C. Wells / Journal of Corporate Finance 6 (2000) 241–289 279

ACT (ERISA), that permitted venture capital investing for pension funds.[13] In Australia, a similar measure was undertaken in 1985, when the Reserve Bank changed its rules to allow banks to make equity investments in small and medium sized enterprises.[14] The Italian government has also recently given pension funds permission to invest in privately held small and medium sized enterprises.[15] In Finland, banks and pension funds were also encouraged to invest in venture capital and in 1995, the share of these institutions in total venture capital raised went to 79%, up from 20% in 1994.[16]

While government funding of private equity is minimal in the UK, government support of the industry occurs through the legislative structure of venture capital. The UK incentive schemes are:[17]

- Venture Capital Trust (VCT): VCTs provide income tax relief on investments and capital gains tax deferral in the case of capital reinvestment.
- Enterprise Investment Schemes (EIS): The EIS, successor program to the Business Expansion Scheme, provides up-front tax relief on investments, along with relief from capital taxation.
- Small Firms Loan Guarantee Scheme (SFLGS): SFGLS was introduced in 1981. Under this scheme, 41,000 loans were made between 1986 and 1996.
- Share option schemes, which allow innovative and precisely tailored incentive compensation plans to be implemented
- Direct financing through grants and awards is also available. These programs, however, are fairly small. Thus, for example, two of the large technology-oriented programs distribute only £50 million (US$75 million) per year.

Another example of government involvement in a mature private equity market is the Netherlands. Government involvement in the Netherlands is still significant, but it is declining. The nominal figure for public investments has not changed substantially since the early 1990s, but its overall importance has declined, as the industry has grown. Thus in 1992, public sector investments were DFl 65 million (US$35.8 million) compared to DFl 55 million (US$34.3 million) in 1995. As a share of total investments, however, the public sector commitment dropped from 12% to 6% over the same time period.[18]

Furthermore, the Netherlands government has scaled back its venture capital commitments in other ways. The guarantee scheme for private venture capital

---

[13] O'Shea (1996).
[14] ibid.
[15] ibid.
[16] ibid.
[17] Bank of England: The Financing of Technology-Based Small Firms.
[18] EVCA Yearbook.

280   *L.A. Jeng, P.C. Wells / Journal of Corporate Finance 6 (2000) 241–289*

companies launched in 1981[19] was a cornerstone of government support. Under this scheme, the government covered up to 50% of losses incurred by venture capital companies. This scheme was reduced in 1990, and discontinued at the end of 1995. However, the reduction of government support programs for venture capital has not reduced the size of the venture capital industry in the Netherlands. On the contrary, over the period from 1990 to 1995, private equity investments as a percentage of GDP grew from 0.11% to 0.15%. Given its level of maturity, the Dutch private equity industry was capable of maintaining its growth, despite the gradual withdrawal of government support.

Thus, whether we consider the legal and tax environment, loss guarantees, direct expenditures, or government encouragement of investment, it is clear that the government can play an important role in the development of private equity. Mature venture capital industries are quite capable of maintaining healthy levels even after this support is withdrawn.

8.2. Israel venture capital case study

Between 1988 and 1992, Israel's venture capital industry was still in its infancy with only one active venture capital fund of US$30 million. At this time, the major suppliers of capital to emerging companies were large established investment companies belonging to holding groups such Hapolain, IDB, Leumi, Israel, Koor, Clal and Elron Groups.

In 1992, the Likud government began to promote the venture capital industry. It set up the Yozma venture capital program to provide financing for venture capital funds and to invest directly in companies. Yozma also encouraged foreign and local corporations to coinvest in high technology startups. In 1993, Yozma provided US$100 million to establish nine venture capital funds. By 1996, Israel's venture capital industry, which had raised more than US$1 billion, had experienced such phenomenal growth that the government decided to exit the market. However, to continue to foster its venture capital industry, the Israeli government enacted a temporary legislation allowing tax-free investing in Israeli venture capital funds by foreign venture funds which had tax-free status in their home countries. Currently, there are 32 venture capital funds with a total of US$500 million invested which represents 50% of raised capital.

Another attribute which fostered the growth of Israeli's venture capital industry is Israel's favorable taxation laws for individual investors. For persons not in the business of trading securities, capital gains on sales of securities on the Tel Aviv Stock Exchange (TASE) or securities of Israeli companies listed on recognized foreign exchanges are exempt from capital gains taxes in Israel. For individual

---

[19] ibid.

L.A. Jeng, P.C. Wells / Journal of Corporate Finance 6 (2000) 241–289   281

residents, dividends are taxed at a maximum of 25% and interest is taxed at a maximum of 45%. Furthermore, some resident corporations receive a tax break on dividends. Finally, foreign investors face a maximum tax rate of 25% on dividends and interest. These laws made investing in equity securities extremely attractive which, in turn, produced a vibrant equity securities market. For reasons mentioned earlier, this provides a conducive environment for venture capital.

A record number of Israeli firms have successfully gone public. Some recent examples are M-Systems, Gilat Satellite, Mercury Interactive and DSP Group. The TASE is by far the strongest Middle East capital market with 654 listed companies in 1995. Total equity market capitalization as of December 1995 was US$37 billion, approximately 42% of Israel's GDP. Between 1991 and 1995, Israel's growth in market value was 589% in local currency. At the same time, Israel's economy had been very strong with GDP growth averaging 5.5% per year since 1991.

Initial public offerings for Israeli companies are not limited to TASE. In 1996, approximately 50 Israeli companies raised US$1.5 billion on US exchanges. In addition, trade sales are a very popular exit mechanism for venture capital startups. In 1995, foreign companies acquired a significant number of Israeli startups. Some recent examples are America-on-Line's acquisition of Ubique, Boston Scientific's acquisition of Medinol and Intel's acquisition of Shamy.

Most portfolio companies in Israel's venture capital funds are in the early stage with an average company age of approximately 1.5–2 years. Currently, Israeli venture capital funds are primarily invested in technology companies such as telecommunications, data communications, industrial electronic equipment, software, multimedia and medical technology.

The bulk of these startup companies were founded by scientists and engineers who left their previous jobs to start their own companies. Also, the immigration of many skilled scientists and researchers from the former Soviet Union fueled Israel's boom in technology research. Venture capitalists are especially attracted to these R&D startups because many of these new enterprises received grants from the Office of the Chief Scientist (OCS) of the Ministry of Industry and Trade. The OCS administers the Law for Encouragement of Industrial Research and Development which targets developing science intensive industry and expands the technology infrastructure of the state. The OCS's 1995 annual budget was US$370 million, up from US$110 million in 1990. Currently, it supports close to one thousand companies.

Finally, the BIRD Foundation (Binational Industrial Research and Development) promotes US/Israeli corporate partnership investments in Israeli high technology startups. The average budget is US$1 million over a 12–15 month period. BIRD typically provides half of all R&D expenses, but does not take an equity position in the enterprise. Instead, BIRD receives 150% repayment from successful projects. Currently, BIRD invests US$114 million in 391 different projects.

282   *L.A. Jeng, P.C. Wells / Journal of Corporate Finance 6 (2000) 241–289*

The venture capital industry in Israel is becoming a significant part of the country's economy. Several factors have contributed to its success. While the government has played an important role in nurturing the industry, Israel's strong equity markets, and cultural and institutional factors, have allowed venture capital to prosper.

8.3. Germany venture capital case study

Germany's tradition of government support for the business sector dates back to the post-WWII programs dedicated to rebuilding industry. While these programs bolstered the growth of small to medium sized companies in general, they did not focus on venture capital specifically.[20]

One of Germany's most important small and medium enterprise programs is the European Recovery Program (ERP) which was started in 1947. It focuses on growing small businesses, primarily by providing low interest loans. ERP funds are disbursed by the Deutsche Ausgleichsbank (German Bank for Compensation) and the Deutsche Bank fuer Wiederaufbau (German bank for Reconstruction).

The ERP also supports research and development programs, as do state and regionally administered funds. In addition to the federally funded and administered programs, the states also have programs intended to support small and medium-sized businesses. Most of these programs emphasize interest rate or loan subsidies to existing businesses, and do not therefore contribute much to the development of startups. Many of the programs weigh non-profit-maximizing objectives, such as labor market or environmental considerations, quite heavily.

Kapitalbeteiligungsgesellschaften (Equity Stock Companies) were initiated in the 1950s and 1960s as yet another government institution intended to foster growth in small and medium-sized companies. Kapitalbeteiligungsgesellschaften (KBGs) are owned and funded by banks and state governments. Depending on whether they are public or private, the KBGs are more or less profit oriented. They provide equity or near-equity to established small firms that require financing for expansion purposes. KBGs are regulated with respect to their portfolio holdings, and for this reason tend to shy away from risky startup ventures. KBG investments are very hands-off. The KBGs provide little management supervision or support even though they might be involved with a company for up to 8 years.

Until the early 1970s, there was no institutional structure available in Germany for the support of more risky startup ventures. When, in the 1970s, Germany's economic growth started to slow, consideration was given to how more growth could be generated in the small business sector. This led to the founding of

---

[20] The following summary of German venture capital relies heavily on Harrison (1990) The West German Venture Capital Market.

L.A. Jeng, P.C. Wells / Journal of Corporate Finance 6 (2000) 241–289 283

Germany's first venture capital company, the Deutsche Gesellschaft fur Wagniskapital (German Society for Venture Capital, WFG).

The founding of the WFG marked the beginning of modern venture capital in Germany. Its members were a group of 29 German financial institutions. Government involvement in the project was significant. The government agreed to cover 75% of capital losses, and also offered the prospect of generous assistance to cover operating expenses, should the need arise.

While it initially focused on startup enterprises, the WFG shifted emphasis somewhat in the early 1980s, when its funds were divided equally among startups — companies earning DM 1 to 10 million (US$0.6 to 6 million) per year — and companies earning between DM 20 and 50 million (US$11.4 to 28.6 million).

In 1984, the WFG was restructured. The emphasis shifted toward later stage investments, and the number of partners was reduced to five. The specific industry focus (on high technology) from earlier years was abandoned, and non-technology investments came to represent a larger portion of the portfolio. Involvement in management decisions was still fairly limited.

In 1988, the WFG underwent another organizational change. Deutsche Bank, one of the partners in the WFG venture, bought out the other partners and integrated the WFG into its own subsidiary.

Other players gradually entered the scene. The initial entrants all had government backing. The second venture capital firm to enter the scene was the Hannover Finanz, in 1979. The third venture capital firm appeared in 1982: the Landesfonds des Landes Berlin. In 1983, eight new companies entered the growing field of competitors. By 1995, the German Venture Capital Association had over 100 members.

From 1989 to 1995, Germany had a program called Beteiligungskapital fur Junge Technologieunternehmen (Equity Participation for Young Technology Companies, BJTU),[21] administered by a subsidiary of the government owned Deutsche Ausgleichsbank. This was a co-investment scheme which gave the owner of the business the option of buying out the government share at a premium over the initial investment. If the company did not fare well, the founder was given the option of selling his share to the government at a discount to book value.

A successor was created to the popular BJTU program. The Beteiligungskapital fur Kleine Technologieunternehmen (Equity Participation for Small Technology Companies, BTU) was created in 1995, and slated to last through 2000.[22] The BTU focuses on new firms. BTU funds will only be brought in at a level that matches the investment of a private investor. The program also contains a guarantee scheme which covers up to 50% of losses to the private investor.

---

[21] O'Shea, 1996.

[22] ibid.

284   *L.A. Jeng, P.C. Wells / Journal of Corporate Finance 6 (2000) 241–289*

The institutional structures in place in Germany over the 1980s and, to a lesser extent, the 1990s have hindered the development of a venture capital industry on the scale of the UK or the US. The tax system in Germany does not favor venture capital investments by corporations. They cannot obtain a capital gains tax rates reduction. Corporate investments are taxed at the 56% corporate tax rate. Trade taxes and capital transaction taxes provide an additional burden.

In 1987, the Geregelter Markt was established as a means to provide an exit mechanism for startup firms. The other two markets already available in Germany at this time, the Amtlicher Handel (main stock market) and the Telefonverkehr (an unregulated market similar to the US OTC market), did not provide a sufficiently liquid exit mechanism. However, listing companies on the Geregelter Markt is still not easy, and is subject to stringent requirements. The companies that satisfy these criteria tend to do well, but only a small number of companies can qualify. In 1995 plans were introduced to provide a new exchange, called the Neuer Markt, which would offer young and fast-growing companies a way to raise capital.

Germany has also experimented with regulatory incentives for venture capital. In 1987, Unternehmensbeteiligungsgesellschaften (Societies for Enterprise Participation, UBGs) were introduced, which benefit from a somewhat more favorable tax status than other types of investment vehicles. The pace of regulatory change increased in the 1990s, but still failed to introduce sweeping changes to the system. Regulations for public promoted venture capital companies were loosened in 1991. In 1994, the operating environment for UBGs was improved.

Despite government programs intended to encourage venture capital, venture capital in Germany is still relatively insignificant. New and early stage investments as a percentage of GDP were only 0.0063 in 1995. Part of the problem in Germany appears to be both a cultural and institutional[23] aversion to risk taking. While some recent success stories[24] on the German venture capital market indicate that this might be changing, Germany has still not evolved into a hotbed of venture capital activity.

9. Conclusion

Private equity and venture capital markets have been subject to strong cyclical fluctuations over the years. Bygrave and Timmons (1992) describe several cycles that have marked the US venture capital experience. A very slow start in the 1940s eventually led to a boom in the 1960s. A downturn through most of the 1970s gave way to another successful period in the 1980s. A brief but sharp downturn at

---

[23] An example of an institutional barrier is the ban on a person becoming a director again, if a company goes bankrupt.
[24] *The Economist*, June 28, 1997.

L.A. Jeng, P.C. Wells / Journal of Corporate Finance 6 (2000) 241–289 285

the start of the 1990s has been followed by another boom. The experience outside the US has been marked by similar ups and downs, albeit over a shorter period of time, stretching back to the 1970s. We have compiled a statistical track record that allows us to not only understand these swings over time, but that also gives us insight into the differences in private equity and venture capital across countries.

We show that, over time, IPOs are the main force behind the cyclical swings in venture capital. This result confirms the conventional wisdom on venture capital. We also discover a surprising result, which is that early and later stage venture capital investments are affected quite differently by the determinants of venture capital. Over time, IPOs explain less of the year to year fluctuations in early stage than in later stage investments. Our finding across countries is even more surprising: while later stage venture capital investments respond strongly to different levels of IPOs across countries, early stage investments are unaffected.

These results point to the need for further research focusing on early stage venture capital investments, and reinforce the notion that the distinct stages of venture capital are fundamentally different. We believe that there are several factors that are determinants of early, but not later, stage venture capital. One of these factors which we have been able to identify is labor market rigidities. Labor market rigidities affect variation in early stage venture capital across countries, but do not explain variation in later stage venture capital.

Given the importance of IPOs it is surprising that venture capitalists in countries with underdeveloped IPO markets do not avail themselves of the more developed IPO markets in countries like the US. This strategy of bringing companies to the US for the purpose of an IPO has been pursued successfully by the Israeli venture capital industry. A number of Israeli firms have had IPOs on the NASDAQ. It is not clear why venture capitalists in other countries have not pursued a similar strategy.

There still appears to be a very strong home bias in the venture capital industry in general. This is expressed in two ways. First, venture capitalists tend to invest in their home country. The costs of monitoring distant companies (Lerner, 1995a,b) can at least partially explain why the home bias might affect investments. Second, venture capitalists also seek to exit their investments in the home country. This can again be partially explained by the time and effort it takes to sell a business. An IPO in a foreign country involves more cost and effort than an IPO in the home country.

The additional costs incurred do not appear very high, and are unlikely to be as high as the monitoring costs incurred by investing in a foreign country. There may also be certain fixed costs associated with exiting through a non-domestic IPO. Once the barrier is breached, as it clearly is the case with Israel's many successful IPOs in the US market, additional IPOs might become easy to arrange. For venture capital industries that have not yet had many foreign IPOs, as is the case with Germany's, it might still be very costly to arrange these transactions. Given the importance of IPOs and the apparent solution for low IPO countries of listing on markets like the NASDAQ, the question of why there is such a strong home bias needs to be further addressed.

Our results on private pension fund levels and growth rates point to a need for a greater understanding of cross-country determinants. In our analysis of new private equity funds raised, we find that pension fund levels are significant over time, but insignificant across countries. We believe that some of these additional determinants, which would help explain differences across countries, can be found in regulatory and policy structures.

Our qualitative analysis shows that government policies can act as catalysts to galvanize private fund flows and investments. On a more quantitative, statistical level, our study of government involvement has produced some interesting results. We show that, compared to private venture capital, government-funded venture capital is less sensitive to IPOs across countries. Once again, the story for early stage investing is different: the difference in sensitivity of government-backed and non-government-backed early stage investments to IPOs drops by half in some specifications. These differences are only present when we compare across countries. Over time, the differences between the sensitivity of private and public venture capital to IPOs are negligible.

Our observation that government-backed venture capital is less sensitive to IPOs across countries than non-government-backed venture capital indicates a direction for future research. Governments appear to be willing to finance early stage projects that would not be funded privately. To evaluate the usefulness of the government role, it is important to understand the economic value of these projects. If more data on returns were available, they could be used to better understand the role of government in venture capital.

By providing an empirical analysis of private equity and venture capital across countries, we have been able to confirm the value of having a well-functioning exit mechanism in the form of a strong IPO market. We have also shown that some segments of the venture capital market behave quite differently from others. Our findings regarding the need for a more differentiated approach to venture capital are especially important, in that they concern two areas — early stage investing and government involvement — that are of particular interest to policy makers today.

Acknowledgements

We thank Paul Gompers, Josh Lerner, and Andrei Shleifer for helpful conversations. We also thank Carl Kester and the participants of the Harvard Industrial Organization seminar for comments. Furthermore, we gratefully acknowledge Chris Allen, the Bureau of Labor Statistics, the European Venture Capital Association, FIBV, The Giza Group, InterSec Research, Macdonald and Associates, Nomura Securities, OECD and the Toronto Stock Exchange for help in obtaining data. We appreciate the financial support of the Division of Research at Harvard Business School. All errors and opinions are our own.

References

Acs, Z.J., Audretsch, D.B., 1994. New-firm startups, technology, and macroeconomic fluctuations. Small Business Economics 6.

Black, B., Gilson, R., 1998. Venture capital and the structure of capital markets: banks versus stock markets. Journal of Financial Economics 47.

Bygrave, W.D., Timmons, J.A., 1992. Venture Capital at the Crossroads. Harvard Business School Press, Boston, MA.

The Economist, 1997. Venture Capitalists: A Really Big Adventure. 1/15.

Edwards, J., Fischer, K., 1994. Banks, Finance and Investment in Germany. Cambridge Univ. Press.

Evans, D.S., Jovanovich, B., 1989. An estimated model of entrepreneurial choice under liquidity constraints. Journal of Political Economy 97 (4).

Fama, E., 1985. What's different about Banks? Journal of Monetary 15.

Gompers, P., 1995. Optimal investment, monitoring, and the staging of venture capital. Journal of Finance L (5).

Gompers, P., 1994. The rise and fall of venture capital. Business and Economic History 23 (2).

Gompers, P., Lerner, J., 1996. The use of covenants: an empirical analysis of venture partnership agreements. The Journal of Law and Economics.

Hardymon, G.F., DeNino, M.J., Salter, M.S., 1983. When corporate venture capital doesn't work. Harvard Business Review 114.

Harrison, E.M., 1990. The West German Venture Capital Market: An Analysis of its Market Structure and Economic Performance. Peter Lang.

Holmes, T.J., Schmitz, J.A. Jr., 1990. A theory of entrepreneurship and its application to the study of business transfers. Journal of Political Economy 98, 265–294.

Hurry, D., Miller, A.T., Bowman, E.H., 1991. Calls on high-technology: Japanese exploration of venture capital investments in the United States. Strategic Management Journal 13.

Jensen, M.C., 1993. Presidential address: the modern industrial revolution, exit and the failure of internal control systems. Journal of Finance 48 (3).

La Porta, R., Lopez-de-Silanes, F., Shleifer, A., Vishny, R.W., 1996. Law and finance. Journal of Finance, forthcoming in the.

Lerner, J., 1999. The Government as Venture Capitalist: The Long-Run Impact of the SBIR Program, NBER Working Paper.

Lerner, J., 1995a. The European association of security dealers: November 1994, Harvard Business School Case Study.

Lerner, J., 1995b. Venture capitalists and the oversight of private firms. The Journal of Finance L (1), March.

Mayer, C., 1988. New issues in corporate finance. European Economic 32.

Myers, S., Majluf, N., 1984. Corporate financing and investment decisions when firms have information that investors do not have. Journal of Financial Economics 13.

National Venture Capital Association, 1997. Seventh Annual Economic Impact of Venture Capital Study. Venture One, Coopers and Lybrand L.L.P.

OECD, 1997. Employment Outlook. Chap. 5 Draft.

O'Shea, M., 1996. Government programs for venture capital, OECD Working Group on Innovation and Technology Policy.

Roe, M.J., 1990. Political and legal restraints on ownership and control of public companies. Journal of Financial Economics 27.

Sahlman, W.A., 1990. The structure and governance of venture-capital organizations. Journal of Financial Economics 27.

Sahlman, W.A., 1991. Insights from the American Venture Capital Organization, Working Paper.

Siegel, R., Siegel, E., MacMillan, I.C., 1988. Corporate venture capitalists: autonomy, obstacles, and performance. Journal of Business Venturing 3.

Sykes, H.B., 1990. Corporate venture capital: strategies for success. Journal of Business Venturing 5.

Venture Economics, 1988. Exiting Venture Capital Investments.

Wright, M., Robbie, K., 1996. Venture capitalists, unquoted equity investment appraisal and the role of accounting information. Accounting and Business Research 26 (2).

Further reading

Asian Venture Capital Journal, 1991. The Guide to Venture Capital in Asia.

Acs, Z.J., Audretsch, D.B., 1991. Innovation and Technological Change: an International Comparison. Harvester Wheatsheaf, England.

Acs, Z.J., Audretsch, D.B., 1988. Innovation in large and small firms: an empirical analysis. American Economic Review 78 (4).

Bank of England, 1996. The Financing of Technology-Based Small Firms. October.

Brav, A., Gompers, P., 1997. Myth or reality? The long-run underperformance of initial public offerings: evidence from venture- and nonventure-capital-backed companies. Journal of Finance 52 (2).

Bureau of Industry Economics, 1993. Venture and Development Capital in Australia and Japan. Australian Government Publishing Service, Canberra.

Cohen, W.M., Levin, R.C., 1989. Empirical studies of innovation and market structure. Handbook of Industrial Organization 2, Chap. 18.

EVCA, 1986. European Venture Capital Journal.

Freear, J.E.S., Wetzel, W.E. Jr., 1995. Angels: personal investors in the venture capital market. Entrepreneurship and Regional 7.

The GIZA Group, 1996. Survey of Investment and Venture Capital Funds in Israel.

Gompers, P., 1996. Grandstanding in the venture capital industry. Journal of Financial Economics 42 (1).

Gompers, P., 1998. Venture capital distributions: short-run and long-run reactions. Journal of Finance, forthcoming.

Grisebach, R., 1989. Innovations-Finanzierung durch Venture Capital. Verlag V. Florentz.

GT Management, 1995. The GT Guide to World Equity Market. Euromoney Publications.

Hellwig, M., in press. Banking, Financial Intermediation and Corporate Finance. European Financial Intergration, Cambridge Univ. Press, Chap. 3.

Holmes, T.J., Schmitz, J.A. Jr., 1995. On the turnover of business firms and business managers. Journal of Political Economy 103 (5).

Holtz-Eakin, D., Harvey Rosen, D.J., 1994. Entrepreneurial decisions and liquidity constraints. Rand Journal of Economics 25 (2).

International Finance, 1995. Emerging Stock Markets Factbook.

International Monetary Fund, 1996. International Financial Statistics Yearbook 1996.

Israel Suspends Capital Gains Tax, 1996. Venture Capital Journal. Securities Data publishing.

Jensen, M.C., 1989. Active investors, LBOs, and the privatization of bankruptcy. Journal of Applied Corporate Finance.

Jensen, M.C., Meckling, W.H., 1976. Theory of the firm: managerial behavior, agency costs and ownership structure. Journal of Financial Economics 3.

Kester, W.C., Luehrman, T.A., 1993. The LBO Association as a Relational Investment Regime: Clinical Evidence from Clayton, Dubilier and Rice, Working Paper.

L.A. Jeng, P.C. Wells / Journal of Corporate Finance 6 (2000) 241–289 289

Kroszner, R.S., 1995. The evolution of universal banking and its regulation in Twentieth Century America, Financial System Design: Universal Banking Considered. Forthcoming in.

Lerner, J., 1994a. The syndication of venture capital investments. Financial Management 23 (3).

Lerner, J., 1994b. Venture capitalists and the decision to go public. Journal of Financial Economics 35.

Marcus, A.D., 1993. Global promise of israeli technology spurs growth of venture capital funds, The Wall Street Journal. 8/4.

OECD, 1994. Employment Outlook.

Ooghe, H., Manigart, S., Fassin, Y., 1991. Growth patterns of the European venture capital industry. Journal of Business Venturing 6, 381–404.

Pavitt, K., Robson, M., Townsend, J., 1987. The size distribution of innovating firms in the UK: 1945–1983. The Journal of Industrial Economics 35 (3).

Pound, J., 1991. Proxy voting and the SEC: investor protection versus market efficiency. Journal of Financial Economics 29.

Reinganum, J.R., 1989. The timing of innovation: research, development, and diffusion. Handbook of Industrial Organization 1.

Robbie, K., Wright, M., 1997. Venture Capital. Dartmouth Publishing.

Rosen, S., 1974. Hedonic prices and implicit markets: product differentiation in pure competition. Journal of Political Economy 82 (1).

Securities Data Publishing, 1996a. Land of milk and money as tech ideas flow out of Israel, venture capital pours. Venture Capital Journal.

Securities Data Publishing, 1996b. Venture Capital Journal 36 (7).

Venture Economics, 1996. Venture Capital Yearbook.

Venture Economics, 1995. Investment Benchmark: Venture Capital.

Part III
Policy Issues and Technology-Based Ventures

[9]

PREDICTORS OF SUCCESS

IN NEW TECHNOLOGY

BASED VENTURES

JUAN B. ROURE
University of Navarra, Barcelona, Spain

ROBERT H. KEELEY
Stanford University

EXECUTIVE SUMMARY

Several recent studies have examined the causes of success and failure in new ventures. From these a three-level analysis has evolved, which considers the management, the venture's strategy, and its competitive environment. Empirical testing is still at an early stage, but results have generally supported the three-level approach. However, the findings are not very strong.

This study considers only high potential, technology based new ventures—the companies on which venture capitalists concentrate. It suggests that such firms face unusual time pressures and uncertainty, and that their responses to these forces are major determinants of success or failure. We propose 11 easily measured qualities—describing management, the firm's strategy, and its environment—which should influence how quickly the venture can act. These should predict a new venture's performance.

The 11 attributes are tested on 36 new ventures, representing essentially all of the startup investments of a major venture capital firm between 1974 and 1982. The data are taken from the firms' original business plans. Performance is measured from the subsequent financial history, using the compound rate of return to all shareholders (founders, employees, and investors).

The ventures in this sample are primarily based on electronic or information technologies. They are highly successful as a group, with an average compound rate of return of 98% per year. They are also very risky; the standard deviation of returns is 171% per year, and in 11 of 36 cases the shareholders lost on their investments.

Results from a single sample must always be treated cautiously. However, several findings are strong enough to merit further study and to be incorporated as a part of a process for evaluating new ventures:

1. A set of four measures—representing all three areas—explains 57% of the variance. The four—completeness of the founding team, technical superiority of the product, expected time for product development, and buyer concentration—all behave as expected. The first two have a positive effect; the latter two have an inverted U-shaped relationship with an optimum

Address correspondence to Robert H. Keeley, Department of Industrial Engineering and Engineering Management, Stanford University, Stanford, CA 94305.

The authors gratefully acknowledge support from the Center for Entrepreneurial Studies of New York University. The authors also acknowledge the helpful comments of the reviewers of this paper.

Journal of Business Venturing 5, 201–220

0883-9026/90/$3.50

development time of 12 months and an optimum number of customers of approximately 60. Three other measures—prior shared experience of the founders, competitive conditions, and projected market share—show an influence when management, strategy, and environment are examined one area at a time.

2. *These relatively simple measures predict success well, probably at least as well as any other study has done using more subtle measures.*

3. *The measures used in this study, though they have strong predictive power, apparently did not influence the young capitalists. Otherwise the relationships should have been different when the return to venture capital investors was used in place of the total return; in fact they were the same. This suggests that the venture capital investors did not give sufficient weight to the qualities that we consider, and could make better choices by giving greater attention to those measures.*

4. *Prospective entrepreneurs and investors should benefit from using our model as part of their screening processes. Specifically, they might calculate a predicted rate of return. If it is low—say, below 30% per year—they should examine the reason for the low score and consider whether circumstances exist which outweigh or invalidate that apparent weakness.*

5. *An "additive" model seems realistic. That is, one can combine dissimilar qualities (with appropriate weighting for relative importance) to arrive at an overall figure of merit with strong predictive power. The specific parameters imply that a company must have a complete management team and score well on two of the remaining three measures in order to be an attractive opportunity. More generally, the model allows a practitioner to make a rough assessment of the tradeoffs among management, product, and industry. This is important because few, if any, new companies have all the qualities an investor may desire.*

6. *Although individual qualities of the founders are no doubt important, this remains a difficult matter to demonstrate statistically.*

7. *Firms exist in an ever changing competitive environment. To the extent that these findings are valid beyond this sample, they may have been recognized and incorporated in more recent new ventures. If so this may change the nature of competition, and alter the key determinants of success or failure.*

INTRODUCTION

Several recent papers have examined the causes of success or failure of new ventures, using a variety of approaches. Khan (1987), MacMillan et al. (1987), and Tyebjee and Bruno (1984) examine the problem indirectly by considering how venture capitalists make investment decisions. Stuart and Abetti (1987) adapt studies of new product success to apply to new ventures. Van de Ven et al. (1984) focus on management processes during the early years of 12 software companies, looking for attributes that separate the successful firms from the others. Sandberg and Hofer (1987) embody the viewpoint of strategic management. Using the business plans of 17 new firms, they identify attributes of the business strategies, and industry structures, which are related to subsequent success.

Although Sandberg and Hofer are the most explicit, all of the above studies employ a "multi-level" framework which considers the firm from the viewpoints of the managers, the business idea, and the environment. Their implicit hypothesis is an extension of American folklore: "being in the right place at the right time." That is, a successful firm exhibits compatibility among its business environment, its products, and its managers. Such a hypothesis is intuitively plausible, and the empirical results generally support it. But there are important limitations and contradictions. For example, none of the studies can simultaneously show the importance of management, environment, and business strategy.

This study builds on the work of Roure and Maidique (1986) to modify the analytical framework discussed above. Roure and Maidique's exploratory study proposed 10 predictors of success and applied them to a sample of eight new ventures. This study extends their work in several ways:

1. It augments their theoretical framework with concepts from organizational development and from strategic management.
2. It develops scales for their qualitative variables and adds a new measure of product strategy—projected product development time.
3. It adds 28 companies to the original sample, making a total of 36 high potential, technology based companies.[1] This allows statistical analysis to replace the qualitative comparisons of their exploratory study.
4. It incorporates measures of performance that permit the use of multiple regression analysis. This facilitates assessment of the relative importance of each explanatory variable, not just its statistical significance in a bivariate comparison.

Our sample includes several industries. In the next section we discuss why our newness itself should produce a set of common influences on performance, which transcend industry differences. The section on Methodology describes the selection of variables, the sample, and the linear regression model used in the analysis. A section on Results presents our findings, and the Conclusion suggestions why certain hypotheses were not confirmed and summarizes the strongest findings.

A FRAMEWORK FOR PREDICTING SUCCESS

A new, high potential venture enters a market large enough to attract competition from firms in related industries and from other startups. It must establish a position quickly in the face of high uncertainty. This involves a series of challenges,[2] including

- Identifying an attractive market opportunity, and developing a plan to obtain a large share of it.
- Obtaining sufficient funds to begin execution of the plan.
- Attracting additional key employees and achieving quick technical progress on the new product.
- Making arrangements with key customers and suppliers.
- Obtaining added funding in order to build manufacturing, marketing, and administrative capabilities.
- Modifying the business strategy in response to changing conditions.
- Broadening the product line, obtaining additional funding, and continuing to build the organization.

---

[1]"High potential" signifies an objective of achieving annual sales of well over $10,000,000 within a few years. "Technology based" implies that the firms rely on a technological advantage as a key element of their initial strategies.

None of the prior studies focuses on high potential, technology based ventures—a very important group in our society. Two (Stuart and Abetti 1987; Van de Ven et al. 1984) study small, technology based ventures—sales averaged $300,000 three years after formation. The others used samples with a mixture of technologies and potential firm sizes.

[2]Ruhnka and Young (1987) survey 73 venture capital firms regarding the tasks confronting new firms. Terminology and timing of activities varies among the respondents, but all of the tasks listed here are clearly identified by them as being important during a firm's early years.

204   J.B. ROURE AND R.H. KEELEY

Success is a matter of degree. The greater the number of tasks that are accomplished rapidly and efficiently, the larger market share, profitability, and return on investment expected. This implies that the three viewpoints—namely, the qualities of the founders, the environment, and the business strategy—should explain success or failure to the degree they reflect how rapidly, efficiently, and effectively a firm accomplishes the above tasks. We believe the three areas are "additive," in the sense that strength on one attribute can compensate for weakness on another. This creates an eclectic framework; we can not rely solely on social psychology, industrial economics, or strategic management.[3] Nonetheless, the idea of urgency in the face of high uncertainty provides a unifying theme—a theme that we expect to override the influence of the particular industries (within the limited range of technology based industries) of our new ventures.

The Founding Management

The founders may be analyzed as individuals and as a team. Regarding individual traits, one would expect the fastest progress from ventures whose managers have all of the skills, knowledge, and relationships needed to excel at their jobs. There would be minimal on-the-job training during the startup period. This expectation is supported by several studies, although the results are tentative. MacMillan et al. (1987) and Vesper (1980) state that relevant experience is a characteristic of successful entrepreneurs. Cooper and Bruno (1977) report that successful firms have founders with relevant experience more frequently than unsuccessful ones, a finding that is supported by Van de Ven et al. (1984).

The value of relevant experience seems clear from theory and from empirical studies; however, business plans vary widely regarding availability of biographical data. Thus we must compromise between the information we would really prefer to have and what is available. "Relevant experience" will be measured in two ways:

- By the percentage of founders who have held a position similar to the one being assumed in the new company (with "similar" being defined as the same function and within one level of that being assumed), and

- By the percentage of founders who have worked in high growth (defined as sales growth over 25% annually) organizations.

In addition to individual qualifications, the ability of the founders as a team should influence performance. For example, if the founders have complementary expertise, they are more likely to avoid errors in key choices such as selecting suppliers or distribution channels. Additionally, smooth interaction among the members should enhance efficiency. These views receive support from organization researchers. Hackman and Oldham (1980) believe a group's performance is influenced by its composition. Specifically, it must be large enough to do its task, but not much larger. Its members must have at least a moderate level of interpersonal skill in addition to their task-relevant skills. And there must be a balance between the shared values and diversity of the members' skills and knowledge.

In this study's exploratory phase (Roure and Maidique 1986), two characteristics of the team seem to distinguish between success and failure: (1) the degree of completeness, or the percentage of essential functions in the new company that are filled by the founders' team at the time of funding; and (2) the extent to which founders had previously worked in the same organization.

---

[3]This is discussed by Roure (1986) in an extensive literature review.

Completeness of the team fits Hackman and Oldham's idea that a group must be large enough to do its task. In addition the more complete the team the broader its set of contacts with customers, suppliers, potential employees, consultants, and investors. As Aldrich and Zimmer (1986) suggest, this should increase the efficiency and adaptability of a young firm.

The importance of prior shared experience receives support from theories of group development. Tuckman (1965) suggests that a group evolves through four stages: forming, storming, norming, and performing. That is, members of a newly formed group must initially reach agreement about how they will proceed in developing a task. As Hackman and Oldham (1980) suggest, group members already familiar with one another may not need to talk at all about their roles, since all members know from previous experience how to proceed in most situations. Katz (1982), in his study of R&D groups' effectiveness, explains the upward slope noticed in teams' performance during the initial months of working together as positive effects of learning and team building.

If the founders have previously worked in the same firm, they can hasten the integrating and developing process described above, and move on to performance. There may be a negative side as well. Common backgrounds may decrease the diversity of experience and contacts. Thus some prior joint experience may be better than having all team members come from a common employer. The same may be said of team completeness. Hackman and Oldham suggest that a team can be too large, becoming inefficient as well as expensive. In our empirical work, we will examine whether both team variables have their maximum influence at less than 100%.

The Environment

The environment, particularly the structure of the company's industry, is widely recognized as an influence on new organizations. Theoretical treatments include population ecology, resource dependency, and industrial economics, with competition being perhaps the most widely studied environmental factor. Brittain and Freeman (1980), in their study of the semiconductor industry, suggest that significant technological innovations or changes in the social system create new niches, which provide opportunities for the formation of new organization. Such situations are characterized by low competition. Under such conditions the authors argue that new companies adopting a first mover approach (or r-strategist type of organizational form proposed by Hannan and Freeman 1977) will have a temporary competitive advantage. Technological change may also create conditions of high "variability" and the alteration of "selection criteria," factors that Aldrich (1979) argues will promote the emergence of new organizations.

Pfeffer and Salancik (1978) pursued a related argument. They suggest that organizations enhance their odds of success if they can control external contingencies. New companies may try to control their destinies by locating market niches with low levels of competition, markets in which they anticipate a major role in shaping standards and customer expectations.

In this study's exploratory stage (Roure and Maidique 1986), three successful firms entered markets that had no dominant competitor. The fourth entered a market with two strong competitors, but did not challenge them directly. Instead, it would be a "second source" for their products. In contrast, two unsuccessful ventures tried to compete head-on with a strong leader. The two other failures entered markets with several existing competitors and other major firms clearly planning to enter.

The exploratory research also found that the successful companies targeted higher market shares than the unsuccessful ones. This is consistent with Pfeffer and Salancik's theory that firms try to influence customer expectations. A high market share may also reflect competitive conditions—the higher the market share, the less important the competition. On the other hand, it may imply excessive ambition in a firm where time and funds are limited, suggesting that a moderate share may be better than a very large or a very small one. In addition, market share is subject to measurement problems in segmented markets—which most of ours are.

We view the level of competition and the projected market share as overlapping, but not identical, indicators of how attractive a firm's environment is. Competition should be monotonically related to success; market share may not be.

A third environmental factor is the level of buyer concentration. Very low buyer concentration means that the new venture will serve a large number of potential customers of limited individual buying capacity. Very high concentration implies the opposite. All four successful companies in the exploratory research (Roure and Maidique 1986), but only one of four failures, have high levels of buyer concentration. This result is consistent with two arguments of Pfeffer and Salancik's (1978) resource dependency theory. First, in the face of high uncertainty an organization attempts to control its fate through close linkages with its environment (e.g., customers). Second, the broader the demands on a firm the more difficult it is to manage.

This suggests that successful startups will establish close links with their potential customers, which is not possible with large numbers of customers. On the other side, as Porter (1980) notes, to depend on a very small number of buyers will increase their bargaining power, and may lower the probability of success for the new company. Thus we expect the success of a new venture to have an inverted U-shaped relationship to the number of potential buyers.

The resource dependency theory of Pfeffer and Salancik (1978) suggests another environmental linkage: ownership. Companies with high growth potential require substantial funding, which they secure through venture capital. Venture capitalists, in addition to providing funds, act as links with the business community, providing access to customers, suppliers, financial institutions, and key people who could collaborate with the venture. The proportion of equity owned by the external investors may influence their eagerness to provide such access. A competing need is that the founders' incentives may be similarly influenced. Interviews with venture capitalists during the exploratory research indicate that external investors and entrepreneurs must both be highly motivated in order for a venture to succeed. This implies the equity should be structured such that both benefit significantly from the venture's success—a hypothesis that was not supported in the exploratory study of eight companies (Roure and Maidique 1986). This study provides a further opportunity to test whether the share of equity owned by the founders will have an inverted U-shaped relationship to the success of the venture, as the resource dependency theory and the preliminary interviews suggest.

The Firm: Strategic Choices

Of the firm's strategic choices, product policy is often the most important for technology based ventures, and is the main subject of this section. The technological advantage of a product can be estimated from its projected performance and cost vis a vis its competitors. Studies (e.g., Cooper 1979) find that products that are unique or superior in the eyes of the customer tend to be successful. Maidique and Zirger (1984) support the value of technical superiority as well as finding an advantage for lower cost. The exploratory phase of this study (Roure and Maidique 1986) finds that expected performance improvement differentiates successful companies from unsuccessful ones, but cost reduction does not. We speculate that performance improvements (usually based on technological changes in the design) are less easily matched by established firms than are cost reductions, and are less likely to meet an effective competitive response. Thus we expect the success of a new venture to be positively related to its product's projected level of performance improvement.

Related to technological superiority is the question of how much time to spend on product development. Given the emphasis on urgency, a short development time seems desirable; however, this may be overdone. If the development time is very short, the product may be easily imitated. Therefore, we expect the estimated development time for the first product to have an inverted U-shaped relationship to the success of the venture.

A third aspect of a new firm's strategy, which has been important in other studies, is the way it plans. Van de Ven (1980) finds that the conditions of the planning process during the creation of new organizations affect their startup performance. His study highlights the importance of a systematic planning process. Furthermore, Bourgeois and Eisenhardt (1985) also find that in rapidly changing environments the more successful technological firms use a rational, analytic planning process. New, high potential ventures may have a particular need for a well stated plan, because their organizations expand rapidly and they need to communicate their mission effectively to new employees, potential suppliers, investors, and others.

The value of a plan may be difficult to demonstrate, because there is little variation among plans in our sample. Even so, the preliminary phase of this research shows a qualitative difference between the plans of successful and unsuccessful firms (Roure and Maidique 1986). Successful technological ventures seem to plan product development in greater detail. This finding coincides with a major conclusion of the Stanford Innovation Project (SINPRO) on new product success and failure (Maidique and Zirger 1984). Therefore, we expect that the level of detail in planning the development of the technology will be positively related to the success of the venture.

METHODOLOGY

Having suggested why a set of common influences should exist and what they should be, we turn to empirical testing. Two prominent venture capital firms (who requested anonymity) provided business plans and investment documents on 36 new, technology-based companies, in which they had invested.[4] From these we recorded the necessary data.

Only firms that received financing are included in the study. This may produce certain limitations in our findings. For example, if these two venture capitalists invest only in management teams with adequate experience, experience may not explain performance in this sample, even though it would have a powerful effect in a more diverse population. This limitation works only in one direction. If one of our measures affects performance, we can say that it is important. But the absence of an effect does not imply irrelevance of a measure for values beyond the range of our sample.

We will use a multivariate linear regression because it fits the theory that perfor-

---

[4]Two business plans were obtained from one fund in a preliminary stage of the study. The other 34 were obtained from the second, which was closer and therefore easier to work with. The 34 represent all but four (whose business plans were missing) of the startup investments of this fund between 1974 and 1982. Performance of the four with missing plans was available and seemed typical of the others. One was a highly successful public company, one had failed, and two were doing moderately well.

mance is an additive result of many influences. Such a model implies that the performance of every company in the population is a single additive function of the independent variables plus a normally distributed error term. An obvious concern is whether a cross sectional sample from several industries can be described by a single function. We have tried to control this a priori by using a single venture capital firm as the source of virtually all of our data (each venture capitalist we interviewed invested in a limited range of industries, technologies, and risks). Another concern is whether the ordinal measures we use in some cases (e.g., product superiority) will have a linear relationship with performance. Such concerns are best addressed empirically, and we perform several tests: (1) the residuals are tested for normality and for heteroskedasticity; (2) the independent variables are tested for interactions (non-additivity), for non-linearity—except where we expect it, and for high intercorrelations; (3) possible influence based on industry or holding period is tested using additional variables.

Three separate regressions, one each for management, environment, and strategy, are used to examine the relative influence of variables within each point of view. Additionally, a regression combining variables from all points of view examines the extent to which some may dominate others.

Description of the Sample

All 36 companies studied were started after 1974, 30 between 1978 and 1982. Usually, they existed for some time before receiving their first major funding ($300,000 or more). Twenty eight companies make electronic or electromechanical products, including five semiconductor companies and 14 makers of computer equipment. Three firms produce computer software. Four are in biotechnology or medical equipment.

All were started in the United States in regions with a supportive local infrastructure. Twenty five were in California. They received an average of four rounds of venture capital funding from an average of six venture capital investors. Altogether 119 venture capital firms invested in these companies. Unsuccessful companies average more rounds of financing from venture capitalists (5.7 rounds) than successful ones (3.7 rounds), and remain in the venture capitalists' portfolios longer (59 months versus 44 months).

Measuring Financial Performance

A principal purpose of a new venture is to create value, which we measure by the internal rate of return realized by shareholders (i.e., founders, subsequent employees, and investors). We consider two rates of return: that realized by the venture capital investors, and that realized by the shareholders as a whole. In principle, the explanatory variables may influence these quite differently. For example, if the effect of team completeness were well known and the venture capital market were highly competitive, investors would attach higher values to ventures with complete teams and would receive (on the average) a return which is just enough to compensate for their risks. The founders and employees would capture all of the excess value. In such a case team completeness might predict the internal rate of return for the firm as a whole, but not for the investors.

We view a measure based on a company's market value as superior to the more common subjective assessments of success or to accounting measures such as sales or market share. The shortcomings of accounting measures are well summarized by Benston (1985) and Beaver (1981). Beaver also reviews the major advantages of market value measures. Market values are themselves subjective assessments, but they may be viewed as "best subjective assessments" in the sense that they represent a pooling of expert judgments, take account of varying circumstances, incorporate information from all sources, and embody strong economic incentives.

The rate of return is calculated by considering the funds invested in each financing round as negative cash flows. A single positive cash flow is assigned to the time when the company holds an initial public offering, is sold, or is written off—using the price at which the event occurs. Companies still in the venture capital firms' portfolios in June 1988 are assigned a value at the time of their last investment equal to the price per share of that round multiplied by the number of shares existing prior to the round. Of the 36 firms 12 were public, nine had been acquired, three had been written off, and 12 were still in the portfolios.

Independent Variables

Our earlier discussion of management, environment, and strategy identified 11 independent variables that we expect to influence the success of new ventures. They are shown in Table 1. They are designed to be easily measured and, hence, replicated in other samples. Summary statistics for each variable are shown in Table 2.

TABLE 1   Description of Independent Variables

Job experience (SIMEXP):   The percentage of founders* with experience in a position similar (i.e., the same function and within one organizational level) to the one to be assumed.

High growth experience (HIGROW):   The percentage of founders* with experience in rapidly growing (over 25% annual growth in sales) companies.

Team completeness (COMPL):   The percentage of key positions which were filled at the time of the first major (over $300,000) outside funding. Key positions are the president and functional managers for marketing, engineering, operations, finance (or a second technical manager in place of one of the latter two if the venture involved two technologies—such as electronic and mechanical design).

Prior joint experience (JTEXP):   This reflects the extent to which founders* had previously worked in the same organization for at least six months. Several measures were tested; the one used here considers the leader (usually the CEO) and the three other founders with the greatest joint experience. For each common employer between the leader and another founder a value of 20 is given. For each common employer among the three other founders a value of 10 is given. The combination produces a range of 90 points which is arbitrarily set from 10 to 100.

Quality of the technical development plan (PLAN):   The technical plan is selected as a variable rather than the business plan because almost every firm in this sample has a complete, high quality business plan. The approach to technical development plans varies considerably, allowing the following measures:
  1 = no mention of how the venture will develop its technology
  2 = general statement about how the technology will be developed without milestones or schedules
  3 = milestones, schedules, and tasks are described in a general way
  4 = a detailed development program has quarterly schedules with an outline of the more important tasks
  5 = a monthly development program includes details of important tasks.

Product development time (DEVTM):   The number of months from the initiation of development to the initial sale as forecast in the business plan.

TABLE 1   (*Continued*)

Product superiority (SUP):   Measured on a five-point scale:
      1 = a product's benefits match those of its competitors or potential substitutes
      2 = a product incorporates minor improvements
      3 = it incorporates significant improvements in performance
      4 = it represents a major improvement
      5 = it will clearly be the industry leader.

Competitor strength (COMPETE):   Assessed on a five-point scale (using information in the business plans):
      1 = no existing competition
      2 = one competitor exists, or a few potential competitors are identified
      3 = a few (2–4) competitors exist, but are either small or not attentive to the market niche
      4 = several small, or a few large, competitors exist, but no clear leader has emerged
      5 = several companies are serving the market and a clear leader exists.

Forecast market share in the fifth year (MKTSHR):   An indirect measure of competitive conditions:

Buyer concentration (CONC):   A measure of the number of potential customers in the target market during the
first two years of sales. It is rated on a five-point scale:
      1 = very low concentration (over 300 customers)
      2 = low concentration (100 to 300 customers)
      3 = medium concentration (30 to 99 customers)
      4 = high concentration (10 to 29 customers)
      5 = very high concentration (less than 10 customers).

Founders' Equity Share (FDRSH):   The share of the company retained by the founders* after the first
financing.

---

  *Founders are those employees, who, as indicated by the business plan, are expected: (1) to play a key role in the development
of the firm, (2) to become employees of the company within the first year after the initial funding date, and (3) to share in the
ownership of the company in a significant manner.

     The measures are taken directly from the business plans. Any inaccuracies in the plans
will carry over to the data. With four possible exceptions discussed below, we believe such
inaccuracies are not common, because the venture capitalists' notes show extensive verifi-
cation of the plans and corrections are rare.

     Two variables, projected market share and projected time of product development, are
inherently subject to error (compared to the plan writer's true belief or compared to the
actual outcome). This may diminish their predictive ability. Two other variables, competition
and product superiority, are the researcher's assessment from evidence in the plan. To
minimize possible biases a set of guidelines are followed (which are summarized in Table
1), and these variables were assessed prior to collection of financial results. Nonetheless,
some of the ventures are very well known, and possible bias from knowledge of actual
performance remains a possibility. We will return to this during the discussion of results.

RESULTS AND ANALYSIS

Five multiple regression analyses, shown in Tables 3 to 7, test the model. Table 3 deals
with the characteristics of the founders. Table 4 deals with the environment, and Tables 5
and 6 with the firm's strategic choices. Table 7 combines the three areas.

     Each equation includes three lines. The first shows the coefficients. The second shows
the standardized coefficients (in which all variables are standardized to zero mean and unit

PREDICTORS OF TECHNOLOGY BASED VENTURE SUCCESS **211**

TABLE 2   Means and Standard Deviations of the Variables

	Variable	Type*	Mean	Standard Deviation
1.	Experience in Similar Position (SIMEXP)	M	85.58	16.53
2.	High Growth Experience (HIGROW)	M	89.39	24.12
3.	Team Completeness (COMPL)	M	70.96	19.02
4.	Principals' Joint Experience (JTEXP)	M	55.56	29.03
5.	Founder Equity Share (FDRSH)	E	47.83	19.10
6.	Competition in Market Segment (COMPETE)	E	3.06	1.07
7.	Projected Market Share (MKTSHR)	E	9.36	6.20
8.	Buyer Concentration (CONC)	E	2.78	1.22
9.	Product Superiority (SUP)	F	3.42	1.18
10.	Quality of Technical Plan (PLAN)	F	3.67	1.21
11.	Time for Product Development (DEVTM)	F	12.28	6.10
12.	Rate of Return (IRR$_{ALL}$)		98.50	171.10
13.	Rate of Return–Investors (IRR$_{INV}$)		68.30	137.60
14.	Time in Portfolio-Years (T)†		4.57	2.09
15.	Rate of Return · Time (IRR$_{ALL}$ · T)†		317.00	527.80

*"M" refers to management variables, "E" refers to environmental variables, "F" refers to firm (strategy and plan) variables.
†Variables 14 and 15 are used to make technical improvements in the analysis.

variance). The third indicates the t statistics and significance levels of the coefficients. All variables are identified by the symbols shown in Tables 1 and 2.

Each table presents at least three relationships. The first regresses the explanatory variables on rate of return to all owners (IRR$_{ALL}$). The second incorporates a time variable (the inverse of the holding period, 1/T), because the rates of return (and their variation) tend to fall as the holding period increases. This helps eliminate any spurious effects caused by a correlation between an explanatory variable and time. The third equation multiplies the holding period by the IRR to all owners.[5] It corrects effectively for heteroskedasticity of the residuals, which creates a possibility that significance levels are misstated in other equations. The significance levels and standardized coefficients of the corrected equation are very similar to the others, which indicates that the coefficients and significance levels are probably reasonable in all equations.

In Tables 3 and 7 a fourth equation shows the regression on the IRR to investors only (it is omitted in the other tables because these examples sufficiently illustrate the result). As noted earlier these results could be quite different from the regression on IRR to all shareholders, but they are not. Standardized coefficients are very similar, and no variable that explains overall returns fails to explain investor returns at about the same significance level. Apparently the explanatory variables do not have much effect on an investment's price (i.e., the relative ownership of founders and investors).

Except for heteroskedasticity, the models seem reasonably well specified. Residuals are probably not normal—in most regressions normality is rejected at about 0.15 level. But they do not exhibit the "fat tails" that tend to invalidate significance tests. Some explanatory variables have intercorrelations as high as 0.6, but tests of multicollinearity do not show this to be unduly high. Possible nonlinear relationships are considered by including the

---

[5]If a firm had only one financing round, the dependent variable—IRR$_{ALL}$·T—would be the logarithm of the multiple on investment. With more rounds of funding it is less easily interpreted, though it remains an indicator of performance.

squared values of the explanatory variables. None added significant explanatory power in any question (except with development time and buyer concentration where it was expected). In some cases the second power alone was as good as the linear term alone. Dummy variables for each industry were not significantly different from zero, which supports the view that the sample is homogeneous.

Relationship Between Managers' Characteristics and Success

Table 3 provides no support for the importance of individual characteristics on the firm's success. The measures of high growth experience (HIGROW) and similar functional experience (SIMEXP) have very low t statistics in all equations. This should be interpreted cautiously. The high mean values and low standard deviations of the explanatory variables, as shown in Table 2, suggest that most of the firms in the sample may be amply qualified on both measures, and that above some threshold additional qualifications add no value. Informally supporting this interpretation is the founders' average experience of 11 years in their industries, in positions similar to the ones they assumed in their new companies. Only 19 of 144 founders had not served previously in a similar position, and those 19 became general managers for the first time.

In contrast to individual traits the team measures, completeness (COMPL), and prior joint experience (JTEXP), are related to success. These relations appear to be linear.

Relationship Between the Environment and Success

Table 4 indicates that environmental characteristics are effective predictors of success. Three of the four influences that we proposed are significant. Competition in the targeted market segment (COMPETE) is negatively related to success, and projected market share (MKTSHR) has a positive relationship. As noted earlier, competition is assessed by the researcher and is subject to bias based on ex post facto knowledge. The standardized coefficient of competition is about the same as that of projected market share, which suggests any bias is modest—otherwise competition should have the stronger explanatory power.

Table 4 also shows that the number of potential buyers (CONC) targeted by the new company has an inverted U-shaped relationship to the success of the venture ($p < .05$). By taking the derivative of performance with respect to buyer concentration we find the optimal concentration to be about three, implying a customer group numbering 30 to 99.

The postulated relationship between the share of equity owned by the founders (FDRSH) and the new company's success is apparently not true. None of the coefficients of founders' equity are significant. As with the measures of individual qualifications, our finding may occur because all firms in the sample arranged a division of equity with adequate incentives for both founders and investors. More extreme divisions might influence performance.

Relationship Between Strategic Choices and Success

Table 5 suggests that of the variables describing the firm—planning of the technology development, projected time of product development, and product superiority—only product superiority is a good predictor of success. Development time has the expected behavior in Equations 8 and 10, but it is not significant in combination with product superiority.

Product superiority is a judgmental measure, and we would like to have a nonjudgmental measure of product strategy to support it. Accordingly, we analyzed development

PREDICTORS OF TECHNOLOGY BASED VENTURE SUCCESS   **213**

TABLE 3   Multiple Regression of Individual and Team Characteristics on Success[a,b,c,d]

1) IRR_{ALL} =   −252.96   −0.08(HIGROW)   −0.30(SIMEXP)   +3.84(COMPL)   +2.12(JTEXP)
     (−1.45)   [−0.01]   [0.03]   [0.41]   [0.35]
     (−0.07)   (−0.21)   (2.28)*   (1.85)†
     S.E. = 136.85,   adj R^2 = 0.40**, df = 31

2) IRR_{ALL} =   −297.64   −0.64(HIGROW)   −1.02(SIMEXP)   +3.87(COMPL)   +1.87(JTEXP)   +635.12(1/T)
     (−2.06)   [−0.09]   [−0.09]   [0.41]   [0.31]   [0.44]
     (−0.75)   (−.85)   (2.78)**   (1.98)†   (3.90)**
     S.E. = 113.30,   adj R^2 = 0.59**, df = 30

3) $IRR_{ALL} \cdot T$ =   −594.35   −0.46(HIGROW)   −0.12(SIMEXP)   +13.22(COMPL)   +5.97(JTEXP)
     (−1.20)   [−0.02]   [−0.12]   [0.48]   [0.33]
     (−0.15)   (−0.90)   (2.75)**   (1.83)†
     S.E. = 391.15,   adj R^2 = 0.45**, df = 31

4) $IRR_{INVESTORS}$ =   −188.62   −0.12(HIGROW)   −0.45(SIMEXP)   +2.85(COMPL)   +1.87(JTEXP)
     (−1.43)   [−0.02]   [−0.05]   [0.39]   [0.39]
     (−0.16)   (−0.41)   (2.24)*   (2.17)*
     S.E. = 103.47,   adj R^2 = 0.43**, df = 31

[a]Standardized coefficients shown in brackets.
[b]t statistics in parentheses. Two tail significance is (†) $p < 0.10$, (*) $p < 0.05$, (**) $p < 0.01$.
[c]Equations 1, 2, and 4 show evidence of heteroskedastic residuals ($p = 0.01$). Equation 3 does not ($p = 0.60$).
[d]Tested for non-linearity by adding second powers of each variable to Equation 1. None was significant at $p < 0.10$.

TABLE 4 Multiple Regression of Environment Characteristics on Success^{a,b,c,R}

5) IRR_{ALL} = −220.74 −46.42(COMPETE) +286.92(BUYCONC) +46.09(BUYCONC)^2 +8.43(MKTSHR) −1.34(FDRSH)
(−1.06) [−0.28] [1.98]^d [−1.79]^d [0.29] [−0.14]^d
(−1.93)† (2.97)*^{d,e} (−2.70)*^{d,e} (2.07)* (−0.25)^{d,f}
 +0.03(FDRSH)^2
[0.35]^d
(0.61)^{d,f}
S.E. = 137.17
adj R^2 = 0.40**
df = 29

6) IRR_{ALL} = −297.56 −37.28(COMPETE) +234.82(BUYCONC) −37.24(BUYCONC)^2 +9.05(MKTSHR) −2.24(FDRSH)
(−1.58) [−0.23] [1.62]^d [−1.44]^d [0.32] [−0.24]^d
(−1.71)† (2.66)*^{d,e} (−2.39)*^{d,e} (2.48)** (−0.47)^{d,f}
 +0.03(FDRSH)^2 +511.16(1/T)
[0.41]^d [0.35]
(0.79)^{d,f} (2.48)**
S.E. = 122.82
adj R^2 = 0.52**
df = 28

7) $IRR_{ALL} \cdot T$ = −552.83 −161.31(COMPETE) +742.67(BUYCONC) −121.38(BUYCONC)^2 +26.54(MKTSHR) +2.87(FDRSH)
(−0.88) [−0.33] [1.72]^d [−1.58]^d [0.31] [0.10]^d
(−2.23)* (2.55)*^{d,e} (−2.36)*^{d,e} (2.16)** (0.18)
 +0.10(FDRSH)^2
[0.04]^d
(0.07)
S.E. = 414.28
adj R^2 = 0.38**
df = 29

^{a} Standardized coefficients in brackets.
^{b} t statistics in parentheses. Two tail significance is (†) $p < 0.10$, (*) $p < 0.05$, (**) $p < 0.01$.
^{c} Equations 5 and 6 show evidence of heteroskedactic residuals ($p = 0.01$). Equation 7 does not ($p = 0.73$).
^{d} For variables entering at first and second power std coeficients and t statistics are of limited value.
^{e} F test on BUYCONC and (BUYCONC)^2 is $p = 0.02$ in Equation 5, $p = 0.03$ in Equation 6 and $p = 0.045$ in Equation 7. Asterisks refer to F test, not t statistic. Optimum value of BUYCONC is 3.11 in Equation 5, 3.15 in Equation 6 and 3.06 in Equation 7.
^{f} F tests on FDRSH and (FDRSH)^2 are not significant.
^{R} Tested for non-linearities of COMPETE and MKTSHR by adding second power terms—they were not significant.

TABLE 5 Multiple Regression of Firm's Management Processes/Strategic Choices for Success[a,b,c]

8) IRR_{ALL} =   −217.65   +54.99(PRODSUP)   +33.02(DEVTM)   −1.39(DEVTM)^2 +35.47(PLAN)

     (−1.84)†   [0.37]   [1.14]^d [−1.23]^d [−0.02]

           (2.11)*   (1.52)^{d,e} (1.73)^{d,e} (−0.10)

     S.E. = 153.04   adj R^2 = 0.25** df = 31

9) IRR_{ALL} =   −418.61   +78.02(PRODSUP)   −7.76(DEVTM)   +0.12(DEVTM)^2 +35.47(PLAN)   +751.31(1/T)

     (−3.56)**   [0.52]   [0.27]^d [0.10]^d [0.23]   [0.52]

           (3.33)**   (−0.35)^{d,e} (0.14)^{d,e} (1.34)   (3.41)**

     S.E. = 132.05   adj R^2 = 0.44** df = 30

10) $IRR_{ALL} \cdot T$ =   −735.69   +185.319(PRODSUP)   +96.02(DEVTM)   −4.04(DEVTM)^2 −1.32(PLAN)

     (−2.16)*   [0.41]   [1.11]^{d,e} [−1.20]^d [0]

           (2.47)*   (1.53)^{d,e} (−1.74)^{d,e} (−0.02)

     S.E. = 440.79   adj R^2 = 0.30** df = 31

[a]Standardized coefficients shown in brackets.

[b]t statistics in parentheses. Two tail significance is (†) $p < 0.10$, (*) $p < 0.05$, (**) $p < 0.01$.

[c]Equations 8 and 9 show evidence of heteroskedastic residuals ($p = 0.01$). Equation 10 does not ($p = 0.43$).

[d]Standardized coefficients and t statistics are of limited value for variables entering at first and second power.

[e]F test on DEVTM and DEVTM^2 is not significant.

216 J.B. ROURE AND R.H. KEELEY

TABLE 6 Polynomial Regression of Development Time on Success[a,b]

11) $IRR_{ALL} =$	-141.24	$+52.36(DEVTM)$ $[1.80]^c$	$-2.12(DEVTM)^2$ $[-1.88]^c$		S.E. = 159.72 adj R^2 = 0.29**
	(-1.41)	$(3.03)**^{c,d}$	$(-3.16)**^{c,d}$		df = 32
12) $IRR_{ALL} =$	-211.82	$+37.59(DEVTM)$ $[1.29]^c$	$-1.53(DEVTM)^2$ $[-1.35]^c$	$+526.57\ (1/T)$ $[0.36]$	S.E. = 149.68 adj R^2 = 0.29**
	$(-2.15)*$	$(2.16)\dagger^{c,d}$	$(-2.25)\dagger^{c,d}$	$(2.36)*$	df = 32
13) $IRR_{ALL} \cdot T =$	-463.91	$+163.61(DEVTM)$ $[1.89]^c$	$-6.58(DEVTM)^2$ $[-1.95]^c$		S.E. = 470.56 adj R^2 = 0.21**
	(-1.57)	$(3.21)**^{c,d}$	$(-3.22)**^{c,d}$		df = 33

[a] Standardized coefficients in brackets.

[b] t statistics in parentheses. Two tail significance is $(\dagger)p < 0.10$, $(*)p < 0.05$, $(**)p < 0.01$.

[c] Standardized coefficients and t statistics are of limited value for variables entering at first and second power.

[d] F test on DEVTM and $DEVTM^2$ is $p = 0.01$ in Equation 11, $p = 0.09$ in Equation 12, and $p = 0.01$ in Equation 13. Symbols on t statistics refer to F test on both coefficients, not to t statistic. Optimum value of DEVTM is 12.34 months in Equation 11, 12.28 months in Equation 12, and 12.43 months in Equation 13.

time alone. The results, shown in Table 6 are significant ($p < .01$ in Equations 11 and 13 and $p < .10$ in Equation 12) and show the inverted U-shaped relationship. Setting the derivative of performance equal to 0 indicates an optimal development time of 12.2 to 12.4 months in the three equations.[6] A comparison of R^2 in Tables 6 and 7 suggests that development time is roughly as strong a predictor as product superiority. Product superiority is subject to the researcher's judgment and is therefore potentially biased. Its parity with the more objective development time suggests that any bias is minor.

The quality of the technical development plan does not influence success according to Table 5. This should be interpreted cautiously, it could mean that technical planning is important, but that business plans do not accurately reflect technical planning.

Combining the Team, Firm, and Environmental Viewpoints

The significant variables of Tables 3 through 6 are combined in a single regression in Table 7, showing only the variables that generally remain significant at a 10% level or better. They include measures from each area—the team, the firm's strategic choices, and the environment—indicating that all three contribute to success. In Equation 14, four predictive variables (team completeness, product superiority, buyer concentration, and development time—the latter two as quadratic functions) explain 57% of the variance, a considerable improvement over the regressions with only one viewpoint. Equation 15, which incorporates time as a variable, and Equation 16, which uses the product of return and time as a measure of success, are similar to Equation 14. Equation 17 illustrates again that the IRR to investors behaves similarly to the IRR for all shareholders—the explanatory variables apparently do not measurably influence pricing, even though they can predict results.

Three variables—prior joint experience, industry competitiveness, and projected market share—no longer show any explanatory power. Given our limited sample, these should not be discarded as influences on success; further tests on other samples are needed.

Table 7 shows the advantages of simultaneously considering management, strategy,

---

[6] We also examined an interactive form in which product superiority and a quadratic function of development time are multiplied. This had stronger explanatory power than the forms shown in Tables 5 and 6. The implication is that superiority has enhanced value if obtained in the optimum amount of time (probably this also corrects as well for erroneous overestimates of product superiority combined with a short development time).

TABLE 7 Multiple Regression of Team, Firm, and Environment Characteristics on Success[a,b,c]

14) IRR_{ALL} = -598.09 + 3.70(COMPL) + 35.37(SUP) + 247.71(CONC) − 43.04(CONC)^2 + 17.34(DEVTM) − 0.93(DEVTM)^2 S.E. = 116.97
  [0.40]   [0.24]   [1.71]^d [−1.72]^d [0.60]   [−0.82]   adj R^2 = 0.57**
  (−5.35)**   (2.95)*   (1.65)   (2.73)*^{d,e} (−2.82)*^{d,e} (1.14)†^{d,f} (−1.60)†^{d,f} df = 29

15) IRR_{ALL} = -639.35 + 3.65(COMPL) + 44.03(SUP) + 204.91(CONC) − 36.93(CONC)^2 + 1.95(DEVTM) − 0.29(DEVTM)^2 + 563.37 (1/T)
  [0.39]   [0.29]   [1.41]^d [−1.43]^d [0.07]   [−0.26]   [0.35]
  (−6.57)**   (3.38)**   (2.36)*   (2.58)*^{d,e} (−2.67)*^{d,e} (0.14)^{d,f} (−0.55)^{d,f} (3.30)**
  S.E. = 100.23   adj R^2 = 0.68**   df = 28

16) $\text{IRR}_{\text{ALL}} \cdot \text{T}$ = -1768.26 + 12.2(COMPL) + 119.23(SUP) + 590.85(CONC) − 110.36(CONC)^2 + 61.24(DEVTM) − 3.05(DEVTM)^2 S.E. = 331.38
  [0.44]   [0.27]   [1.37]^d [−1.43]^d [0.71]   [−0.91]   adj R^2 = 0.61**
  (−5.54)**   (3.42)**   (1.95)†   (2.28)†^{d,e} (−2.45)†^{d,e} (1.40)*^{d,f} (−1.85)*^{d,f} df = 29

17) IRR_{INV} = -486.27 + 2.91(COMPL) + 24.63(SUP) + 183.96(CONC) − 32.30(CONC)^2 + 15.88(DEVTM) − 0.78(DEVTM)^2 S.E. = 90.38
  [0.40]   [0.21]   [1.63]^d [−1.61]   [0.70]   [−0.89]   adj R^2 = 0.57**
  (−5.58)**   (3.00)**   (1.47)   (2.60)*^{d,e} (−2.63)*^{d,e} (1.34)†^{d,f} (−1.74)†^{d,f} df = 29

[a]Standardized coefficients in brackets.

[b]t statistics in parentheses. Two tail significance is (†) $p < 0.10$, (*) $p < 0.05$, (**) $p < 0.01$.

[c]Equations 14 and 17 show evidence of heteroskedastic residuals ($p = 0.03$); Equation 15 shows little ($p = 0.30$); Equation 16 shows less ($p = 0.48$).

[d]Standardized coefficients and t statistics are of limited value for variable entering at first and second power.

[e]F test on CONC and CONC^2 is $p = 0.03$ in Equation 14, $p = 0.04$ in Equation 15, $p = 0.06$ in Equation 16, and $p = 0.05$ in Equation 17. Symbols beside t statistics refer to significance of F test on both coefficients. Optimum values of CONC are 2.78, 2.77, 2.68, and 2.85 in Equations 14, 15, 16, and 17, respectively.

[f]F test on DEVTM and DEVTM^2 is $p = 0.06$ in Equation 14, $p = 0.16$ in Equation 15, $p = 0.05$ in Equation 16, $p = 0.07$ in Equation 17. Symbols beside t statistics refer to significance of F test on both coefficients. Optimum values of DEVTM are 9.32, 3.36 (note the coefficients are not significant), 10.0, and 10.2 in Equations 14, 15, 16, and 17, respectively.

and environmental dimensions. Explanatory power jumps substantially. A comparison of variables from different areas is possible. The relative importance of variables can be assessed, which is much stronger than just knowing their effects are non-zero; and the multivariate approach strengthens some findings (development time) while suggesting others may be spurious (market share, prior joint experience, and competition).

CONCLUSION

The study of new venture performance is still at an early stage, and our findings must be viewed as tentative. In addition, the nature of the competition implies that successful approaches will be imitated and that such imitation will tend to change the relationships reported here. While acknowledging the need for caution, we are encouraged by the results:

1. Success in new ventures is explainable using theories developed for other purposes—organizational behavior, industrial organization, and strategic management. By selecting among them for attributes that allow an organization to move quickly, we obtained a preliminary set of 11 qualities. Our sample confirms that seven of them behave as expected. Three others show no influence, perhaps because of a lack of sufficient variation in this sample. Only one, technical planning, seems conclusively to have no influence, possibly because business plans do not reflect the underlying amount of technical planning.
2. Success requires appropriate choices of management, industry, and strategy. Weakness in one can be offset by strength in another.
3. A multi-industry sample, united by a common investor (who has relatively uniform selection criteria), appears to be reasonably homogeneous. This is fortunate because single industry samples of new ventures are possible in only a few industries (e.g., disk memories and some types of software). The apparent absence of industry-specific results suggests that common elements, such as urgency and uncertainty, may determine the performance of many new ventures.
4. If our model extends to multiple funds—which we are testing with a follow-up study—it would be transferrable across industries and investors, at least within the family of high potential, technology-based new ventures. This would strengthen the results of multi-investor studies (such as MacMillan et al. 1987; or Sandberg and Hofer 1987), which are necessary in many cases to obtain adequate sample sizes.
5. Success may be predictable to some extent with simple variables that do not require expert assessment. This allows easy replication across time and across samples, permitting the detection of trends, changes in the relative importance of variables, and so forth. Detection of variations across funds, industries, and time has special value in a field such as new ventures where many studies are questionnaire-based and not easily replicated. It helps calibrate the range over which other studies may be applied.
6. An unambiguous measure of success—the internal rate of return on investment—has been shown to perform well as a dependent variable. It produces a well specified linear regression model and transcends the industry-specific variations one finds in accounting measures.

We believe the study can be extended in several directions, some of which are indicated above. We also plan to study these firms over time to verify the ways in which the explanatory variables exert their influence.

REFERENCES

Aldrich, H. 1979. *Organizations and Environments*. Englewood Cliffs, NJ: Prentice-Hall.

Aldrich, H., and Zimmer, C. 1986. Entrepreneurship through social networks. In *Population Perspectives on Organizations*. Uppsala: University of Uppsala.

Beaver, W.H. 1981. *Financial Reporting: An Accounting Revolution*. Englewood Cliffs, NJ: Prentice Hall.

Benston, G.J. 1985. The validity of profits-structure studies with particular reference to the FTC's line of business data. *American Economic Review* 75(1):37–67.

Bowman, K.O., and Shenton, L.R. 1986. Moment (b1,b2) techniques. In R.B. D'Agostino and M.A. Stephens, eds., *Goodness-of-Fit Techniques*. New York: Marcel Dekker, pp. 217–329.

Bourgeois, L.J., III, and Eisenhardt, K.M. 1985. *Strategic Decision Processes in High Velocity Environments: Four Cases in the Microcomputer Industry*. Research Paper No. 852, Graduate School of Business, Stanford University.

Brittain, J.W., and Freeman, J.H. 1980. Organizational proliferation and density dependent selection. In J.R. Kimberly and R. Miles, eds., *The Organizational Life Cycle*. San Francisco: Jossey-Bass, pp. 291–338.

Cooper, R.G. 1979. The dimensions of industrial new product success and failure. *Journal of Marketing* 9(3):93–103.

Cooper, A.C., and Bruno, A.V. 1977. Success among high-technology firms. *Business Horizons* April:16–23.

Hackman, J.R., and Oldham, G.R. 1980. *Work Redesign*. Reading, MA: Addison-Wesley.

Hannan, M.T., and Freeman, J.H. 1977. The population ecology of organizations. *American Journal of Sociology* 32:929–964.

Katz, R. 1982. The effects of group longevity on project communication and performance. *Administrative Science Quarterly* 27:81–104.

Khan, A.M. 1987. Assessing venture capital investments with noncompensatory behavioral decision models. *Journal of Business Venturing* 2(3):193–205.

MacMillan, I.C., Zemann, L., and Narasimha, P.N.S. 1987. Criteria distinguishing successful from unsuccessful ventures in the venture screening process. *Journal of Business Venturing* 2(2):123–137.

Maidique, M.A., and Zirger, B.J. 1984. A study of success and failure in product innovation: The case of the U.S. electronic industry. *IEEE Transactions in Engineering Management* EM-31(4):192–203.

Pfeffer, J., and Salancik, G. 1978. *The External Control of Organizations*. New York: Harper and Row.

Porter, M. 1980. *Competitive Strategy: Techniques for Analyzing Industries and Competitors*. New York: The Free Press.

Roure, J.B. 1986. *Success and Failure of High-Growth Technological Ventures: The Influence of Prefunding Factors*. Doctoral dissertation, Stanford University.

Roure, J.B., and Maidique, M.A. 1986. Linking prefunding factors and high-technology venture success: An exploratory study. *Journal of Business Venturing* 1(3):295–306.

Ruhnka, J.C., and Young, J.E. 1987. A venture capital model of the development process for new ventures. *Journal of Business Venturing* 2(2):165–184.

Sandberg, W.A., and Hofer, C.W. 1987. Improving new venture performance: The role of strategy, industry structure and the entrepreneur. *Journal of Business Venturing* 2(1):5–28.

Stuart, R., and Abetti, P.A. 1987. Start-up ventures: Towards the prediction of initial success. *Journal of Business Venturing* 2(3):215–229.

Tuckman, B.W. 1965. Developmental sequence in small groups. *Psychological Bulletin* 63(6):384–399.

Tyebjee, T.T., and Bruno, A.V. 1984. A model of venture capitalist investment activity. *Management Science* 9:1051–1066.

Van de Ven, A.H. 1980. Early planning, implementation, and performance of new organizations. In
    J.R. Kimberly, R.H. Miles and Associates, eds. *The Organizational Life Cycle*. San Francisco:
    Jossey-Bass, pp. 83–133.

Van de Ven, A.H., Hudson, R., and Schroeder, D.M. 1984. Designing new business start ups:
    Entrepreneurial, organizational, and ecological considerations. *Journal of Management* 10(1):87.

Vesper, K.H. 1980. *New Venture Strategies*. Englewood Cliffs, NJ: Prentice Hall.

[10]

Regional Studies, Vol. 32.5, pp. 405–419

A Policy Response to Regional Disparities in the Supply of Risk Capital to New Technology-based Firms in the European Union: The European Seed Capital Fund Scheme

GORDON C. MURRAY

Warwick Business School, University of Warwick, Coventry CV4 7AL, UK

(Received October 1995; in revised form January 1997)

MURRAY G. C. (1998) A policy response to regional disparities in the supply of risk capital to new technology-based firms in the European Union: the European Seed Capital Fund Scheme, *Reg. Studies* 32, 405–419. The European Seed Capital Fund Pilot Scheme (1988–95) was a European Commission response to two primary concerns that: (1) private venture capital firms in Europe were increasingly retreating from the financing and support of start-up, early-stage and, particularly, technology-based enterprises; and (2) existing spatial concentrations in the supply of venture capital prejudiced the formation of new, innovative businesses in less economically developed regions of the Union. This paper presents the updated results of a study of this Scheme in 1992. The comparative internal dynamics of the Seed Funds are explored. The Scheme realized its goal of encouraging private investment into innovative, technology-based young firms. However, the continued ability of the funds to meet longer-term commercial and/or regional developmental objectives is questioned given scale-related problems of economic viability.

Venture capital   High technology   Regional development   Small firms

MURRAY G. C. (1998) La réponse politique aux écarts régionaux de l'offre de capital-risque aux entreprises basées sur les nouvelles technologies et situées au sein de l'Union européenne: le programme en faveur d'un fonds européen de capitaux de lancement, *Reg. Studies* 32, 405–419. Le programme en faveur d'un fonds européen de capitaux de lancement (European Seed Capital Fund Pilot Scheme 1988–95), a été une réponse de la part de la Commission européenne à deux soucis primordiaux. Primo, en Europe les entreprises de capital-risque privées se retiraient de plus en plus du financement et du soutien des pépinières d'entreprises, des entreprises dans les phases initiales de développement et des entreprises basées sur les nouvelles technologies. Secundo, Les concentrations géographiques existantes de l'offre de capital-risque entravaient la création de nouvelles entreprises innovatrices dans les zones défavorisées de l'Union. Cet article cherche à présenter les résultats mis à jour d'une étude de ce programme faite en 1992. On examine la dynamique interne comparative du fonds. Le programme a réussi à encourager l'investissement privé dans de nouvelles entreprises innovatrices, basées sur les nouvelles technologies. Cependant, on remet en question la capacité des fonds à répondre aux objectifs commerciaux et/ou régionaux à plus long terme étant donné le problème de leur viabilité économique lié à la notion d'échelle.

Capital-risque   Technologie de pointe
Aménagement du territoire   Petites entreprises

MURRAY G. C. (1998) Eine grundsätzliche Antwort auf regionale Ungleichheiten im Angebot von Risikokapital für auf neuer Technologie aufgebaute Firmen in der Europäischen Union: das europäische Saatkornkapitalfond Project, *Reg. Studies* 32, 405–419. Das europäische Saatkornkapitalfond Versuchsprojekt (1988–1995) stellte eine Antwort der europäischen Kommission auf zwei grundlegende Anliegen dar: (1) private Risikokapitalfirmen in Europa zogen sich zunehmend von der Finanzierung und Unterstützung neu gegründeter, in Anfängen begriffener und vorallem von auf Technologie aufgebauten Unternehmen zurück, und (2) bestehende räumliche Konzentrationen beim Aufbringen von Risikokapital beeinträchtigten die Bildung neuer, innovativer Geschäftsunternehmungen in weniger entwickelten Gebieten der Union. Dieser Aufsatz stellt die auf den neuesten Stand gebrachten Ergebnisse einer Studie dieses Projektes vom Jahre 1992 vor. Die vergleichsweise interne Dynamik der Saatkornfonds wird untersucht. Das Projekt verwirklichte das ihm gesteckte Ziel, private Investierungen in innovativen, auf Technologie aufgebauten jungen Firmen zu ermutigen. Die anhaltende Fähigkeit des Fonds, das Kapital für längerfristige kommerzielle und/oder regionale Entwicklungsobjekte aufzubringen, wird jedoch angesichts der Größenordnung bezogenen Probleme wirtschaftlicher Realisierbarkeit wegen in Frage gestellt.

Risikokapital   Hochtechnologie
Regionale Entwicklung   Kleinfirmen

0034-3404/98/050405-15 ©1998 Regional Studies Association

INTRODUCTION

The effective economic and social convergence of the, now 15, Member States of the European Union was reconfirmed at Maastricht in 1991. However, a significant barrier to realizing the scale and scope economies of European-wide activity remains the disparate economic development both across and within individual Member States. The Commission's commitment to 'spatial justice' (GIANNAKOURU, 1996) has engendered a wide range of initiatives targeted to less developed areas of the Union.

SMALL AND MEDIUM SIZED ENTERPRISES: THE SPECIAL CASE OF NEW TECHNOLOGY-BASED FIRMS (NTBFs)

Since the late 1970s, small and medium sized enterprises (SMEs) have been seen as an increasingly important policy vehicle for economic and regional development goals within the Union. This interest has come about through an increasing recognition of the major contribution of SMEs to total employment and to the net creation of new jobs (BIRCH, 1979; GALLAGHER and STEWART, 1986; STOREY *et al.* 1989). SMEs are now firmly established as a major focus of the Commission's economic, technological and regional policies (EUROPEAN COMMISSION (EC), 1994, 1995).

Within the wider corpus of SMEs, new technology-based firms represent a peculiarly attractive focus for policy makers. NTBFs are seen as offering significant potential benefits in four cardinal areas of Union interest: employment creation; innovation; export sales growth; and regional development (ROTHWELL and ZEGVELD, 1982; FREEMAN, 1983; OECD, 1986; OAKEY *et al.*, 1988; ROTHWELL, 1989; ROBERTS, 1991; COOPERS & LYBRAND, 1996). Interest in NTBFs has, in part, stemmed from an appreciation of their critical role from the early 1970s in the economic growth of regions of high technology activity in the USA, particularly Silicon Valley, California, and Route 128 around Boston, Massachusetts (OAKEY, 1984; FLORIDA and KENNY, 1988; ROBERTS, 1991; BYGRAVE and TIMMONS, 1992), as well as their contribution to fast growth European regions (MEYER-KRAMER, 1985; KEEBLE, 1989).

However, while successful NTBFs potentially offer material advantages to the economic prosperity of a location, their genesis and early years are fraught with extremely high levels of uncertainty and risk in virtually all areas of activity including financing, technology and marketing (OAKEY, 1984; ROBERTS, 1991; MURRAY, 1995). For the individual NTBF, an exceptional technological offering is a necessary but not sufficient condition for economic success. Their entrepreneurial founders have also to manage organizational and pro-

duct/market demands in both internal and external environments characterized by their complexity and rapid rate of change.

THE FINANCING OF NTBFs

Financing difficulties are particularly acute for NTBFs on formation and at their earliest stages of development (ROBERTS, 1991; MOORE, 1993; MURRAY and LOTT, 1995). Limited tangible assets reduces their opportunity for collateral-based lending from retail banks, which are the predominant source of external finance to European SMEs (EUROPEAN NETWORK FOR SME RESEARCH, 1993; STOREY, 1994). The economic value of intellectual property rights created by the entrepreneur is, as yet, unproven and thus unexploitable (RUMELT, 1984). The ability of new entrepreneurs from a technology/scientific background to attract external equity finance, i.e. formal venture capital, is also prejudiced by their frequent lack of commercial experience and the absence of an established track record of successful enterprise (TYEBJEE and BRUNO, 1984; MACMILLAN *et al.*, 1985; GOSLIN and BARGE, 1986). In consequence, owner-managers of NTBFs are, per force, very heavily dependent on own and family personal finance for initial capitalization (OAKEY, 1984; ROBERTS, 1991; MOORE, 1993) in addition to relying on trade credit and, to a lesser extent, government grants (UTTERBACK *et al.*, 1988; MOORE and GARNSEY, 1991).

The imperfections of capital markets have featured largely in the debates on SME developmental constraints. The proposition of the existence of an 'equity gap', i.e. a market failure in the adequate provision of external risk capital, has been part of the economic literature for over 60 years (see MACMILLAN, 1931). A succession of official committees and research exercises since that date (see, for example, BOLTON, 1971; WILSON, 1979; BURNS and DEWHURST, 1993; CONFEDERATION OF BRITISH INDUSTRY, 1993) have each cited evidence of the existence of equity gaps and their deleterious effect on the viability of smaller businesses which are generally characterized as having weaker liquidity, more volatile levels of profitability, an over-dependence on short term sources of finance and an insufficiency of shareholders' funds or equity. NTBFs are seen as particularly vulnerable to capital constraints given that initial investment costs, particularly R&D, are incurred before any prospect of consequent revenues.

THE IMPORTANCE OF VENTURE CAPITAL

It is within the context of innovative firms seeking early-stage, external finance with the potential promise of substantial returns but at a concomitant high level

Table 1. *Allocation of European venture capital investments by stage, 1993–95*

Stages of venture capital investment	1993 ECU million	1993 % total	1994 ECU million	1994 % total	1995 ECU million	1995 % total
Seed	20·8	0·5	37·1	0·7	34·4	0·6
Start-up and early stage	179·7	4·4	273·3	5·0	286·5	5·2
Expansion	1,888·5	45·9	2,294·2	42·2	2,298·6	41·4
Replacement	345·9	8·4	434·1	8·0	354·5	6·4
MBO/MBI	1,680·2	40·8	2,401·0	44·1	2,572·0	46·4
Total investment	4,115	100·0	5,440	100·0	5,546	100·0

Sources: BVCA, 1995; EVCA, 1995.

Table 2. *Technology investments as a percentage of 'adjusted' total annual venture capital investment (i.e. excluding MBOs/MBIs and LBOs/acquisitions in Europe and the USA, respectively), 1986–94*

	USA: NVCA statistic		Europe: EVCA statistic[1]	
	Annual 'adjusted' investment value ($ million)	Technology investments as % total 'adjusted' investment	Annual 'adjusted' investment value (ECU m)	Technology investments as % total 'adjusted' investment
1986	2,641	87	1,075	38
1987	3,173	80	1,892	36
1988	2,720	86	2,120	34
1989	2,685	85	2,360	37
1990	1,887	85	2,608	31
1991	1,312	92	3,028	25
1992	2,367	85	2,832	27
1993	2,899	86	2,439	28
1994	2,575	88	3,039	28
1995[2]	—	—	2,974	45

Notes: 1. EVCA statistics aggregate 16 European countries including the UK.

2. NVCA figures were complied in a different format from 1995 and this year is excluded (the technology element is 83%).

These trends should only be seen as indicative given broad definition of technology-based investments employed.

Sources: European Venture Capital Association Annual Statistics 1985–95, and the National Venture Capital Association Annual Reports 1990–95.

of risk that the potential of venture capital as a source of entrepreneurial support appears most relevant. Yet, almost without exception in the 16 member countries of the European Venture Capital Association (EVCA), there has been a declining interest in the support of start-up and early-stage investment since the mid 1980s. The European *venture* capital industry has metamorphosed into a *development* capital industry primarily occupied with the restructuring and refinancing of extant businesses (Table 1).

'Fast-track' NTBFs, with their predominant reliance on external equity finance, are particularly disadvantaged by such structural changes in the venture capital market. Even if management buy-out/management buy-in (MBO/MBI) statistics are removed from the European figures, the percentage of total investment allocated to technology-based enterprises has remained largely constant over a decade of enormous technological change in the world's developed economies (Table 2). The proportion of venture finance allocated to NTBFs in Europe is in stark contrast to the preeminence of technology-based investments in the US. (Note: while this paper is exclusively concerned with 'formal' venture capital, an exhaustive treatment of NTBF financing must necessarily address the potentially critical role played by informal investors or 'business angels' particularly within a regional development context (WETZEL, 1993; MASON and HARRISON, 1994)).

REGIONAL DISCONTINUITIES IN THE SUPPLY OF EUROPEAN VENTURE CAPITAL

The existence of a regional dimension to the supply and demand for equity has become a theme of increasing interest to economic geographers (MCNAUGHTON and GREEN, 1988; MARTIN, 1989; THOMPSON, 1989; MASON and HARRISON, 1991; MASON, 1992), given the consequent implications for development in regions with poorly developed capital markets.

THOMPSON, 1989, argues that venture capital is a subject of particular interest for four reasons: its role in new investment processes including regional development disparities; its pivotal importance to high-technology industries; the involvement by (US) public agencies in influencing the supply of venture capital particularly to address regional 'gaps'; and the 'spatial choreography' of venture capital occasioned by behavioural, institutional and distance constraints. Yet, as MARTIN, 1989, and others have noted, given that few robust analyses exist on the processes or outcomes of regional capital formation, theoretical understanding of the spatial organization of capital markets remains unsatisfactory.

The European distribution of venture capital is highly skewed. Some five countries (in rank order: the UK, France, Germany, Italy and the Netherlands) represented 83% of the cumulative funds raised to 1995 (ECU 46·7 billion) by the membership of the EVCA. The UK is the oldest and largest centre of venture capital activity in Europe. It alone represents 45% of cumulative funds, a sum over twice the size of its nearest competitor, France (ECU 10·6 billion).

The considerable regional disparities in venture capital provision between European Member States is further mirrored at the sub-country level. Venture capital firms are clustered in areas characterized by both established financial centres and high concentrations of economic activity (see, for example, LEINBACH and

AMRHEIN, 1987; MCNAUGHTON and GREEN, 1988; MARTIN, 1989; MASON and HARRISON, 1991; SÁNCHEZ, 1992; MINNS, 1993). Critically, the information and governance advantages of a close proximity between investors and investees result in capital being primarily allocated *within* these clusters (FLORIDA and KENNY, 1988).

MASON and HARRISON, 1991, supporting the case for a regional equity gap in the UK, further note that depressed regions in the Midlands and northern England are also net exporters of equity finance to the more successful southern regions, such as Cambridge-shire in East Anglia (KEEBLE, 1989). FLORIDA and KENNY, 1988, and LEINBACH and AMRHEIN, 1987, similarly demonstrate the migration of US finances from less developed central and mid Western states to the East and West coast areas. The empirical literature is uniform in its conclusion that venture capital avail-ability and usage remains highly concentrated in regions of established and growing economic advantage.

A POLICY RESPONSE FROM THE EUROPEAN COMMISSION: THE EUROPEAN SEED CAPITAL FUND SCHEME

Concern at the apparent paucity and limited regional distribution of third party equity finance for European NTBFs engendered a policy response from the Euro-pean Commission. In October 1988, the Commission adopted a Community pilot scheme to stimulate seed capital. The stated objectives of the Scheme were:

> ... to foster enterprise creation in the Community by strengthening the financing opportunities available to new enterprises, through the creation of 24 new seed capital funds throughout the Community, and by improving the quality and survival rate of seed capital projects, through the services the funds will provide to the projects. This pilot scheme aims to stimulate private sector and start-up investment by providing financial incentives to these new funds (CEC document (SEC/88/1496), 1988).

The focus of the pilot scheme was 'new or embryonic companies that require financial and/or management support for development into companies capable of raising first round finance' (*ibid.*). Importantly, while the Scheme was subsequently translated by the partici-pant funds as to be primarily concerned with NTBFs, the original documentation did not specifically state an exclusive technological focus.

The sponsoring Directorates General for the pilot scheme were DG XXIII (Enterprise) and DG XVI (Regional Development). While the objectives of the Scheme did not directly allude to distributional inequalities in capital provision, the involvement of DG XVI ensured a regional dimension to the pilot scheme and the specific inclusion of new funds in Objective 1, 2 and 5b areas.

Each of the supported funds in the scheme received a reimbursable, interest-free advance of up to 50% of the annual operating costs of the fund over a three to five year period. This loan is due for repayment after 10 years when it was deemed that sufficient investment realizations would have been made to enable the return of the advance. Those funds which have not achieved net investment returns above a 'hurdle' (referenced to long term treasury bonds plus five percentage points during the period of the fund's existence) are to be absolved from repaying the loan.

The operating subsidy was paid by DG XXIII to all funds. For those 14 funds which operated in selected assisted areas of the Union, DG XVI paid a further capital contribution of up to 25% of the funds under management – a minimum of ECU 125,000 and a maximum of ECU 250,000. This additional capital loan was a recognition of the likely difficulties in attracting private investors which would be faced by small regional funds. This interest-free advance is only returnable if the fund has made a capital gain at the end of the term.

OBJECTIVES OF THE STUDY

Three years after the Scheme's inception, the author was invited to review the progress of the Scheme to date. By January 1992, 22 funds had been created in 10 countries and had started to invest in SMEs. In agreement with the Commission sponsors, the study embraced the following objectives:

1. To review progress to date of the supported funds including their ability to attract additional private sources of investment capital
2. To ascertain indicative evidence of the funds' ability to meet desired goals of enterprise and job creation via technology-based new firms
3. To address the inter-relationship between economic and (regional) developmental objectives of the funds
4. To appraise the continued viability of the funds created after the five-year period of Commission support.

THE SURVEY METHODOLOGY

It was decided to interview personally the senior invest-ment manager of each of the 22 funds from the 10 Member States in the Scheme as of January 1992. A semi-structured overview schedule was prepared in English and French. Only one fund declined to be interviewed. (A further postal survey of the investee firms was also completed but does not form part of the present paper.)

A FUND TYPOLOGY

The two types of fund, primary supported by DG XXIII and DG XVI respectively, were termed *regional*

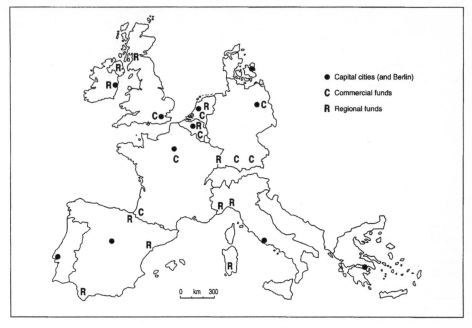

Fig. 1. Location of 21 ESCF scheme supported funds surveyed in 1992

funds and *commercial funds*. Their characteristics are summarized in Table 3.

The following results from the study, and subsequent Commission updates, address fund behaviour primarily from the perspective of the regional funds. Their actions are contrasted with the commercial funds particularly to illustrate the nature and consequences of the additional or different policy objectives placed on regional funds as vehicles for local development.

BASIC FUND CHARACTERISTICS

Size and investment disparities in commercial and regional funds

By 1992, the extant funds had already started to exhibit material differences based on both the resources employed and their regional or commercial logic (Table 4). The average size of investment in individual firms by the commercial funds was four times higher than

Table 3. Typology of regional and commercial seed capital funds

	Regional funds	Commercial funds
Primary fund objective	Encouragement of new firm formation and employment in location of fund	Attractive capital gain to investors fully reflecting premia for risk and illiquidity
Secondary fund objective	Positive and acceptable financial return to investors	New NTBF formation
Capitalization	Public funds and 'social' investment by private sector	Primarily commercial investors but including some social investors
Investee focus	New and early stage enterprises with some technology component	Exclusively, NTBFs with exploitable intellectual property rights in attractive and fast growing markets
Locus of operation	Development region	Area determined by practicability of regular investor/ investee contact
Support infrastructure	Business Innovation Centre and other public enterprise support agencies, public and commercial networks	Private commercial networks and commercial consultants

Table 4. *Statistics of seed capital funds in ESCF scheme, 1992*

ECU(000s)	Regional funds N = 13	Commercial funds N = 8
Average fund size (ECU000s)	1,345·4	2,341·3
Range of funds raised (ECU000s)	500–2,575	750–7,000
Number of investee firms	48	31
Average investment per firm (ECU)	58,922	232·777
Annual operating costs(ECU)	157,176	189,162
Range of annual operating cost (ECU000s)	21–195	87–406
Operating costs as % funds under management	11·7	8·1

their regional counterparts. Commercial funds managed their investee portfolio more intensely. Accordingly, the operating costs of commercial funds were 20% higher than their regional counterparts. However, when expressed as a percentage of funds under management, these costs were one-third lower for commercial funds. This illustrates a fundamental issue for small scale investor groups of the penal effect of invisible, fixed governance costs.

The figures suggest that regional funds were pursuing a diversified portfolio approach by making modest investments among a larger number of client firms. In contrast, commercial funds had restricted their activities to relatively few but larger investments, thereby allowing for contingencies and planned follow-on finance to existing investees. This latter strategy is consistent with the practice in private venture capital firms with a technology focus (BYGRAVE and TIMMONS, 1992; MURRAY, 1994). It was not possible to determine if the regional funds' policy was purposeful or contingent on supply-side limitations, i.e. fewer attractive candidates available in which to invest larger sums.

FINANCE RAISING BY THE FUNDS

Some two years after the inception of the Scheme, the funds had raised ECU 36·2 million of new finances for equity investment. This figure excludes the capital subvention of approximately ECU 2·6 million made to regional funds by DG XVI. The small scale of this sum is put into context when it is recognized that 15 (71%) of the funds had total financing of under ECU 2 million. The average external finance raised per fund was ECU 1·72 million (range: ECU 0·5–7·0 million). The importance of this figure is apparent if referenced to average operating costs of the funds. *Without making any investments whatsoever, the regional and commercial funds would have exhausted their original capital in eight and 12 years, respectively.*

The leverage effect of European Commission subsidy

The effectiveness of the *imprimatur* of the EU in assisting the process of fund raising was significant,

particularly for the regional funds. Fund managers were asked to estimate the amount of finance they believed they would have been able to raise from private investors without the existence of the Scheme. *Only two of the 13 regional funds reported that they would have been able to raise any finance.* The total fund raising estimate of the regional managers, in the absence of the Scheme, was ECU 2·8 million compared to the actual sum raised of ECU 13·5 million. The 'pump-priming' role of the Commission resulted in an increase of finances raised by the 13 regional funds of 382%. Conversely, only three of the eight commercial funds believed that they would not have been able to raise finance unaided. Their views as to the Commission's influence was that it represented an additional ECU 4 million – a 27% increase in funds raised.

Thus, the Scheme had met initially one of its objectives of stimulating private sector financial transfers. However, the effectiveness of the Commission's intervention, more pessimistically, may conversely be seen as an indication of private investors' circumspection as to the economic viability of regional seed capital investment in the absence of significant EU subsidy.

Sources of private investment

The proportion of finance provided by private sources for the regional funds was 64%, although government agencies represented the largest category (28·9%) of contributor (Table 5). Over three-quarters (77·3%) of the commercial funds' finances came from institutional and private investors, i.e. the source from which most mainstream venture capitalists attract finance.

Investors' reasons for and against supporting Seed Funds (respondents' opinions)

However, only one-quarter (six) of regional fund managers believed that investors contributed to their funds for predominantly commercial reasons (Table 6). This makes the material contribution of venture capital firms to regional funds surprising (although several of these firms were owned by regional banks.). Conversely, nearly half (48%) of commercial fund managers believed that profit was the primary reasoning of their investors. None the less, both types of fund managers acknowledged the critical importance of non-economic reasons in motivating institutional investors. This has implications for further finance raising. In the absence of tangible evidence of attractive investment performance, initial fund supporters may not be a reliable source of further finance. Critically, all funds are likely to require further finance raising before tangible evidence of their investment performance is available. Investors who declined to participate were, in the opinion of the fund managers, discouraged by the high risk and poor prospects for attractive returns from seed capital investment.

Table 5. *Types of institutional investors in seed capital funds, 1992*

Source	Investment in regional funds (ECUs)	% total investment	Investment in commercial funds (ECUs)	% total investment
Private banks	1,569,000	12·3	3,063,040	16·4
State banks			2,500,000	13·3
Business Innovation Centres	132,000	1·0	—	—
Chambers of Commerce	120,000	0·9	1,000,000	5·3
Churches	556,000	4·4	—	—
Private financial intitutions	2,775,000	21·7	8,751,960	46·7
National government agencies	2,886,650	22·6	—	—
Regional government agencies	805,600	6·3	750,000	4·0
Private companies	402,000	3·1	—	—
Venture capitalists	2,748,650	21·5	1,480,000	7·9
Universities	77,250	0·6	—	—
Individuals	693,000	5·4	1,185,000	6·3
Total funds raised	12,765,150		18,730,000	

Table 6. *Investors' reasons for and against contributing to a seed capital fund*

Reasons for	Ranking	No.	Reasons against	Ranking	No.
Regional development/job creation/social responsibilities	1	13	Excessive risk poor expected returns	1	11
SME development	2	7	Alternative investment opportunities	2	3
EC financial support for the fund	3	6	No seed capital experience/interest	3=	2
Growth opportunities	4	4	No track record by seed fund	3=	2
New products/technologies	5=	3	Already investing in seed capital	3=	2
Attractive potential returns	5=	3			

Fund performance evaluation by their managers

The regional fund managers appeared to give little priority to quantitative performance variables in their own individual benchmarks for their fund's performance (Table 7). The absence of formal monitoring/evaluation criteria for nearly half the funds in the Scheme was potentially alarming given the managers' fiduciary accountability to their public and private investors. Particularly for regional fund managers, the interim results of substantial investment activity appeared to have received little explicit analysis.

THE IMPORTANCE OF DEAL FLOW

A key prerequisite of success for a venture capital firm is its ability to attract a flow of attractive, potential investee businesses. Only six of the 21 funds admitted to having a formal marketing strategy for attracting

Table 7. *Primary criteria for fund performance evaluation*

Fund performance criteria	Regional funds *N* = 13	Commercial funds *N* = 8
No. of jobs created	—	1
No. businesses created	1	—
Return on capital	4	5
No formal evaluation criteria	8	2

deal flow. However, the funds did not appear to have suffered from a limited supply of entrepreneurial firms seeking equity finance in the period 1990–92. Collectively, the respondents' funds had received a total of 1,410 approaches, from which 69 investments had been made in total. While no data were collected on the quality of this deal flow, the overall acceptance rate of 5·6% accords closely to the other researchers' findings of venture capital acceptance rates (BANNOCK, 1991; DIXON, 1991; ROBERTS, 1991). For the 669 deals on which specific information was available, there appeared to be little difference in summary acceptance rates between the two types of fund.

Sources of referrals

The apparent ease with which the funds had managed to engender interest among entrepreneurs is arguably a recognition of the strong networking skills applied by managers within often strictly defined regional locations or specific product/technology markets.

Table 8 illustrates the wide spread of sources of referral employed by managers of both types of fund. HUSTEDDE and PULVER, 1992, in the US have indicated that the source of the advice and referral can be an important indicator as to the likely outcome of the subsequent investment. These authors reported that public sector conduits tend to be associated with,

412   *Gordon C. Murray*

Table 8. Sources of funds' deal flow, 1992

Deal channels	Regional funds, N = 13		Commercial funds, N = 8	
	Proposals (%)	Acceptances (%)	Proposals (%)	Acceptances (%)
Banks/financial institutions	6·4	0	15·3	27·2
Business Innovation Centres	40·5	50·0	7·6	9·1
Development agencies	0·7	0	—	—
Chambers of Commerce	—	—	7·3	9·1
Government	8·1	0	3·1	9·1
Consultants	—	—	5·3	4·5
Fund investors	1·2	0·7	—	—
European Commision	—	—	0·4	4·5
Universities/SCI parks	3·7	3·3	0·1	4·5
Venture capitalist	3·9	10·0	2·7	9·1
Unspecified dealflow	24·9	30·0	57·3	22·7
Total numbers	407	30	262	22
Acceptance rate (%)		7·4		8·4

subsequently, less successful investee firms in the US. If valid in a European context, these findings will be a cause for concern to the regional funds which largely employ public sector channels for prospective deal flow.

Different fund types, different networks

The close relationship between the regional funds and the Business Innovation Centres (BICs) is evident. (BICs were set up by DG XVI in 1984 and were originally designed to assist areas undergoing economic restructuring and/or economically less advantaged areas of the Community.) BICs are normally represented on the board of the regional seed funds.

The limited data suggest that commercial funds employed wider and more heterogeneous sources of referral, and non-public contacts were particularly important. Bank and financial institution originated enterprises represented over one-quarter of the commercial funds' investment portfolios. In contrast, none of the 26 firms introduced by banks to the regional funds resulted in an investment. The lack of locational/developmental constraints on commercial funds may represent an advantage in deal sourcing.

PROJECT APPRAISAL AND SELECTION CRITERIA

The would-be investor has to reach a judgement on three critical sources of uncertainty: the viability of the technology; the existence of an attractive product/market opportunity; and the abilities of the entrepreneur/management team. It is in the area of project evaluation that the regional and commercial funds exhibited most commonality. Asked to cite the five most important project selection criteria, the two types of funds only differed in the importance given to the

Table 9. Fund managers' rating of key project selection criteria

Key acceptance criteria	Regional funds' ratings[1] N = 13	Commercial funds' ratings[1] N = 8
Entrepreneur's character	4·9	4·8
Entrepreneur's experience	4·1	3·9
Degree of expected competition	4·0	4·1
Legal protection of technology	3·2	3·0
Nature of technology	2·8	3·6

Note: 1. Rating scale: not important, 1; very important, 5.

'nature of the technology' (Table 9). This likely reflects the commercial funds greater focus on technology investments. Their responses also confirmed the findings of several other studies which have indicated that the essentially subjective appraisal of the entrepreneur or management team dominates more formal financial appraisals in early-stage investments (see TYEBJEEE and BRUNO, 1984; MACMILLAN et al., 1985, 1987; GOSLIN and BARGE, 1986; SAPIENZA, 1992; HALL and HOFFER, 1993).

The commonality of the two types of fund managers' response was also reflected in their reasons for refusing a new project proposal (Table 10). However, the views of the two types of fund managers did diverge markedly on the minimum level of financial attractiveness of a project proposal as assessed by the target Internal Rate of Return (IRR) acceptable to the fund. Only three (23%) of the regional fund managers would impose a rate of return at > 20% per annum, i.e. a level significantly below the threshold of 57% imposed by UK technology investors (MURRAY and LOTT, 1995). Half of the commercial funds stipulated this minimum IRR target. That nearly half of all managers did not have a defined financial performance target was arguably a reflection of the extreme practical difficulty

Table 10. *Fund managers' reason for refusing new projects*

Unprompted reasons	Regional funds % total N = 29		Commercial funds % total N = 22	
Entrepreneur's lack of experience	20·7	} Σ 34·5	13·6	} Σ 36·3
Character of entrepreneur	13·8		22·7	
Market/growth potential of product	24·1		27·3	
Technology potential	10.3		13·6	
Other	30·1		22·8	

Table 12. *Percentage distribution of investee firms by level of technological innovation*

Technology innovation:	Low	Medium	High	No. of responses
Regional funds				
Preferred	23·1	53·8	23·1	13
Actual[1]	11·4	61·3	27·2	48
Commercial funds				
Preferred	25	62·5	12·5	8
Actual[1]	9·5	46·9	43·6	31

Note: 1. Estimated from investments made.

of setting an *ex ante* target given the imperfect information available for early-stage technology investments. However, this omission may also reflect, especially for regional fund managers, the subordination of financial objectives to wider developmental goals.

INVESTMENT FOCUS OF FUNDS

Targeted stage of investment

As noted, the history of the European venture capital industry illustrates a marked movement away from early-stage investment (MURRAY, 1995). The logic of the Scheme was to encourage the supply of finance dedicated to enterprise formation and growth. The actions to date of the two types of funds show that their activities remain exclusively directed to early-stage investment (Table 11). There was no evidence of a 'creep' to later stage, less risky development capital investments.

Commercial funds were particularly likely to invest in young businesses before any sales had been made. That the regional funds had, on average, over one-third of their portfolio in firms which had already started making sales could be a reflection of their close relationship to existing supporting agencies, e.g. BICs. This relationship is also likely to explain the greater proportion of low/medium technology firms within their portfolios when compared to commercial funds. Given the geographical constraints of regional funds, it is also highly probable that the supply of early-stage

Table 11. *Percentage of investments made by stage of investee firm development*

	Concept testing	Pre-pro- duction sales	Initial sales	Early growth	No. of responses
Regional funds					
Preferred	32	32	36	0	13
Actual[1]	12·5	52·1	33·3	2·1	48
Commercial funds					
Preferred	20	33	47	0	8
Actual[1]	28·1	56·3	15·6	0	31

Note: 1. Estimates from investments made.

NTBF opportunities was significantly more constrained than for their commercial fund counterparts.

Targeted level of technology investments

Within broad definitions, the respondents were asked to 'self code' their portfolio of investee firms regarding the degree to which they incorporated advanced and novel/innovative technology processes or product features. Such a process of categorization is less robust than that employed by BUTCHART, 1987, and OECD, 1992, but the researchers were primarily interested in a broad classification of the existing investments rather than determining the technology status of a single firm.

Two particular observations resulted from this enquiry. The regional funds espoused a greater preferred interest in advanced technology investments but it was the commercial funds that had assumed this role in practice (Table 12). This, as noted, may be a reflection of the limited supply of such investments in funds constrained by regional boundaries. Secondly, while both types of fund indicated a preference for including between a quarter and a fifth of low technology investments, in practice, these investments represented around 10% of the average portfolio. Managers observed that technology-based firms were potentially more attractive from either the perspective of job creation or capital gain.

EXIT ARRANGEMENTS

Central to the logic of venture capital investment is the ability for the investors eventually to liquidate/realize their investment at a capital gain reflecting risk and illiquidity premia. (It has been argued that the limited role of small firm stockmarkets in Europe has been a major disincentive to potential investors in growth SMEs – see EVCA, 1993; BANNOCK, 1991).

Managers were asked to give their assessment of the most likely exit routes for their present and future portfolio companies. Table 13 indicates that trade sales remain the most likely source of a project exit for both types of funds. This is in line with general venture

Table 13. *Planned exit route for investee companies (weighted by rank ordering).*

Planned exit routes	Regional funds (% exits)	No. of responses	Commercial funds (% exits)	No. of responses
Trade sale	34·4	21	34·3	37
Entrepreneur share repurchase	33·3	36	31·1	19
Sale to a venture capitalist	30·6	33	27·9	17
Initial public offering	1·8	2	6·6	4

capital behaviour (RELANDER and SYRJÄNEN, 1992). The two categories of funds are similar in their exit expectations. The exception is the relatively greater importance given to an Initial Public Offering by the commercial funds. However, such a route is only feasible for the commercially most successful NTBFs. The limited importance given to a stockmarket exit suggests that only a small minority of investments are regarded as being of the highest commercial potential or, conversely, the inappropriateness of existing stock exchanges for NTBFs in several European countries.

The importance of a repurchase of the investors' equity by the original entrepreneur(s) reflected the peculiarities of investing in small businesses which were faced by several funds. These managers noted that entrepreneurs would not accept seed capital investment without the contractual right to subsequently repurchase the investor's portion of the equity. Such an exit channel is of no interest to commercial investors as the entrepreneur has a direct incentive in discouraging or delaying the growth in the value of the enterprise in order to repurchase the equity he/she does not control (an 'agency cost' problem, see AMIT *et al.*, 1990). For most funds, this route remained the 'exit of last resort'.

Venture capitalists were also seen as a potentially important source of follow-on finance as co-investors in growing enterprises needing significant increases in capitalization. However, MURRAY, 1994, has noted the limited interest of UK later stage venture capitalists in providing follow-on finance for seed capitalist derived projects. It is also noteworthy that there was a negligible incidence of syndicated financing of the original investments. MASON and HARRISON, 1991, have observed that interregional co-investment is one

means by which regional equity gaps may be ameliorated.

CONTEMPORARY PERFORMANCE OF THE ESCF SCHEME

Subsequent to the original study in 1992, the Commission has provided updated statistics on both the participating funds and their investee companies on an annual basis. Two additional funds have been introduced and the non-respondent Greek fund has been removed from the Scheme.

Importantly, the author's original classification has been refined by the Commission. Funds are now segregated into exclusively commercial, high-tech funds, and two regional categories which are defined by the nature of the predominant sources of finance. This re-classification serves to increase the differences cited in this paper between the commercial and the regional funds in 1992:

Commercial funds
Private high-tech funds ($n = 4$): investment raised exclusively from private investors and directed only to high technology projects irrespective of location
Regional funds
1. Private regional funds ($n = 8$): > 50% of funds raised from private investors with investments directed to one or more well defined regions
2. Public regional funds ($n = 11$): < 50% of funds raised from private investors with investments directed to one or more well defined regions

FUND CAPITALIZATION AND INVESTMENT ACTIVITY, POST 1992

There has been relatively little additional fund raising in the three-year period. However, nine funds have noted an intent to raise a further ECU 20 million, two-thirds of which will be via new shareholders. This imperative is greatest for the high-tech funds which are almost fully invested. Their average investment values and the costs associated with a 'hands-on' method of governance remain significantly higher than for all regional funds. Additional demands on their funds from existing, or new investees, cannot be sustained from extant resources. This places these funds

Table 14. *Growth of total ESCF scheme funds under management*

	January 1992	January 1993	January 1994	January 1995
Number of funds	21	24	24	23
Total (non-EC) capital raised	36·2	37·7	39·9	41·0
Average capital per fund	1·72	1·57	1·66	1·78
Average fund operating cost (ECU)	142,685	155,441	174,254	176,126

Table 15. *Total investment activity by type of fund by January 1995*

	Private regional funds $N = 8$	Public regional funds $N = 11$	Private high-tech funds $N = 4$
Average capitalization (ECU m)	1·3	1·3	4·06
Percentage of fund invested	45	47	92
Annual fund operating costs (ECU)	145,997	122.618	259,762
Total number of investments	62	85	41
Average investment value (ECU)	59,736	68,836	333,576
Percentage high-tech investments	31	42	85
Percentage medium-tech investments	45	45	15
Percentage low-tech investments	24	13	0
Number of business failures	21	15	4
Failures as a % of total investments	33·9	17·6	9·8

and their existing investees in a position of vulnerability in the event of unforeseen problems.

The continued structural differences between regional and high technology funds is a recognition of the diversity of their respective goals (Table 15). Significantly, interim figures show the firm failure rate of commercial funds to be nearly one-third of that of all regional funds. This may be a consequence of the 'better' stock of available investee businesses, more discriminating investment policies of commercial funds and/or their greater investee support activities. However, it is still premature to draw strong conclusions.

EMPLOYMENT CREATION

Table 16 serves to reinforce the importance of NTBFs as a potentially attractive source of employment creation relative to SMEs embracing less innovative technologies. The degree of technological sophistication of the investee firms appears directly related to the firms' potential to create new jobs. The figures also illustrate a paradox. The regional funds were created for developmental objectives including additional employment generation. In contrast, the high technology funds remain primarily an economic activity. Yet, it is the high technology firms which have recorded the greatest employment growth per investee firm and per fund. The Commission (DG XXIII) has drawn the conclusion from the Pilot Scheme results to date that its future policy focus should concentrate exclusively on commercial funds, which target high technology enter-

prises and employ finance from the private sector, *regardless of their location*.

On a Commission assumption of a 30% loan default, the cost *to the EU* of the Scheme per job and enterprise created was ECU 1,260 and 13,979, respectively (Table 17). These figures appear to be remarkably attractive. STOREY's, 1994, analysis of the Enterprise Allowance Scheme in the UK estimated a public cost of ECU 2,600 per job and ECU 78,000 per firm. The cost per job of the Urban Development Corporations in England and Wales has been cited as ECU 28,000 per job (*The Guardian*, 19 August 1995, p. 9). Statistics (1980–96) from the Massachusetts Technology Development Corporation (MTDC) in Boston, an arguably more relevant comparison given its NTBF focus, show similarly effective public funds leverage with a cost per job of ECU 1,055 and cost per enterprise of ECU 110,000. MTDC has created relatively fewer, larger enterprises (60 active) but with a higher average employment growth at 104 new jobs per firm.

The efficacy of the Scheme is in part a result of the leverage effect of public loans on private investment. While high-tech funds created the most jobs in advanced technologies, the greatest total number of jobs and enterprises created by the regional funds relative to the public subsidies given significantly increased their comparative performance. However, a more rigorous analysis of the employment impact of the Scheme will necessarily have to address deadweight arguments regarding the actions of entrepreneurs in the absence of the Scheme. Further and critically, the

Table 16. *Number of jobs created by category of fund and technology status, 1992–94*

	Public regional funds $N = 11$	Private regional funds $N = 8$	Private high-tech funds $N = 4$	Total jobs by technology status	No. of firms by technology status	Jobs/firm by technology status
High-tech companies	261	360	514	1,135	90	12·6
Medium-tech companies	239	377	119	735	72	10·2
Low-tech companies	118	97	0	215	26	8·3
Total jobs created	618	834	633	2.085	188	
Number of jobs/fund	56·2	104·3	158·3			
Number of jobs/firm	7·3	13·5	15·4			

Table 17. *Cost of community support per job and enterprise created*

Assumption of 30% repayment default	Overall scheme N = 23	All regional funds N = 19	Private high-tech funds N = 4
Total cost of repayable operating and capital subsidies (ECU m)	8·76	4·77	3·99
Estimated real total subsidy cost (ECU m)	2·628	1·43	1·20
Cost per job (2,085 jobs created) (ECU)	1,260	985	1,892
Cost per enterprise (188 enterprises created) (ECU)	13,979	9,731	29,210

longer-term viability of fledgling NTBFs cannot yet be assumed.

THE THREAT OF INVESTMENT/ REALIZATION DISCONTINUITIES

The interim success of the high technology/commercial funds has produced one area of considerable threat. In early-stage venturing, the investment cycle is generally seen as seven to 10 years (BANNOCK, 1991). During this period, successful investees will frequently require several rounds of finance as the business grows and develops but remains insufficiently profitable in the short-medium term to fund growth and R&D investment exclusively from retained earnings (MURRAY, 1994). The cycle of costs and returns are not synchronized and the fund needs to be able to have recourse to substantial finance prior to a profitable realization of its investments. The ability of the Scheme's high-tech funds to meet future cash demands is, at present, highly constrained in the absence of further sources of finance.

Table 18 takes no consideration that the existing investments of the technology funds may require additional finance over the remaining six-year average life of the funds. Nor are the substantial costs for an investee firm of a market flotation or a trade sale included in the above calculations. *In short, for the most successful fund category, there is a present danger that the funds will imminently run out of operating finances before the majority of their investments can be successfully realized.* In these critical circumstances, any attempt to obtain additional fund finance from investors is likely to be problematic given the parlous negotiating position of a financially weak fund.

CONCLUSIONS AND DISCUSSION

Problems in the supply of seed and early-stage venture capital remain endemic in Europe. In the absence of professional investors or the complementary, informal investor/business angel sector, prescriptions to address 'equity gap' issues are heavily dependent on public initiatives. The ESCF Scheme represents a European response. It is properly judged according to its objectives. Yet, as a *pilot* programme, its findings have their greatest import in influencing subsequent EU regional and enterprise policies.

By February 1995, at a budgeted public investment of ECU 8·76 million, 23 funds (and a support network) had been created and had attracted ECU 41 million of institutional finance. The 188 extant, early-stage enterprises had created 2,085 direct jobs, predominantly in technology-related activities. Failed enterprises currently represent 17·5% of investments. Under the EU's revised fund definitions, the 19 regional funds representing 60% of the finance raised ECU 24·8 million and had supported 147 enterprises. The explicit objectives of the Scheme had been successfully realized and the estimated subsidies per job and enterprise created appeared highly cost effective. EU intervention cannot be challenged on either opportunity cost grounds, or as displacing (crowding-out) established private markets for venture capital (FISHER, 1988).

However, conclusions must remain circumspect until the longer term viability of both the new enterprises and the funds as economic entities are proven. The urgent need of the high-tech funds for additional finance raises serious concerns as to future viability. Without exception, the small scale of all funds prejudices viability given the penal effect of fixed management costs. This future viability may well be

Table 18. *Fund statistics in January 1995*

	Private regional funds N = 8	Public regional funds N = 11	Private high-tech funds N = 4
Total funds raised (ECU m)	10·4	14·4	16·2
Percentage of available finance per fund invested	47·4	45·0	92·4
Average uninvested finance per fund (ECU m)	0·68	0·72	0·31
Annual operating costs (ECU)	122,618	1245,997	259,762
Time in years to exhaustion of present finance (excluding new investment) for an average fund	5·6	4·9	1·2

conditional on the development of what FLORIDA and KENNY, 1988, describe as indigenous 'technology infrastructures' and by which additional finance, information and advice is efficiently provided to NTBFs and their investors through symbiotic local linkages.

All funds raised institutional finance on the basis of securing an acceptable return for their investors. This return can only be met by the subsequent, profitable sale of their portfolio companies. At the end of the 10-year funding period, if the investors do not receive a risk and time adjusted return on their capital, they have in effect subsidized the social goals of enterprise creation. This is likely to severely curtail future private fund raising in addition to increasing significantly the real cost of the Scheme.

There is an evident quantity/quality divide between regional and commercial (high-tech) funds. The latter actively discriminated by investing greater finance and managerial support in a smaller number of attractive (by sales and employment growth) firms. Unencumbered by developmental goals, the four high-tech funds appeared demonstrably more professional in managerial behaviour. The separateness of the regional funds from private communities of finance, information and deal flow is potentially problematic if these agents are to be judged ultimately as commercial organizations.

The funds had established effective networks as evidenced by the availability of initial funding and a robust deal flow. There does not appear circumstantial support for BENNETT and KREBS', 1994, assertion of the more fragmented networks in less developed regions. However, the regional funds were not sited in the most economically and socially disadvantaged areas of the Union. The ability of the regional funds to make technology investments would suggest that a latent demand exists and is frustrated by supply side constraints of finance. However, that investees are willing to accept finance allows no observation on the *quality* of these enterprises. Indeed, the limited evidence from the study suggests that regional investees are smaller, grow less quickly, are less technologically intensive and are more liable to fail than the recipients of commercial fund investments.

That these funds had to be created *de novo* lends support to THOMPSON's, 1989, questioning of neo-classical diffusion arguments regarding the correction of either regional or early-stage investment shortages. The steeply sloped 'distance decay curves' witnessed by MCNAUGHTON and GREEN, 1988, in Canada remain evident in Europe. Governance and information demands ensure the continued spatial concentration of venture capital activity. The materiality of these constraints present a powerful argument for the logic of public initiatives which address barriers to the local supply of additional private venture capital finance. However, such schemes are likely to be necessary but not sufficient catalysts for continued regional enterprise/employment growth in the absence of complementary, techno-commercial networks to assist the subsequent development of the new firms.

Acknowledgements − The author would like to thank the European Commission (DGs XXIII and XVI) for their financial support of the original 1992 study, and David Francis whose participation in the fieldwork and subsequent analysis was invaluable. Any errors of fact, interpretation or omission remain the sole responsibility of the author.

REFERENCES

AMIT R., GLOSTEN L. and MULLER E. (1990) Does venture capital foster the most promising entrepreneurial firms?, *Calif. Mgt. Rev.* Spring, pp. 102–111.

BANNOCK G. (1991) *Venture Capital and the Equity Gap.* National Westminster Bank, London.

BENNETT R. J. and KREBS G. (1994) Local economic development partnerships: an analysis of policy networks in EC-LEDA local employment development strategies, *Reg. Studies* 28, 119–40.

BIRCH D. (1979) The job creation process, in *MIT Program on Neighbourhood and Regional Change.* MIT Press, Cambridge, MA.

BOLTON J. E. (1971) *Report of the Committee of Enquiry on Small Firms*, Cmnd. 4811. HMSO, London.

BRITISH VENTURE CAPITAL ASSOCIATION (BVCA) (1996) *Report on Investment Activity 1995.* BVCA, London.

BURNS P. and DEWHURST J. (1993) *Financial Characteristics of Small Companies in Britain.* 3i plc/Cranfield School of Management, Bedford.

BUTCHART R. L. (1987) A new definition of the high technology industries, *Econ. Trends* 400, February, pp. 82–88.

BYGRAVE W. D. and TIMMONS J. A. (1992) *Venture Capital at the Crossroads.* Harvard Business School Press, Boston, MA.

COMMISSION OF THE EUROPEAN UNION (1995) *Fourth Progress Update on the Seed Capital Pilot Scheme.* DG XXIII, Brussels.

CONFEDERATION OF BRITISH INDUSTRY (1993) *Finance for Growth.* CBI, London.

COOPERS & LYBRAND (1996) *Sixth Annual Economic Impact of Venture Capital Study.* Coopers & Lybrand, Boston, MA.

DIXON R. (1991) Venture capital and the appraisal of investments, *Omega* 19(5), 333–44.

EUROPEAN COMMISSION (1994) *Growth, Competitiveness, Employment: The Challenges and Way Forward into the 21st Century,* White Paper. EC, Brussels.

EUROPEAN COMMISSION (1995) *Green Paper on Innovation.* EC, Brussels.

EUROPEAN NETWORK FOR SME RESEARCH (1993) *The European Observatory for SMEs: First Annual Report.* Commission of the European Union, DG XXIII, Brussels.

EUROPEAN VENTURE CAPITAL ASSOCIATION (EVCA) (1996) *Venture Capital in Europe: 1995 EVCA Handbook*. Ernst & Young, London.

EUROPEAN VENTURE CAPITAL ASSOCIATION (1993) *Special Paper: Capital Markets for Entrepreneurial Companies – a European Opportunity for Growth*. EVCA, Zaventem.

FISHER P. S. (1988) State venture capital funds as an economic development strategy, *APA Journal*, Spring, pp. 166–177.

FLORIDA R. and KENNEY M. (1988) Venture capital, high technology and regional development, *Reg. Studies* 22, 33–48.

FREEMAN C. (1983) *The Economics of Industrial Innovation*. MIT Press, Cambridge, MA.

GALLAGHER C. and STEWART H. (1986) Jobs and the business life cycle in the UK. *Appl. Econ.* 18, 875–900.

GASTON R. J. (1989) *Finding Private Venture Capital for your Firm: A Complete Guide*. Wiley, New York.

GIANNAKOUROU G. (1996) Towards a European spatial planning policy: theoretical dilemmas and institutional implications, *Europ. Plann. Studies* 4(5), 595–613.

GORMAN M. and SAHLMAN W. A. (1989) What do venture capitalists do?, *J. Bus. Venturing* 4, 231–48.

GOSLIN N. L. and BARGE B. (1986) Entrepreneurial qualities considered in venture capital support, Frontiers of Entrepreneurial Research, Babson College, Wellesley, MA.

HALL J. and HOFFER C. W. (1993) Venture capitalists' decision criteria in new venture evaluation, *J. Bus. Venturing* 8, 25–42.

HUSTEDDE R. J. and PULVER G. (1992) Factors affecting equity capital acquisition: the demand side, *J. Bus. Venturing* 7, 363–74.

KEEBLE D. E. (1989) High-technology industry and regional development in Britain: the case of the Cambridge phenomenon, *Environ. Plann. A* 7, 153–72.

LEINBACH T. R. and AMRHEIN C. (1987) A geography of the venture capital industry in the US, *Prof. Geogr.* 39(2), 146–58.

MCNAUGHTON R. B. and GREEN M. B. (1988) Spatial patterns of Canadian venture capital investment, *Reg. Studies* 23, 9–18.

MACMILLAN H. (1931) *Report of the Committee on Finance and Industry*, Cmd. 3897. HMSO, London.

MACMILLAN I. C., SIEGAL R. and NARISHIMA P. N. S. (1985) Criteria used by venture capitalists to evaluate new venture proposals, *J. Bus. Venturing* 1, 119–28.

MACMILLAN I. C., ZEHMANN L. and SUBBANARASIMHA P. N. (1987) Criteria distinguishing successful from unsuccessful ventures in the venture screening process, *J. Bus. Venturing* 2, 123–37.

MARTIN R. (1989) The growth and geographical anatomy of venture capitalism in the United Kingdom, *Reg. Studies* 23, 389–403.

MASON C. M. and HARRISON R. T. (1991) Venture capital, the equity gap and the 'north–south divide' in the United Kingdom, in GREEN M. (Ed) *Venture Capital: International Comparisons*. Routledge, London.

MASON C. M. (1992) The supply of equity finance in the UK: a strategy for closing the equity gap, *Entrepreneurship & Reg. Dev.* 4, 357–80.

MASON C. and HARRISON R. (1994) The role of informal and formal sources of venture capital in the financing of technology-based SMEs in the United Kingdom, in OAKEY R. (Ed) *New Technology-based Firms in the 1990s*. Paul Chapman, London.

MEYER-KRAMER F. (1985) Innovation behaviour and regional indigenous potential, *Reg. Studies* 19, 523–34.

MINNS R. (1993) The value added by Community interventions to enhance the access of SMEs to capital, in the context of regional policy, paper given at the European Seminar on Financial Engineering and Regional Development, DG XIII, Commission of the European Communities, June, Luxembourg.

MOORE B. (1993) *Financial Constraints to the Growth and Development of Small, High-technology Firms*. Small Business Research Centre, University of Cambridge.

MOORE I. and GARNSEY E. (1991) *Funding for Innovation in Small Firms: the Role of Government*. Department of Engineering, University of Cambridge.

MURRAY G. C. (1994) The second 'equity gap': exit problems for seed and early-stage venture capitalists and their investee companies, *Int. Small Bus. J.* 12(4), 59–76.

MURRAY G. C. (1995) Evolution and change: an analysis of the first decade of the UK venture capital industry, *J. Bus. Fin & Accounting* 22(8), 1,077–107.

MURRAY G. C. and LOTT J. (1995) Have UK venture capital firms a bias against investment in new technology based firms?, *Res. Policy* 24, 283–99.

NATIONAL VENTURE CAPITAL ASSOCIATION (1996) *Annual Report 1995*. Venture Economics, Arlington, VA.

OAKEY R. O. (1984) *High Technology Small Firms*. Frances Pinter, London.

OAKEY R. O., ROTHWELL R. and COOPER S. (1988) *Management of Innovation in Small Firms*. Frances Pinter, London.

ORGANIZATION OF ECONOMIC CO-OPERATION AND DEVELOPMENT (OECD) (1986) *R&D Innovation and Competitiveness*, Science Technology Indicators 2. OECD, Paris.

ORGANIZATION OF ECONOMIC CO-OPERATION & DEVELOPMENT (1992) *Industrial Policy in OECD Countries: Annual Review*. OECD, Paris.

RELANDER K. E. and SYRJÄNEN A. P. (1992) Analysis of the trade sale as a venture capital exit route, paper given at the 1992 European Foundation for Entrepreneurship Research Conference, December, London.

ROBERTS E. B. (1991) *Entrepreneurs in High Technology*. Oxford University Press, New York.

ROTHWELL R. (1989) Small firms, innovation and industrial change, *Small Bus. Econ* 1, 51–64.

ROTHWELL R. and ZEGVELD W. (1982) *Industrial Innovation and Small and Medium Sized Firms*. Frances Pinter, London.

RUMELT R. P. (1984) Towards a strategic theory of the firm, in LAMB R. B. (Ed) *Competitive Strategic Management*, pp. 556–71. Prentice Hall, Englewood Cliffs, NJ.

SÁNCHEZ A. M. (1992) Regional innovation and small high technology firms in peripheral regions, *Small Bus. Econ.* 4, 153–68.

SAPIENZA H. J. (1992) When do venture capitalists add value?, *J. Bus. Venturing* 7, 9–27.

STOREY D. J. (1994) *Understanding the Small Business Sector.* Routledge, London.

STOREY D. J. and JOHNSON S. (1987) *Are Small Firms the Answer to Unemployment?* Employment Institute, London.

STOREY D., WATSON R. and WYNARCZYK P. (1989) Fast growth businesses: case studies of 40 small firms in the North East of England, Paper No. 67, Department of Employment, London.

THOMPSON C. (1989) The geography of venture capital, *Progr. Hum. Geogr.* 13(1), 62–99.

TYEBJEE T. T. and BRUNO A. V. (1984) A model of venture capital investment activity, *Mgt. Sci.* 30, 1,051–66.

UTTERBACK J. M., MEYER M., ROBERTS E. and REITBERGER G. (1988) Technology and industrial innovation in Sweden: a study of technology-based firms formed between 1965 and 1980, *Res. Policy* 17, 15–26.

WETZEL W. E. (1993) Angels and informal risk capital, *Sloan Mgt. Rev.* 24, Summer, pp. 23–34.

WILSON H. (1979) *The Financing of Small Firms*, Cmnd. 7503. HMSO, London.

[11]

ELSEVIER

Research Policy 29 (2000) 1135–1155

www.elsevier.nl/locate/econbase

Venture capital and the birth of the local area networking industry

Urs von Burg [a,1], Martin Kenney [b,c,*]

[a] *University of St. Gallen, St. Gallen, Switzerland*
[b] *Department of Human and Community Development, Davis, CA 95616, USA*
[c] *Berkeley Roundtable on the International Economy, USA*

Received 17 September 1998; received in revised form 11 November 1998; accepted 6 September 1999

Abstract

Venture capital has played an important role in funding the development of a number of US high-technology industries. Economists and business scholars utilizing models based in traditional economics have studied venture capital from the perspective of investment decision-making. These models provide significant insights, and yet they do not explain the actual operation of venture capital. This case study of the creation of LAN industry utilizes a synthesis of the dominant design and social constructionist perspectives to create a more nuanced explanation of how the practice of venture capitalists operates to create firms and industries. © 2000 Elsevier Science B.V. All rights reserved.

Keywords: Venture capital; Local area networking; Industry; Dominant design; Social construction

1. Introduction

In the mid 1990s, personal computers and other devices linked through a local area network (LAN) had become the dominant computer architecture in institutions. Twenty years earlier, LANs were nearly non-existent with their deployment almost exclusively confined to mainframe computers and terminal-to-host switching. Only a few engineers envisioned the demise of the then-dominant computing paradigm based on central computers serving many dumb terminals and its replacement with an alterna-

tive architecture of large numbers of networked, distributed computers. The deployment of a new technology in a set of newly created firms, which then becomes a new industry, is often accepted as unproblematic or natural. But, the manner by which a technology is embedded in social institutions is not predetermined. The expression of a technology in new firms entails the creation of firms and products simultaneously. This paper examines the role venture capitalists played in facilitating the emergence of the local area computer networking (LAN) industry in the United States and the issues they faced in funding startups. [2]

---

* Corresponding author. Department of Human and Community Development, University of California, Davis, CA 95616, USA.
E-mail: mfkenney@ucdavis.edu
[1] E-mail: uavonburg@ucdavis.edu.

[2] Some of the major inventions in the development of LAN industry, such as Token Ring were developed in Europe, however, few significant European firms were created. The most important European startup was the Token Ring-based Madge Networks, established in 1986.

1136 *U. von Burg, M. Kenney / Research Policy 29 (2000) 1135–1155*

For a study of the firm and industry formation process the LAN industry is a particularly appropriate, because it is a clear case in which entrepreneurs funded by venture capital out-maneuvered the large established companies. This paper shows the myriad ways in which the venture capitalists were actively involved in creating new firms in conjunction with entrepreneurs, and how the investment decisions were contingent and often hinged upon quite idiosyncratic criteria. In larger terms, this is an examination of how venture capitalists contributed to the construction of an entire industry.

We use the structural theories that trace their lineage to Joseph Schumpeter and its inheritors, especially those of the "dominant design" paradigm (see Abernathy, 1978 for an early exposition), and the social construction of technology line of study (Bijker et al., 1987). Henderson (1995) articulated the compatibility of these perspectives and we follow her line, with the exception of extending it to a new industry and the role of venture capital. Neither of these lines of explanation have been explicitly been applied to the role of venture capitalists in the construction of innovatory firms or new industries. Our particular interest is the venture capital decision-making in the pre-dominant design phase, when no industry exists, and then later when the industry is taking shape.

To understand the venture capitalists' role in the creation of the LAN industry, this paper is organized in roughly chronological order. Section 2 reviews previous theories of new industry formation. Section 3 briefly describes the research methodology. Section 4 provides an overview of the role of venture capital in funding new firms. Section 5 sketches the institutional roots of local area computer communication. Section 6 describes the beginnings of LAN industry, as the established firms grasped for a strategy to succeed in this new business space.

Section 7 examines the movement to create networking protocols and the standardization of Ethernet, which set the stage for a wave of startups exploiting Ethernet. Section 8 describes the venture capital process experienced by 3Com, the first startup dedicated to Ethernet. Section 9 examines other startups established slightly later to exploit the Ethernet standard, which resulted in the creation of the LAN industry. Section 10 discusses the role of venture

capitalists in funding the final critical innovation in the emergence of Ethernet as the dominant design and the defeat of the IBM-supported alternative of Token Ring. The conclusion summarizes the role of venture capitalists played in the construction of the LAN industry based on Ethernet, and how the LAN industry evolved into the highly dynamic computer networking business today.

2. Dominant design, social construction, and new firms

Social scientists, at least, as long ago as Schumpeter (1964) recognized the role of technical innovation as a powerful trigger for new firm formation and, in some cases, entire new industries. Despite the emergence of multidivisional firms investing enormous sums in R & D and committed to offering new products (Schumpeter, 1975; Chandler, 1977; Chandler, 1990), there has been a counter-tendency of an increasingly complex industrial division of labor and the emergence of a number of new industries (Hounshell, 1995). Often, new fast-growing firms have constituted industries in fields directly adjacent to those of existing large corporations and established industries, e.g., the relationship between the computer industry and the new computer networking industry. [3] The established companies had the technical core competencies necessary internally, but were unable to mobilize these capabilities and to deter entry by swarms of independent startups. As Schumpeter repeatedly pointed out, the firm is not the only institution that might be created. If the economic space is sufficiently large, this wave of creation can be so powerful as to launch an entirely new industry, thereby deepening the industrial division of labor (Smith, 1776; Young, 1928). Schumpeter (1964; 1968) termed this the creation of "new economic spaces."

Explaining the linkages between sociotechnical innovation and new firms is a difficult task for the social sciences. One model for explaining technological innovation and industrial organization is associ-

---

[3] For a discussion of this process in the biotechnology industry, see Kenney (1986a).

U. von Burg, M. Kenney / Research Policy 29 (2000) 1135–1155   1137

ated with William Abernathy and his colleagues who coupled Schumpeterian insights with product-cycle theory observing that at different stages in the cycle different types of innovations and industrial organization were prevalent (Abernathy, 1978; Abernathy and Utterback, 1978; Abernathy and Clark, 1985). [4] The cycle begins with a discontinuity resulting from a technological development that creates an environment with low entry barriers facilitating new entrants and much experimentation and uncertainty. In these periods it is difficult to forecast demand, prices, or even the eventual technological outcome (Tushman and Anderson, 1986). This period of ferment ends when one design becomes the standard (or dominant) and innovation shifts to incremental product and process innovations. At this stage there are far fewer new entrants to the industry (Utterback and Suarez, 1993).

Schumpeter carefully separated the role of the entrepreneur from that of the financier, but treated the financier as a relatively passive participant in the new firm formation process (Kenney, 1986b). In more recent literature the financial backers of new firms are treated as unproblematic. If an innovation is sufficiently attractive, then it is assumed that the financial backing will be available — it is simply a matter of understanding the investment criteria of venture capitalists. Given the level of analysis and topics of interest at which this perspective operates it is understandable, however, if the black box of the new firm formation process is examined more closely and from the perspective of the participants, then it can be seen that the attraction of financial support is far more tenuous and open to the forces of vagary, chance, and agency. The entrepreneur must recruit the venture capitalist.

In contrast to the previous rather structuralist positions, a group of sociologists argue that technology is socially constructed (Bijker et al., 1987). For them, the macrolevel forces detected, when analyzing technological evolution in broad terms, are not nearly so visible at the microlevel (Misa, 1994). A closer examination of the black box of technology development and adoption reveals that the dominant design of a particular technology or technological artifact is the product of an interaction between its social environment and technological development — with neither determinant. Rather than being invented or innovated, they found it more descriptive to say an artifact is socially constructed. The adoption of a new artifact should be seen as the creation of a network of linkages between human actors and artifacts (Cowan, 1987; Latour, 1993; Latour, 1996). This is a process of trying to both create an environment for the artifact and create an artifact for the environment. In this sense, the social construction of technology is the creation of networks including various actors, such as producers, consumers, and others. Within these networks there is a bargaining process through which an artifact and an economic arrangement to supply the artifact emerges (Bijker, 1993). As part of this process the supporters of the artifact must recruit resources and adherents (Foray, 1991). To pursue economic activities, one of the most important resources to be recruited is financial support, because of its role in binding actual productive resources such as employees and inputs to the project. This makes social actors such as venture capitalists important constituents for the entrepreneur wishing to actualize an innovation in a freestanding firm.

The concept of "embeddedness" developed by Granovetter (1985), which has never been applied to the relationship between venture capitalists and entrepreneurs, offers powerful insight because the actors are actually trying to embed the technology and the firm into the environment. Reputations and social connections are vital in securing funding and in facilitating the startup's success. [5] From a different but congruent perspective, Van de Ven and Garud (1989) propose an "accumulative theory of industry formation" based on conceptualizing an industry "as a social system consisting of three loosely coupled hierarchical subsystems: Instrumental, resource

---

[4] An important further extension to this line of thought explaining the industrial organization of regions such as Silicon Valley is Langlois and Robertson (1995, especially Chap. 7).

[5] For discussions relevant to this idea, see Kenney and von Burg (1999), Suchman (2000), Cohen and Fields (2000) and Kenney and von Burg (2000).

procurement and institutional subsystems.'' This study of the formation of the LAN industry focuses only on the resource procurement subsystem and the role of financiers, the venture capitalists. However, to adequately explain the role of the venture capitalists, we must repeatedly refer to the other subsystems.

3. Research methodology

Our research methodology comprised of two components. The first component was a review of all the industry journals, consultant's reports, and other written materials available. Of particular use were the US Securities and Exchange Commission (SEC) S-1 files. However, these were not sufficient to understand the industry and were often contradictory, especially in the details. The second component were telephonic interviews with entrepreneurs, venture capitalists, and senior corporate officials (who were not entrepreneurs). Our requests for interviews were largely successful, but five persons rejected our requests. However, for every firm we interviewed at least one founder and one of the original investors (except in the case of Interlan). We conducted 46 interviews with entrepreneurs, venture capitalists, and LAN industry executives from 1995 to 1999, all of which were taped and transcribed (a list is available from the authors by request). None of the interviewees asked for anonymity; however, each one quoted was sent the entire article for vetting, but only three responses were received clarifying errors of fact. In two cases, the entrepreneurs sent us copies of their business plans. We have no reason to suspect bias, but the difficulty of recalling events nearly 20 years ago could introduce inaccuracies, though all answers did agree with archival materials especially with the SEC S-1 files.

4. Venture capital

A striking feature of the postwar US national system of innovation has been the emergence of a set of financiers, the venture capitalists, specializing in providing the capital to entrepreneurs founding new firms. In quite a number of cases, these firms coa-

lesced into an industry. [6] Before the emergence of organized venture capital, the only sources of capital for an entrepreneur were informal, such as family, friends, and wealthy individuals. Financial institutions, such as banks or stockbrokers, generally were not organized to take risks on firms with little or no collateral (for further discussion, see Wilson, 1985; Florida and Kenney, 1988; Bygrave and Timmons, 1992). [7]

The venture capitalists only invest when they believe that the firm has potential to grow, and thereby rapidly increase the value of their equity investment. Venture capitalists aim to be at what the venture capitalist, Carano (1995), termed, ''the intersection of a dislocating long-term advantage and an explosive or compelling market application.'' The firms funded by venture capitalists include some of the fastest growing technology firms, many of which were key for constituting entirely new industries, such as biotechnology, hard disk drives, relational databases, workstations, and minicomputers, to name a few. Chronologically from a relatively inchoate group of private investors, venture capital coevolved with the growth of high-technology businesses in Silicon Valley and Route 128 to become an organized set of financiers (Kenney and von Burg, 1999).

The current scholarly research on venture capital concentrates upon the investment decisions and their outcomes. For the most part, this has been treated as a principal–agent problem. As Sahlman (1990) notes in venture capital there are actually two investments involved: investment in the venture capital limited partnership and by the limited partnership in startups. The various contract provisions and procedures help sort out the skills and intentions of the participants (Sahlman, 1990, p. 518). Gompers and Lerner (1996) examined limited partnerships covenants and found that both agency problems and supply and demand for fund managers, i.e., labor availability, were sig-

---

[6] Venture capital-financed entrepreneurial innovation has been so successful that it became a part of the US national system of innovation, see Lundvall (1992) and Nelson (1993).

[7] Though the bulk of formal venture capital investments are in the high-technology arena, they do not confine themselves to technology investments. For example, Federal Express was started with venture capital funds and a number of funds invest in franchising startups.

nificant factors in the use of covenants. Hellmann (1998) shows through an abstract mathematical model that entrepreneurs with less financial means are likely to surrender more control to venture capitalists, i.e., give the principal more power. These contributions by economists to understanding the investment decision are significant, however, they address neither the larger issue of how venture capitalists actually undertake their activities nor their role in the creation of firms and industries.

From the venture capitalists' perspective investment decisions occur in an environment of imperfect information, entrepreneurial visions, and educated guesses — it is exactly here that the entrepreneurs construct their firm. In contrast to neoclassical models in which time is largely irrelevant for venture capital investing time and timing are critical (Freeman, 1999). Not surprisingly, there is also an important evolutionary and path-dependent element in the activities of venture capitalists as they continually seek to build upon previous investments by funding the next step in the progress of the technology (Nelson and Winter, 1982; David, 1986; Arthur, 1994).

Venture capitalists differ from traditional investors in that they are not passive. In effect, after being recruited (or recruiting themselves into the deal) they become active social constructors. In other words, they try to shape the future in ways that improve the outcome of their investments. To do this they offer advice, become involved in critical corporate decisions, assist in corporate recruiting, even at times reassure an important prospective customer or supplier that they stand behind the firm, and undertake various other tasks (MacMillan et al., 1988; Sapienza, 1992). In effect, they try to influence the market outcome in favor of their investment.

The common view is that the venture capitalists are risk takers and, at one level, it is correct that they take larger risks than do ordinary bankers. But as our study of the LAN industry indicates, generally speaking, most venture capitalists are risk averse. The venture capitalist's craft is to balance between errors of omission, not investing when one should, and errors of commission, investing when one should not. There is another twist, namely that the greatest successes are almost always those in which the market growth is unforeseen by most investors, be-

cause if the success was foreseen the true value of the firm could have been judged. Not unexpectedly, those "foreseeing" the future have a high likelihood of being wrong.

5. Early networking and the invention of LAN technology

The history of networking goes back one and a half decades before the invention of LAN technology in the early 1970s. In 1958, the US Air Force installed the SAGE network, an air defense system that connected radars to central mainframe computers over telephone lines. Eventually, the SAGE network spanned over one million miles. Based on the innovative SAGE technology, in 1964 American Airways installed the SABRE network, which connected terminals to a mainframe for reservation purposes. Similarly structured reservation and transaction networks followed in other industries including banking and hotels, but SAGE's most critical contribution to networking was the development of the time-sharing concept. Like the SAGE and SABRE systems, time-sharing used terminals to connect users to the computer, but in contrast to the former two systems, time-sharing was implemented on generic computers that could be used for any application (Abbate, 1994). Then in 1969–1970 ARPA installed the ARPANET, which later evolved into the Internet. Many technologies that were adopted in LANs can be traced to the ARPANET (Hafner and Lyon, 1996).

Despite the development of networks in the late 1950s and 1960s, there was little commercial interest in networks. In fact, most computer manufacturer did not expand into networking adjacent to their product, nor did they set up network divisions in their enterprises. [8] Likewise, the development of the early networks did not trigger the formation of start-ups attempting to capitalize on the new technology. [9] To

---

[8] The important exception was IBM, which had developed the SAGE concept for the Air Force and then commercialized it by developing SABRE for American Airlines.

[9] The most significant exception is the Boston-area firm, Bolt, Beranek and Newman, which was the primary commercial firm involved in the ARPANET.

1140 *U. von Burg, M. Kenney / Research Policy 29 (2000) 1135–1155*

a large extent, the reasons for this commercial neglect can be found in the computer paradigm and industry of the 1960s. Compared to the hundreds of millions of computers installed today, in the 1960s, the installed base of computers was quite small — in 1960 only 5950 mainframe computers were shipped and in 1970, the number roughly doubled to 11,760 (Juliessen and Petska-Juliessen, 1994, p. 317). At the time, most computers, even when manufactured in large numbers, were conceived of as stand-alone machines and in the era of batch-processing typically lacked the means for communication with the outside world. This meant that the market potential for networking was small.

Only when time-sharing appeared, did commercial interest in networks begin growing. So, in the early and mid 1970s as time-sharing replaced the previous batch-processing mode, networking became an integral concept for computing. Most computer manufacturers developed protocols to connect terminals to host computers and to build hierarchies of terminals, front-end processors, and host computers. In 1974, for example, IBM introduced its SNA protocol, followed by DEC's DECnet in 1976, as did other major computer vendors. This made networking an integral part of computer manufacturers' business, but their employment of time-sharing did not lead to LAN technology. [10] The communication between terminals and hosts was not very data-intensive and thus did not require high bandwidth. Besides, the early systems were still relatively small. As the following discussion shows, LAN technology only emerged when users began interconnecting computers instead of terminals.

Given this lack of interest in LANs in the late 1960s and early 1970s, it is not surprising that researchers outside the corporate sector developed the first LAN technologies. For example, in 1971, David Farber of UC Irvine built the first operational LAN, which was based on a Token Ring technology. His LAN, transmitted at 2.3 Mbps, that is, 46 times faster than the ARPANET, itself a relatively fast wide area network (Farber, 1972; Farber, 1975). Farber designed a relatively high-speed network because he built a locally distributed computing system based on minicomputers. In other words, his system connected computers instead of terminals and distributed the processing over several machines. In 1973, Robert Metcalfe at Xerox PARC developed the second major LAN type, Ethernet. [11] Ethernet used a fundamentally different topology and transmission and access method, but it transmitted at a similar speed, namely 2.94 Mbps. Like Farber, Metcalfe needed the high networking speed because he built a distributed computing system, but unlike the system of Farber, PARC's system was based on connecting Xerox Alto personal workstations. PARC commissioned the development of a LAN because it needed the means to link the Alto computers with laser printers, which were the output devices for its "office of the future." With this distributed computing system, based on personal computers and intended for the office use, PARC had invented what eventually became the dominant environment in which LANs would be deployed (Hiltzik, 1999). LANs were initially used to connect minicomputers and to switch terminals to a host computer, but the LANs' main application would eventually be the connection of personal computers (that, is, IBM PCs) in the office environment. This client/server architecture would overthrow minicomputers and time-shared systems.

As in the case of the initial (wide area) networks, Farber's and Metcalfe's invention of LAN technology failed to trigger the rapid commercialization of the new technology. Farber had no commercial interest in his LAN technology, which was only a side product in his distributed system. Simultaneously, Xerox delayed the introduction of the office system developed by PARC. Moreover, in the mid 1970s, the incumbent computer manufacturers were focused upon central time-shared systems.

---

[10] LAN technology differs from time-sharing and the wide area networking technologies, because LANs must transmit at very high speeds but need only cover short distances.

[11] Metcalfe could have adopted Farber's Token Ring, but in this experimental stage, he rather wanted to invent something different (Farber, 1997).

U. von Burg, M. Kenney / Research Policy 29 (2000) 1135–1155 1141

6. The beginning of LAN commercialization

In the late 1970s, most computer manufacturers finally began experimenting with the new LAN technology or even prepared their introduction. In 1977, Datapoint offered a LAN technology called ARCnet to integrate its small business computers into a homogeneous computing environment, allowing users to share files and peripherals. In 1980, the computer workstation startup, Apollo Computer, introduced a line of workstations using a LAN technology called DOMAIN to connect its workstations together. Likewise, in 1979, minicomputer manufacturer Prime Computer introduced a LAN called Primenet with the express purpose of networking their minicomputers (Clarke, 1998). Contemporaneously, IBM at its Zurich research lab began experimenting with the technology in 1979, but for a number of reasons this project did not receive the highest priority.

It is not surprising that the computer manufacturers should begin developing LANs. Customers with more than one computer at a site wanted them to communicate at speeds greater than that available over modems connected to the telephone system. Moreover, by the late 1970s, the number of terminals had increased so dramatically that higher network speeds to connect terminals to a host computer became very desirable. At the time, to most observers, networking appeared to be mere extension of the computer industry's existing a business, and from this, it seemed natural that the computer manufacturer would dominate the networking space. They had the technical skills, they controlled the LANs' primary market including the interfaces, they interacted with the customers, and they controlled the machines to be networked.

Despite the overwhelming advantages of the computer makers, a few entrepreneurs believed there were market opportunities, which prompted them to establish firms and to launch LAN products. The computer makers though proclaiming their decisions to provide LANs were slow at introducing products. Moreover, they aimed to provide proprietary systems capable of only connecting their own computers. In other words, the LAN would be used to lockout competitors and lock-in their customers. Thus, a space for the entrepreneurs opened as customers searched for solutions to their on-site interconnection problems, which involved multiple computer brands.

The first start-up to offer LANs was Network Systems, which was established in 1974 in Minnesota by some former employees of Control Data and Univac. The founders believed that data centers would be interested in a technology allowing them to connect their various mainframes. Network Systems believed it would be possible to compete successfully with the computer manufacturers especially IBM because as a specialized LAN vendor they could interconnect the vendors' incompatible mainframe computers, a gateway function the computer manufacturers did not want to offer. Network Systems experienced much difficulty raising venture capital. Despite being established in 1974, only in 1976 did the firm receive funding from the local Minneapolis venture capital fund, Norwest Venture Capital Management. This meant that for nearly 2 years the entrepreneurs had to bootstrap the firm. However, the mainframe networking market remained small, thus limiting Network Systems' growth.

In 1979, Ungermann–Bass (UB) was established by Zilog alumni Ralph Ungermann and Charles Bass to create high-speed local area access between terminals and minicomputers. However, before discussing UB, the role of Zilog in the creation of the LAN industry should be highlighted. Zilog was established in 1974 by Frederico Faggin (one of the co-designers of Intel's microprocessor) and Ralph Ungermann with venture capital from Exxon as part of its quixotic attempt to use its oil crisis-related windfall profits to design the "office of the future." In the late 1970s, Zilog developed a LAN based on its already successful communications peripheral chip for input/output devices (Ungermann, 1995). A group of engineers including Charles Bass developed not only an operating system called Leo for controlling a number of microprocessors, but also a personal computer LAN, the ZNet. However, ZNet had technical problems and was not marketable (Ungermann, 1995). Then Ungermann and Bass left in 1979. Zilog hired William Carrico, Judith Estrin, and Eric Benhamou continued working on the Znet until they left to establish Bridge Communications in 1981. Whereupon Zilog hired a group of engineers including Kanwal Rekhi, who left within a year to join a team

1142 *U. von Burg, M. Kenney / Research Policy 29 (2000) 1135–1155*

of Indian engineers to start Excelan. Zilog proved to be an important seed company for an entire generation of LAN companies (see Fig. 1) and, as is so often the case, Exxon reaped little benefit from its large investments.

Upon leaving Zilog, Ungermann and Bass wrote their business plan with the venture capitalist, Neill Brownstein of Bessemer Ventures. Their explicit strategy was to start the company in a field with great potential but no entrenched competition (Ungermann, 1995), while avoiding an extended pioneering effort (Electronics News, 1980: 17). [12] This strategy, though excellent from an entrepreneurship perspective, made it difficult to secure venture capital, since there were no benchmarks or other LAN companies against which to value the company and there was no obvious market. Technically, the lack of a protocol or standard to be used for data transmission meant that there was no way to predict which protocol would be adopted. Obviously, few observers believed a startup would successfully induce larger players to adopt its protocol. According to Ralph Ungermann (1995), "everybody in the venture community turned us down because they believed that the International Standards Organization (ISO) standard was coming and the computer companies would build the network that would interconnect each other's equipment. So, there [would be] no room for a stand-alone networking company."

Not surprisingly, most venture capitalists could not envision the economic space and could not believe that a startup could construct such a market. Ungermann (1995) contacted virtually "every venture capitalist in the United States and in the world really" with little success. It took 8 months to close the deal. The market and technical problems were one set of issues, but Brownstein (1998) recalled that some venture capitalists believed Ungermann's association with Zilog was also negative because of its

relative lack of success, though Brownstein now believes this was a rationalization for not wanting to invest. This agrees with Burton et al. (1998), who found that an entrepreneur's past employer had a significant impact on the venture capital funding decision.

Because Brownstein assisted in developing the business plan, he was committed to the venture, but his policy was only to coinvest, so other investors were required. The other lead investor came to UB by a very different route. In the Fall of 1979, James Swartz, a venture capitalist, attended a McGraw-Hill Conference on data communications in New York, where Robert Metcalfe, the inventor of Ethernet at Xerox PARC, presented a seminar and proselytized for the adoption of the Ethernet protocol. One slide listed the small companies that had adopted Ethernet, which included UB. Since Swartz was interested in computer networking, he decided to visit the listed companies.

Swartz was uniquely prepared to see the potential of LANs because in 1978, he had made an investment in Amdax, a company commercializing a broadband technology for factory automation. Soon after the investment, the founder died and Swartz managed the company until a successor could be found. As the temporary CEO, he was immersed in the networking business and was convinced of its potential. [13] So, by the time he visited UB, he was primed to make an investment. Swartz (1995) described his meeting with the two founders:

I met Ralph and Charlie [and discussed their business]. At the end of the day I said, 'Jesus, this is terrific. I really like what you guys are doing. You are absolutely right on everything. I can tell you I want to do this.' So, I called Fred (Fred Adler, his partner) that evening and told him what I was doing. He said, 'fine go do it.' And so that evening or the next day, I called Ralph and committed to him.

Since Bessemer Securities had already committed, the deal was quickly finalized with Oak Investment

---

[12] UB's business plan listed the following potential customers: Ford, Hughes Aircraft, State Island Hospital, Sytek, LII, TRW, Chase Manhattan, Chemical Abstract Service, Library of Congress, Western Union, Employers Insurance of Wausau, Boeing Aerospace and Boeing Computer Services, Wells Fargo, US Navy Ship R&D Center, Martin Marietta, Citibank, Tymshare, Control Data, Shell, GTE Services, University of California, San Diego. See Ungermann–Bass (1979).

[13] In 1983, UB acquired Amdax.

U. von Burg, M. Kenney / Research Policy 29 (2000) 1135–1155   1143

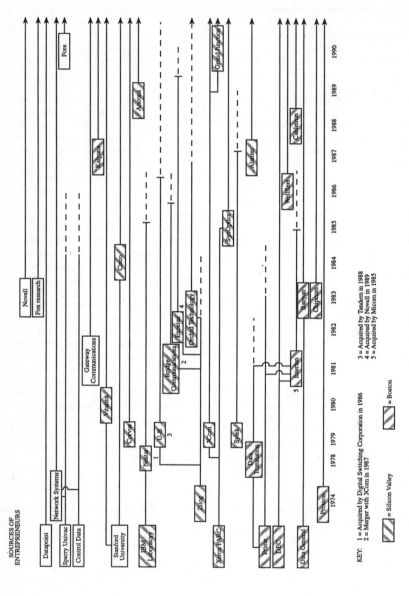

Fig. 1. Genealogy of startup LAN companies.

also joining (Ungermann, 1995). Swartz, Neill Brownstein of Bessemer Venture Partners, and Stewart Greenfield of Oak Investment Partners invested an initial US$1.5 million in February 1980. In total, the investors committed US$10 million before the company went public in June 1983 with a total valuation of US$48 million (Hofmeister, 1989).

In sectors where there is no industry and no market, the investment decision is inherently difficult. Swartz (1995), when asked about whether he contacted personnel in large companies, such as IBM, DEC, or Xerox regarding the feasibility of the business plan said, ''if I had tried to do that kind of due diligence, I would have been absolutely convinced that [the UB investment] was something I should not do.'' Since Swartz believed in the potential inherent in the technology, he described the decision-making process in this way, ''[the investment] became a people thing, who [the founding team] are and what they have done — classic resume tracking. And then it becomes a very gut-level feel of, 'gee, are these credible people. Do they have the right integrity and right ethics?''' Brownstein also said it was difficult to effectively research an almost infant technology, but he was sensitized to the possibilities of LANs due to Bessemer Ventures involvement with Telenet Communications, which was founded in 1979 (Brownstein, 1999).

Despite great difficulty, Network Systems and UB succeeded in securing venture capital. However, funding was not a foregone conclusion. During the same period another firm, Nestar, established in October 1978, never found venture capital. Inspired by the feverish experimentation with microcomputers in the Silicon Valley area, Nestar's founders, Harry Saal and Leonard Shustek, recognized that an important limitation for these microcomputers was the high cost of peripherals such as hard disk drives and printers. At the time, Saal was developing interactive time-sharing systems for mainframes at the IBM Palo Alto Laboratory and then later the IBM Santa Teresa Laboratory. They were intrigued by ''the idea of building large distributed systems of personal computers, networking them, and connecting them together'' (Saal, 1995). He tried to convince IBM to let him work on these ideas, but IBM was uninterested. So, Saal resigned and convinced Shustek (1999), a Stanford physics graduate student

who had become an assistant professor at Carnegie Mellon University, to found Nestar to develop and market microcomputer LANs.

In 1978, while building their first LAN prototype for the Commodore PET, they tried fruitlessly to raise venture capital in Silicon Valley and New York. They later began networking Apple II computers, but as Saal recalled, ''[the venture capitalists] really did not believe that these types of computers would ever be used in a real commercial-type environment or that people would have large numbers of them networked together. I got a fantastic rejection from all of them. They said this [company would] not go anywhere, that these toy computers were never going to be serious and if they were serious, nobody would have many of them at a time together'' (Saal, 1995). Further, they questioned the reasons IBM did not invest, if the idea was so good. [14] Only later, did Nestar receive capital from the Rank organization in the United Kingdom.

Nestar was too early. The microcomputer was still the province of hobbyists, and there was not a large installed base (see Fig. 2). To be legitimate in the business world, microcomputer LANs would have to wait until IBM introduced the PC. Nestar never had revenues greater than US$10 million and was eventually merged with another company and closed in 1986. [15] Saal and Shustek were the typical pioneers that had all the elements right, but they were unable to recruit resources and to unify them into an economically viable system. Since it was early, Nestar had to wait for the microcomputer market to grow sufficiently large, and it had to develop all of its own hardware and software. Nestar provides an interesting example of how venture capitalists often are unwilling to support an entrepreneur's vision that ultimately proves to be quite accurate. With suffi-

---

[14] This was the period when IBM appeared invincible.

[15] Failure is often not final. In 1986, Harry Saal and Leonard Shustek left Nestar to start another LAN, Network General, with ''with a blank piece of paper (Saal, 1995).'' At Network General, Saal and Shustek controlled nearly 60% of the stock. For the most part, they boot strapped the company and only brought in TA Associates of Boston later. Network General went public in 1987 and merged with McAfee Associates in the late 1990's. Both Saal and Shustek have since left Network General.

U. von Burg, M. Kenney / Research Policy 29 (2000) 1135–1155   1145

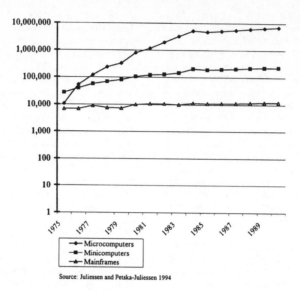

Fig. 2. Annual US shipments of microcomputers, minicomputers, and mainframes, 1975–1990.

cient funding Nestar might have had the wherewithal to find a market for their LAN.

There were other early startups, which had proprietary LANs that met with limited success. For example, another early startup, Corvus, was a hard disk drive manufacturer, which had a LAN system meant to link its hard disk drives to an office network. The LAN sold well especially for linking Apple II computers. Because of its internal status, it did not need venture capital. However, when the disk drive business failed, the LAN business also failed. Another very early Boston-area LAN firm, Proteon, was established in 1972 by Howard Salwen. Initially, the firm consulted on networking for the U.S Department of Defense. In the late 1970s and early 1980s, Proteon developed a Token Ring LAN system and began marketing it. It only began looking for venture capital in 1983, and the deal was closed in 1984 (Proteon, 1991; Bayless, 1998).

There were a number other startups with proprietary protocols. Examples include Sytek (1984), a Silicon Valley spin-off of Ford Aerospace incorporated in 1979, with funding from General Instrument

(50.8% of total equity at time of IPO). Another firm was Gateway Communications (1985) of Irvine, California, which was financed by the entrepreneurs and the Noorda family trust of which Raymond Noorda, the president of Novell, was the trustee. Gateway also had a proprietary protocol that was not accepted in the market. Still another firm was Xyplex (1991) established in the Boston area in 1981, which at its inception focused connecting DEC computer systems using a proprietary LAN protocol. Xyplex received funding from a number of Boston-area venture capital partnerships, including Claflin Capital, Matrix Partners, BancBoston Ventures, and Charles River, and the California partnerships, Menlo Ventures and Sigma Group. It only went public in 1991, after a long period of continually losing money.

To conclude, by 1980, a few LAN startups had been founded and even had begun shipping some products. But by large, the computer manufacturers appeared far better positioned to capture this economic space. They controlled interfaces and customer base, and had all the required financial and technical capabilities. The computer manufacturers' better position clearly reflected on the venture capitalist's assessment of the business opportunities of startups. There was no standard at the time, and the various proprietary LANs introduced by the startups had significant difficulty gathering outside support. Not surprisingly, though the venture capitalists funded a few firms, they were hesitant and did not see LANs as a promising investment field.

7. Xerox changes the equation

In the late 1970s and early 1980s, two events occurred that changed the prospects for new entrants. Like IBM and the other computer manufacturers, DEC became interested in LAN technology. However, rather than designing its own protocols, in 1979, DEC began to discuss licensing Ethernet from Xerox for networking their forthcoming VAX computers. As an outcome of discussions, Xerox came to believe its strategic interest would be served, if Ethernet was adopted widely. Therefore, it eschewed royalties and set a low licensing fee of US$1000 (Liddle, 1995). The widespread adoption of Ethernet was in Xerox's interest because at the time most customers were locked into the proprietary systems offered by Wang, DEC, and IBM (Sirbu and Hughes, 1986). Adoption of the open Ethernet system would free customers to purchase eclectically. [16] To assist in popularizing Ethernet, Xerox and DEC recruited Intel to form the DIX group. DEC and Xerox, which intended to sell minicomputers and printers, respectively, hoped an open network protocol would ignite competition in component manufacturing, thereby lowering price and encouraging innovation. Also, for DEC it solved the problem of having to design its own protocol.

While the DIX group was preparing to announce Ethernet as an open standard, a second critical process was underway, namely an Institute of Electrical and Electronics Engineers (IEEE) committee meeting (called IEEE 802) on creating a LAN standard. The DIX group decided to offer Ethernet to the IEEE. However, this created a rift between the DIX

group and another group led by IBM advocating a Token Ring standard. Very soon, the IEEE committee divided into two separate groups, each of which issued their own standard. Ethernet's advantage was its openness and that it was already available. Token Ring was not yet in production but it had support from IBM and had superior network management technology (von Burg, 1999). The decision to create open standards doomed the proprietary firms.

In hindsight, the IEEE 802 standardization was a fundamental event in the creation of the LAN industry. The Ethernet standard shifted the balance of power between the LAN specialists and the incumbent computer manufacturers, as the licensing and standardization of Ethernet provided a "language" around which an economic community could coalesce. Whereas most early LAN entrants excluded other firms from using their standard, Ethernet welcomed all. For startups this meant they did not have to develop a protocol from scratch. Also, DEC and Xerox systems were now a market, and for suppliers uncertainty was reduced. Also, there was the promise of being freed from the control of computer makers' proprietary systems. DIX had issued an open invitation to entrepreneurs to begin developing Ethernet-compatible products.

8. Ethernet startups

Although IBM's and DEC's adoption of an open standard put the startups on an equal basis, from a theoretical perspective the computer manufacturers still had significant advantages vis-à-vis startups. They had enormous marketing power and had access to potential customers. Also, they had strong research and engineering capabilities, so it was reasonable to expect them to overwhelm the startups and occupy the industrial space. Yet, both were relatively slow in getting products to the market. In its insistence on developing a perfect technology, IBM spent several additional years at the IEEE standardizing Token Ring. Hence, standard Token Ring did not become available before 1986. Given Ethernet's faster standardization, DEC could have acted faster, but it also responded slowly and did not ship products until late 1983.

---

[16] For a discussion of standards and lock-in, see Farrell and Saloner (1986), Katz and Shapiro (1986) Arthur (1989), David and Greenstein (1990) and Shapiro and Varian (1999).

U. von Burg, M. Kenney / Research Policy 29 (2000) 1135–1155   1147

While the two computer giants moved very slowly, startups were very fast. UB immediately switched to the Ethernet version and introduced an Ethernet-compatible product in 1981 months before anybody else. UB's reaction to Ethernet was not surprising as DEC systems were a very important part of their business, and a standard legitimized them to their Fortune 500 customers. Ethernet was the logical choice for UB because it was available, whereas the ultimate Token Ring standard was still being developed. Finally, the UB founders were well acquainted with Metcalfe and Xerox PARC.

The Ethernet market was far more attractive than Token Ring because it was far nearer to becoming a defacto standard. Ethernet clearly had the backing to become a dominant design, but there was no guarantee that startups could be successful in competition with larger established firms such as DEC. If the startups were to be successful, it would be necessary to recruit the capital that could be used to develop an operational firm. Given the support by the DIX group and the IEEE standardization process underway, one might expect venture capitalists to leap at the opportunity to participate in the construction of a new industry space and, if fortunate, an entire dominant design. However, as we shall show, at this early stage venture capitalists were reluctant to invest.

3Com was the first of the new Ethernet-dedicated startups. It was founded by Robert Metcalfe, the inventor of Ethernet, and Gregory Shaw on June 4, 1979 (Crane, 1995). After leaving Xerox PARC and prior to founding 3Com, Metcalfe had consulted for DEC and helped make DEC's new VAX minicomputer product line compatible with Ethernet. Metcalfe established 3Com to exploit the Ethernet standard, which he had encouraged Xerox to license at favorable terms. The 3Com founders had never started or managed a company. Metcalfe's experience had been in the university and research environment, and he had no experience as a business manager.

The founding team had never raised venture capital or written a business plan. Charney (1995), the original Secretary and Vice President of Operations, described their presentations to the venture capitalists as "meandering." They intended to target desktop computers, but in October 1980, there was only a small installed base, as the IBM PC had not yet been introduced. Written in the last quarter of 1980, 3Com's business plan was necessarily vague, because the market was not yet formed. According to the October 6, 1980 3Com briefing document for David Arscott and Leal Norton, a venture capital partnership, 3Com planned to capitalize on Xerox's Ethernet to provide multi-vendor compatibility in local networks [3Com, 1980]. Given the vagueness of the business plan, the lack of a clear market, and fears that large companies such as IBM and DEC would control the market, Arscott and Norton and many others decided against investing (Richman, 1989). This was not surprising. One of the original venture capital backers, Richard Kramlich, remembered his first meeting with Metcalfe:

> He [Metcalfe] told me about his background and where he had been. He sketched out his Ethernet idea. I will never forget because he brought in his business plan and it amounted to a series of clouds. I was trying my best to understand what he was talking about and I had a vague understanding of it. But I did not know any of the technology at the time.

Fig. 3 is a reproduction of a page in the original business plan and shows that 3Com was proposing to undertake a large variety of tasks. In fact, another very successful venture capitalist, Dougery (1998), said he had met Metcalfe and remembers talking "with people at Mayfield (a very successful venture fund) who looked at it and they didn't understand what the hell Metcalfe was saying." This provides an indication of how great the task was, not of building, but simply of explaining what a useful LAN was at the time.

Because of Metcalfe's reputation at Xerox PARC, there was interest in the venture capital community. Wallace Davis at Mayfield offered US$7 per share to Metcalfe who rejected the offer as too low. Richard Kramlich at New Enterprise Associates put together an offer for US$13 a share, and Metcalfe turned him down, also. Metcalfe then managed to secure a US$21 per share offer from a Boston venture capitalist. However, the Boston firm never closed the deal. After presentations to nearly 40 venture capital

1148   *U. von Burg, M. Kenney / Research Policy 29 (2000) 1135–1155*

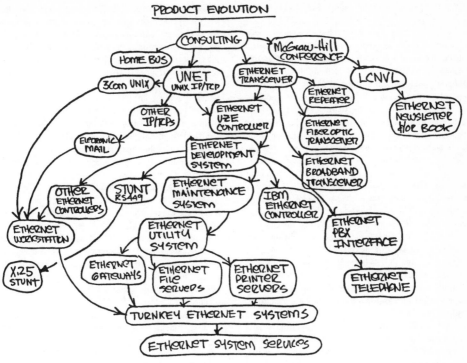

Source: 3Com Corporation. 1980. "Confidential Briefing for David Arscott and Leal F. Norton"

Fig. 3. Product evolution.

groups, Metcalfe returned to the Silicon Valley venture capitalists; Jack Melchor of Melchor Venture Management, Richard Kramlich, and Wallace Davis, and closed the deal (Wilson, 1985, pp. 177–179). At the end of this 6-month search period, 3Com received US$1.05 million on February 28, 1981 — the same day 3Com actually ran out of money (Charney, 1995).

Kramlich invested in 3Com because Metcalfe and the technical expertise of the team impressed him. Kramlich (1995) attributes his decision to invest to his involvement in Apple Computer, which alerted him to "the logic of going from a personal computer to a network. Resource sharing was going to be the wave of the future." As with Swartz and Brownstein

in the UB deal, Kramlich appears to have had an experience that prepared him for his pioneering investment.

The venture capitalists were intent upon building a complete firm. One important stipulation in closing the 3Com financing was that 3Com hire a seasoned manager to handle the general management issues. The venture capitalists were actively involved in this recruitment, which brought in an executive from Hewlett Packard, William Krause, as the CEO. [17] In this recruitment, the venture capitalists undertook to

---

[17] In 1995 *Business Week* reported incorrectly that Krause was a 3Com founder.

U. von Burg, M. Kenney / Research Policy 29 (2000) 1135–1155   1149

assist the company in the search and selection process.

Initially, 3Com grew slowly, but changed its strategy dramatically in August 1981 when IBM introduced the IBM personal computer. Almost immediately, Metcalfe decided 3Com should design an Ethernet adapter card for the IBM PC using VLSI circuitry. The reason Metcalfe gave for focusing 3Com's resources upon the IBM PC was that 3Com had not been established to support what Metcalfe believed were the "dying" technologies of minicomputers and mainframes. For him connecting terminals and hosts was a poor utilization of the technology. Of course, providing Ethernet connections for the only recently released IBM PC was not immediately a large business because of the paucity of installed IBM PCs. There is another interpretation, Brownstein (1998), an investor in UB, said UB with its headstart had already occupied the existing minicomputer market, so 3Com had little to lose by moving to the PC. Whatever the motivation, this proved to be a brilliant and fortuitous move as 3Com's sales accelerated after 1984, as the installed base of IBM PCs and PC-compatibles grew dramatically.

In the 3Com deal, Metcalfe's reputation was a significant factor in attracting capital, but the process remained difficult. Notice the large spread in valuations and the inability or unwillingness of the Boston-based venture capitalist to close the deal. At this time, there was no consensus or community; finally 3Com looked like a "me-too" company as UB was already selling into the existing minicomputer market. Still it was clear that 3Com would adopt Ethernet, so in this sense, the technological question was solved, though it was not yet certain that Ethernet would become the dominant standard.

9. Other early entrants

There were other early startups that entered the LAN business. As mentioned earlier one of the most significant, Bridge Communications, was established in September 1981 by William Carrico, Judith Estrin, and Eric Benhamou, alumni of Zilog's Z-Net (Bridge Communications, 1985). Bridge Communications addressed the incompatibility of the wide variety of LANs using different protocols by building electronic "bridges" between them, hence the name, Bridge Communications. During the funding process the entrepreneurs realized that their business plan was flawed because there were not yet enough LANs to interconnect (Brinton, 1981). In this case, the venture capital process uncovered a flaw in the entrepreneur's plans. This did not prevent funding, rather Bridge had to offer other networking equipment and not just focus upon internetworking (Estrin, 1995). Bridge adopted Xerox's Ethernet standard from its establishment (Bridge Communications, 1986). Finding venture funding was a slow process, but after a 6-month search in December 1981, they closed the deal and received US$1.8 million for 60% of the firm's equity from Weiss, Peck and Greer Venture Partners (WPG); Merrill, Pickard, Anderson and Eyre (MPA&E); and later Warburg, Pincus Investors (Hofmeister, 1989). Estrin (1995) felt that, in the case of Bridge Communications, the venture capitalists made their decision on the basis of the people involved, because she thought most of the venture capitalists initially did not understand the technology. [18]

Another important Ethernet startup was Excelan, a Zilog spinout, which was founded in January 1982 by four Indian entrepreneurs, but received venture capital funding only in November 1984. Excelan was formed with the idea of interconnecting various LANs using the TCP/IP protocol. According to one of its founders, Kanwal Rekhi, Excelan had great difficulty securing funding, which he attributed to the entire founding team being from India. When this was mentioned to Dougery (1998), one of the lead venture capitalists in the deal, he said he had heard this rumor, but his response was:

> It [their being Indian] wasn't [a problem] for me. First [sic] immigrants I love it. All they have to do is work hard and they are obviously self-selected being here and, great education, and are highly motivated. I love it. That is a positive for me.

---

[18] Philip Greer (1996), a co-founder of WPG, readily agreed with Estrin's assessment that he did not completely understand the technology. However, he apparently did understand good entrepreneurs.

1150   *U. von Burg, M. Kenney / Research Policy 29 (2000) 1135–1155*

Almost immediately after investing the venture capitalists had to fire the CEO, one of the founding team, because of an internal "revolt." To replace him, they found a manager, who helped them go public before leaving. In essence, the venture capitalists were intimately involved in the firing of two CEOs. Ultimately, due to the management turmoil and an enticing offer Excelan was sold to Novell to which it brought LAN knowledge and the focus upon the TCP/IP protocol.

Another important Ethernet startup in this period was the Boston-area firm, Interlan, founded in May 1981, to network minicomputers. It only became involved in PCs in late 1983 (Seifert, 1995). One of Interlan's founders had already been a successful entrepreneur at Data Translation so he was able to secure capital relatively easily from four East Coast partnerships.

After 1981, few startups chose to develop a proprietary standard. Though not yet dominant, Ethernet was fast creating a community and being accepted as a standard. By 1983 proprietary LANs were fading from the scene as a "bandwagon" formed around Ethernet. [19] Increasingly, new startups concentrated on developing products that were Ethernet-compatible, and venture capitalists would no longer back non-Ethernet firms. In 1983, Ethernet was an adequate, low-cost solution, but it was threatened by a well-designed alternative, Token Ring, supported by IBM. Though the vendors had established a thriving and rapidly growing industry based on the Ethernet standard, it still was not clear that they could survive an IBM-supported Token Ring standard that had significant technical advantages.

10. Fixing Ethernet — the second great wave

The Ethernet startups quickly captured market share, and the proprietary LAN vendors and minicomputer makers such as DEC were becoming increasingly dependent upon them. But in the mid 1980s, IBM had a real chance to recapture industry-

dominance. Ethernet, in fact, had serious technological shortcomings. It was difficult to connect a node to the cable; the cable did not bend easily around corners; connections were often unreliable; an ill-connected node could take down the entire network; and finally, Ethernet's bus topology made it difficult to locate network failures. This gave IBM's Token Ring a critical window of opportunity. Designed as an enterprise LAN, Token Ring was far better suited to accommodate the growing networks, and due to its hub topology it also offered better network management and troubleshooting features. If Ethernet failed to improve, there was the potential for Token Ring to become the dominant design. Since IBM tightly controlled the Token Ring standard, it was likely that Token Ring's victory would have shifted the power balance back to the computer manufacturers.

In 1980, Xerox PARC hired Ronald Schmidt to develop an Ethernet version for fiber optic cable. While experimenting with fiber optic Ethernet, Schmidt replaced Ethernet's bus topology with a star topology, in which the cables from each node ran through a central hub. To publish a few academic papers and to help Xerox PARC, which had come under attack in the press for its unsuccessful commercialization track record, he built a prototype. Schmidt even developed a business plan aimed at interesting Xerox's management in commercializing his invention. After some consideration, Xerox decided not to commercialize this new topology, even though Xerox's own real estate consulting unit argued that the new configuration could solve the Ethernet cabling difficulties in their office buildings (Schmidt, 1995).

In 1985, after deciding it did not want to commercialize the hub, Xerox permitted Schmidt and Ludwick to resign, license the technology, and establish a firm. In return for using its intellectual property Xerox received equity in the start-up (Borsook, 1988; Schmidt, 1995). The company was incorporated in June 1985 by Andrew Ludwick, Ronald Schmidt, Shelby Carter, and Xerox as Astra Communications, but soon changed its name to SynOptics (SynOptics, 1988). Almost immediately SynOptics was profitable (SynOptics, 1988). In fiscal year 1985, it earned US$485,000 on US$1.18 million in sales and grew rapidly thereafter.

---

[19] For a discussion of standards and bandwagon effects, see Arthur (1989), Bresnahan and Chopra (1990) and Katz and Shapiro (1994).

U. von Burg, M. Kenney / Research Policy 29 (2000) 1135–1155 1151

In the early 1986, SynOptics sought venture capital. As with the previous companies, SynOptics had considerable difficulty finding investors. Many prestigious venture capitalists turned the deal down or missed it. For example, Richard Kramlich at New Enterprise Associates saw the SynOptics deal early because one of his partners was a fraternity brother of one of the founders. Kramlich (1995), a successful 3Com investor and very successful venture capitalist, recalled, "we should have done it. I knew it was going to be a great deal." However, for a variety of reasons, many of which had to do with valuation and disagreements among the partners, NEA did not invest. Donald Valentine also saw the deal and says he believed it was a good opportunity. But he also did not invest (Valentine, 1995).

There were various reasons for the decisions not to invest in SynOptics. Many venture capitalists believed that the market for an Ethernet system running on fiber optic cable networks and the IBM Cabling System would be small (Jeffery, 1986). In this, they were correct, but SynOptics soon developed a hub-based, 10 Mbps Ethernet LAN on telephone wire. Because the hub was a relatively low technology product, many venture capitalists were concerned that the low barriers to entry would not allow SynOptics sufficient profitability or that competitors would quickly erode its first-mover advantages. These venture capitalists were correct, the hub was not high technology or software-intensive enough to deter the larger, incumbent LAN vendors such as 3Com, Hewlett Packard, or UB. What many did not envision was that the hub could become a platform upon which high-value software and firmware could be added and that the first-mover advantage combined with rapid innovation would permit SynOptics to outrun its competitors in the hub business (Bredt, 1995).

When the venture capitalists investigated the business plan, their concerns were reinforced by the incumbent LAN vendors. These companies thought the hub was trivial and easy to imitate. Ronald Schmidt (1995) described the situation:

The VC all [talk to] the winners. They went and talked to 3Com. 3Com said it's trivial what they are doing, we can do it with our hands tied behind our back and one-eye blindfolded. And then, that went out to the entire VC community. So you had to find people who would not think as part of the herd instinct.

They escaped this "herd" instinct when John Lewis of Paragon Partners agreed to invest. Lewis was then joined by Thomas Bredt of Menlo Ventures, a prestigious Silicon Valley partnership, and this solidified the deal. The other venture capital firm to join the deal was Rust Ventures from Austin, TX and the investment closed in August 1986.

So why did Thomas Bredt invest when the others did not? Due to his experience with LANs from his previous employment at HP and Dataquest, he said it was obvious that the SynOptics' implementation of Ethernet had significant advantages over the existing technology. The hub and adoption of telephone wire radically simplified the installation and maintenance of an Ethernet LAN. Also, SynOptics inherited a powerful patent position from Xerox, though this proved of little value because securing approval from the IEEE meant freely licensing to all interested parties (Bredt, 1995).

As with the other firms, the SynOptics deal was shopped to many venture capitalists, but most declined to invest. Since the technology was simple, it was difficult to envision how the product's benefits would combine with the increasing number of PCs in such a way as to create an explosion of demand. Further, few foresaw the hub as a site for embedding high value-added software and specialized integrated circuitry, thereby increasing its value to the customer. Finally, they did not grasp the advantage SynOptics would have as the first mover. [20] The decision to fund SynOptics differed significantly from the decisions to fund LAN startups in the earlier period. The investment decision was based not so much on the entrepreneurs, but rather on the technology. The SynOptics' solution addressed two important Ethernet deficiencies. The character of the investment decision changed during this period because now Ethernet was a winning technology, there was a community of firms and individuals to consult (though many offered the wrong advice), and

---

[20] In today's Internet market, this is simply an environmental condition.

there were some measures with which to evaluate SynOptics (i.e., the previous successes of UB, 3Com, and Bridge). At least some venture capitalists claimed they wanted to invest, though they did not, indicating some awareness of the technology's value. Ultimately, investment decisions were based upon beliefs regarding whether the hub provided a profitable opportunity. The parameters of variation to be considered had narrowed significantly from the 1978–1986 period. Risk, of course, still existed, but the preeminent issues had shifted to execution, moving faster, and adding value.

With SynOptics and Ethernet's improvement, Ethernet prevailed over Token Ring. This meant the startups, then firms with US\$100–500 million sales, continued to dominate the industry, and LAN technology was definitely embedded in an industry separate from the computer industry. This would have significance in a myriad of other ways. The venture capitalists' success in these early networking startups dramatically increased their interest in funding other startups such as Cisco and various infrastructure firms and, in the mid 1990s the Internet phenomenon.

11. Discussion

The investment decision and the building of the firm are better understood as an attempt to construct an entity and space. The entrepreneurs recruit resources from the environment and unite them into a working entity. They must convince investors that their vision of the future has the possibility of being actualized. With the venture capitalist, the entrepreneur recruits an active investor who will assist in the construction process.

The construction of these LAN firms was not orderly, rather it had an emergent quality. Rather than constructing, the process seems far less rational, often the actors cobbled things together and engaged in leaps of faith. Venture capitalists undertook due diligence and even calculated possible rates of return, but then they attributed investments to their "gut feelings" about the people involved. Since these investments demand an envisioning process, there is a significant component of tacit knowledge in the investment decision that cannot be easily made

explicit. If the cobbled together firm experiences some success in attracting capital and sales, i.e., it grows, then it will become concretized, rewarding the cobblers. Success also attracts imitators and extenders (both entrepreneurs and venture capitalists), these create the community — as in the case of Ethernet.

The utility of the dominant design schema for thinking about the venture capital decision-making process is illustrated by the difficulties of the earliest startups in securing financing. With no dominant design the situation was difficult for investors; there was no industry or market for these startups, making it difficult to envision firms dedicated to producing LANs. For many venture capitalists, the claims by the large established companies such as IBM, DEC, Wang, and HP that they could and would provide computer networking appeared all too plausible. The idea of an independent industry became easier to accept after the decision by Xerox to license Ethernet and DEC's adoption of Ethernet. This certified there could be a market. As important, it provided the first indication that Ethernet might become dominant, thereby removing a source of uncertainty.

Before a dominant design emerged, the venture capitalists had to bet on the entrepreneurs presenting the business plan, i.e., bet on people. The difference between a radical innovation with massive capital gains and a mistake with no chance of success is not always easy to discern a priori. Many apparently sure things and great entrepreneurial visions ultimately look foolish, because they find no customers, encounter problems that cannot be solved technically, or come to fruition only years or even decades after the first investments. Thus, often the initial chaos and opaqueness of a technology or market is sufficient to discourage venture capital investors as a group. The critical point, however, is that venture capitalists are evaluated as individuals in partnerships, therefore an individual or partnership can break ranks and provide funding. This means that many alternatives can be tried and failures do not destroy the system.

Drawing upon a synthesis of the theories about design and social constructionism, we used a case study of the creation of the LAN industry to provide a new and richer framework for considering the venture capital process. Our formulation, though not

U. von Burg, M. Kenney / Research Policy 29 (2000) 1135–1155

1153

as tightly determined as many more economics-inspired studies, is more appreciative of the contingent and emergent features of economic activity seeking to construct a firm de novo. Hopefully, this contribution will encourage more research on the interaction between venture capital, firm formation, the lock-in of a dominant design, and the creation of new industries.

Acknowledgements

The authors thank the three anonymous reviewers for their valuable comments. We also thank those entrepreneurs and venture capitalists that took time from their schedules to grant us interviews. Special thanks must go to James Swartz of Accel Partners and Neill Brownstein of Bessemer Ventures for taking time to read and comment on the paper. Obviously, the authors are solely responsible for all of the positions and opinions expressed in this paper.

References

Abbate, J., 1994. From ARPANET to Internet: A History of ARPA-sponsored Computer Networks, 1966–1988, PhD dissertation, University of Pennsylvania.

Abernathy, W., 1978. The Productivity Dilemma: Roadblock to Innovation in the Automobile Industry. Johns Hopkins Univ. Press, Baltimore.

Abernathy, W., Clark, K., 1985. Innovation: mapping the winds of creative destruction. Research Policy 14, 3–22.

Abernathy, W., Utterback, J., 1978. Patterns in innovation in technology. Technology Review 80 (7), 40–47.

Arthur, W.B., 1989. Competing technologies, increasing returns, and lock-in by historical events. The Economic Journal (March) 116–131.

Arthur, W.B., 1994. Increasing Returns and Path Dependence in the Economy. University of Michigan Press, Ann Arbor.

Bayless, J., (general partner) 1998. Sevin Rosen Ventures, Personal interview (March 17).

Bijker, W., 1993. Do not despair: there is life after constructivism. Science, Technology, and Human Values 18 (1), 113–138.

Bijker, W., Hughes, T., Pinch, T. (Eds.), 1987. The Social Construction of Technological Systems. MIT Press, Cambridge.

Borsook, P., 1988. An engineer scores with "low-class" technology: twisted-pair Ethernet. Data Communications, (June 1988) 113–114.

Bredt, T. (cofounder, Menlo Ventures), 1995. Personal interview (July 2).

Bresnahan, T., Chopra, A., 1990. The development of the local area network market as determined by user needs. Economics of Innovation and New Technology 1, 97–110.

Bridge Communications, 1985. Securities and Exchange Commission S-1 File, Mountain View, CA.

Bridge Communications, 1986. Annual Report, Mountain View, CA.

Brinton, J., 1981. Market forms for local-net bridges. Electronics, (July 28) 97–100.

Brownstein, N., 1998. Personal interview (April 8).

Brownstein, N. (cofounder and general partner, Bessemer Venture Partners), 1999. Personal communication (July 24).

Burton, M., Sorensen, J., Beckman, C., 1998. Coming from Good Stock: New Histories and New Venture Formation. Harvard Business School, Division of Research Working Paper, 99-010.

Bygrave, W., Timmons, J., 1992. Venture Capital at the Crossroads. Harvard Business School Press, Boston.

Carano, B. (general partner, Oak Investment Partners) 1995. Personal interview (June 3).

Chandler, A., 1977. The Visible Hand: The Managerial Revolution in American Business. Belknap Press, Cambridge.

Chandler, A., 1990. Scale and Scope: The Dynamics of Industrial Capitalism. Belknap Press, Cambridge.

Charney, H. (ex-secretary and vice president of operation, 3Com; cofounder, Grand Junction), 1995. Personal interview (July 14).

Clarke, R., 1998. Prime Computer FAQ http://www.malch.com/prime/primefaq.txt.

Cohen, S., Fields, G., 2000, Social capital and capital gains or virtual bowling in silicon valley. In: Kenney, M. (Ed.), Anatomy of Silicon Valley. Stanford Univ. Press, Stanford.

Cowan, R., 1987. The consumption junction: a proposal for research strategies in the sociology of technology. In: Bijker, W., Hughes, T., Pinch, T. (Eds.), The Social Construction of Technological Systems. MIT Press, Cambridge, pp. 261–280.

Crane, R. (designer of 3Com's PC adapter card), 1995. Personal interview (May 17).

David, P., 1986. Clio and the economics of QWERTY. American Economic Review Proceedings 75, 332–337.

David, P., Greenstein, S., 1990. The economics of compatibility standards: an introduction to recent research. Economics of Innovation and New Technology 1, 3–41.

Dougery, J. (ex-Citicorp Venture Capital; cofounder, Dougery Jones and Wilder Ventures; principal, Dougery Ventures), 1998. Personal interview (March 20).

Electronics News, 1980. Ungermann–Bass obtains venture capital funding (March 17), p. 17.

Estrin, J. (ex-Zilog; ex-Ungermann–Bass; cofounder, Bridge Communications, executive, Network Computing Devices, founder, Precept Software), 1995. Personal interview (April 24).

Farber, D., 1972. Networks: an introduction, Datamation (April) 36–39.

Farber, D., 1975. A ring network. Datamation (February) 44–46.

Farber, D., 1997. Personal interview (January 31).

Farrell, J., Saloner, G., 1986. Installed base and compatibility: innovation, product preannouncements, and predation. American Economic Review 76 (5), 940–955.

Florida, R., Kenney, M., 1988. Venture capital-financed innovation and technological change in the US. Research Policy 17 (3), 119–137.

Foray, D., 1991. The secrets of industry are in the air: industrial cooperation and the organizational dynamics of the innovative firm. Research Policy 20, 393–405.

Freeman, J., 1999. Venture capital as an economy of time. In: Leenders, R., Gabbay, S. (Eds.), Corporate Social Capital. Addison Wesley, New York, pp. 400–419.

Gompers, P., Lerner, J., 1996. The use of covenants: an empirical analysis of venture partnership agreements. Journal of Law and Economics 39 (October), 463–498.

Granovetter, M., 1985. Economic action and social structures: the problem of embeddedness. American Journal of Sociology 91 (5), 481–510.

Greer, P. (cofounder, Weiss, Peck and Greer Venture Associates), 1996. Personal interview (November 14).

Hafner, K., Lyon, M., 1996. Where Wizards Stay Up Late. Simon & Schuster, New York.

Hellmann, T., 1998. The allocation of control rights in venture capital contracts. RAND Journal of Economics 29 (1), 57–76.

Henderson, R., 1995. Of life cycles real and imaginary: the unexpectedly long old age of optical lithography. Research Policy 24, 631–643.

Hiltzik, M., 1999. Dealers of Lightning. HarperBusiness, New York, 1999.

Hofmeister, S., 1989. Two men and a merger. Venture (January) 40–43.

Hounshell, D., 1995. Hughesian history of technology and Chandlerian business history: parallels, departures, and critics. History and Technology 12, 205–225.

Jeffery, B., 1986. A look at IBM's token-ring network. Computerworld 20 (2), 33–36.

Juliessen, E., Petska-Juliessen, K., 1994. The 7th Annual Computer Industry Almanac. Computer Industry Almanac, Austin, TX.

Katz, M., Shapiro, C., 1986. Technology adoption in the presence of network externalities. Journal of Political Economy 94, 822–841.

Katz, M., Shapiro, C., 1994. Systems competition and network effects. Journal of Economic Perspectives 8 (2), 93–115.

Kenney, M., 1986a. Biotechnology: The University–Industrial Complex. Yale Univ. Press, New Haven, CT.

Kenney, M., 1986b. Schumpeter's theory of innovation in capitalism: a case study of the genetic engineering industry. Research Policy 15, 21–31.

Kenney, M., von Burg, U., 1999. Bringing technology back in: explaining the divergence between Silicon Valley and Route 128. Industrial and Corporate Change 8 (1).

Kenney, M., von Burg, U., 2000. Institutions and economies: creating Silicon Valley. In: Kenney, M. (Ed.), Anatomy of Silicon Valley. Stanford Univ. Press, Stanford.

Kramlich, R. (managing general partner, New Enterprise Associates), 1995. Personal interview (July 17).

Langlois, R., Robertson, P., 1995. Firms, Markets and Economic Change. Routledge, London.

Latour, B. (translated by C. Porter), 1993. We Have Never Been Modern. Harvard Univ. Press, Cambridge.

Latour, B. (translated by C. Porter), 1996. ARAMIS or the Love of Technology. Harvard Univ. Press, Cambridge.

Liddle, D., 1995. Xerox PARC; founder, president and CEO of Metaphor, president and CEO of Interval Research, Personal interview (June 21).

Lundvall, B. (Ed.), 1992. National Systems of Innovation: Towards a Theory of Innovation and Interactive Learning. Pinter Publishers, London.

MacMillan, I., Kulow, D., Khoylian, R., 1988. Venture capitalists involvement in their investments: extent and performance. Journal of Business Venturing 4, 27–47.

Misa, T., 1994. Retrieving sociotechnical change from technological determinism. In: Marx, L., Smith, M., (Eds.), Does Technology Drive History? MIT Press, Cambridge, pp. 115–142.

Nelson, R. (Ed.), 1993. National Systems of Innovation: A Comparative Study. Oxford Univ. Press, New York.

Nelson, R., Winter, S., 1982. An Evolutionary Theory of the Economic Change. Harvard Univ. Press, Cambridge, 1982.

Proteon, 1991. Form S-1, Securities and Exchange Commission, Washington, DC.

Richman, T., 1989. Who's in charge here. Inc (June) 36–46.

Saal, H. (cofounder, Nestar; cofounder Network General), 1995. Personal interview (August 5).

Sahlman, W., 1990. The structure and governance of venture capitalist organizations. Journal of Financial Economics 27, 473–521.

Sapienza, H., 1992. When do venture capitalists add value. Journal of Business Venturing 3 (7), 9–27.

Schmidt, R. (cofounder, SynOptics), 1995. Personal interview (June 5).

Schumpeter, J. (as abridged by R. Fels), 1964. Business Cycles. McGraw-Hill, New York.

Schumpeter, J., 1968. The Theory of Economic Development. Harvard Univ. Press, Cambridge.

Schumpeter, J., 1975. Capitalism, Socialism, and Democracy. Harper Colophon Books, New York.

Seifert, W. (cofounder, Interlan; cofounder, WellFleet Communications; and cofounder, Agile Networks), 1995. "Personal interview." (June 28).

Shapiro, C., Varian, H., 1999. Information Rules. Harvard Univ. Press, Boston, MA.

Shustek, L. (cofounder, Nestar; cofounder, Network General), 1999. Personal interview (June 23).

Sirbu, M., Hughes, K., 1986. Standardization of local area networks, Presented at the Fourteenth Annual Telecommunications Policy Research Conference, Airlie, VA, (April).

Smith, A., 1776. The Wealth of Nations. University of Chicago Press, Chicago.

Suchman, M., 2000. Dealmakers and counselors: law firms as intermediaries in the development of Silicon Valley. In: Kenney, M. (Ed.), Anatomy of Silicon Valley. Stanford Univ. Press, Stanford.

Swartz, J. (vice president of Citicorp Venture Capital; cofounder of Adler and Company; cofounder of Accel Partners), 1995. Personal interview (June 22).

SynOptics, 1988. Securities and Exchange Commission S-1 File, Mountain View, CA.

3Com, 1980. Confidential Briefing for David Arscott and Leal F. Norton given by Robert and Howard Charney (October 6).

Tushman, M., Anderson, P., 1986. Technological discontinuities and organizational environments. Administrative Science Quarterly 31, 439–465.

Ungermann, R. (cofounder, Zilog, cofounder, Ungermann-Bass; cofounder, First Virtual), 1995. Personal communication (November 8).

Ungermann–Bass, 1979. Customer Prospect List (December 17).

Utterback, J., Suarez, F., 1993. Innovation, competition, and industry structure. Research Policy 22, 1–21.

Valentine, D. (cofounder, Sequoia Capital), 1995. Personal interview (June 29).

Van de Ven, A., Garud, R., 1989. A framework for understanding the emergence of new industries. Research on Technological Innovation, Management and Policy 4, 195–225.

von Burg, U., 1999. Plumbers of the Internet: The Creation of the Local Area Networking Industry, PhD Dissertation, University of St. Gallen, St. Gallen, Switzerland.

Wilson, J., 1985. The New Venturers. Addison-Wesley Publishing, Reading, New York.

Young, A., 1928. Increasing returns and economic progress. The Economic Journal 38 (152), 527–542.

[12]

RAND Journal of Economics
Vol. 31, No. 4, Winter 2000
pp. 674–692

Assessing the contribution of venture capital to innovation

Samuel Kortum*

and

Josh Lerner**

We examine the influence of venture capital on patented inventions in the United States across twenty industries over three decades. We address concerns about causality in several ways, including exploiting a 1979 policy shift that spurred venture capital fundraising. We find that increases in venture capital activity in an industry are associated with significantly higher patenting rates. While the ratio of venture capital to R&D averaged less than 3% from 1983–1992, our estimates suggest that venture capital may have accounted for 8% of industrial innovations in that period.

1. Introduction

■ Governments around the globe have been eager to duplicate the success of the fast-growing U.S. venture capital industry. These efforts share a common rationale: that venture capital has spurred innovation in the United States, and can do so elsewhere (see, for instance, European Commission (1995)).

The purported relationship between venture capital and innovation, however, has not been systematically scrutinized. We address this omission by exploring the experience of twenty industries covering the U.S. manufacturing sector over a three-decade period. We first examine in reduced-form regressions whether, controlling for R&D spending, venture capital funding has an impact on the number of patented innovations. We find that venture capital is associated with a substantial increase in patenting. The results are robust to a variety of specifications of how venture capital and R&D affect patenting and to different definitions of venture capital.

We then consider the limitations of this approach. We present a stylized model of the relationship between venture capital, R&D, and innovation. This model suggests

* Boston University and NBER; kortum@bu.edu.

** Harvard University and NBER; jlerner@hbs.edu.

We thank Chris Allen, Ben Conway, Kay Hashimoto, Justin Jow, Bac Nguyen, and Patty Pitzele for research assistance. Jim Hirabayashi, Adam Jaffe, Jesse Reyes, and F.M. Scherer generously provided assistance with patent and venture capital data. Helpful comments were provided by Eli Berman, Jonathan Eaton, Simon Gilchrist, Zvi Griliches, Kevin Lang, Kaivan Munshi, Robert Porter (the Editor), Joel Waldfogel, three anonymous referees, and various seminar participants. The U.S. National Science Foundation and the Harvard Business School's Division of Research provided financial support. An earlier version of this article was entitled "Does Venture Capital Spur Innovation?" All errors are our own.

that simple reduced-form regressions may overstate the effect of venture funding. Both venture funding and patenting could be positively related to a third unobserved factor, the arrival of technological opportunities.

We address this concern in two ways. First, we exploit the major recent event in the venture capital industry. In 1979, the U.S. Department of Labor clarified the Employee Retirement Income Security Act, a policy shift that freed pensions to invest in venture capital. This shift led to a sharp increase in the funds committed to venture capital. This type of exogenous change should identify the role of venture capital, because it is unlikely to be related to the arrival of entrepreneurial opportunities. We exploit this shift in instrumental-variable regressions. Second, we use R&D expenditures to control for the arrival of technological opportunities that are anticipated by economic actors at the time, but that are unobserved to us as econometricians. In the framework of our model, we show that the causality problem disappears if we estimate the impact of venture capital on the patent-R&D ratio, rather than on patenting itself.

Even after addressing these causality concerns, the results suggest that venture funding does have a strong positive impact on innovation. The estimated parameter varies according to the techniques we employ, but focusing on a conservative middle ground, a dollar of venture capital appears to be about three times more potent in stimulating patenting than a dollar of traditional corporate R&D. Our estimates therefore suggest that venture capital, even though it averaged less than 3% of corporate R&D from 1983 to 1992, is responsible for a much greater share—about 8%—of U.S. industrial innovations in this decade.

One natural concern is that changes in the legal environment may be confounding our results. In earlier work (1998), we have highlighted how the creation of a centralized appellate court for patent cases in 1982 nearly coincided with an increase in the rate of U.S. patent applications. To address this concern, we employ in all regressions dummy variables for each year, which should control for changes in either the propensity to file for patents or for these applications to be granted. Year effects control for changes in the overall legal environment unless the 1982 policy shift boosted patenting disproportionately in particular industries, which does not appear to have been the case (Kortum and Lerner, 1998).

The final section of the article addresses concerns about the relationship between the dependent variable in our analyses (patents) and what we really wish to measure (innovations). Venture capital may spur patenting while having no impact on innovation if venture-backed firms simply patent more of their innovations to impress potential investors or to avoid expropriation of their ideas by these investors. To investigate this possibility, we compare indicators of the quality of patents between 122 venture-backed and 408 non-venture-backed companies based in Middlesex County, Massachusetts. Venture-backed firms' patents are more frequently cited by other patents and are more aggressively litigated: venture backing does not appear to lead to lower-quality patents. Furthermore, the venture-backed firms are more frequent litigators of trade secrets, which suggests that they are not simply patenting more in lieu of relying on trade secret protection.

It is important to acknowledge the limits of our analysis. We have followed a somewhat crude "production function" approach to assess the contribution of venture capital. In so doing, we face many of the fundamental issues raised by Griliches (1979) in his critique of attempts to assess the contribution of R&D to productivity. Due to the lack of previous research in this arena, our article should be seen as a first cut at quantifying venture capital's impact on innovation. We hope that it will stimulate additional investigations of the relationship between the institutions through which innovative activities are financed and the rate and direction of technological change.[1]

The plan of the article is as follows. Section 2 provides an overview of the U.S. venture capital industry.[2] Section 3 presents the data and a set of reduced-form regressions. In Section 4 we build a simple model of venture capital, R&D, and innovation, in light of which we refine our estimates of the potency of venture capital. We address concerns about patenting as a measure of innovation in Section 5. The final section concludes.

2. Venture capital and the financing of young firms

■ Venture capital—defined as equity or equity-linked investments in young, privately held companies, where the investor is a financial intermediary who is typically active as a director, an advisor, or even a manager of the firm—dates back to the formation of American Research and Development in 1946. A handful of other venture funds were established in subsequent decades. The flow of money into new venture funds between 1946 and 1977 never exceeded a few hundred million dollars annually and usually was much less.

As Figure 1 demonstrates, funds flowing into the venture capital industry increased dramatically during the late 1970s and early 1980s. An important factor behind this increase was the 1979 amendment to the "prudent man" rule governing pension fund investments. Prior to 1979, the Employee Retirement Income Security Act (ERISA) limited pension funds from investing substantial amounts of money into venture capital or other high-risk asset classes. The Department of Labor's clarification of the rule explicitly allowed pension managers to invest in high-risk assets, including venture capital.[3] The fundraising patterns are mirrored in the investments by venture capitalists into young firms, also depicted in Figure 1. In the second half of the 1990s, there was another leap in venture capital activity, which emerged as the dominant form of equity financing in the United States for privately held high-technology businesses.

3. Reduced-form regressions

■ We begin our empirical analysis by investigating whether, conditional on R&D spending, venture capital funding influences innovation. After describing the dataset, we estimate and report on patent production functions in the next two subsections. In undertaking this analysis, we will employ many of the conventions of the literature on "innovation production functions" reviewed in Griliches (1990).[4] In the last subsection, we estimate a simpler linear specification that we will return to later in the article. Throughout Section 3, we treat venture financing as exogenous, deferring the discussion of its determinants until the next section.

---

[1] In addition to the literature on the contribution of R&D to productivity (Griliches, 1979) and on the relationship between R&D and patenting (reviewed in Griliches, 1990), our article also relates to the empirical literature on the relationship between cash flow and R&D expenditures at the firm level (e.g., Bernstein and Nadiri, 1986; Himmelberg and Petersen, 1994). But as far as we are aware there is only one other study examining the relationship between innovation and the presence of particular financial institutions: Hellmann and Puri (1998) compare the survey responses of 170 venture-backed and non-venture-backed firms.

[2] This section is based in part on Gompers and Lerner (1998, 1999).

[3] In 1978, when $424 million was invested in new venture capital funds, individuals accounted for the largest share (32%). Pension funds supplied just 15%. Eight years later, when more than $4 billion was invested, pension funds accounted for more than half of all contributions.

[4] As in this literature, we initially ignore the impact of such factors as the uncertainty about technological success on the propensity to patent innovations. In Section 5 we show that the results are robust to the use of alternative measures that at least partially address these problems.

FIGURE 1

VENTURE CAPITAL FUNDRAISING AND DISBURSEMENTS, 1965–1999

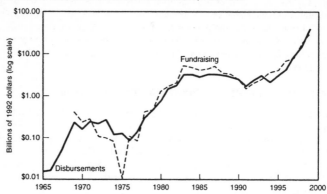

Note: Data on venture capital fundraising are not available prior to 1969. No capital was raised by venture funds in 1975.

□ **The dataset.** We analyze annual data for twenty manufacturing industries between 1965 and 1992. The dependent variable is U.S. patents issued to U.S. inventors by industry and date of application. Our main explanatory variables are measures of venture funding collected by Venture Economics and industrial R&D expenditures collected by the U.S. National Science Foundation (NSF).

Before discussing the use of this data, we should acknowledge two challenges that these measures pose. First, our dependent variable is problematic. Since the U.S. Patent and Trademark Office (USPTO) does not compile patent statistics by industry and many firms have multiple lines of business, patenting in each industry can be only be indirectly inferred. We rely on a concordance that relates a patent's industry to the primary technological classification to which it is assigned by the patent examiner.[5]

Second, while we distinguish conceptually between R&D financed by corporations and R&D financed by venture capital organizations, the data do not allow a clean division. The industrial R&D data that we use, while based on a survey that overlooks the activities of many smaller firms, undoubtedly includes some research financed by venture capital organizations. Similarly, while the bulk of venture financing supports innovative activities at technology-intensive firms, some is used for other purposes. For instance, some of the venture financing goes to low-technology concerns or is devoted to marketing activities. It should be noted that by leaving some venture funding in our measure of corporate R&D, it is less likely that we will find an impact of venture capital on patenting conditional on the R&D measure.

---

[5] This concordance relies on industry assignments of patents issued by Canada (the majority of which are issued to U.S. inventors) to determine the likelihood of a particular industry assignment given a patent's technological classification (Kortum and Putnam, 1997). Industry counts for the United States are based on the International Patent Classification assigned to each patent issued by the USPTO. The patent counts differ depending on whether the assigned industry corresponds to the user or the manufacturer of the patented invention. We focus on the industry of use series, but our results about the impact of venture capital are robust to replacing industry of use with industry of manufacture. In either case, the industry assignment of patents may not correspond precisely to the industry doing the R&D or receiving the venture capital funding that led to the underlying invention.

Venture funding and patents are then aggregated into essentially the industry scheme used by the NSF in tabulating its survey of industrial R&D. We consolidate a few NSF industries that account for little R&D.[6] The data are described in detail in the supplement to this article (available at http://www.rje.org/main/sup-mat.html).

Table 1 summarizes the main data series. The table highlights the rapid growth of the venture capital industry. The ratio of venture capital to R&D jumped sharply in the late 1970s and early 1980s, and fell a bit thereafter. Patenting declined from the early 1970s to the mid-1980s, but then rose sharply.[7] It should be noted that disbursements are concentrated in certain industries. The top three industries—drugs, office and computing, and communication equipment—represent 54% of the venture disbursements. The comparable figure for R&D expenditures is 39%.

□   **The patent production function.** We estimate a patent production function of the form $P_{it} = (R_{it}^{\rho} + bV_{it}^{\rho})^{\alpha/\rho}u_{it}$. Patenting ($P$) is a function of privately funded industrial R&D (R) and venture disbursements (V), while an error term (u) captures shifts in the propensity to patent or technological opportunities, all indexed by industry (i) and year (t). We focus on the parameter b, which captures the role of venture capital in the patent production function. For any $b > 0$, venture funding matters for innovation, while if b equals zero, the patent production function reduces to the standard form, $P_{it} = R_{it}^{\alpha}u_{it}$. The parameter α captures returns to scale, i.e., the percentage change in patenting brought about by a 1% increase in both R and V. The parameter ρ measures the degree of substitutability between R and V as means of financing innovative effort. When ρ equals one, the function reduces to $P_{it} = (R_{it} + bV_{it})^{\alpha}u_{it}$. As ρ goes to zero, the patent production function approaches the Cobb-Douglas functional form, $P_{it} = R_{it}^{\alpha/(1+b)}V_{it}^{\alpha b/(1+b)}u_{it}$.

□   **Estimates.** Nonlinear least-squares estimates of the patent production function are shown in Table 2. The dependent variable is the logarithm of the number of (ultimately successful) patent applications filed by U.S. inventors in each industry and year. The two independent variables of interest are privately financed R&D in that industry and year and either the dollar volume of venture disbursements or the number of firms in the industry receiving venture backing.[8] We use as controls the logarithm of the federally funded R&D in the industry, as well as dummy variables for each industry (to control for differences in the propensity to patent) and year.

---

[6] We focus on the manufacturing industries, since survey evidence (summarized in Cohen (1995)) suggests that the reliance on patenting as a means of appropriating new technological discoveries is much higher in these industries (as opposed to, for instance, trade secrecy or first-mover advantages). Patenting is thus likely to be a better indicator of the rate of technological innovation in the manufacturing sector. The time period is determined on one end by the availability of data on venture capital investment and on the other end by our inability to observe the detailed technological classifications of U.S. patent applications before they are issued (applications are held confidential until issue).

[7] A natural concern is the extent of correlation between the venture capital and private R&D measures. While the two variables are positively correlated, the extent of correlation is less than the aggregate numbers in Table 1 might lead one to believe. In particular, the correlation coefficient between the logarithms of the dollar volume of venture financings and private R&D in each industry is .43. The partial correlation, once the year and industry are controlled for, is .31. The correlation between the number of companies receiving venture financing and private R&D is even lower.

[8] The parameter b is generally not invariant to the units in which venture activity is measured. To facilitate comparisons across regressions, we scale our measure of the number of companies funded by venture capitalists to have the same overall mean as the dollar disbursements measure (in 1992 dollars). For both measures of venture finance, we add a minuscule amount (the equivalent of $1,000) to each observation so that we can consider the Cobb-Douglas limiting case in which the log of venture funding is what matters.

TABLE 1   Patenting Activity of, R&D Expenditures by, and Venture Capital Disbursements for U.S. Manufacturing Industries, by Year

Year	Number of Patent Applications	R&D Expenditures ($M)	Venture Capital Disbursements		Ratio of Venture Capital to R&D	
			Number of Firms	Amount ($M)	All VC	Early-Stage Only
1965	50,278	25,313	8	13	.05%	.02%
1966	48,740	27,573	3	2	.01%	.00%
1967	48,900	29,515	9	24	.08%	.07%
1968	49,980	31,387	25	37	.12%	.08%
1969	51,614	33,244	66	149	.45%	.38%
1970	53,950	32,883	63	126	.38%	.24%
1971	54,776	32,360	57	224	.69%	.41%
1972	49,777	33,593	52	209	.62%	.44%
1973	45,807	36,169	74	235	.65%	.30%
1974	44,465	37,323	42	81	.22%	.13%
1975	44,082	35,935	41	118	.33%	.24%
1976	44,026	38,056	47	83	.22%	.10%
1977	41,550	39,605	57	138	.35%	.21%
1978	42,648	42,373	116	255	.60%	.37%
1979	44,941	45,318	152	301	.66%	.28%
1980	41,726	48,700	231	635	1.30%	.80%
1981	39,137	52,012	408	1,146	2.20%	1.39%
1982	38,039	55,033	466	1,388	2.52%	1.29%
1983	34,712	58,066	656	2,391	4.12%	1.97%
1984	33,905	63,441	709	2,347	3.70%	1.95%
1985	36,732	66,860	646	1,951	2.92%	1.42%
1986	41,644	68,476	639	2,211	3.23%	1.62%
1987	46,434	67,700	713	2,191	3.24%	1.57%
1988	51,355	69,008	660	2,076	3.01%	1.54%
1989	55,103	70,456	669	1,995	2.83%	1.56%
1990	58,358	69,714	557	1,675	2.40%	1.11%
1991	58,924	69,516	422	1,026	1.48%	.71%
1992	60,771	70,825	469	1,571	2.22%	1.05%

Notes: Patent applications refer to the number of ultimately successful patent applications filed in each year. All dollar figures are in millions of 1992 dollars. The ratios of venture capital disbursements to R&D expenditures are computed using all venture capital disbursements and early-stage venture disbursements only.

The results suggest that venture funding matters. The magnitude of b estimated in the unconstrained equation is substantial, in fact implausibly large, an issue we will return to below. Although the estimates are imprecise, a likelihood ratio test overwhelmingly rejects the special case of b equal to zero (with a p-value of less than .005).

TABLE 2   Nonlinear Least-squares Regression Analysis of the Patent Production Function

	Using Firms Receiving Venture Backing		Using Venture Disbursements	
	Unconstrained	Constrained ($\rho = 1$)	Unconstrained	Constrained ($\rho = 1$)
Returns to scale parameter (α)	.22	.23	.20	.20
	(.02)	(.02)	(.02)	(.02)
Venture capital parameter (b):				
Firms receiving funding	58.51	39.57		
	(67.31)	(10.97)		
Venture disbursements			58.71	46.94
			(77.52)	(13.66)
Substitution parameter (ρ)	1.08	1.00	1.04	1.00
	(.24)	—	(.26)	—
Federally funded industrial R&D	.01	.01	.01	.01
	(.01)	(.01)	(.01)	(.01)
R^2	.99	.99	.99	.99
R^2 relative to dummy variable only case	.26	.26	.27	.27
Number of observations	560	560	560	560
Likelihood ratio statistic		.2		.0
p-values, likelihood ratio test		.65		.99

Notes: Standard errors are in parentheses. The dependent variable is the logarithm of the number of patents. Year and industry dummy variables are included in each regression.

We also find that R&D and venture capital are highly substitutable, with the point estimate of ρ close to one. A likelihood ratio test does not come close to rejecting the restriction that $\rho = 1$. On the other hand, $\rho = 0$ (the Cobb-Douglas special case) is strongly rejected (with a p-value of less than .005). As a consequence, in the remainder of the article we focus on the restricted equation, $\ln P_{it} = \alpha \ln(R_{it} + bV_{it}) + \ln u_{it}$, in which R&D and venture funding are perfect substitutes. In the restricted equation, b has the interpretation of the potency of a dollar of venture funding relative to a dollar of R&D (this interpretation of b holds for either measure of venture funding, as discussed in footnote 8).

The results for the restricted equation are shown in the second and fourth columns of Table 2. Together, variation in R&D and venture funding explain over one-fourth of the variation in the logarithm of patenting not captured by industry or time effects.[9] The returns-to-scale parameter α is about one-fourth, small but not implausible. What does strain credibility, however, are the point estimates of b in the two regressions, implying as they do that venture funds are about 40 times as potent as R&D. Below we explore a number of reasons why these estimates might be biased upward.

□   **A linear specification.** Before turning to the more difficult issues arising from the endogeneity of venture funding (which we address in Section 4), we first consider

---

[9] In all of the regression tables we present two measures of the goodness of fit: the overall R^2 and the R^2 when compared against a regression with just year and industry dummies. The latter is computed as (SSR$_{\text{dummy only}}$ − SSR$_{\text{new regression}}$)/SSR$_{\text{dummy only}}$, where SSR refers to the sum of squared residuals of the various regressions.

estimating *b* through a linear approximation of the patent production function (again with $\rho = 1$). Such an approximation is valid when venture funding is small relative to R&D. The linear specification has the advantage of simplicity. It is also inherently conservative in its empirical implications for the potency of venture capital. It interprets the observed average impact of *V/R* on patenting as the maximum marginal impact (i.e., the marginal impact as *V/R* approaches zero). Since our task is to evaluate the null hypothesis that venture capital is impotent, we find this inherent conservatism reassuring.

After linearizing the equation, we get $\ln P_{it} = \alpha \ln R_{it} + \alpha b(V_{it}/R_{it}) + \ln u_{it}$. This approximation is analogous to that employed by Griliches (1986) in his analysis of the impact of basic research, which like venture capital represented a small fraction of total R&D expenditures, on productivity growth. Note that in this equation, the potency of venture funding is calculated by dividing the coefficient on *V/R* by the coefficient on ln *R*. Table 3 presents regressions employing the linear specification. The basic equations are in the first two columns. Consider the second regression, which estimates the coefficient on venture capital as 1.73. Because this is an estimate for the product of α and *b*, we must divide by our estimate of α, .24, to obtain the implied potency of venture funding, $b = 7.26$. The implied estimates of potency and the associated standard errors (calculated using the delta method) are shown in the last two rows. In both regressions, the estimate of potency is significantly positive.[10] The estimates suggest that a dollar of venture capital is over seven times more powerful in stimulating patenting than a dollar of corporate R&D. Although these estimates are large, note that they are substantially more modest than the estimates of *b* from the nonlinear regressions.

These linear results appear to be quite robust. We have explored changing the specification,[11] the measures of venture capital,[12] and the sample,[13] adding additional controls,[14] and using lags of the explanatory variables.[15]

---

[10] Our error term consists of shocks to the propensity to patent and technological opportunities, which are likely to be persistent over time. To avoid inflating the statistical significance of the results, we calculate the standard errors using the autocorrelation-consistent covariance estimator of Newey and West (1987), with a maximum lag of three years.

[11] If the errors in the patent production function follow a random walk, then the equation should be estimated in differences rather than in levels. The difference regressions are shown in the last two columns of Table 3. To reduce the errors-in-variables problem, which tends to be magnified in a first-difference approach (Griliches and Hausman, 1986), we compute averages of the logarithm of each variable over a four-year period. We then compute the change in the industry measures at eight-year intervals. Since we difference out the industry effects, we drop industry dummies from these regressions but maintain a set of period dummies (not shown). The results of the long-difference regressions are very similar to those of the levels regressions except that the precision of the estimates declines.

[12] It might be thought that the financing of startups and very young companies would pose the greatest information problems, and that the contributions of the venture capitalists would be most valuable here. In regressions reported in the supplement, we replace the venture funding measures with the count and dollar volume of only seed and early-stage financings. The estimated potency of a dollar of venture funding increases by 45% to 80%.

[13] Our analysis may be distorted by the inclusion of numerous industries with very little innovative activity. In the supplement, we report regressions in which we drop industries whose R&D-to-sales ratio was below the median in 1964, the year before the beginning of the analysis. Once again, there is an increase in the estimated potency of venture funding relative to our baseline regressions.

[14] In unreported regressions, we also control for the logarithms of gross industry product or of industry employment. The effect of adding these controls is to reduce the coefficient on the logarithm of R&D, α (although it remains significantly positive). Both the magnitude and significance of the coefficient on *V/R* are essentially unchanged by the addition of either control.

[15] Another robustness check concerns possible lags between R&D spending, venture financing, and patenting. The empirical literature suggests that R&D spending and patent filings are roughly contempora-

TABLE 3   Ordinary Least-squares Regression Analysis of the Linear Patent Production
             Function

	Levels with Year and Industry Effects		Long Differences with Period Effects	
Privately funded industrial R&D (α)	.25	.24	.24	.22
	(.06)	(.06)	(.07)	(.07)
Venture capital/privately funded R&D (αb):				
Firms receiving funding	2.13		2.42	
	(.63)		(1.21)	
Venture disbursements		1.73		2.29
		(.69)		(1.04)
Federally funded industrial R&D	.01	.01	.03	.02
	(.01)	(.01)	(.02)	(.02)
R^2	.99	.99	.81	.82
R^2 relative to dummy variable only case	.21	.20	.24	.25
Number of observations	560	560	60	60
Implied potency of venture funding (b)	8.49	7.26	9.98	10.39
	(2.62)	(3.16)	(5.82)	(6.21)

Notes: Standard errors are in parentheses. For the levels specifications they are based on the Newey-West autocorrelation-consistent covariance estimator (with a maximum of three lags). The standard errors for the parameter b are calculated using the delta method.

4. Addressing the causality problem

■   The empirical results in Section 3 suggest that there is a strong association between venture capital and patenting and that corporate R&D and venture funding are highly substitutable in generating innovations. The mechanisms behind this relationship and the extent to which our estimates of the impact of venture funding may be inflated by unobserved factors, however, are not addressed by our reduced-form regressions.

To explore these issues, we build a theoretical model of venture capital, corporate research, and innovation. We then use the model to illustrate under what conditions the approach of Section 3 is appropriate and when it may be problematic. The final two subsections present refinements of our empirical approach, motivated by the model. We do not seek to determine which single empirical specification is the best representation of the impact of venture capital on innovation. Rather, we seek to demonstrate the robustness of the results in Section 3 by showing that they hold up across a variety of specifications.

□   **Modelling the relationship.** We consider an industry in which inventions can be pursued through either corporate R&D funding or venture capital. We make four major

---

neous (Hall, Griliches, and Hausman, 1986). Furthermore, there is an institutional reason why there should not be long lags between venture capital and patenting: the ten-year life spans of venture partnerships lead to pressure on companies to commercialize products quickly after obtaining venture financing. Nevertheless, to explore this issue empirically, in unreported regressions we repeat the analyses in Table 3, including one-year and two-year lagged values of the R&D and venture capital variables along with the contemporaneous variables. We find that the contemporaneous variables have the bulk of the explanatory power (and their coefficients are significantly positive), while the lagged variables have coefficients that are smaller (and insignificantly different from zero).

assumptions. First, we assume that the production function for innovations I in each industry i and time period t is essentially the one we settled upon empirically:

$$I_{it} = (R_{it} + bV_{it})^\alpha N_{it} = H_{it}^\alpha N_{it},$$ (1)

where $0 < \alpha < 1$ and, for expositional ease, total innovative effort is denoted by H_{it}. The final term N_{it} represents a shock to the invention production function, which we interpret as the exogenous arrival of innovative opportunities.

Second, we assume that innovations, on average, translate into patents in a proportional manner. Thus $P_{it} = I_{it}\epsilon_{it}$, where P_{it} is the number of patented innovations generated in a particular industry and year and ϵ is an independent shock determining the propensity to patent innovations. Combining this equation with (1), we obtain

$$P_{it} = H_{it}^\alpha N_{it}\epsilon_{it}.$$ (2)

The unobserved factor driving patenting is thus $N\epsilon$, the product of technological opportunities and the propensity to patent.

Third, we assume that the expected value of a new innovation for a given time period and industry is Π_{it}. We take a simple partial equilibrium approach and do not model the determinants of Π, although we have in mind that it evolves with the size of the market, as in Schmookler (1966). We assume that individual firms are small relative to the industry, and therefore we take Π as given. The expected value of a new invention incorporates the fact that some, but not all, innovations will be worth patenting.

Finally, we make assumptions about the marginal costs of innovating that deserve discussion at greater length. In addition to the direct expenditures on R&D and venture disbursements, we assume that there are associated indirect expenses. These might include the cost of screening opportunities, recruiting managers and researchers, and undertaking the crucial regulatory approvals to sell the new product. We argue that at each point of time, there is likely to be a spectrum of projects: some will be very appropriate for a corporate research laboratory, while others will be more suited for funding by a venture capitalist in an entrepreneurial setting. Raising venture activity as a fraction of total innovative effort pushes venture capitalists into areas farther from their comparative advantage, raising their costs, while corporate researchers are able to specialize in areas they have the greatest advantage in exploiting.

More specifically, we assume that given total research effort H, and venture financing V, the venture capitalist's cost of managing the last venture-backed project is $v_t f_v(V_{it}/\lambda_{it}H_{it})$, while the corporation's cost of managing the last corporate-backed project is $f_R(V_{it}/\lambda_{it}H_{it})$. We assume that the venture capitalist's function f_v is strictly increasing while the corporation's f_R is strictly decreasing in $V/\lambda H$. The term λ_{it} governs the extent to which opportunities are conductive to venture finance. We interpret a rise in λ to mean that technological opportunities have become more radical in nature, a shift that should lower the management costs of pursuing such projects in an entrepreneurial rather than a corporate setting. The v_t term represents the venture capitalist's cost of funds, which we enter explicitly to enable us to consider the impact of the 1979 clarification of the prudent man rule (a fall in v).

From this set of assumptions, we derive several equilibrium conditions. The equilibrium level of venture capital and corporate R&D will equate the marginal cost of additional spending to the marginal benefit. Assuming that we are not at a corner solution where V or R is equal to zero,[16] the conditions are

$$\Pi_{it}\frac{\partial I_{it}}{\partial V_{it}} = \alpha\Pi_{it}N_{it}bH_{it}^{\alpha-1} = v_t f_V\left(\frac{V_{it}}{\lambda_{it}H_{it}}\right) \tag{3}$$

$$\Pi_{it}\frac{\partial I_{it}}{\partial R_{it}} = \alpha\Pi_{it}N_{it}H_{it}^{\alpha-1} = f_R\left(\frac{V_{it}}{\lambda_{it}H_{it}}\right). \tag{4}$$

Through a series of mathematical manipulations,[17] we obtain the expressions

$$H_{it} = \left[\frac{\alpha\Pi_{it}N_{it}}{g_1(v_t)}\right]^{1/(1-\alpha)} \tag{5}$$

$$\frac{V_{it}}{R_{it}} = \lambda_{it}\left[\frac{g_2(v_t)}{1 - b\lambda_{it}g_2(v_t)}\right], \tag{6}$$

where g_1 is an increasing function and g_2 a decreasing one. According to (5), total innovative effort is decreasing in the cost of venture funds, v, but stimulated by positive shocks to either the value of inventions or the arrival of technological opportunities. Venture funding relative to corporate R&D, (6), is increasing in the degree to which the opportunities are radical in nature, λ, and decreasing in the cost of venture funds.

A positive shock to λ favors venture capital relative to corporate R&D, while a jump in N not only stimulates both forms of finance but also leads to a jump in patenting conditional on the amount of innovative effort. Complicating matters, we suspect that the two shocks, λ and N, will be positively correlated. A burst of innovative opportunities will often be associated with a radical shift in the technology, a shift that small venture-financed entrepreneurs rather than large corporations will be better able to exploit. It is this potential correlation between a shock to the patent equation and a shock that favors venture finance that leads us to be skeptical of our reduced-form regression results.

□ **Implications for the estimation.** This set of equations allows us to illustrate the issues that we face in estimating the linear form of the patent production function,

$$\ln P_{it} = \alpha\ln R_{it} + \alpha b(V_{it}/R_{it}) + \ln N_{it} + \ln \epsilon_{it}, \tag{7}$$

with industry dummies, year dummies, and federally funded R&D included as controls. If technological opportunities, N, are totally captured by our controls, our estimates in Tables 2 and 3 should be valid. Variation in Π_{it}, according to (5), will lead to variation

---

[16] An attractive feature of the model is that it can also address the empirically relevant case of $V = 0$. In that case, $\alpha\Pi_{it}N_{it}bR_{it}^{\alpha-1} \leq v_t f_V(0)$, where $R_{it} = \{\alpha\Pi_{it}N_{it}/[f_R(0)]\}^{1/(1-\alpha)}$.

[17] Specific steps were to (i) define $x \equiv \alpha\Pi_{it}N_{it}H_{it}^{\alpha-1}$, (ii) combine (3) and (4) to get

$$b/v = (1/x)f_V(f_R^{-1}(x)) \equiv h(x),$$

where $h(x)$ is a strictly decreasing function, (iii) solve for $x = h^{-1}(b/v) \equiv g_1(v)$, (iv) plug into (4) to get $V/H = \lambda f_R^{-1}(g_1(v)) \equiv \lambda g_2(v)$, (v) use $x \equiv g_1(v)$ to solve for H, and (vi), recalling that $H = R + bV$, solve for V/R.

in H and hence R, which identifies α. Variation in the cost of funds to venture capitalists, v_t, interacted with differences across industries in λ, will cause variation in V/R, which identifies b.

The more likely scenario, however, is one in which variation in technological opportunities is only partially explained by the controls. In that case, variations in H, and hence R, will be correlated with the disturbance. Similarly, variations in V/R will also be correlated with the disturbance (if λ and N are in fact correlated). Simply regressing patents on R&D and venture funding could yield biased estimates of both α and b and will probably overstate the potency of venture capital.

We consider two approaches to get around potential biases in our estimates of the potency of venture funding. First, we attempt to find good instruments. Our instrument for venture funding relative to corporate R&D relies on the U.S. Department of Labor's 1979 clarification of the "prudent man" rule (discussed in Section 2). We argue that this clarification lowered the cost of funds to venture capitalists, much like a drop in v_t in our model. We propose an instrument based on the interaction of this 1979 change with the historical differences across industries in venture funding relative to corporate R&D.[18]

Our second approach is to use R&D to control for the unobservable term N, which is the source of our identification problems when estimating the patent production function. The basic idea is similar to Olley and Pakes (1996) and more recently to Levinsohn and Petrin (2000), who respectively use capital investment and purchased materials to control for unobservables in a standard production function. Combining (2) and (5), while noting that $R_{it} = H_{it}/(1 + bV_{it}/R_{it})$, we can solve for the patent-R&D ratio,

$$\frac{P_{it}}{R_{it}} = \left[\frac{\alpha \Pi_{it}}{g_1(v_t)} \right]^{-1} \left(1 + b\frac{V_{it}}{R_{it}} \right) \epsilon_{it}. \qquad (8)$$

The striking feature of (8) is that normalizing patents by R&D eliminates technological opportunities N from the right side of the equation. We no longer identify α (which was not essential in any case), but we can now estimate the potency of venture funding b without worrying (subject to some caveats in how we treat Π) about correlation between V/R and the disturbance in the equation.

☐   **Instrumental-variables estimation.** We now turn to a more complete discussion of our instrument choice and to the results we obtain using instrumental-variables (IV) techniques to estimate (7). We start with our instrument for V/R. It is based on the Department of Labor's clarification of a rule that, prior to 1979, limited the ability of pension funds to invest in venture capital. One might first think of capturing this shift empirically through a dummy variable taking on the value of zero through 1979 and one thereafter. The problem with this simple approach is that patenting rates across all industries may change over time for a variety of reasons, including swings in the judicial enforcement of patentholder rights and antitrust policy. We are unlikely to be able to disentangle the shift in venture fundraising from that in the propensity to patent. As Table 1 makes clear, the filing of successful patent applications actually fell in the

---

[18] This approach also faces another challenge, which we explore in depth below. Even if our instrument for V/R is convincing, we are still faced with the endogeneity of total innovative effort. To address this issue, we consider demand-side instruments that are correlated with the value of inventions, Π_{it}, but potentially unrelated to technological opportunities.

years after 1979. But this was also a period during which the ability of firms to enforce intellectual property rights was under attack (Kortum and Lerner, 1998).

The 1979 policy shift, however, should have had a predictably greater impact on patenting in some industries than others. Industries with a high level of venture capital before the policy change should have experienced a greater increase in funding and, thus, a greater burst in patenting. Thus, in certain circumstances, we can use the level of venture financing before the shift, interacted with a dummy variable taking on the value zero through 1979 and one thereafter, as an instrumental variable.[19]

We can motivate the proposed instrument more formally by returning to the model. From (6) we see that the impact on V_{it}/R_{it} of a change in v_t (we argue above that v declined dramatically in the late 1970s) is increasing in V_{it}/R_{it} itself. In particular, the derivative of V/R with respect to a change in v in 1979 is $D_i = (-g_2'/g_2)(V_{i79}/R_{i79})(1 + bV_{i79}/R_{i79})$. Historically, differences between industries in venture funding relative to R&D have been highly persistent over time. Hence the industry-specific average of V/R from 1965 through 1978, denoted A_i, should be highly correlated with D_i. To exploit this result, we propose an instrument that takes on the value of zero up through 1979 (before the effect of the policy shift is seen) but in each year after 1979, and for each industry i, takes on the value A_i.[20]

The validity of the instrument, however, requires that λ_{it} not deviate for too long from its industry-specific mean. To ensure this property, we assume that $\ln \lambda_{it}$ can be decomposed into the sum of a permanent industry component λ_i (which accounts for the persistent differences between industries in V/R) and a transitory component ω_{it}. If the transitory component is independent across time, then from 1980 on it will not be correlated with A_i. Under this assumption, our instrument will not be correlated with technological opportunities ($\ln N_{it}$) as they vary from their industry-specific means (industry and year dummies will always be included in the regressions). More generally, if ω_{it} is a moving average process of order m, then the instrument is still valid as long as it is amended by calculating A_i as the industry-specific average of V/R from 1965 only up to m years prior to 1980. We consider this extension in two of the regressions below, for the case of $m = 5$.

As noted above, we must also contend with the endogeneity of R&D expenditures. There is no point in instrumenting for V/R while ignoring the potential correlation between R&D expenditures and the disturbance in the patent equation. The endogeneity problem, however, would be irrelevant if we already knew the value of the parameter α. Thus, before undertaking the daunting task of searching for a valid instrument for R&D, we simply fix the parameter α at some preassigned values and instrument for V/R.

The results are shown in Panel A of Table 4. Here we have instrumented for V/R in the linear specification of the patent production function, while fixing $\alpha = .2$ or $\alpha = .5$

---

[19] The empirical relevance of this instrument is based on the observation that the increase in the ratio of venture capital activity to R&D following the 1979 shift was positively correlated with the level of V/R prior to the shift. A regression of y_i (the industry-specific change in the average ratio of venture capital disbursements to R&D spending between the 1985–1990 period and the 1965–1975 period) on x_i (the average ratio in the 1965–1975 period) yields an R^2 of .42. The observed relationship is likely to derive from the inelastic supply of venture capitalists and the industry specialization of individual venture capitalists.

[20] Note that our instrument for V/R is based on an average of the level of venture capital financing, A_i, over a number of years. Venture capital disbursements in each industry are "lumpy": a single large later-round financing may account for a substantial fraction of the total financing in a given industry and year. By better capturing the mean level of financing activity in a given industry, the instrument may alleviate errors-in-variables problems, and may even lead to an increase in the coefficient on venture capital.

TABLE 4   Instrumental-Variable (IV) Regression Analysis of the Linear Patent Production Function

Panel A: IV Regressions, Constraining α

	IV: 1965–1978 Period α = .20		IV: 1965–1978 Period α = .50	
Privately funded industrial R&D (α)	.20 —	.20 —	.50 —	.50 —
Venture capital/privately funded R&D (αb):				
Firms receiving funding	3.06 (.92)		2.51 (1.06)	
Venture disbursements		3.38 (1.13)		1.72 (1.10)
Federally funded industrial R&D	.01 (.01)	.01 (.01)	.02 (.01)	.02 (.01)
R^2	.99	.98	.98	.98
R^2 relative to dummy variable only case	.19	.14	.07	.07
Number of observations	560	560	560	560
Implied potency of venture funding (b)	15.28 (4.59)	16.89 (5.63)	5.02 (2.12)	3.45 (2.21)

Panel B: IV Regressions, Instrumenting for R&D

	IV: 1965–1978 Period and Industry GDP		IV: 1965–1975 Period and Industry GDP	
Privately funded industrial R&D (α)	.52 (.10)	.48 (.12)	.52 (.10)	.54 (.13)
Venture capital/privately funded R&D (αb):				
Firms receiving funding	2.48 (1.13)		2.12 (1.14)	
Venture disbursements		1.81 (1.40)		.13 (1.70)
Federally funded industrial R&D	.02 (.01)	.02 (.01)	.02 (.01)	.02 (.02)
R^2	.98	.98	.98	.98
R^2 relative to dummy variable only case	.07	.07	.05	−.04
Number of observations	560	560	560	560
Implied potency of venture funding (b)	4.81 (2.67)	3.74 (3.56)	4.08 (2.58)	.25 (3.21)

Notes: Standard errors (in parentheses) are based on the Newey-West autocorrelation-consistent covariance estimator (with a maximum of three lags). The standard errors for the parameter *b* are calculated using the delta method. Year and industry dummy variables are included in each regression.

(which straddle our estimates from Tables 2 and 3).[21] We still obtain large and statistically significant estimates of the potency of venture funding. The magnitude of the

----

[21] All of the instrumental-variable (IV) regressions that we report are based on the linear specification used in Table 3. We also experimented with nonlinear IV estimation based on the specification in the second and fourth regressions in Table 2. A feature of nonlinear IV is ambiguity about which functions of the

estimated parameter, however, is sensitive to the assumed value of α. We find that venture capital is about fifteen times as potent as corporate R&D if $\alpha = .2$, but only three to five times as potent as R&D if $\alpha = .5$. In light of our uncertainty about the actual value of α, and given its substantial impact on the results, we attempt to instrument for R&D as well as venture capital.

The perfect instrument for R&D would be a measure of shifts in industry demand that affect the value of an invention Π_{it}, but are unrelated to technological opportunities. Since this ideal instrument is not available, we settle on an instrument that we can measure—the value of the gross industry product Y_{it}—which under certain assumptions is the same as the ideal instrument. The value of industry product is almost certainly relevant, since the amount of R&D in an industry will be stimulated by an increase in the size of the market. Its validity as an instrument is less of a sure thing. In particular, the instrument will be valid only if technological opportunities (and the innovations stimulated by those opportunities) do not affect the size of the market.[22]

The regressions reported in Panel B of Table 4 use instruments both for venture funding relative to R&D and for R&D itself. The last two regressions in the panel also apply a modification of the instrument for V/R, as suggested above, to allow for the transitory component in entrepreneurial opportunities ω_{it} to be correlated for up to five years. Using the value of industry product as an instrument for R&D approximately doubles the estimate of α. The effect is to lower our estimates of the potency of venture funding, much like in the last two regressions in Panel A (in which α is constrained to be .5). The large increase in α when we instrument for R&D can be understood in two ways. One possibility is that our earlier estimates of α are biased downward (due to errors in our measure of R&D, similar to the problem discussed in footnote 20). A second possibility is that gross industry product is not a valid instrument, because it is positively correlated with technological opportunities. Since we cannot resolve these issues within the context of our IV approach, we pursue instead a very different technique for dealing with the endogeneity of venture funding.[23]

☐ **Controlling for technological opportunities.** Our second approach for dealing with the endogeneity problem is to use R&D to control for unobserved technological opportunities. The basic idea follows from (8): conditional on the ratio of venture capital to R&D and the expected value of an innovation, the patent-R&D ratio does not depend on technological opportunities. Taking logarithms of (8) and linearizing around $V/R = 0$, we have

$$\ln P_{it} - \ln R_{it} = b(V_{it}/R_{it}) - \ln \Pi_{it} + \ln \epsilon_{it}. \qquad (9)$$

(The term $\ln[g_1(v_t)/\alpha]$ is subsumed in year effects. Industry effects are also included.) One approach to estimating this equation is to subsume any variation in the expected

---

underlying instruments should be included in the instrument set. In some cases we obtained estimates of the potency of venture capital similar to the estimates reported in Table 4, but these estimates were not robust to dropping or adding powers of the underlying instruments. Since a comparison of Table 2 and Table 3 suggests that the linear specification is more conservative in its implications about the potency of venture funding, we decided to focus on that specification.

[22] Such a feedback will not exist if the price elasticity of industry demand is equal to one. In this case, a fall in quality-adjusted prices associated with a process or product innovation will be just offset by the increase in demand, leaving the value of industry output unchanged.

[23] If we accept $\alpha = .5$, we can resolve the puzzle of the high estimates of venture-capital potency shown in Table 2. Redoing those nonlinear regressions under the restriction that $\alpha = .5$ (and $\rho = 1$) yields much lower estimates of the potency of venture capital, in the range of four to five.

value of inventions in the disturbance. This approach implicitly assumes, however, that shocks to venture funding relative to R&D are uncorrelated with shocks to the expected value of an invention.

Our other approach begins with (9) but uses industry output as a proxy for the expected value of an invention, $\ln \Pi_{it} = a_0 + a_1 \ln Y_{it}$. Assuming $a_1 = 1$ (footnote 24 relaxes this assumption), we obtain the equation

$$\ln P_{it} - (\ln R_{it} - \ln Y_{it}) = b(V_{it}/R_{it}) + \ln \epsilon_{it}. \tag{10}$$

The dependent variable is simply the logarithm of the ratio of patents P to R&D intensity, R/Y. Note that our use of the value of industry output as a proxy for the expected value of an invention does not require the value of industry output to be independent of technological opportunities. Thus, we are able to avoid the most problematic assumption that was required in our IV approach.

The results from estimating (9) and (10), shown in Table 5, are largely consistent with our findings in Tables 3 and 4. In all cases, venture funding is significantly more potent than corporate R&D. The estimates of b are more modest, suggesting that venture funding is between 1.5 and 3 times as potent as corporate R&D.[24]

5. Patenting or innovation?

■   While the analyses above suggest a strong relationship between venture capital and patenting on an industry level, one major concern remains. In particular, it might be thought that the relationship between venture capital disbursements and patent applications is not indicative of a relationship between venture disbursements and innovative output. It may be that the increase in patenting is a consequence of a shift in the propensity to patent innovations stimulated by the venture financing process itself. In the terms of (7), there may be a positive correlation between the ϵ_{it} and V_{it}/R_{it} terms.

Two reasons might lead venture-backed firms—or companies seeking venture financing—to patent inventions that other firms would not. First, they may fear that the venture investors will exploit their ideas. Firms seeking external financing must make extensive disclosure of their technology. While potential investors may sign nondisclosure agreements (and may be restrained by reputational concerns), there is still a real possibility that entrepreneurs' ideas will be directly or indirectly transferred to other companies. Alternatively, venture or other investors may find it difficult to discern the quality of firms' patent holdings. To enhance their attractiveness (and consequently increase the probability of obtaining financing or the valuation assigned in that financing), firms may apply for patents on technologies of marginal worth.

The industry-level data do not give us much guidance here, but we can explore these possibilities by examining a broader array of behavior by venture-backed and non-venture-backed firms. Using a sample of 530 Middlesex County firms, we examine three measures of innovative activity.

Trajtenberg (1990) has demonstrated a strong relationship between the number of patent citations received and the economic importance of a patent. Using only those

---

[24] We can generalize by including $-a_1 \ln Y_{it}$ on the right-hand side of (9). Restricting $a_1 = 0$, we get back the specification shown in the first two columns of Table 5, while restricting it to be one yields the specification in the last two columns. If we estimate a_1, we get a value of about .4 while the corresponding estimate of b remains statistically significant and within the range reported in Table 5. We have also run regressions corresponding to the nonlinear versions of equations (9) and (10). The estimates of b are somewhat larger than those reported in Table 5: 3.23 [.74], 1.86 [.58], 4.55 [.91], and 4.81 [.84].

690 / THE RAND JOURNAL OF ECONOMICS

TABLE 5 Ordinary Least-squares Regression Analyses of the Patent-R&D Ratio

	Dependent Variable			
	$\ln P_{it} - \ln R_{it}$		$\ln P_{it} - (\ln R_{it} - \ln Y_{it})$	
Venture capital/privately funded R&D (b):				
Firms receiving funding	2.39		2.96	
	(.82)		(.87)	
Venture disbursements		1.45		2.70
		(.55)		(.85)
R^2	.97	.97	.97	.97
R^2 relative to dummy variable only case	.04	.02	.06	.07
Number of observations	560	560	560	560

Notes: Standard errors (in parentheses) are based on the Newey-West autocorrelation-consistent covariance estimator (with a maximum of three lags). Year and industry dummy variables are included in each regression.

firms that received any patent awards before 1990, we compute the ratio of the number of U.S. patent citations during the period between 1990 and June 1994 to U.S. patents awarded between 1969 and 1989. Citations per patent provides a largely external measure of the average importance of the firms' patent awards.

The second and third measures of the intellectual-property activity of firms are the frequency and extent of patent and trade-secret litigation in which the firm has engaged. Models in the law-and-economics literature suggest that parties are more likely to file suits and pursue these cases to trial when (i) the stakes of the dispute are high relative to the costs of the litigation or (ii) the outcome of the case is unclear (Cooter and Rubinfeld, 1989). Thus, litigation may serve as a rough proxy for economic importance, a suggestion verified empirically by Lanjouw and Schankerman (1997). We present

TABLE 6 Comparisons of Intellectual Property Activities of Venture-Backed and Non-Venture-Backed Firms

	Mean for Firms		p-Value, Comparison	
	Venture-Backed	Non-Venture	Means	Medians
Patents, 1990 to mid-1994	12.74	2.40	.029	.000
Citations/patent	6.44	4.06	.016	.004
Intellectual property suits:				
Number of suits	.79	.18	.000	.000
Number of docket filings	30.29	4.21	.000	.000
Patent suits only:				
Number of suits	.36	.08	.000	.000
Number of docket filings	15.35	2.04	.000	.000
Trade-secret suits only:				
Number of suits	.34	.08	.000	.000
Number of docket filings	6.43	1.86	.007	.000

Notes: The sample consists of 530 firms based in Middlesex County, Massachusetts, of which 122 are venture-backed.

these tabulations separately for patent and trade-secret suits. These measures may provide a rough indication of the importance of both patents and trade secrets to the firm.

Table 6 presents univariate comparisons. There are substantial differences between the 122 venture-backed and 408 non-venture-backed firms: the venture firms are more likely to patent, have previous patents cited, and engage in frequent and protracted litigation of both patents and trade secrets. All the tests of differences in means and medians in these three categories are significant at least at the 5% confidence level, as well as when we employ regression specifications. These findings help allay fears that differences in the propensity to patent drove our findings in Sections 3 and 4. At the same time, it is important to acknowledge that while the firm-level analysis allows us to examine whether the innovative behavior of venture-backed and non-venture-backed firms differs on measures other than patent counts, it does not allow us to address endogeneity issues as in the industry-level analysis.

6. Conclusions

■   This article examines the impact of venture capital on technological innovation. Patenting patterns across industries over a three-decade period suggest that the effect is positive and significant. The results are robust to different measures of venture activity, subsamples of industries, and representations of the relationship between patenting, R&D, and venture capital. Averaging across our preferred regressions, we come up with an estimate for b (the impact on patenting of a dollar of venture capital relative to a dollar of R&D) of 3.1. This estimate suggests that venture capital accounted for 8% of industrial innovations in the decade ending in 1992.[25] Given the rapid increase in venture funding since 1992, and assuming that the potency of venture funding has remained constant, the results imply that by 1998, venture funding accounted for about 14% of U.S. innovative activity.[26]

In our earlier work (1998), we argued that the recent surge in patenting in the United States was most likely explained by changes in the management of innovative activities. Interpreted broadly, the growth of venture capital is one such management change. While our results help answer some questions, they pose in turn additional questions:

First, what are the sources of the venture capitalists' advantage in funding innovation? Is the key source of advantage the process by which projects are chosen *ex ante*, or is it the monitoring and control after the investment is made?

Second, the finding of the apparently greater efficiency of venture funding in spurring innovation raises the question of why industrial R&D managers have not adopted some of the same approaches to financing innovation. Jensen (1993), for one, has argued that agency problems have hampered the effectiveness of major corporate industrial research facilities over the past several decades. What barriers have limited the diffusion of the venture capitalists' approaches?

---

[25] We get the estimate of $b = 3.1$ by averaging the estimates in the regressions reported in Panel B of Table 4, Table 5, and footnote 24. The ratio of venture capital disbursements to R&D (V/R) averaged over the years 1983 to 1992 is 2.9% (see Table 1). Our calculation of the share of innovations due to venture capital is $b(V/R)/(1 + b(V/R))$.

[26] Based on estimates of venture capital disbursements to all industries in 1998 (from Venture Economics) and preliminary estimates of R&D performed and funded by industry (from the National Science Foundation), we calculate that V/R increased at a 14% annual rate from 1992 to 1998. Given that V/R was 2.22% in 1992, we project that it had risen to 5.1% by 1998. Applying the same venture funding potency b of 3.1, we get the 14% number noted in the text.

Finally, other innovations in organizing research occurred contemporaneously. For example, central R&D facilities of large corporations have been redirected toward more applied problems (for an overview, see Rosenbloom and Spencer (1996). Is it possible to disentangle the distinct effects of the rise of venture capital from other R&D management innovations?

References

BERNSTEIN, J. AND NADIRI, M.I. "Financing and Investment in Plant and Equipment and Research and Development." In M.H. Peston and R.E. Quandt, eds., *Prices, Competition and Equilibrium.* Oxford: Philip Allan, 1986.

COHEN, W.M. "Empirical Studies of Innovative Activity." In P. Stoneman, ed., *Handbook of the Economics of Innovation and Technical Change.* Oxford: Blackwell, 1995.

COOTER, R.D. AND RUBINFELD, D.L. "Economic Analysis of Legal Disputes and Their Resolution." *Journal of Economic Literature,* Vol. 27 (1989), pp. 1067–1097.

EUROPEAN COMMISSION. *Green Paper on Innovation.* The European Union, 1995. http://europa.eu.int/en/record/green/gp9512/ind_inn.htm.

GOMPERS, P.A. AND LERNER, J. "What Drives Venture Capital Fundraising?" *Brookings Papers on Economic Activity, Microeconomics* (1998), pp. 149–192.

——— AND ———. *The Venture Capital Cycle.* Cambridge, Mass.: MIT Press, 1999.

GRILICHES, Z. "Issues in Assessing the Contribution of Research and Development to Productivity Growth." *Bell Journal of Economics,* Vol. 10 (1979), pp. 92–116.

———. "Productivity, R&D, and the Basic Research at the Firm Level in the 1970's." *American Economic Review,* Vol. 76 (1986), pp. 141–154.

———. "Patent Statistics as Economic Indicators: A Survey." *Journal of Economic Literature,* Vol. 28 (1990), pp. 1661–1707.

——— AND HAUSMAN, J.A. "Errors in Variables in Panel Data." *Journal of Econometrics,* Vol. 31 (1986), pp. 93–118.

HALL, B.H., GRILICHES, Z., AND HAUSMAN, J.A. "Patents and R&D: Is There a Lag?" *International Economic Review,* Vol. 27 (1986), pp. 265–283.

HELLMANN, T. AND PURI, M. "The Interaction Between Product Market and Financing Strategy: The Role of Venture Capital." Mimeo, Stanford University, 1998.

HIMMELBERG, C.P. AND PETERSEN, B.C. "R&D and Internal Finance: A Panel Study of Small Firms in High-Tech Industries." *Review of Economics and Statistics,* Vol. 76 (1994), pp. 38–51.

JENSEN, M.C. "Presidential Address: The Modern Industrial Revolution, Exit, and the Failure of Internal Control Systems." *Journal of Finance,* Vol. 48 (1993), pp. 831–880.

KORTUM, S. AND LERNER, J. "Stronger Protection or Technological Revolution: What Is Behind the Recent Surge in Patenting?" *Carnegie-Rochester Conference Series on Public Policy,* Vol. 48 (1998), pp. 247–304.

——— AND PUTNAM, J. "Assigning Patents to Industries: Tests of the Yale Technology Concordance." *Economic Systems Research,* Vol. 9 (1997), pp. 161–175.

LANJOUW, J. AND SCHANKERMAN, M. "Stylized Facts of Patent Litigation: Value, Scope and Ownership." Working Paper no. 6297, National Bureau of Economic Research, 1997.

LEVINSOHN, J. AND PETRIN, A. "Estimating Production Functions Using Inputs to Control for Unobservables." Working Paper no. 7819, National Bureau of Economic Research, 2000.

NEWEY, W.K. AND WEST, K.D. "A Simple, Positive Semi-definite, Heteroskedasticity and Autocorrelation Consistent Covariance Matrix." *Econometrica,* Vol. 55 (1987), pp. 703–708.

OLLEY, S. AND PAKES, A. "The Dynamics of Productivity in the Telecommunications Industry." *Econometrica,* Vol. 64 (1996), pp. 1263–1297.

ROSENBLOOM, R.S. AND SPENCER, W.J., eds. *Engines of Innovation: U.S. Industrial Research at the End of an Era.* Boston: Harvard Business School Press, 1996.

SCHMOOKLER, J. *Invention and Economic Growth.* Cambridge, Mass.: Harvard University, 1966.

TRAJTENBERG, M. "A Penny for Your Quotes: Patent Citations and the Value of Innovations." *RAND Journal of Economics,* Vol. 21 (1990), pp. 172–187.

Part IV
Funds Providers

[13]

Journal of Financial Economics 27 (1990) 473–521. North-Holland

The structure and governance of venture-capital organizations

William A. Sahlman*

Harvard Business School, Boston, MA 02163, USA

Received August 1989, final version received December 1990

Venture-capital organizations raise money from individuals and institutions for investment in early-stage businesses that offer high potential but high risk. This paper describes and analyzes the structure of venture-capital organizations, focusing on the relationship between investors and venture capitalists and between venture-capital firms and the ventures in which they invest. The agency problems in these organizations and to the contracts and operating procedures that have evolved in response are emphasized. Venture-capital organizations are contrasted with large, publicly traded corporations and with leveraged buyout organizations.

1. Introduction

The venture-capital industry has evolved operating procedures and contracting practices that are well adapted to environments characterized by uncertainty and information asymmetries between principals and agents. By venture capital I mean a professionally managed pool of capital that is invested in equity-linked securities of private ventures at various stages in their development. Venture capitalists are actively involved in the management of the ventures they fund, typically becoming members of the board of directors and retaining important economic rights in addition to their ownership rights. The prevailing organizational form in the industry is the limited partnership, with the venture capitalists acting as general partners and the outside investors as limited partners.

Venture-capital partnerships enter into contracts with both the outside investors who supply their funds and the entrepreneurial ventures in which

*The author gratefully acknowledges the useful comments of Bruce Greenwald, Michael Jensen, Christopher Barry, Clifford Smith, Kenneth French, Richard Ruback, two anonymous referees, Geoff Barss, Howard Stevenson, Jeffry Timmons, Regina Herzlinger, Andre Perold, Peter Wendell, Tench Coxe, and Christina Darwall. All errors and omissions remain the responsibility of the author.

they invest. The contracts share certain characteristics, notably:

(1) staging the commitment of capital and preserving the option to abandon,
(2) using compensation systems directly linked to value creation,
(3) preserving ways to force management to distribute investment proceeds.

These elements of the contracts address three fundamental problems:

(1) the sorting problem: how to select the best venture capital organizations and the best entrepreneurial ventures,.
(2) the agency problem:[1] how to minimize the present value of agency costs,
(3) the operating-cost problem: how to minimize the present value of operating costs, including taxes.

From one perspective, venture capital can be viewed as an alternative model for organizing capital investments. Like corporations, venture-capital firms raise money to invest in projects. Many projects funded by venture capitalists (for example, the development of a new computer hardware peripheral) are similar to projects funded within traditional corporations. But the governance systems used by venture-capital organizations and traditional corporations are very different. This paper addresses some of the differences.

The information and analysis in the paper comes from two basic sources. Most of the data cited come from Venture Economics, the leading information source on the venture-capital industry. Venture Economics publishes the *Venture Capital Journal* (VCJ), a monthly magazine on trends in the industry, as well a number of specialized studies. The second major source is extensive field research I have done over the past eight years. This effort has resulted in 20 Harvard Business School cases based on decisions in venture-capital firms or in the companies they fund [e.g., Sahlman (1986c), Knights and Sahlman (1986d)], four technical and industry notes [e.g., Sahlman and Scherlis (1988)], and several articles [e.g., Sahlman and Stevenson (1985)]. The field research embodied in the cases and notes has been supplemented with on-site interviews with 25 venture-capital-firm management teams, over 150 venture capitalists, and approximately 50 venture-capital-backed entrepreneurial management teams.

Section 2 provides background information on the venture-capital industry, emphasizing the great uncertainty about returns on individual venture-capital projects. Sections 3, 4, and 5 discuss the general structure of a venture-capital firm and the contracts between external investors and venture capitalists. Sections 6 and 7 examine the contractual relationship between the venture-

---

[1]See Jensen and Meckling (1976), Fama (1980), and Fama and Jensen (1985) for background on the theory of agency costs. See also Williamson (1975, 1988) for background on transaction-cost theory. For related articles using the same basic framework to analyze organizational forms, see Wolfson (1985) on oil and gas limited partnerships and Brickley and Dark (1987) on franchises. Smith and Warner (1979) provide a similar analysis of financial contracts.

capital firm and the companies in which it invests. Venture-capital organizations are compared with other organizational forms for corporate or project governance in section 8. Section 9 summarizes the paper.

2. General industry background

Table 1 presents historical data on the venture-capital industry from 1980 to 1988. In 1988 an estimated 658 venture-capital firms in the U.S. managed slightly over $31 billion in capital and employed 2,500 professionals (panel A, table 1).[2] Industry resources were concentrated: the largest 89 firms controlled approximately 58% of the total capital. The average amount controlled by these 89 firms was just under $200 million [VCJ April 1990, p. 13)].

In each of the last several years, venture capitalists disbursed approximately $3 billion to fewer than 2,000 companies, most in high-technology industries (panel C, table 1). Although a typical large venture-capital firm receives up to 1,000 proposals each year, it invests in only a dozen or so new companies.

Venture capitalists invest at reasonably well-defined stages (panel C, table 1). The seed stage typically precedes formation of a complete management team or completion of a product or service design. Each successive stage is generally tied to a significant development in the company, such as completion of design, pilot production, first profitability, introduction of a second product, or an initial public offering [Plummer (1987), Kozmetsky et al. (1985)]. The stages of investment are described more completely in table 2.

Approximately 15% of the capital disbursed in each of the last three years went to ventures in early stages, whereas 65% was invested in later-stage companies, typically still privately held. The remaining 20% was invested in leveraged buyout or acquisition deals. In recent years venture capitalists have channeled roughly two-thirds of the capital invested each year into companies already in their portfolios, and one-third into new investments. Venture capitalists often participate in several rounds of financing with the same portfolio company, as illustrated in table 3.

Venture-capital investing plays a small role in overall new-business formation. According to Dun & Bradstreet, approximately 600,000 to 700,000 new businesses are incorporated in the United States each year [Council of Economic Advisors (1990)]. The vast majority of those that seek external funding do so from sources other than venture capitalists. Some analysts

---

[2] Venture Economic's estimate of total industry capital is based on commitments of capital and is measured at cost rather than market value: thus, the $31.1 billion cited in table 1 consists of capital that has been committed to venture-capital funds but not yet invested, some cash, and portfolio investments in individual ventures by venture-capital funds. The market value of the assets under management in the industry probably exceeds book value.

Table 1

Selected data on the United States venture-capital industry, 1980–1988.[a]

	1980	1981	1982	1983	1984	1985	1986	1987	1988
Panel A: Aggregate venture-capital industry statistics									
1 Total venture-capital pool ($M)	$4,500	$5,800	$7,600	$12,100	$16,300	$19,600	$24,100	$29,000	$31,100
2 Number of venture-capital firms	NA	NA	331	448	509	532	587	627	658
3 Number of industry professionals	NA	NA	1,031	1,494	1,760	1,899	2,187	2,378	2,474
4 Net new commitments to the venture-capital industry ($M)	$700	$1,300	$1,800	$4,500	$4,200	$3,300	$4,500	$4,900	$2,900
Panel B: Data on the independent private sector *(noncorporate and non-SBIC venture capital organizations)*									
1 Net new commitments to the independent private sector ($M)	$661	$867	$1,400	$3,400	$3,200	$2,300	$3,300	$4,200	$2,100
Sectoral analysis (% of total capital)									
2 Independent private	40.0%	44.0%	58.0%	68.7%	72.0%	73.0%	75.0%	78.0%	80.0%
3 Corporate	31.1%	28.0%	25.0%	21.0%	18.0%	17.0%	16.0%	14.0%	13.0%
4 SBIC	28.9%	28.0%	17.0%	11.0%	10.0%	10.0%	9.0%	8.0%	7.0%
Sectoral analysis – Average capital per firm ($M)									
5 Independent private	NA	NA	$27	$36	$45	$52	$57	$65	$65
6 Corporate	NA	NA	$30	$37	$36	$37	$34	$32	$29
7 SBIC	NA	NA	$6	$5	$5	$5	$5	$6	$5
8 Median size of independent private firms ($M)	NA	NA	$22	$18	$21	$25	$30	$30	$30

Independent private-sector partnership formation									
9 Total # of funds raising capital	22	37	54	89	101	77	77	110	84
10 Total capital raised ($M)	$661	$866	$1,423	$3,460	$3,300	$2,327	$3,320	$4,184	$2,810
11 # of follow-on funds	12	13	18	47	58	40	44	66	59
12 Capital raised by follow-on funds ($M)	$418	$477	$628	$2,383	$2,300	$1,396	$2,800	$3,347	$2,422
13 # of new funds	10	24	36	42	43	37	33	44	25
14 Capital raised by new funds ($M)	$243	$389	$795	$1,077	$1,000	$931	$520	$837	$388
Sources of capital to the independent private sector (%)									
15 Corporations	19.0%	17.0%	12.0%	12.0%	14.0%	12.0%	11.0%	10.0%	12.0%
16 Individuals	16.0%	23.0%	21.0%	21.0%	15.0%	13.0%	12.0%	12.0%	8.0%
17 Pension funds	30.0%	23.0%	33.0%	31.0%	34.0%	33.0%	50.0%	39.0%	47.0%
18 Foreign	8.0%	10.0%	13.0%	16.0%	18.0%	23.0%	11.0%	14.0%	13.0%
19 Endowments	14.0%	12.0%	7.0%	8.0%	6.0%	8.0%	6.0%	10.0%	11.0%
20 Insurance companies	13.0%	15.0%	14.0%	12.0%	13.0%	11.0%	10.0%	15.0%	9.0%
Panel C: Investment activity of venture capitalists									
Disbursements									
1 Estimated value of disbursements ($M)	$610	$1,160	$1,450	$2,580	$2,760	$2,670	$3,230	$3,940	$3,650
2 Number of companies financed	504	797	918	1,320	1,469	1,377	1,504	1,729	1,474
3 Average investment per company	$1.21	$1.46	$1.58	$1.95	$1.88	$1.94	$2.15	$2.28	$2.48
Allocation of investments									
4 New company commitments as a % of total	58.0%	55.0%	39.0%	34.0%	31.0%	23.0%	37.0%	39.0%	33.0%
5 Follow-on financings as a % of total	42.0%	45.0%	61.0%	66.0%	69.0%	77.0%	63.0%	61.0%	67.0%
Stages of financing									
6 Seed and startup as a % of total	25.0%	22.6%	20.0%	17.2%	21.0%	15.0%	19.0%	13.0%	12.5%
7 Expansion and later-stage as a % of total	75.0%	77.4%	68.0%	70.8%	67.0%	69.0%	58.0%	69.0%	67.5%
8 Leveraged buyouts as a % of total	NA	NA	12.0%	12.0%	12.0%	16.0%	23.0%	18.0%	20.0%

continued overleaf

Table 1 (continued)

		1980	1981	1982	1983	1984	1985	1986	1987	1988
Panel D: Exiting venture-capital investments										
1	# of venture-capital-backed companies that are acquired	28	32	40	49	86	101	120	147	106
	Venture-capital-backed initial public offerings (IPOs)										
2	# of companies	27	68	27	121	53	46	97	81	35
3	Total amount raised ($M)	$420	$770	$549	$3,031	$743	$838	$2,118	$1,840	$756
4	Total market value of companies with IPO in each year ($M)	$2,626	$3,610	$2,374	$14,035	$3,495	$3,258	$8,434	$6,893	$3,122
	All IPOs										
5	# of companies	95	227	100	504	213	195	417	259	96
6	Total amount raised ($M)	$1,089	$2,723	$1,213	$9,580	$2,545	$3,166	$8,190	$5,220	$2,392
7	Total market value of companies ($M)	$5,717	$10,922	$5,466	$40,473	$10,792	$11,618	$31,616	$23,813	$11,759
	Venture capital backed IPOs as % of total IPOs										
8	# of companies	28.4%	30.0%	27.0%	24.0%	24.9%	23.6%	23.3%	31.3%	36.5%
9	Total amount raised	38.6%	28.3%	45.2%	31.6%	29.2%	26.5%	25.9%	35.2%	31.6%
10	Total market value of companies	45.9%	33.1%	43.4%	34.7%	32.4%	28.0%	26.7%	28.9%	26.5%

[a]*Source*: Various publications of Venture Economics (Needham, MA).
NA: not available.
Total capital (for example, panel A, row 1) is the book value of all commitments to professional venture-capital firms (net of fund liquidations). See also footnote 2 in text.
Data on initial public offerings in panel D, rows 5–7, come from Securities Data Corporation (see footnote 3 in the text).

Table 2

The stages of venture-capital investing.[a]

1. *Seed investments*

   Although the term is sometimes used more broadly, the strict meaning of 'seed investment' is a small amount of capital provided to an inventor or entrepreneur to determine whether an idea deserves of further consideration and further investment. The idea may involve a technology, or it may be an idea for a new marketing approach. If it is a technology, this stage may involve building a small prototype. This stage does not involve production for sale.

2. *Startup*

   Startup investments usually go to companies that are less than one year old. The company uses the money for product development, prototype testing, and test marketing (in experimental quantities to selected customers). This stage involves further study of market-penetration potential, bringing together a management team, and refining the business plan.

3. *First stage – early development*

   Investment proceeds through the first stage only if the prototypes look good enough that further technical risk is considered minimal. Likewise, the market studies must look good enough so that management is comfortable setting up a modest manufacturing process and shipping in commercial quantities. First-stage companies are unlikely to be profitable.

4. *Second stage – expansion*

   A company in the second stage has shipped enough product to enough customers so that it has real feedback from the market. It may not know quantitatively what speed of market penetration will occur later, or what the ultimate penetration will be, but it may know the qualitative factors that will determine the speed and limits of penetration. The company is probably still unprofitable, or only marginally profitable. It probably needs more capital for equipment purchases, inventory, and receivable financing.

5. *Third stage – profitable but cash poor*

   For third-stage companies, sales growth is probably fast, and positive profit margins have taken away most of the downside investment risk. But, the rapid expansion requires more working capital than can be generated from internal cash flow. New VC capital may be used for further expansion of manufacturing facilities, expanded marketing, or product enhancements. At this stage, banks may be willing to supply some credit if it can be secured by fixed assets or receivables.

6. *Fourth stage – rapid growth toward liquidity point*

   Companies at the fourth stage of development may still need outside cash to sustain growth, but they are successful and stable enough so that the risk to outside investors is much reduced. The company may prefer to use more debt financing to limit equity dilution. Commercial bank credit can play a more important role. Although the cash-out point for VC investors is thought to be within a couple of years, the form (IPO, acquisition, or LBO) and timing of cash-out are still uncertain.

7. *Bridge stage – mezzanine investment*

   In bridge or mezzanine investment situations, the company may have some idea which form of exit is most likely, and even know the approximate timing, but it still needs more capital to sustain rapid growth in the interim. Depending on how the general stock market is doing, and how given types of high-tech stocks are doing within the stock market, 'IPO windows' can open and close in very unpredictable ways. Likewise, the level of interest rates and the availability of commercial credit can influence the timing and feasibility of acquisitions or leveraged buyouts. A bridge financing may also correspond to a limited cash-out of early investors or management, or a restructuring of positions among VC investors.

8. *Liquidity stage – cash-out or exit*

   A literal interpretation of 'cash-out' would seem to imply trading the VC-held shares in a portfolio company for cash. In practice, it has come to mean the point at which the VC investors can gain liquidity for a substantial portion of their holdings in a company. The liquidity may come in the form of an initial public offering. If it does, liquidity is still restricted by the holding periods and other restrictions that are part of SEC Rule 144, or by 'stand-off' commitments made to the IPO underwriter, in which the insiders agree not to sell their shares for some period of time after the offering (for example, 90 or 180 days). If acquisition is the form of cash-out, the liquidity may be in the form of cash, shares in a publicly traded company, or short-term debt. If the acquisition is paid for in shares of a nonpublic company, such shares may be no more liquid than the shares in the original company. Likewise, if the sellers take back debt in a leveraged buyout, they may wind up in a less liquid position than before, depending on the liquidity features of the debt.

   ---
   [a] This table is drawn from Plummer (1987, pp. I-11 to I-13).

Table 3

Participation in multiple financing rounds by a venture-capital fund.[a,b]

Company/ Date of purchase	Security purchased	Price per share	Number of shares	Total cost
Company 1				
5/1/85	Convertible preferred series B	$0.68	525,145	$354,473
8/1/85	Convertible preferred series B	$0.68	972,531	$656,458
3/1/86	Convertible preferred series C	$2.25	444,445	$1,000,001
4/1/87	Convertible preferred series D	$4.50	66,667	$300,002
	Totals (average price per share)	$1.15	2,008,788	$2,310,934
7/24/90	Estimated value	$23.00		$46,202,124
Company 2				
6/1/85	Convertible preferred series A	$15.00	20,833	$312,500
11/1/85	Convertible preferred series A	$15.00	20,833	$312,495
4/1/86	Convertible preferred series A	$15.00	25,000	$375,000
5/2/88	Convertible preferred series B	$8.60	28,588	$245,857
	Totals (average price per share)	$13.08	95,254	$1,245,852
	Note: Loans totalling $206,500 were made in 1987 and these were converted to series B preferred on 5/2/88			
7/24/90	Estimated value	$3.27		$311,463
Company 3				
2/1/87	Convertible preferred series B	$1.15	347,827	$400,001
7/1/87	Convertible preferred series C	$1.90	131,579	$250,000
3/16/88	Convertible preferred series D	$1.60	283,326	$453,322
	Totals (average price per share)	$1.45	762,732	$1,103,323
	Note: Loans totalling $200,000 were made in 1987 and these were converted to series D preferred on 3/16/88			
7/24/90	Estimated total value	$1.45		$1,103,323

W. A. Sahlman, *Structure of venture-capital organizations* 481

Company 4				
2/1/86	Convertible preferred series B	$0.95	1,473,684	$1,400,000
12/1/86	Convertible preferred series D	$1.85	461,808	$854,345
7/22/87	Convertible preferred series D	$1.85	141,829	$262,384
	Totals (average price per share)	$1.21	2,077,321	$2,516,728
7/24/90	Estimated value	$4.34		$9,005,259
Company 5				
11/1/85	Convertible preferred series A	$0.34	1,470,588	$500,000
3/1/86	Convertible preferred series B	$0.45	2,083,333	$937,500
3/1/87	Convertible preferred series C	$0.75	1,333,333	$1,000,000
	Totals (average price per share)	$0.50	4,887,254	$2,437,500
7/24/90	Estimated value	$0.00		$0
Total cost for 5 companies			$9,614,336	
Total estimated value for 5 companies			$56,622,169	
Total gain for 5 companies			$47,007,832	

Source: An interim report to the limited partners of a venture-capital fund with more than $20 million in capital.
[b]The amounts listed do not include investments made by others at the same time or at other times.

estimate that the amount invested by so-called angels is an order of magnitude larger than the amount invested by professional venture capitalists [see, for example, Wetzel (1983) and Freear and Wetzel (1990)].

Venture-capital investing is also modest in comparison with the level of capital investment in the domestic corporate sector: total capital expenditures in 1988 by the nonfinancial, nonfarm sector exceeded $380 billion [Economic Report of the President (1990)]. Total expenditures on research and development in the U.S. each year are estimated to top $150 billion, of which $74 billion is invested by private industrial concerns [Studt (1990)]. Finally, the $3 billion disbursed by all professional venture capitalists in 1988 was only slightly less than one-third the amount invested by IBM in capital expenditures and R & D in the same year, and 25% of the amount invested by General Motors.

Despite its modest scope, the industry has helped create many successful enterprises, including Apple Computer, Intel, Federal Express, People Express, Businessland, Lotus Development, Microsoft, Sun Microsystems, Digital Equipment, Compaq Computer, Teledyne, Tandem, Tandon, Hybritech, and Genentech. Each of these companies received venture capital early in its development and later went public. In aggregate, 579 venture-capital-backed companies went public during the 11 years ending in 1988. Their total market value exceeded 30% of the total market value of all comparable companies going public during the same period (panel D, table 1).[3]

The payoff to venture capitalists has been handsome in some cases. During 1978 and 1979, for example, slightly more than $3.5 million in venture capital was invested in Apple Computer. When Apple went public in December 1980, the approximate value of the venture capitalists' investment was $271 million, and the total market capitalization of Apple's equity exceeded $1.4 billion. Similarly, several venture capitalists invested slightly over $4.7 million in Lotus Development Corporation in two rounds of financing in 1982: their equity was assigned a market value of almost $130 million in October 1983. The lead venture capitalist, Ben Rosen of Sevin-Rosen Partners, played a very important role in the formation and evolution of the company [see Sahlman (1985e) for background on the Sevin-Rosen investment in Lotus].

The industry has also been involved in some spectacular failures. Well-known examples include Ovation Technologies, Osborne Computer, Ztel, and Gavilan. In each case, venture capitalists lost their entire investment. In late 1983 Ovation Technologies raised almost $6 million in venture capital to compete with Lotus Development in microcomputer software. The product proved far more difficult and costly to complete than anticipated, however,

---

[3]Venture Economics provides the data on the venture-capital-backed companies. Data on all initial public offerings (IPOs) during the period come from Securities Data Corporation. The specific comparison sample excludes all closed-end investment companies, savings and loan conversions. and companies with an offering price under $5.00 per share.

and the venture-capital firms chose to liquidate the company rather than continue funding development. Ovation closed its doors in late 1984 without having generated one dollar of revenues. [For further information on Ovation, see Knights and Sahlman (1986a).]

Although comprehensive data are difficult to obtain, the overall rate of return on venture capital seems to have been high from the mid-1960s through the mid-1980s, the only period for which reliable data are currently available. Between 1965 and 1984, for example, the median realized compound rate of return on 29 venture-capital partnerships over the life of each partnership (an average of 8.6 years) exceeded 26% per year [Venture Economics (1985, p. 69)]. The minimum compound annual rate of return for the 29 funds was 6%.[4]

A more recent and comprehensive study [Venture Economics (1988c)] suggests that funds started before 1981 experienced generally positive returns through 1987. For example, the average annual rate of return (weighted by initial investment) on the 13 funds started in 1980 was 20.6% for the period ending December 31, 1987, compared with 16% for the Standard & Poor's 500 and 16% for smaller capitalization stocks during the same period [Ibbotson Associates (1988)]. These 13 funds represented 50% of the total funds raising money in 1980 and 66% of the capital raised that year. This study also reveals that rates of return have declined since 1983, particularly for funds started later in the period. It is extremely difficult to estimate the extent to which returns have declined, however, because accounting practices in the industry typically reflect a downward bias. [See also VCJ (August 1989) and Sahlman (1989).]

Returns on individual investments in a venture-capital portfolio vary widely. According to Huntsman and Homan (1980), slightly more than half of the 110 investments made by three venture-capital firms from 1960 to 1975 resulted in a realized rate of return of less than 10%; over one-quarter resulted in an absolute loss. According to Venture Economics (1988c), more than one-third of 383 investments made by 13 firms between 1969 and 1985 resulted in an absolute loss. More than two-thirds of the individual investments made by these same firms resulted in capital returns of less than double the original cost.

Nevertheless, the returns on a few investments have more than offset these disappointments. Venture Economics (1988c) reports, for example, that 6.8% of the investments resulted in payoffs greater than ten times cost and yielded 49.4% of the ending value of the aggregate portfolio (61.4% of the profits).

---

[4]The findings reported in Venture Economics (1985) are supported by Huntsman and Homan (1980), Chiampou and Kellet (1989), Bygrave et al. (1987), Horsley Keogh (1988), and analysis of the returns reported by 20 venture-capital funds in offering memoranda used to raise new capital. No attempt was made in these studies to adjust for the systematic risk incurred in venture-capital investing.

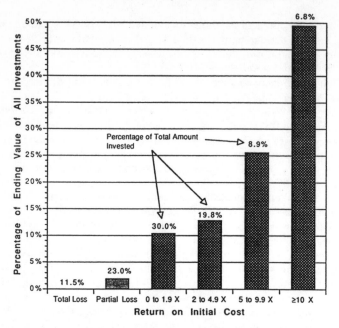

Fig. 1. Payoffs from venture-capital investing.

This graph shows the distribution of gains and losses on a group of investments made by venture-capital firms. The data are taken from Venture Economics (1988c) and cover investments by 13 venture-capital partnerships in 383 companies from 1969 to 1985. In total, $245 million was invested, which resulted in total value of $1.049 billion (4.3 times cost). The vertical axis shows the percentage of total ending value (that is, the $1.049 billion) resulting from six groups of investments, comprising investments with differing returns on capital invested (from total loss to more than 10 times capital invested). At the top of each bar the percentage of total cost represented by each group is shown. Thus, 6.8% of the capital invested resulted in payoffs of more than 10 to 1 and contributed almost 50% of the total ending value. Similarly, 11.5% of the cost was invested in companies that experienced a total loss.

Fig. 1 shows the distribution of outcomes analyzed in Venture Economics (1988c). An earlier Venture Economics report (1985) reached similar conclusions: investments in 22 of 216 companies yielded more than ten times cost, and the profits realized were more than 40 times larger than the losses incurred on the 70 companies that failed to return the amount invested. The same basic patterns are found by Keeley (1986) and Horsley Keogh (1988). See also Stevenson et al. (1987) and Sahlman and Soussou (1985a).

Even companies that are successful in the long run sometimes flirt with failure. For example, an analysis of various documents filed with the Securities and Exchange Commission (SEC) reveals that Federal Express raised

Table 4

Multiple financing rounds for selected venture-capital-backed firms.[a]

Company (business)	Investor[b]	Date	Amount raised ($000)	Cumulative funding ($000)	Stock received (000)	Total shares outstanding (000)	% ownership acquired	Fully diluted valuation ($000)	Price per share ($)	Estimated ending ownership %[c]
Apple Computer (computer)	Founders	Mar-77	1	1	16,640	16,640	100.0%	1	0.00	30.7%
	Founders	Nov-77	115	116	10,480	27,120	38.6%	298	0.01	19.3%
	Venture 1	Jan-78	518	634	5,520	32,640	16.9%	3,063	0.09	10.2%
	Founders	Jul-78	426	1,060	4,736	37,376	12.7%	3,362	0.09	8.7%
	Venture 2	Sep-78	704	1,764	2,503	39,879	6.3%	11,216	0.28	4.6%
	Venture 3	Dec-80	2,331	4,095	2,400	43,306	5.5%	42,061	0.97	4.4%
	IPO	Dec-80	101,200	105,295	4,600	54,215	8.5%	1,192,730	22.00	8.5%
Cray Research (computer)	Founders	Aug-72	2,550	2,550	2,869	2,794	102.7%	2,483	0.89	24.3%
	Venture 1	Jan-74	2,675	5,225	2,006	4,875	41.1%	6,501	1.33	17.0%
	Venture 2	Jan-75	642	5,867	387	5,302	7.3%	8,796	1.66	3.3%
	Venture 3	Apr-75	2,720	8,587	1,530	6,832	22.4%	12,146	1.78	13.0%
	IPO	Mar-76	10,890	19,477	4,950	11,783	42.0%	25,923	2.20	42.0%
Federal Express (transportation)	Founders	Jan-72	4,745	4,745	100	100	100.0%	4,745	47.45	0.7%
	Venture 1	Sep-73	12,250	16,995	60	160	37.5%	32,667	204.17	0.4%
	Venture 2	Mar-74	6,400	23,395	872	1,032	84.5%	7,574	7.34	6.4%
	Venture 3	Sep-74	3,876	27,271	6,200	7,232	85.7%	4,521	0.63	45.8%
	IPO	Apr-78	25,800	53,071	4,300	13,535	31.8%	81,210	6.00	31.8%
Genentech (biotechnology)	Founders	Jan-76	126	126	3,200	3,200	100.0%	126	0.04	41.4%
	Venture 1	Apr-76	850	976	1,180	4,280	27.6%	3,083	0.72	15.3%
	Venture 2	May-78	950	1,926	475	4,945	9.6%	9,890	2.00	6.1%
	Corporate	Sep-79	10,000	11,926	1,000	6,348	15.8%	63,480	10.00	12.9%
	IPO	Oct-80	38,500	50,426	1,100	7,724	14.2%	270,340	35.00	14.2%

Table 4 (continued)

Company (business)	Investor[b]	Date	Amount raised ($000)	Cumulative funding ($000)	Stock received (000)	Total shares outstanding (000)	% ownership acquired	Fully diluted valuation ($000)	Price per share ($)	Estimated ending ownership %[c]
Lotus Development (software)	Founders	Apr-82	13	13	4,410	4,410	100.0%	13	0.00	30.9%
	Venture 1	Apr-82	1,000	1,013	3,500	7,910	44.2%	2,260	0.29	24.5%
	Venture 2	Dec-82	3,755	4,768	3,767	11,677	32.3%	12,044	1.03	26.4%
	IPO	Oct-83	46,800	51,568	2,600	14,277	18.2%	256,988	18.00	18.2%
Midway Airlines (transportation)	Founders	Jun-76	7	7	700	700	100.0%	7	0.01	19.2%
	Venture 1	Jul-79	5,739	5,746	1,380	2,080	66.3%	8,650	4.16	37.9%
	Venture 2	Sep-80	6,000	11,746	789	2,789	28.3%	23,620	7.60	21.7%
	IPO	Dec-80	11,475	23,221	850	3,639	23.4%	53,433	13.50	23.4%
Seagate (disk drives)	Founders	Oct-79	161	161	11,723	11,723	100.0%	161	0.01	64.1%
	Venture 1	Jun-80	1,000	1,161	3,125	14,848	21.0%	4,751	0.32	17.1%
	IPO	Sep-81	25,000	26,161	2,500	18,277	13.7%	182,770	10.00	13.7%
Staples (retailing)	Founders/ Venture 1	Jan-86	4,425	4,425	1,844	1,844	100.0%	4,425	2.40	20.2%
	Venture 2	Jan-87	13,927	18,352	2,211	4,054	54.5%	25,543	6.30	24.2%
	Venture 3	Dec-87	13,597	31,950	1,563	5,617	27.8%	48,871	8.70	17.1%
	Venture 4	Sep-88	2,800	34,750	267	5,884	4.5%	61,782	10.50	2.9%
	IPO	Apr-89	61,750	96,500	3,250	9,134	35.6%	173,546	19.00	35.6%

[a] *Sources:* Annual reports, prospectuses.
[b] Venture 1, etc., represent rounds of financing from venture capitalists; IPO = Initial Public Offering.
[c] Ending ownership is based on final total shares outstanding. The figures do not always add exactly to 100%, which reflects stock options issued and other capital structure changes, including share repurchases, warrants issued, and debt conversions.

three rounds of venture capital in 1973 and 1974. With the company behind plan and over budget, the price paid per share in the third round was $0.63, compared with the adjusted price of more than $200 in the first round and just over $7 per share in the second round. By 1976, when the company made its first public offering of shares, the adjusted price per share was $6; by 1981, it was $47.45. Table 4 shows the prices paid and capital raised in Federal Express and seven other ventures.

Conversely, companies that give venture capitalists and their investors high rates of return do not always succeed in the long run. Priam Corporation, a disk-drive manufacturer, received five rounds of venture capital before it went public. In the initial round of financing in 1978 the price per share was less than $1, whereas the per-share value assigned soon after the company went public in 1983 was $23. Every intervening round had taken place at a higher price per share, but although it raised more than $70 million in its IPO, Priam filed for bankruptcy in 1989. [See Sahlman (1984), Knights and Sahlman (1986c, 1986d), and Sahlman and Stevenson (1985) for details on Priam and other disk-drive manufacturers.]

An important variable in venture-capital investments is the time that elapses between the initial investment and the return of capital. According to Venture Economics (1988c), the average holding period for an investment is 4.9 years. Roughly one-third of the individual investments studied are held for more than six years. Investments with payoffs greater than five times the invested capital are held significantly longer than investments that fail completely. The average investment in companies with high payoffs is approximately $1 million, versus $366,000 for the losers.

3. The most common structure of venture-capital firms[5]

By 1988 the typical venture-capital firm was organized as a limited partnership, with the venture capitalists serving as general partners and the investors as limited partners. According to Venture Economics (1987), 500 firms with $20 billion in capital in 1987 were structured as limited partnerships. The remaining one-third of industry capital was invested in independent private venture-capital firms not organized as limited partnerships (for example, incorporated venture-capital companies and publicly traded closed-end funds) (9% in 1987); in venture-capital subsidiaries of industrial and financial corporations (14%); and in independent small-business investment companies (SBICs) (8%), which had access to government-guaranteed debt to

---

[5]For background information on the venture-capital industry and the structure of venture-capital firms, see Gorman and Sahlman (1989), Sahlman and Stevenson (1985), Sahlman (1988, 1989), Wilson (1985), Morris (1988a), Bartlett (1988), and Venture Economics (1985, 1987, 1988a, 1988b, 1988c).

leverage their equity capital (panel B, table 1). The share of total industry capital managed by the independent private sector, which comprises mostly limited partnerships, increased dramatically over the nine years ending in 1988.

Table 1 (panel B) also reveals that in 1988 12% of the new capital committed to the private independent sector (i.e., noncorporate subsidiaries and non-SBICs) came from individuals, whereas 64% came from pension funds, endowments, and insurance companies. Typically, the general partners provide only a small proportion (about 1%) of the capital raised by a given fund. Most venture-capital firms are structured as management companies responsible for managing several pools of capital, each representing a legally separate limited partnership.

In each new fund, the capital is invested in new ventures during the first three to five years of the fund. Thereafter few if any investments are made in companies not already in the portfolio, and the goal is to begin converting existing investments to cash. As investments yield cash or marketable securities, distributions are made to the partners rather than reinvested in new ventures.

Typically, well before all of the capital from a venture-capital pool is distributed to the partners, a new fund is raised and invested in new ventures. For example, Institutional Venture Partners (IVP), a California-based venture-capital firm, raised $16.5 million in 1980, the year it was formed. In 1982 the IVP management company raised $40 million in a fund called IVP II. The group raised $96 million in 1985, launching IVP III, which was followed in 1988 by IVP IV, a $115 million fund [VCJ (May 1989, pp. 26–29)]. Thus investment and distribution periods overlap. Approximately 72% of the increase in capital controlled by the private independent sector from 1977 to 1988 was attributable to so-called follow-on funds, new venture-capital pools raised by existing firms.

The average firm in 1988 had $65 million in committed capital (measured at cost rather than market value). The largest 89 firms, as noted earlier, had average committed capital of almost $200 million and controlled almost 60% of the industry's assets. A fund with $200 million in committed capital is typically managed by a professional staff of between 6 and 12, who invest approximately $15 to $35 million each year in new companies and companies already in the portfolio.

Most venture-capital firms have several general partners and a staff of associates and administrative support personnel. Associates function as apprentices to the general partners and often become general partners themselves in later funds. In 1988, the average capital managed per professional (partner or associate) was $12.6 million. For the independent private sector, the figure was $15 million per professional [Venture Economics (1989)]. The capital managed by each professional is a function of total capital under management. For independent private firms with total committed capital of more than $200 million, each professional was responsible for managing $34 million.

Institutional Venture Partners, for example, had six general partners and two associates responsible for managing the various active funds. In 1988 IVP invested $11.2 million in 11 new companies not already in one of the fund portfolios and $19.2 million in 27 follow-on deals.

By 1988 roughly one-third of all venture-capital firms had at least one partner with more than 10 years of experience, and these firms managed almost 60% of total industry capital. In the independent private sector, which was characterized by more experience, roughly 68% of the firms (managing 89% of the capital) had one partner with at least five years of experience in the industry [Venture Economics (1989)].

Venture-capital firms tend to specialize by industry or stage of investment. Some firms focus on computer-related companies, others on biotechnology or specialty retailers. Some will invest only in early-stage deals, whereas others concentrate on later-stage financings. Many firms also limit their geographic scope.

4. The contract between the investors and the venture-capital firm

The relationship between investors and managers of the venture funds is governed by a partnership agreement that spells out the rights and obligations of each group. Key elements of the contract are described in this section, and an economic analysis follows in section 5. The description of the legal structure of a venture-capital firm is based primarily on Venture Economics (1987), which studied contracts for 76 funds raised between January 1986 and August 1987. These funds represented 76% of all venture-capital funds raised during this period. Of the 76, 40 were initial funds and 36 were follow-on funds started by firms already managing other pools. The findings in that report were checked against primary-source documents from 25 venture capital firms. See also Bartlett (1988).

4.1. Legal structure

The limited-partnership organizational form has important tax and legal considerations. Limited-partnership income is not subject to corporate taxation; instead income is taxable to the individual partners. Also, partnerships can distribute securities without triggering immediate recognition of taxable income: the gain or loss on the underlying asset is recognized only when the asset is sold. To qualify for this form of tax treatment, partnerships must meet several conditions:[6]

(1) A fund's life must have an agreed-upon date of termination, which is established before the partnership agreement is signed.
(2) The transfer of limited partnership units is restricted; unlike most registered securities, they cannot be easily bought and sold.
(3) Withdrawal from the partnership before the termination date is prohibited.
(4) Limited partners cannot participate in the active management of a fund if their liability is to be limited to the amount of their commitment.

General partners, in contrast, bear unlimited liability, so they can conceivably lose much more than they commit in capital. The consequences of unlimited liability are minor, however, because venture-capital partnerships typically do not borrow, nor are they exposed to the risk of having liabilities in excess of assets.

Despite restrictions on their managerial rights, limited partners are almost always permitted to vote on key issues such as amendment of the limited-partnership agreement, dissolution of the partnership before the termination date, extension of the fund's life, removal of any general partner, and valuation of the portfolio. Contracts vary, but typically a two-thirds majority of limited-partnership votes is required to effect change.

4.2. General-partner contribution

Of the 76 partnerships surveyed in Venture Economics (1987), 61% report general-partner contributions of exactly 1% of committed capital. This contribution can be, and often is, in the form of a promissory note rather than cash. Some tax advisors counsel those forming venture-capital partnerships to have the general partners contribute at least 1% in order to be assured of favorable tax treatment.

4.3. Economic life

For the Venture Economics (1987) sample, the economic life of 72% of the funds is set at ten years. All of the partnerships include provisions to extend the life of the funds, with 52% requiring some level of consent by the limited partners and 48% leaving the decision up to the general partners. The most frequent extension period is three years maximum in one-year increments. At the end of a fund's legal existence, all cash and securities are distributed and a final accounting is rendered.

---

[6]The list below is replicated from Venture Economics (1987, p. 7). See also Wolfson (1985), who describes the use of the limited-partnership organization form in the oil and gas industry, which is driven primarily by tax considerations.

4.4. Takedown schedules

In the survey sample the limited partners typically are required to invest a certain amount at the outset, but can phase in the remainder of their investment over time. Most fund agreements call for a cash commitment of between 25% and 33% at the close, with additional capital to be invested at some future date or dates (for example, 25% each year). The venture capitalists exercise considerable control over the timing of capital infusions by the limited partners.

If limited partners renege on a funding commitment, severe penalties are imposed on the ownership percentages associated with the partners' earlier investments and their ability to withdraw already invested funds. The kinds of penalties imposed vary considerably, though a common clause calls for the limited partner to forfeit one-half of the partner's capital account in the partnership and therefore one-half of the profits to which the partner would have been entitled.

4.5. Compensation

Venture-capital management companies typically receive compensation from two sources for managing the investments in each limited partnership. They are entitled to a management fee, and they receive some percentage of the profits over the life of each fund. More than 50% of the contracts surveyed by Venture Economics call for an annual management fee equal to 2.5% of committed capital through the life of the fund. Most of the remaining partnerships base the management fee on capital committed, though the formula varies. Only seven of the funds base the fee directly on the estimated value of the portfolio. Typically the base management fee increases annually by the rate of consumer price inflation. The survey finds little evidence that the percentage fee declines with the amount of capital under management.

In 88% of the funds surveyed, venture capitalists are entitled to 20% of the realized gains on the fund. In the remaining partnerships, the general partner's share of realized gains ranges from 15% to 30%. Given the diversity of fund organizers and their differing stated purposes, this seems remarkably consistent, in sharp contrast to the widely varying contract terms found in oil and gas partnerships [Wolfson (1985)].

4.6. Distributions

Half of the partnership agreements studied by Venture Economics require annual distributions from realized profits. In 18% of the agreements, the general partners state their intentions to make annual distributions, whereas the remaining partnerships leave the issue of distribution to the discretion of the general partners.

In 29% of the contracts studied, the general partners are entitled to take their profit participation (called the 'carried interest') – in income or gains without restriction. In the other partnerships the general partners are not entitled to take the carried interest until the limited partners have received an amount at least equal to their cumulative capital contribution.

General partners generally have the option to make distributions in the form of securities, cash, or both. Often when a portfolio company becomes successful, its shares are registered with the SEC and a public offering takes place [see Barry et al. (1990)]. Typically, the venture-capital firm does not or cannot liquidate its shareholdings on the offering. The shares can be distributed to the limited partners in proportion to their ownership of the fund, or the fund can continue to hold the shares, taking responsibility for distributing them at some future date, or converting them to cash through a transaction such as a secondary offering. If the shares are distributed to the limited partners, the value assigned is the last price in the stock market before the distribution.

4.7. Reporting and accounting policies

All venture-capital firms surveyed agree to provide the limited partners with periodic reports on the value and progress of portfolio companies, including an annual meeting with the general partners and selected portfolio-company management teams. Because most investments are made in private companies with highly uncertain prospects, assigning values is very difficult. Often the partners agree to recognize losses quickly and to write up the value of an investment only if there is a significant arms-length transaction at a higher value. If no such transactions have occurred and no loss seems likely, cost is used as a basis for reporting. As a result of these policies, most venture-capital firms report negative rates of return during the first few years of the fund [see also Venture Economics (1988c)].

4.8. Specific conflicts of interest

Most contracts specify the percentage of time the venture capitalists propose to devote to the management of the fund being raised. A small number of partnership agreements restrict the ability of general partners to coinvest or receive securities from portfolio companies. Some partnerships restrict follow-on funds from investing in securities held by a previous fund managed by the same venture capitalists. Other fund agreements prevent the general partner from raising a new fund until some percentage (for example,

50%) of the capital raised in the existing fund has been invested in portfolio companies.

4.9. Special advisory committees

Of the 76 funds studied by Venture Economics (1987), 41 establish formal advisory boards; another 17 create informal advisory boards. Of those with formal advisory boards, 19 require limited-partner representation. An additional 18 funds establish boards composed solely of representatives of the limited partners; these boards are separate and distinct from the advisory board.

Advisory boards and boards composed of limited partners are often designed to provide access to deals or technical expertise. Some boards are structured like traditional boards of directors, providing guidance and oversight for the operation of the venture-capital fund. Still other advisory committees are assigned specific responsibilities, the most important of which is determining the value of the portfolio.

5. Analyzing the relationship between external investors and venture capitalists

Venture capitalists act as agents for the limited partners, who choose to invest in entrepreneurial ventures through an intermediary rather than directly. In such situations, conflicts arise between the agent and the principal, which must be addressed in the contracts and other mechanisms that govern their relationship.

In the venture-capital industry, the agency problem is likely to be particularly difficult. There is inevitably a high degree of information asymmetry between the venture capitalists, who play an active role in the portfolio companies, and the limited partners, who cannot monitor the prospects of each individual investment as closely.

The contractual provisions outlined in section 4 can be explained as attempts to resolve the agency problem, the operating cost problem, and the sorting problem simultaneously.

5.1. Agency costs

Venture capitalists have many opportunities to take advantage of the people who invest with them. To a degree, the agency problem is exacerbated by the legal structure of limited partnerships, which prevents limited partners from playing a role in the management of the venture-capital partnership.

Contracts are designed with several key provisions to protect the limited partners from the possibility that the venture capitalists will make decisions against their interests. First, the life of a venture-capital fund is limited; the venture capitalist cannot keep the money forever. Organizational models like mutual funds or corporations, in contrast, have indefinite life spans. Implicitly, the investors also preserve the right not to invest in any later fund managed by the same venture capitalists.

Second, the limited partners preserve the right to withdraw from funding the partnership by reneging on their commitments to invest beyond the initial capital infusion as described in section 4.4. Third, the compensation system is structured to give the venture capitalists the appropriate incentives. The fund managers are typically entitled to receive 20% of the profits generated by the fund. For reasons which will be explored more fully below, the profit participation and other aspects of the contract encourage the venture capitalist to allocate the management fee to activities that will increase the total value of the portfolio.

Fourth, the mandatory distribution policy defuses potential differences of opinion about what to do with the proceeds from the sale of assets in the portfolio. The general partners cannot choose to invest in securities that serve their own private interests at the expense of the limited partners.

Finally, the contract addresses obvious areas of conflict between the venture capitalist and the limited partner. Thus, the venture capitalist is often explicitly prohibited from self-dealing (for example, being able to buy stock in the portfolio on preferential terms or receiving distributions different from those given to the limited partner). Also, the venture capitalists are contractually required to commit a certain percentage of their effort to the activities of the fund. Although this requirement is difficult to monitor, egregious violations can be the subject of litigation if fund performance is poor.

5.2. Further analysis of the compensation system

The compensation system plays a critical role in aligning the interests of the venture capitalists and the limited partners. To understand the implicit incentives, consider a $200 million fund with eight general partners that receives a management fee of 2.5% of total capital committed. Annual revenues are $5 million and revenues per partner are $625,000. Various expenses must be subtracted, including partner base salaries, office expenses, travel, insurance, and support staff. A reasonable estimate of the partners' base pay is $250,000 per year per partner, equivalent to 40% of total revenues. An informal survey of five venture-capital firms with this amount of capital under management revealed that the firm can be expected to clear a profit each year. If total expenses are 2.1% of the capital committed (the average reported in the informal survey), the annual operating profit is $800,000, or $100,000 per partner. Such profits are typically distributed to partners at the end of the year as a bonus.

If this hypothetical $200 million fund is successful and achieves a 20% rate of return on committed capital over its five-year duration (before consideration of the profit participation but after taking into account the management fee), the ending value will be approximately $498 million. The general partners will be entitled to 20% of the $298 million profit, or $59 million, equivalent to $7.4 million per partner. This figure translates to a $4.2 million present value per partner, assuming payment at the end of the last year and a 10% discount rate, or roughly $1.2 million per year per partner on a comparable annuity basis (also assuming a 10% discount rate). This figure far outweighs each general partner's combined base salary and annual bonus, estimated at $350,000 per year. An extra 1% in compound rate of return increases the present value of the carried interest from $4.2 million to $4.5 million, based on the assumptions used earlier. As long as the compound annual rate of return on the fund is positive, the percentage increase in the venture capitalists' share exceeds the percentage increase in the total value of the portfolio.[7]

Gathering hard data on venture-capital compensation is very difficult: many firms do not reveal key statistics about their business. According to a survey of 63 private independent venture-capital firms with over $5 billion in total committed capital in 1988 [Hay Management Consultants (1988)], how-ever, the average 1987 base pay of a managing partner of a private, independent venture-capital firm was $223,000. The annual operating bonus was $51,000 and the average realized profits distribution was $163,000, resulting in total compensation of $437,000. These figures are not as dramatic as the simple numerical calculation used above, which accurately reflects the data provided by the four venture firms interviewed specifically about compensation. Also, the Hay Management Consultants data are difficult to interpret in light of the poor overall returns for most venture-capital funds in 1987 and the tendency for general partners to defer as long as possible the recognition of income for tax purposes. Nevertheless, the carried interest component of compensation is large in relation to the other components.[8] The implication is that the venture capitalists have incentives to engage in activities that increase the value of the carried interest, which is precisely what benefits the limited partners.

[7]These calculations ignore the return the venture capitalists receive on their direct investments in the partnership (for example, on the 1% investment described in section 4.2).

[8]The informal survey cited earlier also revealed that a number of successful venture-capital firms operate on an annual budget, which is negotiated each year with the limited partners. Examples include Greylock, Sutter Hill, and Charles River Partners. In these firms, the partners receive modest cash salaries and the venture-capital management company does not realize an annual profit. The partners are dependent on the carried interest to supplement current salaries. It is difficult to find evidence of a correlation between compensation structures and performance, however. For example, one highly regarded firm, Kleiner Perkins, receives a management fee of 3% and a carried interest percentage of 30%.

Although the compensation system seems to provide appropriate incentives, there are some difficult issues. One area of potential conflict between the limited and general partners relates to risk. The venture capitalist's equity participation may be thought of as an option that entitles the venture-capital management firm to 20% of the increase in value of the underlying fund. The exercise price of the option is the cost basis of the fund, and the life of the option equals the life of the fund.

Numerical analyses, based on a simple Black–Scholes model, suggest that the ex ante value of the venture-capital contract might be as high as 10% of the initial total capital of the fund. Thus the value of the contract on a $100 million fund might be $10 million at the time of signing. Table 5 presents estimates of the value of the contract (as a fraction of the original cost of the fund assets) based on different assumptions about the volatility of returns, current fund value, the carried interest percentage, and the life of the fund.

The fact that the management contract can be viewed as an option suggests the inherent agency problem: if one party has a contingent claim on value, there is an implicit incentive to increase risk [Myers (1986)]. The value of the contingent claim increases as risk increases. In the example above, the value of the contract would rise from approximately $13.2 million to $16 million if the assumed annual volatility were increased from 50% to 80%. In some situations, it will pay a venture capitalist to make negative-net-present-value investments because doing so increases the value of the option by more than the loss in value on his portion of the equity claim.

Partnership agreements respond in several ways to the possibility that the venture capitalist will take undue risks. Since the contract can be cancelled by the limited partners at any point in the life of the fund, the venture capitalist's incentive to incur such uncompensated risks is reduced. Although this solution helps resolve the agency problem from the limited partners' perspective, however, it can be abused. In one situation [Sahlman (1988c)], for example, a contract was cancelled by the sole limited partner after three years of a ten-year term. At the time of cancellation, the estimated value of the fund's underlying assets was close to the cost of those assets. The contract stipulated that the only payment due the venture-capital management company by the limited partner upon cancellation was the 20% share of estimated realized and unrealized gains on the portfolio. The limited partner was not contractually required to pay anything to the venture-capital management company for canceling the contract per se, even though from an option-valuation perspective the contract was clearly valuable. Most contracts, however, make cancellation more difficult than this (for example, by defining a narrow set of circumstances – such as fraud – under which the general partner can be fired).

Other mechanisms are also used to manage the perverse incentives of the contract. For example, the partnership agreement usually limits the amount

Table 5

Sensitivity of the present value of the carried interest of a venture-capital fund (as a fraction of original cost) to changes in volatility, current market value of fund assets, carried interest percentage, and life of the fund.

Assumptions:

Total original capital of the fund (cost)	$100,000,000
Current market value of fund assets	$100,000,000
Profit participation % – Carried interest	20%
Time to maturity – Economic life in years	7
Risk-free interest rate	10.0%
Volatility – Standard deviation of annual returns	50.0%

Results:

Estimated present value of carried interest	13,212,516
Estimated value of carried interest as a % of original capital (cost)	13.2%

Present value of the carried interest as a fraction of the original capital of the fund as a function of volatility and the current market value of the fund assets

Volatility	Current market value of fund (millions)						
	$70.00	$80.00	$90.00	$100.00	$110.00	$120.00	$130.00
10.0%	4.2%	6.1%	8.1%	10.1%	12.1%	14.1%	16.1%
20.0%	5.0%	6.7%	8.5%	10.4%	12.3%	14.2%	16.2%
30.0%	6.0%	7.7%	9.4%	11.2%	13.0%	14.9%	16.7%
40.0%	7.1%	8.7%	10.4%	12.2%	14.0%	15.8%	17.6%
50.0%	8.1%	9.8%	11.5%	13.2%	15.0%	16.8%	18.6%
60.0%	9.0%	10.7%	12.5%	14.2%	16.0%	17.8%	19.7%
70.0%	9.9%	11.6%	13.4%	15.2%	17.0%	18.8%	20.7%
80.0%	10.6%	12.4%	14.2%	16.0%	17.9%	19.7%	21.6%
90.0%	11.3%	13.1%	14.9%	16.8%	18.7%	20.5%	22.4%

Table 5 (continued)

Present value of the carried interest as a fraction of the original capital of the fund as a function of volatility and the profit participation – Carried interest (%)

Volatility	Profit participation – Carried interest (%)						
	5.0%	10.0%	15.0%	20.0%	25.0%	30.0%	35.0%
10.0%	2.5%	5.0%	7.6%	10.1%	12.6%	15.1%	17.6%
20.0%	2.6%	5.2%	7.8%	10.4%	13.0%	15.6%	18.2%
30.0%	2.8%	5.6%	8.4%	11.2%	14.0%	16.8%	19.5%
40.0%	3.0%	6.1%	9.1%	12.2%	15.2%	18.3%	21.3%
50.0%	3.3%	6.6%	9.9%	13.2%	16.5%	19.8%	23.1%
60.0%	3.6%	7.1%	10.7%	14.2%	17.8%	21.3%	24.9%
70.0%	3.8%	7.6%	11.4%	15.2%	19.0%	22.8%	26.6%
80.0%	4.0%	8.0%	12.0%	16.0%	20.0%	24.0%	28.1%
90.0%	4.2%	8.4%	12.6%	16.8%	21.0%	25.2%	29.4%

Present value of the carried interest as a fraction of the original capital of the fund as a function of volatility and the time to maturity (life) of the fund

Volatility	Time to maturity – Life (years)						
	2.5	4.0	5.5	7.0	8.5	10.0	11.5
10.0%	4.5%	6.6%	8.5%	10.1%	11.5%	12.6%	13.7%
20.0%	5.1%	7.1%	8.9%	10.4%	11.7%	12.8%	13.8%
30.0%	6.0%	8.0%	9.7%	11.2%	12.4%	13.4%	14.3%
40.0%	7.0%	9.1%	10.8%	12.2%	13.3%	14.3%	15.1%
50.0%	7.9%	10.1%	11.8%	13.2%	14.3%	15.2%	16.0%
60.0%	8.9%	11.2%	12.9%	14.2%	15.3%	16.1%	16.8%
70.0%	9.9%	12.2%	13.9%	15.2%	16.2%	16.9%	17.5%
80.0%	10.8%	13.2%	14.8%	16.0%	16.9%	17.6%	18.1%
90.0%	11.6%	14.0%	15.7%	16.8%	17.6%	18.2%	18.6%

of capital that can be invested in a single venture, which prevents excessive investments in high-risk ventures with inadequate rewards. As mentioned earlier, many contracts call for mandatory distributions of realized gains. If venture capitalists were allowed to invest realized gains in new ventures, they might increase the risk to the fund without a commensurate increase in return. Mandatory distributions also protect the principals against activities not consistent with the goals of the fund.

One final contractual response to the problem of risk is to force the general partner to invest more in the fund than the customary small amounts mentioned earlier. Then the venture capitalists bear a greater share of the costs of investing in ventures that perform poorly. On the other hand, the risk problem will be intensified if the venture capitalist is required to pay a fee up front for the right to manage the funds of the limited partners.[9] This has the effect of making the excise price on the option higher. The same basic problem arises if there is a rate-of-return hurdle that has to be exceeded before the venture capitalist is entitled to a carried interest. In this case, the exercise price of the option rises each year, which means that an increase in risk has a significant payoff to the option holder.

One other area of concern in the compensation system used in the venture-capital organization relates to incentives to increase the amount of capital under management and/or to manage multiple pools of capital over time. The basic issues are discussed in the next section.

5.3. Operating costs

Two kinds of operating costs deserve analysis when discussing venture capital, taxes, and continuing operating costs. With respect to taxes, partnership gains are not subject to partnership-level taxation. The limited and general partners report the realized gains and losses on their individual tax returns. Second, securities can be distributed without triggering immediate taxable income for the recipient. Thus a limited partner who receives stock in a portfolio company can defer recognizing the gain (or loss) until that security is sold. Third, the venture capitalists do not incur taxable income when they receive their carried interest in the partnership: they report taxable income only as gains and losses are realized on the underlying securities.

Finally, the partnership's compensation scheme can be structured to allocate losses to those who can make best use of them. This feature of partnerships has been used widely in structuring oil-and-gas partnerships [Wolfson (1985)] and research-and-development limited partnerships. Tax

---

[9]In a number of cases, venture-capital management firms have been purchased. Examples include Ampersand Ventures, TA Associates, and Brinson Partners.

incentives in venture capital are less important, however, because many of the investors in venture funds are tax-exempt. More importantly, there are no significant tax losses to be allocated because a fund's unrealized losses are not recognized by the IRS for tax purposes unless the underlying securities are transferred to another party in an arms-length transaction. Often partnerships do allocate these losses to the limited partners, but the economic impact is minimal.

With respect to operating costs, scale economies, scope economies, and learning-curve effects are often very significant to a venture-capital management company that manages one or more funds. Scale economies exist if the unit cost of production and distribution of a product or service declines as volume increases. In the venture-capital organization, production and distribution encompass raising capital, finding and structuring deals, monitoring the investments, and distributing the proceeds. Scope economies exist if unit costs decline if multiple products or services are produced simultaneously (for example, if more than one fund is managed at a time). Learning-curve effects exist if the unit cost of a process declines over time with accumulated volume.

With respect to scale economies, it seems likely that unit costs decline with the absolute size of the venture-capital pool under management because there are a number of fixed (or near-fixed) costs, including items in the overhead budget such as rent, information acquisition, accounting, and certain legal costs. Economies of scope are also likely because the cost of managing multiple pools of capital does not rise linearly with the number of such pools.

Finally, with respect to learning-curve effects, venture-capital firms become repositories of useful institutional knowledge. Venture capitalists and their support staffs benefit from learning-curve effects as they become adept in dealing with each other and with other resource suppliers, such as law firms, accounting firms, investment bankers, and management recruiting firms. They cultivate a deal flow based on networks of contacts and relationships. The venture-capital organization develops a reputation that has economic value. The ultimate effect is to make the firm more efficient as time passes and experience accumulates.

Compensation practices give evidence of scale and/or scope economies as well as experience effects. According to the Hay Management Consultants (1988) survey, the total compensation for the managing partner of a venture-capital fund with less than $25 million in capital averages $163,000. The comparable figure for a managing partner of a fund with more than $200 million under management is $581,000. The annual bonus, which is based on the operating profit of the management company rather than the investment performance of the fund, constitutes 28% of total compensation in the larger funds, compared with 17% in the small funds. These differences suggest that venture capitalists have an incentive to increase the size of the firm. One driving factor in this regard is the fact that the percentage fee charged to manage a venture-capital fund does not appear to decline with the size of the fund [see Venture Economics (1987)].

There can also be incentives to create multiple funds over time, all managed by the same venture capitalists. Doing so accomplishes two goals. First, keeping the venture-capital management company in existence preserves the learning that has taken place. Second, managing multiple funds takes advantage of any scale or scope economies. From 1977 to 1988, new funds averaged less than one-half the size of follow-on funds (panel B, table 1).

Even though unit costs decline as the size of the venture-capital management firm (or number of funds under management) increases, the limited partners and general partners will not necessarily agree about the optimal size and structure of the firm. This is because the unit costs and risk-adjusted rates of return to the limited partners may be negatively correlated, and because the limited and general partners do not have equal stakes in all the income streams generated by the fund. There could easily be situations in which the venture capitalists find it more profitable to have a large firm, one effect of which is lower returns to the limited partners. This would be true if there were diseconomies of scale or scope in the investment-return-generating process.

The possibility that the interests of the general and limited partners will diverge over time is addressed directly by limiting the lifespan of the venture-capital partnership. If the venture capitalists make decisions that aren't in the best interests of the limited partners, they can be denied access to capital. Any learning, scale, or scope economies will then go to waste. The ability to withdraw funding support is the ultimate tool for aligning the interests of the agent and principal in this organizational form, and is reinforced by the existence of the scale or scope economies and learning-curve effects.

5.4. The sorting problem

The final component of this analysis of the economic relationship between the limited partners and the venture capitalists is an examination of how limited partners decide which venture capitalists to back. For obvious reasons, filtering out the 'good' from the 'bad' venture capitalists is extremely important. 'Good' venture capitalists have the skill and intention to generate high risk-adjusted rates of return for the limited partners. Actual rates of return will also depend, of course, on such factors as the capital markets, competition among venture capitalists, and the market for innovation.

502   *W. A. Sahlman, Structure of venture-capital organizations*

Limited partners in venture-capital firms typically invest at least $1 million in each fund. Before committing this amount of capital, the investors spend resources on due diligence. They read the offering memoranda prepared by the venture capitalists in accordance with SEC regulations, and they often check the venture capitalists' credentials. This investigation acts as a preliminary screen on potential investments.

The governance structure also helps potential investors distinguish between good venture capitalists and weak ones. The basic argument is simple: good venture capitalists are more likely than weak venture capitalists to accept a finite life for each new partnership and a compensation system heavily dependent on investment returns. By doing so, they agree explicitly to have their performance reviewed at least every few years: if they engage in opportunistic acts or are incompetent, they will be denied access to funds. In addition, most of their expected compensation comes from a share in the fund's profits. If they perform well, they will participate handsomely in the fund's success. They will also be rewarded by being able to raise additional capital and, most likely, benefit from the various economies characteristic of the business. If they are not confident of performing well, or if they intend to neglect the interests of the limited partners, they will probably not agree to the basic terms of the contract.[10]

5.5. The overall incentives

In sum, the relationship between the limited and general partners in a venture-capital fund is fraught with agency problems. The limited partners structure a contract that creates incentives for mutual gain, and they specifically forbid certain obvious acts of self-interest like buying stock in portfolio companies at prices less than those paid by the fund. The limited partners then expend resources to monitor the fund's progress, often through special committees. At the same time the venture capitalists agree to forego certain self-interested acts and to supply information to the limited partners. The venture capitalists willingly enter into an agreement with a finite life, exposing the contract to renewal. In effect, the limited partners stage the commitment of capital to the venture capitalists while preserving mechanisms to ensure that the profits will be distributed rather than kept inside the venture-capital fund. And the terms of the contract both communicate the

---

[10]This description of the incentives of the venture capitalists is drawn from the signaling literature [Spence (1973), Ross (1977), Leland and Pyle (1977), and Bhattacharya (1979)]. The implicit condition for the sorting process to work is that the short-term payoff (in present-value terms) to the venture capitalist must be less than the opportunity cost for a 'bad' venture capitalist. Note also that each limited partner spends time and resources researching venture capitalists seeking to raise funds, which helps guard against false signaling. From another perspective, accepting these terms may be viewed as a bonding commitment by the venture capitalist, who implicitly agrees not to divert money from the fund.

expectations of the limited partners to the venture capitalists, and filter out those who are unable or unwilling to meet those expectations.

The contracts and operating procedures that have evolved in the venture-capital industry address three issues simultaneously: sorting good from bad venture capitalists, minimizing the present value of agency costs, and minimizing the present value of operating costs. The same basic issues confront the venture capitalists when they invest in entrepreneurial ventures. In this case, the venture capitalists become the principals and the entrepreneurs the agents. Analogous contractual and operating responses to these issues are made by the venture-capital fund.

6. The venture-capital investment process

Once a venture-capital fund is raised, the venture capitalists must identify investment opportunities, structure and execute deals with entrepreneurial teams, monitor investments, and ultimately achieve some return on their capital. For the purposes of this paper, I focus on structuring deals.

Just as venture-capital partnerships have many elements in common, the contracts between the venture capitalists and the companies they invest in are similar in many ways. The basic document that governs the relationship between the venture-capital firm and the venture is the stock-purchase agreement, which is described below.[11] The economic rationale for the terms and conditions of this document and other aspects of the venture-capital process are explored in section 7.

6.1. Amount and timing

Each stock-purchase agreement fixes the amount and timing of the investment. Venture capitalists typically invest more than once during the life of a company, and the amount invested often increases with each round (see tables 3 and 4). They expect the capital invested at each point to be sufficient to take the company to the next stage of development, when it will require additional capital to make further progress.

---

[11]This account of stock-purchase agreements is drawn from a number of sources. First, I have gathered approximately 40 such agreements from a broad range of venture-capital partnerships. Venture capitalists tend to use the same deal structure in all of their deals so that knowing how one deal is structured sheds light on many investments made by the same fund. Some of these materials have formed the basis for case studies used at Harvard Business School, including Knights and Sahlman (1986a, 1986b, 1986c, 1986d), Sahlman (1983a, 1983b, 1984, 1985a, 1985b, 1985c, 1985d, 1985e, 1986a, 1986b, 1986c, 1986d, 1988c, 1989b), Sahlman and Knights (1986), Sahlman and Scherlis (1988), Sahlman and Soussou (1985a, 1985b), and Soussou and Sahlman (1986). See also Sahlman (1988). A broad survey of the characteristics of deals struck by venture-capital firms is included in Plummer (1987). Finally, a number of texts describe standard operating procedures in the industry, including Bartlett (1988) and Morris (1988a).

6.2. Form and terms of investment

Many venture-capital investments are made as purchases of convertible preferred stock. Specific terms concern:

(1) conversion price, which can vary according to the performance of the company;
(2) liquidation preference, including a description of the events that trigger liquidation (for example, a merger or reorganization with a total value less than some predetermined amount);
(3) dividend rate, payment terms, and voting rights (typically on an as-if-converted basis).

Typically, the convertible preferred stock does not pay a dividend on a current basis, but at the discretion of the board of directors. Some preferreds have provisions that call for accruing dividends but deferring the payment of cash. The liquidation preference amount is equal in most cases to the face amount of the convertible preferred issue and all accrued but unpaid dividends.

6.3. Puts and calls

Agreements typically give the venture capitalists the right to put the security by calling for redemption of the preferred stock. Less frequently, contracts give portfolio-company management the right to call the security away from the venture capitalists at some point.

6.4. Registration rights

Most agreements give the venture capitalists the right to register their shares at some point or points in the future. This enables the venture capitalists to demand registration at any two dates in the future, with the expenses of registration paid by the company. Venture capitalists also insist on piggyback registration rights that entitle them to register shares at the same time as the company, subject to limitations imposed by the SEC and the underwriters.

6.5. Go-along rights

Many agreements specify that the venture capitalists can sell shares after conversion at the same time and on the same terms as the key employees.

6.6. Preemptive rights and rights of first refusal

Many agreements entitle the venture-capital investors to participate in new financings by buying newly issued shares from the company, often in proportion to their common-stock-equivalent holdings before the issuance of new equity-equivalent shares. The terms of such financing rounds are not typically negotiated in advance; they reflect the then-current conditions in the capital markets and the performance and prospects of the firm.

6.7. Option pool

Most agreements fix the number of shares outstanding and the size of the pool of shares that can be granted or sold to current and future employees. Provisions for modifying the option pool are also included in the stock-purchase agreement.

6.8. Employment contracts

Most agreements require that key employees execute employment contracts and agree to noncompete clauses. Such contracts usually specify compensation, benefits, and, most important, the conditions under which the contract can be terminated and the consequences of termination.

6.9. Vesting schedules and buy-back provisions

Employees of venture-capital-backed companies often accept modest cash salaries in return for equity ownership. Many agreements set explicit vesting schedules for management shares and also grant the company being financed the right to repurchase shares in the event of an employee's voluntary or involuntary departure. When shares are repurchased under these agreements, the price paid by the company to the departing entrepreneur is often based on book value, which may be below market value.

6.10. Information rights

Most agreements call for regular transmission of information, including financial statements and budgets, and permit the venture capitalists to inspect the company's financial accounts at will. Venture capitalists insist on timely access to such information. They typically receive detailed monthly financial statements and more frequent operating statements. They evaluate this information to anticipate problems and respond expeditiously when performance falls short.

6.11. Board structure

Most agreements call for venture capitalist representation on the company's board of directors [see Barry et al. (1990) for information on venture-capitalist board representation of companies going public]. Often, the agreement calls for other mutually acceptable people to be elected to the board. The venture capitalists typically receive no cash compensation for board duties; if any cash is received for board membership, it is paid into the partnership. Outside members recruited to join the board usually receive inexpensive common stock or warrants to acquire shares, and little or no cash compensation.

7. The relationship between the venture capitalists and the entrepreneurial ventures

Each year venture capitalists screen hundreds of investment proposals before deciding which ideas and teams to support. The success or failure of any given venture depends on the effort and skill of the people involved as well as on certain factors outside their control (for example, the economy), but the capabilities of the individuals involved are difficult to gauge up front.

Once investment decisions are made and deals consummated, it is difficult to monitor progress. The probability of failure is high (see fig. 1, which shows that 34.5% of the capital invested in the survey resulted in a loss). The venture capitalist and the entrepreneur are also likely to have different information. Even with the same information, they are likely to disagree on certain issues, including if and when to abandon a venture and how and when to cash in on investments.

Venture capitalists attack these problems in several ways. First, they structure their investments so they can keep firm control. The most important mechanism for controlling the venture is staging the infusion of capital. Second, they devise compensation schemes that provide venture managers with appropriate incentives. Third, they become actively involved in managing the companies they fund, in effect functioning as consultants. Finally, venture capitalists preserve mechanisms to make their investments liquid.

7.1. Staging the commitment of capital and other control mechanisms

Venture capitalists rarely, if ever, invest all the external capital that a company will require to accomplish its business plan: instead, they invest in companies at distinct stages in their development. As a result, each company begins life knowing that it has only enough capital to reach the next stage. By staging capital the venture capitalists preserve the right to abandon a project whose prospects look dim. The right to abandon is essential because an entrepreneur will almost never stop investing in a failing project as long as others are providing capital.

Staging the capital also provides incentives to the entrepreneurial team. Capital is a scarce and expensive resource for individual ventures. Misuse of capital is very costly to venture capitalists but not necessarily to management. To encourage managers to conserve capital, venture-capital firms apply strong sanctions if it is misused. These sanctions ordinarily take two basic forms. First, increased capital requirements invariably dilute management's equity share at an increasingly punitive rate. (This was the case with Federal Express). Second, the staged investment process enables venture-capital firms to shut down operations completely. The credible threat to abandon a venture, even when the firm might be economically viable, is the key to the relationship between the entrepreneur and the venture capitalist [see also Stiglitz and Weiss (1983) for a similar argument in the banking industry].[12] By denying capital, the venture capitalist also signals other capital suppliers that the company in question is a bad investment risk.

Short of denying the company capital, venture capitalists can discipline wayward managers by firing or demoting them. Other elements of the stock-purchase agreement then come into play. For example, the company typically has the right to repurchase shares from departing managers, often at prices below market value (for example, at book value). The use of vesting schedules limits the number of shares employees are entitled to if they leave prematurely. Finally, noncompete clauses can impose strong penalties on those who leave, particularly if their human capital is closely linked to the industry in which the venture is active.

Entrepreneurs accept the staged capital process because they usually have great confidence in their own abilities to meet targets. They understand that if they meet those goals, they will end up owning a significantly larger share of the company than if they had insisted on receiving all of the capital up front. As discussed below, entrepreneurs also must make conscious choices about who provides capital and what value they can add in addition to capital.

Finally, whereas venture capitalists insist on retaining the option to abandon a particular venture, they also want to be able to invest more if the company requires and warrants additional capital. This option is preserved by insisting on rights of first refusal or pre-emptive rights.

---

[12] The seemingly irrational act of shutting down an economically viable entity is rational when viewed from the perspective of the venture capitalist confronted with allocating time and capital among various projects. Although the individual company may be economically viable, the return on time and capital to the individual venture capitalist is less than the opportunity cost, which is why the venture is terminated.

7.2. The compensation scheme

Entrepreneurs who accept venture capital typically take smaller cash salaries than they could earn in the labor market. The shortfall in current income is offset by stock ownership in the ventures they start. Common stock and any subsequent stock options received will not pay off, however, unless the company creates value and affords an opportunity to convert illiquid holdings to cash. In this regard, the interests of the venture-capital investor and entrepreneur are aligned.

This compensation system penalizes poor performance by an employee. If the employee is terminated, all unvested shares or options are returned to the company. In almost all cases, the company retains the right to repurchase shares from the employee at predetermined prices.

Without sanctions, entrepreneurs might sometimes have an incentive to increase risk without an adequate increase in return. An entrepreneur's compensation package can be viewed as a contingent claim, whose value increases with volatility. The sanctions, combined with the venture capitalists' active role in the management of the venture, helps to mitigate the incentive to increase risk.

7.3. Active involvement of venture capitalists in portfolio companies

No contract between an entrepreneur and venture capitalist can anticipate every possible disagreement or conflict. Partly for this reason, the venture capitalist typically plays a role in the operation of the company.

Venture capitalists sit on boards of directors, help recruit and compensate key individuals, work with suppliers and customers, help establish tactics and strategy, play a major role in raising capital, and help structure transactions such as mergers and acquisitions. They often assume more direct control by changing management and are sometimes willing to take over day-to-day operations themselves. All of these activities are designed to increase the likelihood of success and improve return on investment: they also protect the interests of the venture capitalist and ameliorate the information asymmetry.

According to one survey [Gorman and Sahlman (1989)], lead venture investors visit each portfolio company an average of 19 times per year, and spend 100 hours in direct contact (on site or by phone) with the company. Since each venture capitalist in the survey is responsible for almost nine investments and sits on five boards of directors, the allocation of time to each portfolio company is considerable [see also MacMillan et al. (1989) and Timmons (1987)]. In addition to devoting time to companies already in the portfolio, a venture capitalist must allocate time to raising capital for the venture-capital firm, finding new deals, managing the venture-capital firm, and meeting with various resource suppliers, such as bankers and accountants.

Successful venture capitalists bring instant credibility associated with their capital, their contacts, and their range of projects. A venture-capital-backed company can often gain access to more capital from the fund itself, and the venture capitalist's contacts in the financial community can make it easier to raise new capital from other sources. In addition, resource suppliers form implicit and explicit relationships with venture capitalists in an attempt to piggyback on the data-gathering and monitoring process [see the HBS cases Sahlman (1986d, 1985e) and Knights and Sahlman (1986b)]. Venture capitalists have incentives not to exploit a resource supplier on any individual deal, since the repercussions can affect other deals. At the same time, the resource suppliers have incentives to preserve their relationship with venture-capital firms by avoiding opportunistic behavior on individual deals.

Finally, venture capitalists maintain close ties to investment bankers who can assist companies going public or merging with other companies [Barry et al. (1990)]. Venture capitalists also often have contacts in large companies to which entrepreneurial ventures might be sold.

7.4. Mechanisms related to liquidity

Both venture capitalists and entrepreneurs want eventually to convert their illiquid holdings into cash or cash equivalents, but they can disagree on the timing or the method. The standard stock-purchase agreement has a number of features that control the process by which the venture capitalists and the entrepreneurs achieve their goals. Chief among these is the decision to invest in the form of a convertible preferred.

Using preferred stock with a dividend creates a mechanism for deriving some income from an investment if the company is only marginally successful. Most deals defer payment of the dividend until the board allows it, but because venture capitalists often control the board, they can make the decision. Since the dividends are not tax-deductible, the burden of paying dividends is often onerous, which often leads the entrepreneurs to try to buy out the preferred.

Many agreements also give the venture capitalists the right to force redemption of a preferred stock or the right to put the stock to the company, to achieve liquidity. This option may be exercised if the company is financially viable but too small to go public. Some contracts give entrepreneurs the right to sell stock back to the venture capitalist, as might happen if the venture capitalists terminate the entrepreneur's employment without cause.

Finally, venture capitalists are concerned about situations where the entrepreneurs have an opportunity to sell their shares before the venture capitalists sell theirs. Therefore, the contract typically specifies that the venture capitalists can sell their shares at the same time and on the same terms as the entrepreneur.

7.5. Additional implications of using convertible preferred stock

Using a convertible preferred also provides flexibility in setting the conversion terms. The venture capitalist often can base the conversion ratio for the preferred stock on the company's performance. If the company does well, the conversion price might be higher, with lower dilution for the management team. A similar tool is the 'ratchet', which ensures that the effective price per share paid by the venture capitalist is at least as low as any price paid in the future.

Flexible conversion terms alter the risk-and-reward-sharing scheme. One intent is to discourage entrepreneurs from overstating their projections to increase the initial valuation, and to encourage them to build value. Incorporating these provisions into contracts also serves as a negotiating tool to account for differences of opinion about future prospects.[13]

One final consequence of having preferred stock in the capital structure relates to taxation: using a preferred creates two kinds of securities, one with superior rights. A security that is senior in rights to common stock in effect lowers the economic value of the common. Members of the management team can therefore buy the common stock at low prices without incurring taxable income. Common-stock value is frequently set at 10% of the conversion price of the preferred. If the common stock had the same rights as the preferred, the managers would have to report taxable income on the difference between the price they paid and the price paid by the venture capitalists. There is no immediate tax disadvantage to using preferred stock, however, because the dividend is deferred and many of the ultimate recipients are tax exempt.

7.6. Using the contract to sort out entrepreneurs

A key feature of the contracts and operating procedures is that risk is shifted from the venture capitalists to the entrepreneur. The entrepreneur's response to these terms enables the venture capitalist to make informed evaluations and judgments. It would be foolish for entrepreneurs to accept such contract terms if they were not truly confident of their own abilities and deeply committed to the venture.

For example, by substituting stock ownership for higher current income, the contract shifts the risks of poor performance to the entrepreneur. Similarly, the convertible preferred security shifts some of the costs of poor performance to the entrepreneurial team. Given the liquidation preference

---

[13]See Knights and Sahlman (1986b) for a description of a conditional conversion price. In that situation, the venture capitalists agreed to increase the conversion price (from $0.45 to $0.67) if the company met its business-plan sales-and-profit targets.

Table 6[a]

Stage	Discount rate range (%)
Startup	50 to 70
First stage	40 to 60
Second stage	35 to 50
Third stage	35 to 50
Fourth stage	30 to 40
IPO	25 to 35

[a]*Source:* Plummer (1987, p. I-18).

embodied in the security, the venture capitalists will be entitled to a larger share of total value if total value is low.

Moreover, the entrepreneurs typically hold undiversified portfolios. Much of their wealth is invested in the securities of the company they manage. The entrepreneur's willingness to bear diversifiable risk also conveys useful information to the venture capitalists.

7.7. Evaluation techniques

The methods venture capitalists use to judge the prospects of individual projects are also used to sort out entrepreneurs. In screening potential ventures, venture capitalists use certain standard evaluation techniques, including this simple method for determining the value of the companies[14]:

(a) A forecast is made reflecting successful attainment of achievable long-term goals.
(b) The venture capitalist estimates a possible terminal value that would obtain if the investment in the company were harvested at that point.
(c) The terminal value is converted to a present value by applying a high discount rate, usually between 40% and 60%.
(d) The proportion of company stock to be owned by the venture-capital firm is then calculated by dividing the required investment by the total present value.

The most important element of this process is determining the discount rate. According to Plummer (1987), the discount rates used by venture capitalists vary by the company's stage of development. The results of that study are summarized in table 6 (the stages are defined in table 2):

These discount rates seem high compared with other rates of return in the economy [for example, the returns on publicly traded stocks and bonds as reported in Ibbotson (1988)] or even the actual returns reported by profes-

---

[14]See Plummer (1987), Morris (1988b), and Sahlman and Scherlis (1988) for more detailed descriptions of the method.

sional venture-capital funds [Venture Economics (1985, 1988c)]. In theory the required rate of return on an entrepreneurial investment reflects the risk-free interest rates in the economy, the systematic risk of the particular asset and the market risk premium, the liquidity of the asset,[15] and compensation for the value added by the supplier of capital (including favored access to other resources). This last adjustment is required to compensate venture capitalists for monitoring the company and playing an active role in management, while leaving the limited partner with the appropriate rate of return after taking into account the venture-capital fund's management fees and profit participation.

In practice, the use of high discount rates also reflects a well-known bias in financial projections made by entrepreneurs. Because few companies ever do as well as their founders believe they will, the numerator used in the calculation described above is typically higher than the expected value, though it may be an unbiased estimate conditional on success. To adjust for the bias, projections can be lowered or a higher discount rate can be used. The latter mechanism seems to dominate in the venture-capital industry [Keeley (1986)].

The use of high discount rates, however, means that few projects are feasible. Suppose a venture requires a $2 million capital infusion (the average invested in recent years in each venture) and that in five years the company will be worth $12 million. If the required rate of return is 50% per year, the $2 million investment must be worth approximately $15.2 million by the end of the fifth year, an amount exceeding the likely value of the entire company. Accordingly, venture capitalists are reluctant to back any company that cannot reasonably be expected to generate at least $25 to $50 million in total value in five years [MacMillan et al. (1985)]. The entrepreneurs' willingness to accept high discount rates indicates belief in the prospects of the company.

The use of high discount rates in venture-capital investing seems to fly in the face of conventional wisdom. One often reads that high discount rates discourage investments in highly uncertain, long-term projects [Hayes and Garvin (1982)], but in venture capital high discount rates are part of a more complex process of investing and managing the agency problem.

7.8. Adverse selection

Using very high discount rates might have the unintended effect of driving the most competent entrepreneurs to seek alternative sources of capital, leaving only those with no other financing options.

---

[15] Venture-capital investments are illiquid for a number of reasons, including the existence of information asymmetries and restrictions imposed by regulatory authorities on transfers of unregistered securities.

The adverse-selection problem is a difficult one in venture capital. Venture capitalists argue that by playing a positive role in the venture, they can increase total value by enough to offset the high cost of the capital they provide. To the extent that venture capitalists make good on this claim, the adverse-selection issue is effectively mitigated. In addition, the due diligence conducted before an investment is made is intended partly to make sure the entrepreneurs are qualified.

Although it seems that venture capitalists retain much of the power in the relationship with entrepreneurial ventures, there are checks and balances in the system. Venture capitalists who abuse their power will find it hard to attract the best entrepreneurs, who have the option of approaching other venture capitalists or sources other than venture capital. In this regard, the decision to accept money from a venture capitalist can be seen as a conscious present-value-maximizing choice by the entrepreneur.

7.9. Comparing the venture-capital fund – limited partner and venture capitalist – entrepreneur relationships

The relationship between the limited partners and the venture capitalists shares several elements with that between the venture capitalists and the entrepreneurs. First, each relationship entails staging the commitment of capital and preserving the option to abandon. The limited partners insist on a limited life for the fund, and the venture capitalists invest in stages related to the attainment of specific goals by the venture.

The compensation schemes are similar as well. The venture capitalists have strong incentives to create value because they share in the profits of the fund. The entrepreneurs receive a significant share of the value they help create (see table 4 for evidence about the share held by founders).

Also, in both cases, there are defined mechanisms in place to achieve liquidity. The limited partners insist on distributions of investment returns. The venture capitalists build into their stock-purchase agreements a number of mechanisms for achieving liquidity, such as the right to demand redemption of their convertible preferred stock.

Finally, the venture capitalist and entrepreneur alike face serious consequences if they fail. Entrepreneurs will be denied access to capital, their equity participation will be retracted, and their reputations damaged. Similarly, venture capitalists will find capital more difficult and costly to raise and their reputations will suffer as well, though their penalties are modest in comparison with those confronting entrepreneurs. In both cases, however, the multiperiod nature of the game creates strong incentives to perform well and to forego opportunistic behavior.

These common elements reinforce each other. For example, because venture capitalists capture 20% of their funds' profits, they structure incentives for the entrepreneurs that reward value creation. Similarly, because venture capitalists are legally required to liquidate the fund in ten years or so, they build mechanisms into their contracts with the entrepreneurs to make that feasible.

8. Other organizational forms

The venture-capital organization has evolved in response to the demanding investment environment in which new businesses are built. But, sorting, agency, and transactions cost problems are present in other settings as well.

A venture-capital firm performs economic functions similar to those of a corporation. Both raise capital from outsiders and invest in projects on behalf of the outside investors. The outside investors in both cases create a governance structure for monitoring the decisions made by the agents. When investments are made in individual projects, the managers within the venture-capital fund or within the corporation must monitor performance. Ultimately, the outside investors insist that they receive some return on their capital.

A venture-capital firm is also similar to a leveraged buyout fund. Each organization raises capital to invest in individual projects. In the venture-capital example, the projects tend to be early-stage ventures: in the leveraged-buyout example, the projects are more mature businesses with substantial debt capacity. The following sections compare the venture-capital organization, the corporate organization, and the leveraged-buyout-fund organization.

8.1. Capital budgeting

Corporate managers confront issues similar to those facing venture capitalists, yet their responses are very different. For example, consider an opportunity to invest in a new computer technology that could be funded inside a large company or as a separate business by venture capitalists.

If the project is funded within a corporation, the project initiation and management team probably will not receive a significant share of the value it creates. More likely, if the project is successful, their rank in the company and current compensation will increase [see Baker (1987)]. Team members often own or receive some stock options in the company, but the value of these options does not necessarily reflect the success of the project they undertook.[16] If the project is not successful, on the other hand, team members probably will find other tasks within the corporation, provided they

---

[16]See Jensen and Murphy (1990) for information on the relationship between compensation and value changes for American managers.

were not guilty of gross incompetence or malfeasance. Though the pecuniary rewards for success are modest, so too are the consequences of failure.

During development of the technology, the in-house team receives assistance from other members of company management, who monitor performance and try to increase the chances that the project will succeed. The specific team generally does not need to compensate these advisors. To the extent that the project is charged with the costs of monitoring, the costs reflect standard overhead-absorption charges rather than the amount of assistance provided or its perceived value, and the compensation of the advisors will probably not be dramatically affected by the project's outcome.

In contrast, if the project is financed by a venture-capital fund, the initiators and key members of the team own part of the venture, and they probably receive lower salaries than an in-house management team. If the project succeeds, management participates directly in the value it helped create. The team is not broken up as often occurs in large companies when individual managers in a team are promoted or transferred after a successful venture.[17] If the project fails, management suffers the consequences directly. If the project falters in midstream, entrepreneurial managers stand a good chance of being fired, often losing equity shares because of the vesting schedules used by venture capitalists. Further, the compensation of the venture capitalists (and the other outside directors) mirrors that of the entrepreneurial team: they will benefit only if the company succeeds, and they will suffer the consequences if the venture fails.

There is often one other substantive difference between the two approaches. In the corporate setting, projects are often funded all at once. In the venture-capital situation, the capital is meted out according to perceived performance at each successive project stage. Although in either situation managers will not purposefully pour good money after bad, team managers inside the company feel more secure about access to future capital than managers do in the venture-capital scenario.

If the typical American corporation were organized like a venture-capital fund, its discrete business units would be separated into individual business entities, equity shares in those entities would be awarded to their managers, capital would be meted out according to the attainment of specific business goals, a separate board of directors would be constituted for each business entity, and each board would be compensated according to the value created in each unit. The board would have the right to demand that funds be returned from the operating units to the holding company, and the ultimate

---

[17]The venture capitalists ultimately do leave the team, often when the company goes public, and always when the company is sold. In these instances, however, new directors are recruited who bring skills and resources appropriate to the issues confronting the company as it matures. Also, in many instances (for example, Teradyne, Thermo Electron, New England Business Services, Apple Computer), the venture capitalists remain on the board long after the limited partners have received distributions of shares in the company.

owners of the holding company would also have the right to demand distribution of the rewards of investing (for example, by imposing a finite life on the organization). In contrast to a traditional corporation, the new organization would be structured as a limited partnership, which would eliminate the possibility of adverse tax consequences in distributing the rewards of investing to the ultimate owners. In effect, the entire incentive system for directors and unit managers would be radically altered, as would the process of allocating capital. This model is similar to the leveraged-buyout fund, described in the following section.

8.2. Leveraged-buyout funds

Separation of ownership and management has become a pressing problem in American business [Jensen and Ruback (1983), Jensen (1986, 1988)]. Evidence from the capital markets suggests that corporate managers do not always make value-maximizing decisions. One response to this problem has been the leveraged buyout (LBO). In an LBO, a company or business unit is acquired by a group of managers and financiers who end up owning the equity in the new organization. Most of the capital required to finance the acquisition is raised as debt rather than equity.

The reallocation of equity to management and the imposition of heavy debt burdens (interest and amortization) can be interpreted as a direct response to the agency problems inherent in corporations [Jensen (1989)]. After an LBO, managers have greater incentives to create value than they did when they had little or no equity stake in the outcome. Because of the substantial debt burdens, there is little or no discretionary cash flow that can be dissipated on negative-net-present-value investments, including perquisites.

In LBO organizations the relationships among the company, its management, and financiers are similar to the deal struck between venture capitalists and management teams in entrepreneurial ventures. The compensation scheme is oriented toward equity, whose value depends on the efforts and skills of the managers involved. There are severe penalties for underperformance: for example, managers' equity shares are often vested over time so that, if they are fired before full vesting has occurred, they lose the unvested portion of their claim. The debt used in LBOs is similar in function to the staged-capital-commitment process used in venture-capital deals; in neither is there much discretionary cash flow. The critical characteristic of the debt is really the contractual right to take control of the project by denying access to new funds or changing the terms of that access if the company's performance falters.[18]

---

[18]See Hart and Moore (1989) for a discussion of the nature of control in a firm and the somewhat arbitrary distinction between debt and equity.

Venture-capital funds and LBO funds are also similar in structure; indeed, many venture-capital firms also invest in leveraged buyouts. LBO funds are typically organized as private limited partnerships with the LBO fund managers acting as general partners: each partnership has a finite life, typically ten years. These funds raise capital from larger financial institutions such as pension funds and endowments, and they invest in diversified portfolios of companies. LBO fund managers also raise multiple funds over time; as investment activities wind down in one fund, a new one is raised, often from the same investors. LBO fund managers are active in the operation of the companies in which they invest, typically assuming control of the board of directors, but they are generally less likely than venture capitalists to assume operational control. They bring a great deal of process knowledge to bear, particularly in the area of financing, and they have close contacts with financial institutions and investment bankers. Their compensation is highly sensitive to value creation; like general partners in venture-capital deals, general partners of LBO funds typically receive a 20% share of the value created in addition to a periodic management fee. Most importantly, LBO fund managers are skilled and active monitors of the decisions being made by the company managers. They are the antithesis of the passive institutional investors who have come to dominate ownership of American companies.

Both the venture-capital fund and the LBO fund invest capital on behalf of institutions that could conceivably invest directly rather than through intermediaries. The LBO-fund model is interesting because the same institutions that invest in publicly traded residual claims also choose to participate through the LBO limited partnership in the new structure. Investing through the LBO fund addresses some of the inherent agency problems in publicly traded securities while also minimizing the present value of tax burdens.

There are also some significant differences between the venture-capital model and the leveraged-buyout firm. First, leveraged buyouts are typically restricted to companies that have modest growth rates and stable cash flows, firms in which management would otherwise have significant control over discretionary cash flows. After the LBO, management has an incentive to use its cash flow to pay down debt, thus increasing the value of its equity. In the traditional venture-capital model, there is little discretionary cash flow to begin with. Value is created by building the company to gain access to more resources, which in turn facilitates more growth. A final distinction to be drawn is that leveraged-buyout funds often charge up-front investment banking fees and continuing management fees to the companies in which they invest: venture capitalists rarely if ever charge fees to portfolio companies.

9. Conclusions

The venture-capital industry is a productive place to study organizational responses to agency and other problems. The environment is characterized by substantial uncertainty about payoffs on individual investments and a high degree of information asymmetry between principals and agents. To cope with the challenges posed by such an environment, certain standard operating procedures and contracts have evolved, including staging the commitment of capital, basing compensation on value created, and preserving mechanisms to force agents to distribute capital and profits. These procedures and contracts help sort out the skills and intentions of the participants while simultaneously addressing cost and taxation issues.

The venture-capital organizational form may be applicable in other settings, particularly corporate and project governance. At the corporate level, adopting some aspects of the venture-capital organization, such as the compensation system and the finite-life form of organization, might solve some of the problems that lead to leveraged-buyout transactions in the first place. Then the goals of shareholders, monitors, and managers would be better aligned [see Sahlman (1990) for a description of the specific issue of compensating corporate boards of directors].

At the project level, there are also important insights from studying the organization of venture-capital firms. For example, establishing project boards of directors, with skills and resources specifically tailored to the project, seems to make sense. Also, implementing value-sensitive compensation systems and staging the commitment of capital has potential advantages, particularly for projects designed to exploit new business opportunities.

Much research remains to be done on the venture-capital organization. Though the economic resources under management are modest, the model seems to have been effective. Understanding why it works is in the interests of academics and practitioners alike.

References

Baker, George P., 1987, Incentives in hierarchies: Promotions, bonuses and monitoring, Working paper no. 88-023 (Harvard Business School, Boston, MA).

Barry, Christopher B., Chris J. Muscarella, John W. Peavy III, and Michael R. Vetsuypens, 1990, The role of venture capital in the creation of public companies: Evidence from the going-public process, Journal of Financial Economics, this volume.

Bartlett, Joseph W., 1988, Venture capital law, business strategies, and investment planning (Wiley, New York, NY).

Bhattacharya, Sudipto, 1979, Imperfect information, dividend policy and the 'bird in the hand' fallacy, Bell Journal of Economics 10, 259–270.

Brickley, James A. and Frederick H. Dark, 1987, The choice of organizational form: The case of franchising, Journal of Financial Economics 18, 401–420.

Bygrave, William, Norman Fast, Roubina Khoylian, Linda Vincent, and William Yue, 1987, Early rates of return of 131 venture capital funds started 1978–1984, Journal of Business Venturing 4, 93–106.

Chiampou, Gregory F. and Joel J. Kellet, 1989, Risk/return profile of venture capital, Journal of Business Venturing 4, 1–10.

Council of Economic Advisors, 1990, Economic report of the President (U.S. Government Printing Office, Washington, DC).

Fama, Eugene F., 1980, Agency problems and the theory of the firm, Journal of Political Economy 88, 288–307.

Fama, Eugene F. and Michael C. Jensen, 1985, Organization forms and investment decisions, Journal of Financial Economics 14, 101–119.

Freear, John and William E. Wetzel, Jr., 1990, Who bankrolls high-tech entrepreneurs?, Journal of Business Venturing 5, 77–90.

Gorman, Michael and William A. Sahlman, 1989, What do venture capitalists do?, Journal of Business Venturing 4, 231–248.

Hart, Oliver and John Moore, 1989, Default and renegotiation: A dynamic model of debt, Working paper no. 89-069 (Harvard Business School, Boston, MA).

Hay Management Consultants, 1988, Survey of compensation among venture capital/leveraged buy-out firms (Hay Group, New York, NY).

Hayes, Robert H. and David Garvin, 1982, Managing as if tomorrow mattered, Harvard Business Review, May–June, 70–79.

Horsley Keogh & Associates, 1988, Horsley Keogh venture study (Horsley Keogh & Associates, Pittsford, NY).

Huntsman, Blaine and James P. Homan, Jr., 1980, Investment in new enterprise: Some empirical observations on risk, return, and market structure, Financial Management 9, 44–51.

Ibbotson Associates, 1988, Stocks, bonds, bills, and inflation, 1988 yearbook (Ibbotson Associates, Chicago, IL).

Jensen, Michael C., 1986, The agency costs of free cash flow: Corporate finance and takeovers, American Economic Review 76, 323–329.

Jensen, Michael C., 1988, Takeovers: Their causes and consequences, Journal of Economic Perspectives 2, 21–38.

Jensen, Michael C., 1989, Active investors, LBOs, and the privatization of bankruptcy, Journal of Applied Corporate Finance 2, 35–49.

Jensen, Michael C. and William H. Meckling, 1976, Theory of the firm: Managerial behavior, agency costs and ownership structure, Journal of Financial Economics 3, 305–360.

Jensen, Michael C. and Kevin J. Murphy, 1990, Performance pay and top management incentives, Journal of Political Economy 98, 225–264.

Jensen, Michael C. and R. Ruback, 1983, The market for corporate control: The scientific evidence, Journal of Financial Economics 11, 5–50.

Keeley, Robert, 1986, Risk (over)adjusted discount rates: The venture capitalist's method, Unpublished working paper.

Knights, David H. and William A. Sahlman, 1986a, Horizon Group, 286-058 Rev. 9/86 (Publishing Division, Harvard Business School, Boston, MA).

Knights, David H. and William A. Sahlman, 1986b, Centex Telemanagement, Inc., 286-059 Rev. 9/88 (Publishing Division, Harvard Business School, Boston, MA).

Knights, David H. and William A. Sahlman, 1986c, Vertex Peripherals, 286-069 Rev. 12/87 (Publishing Division, Harvard Business School, Boston, MA).

Knights, David H. and William A. Sahlman, 1986d, Priam Corporation – Vertex Peripherals, 286-103 Rev. 9/86 (Publishing Division, Harvard Business School, Boston, MA).

Kozmetsky, George, Michael D. Gill, Jr., and Raymond W. Smilor, 1985, Financing and managing fast-growth companies: The venture capital process (Lexington Books, Lexington, MA).

Leland, Hayne and David Pyle, 1977, Information asymmetries, financial structure and financial intermediation, Journal of Finance 32, 371–387.

MacMillan, Ian C., David M. Kulow, and Roubina Khoylian, 1989, Venture capitalists' involvement in their investments: Extent and performance, Journal of Business Venturing 4, 27–34.

MacMillan, Ian C., Robin Siegel, and P.N. Subba Narisimha, 1985, Criteria used by venture capitalists to evaluate new venture proposals, Journal of Business Venturing 1, 119–128.

Morris, Jane K., ed., 1988a, Pratt's guide to venture capital sources, 12th ed. (Venture Economics, Inc., Needham, MA).

Morris, Jane K., 1988b, The pricing of a venture capital investment, in: Pratt's guide to venture capital sources, 12th ed. (Venture Economics, Inc., Needham, MA) 55–61.

Myers, Stewart C., 1977, Determinants of corporate borrowing, Journal of Financial Economics 5, 147–176.

Plummer, James L., 1987, QED report on venture capital financial analysis (QED Research, Inc., Palo Alto, CA).

Ross, Stephen, 1977, The determination of financial structure: The incentive signalling approach, Bell Journal of Economics 8, 23–40.

Sahlman, William A., 1983a, Technical Data Corporation, 283-072 Rev. 12/87 (Publishing Division, Harvard Business School, Boston, MA).

Sahlman, William A., 1983b, Technical Data Corporation Business Plan, 283-073 Rev. 11/87 (Publishing Division, Harvard Business School, Boston, MA).

Sahlman, William A., 1984, Priam Corporation, 284-043 Rev. 9/84 (Publishing Division, Harvard Business School, Boston, MA).

Sahlman, William A., 1985a, CML Group, Inc. – Going public (A), 285-003 Rev. 9/86 (Publishing Division, Harvard Business School, Boston, MA).

Sahlman, William A., 1985b, Business Research Corporation (A), 285-089 (Publishing Division, Harvard Business School, Boston, MA).

Sahlman, William A., 1985c, Business Research Corporation (B), 285-090 (Publishing Division, Harvard Business School, Boston, MA).

Sahlman, William A., 1985d, CML Group, Inc. – Going public (B), 285-092 Rev. 9/86 (Publishing Division, Harvard Business School, Boston, MA).

Sahlman, William A., 1985e, Lotus Development Corporation, 285-094 Rev. 11/87 (Publishing Division, Harvard Business School, Boston, MA).

Sahlman, William A., 1986a, CML Group, Inc. – Going public (C), 286-009 (Publishing Division, Harvard Business School, Boston, MA).

Sahlman, William A., 1986b, Note on the venture capital industry – update (1985), 286-060 (Publishing Division, Harvard Business School, Boston, MA).

Sahlman, William A., 1986c, Palladian Software, 286-065 Rev. 11/87 (Publishing Division, Harvard Business School, Boston, MA).

Sahlman, William A., 1986d, Bank of Boston New Ventures Group, 286-070 Rev. 9/86 (Publishing Division, Harvard Business School, Boston, MA).

Sahlman, William A., 1988a, Aspects of financial contracting in venture capital, Journal of Applied Corporate Finance 1, 23–36.

Sahlman, William A., 1988b, Note on financial contracting: 'Deals', 288-014 Rev. 6/89 (Publishing Division, Harvard Business School, Boston, MA).

Sahlman, William A., 1988c, Sarah Jenks-Daly, 288-008 Rev. 9/88 (Publishing Division, Harvard Business School, Boston, MA).

Sahlman, William A., 1989a, Report on the Harvard Business School venture capital conference: September 23–24, 1988, Unpublished manuscript (Harvard Business School, Boston, MA).

Sahlman, William A., 1989b, Tom Volpe, 289-025 Rev. 2/89 (Publishing Division, Harvard Business School, Boston, MA).

Sahlman, William A., 1990, Why sane people shouldn't serve on public boards, Harvard Business Review 90-3, 28–37.

Sahlman, William A. and Howard H. Stevenson, 1985, Capital market myopia, Journal of Business Venturing 1, 7–30.

Sahlman, William A. and David H. Knights, 1986, Analog Devices – Bipolar Integrated Technology, 286-117 Rev. 12/88 (Publishing Division, Harvard Business School, Boston, MA).

Sahlman, William A. and Dan Scherlis, 1988, A method for valuing high-risk long-term investments, 288-006 Rev. 6/89 (Publishing Division, Harvard Business School, Boston, MA).

Sahlman, William A. and Helen Soussou, 1985a, Note on the venture capital industry (1981), 285-096 Rev. 11/85 (Publishing Division, Harvard Business School, Boston, MA).

Sahlman, William A. and Helen Soussou, 1985b, Precision Parts, Inc. (A), 285-131 (Publishing Division, Harvard Business School, Boston, MA).

Smith, Clifford W., Jr. and Jerold B. Warner, 1979, On financial contracting: An analysis of bond convenants, Journal of Financial Economics 7, 117–161.

Soussou, Helen and William A. Sahlman, 1986, Peter Wendell, 286-008 Rev. 1/86 (Publishing Division, Harvard Business School, Boston, MA).

Spence, A. Michael, 1973, Job market signalling, Quarterly Journal of Economics 3, 355–379.

Stevenson, Howard H., Daniel F. Muzyka, and Jeffry A. Timmons, 1987, Venture capital in transition: A Monte Carlo simulation of changes in investment patterns, Journal of Business Venturing 2, 103–122.

Stiglitz, Joseph E. and Andrew Weiss, 1983, Incentive effects of terminations: Applications to the credit and labor markets, American Economic Review 73, 912–927.

Studt, Tim A., 1990, There's no joy in this year's $150 billion for R&D, Research & Development, Jan., 41–44.

Testa, Richard J., 1988, The legal process of venture capital investment, in: Pratt's guide to venture capital sources, 12th ed. (Venture Economics, Inc., Needham, MA).

Timmons, Jeffry A., 1987, Venture capital: More than money, in: Pratt's guide to venture capital sources, 12th ed. (Venture Economics, Inc., Needham, MA).

Venture Economics, 1985, The venture capital industry: Opportunities and considerations for investors (Venture Economics, Inc., Needham, MA).

Venture Economics, 1987, Terms and conditions of venture capital partnerships (Venture Economics, Inc., Needham, MA).

Venture Economics, 1988a, Exiting venture capital investments (Venture Economics, Inc., Needham, MA).

Venture Economics, 1988b, Trends in venture capital – 1988 edition (Venture Economics, Inc., Needham, MA).

Venture Economics, 1988c, Venture capital performance: Review of the financial performance of venture capital partnerships (Venture Economics, Inc., Needham, MA).

Venture Economics, 1989, Venture capital yearbook 1989 (Venture Economics. Inc., Needham, MA).

Wetzel, William E., 1983, Angels and informal risk capital, Sloan Management Review 24, 23–34.

Williamson, Oliver E., 1975, Markets and hierarchies (Free Press, New York, NY).

Williamson, Oliver E., 1988, Corporate finance and corporate governance, Journal of Finance XLII, 567–591.

Wilson, John, 1985, The new venturers: Inside the high stakes world of venture capital (Addison-Wesley, Reading, MA).

Wolfson, Mark A., 1985, Empirical evidence of incentive problems and their mitigation in oil and gas tax shelter programs, in: John W. Pratt and Richard J. Zeckhauser, eds., Principals and agents; The structure of business, (Harvard Business School Press, Boston, MA) 101–126.

ENTREPRENEURSHIP & REGIONAL DEVELOPMENT, 6 (1994), 275-297

Sources of finance for UK venture capital funds: the role of corporate investors

KEVIN N. MCNALLY

Department of Geography, University of Southampton, Southampton SO17 1BJ, UK

A current concern for the UK venture capital industry involves the long-term availability of funds for investment. To date the corporate sector is a relatively under-utilized source of finance for UK funds, particularly in comparison with the USA. Based on a survey of 39 venture capital fund managers in the UK, this paper examines the significance of corporate sources of finance for venture capital funds, and identifies the investment characteristics of these funds. The potential advantages and disadvantages of corporate venture capital (CVC) for venture capitalists, corporate investors and small investee firms are considered along with possible future trends and the scope for development of the activity in the UK. The study finds that on account of both an unwillingness on the part of corporates to invest and a venture capital community that has largely been discouraged by previous experiences to seek finance from the corporate sector, CVC is still underdeveloped in the UK. However, a large majority of venture capitalists support its encouragement and highlight important roles for venture capitalists, large and small companies, and policy makers in increasing its significance.

Keywords: venture capital; corporate venturing; entrepreneurship; small firm finance; technology

1. Introduction

The UK venture capital industry was created in a period of sustained economic growth throughout the 1980s during which time it experienced quite dramatic growth. Now in its second decade, the boom appears to be over leaving the industry in a state of some considerable uncertainty (Murray 1992a). Murray (1991a) identified widespread doubts among members of the British Venture Capital Association (BVCA) that the UK venture capital industry would continue to sustain the growth rates of the 1980s during the first half of the 1990s. The longer term availability of funds was reported to be the single most important concern, particularly with the 'increasing ambivalence of institutional investors to venture capital activity [which has been illustrated by] the growing difficulties experienced by venture capitalists seeking to raise new funds, particularly after 1989' (Murray 1991a: 73).

The amount raised in new funds increased from £112 million in 1983 to £1·68 billion in 1989 (Murray 1994). However, the early 1990s have witnessed the most difficult fund raising environment in the brief history of the UK venture capital industry (Murray 1994), as the total amount of funds raised by independent UK venture capital firms fell to £400 million in 1991 (*Financial Times* 1992a) and then to £347 million in 1992 (BVCA 1993), before increasing slightly to £380 million in 1993 (BVCA 1994). Murray reported expectations of some form of 'shake-out' in the industry, as poorly performing independent venture capitalist, and those specializing in riskier, early-stage financing, are left particularly vulnerable to the increasing bargaining power of the institutional investors. In support of this, accountants Levy Gee reported a decline of about 10% in the number of active UK venture capital funds during the second half of 1991 (*Financial*

Times 1992b). This trend led Murray to suggest that 'if the industry loses the confidence of the institutional investors ... then the industry has no long term future in the absence of substantial alternative funding sources' (Murray 1991b: 19).

2. Corporate Venture Capital (CVC)

A relatively under-utilized source of finance for UK venture capital funds is the corporate sector. Corporate investment in venture capital involves a corporate ('investor') making equity investments in smaller, unquoted, often innovative companies ('investees'). This investment can take two main forms: externally-managed (indirect) investment (i.e., investment in venture capital funds) and internally-managed (direct) investment (ACOST 1990) (Figure 1).

	Corporate Venture Capital			
Type of investment	**Externally Managed (Indirect)** (investment via independently managed venture capital fund)		**Internally Managed (Direct)** (direct subscription for minority equity stakes)	
Investment vehicle	Independently managed fund ('pooled' or 'multi-investor')	Independently managed *captive* fund ('client-based' or 'dedicated')	In-house corporate managed fund	Ad hoc/one-off investments eg: strategic alliances/'spin-offs' from company
Investment characteristics	Funds reinvest in small, innovative, often high-technology companies. Corporate investors may establish further relationships with investee companies (eg: customer, supplier, licensing, research contracts, joint production/marketing, etc).		As well as finance, relationships often involve *venture nurturing* - managerial assistance in marketing, production, R&D, or licensing/research contracts. Investments may be alongside independently managed venture capital funds (*parallel investments*).	
Corporate organisational structure	Corporate investment may be co-ordinated by a separate subsidiary (fully or partially owned) or an in-house department/operating division. In each case, externally and/or internally managed strategies may be the focus. An integrated, in-house venture capital programme may be established combining several CVC vehicles as well as other corporate development strategies.			

Figure 1. Corporate venture capital strategies.

For the investor and investee companies the potential benefits of CVC investment are both financial and strategic. While investment in the equity of small innovative companies can provide a large firm with attractive returns on invested capital, it may also present an opportunity to obtain windows on new technologies and allow assessment of new markets. As Block and MacMillan (1993: 348) explain 'the fundamental idea is for the parent company to get a "window" on potential new growth areas, which is appealing given the historical pattern that major new-business growth has generally originated with small, innovative firms'. In return, corporate investors not only provide investees with a much needed source of risk capital (often early-stage financing in high-technology sectors), but can also allow the small firm to gain access to technical and marketing resources as well as to a wide range of management expertise. Burgelman (1985) recognized the potential for establishing long-term contracting relationships in which the large firm could supply its smaller partner with some of its excess capabilities and skills. NEDO (1986: vi) believed that CVC offered an 'opportunity to combine the different strengths of large and small companies in order to generate opportunities for business development which might not otherwise be fully exploited'.

The relative advantages of direct and indirect CVC have been debated in the corporate venturing literature (for example Sykes 1990, Block and MacMillan 1993). The focus of this paper is specifically on indirect CVC. Through investment in a venture capital fund a corporate can gain access to a far larger portfolio of investee companies than would be the case with direct investment (MacDonald 1991), as well as enjoying greater diversification by geographic region, investment stage and field of interest (Winters and Murfin 1988). Corporate investors can benefit from the venture capitalists' screening process, and have more opportunities for earning attractive returns on investment (MacDonald 1991). Indeed Bailey (1985: 11) stated that 'intelligently planned and executed involvement with the international venture-capital community is by an overwhelming margin the most productive mechanism a corporation can have for providing the corporation with useful numbers of prefiltered business opportunities'.

For the investee company there may also be advantages of indirect CVC as it can provide the smaller firm with access to the financial expertise of the venture capitalist *as well as* the technical expertise of the corporate investor, while being protected from corporate pressure by the venture capitalist who acts as a buffer to corporate investors seeking to offer 'unsolicited "assistance" to the venture' (Bailey 1985: 12).

Finally, indirect CVC can also provide the venture capitalist with many benefits. Perhaps most importantly the corporate sector may be able to provide an alternative source of finance for venture capital funds at a time when the amount received from traditional sources is declining. The article on corporate venturing in *European Venture Capital Journal* (1990) believed there to be scope for the venture capital community to tap vast additional capital sources if it could better meet the needs of corporate investors. In addition, corporate investors possess industry-specific knowledge and can provide an exit route for venture capitalists. Corporates can afford to commission investigations into market sizes, patent validity, etc, which no venture capitalist could ever afford, and, by contributing their marketing skills and networks, can enhance the attractiveness of ventures that otherwise lack competitive advantage (Bailey 1985).

To date, corporate involvement in venture capital has been greatest in the USA, where large corporations have increasingly served as an important source of risk capital (*Journal of Applied Corporate Finance* 1992). Winters and Murfin (1988) noted a general increase in the amount of capital committed to externally-managed, multi-investor US venture capital funds by corporations between 1979 and 1986, and Oakley (1987) stated that over

100 US corporations were involved in such activities. Corporations were still significant fund investors in the late 1980s (Winters and Murfin 1988) when they accounted for 11% of the total finance ($2·95 billion) raised by US venture capital funds (Bygrave and Timmons 1992).

Corporate contributions to venture capital funds in the US reached a peak in 1989 when they accounted for over 20% (> $0·5 billion) of the total funds raised (Vachon 1993). However, owing to the global recession, US corporations have been reducing their exposure to the venture capital sector (Dickson 1993). Since 1989 the amount of finance raised from corporates has consequently declined, as has the relative importance of this source. This downturn paralleled an overall decline in venture capital fund raising in the US, particularly for early stage venture capital, because, as in the UK, institutions tended to shy away from riskier investments. Despite recent reports of a 'bounce-back' in the fortunes of US venture capital firms (*INC* 1993, Vachon 1993), exemplified by the significant resurgence in fund raising activity in 1992, the relative importance of corporates continued to fall as they provided only 3·3% of the $2·548 billion total funds raised during the year (Vachon 1993). However, with increasing anticipation of the recovery of US venture capital, including early stage investment, some experts are already predicting renewed interest from corporations (Vachon 1993).

A very marked difference between the UK and US venture capital industries has been the extremely low level of corporate investment in externally managed funds in the UK (*UK Venture Capital Journal* 1987). Until 1984 no UK corporation had invested in an externally managed venture capital fund, but in that year a modest start was made with £17 million committed (Oakley 1987). Between 1984 and 1986, the mean annual investment by corporates in venture capital funds was £13 million (Oakley 1987). In 1988, Ormerod and Burns tentatively suggested that 18 companies had committed over £30 million to UK venture capital funds, a larger number than estimated by Oakley (1987), who stated that only four UK venture capital groups were known to have raised capital from industrial corporations. Table 1 indicates that the annual corporate contribution has never been >6% of the total capital received from all sources.

While corporations have not been a significant source of finance for UK venture capital funds to date, a recent BVCA annual review reported an absolute increase in corporate investment from £20m in 1991 to £50m in 1992 (at a time when the total amount raised from all sources fell) and an increase in the percentage of funds raised from 5 to 15% (BVCA 1993). This suggests that corporate sources of finance for UK venture capital funds may be growing in significance – albeit from a very small base – at a time when their importance in the US has, at least temporarily, declined.

Table 1.   Capital committed by industrial corporations to UK independent venture capital funds (1986–1991).

Year	Total capital committed by corporations (£m)	Percentage of total venture capital funds raised
1986	11	4
1987	21	3
1988	34	6
1989	62	4
1990	17	2
1991	20	5

Source: UK Venture Capital Journal, 1987-1992.

3. Research aims and methodology

This research attempts to answer five questions concerning indirect CVC investment in the UK:

1. How significant are corporate sources of finance for independent and affiliated venture capital funds in the UK?
2. What are the characteristics of, and motivations behind, the corporate investments?
3. What are the characteristics of the investments of venture capital funds in which corporates have invested?
4. What do venture capitalists perceive to be the advantages and disadvantages of corporate investment in venture capital funds?
5. What are the possible future trends regarding corporate investment in venture capital funds, and the scope for development of the activity in the UK?

The empirical information reported here was derived from a survey of a sample of UK venture capital fund managers. The four major sources used for sample compilation were *The Venture Capital Report: Guide to Venture Capital in the UK and Europe* (Cary 1993), *The British Venture Capital Association Directory 1992/3* (British Venture Capital Association 1992), the *UK Venture Capital Journal* (1989 onwards), and the *European Venture Capital Journal* (1989 onwards). A two-stage selection process was used to identify venture capital firms appropriate for the study. In stage one, firms had to satisfy two criteria:

1. *Independent or affiliated* – To ensure that funds were raised from external sources, venture capital firms had to be 'independent' (i.e., their funds are raised from third parties), or 'affiliated' (they have a close affiliation with a larger group [often a merchant bank] but operate as autonomous associates, raising and managing funds subscribed by external investors). Venture capital firms classified as 'captive' (i.e., those that do not raise their own finance, but instead draw on the resources of a larger financial institution of which they are a part) were excluded from the survey as corporates clearly would not have invested in these funds.
2. *Non MBO/MBI/LBO Specialist* – Recent years have seen an increase in the number of venture capital firms concentrating on investing in management buyout (MBO), management buyin (MBI) and leveraged buyout (LBO) deals (Clark 1987, Murray 1991b, 1993). Corporations tend not to invest in the funds managed by these venture capitalists as they do not meet the corporates' objectives for investing. Therefore, such venture capital firms were considered to be unsuitable for this study.

The five research questions are largely concerned with the experiences of venture capitalists who have raised finance for their funds from corporate sources. As a result, the second stage of the selection process sought to identify venture capital firms that had, or at least were likely to have, raised finance from large companies. In addition, the views of the most experienced venture capitalists were considered also to be of great importance. Therefore, the remaining venture capitalists had to satisfy *one or more* of the following three criteria based on information available in the source material or in industry literature and press reports.

1. According to the source material, the business literature and/or the press the funds managed by the venture capital firm receive finance from the corporate sector.

2 CVC investment in the UK is generally in high-technology sectors owing to the strategic motives of many corporate investors, thus the venture capital firm specializes in making investments in high technology industries.

3 In a survey of Chief Executive Offiers (CEO)s of UK venture capital organizations undertaken by Murray (1991a), it was considered important that the view of experienced venture capitalists were sought. Therefore, the firm is well established and experienced in venture capital.

These procedures resulted in the identification of 49 venture capitalists. Table 2 indicates the basis on which they were selected for the study. All of these firms were contacted by introductory letter and follow-up telephone call and 39 agreed to participate in the survey (80% response rate).

Table 2. Criteria for selection of venture capitalists.

Criterion	Number of venture capitalists* (n = 49)	Percentage
Reports of CVC involvement	26	53
High-tech industry preference	27	55
Established and experienced venture capital firm	21	43

*Venture capitalists could satisfy more than one criterion.
Number of venture capitalists satisfying all three criteria = 3(6%)
Number of venture capitalists satisfying more than one criterion = 22(45%)

The nature of the information required in this survey was both quantitative and qualitative, as well as being commercially sensitive. As a result, face-to-face and telephone interview techniques were considered to be more appropriate than a postal survey design. A mixture of face-to-face and telephone methods was employed to ensure a satisfactory response rate.

4. Significance of corporate sources of finance for UK venture capital funds

Over one-third (16/41%)[1] of the venture capitalists who participated in the survey (n = 39) had raised finance from the corporate sector. While this clearly tells us nothing about the actual amounts raised, it does suggest that the corporate sector is of some significance.

Of those 23 venture capitalists that had not raised finance from corporate sources, approximately one-quarter (n = 6) had actually approached corporates in search of funding but had been unsuccessful. The corporates that had been approached had either disagreed with the concept of corporate venture capital altogether, believed that direct venture capital investment would be more appropriate for them, or felt that it was economically a poor time for them to make any venture capital investments. Consequently they had chosen not to invest. The remaining 17 venture capitalists who had not raised finance from corporate sources had chosen not to target corporates as they had felt that traditional sources of venture capital funding were more accessible and also more appropriate. Several did not believe that corporates would invest even if they were approached, and therefore they had not tried. Others felt that their funds were not suitable for corporates, and recognized the potential exiting problems and conflicts of interest that could result.

5.   Corporate investment in venture capital funds: some characteristics

The 16 venture capitalists that indicated that they had been involved with indirect CVC managed a total of 72 funds, 44 (61%) of which had raised finance from corporate sources. On average each of the 16 venture capital firms had raised finance for $2 \cdot 9$ of the funds that they managed from the corporate sector. Almost all of these funds were closed funds, and just less than half were fully invested. Several characteristics of the corporate investors and their investments can be examined.

5.1   Number of corporate investors

Based on information from 40 of the 44 funds that had received corporate finance, corporates had made a total of 84 investments[2]. The average number of corporate investors in each of the funds was therefore $2 \cdot 1$; however, over half only had one corporate investor, and 93% of funds had a maximum of three corporate investors. The largest number of investors in a single fund was 15 (Table 3).

Table 3.   Number of corporate investors in venture capital funds.

	1	*2*	*3*	*4*	*5–10*	*10 +*
Number of funds	24	5	8	0	2	1
%	60	13	20		5	3

*Number of corporate investors per fund**

*Based on data for 40 funds.

5.2   Corporate investment size

The proportion of total fund value accounted for by corporate investment varies considerably within this sample. Table 4 shows that almost half of the funds in which corporates had invested had not raised finance from any other source. These 'dedicated' or 'client-based' funds (as opposed to 'pooled', 'multi-investor' funds that receive finance from several, often non-corporate, investors) are managed in such a way as to ensure that investments are made in small companies relevant to the strategic development of the corporate investor. Although still externally-managed and therefore distinct from direct, internally-managed CVC, the corporate investor does have much more of an active role, defining its key areas of interest and gaining right of first refusal on any deals identified (*European Venture Capital Journal* 1990). The involvement of a corporate in such a fund is

Table 4.   Corporate contributions to venture capital funds relative to fund size.

	1–9	*10–19*	*20–29*	*30–39*	*40–49*	*50–59*	*60–69*	*70–79*	*80–89*	*90–99*	*100*
Number of funds	4	2	4	3	1	2	1	0	1	1	16
%	11	6	11	9	3	6	3		3	3	46

*Percentage of total funds from corporate sources**

*Based on data for 35 funds.

therefore primarily for strategic purposes. Sykes (1990) reported that sole investor, client-based funds were more strategically effective for investing corporates, and indeed in the US the number of client-based funds grew rapidly during the late 1980s (Mast 1991) because of dissatisfaction with the amount of strategic benefit gained from investment in 'standard' (pooled) venture capital funds.

However, the apparent popularity of dedicated funds in this sample is slightly misleading as 12 of the 16 dedicated funds were managed by just one venture capital firm (Advent International). Indeed, only five venture capital firms managed client-based funds, and one of these firms explained that the corporate's involvement was primarily for reasons of social responsibility rather than for strategic benefit.

The average fund size was £16·7 million, and the average total corporate investment in each fund was just less than half that figure (£8.1 million) suggesting corporate investment to be of particular significance. However, here again this figure is influenced by Advent International and its 12 dedicated funds. If Advent is omitted then the average fund size increases to £17.4 million, but the average corporate investment falls to £4·3 million.

5.3 Countries of origin of corporate investors

A further characteristic that can be examined concerns the countries of origin of the investors (Figure 2). Three-quarters of the 45 corporate investors that were identified by respondents[2] were from either the UK, US or Japan. However, only one-third of the 45 companies were from the UK. The remaining two-thirds were of non-UK parentage, suggesting that UK corporates were of only limited significance.

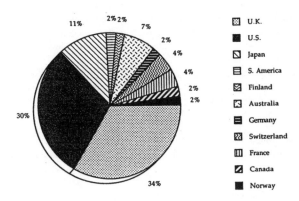

Figure 2.   Countries of origin of named corporate investors.

5.4   Contacts with corporate organizations

Venture capitalists have to make the first move in attracting corporate funding. The overwhelming opinion among the respondents was that large corporate organizations have to be persuaded to invest and they will therefore rarely make contact initially. Only 19% of venture capitalists in this survey that had raised corporate finance indicated that corporates had approached them concerning the provision of finance for funds.

Within the corporate organizations venture capital investments were most commonly co-ordinated by top management at the executive committee level (50% of occasions) and thus venture capitalists were most familiar with relationships with corporates at the board level. New venture divisions and corporate development officers were also used on occasions, and in two cases the investing company employed a venture capital manager. While several respondents indicated the desirability of dealing with a venture capital manager specialized in the field, the opportunity to do so was a rarity.

5.5   Corporate motivations

The motivations of companies for becoming involved in direct CVC can be classified into three types: financial, strategic and social responsibility. Almost half of all venture capitalists that had received corporate finance reported that investing companies specifically sought financial benefit in the form of a high return on investment, while 31% stated that the objectives of corporates were strategically oriented. One-quarter of all respondents felt that individual corporates had both financial and strategic motivations, although findings in the *European Venture Capital Journal* (1990) questioned the compatibility of financial and strategic objectives together. Corporate investors in 19% of the venture capital firms were believed to be investing for reasons associated with social responsibility.

Some interviewees felt that corporate objectives had changed over time, with several suggesting that financial motivations had become more significant as a result of dis-illusionment on the part of many corporates with strategically-oriented investments. Indeed, the increasing trend for corporates to use venture capital investment purely as a vehicle for high rates of return rather than any form of strategic gain suggests that funds have not adequately catered for the strategic needs of corporate investors in the past. The fact that only five of the venture capitalists in this survey manage dedicated funds which, due to their very nature tend to be oriented more towards strategic objectives, perhaps reinforces this point. Alternatively, large companies may feel that strategic objectives can be better met by using other corporate development strategies such as acquisition, internal development, and possibly even internally-managed CVC, and hence the lack of dedicated funds may be more a result of a lack of demand than a lack of supply.

5.6   Corporate involvement in funds

The extent to which corporates became involved with the operations of the venture capital fund in which they had invested varied considerably within the sample. While half of the venture capitalists allowed substantial corporate involvement, usually in the form of a seat on the advisory committee or an influence in the assessment and monitoring of deals, almost as many permitted no corporate involvement at all. The degree of involvement tended to depend upon whether the managed funds were dedicated or pooled. Corporates investing in dedicated funds experienced far greater contact and closer communication with the venture capitalist managing the fund and enjoyed more control over the investment process. In contrast, more than half of the investors in pooled funds were permitted no involvement with the funds.

Two-thirds of the venture capitalists set investment criteria themselves rather than allowing corporate investors to do so. As one respondent explained 'we cannot afford to let the tail wag the dog'. Again, investors in dedicated funds tended to have a greater influence than those in pooled funds, although this influence was often limited to sectors of investment and investment size. It would seem that a possible explanation for the lack of dedicated funds in the UK, and hence the lack of strategically-oriented investment opportunities for large companies, is that venture capitalists are hesitant about allowing corporate investors too much influence over the investment process.

5.7 Corporate involvement with investee companies

A large proportion of corporate investors had become involved with investee firms. Two-thirds of venture capitalists had permitted, and in some cases even encouraged, the establishment of investor/investee links in the belief that they would enable corporates to gain access to windows on technology more easily, help them to establish supply and licensing deals, and also to provide other 'added extras' to investments such as industry expertise. Those venture capitalists that did not allow corporate investors contact with investee firms explained that the investing companies were not interested in strategic benefit and thus had no need to get closer to investees. Some believed that too much direct contact and associated corporate pressure could harm the smaller firm.

6. Characteristics of venture capital fund investments

The nature of the investments of the 44 funds in which corporates have invested are examined under four headings.

6.1 Number and size of investments

In terms of number of investments made, great diversity existed within the sample. While the average number of investments made by each of the 44 funds was 18·4, the figure ranged from 0 to 50. Average investment size for these funds was £840 000, and half of the funds made typical investments of between £500 000 and £1m (Figure 3). Since the MacMillan Report in 1931 the existence of 'equity gaps' in the UK has been regularly debated (Hall 1989, Pratt 1990, Mason and Harrison 1992, Murray 1993). The most frequently discussed equity gap concerns the lack of provision of funds of less than £250 000 to new and small firms. Although 22% of the investments made by the funds in this survey were of less than £500 000, these figures still suggest that the contribution of funds in which corporates have invested to the filling of this particular aspect of the equity gap remains somewhat limited.

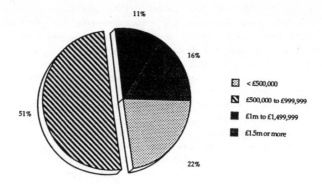

Figure 3.   Typical investment sizes of funds that have raised finance from corporates.

6.2   Investment type

Two further aspects of the equity gap are concerned with the shortage of finance for particular stages of investment – notably seed, start-up and early stage – and specific sectors of industry – notably high-technology industries. The number of venture capitalists specializing in early stage and/or high-technology investments (and the funds at their disposal) remain minimal in the UK (Murray 1992b, 1993, 1994) largely as a result of both the riskiness of such investments and the typically large investment sizes required. Drummond (1993: 13) noted that 'looking at the 115 strong membership of the BVCA we find 26 firms who claim technology specialisation and 29 more who are prepared to consider early stage transactions'. In the *European Venture Capital Journal* (1993) the UK venture capital industry was described as being preoccupied with investments in the consumer (32%) and industrial products (13%) sectors, and also with later stage deals, while Murray (1992a: 81) described the majority of venture capitalists as 'generalists', not willing to invest in specific stages or sectors.

However, a large majority (32/73%) of the funds in this survey that had raised finance from corporates were described by the venture capitalists that manage them as focused rather than general, in that particular stages of development, levels of technology and industrial sector were targeted specifically. These funds are attractive to corporate investors who want to invest in sectors in which they have a strategic interest. Moreover, although most stages of investment, ranging from seed to MBO, were catered for by the 44 funds in this sample, 65% concentrated specifically on early stage investments (usually start-up and other early stage) (Figure 4). In addition, funds that had raised finance from corporates typically invested in high technology sectors such as healthcare, information technology, advanced materials, environmental products and services, and chemicals (Table 5). Corporates with strategic motivations were typically active in these sectors and invested in these funds to obtain windows on early stage technologies in their industries.

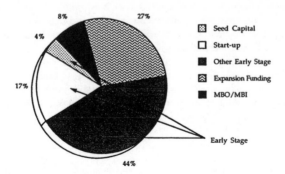

Seed Capital
Start-up
Other Early Stage
Expansion Funding
MBO/MBI

Early Stage

(Based on data for 43 funds)

Figure 4.   Stages of investment of funds that have raised finance from corporates.

Table 5.   Typical sectors of investment of funds receiving corporate finance.

Sector	Number of mentions	Sector	Number of mentions
Healthcare	11	Energy	1
Information technology	5	Industrial automation	1
Advanced materials	4	Food and drink	1
Environmental products and services	4	Defence	1
Chemicals	3	Leisure	1
Communications	2	Data sources	1
Computers	2	Electronics	1
Manufacturing	1		

In the US venture capital funds that have raised finance from corporate sources have been increasingly investing in companies that have been 'spun-out' from their corporate investors (Mast 1991). Corporate investments in spin-out companies are often made to enable the corporate to maintain links with related technologies that have developed within its own R&D laboratories. However, only four of the venture capital firms in this study had invested in companies spun-out from corporate investors, and one of these noted the number of such investments to be declining. It is conceivable that spin-out companies are more likely to attract *direct* venture capital investment from the corporate from which they originated as the parent organization often wants to retain close links.

6.3   *Location of investees*

A majority of the investments made by the venture capital funds in which corporates had invested were in UK companies. However, investments had also been in companies in the USA as well as in several European countries. The provision of finance for overseas companies is evidence of the global scanning process of multinational corporations. At a time of increasing global competition companies need to be aware of technological developments on a global scale and investment in innovative, foreign-based companies provides a way of keeping a watching brief on such developments.

6.4   *Fund performance*

Any measure of the performance of a venture capital fund is relatively meaningless during the course of the fund's life. As a result, performance information is often cursory and subjective (Murray 1994). However, while it is clearly difficult to define, measure, and compare the performance of different funds, a majority (60%) of the venture capitalists in this survey believed that most of their funds that had raised finance from corporates were performing as well as other funds that had not received corporate money; indeed 19% of respondents believed them to be performing better.

7.   Advantages and disadvantages of corporate investment in funds

Corporates will only invest in capital funds if they believe the advantages of making such investments to outweigh the disadvantages. Likewise, venture capitalists will not target corporate investors for their funds if they believe that they will cause more problems than benefits for themselves and their investees. According to the venture capitalists that had received corporate investment in the past, while there are potential advantages of indirect CVC for investor and investee companies, as well as for venture capitalists, there are also many disadvantages.

7.1   *For the venture capital firm*

Almost 90% of the venture capitalists that had received corporate finance stated that there were benefits to them of having corporate investors in their funds. Large industrial corporations can provide an alternative source of finance for venture capital funds at a time when the amount received from institutions is declining. Also, as has been emphasized by several authors (Bailey 1985, Murray 1993), many venture capitalists recognized that the corporate can bring added value to investments such as industrial knowledge, technical knowledge and advice, and can also provide an exit route for the venture capitalist in the form of a trade sale.

However, just over half of the venture capitalists drew attention to various disadvantages such as the propensity for corporate investors to develop unrealistic expectations of their investments, and hence become very disillusioned with the venture capital process when the expected returns and strategic benefits do not materialize. They often become over-obsessed, consequently trying to place far too much pressure on investees and wanting to treat them as subsidiary companies. Large companies are often very short-termist, failing to recognize or understand the long-term nature of venture capital, and often problems arise owing to the conflicting objectives of the venture capitalist and the corporate investors. This final observation has been reported numerous times in the corporate venture capital literature (Hardymon *et al.* 1983, Littler and Sweeting 1987).

7.2 For the corporate investor

All but one of the venture capitalists in the survey believed there to be definite advantages to the corporate investor of investing in externally-managed venture capital funds. Compared to investing directly, investment in a fund allows the corporate to benefit from the expert investment advice of the venture capitalist, as well as the improved deal flow and spread of investments. If the objectives of the investment are financial then investment in a fund can often also provide a better ROI. According to three of the venture capitalists interviewed, corporates rarely understand venture capital well enough to succeed on their own. Lack of understanding of the nature of the venture capital process often leads the corporate to put too much pressure on the investee in direct deals, but by investing indirectly the venture capitalist acts as a buffer that protects the smaller company from direct and possibly damaging contact with the corporate investor.

There may also be several disadvantages of indirect CVC for the corporate investor, and indeed 81% of the venture capitalists that had raised finance from corporate sources recognized areas of potential difficulty. Indirect investment in a venture capital fund may not allow corporates with strategic motivations enough direct contact with investee companies, and hence make it difficult for them to establish close relationships. Particularly when investing in a pooled fund, a corporate may have very little say in the evaluation and selection of investments, and may find itself with stakes in companies totally unrelated to its business activities. However, it was recognized that these potential problems are only really relevant when the corporate objectives are strategic, and even then they may be overcome if funds are dedicated rather than pooled.

7.3 For the investee business

The benefits for investee companies of receiving finance from a venture capital fund in which a corporate has invested were recognized by three-quarters of the respondents. They include the potential for obtaining 'added extras' from the corporate such as industry specific expertise, and also the possibility of forming strategic relationships with corporate investors. The presence of a corporate can help to validate a small firm's products and thus enable it to compete successfully in the global market-place. At the same time, the presence of the venture capitalist provides valuable expertise, as well as acting as a buffer to the corporate which, as mentioned earlier, can stifle the investee. This buffer is clearly not present when corporates invest directly in the equity of small companies.

According to 44% of the venture capitalists interviewed, these advantages must be balanced by a number of potential disadvantages for investee companies. Corporate impatience and the 'Big Brother' effect, whereby the presence of a corporate, even in this indirect form, may make other corporates suspicious and therefore unwilling to establish links themselves with the small firm, were issues mentioned by the survey respondents. In addition, corporate plans for acquisition and commercial confidentiality concerns, relating to what Oakey (1993) terms 'predatory networking' (i.e. the capturing or stifling of small firm ideas by corporate partners), were also seen as possible disadvantages for the investee company. Indeed much of the recent CVC and strategic alliance literature has drawn attention to entrepreneurial distrust of large companies. Block and MacMillan (1993) and Ahern (1993) have observed a suspicion among entrepreneurs that large companies will steal their ideas or control their companies to specifically satisfy corporate objectives if given half a chance. While the venture capitalist buffer may reduce the likelihood of such corporate behaviour, the associated limited corporate exposure to investee companies may in turn inhibit the chances of small companies establishing further strategically beneficial relationships with their corporate investors.

8. Corporate investment in venture capital funds: UK/US comparisons

Although the number of venture capitalists in this survey that have raised finance for their funds from the corporate sector suggests this source to be of significance in the UK (even though the number of corporates investing in each fund is very small), and despite the recent decline in significance of corporate sources of finance for US venture capital funds, the venture capitalists interviewed confirmed the commonly held belief that levels of indirect CVC in the UK are considerbly lower than in the US. Almost all of the 39 venture capitalists in this survey felt that in the UK industrial corporations had been less willing to invest in venture capital funds than in the US (Table 6). The limited involvement of UK corporates in indirect CVC is exemplified by the fact that two-thirds of the corporate investors in this survey were non-UK companies.

A number of reasons were postulated to explain the greater investment levels of corporations in the US. For example, US culture was commonly believed to be far more entrepreneurial and conducive to risk taking than is the case in the UK. In support of

Table 6.   Corporate willingness to invest in UK and US venture capital funds.

Agreement with statement*	Number of respondents	Percentage
Agree	35	90
Disagree	0	0
No opinion	4	10

*'In the UK corporates have been less willing to invest in venture capital funds than in the US'.

this, Pratt (1990) suggested that those taking business risks in the US are held in higher regard than in Europe, and to have tried and failed is deemed better than not to have tried at all. In addition, the US venture capital industry is longer established than that in the UK, dating back to 1946 with the formation of ARD (Bygrave and Timmons 1992), while the UK industry has only developed since the late 1970s. As a result, US corporations are far more aware of the possibilities of becoming involved with equity investments. Numerous US venture capital firms have been established by former corporate managers, and several of the largest corporate players in the US today were originally established during the 1950s to 1970s with the help of venture capital backing (Bygrave and Timmons 1992). Many such companies have since invested in venture capital funds themselves, with Apple, Lotus Development Corp. and Genentech providing good examples.

The venture capitalists in this survey also felt that the greater propensity for US venture capital funds to invest in early stage and high-technology deals helped to explain the increased tendency for corporates to invest in venture capital funds. As was noted in §6.2, the levels of early stage, technology-related investment are particularly low in the UK. However, despite the recent difficult fund raising environment for US venture capitalists specializing in early stage deals, Murray (1994) highlighted the relative significance of seed, start-up and other early stage deals in the US. Such deals accounted for 32% of 1991 disbursements in the US compared with 6% in the UK. Moroever, if MBOs/MBIs are omitted, 84% of total annual disbursements in the US between 1986 and 1991 were in technology-related projects, compared with only 30% in the UK (Murray and Lott 1992).

Conversely, UK companies tend to be more inward looking, less adventurous, hesitant, untrusting, short-termist and extremely prone to the 'Not Invented Here Syndrome'. Such a corporate environment was recognised by Littler and Sweeting (1984) who described large mature companies as highly bureaucratized systems with extensive commitments to established business activities. According to Walker (1993) European business 'is essentially risk averse and frequently arrogant in its approach to small companies'. In addition, several respondents echoed the views of Littler and Sweeting (1987) who believed it to be 'doubtful that many companies contain the requisite expertise not only to perform it [CVC] effectively but also to capitalise on any opportunities that it may yield'. Many UK corporations cannot justify risk to their share-holders, and are consequently more interested in outright acquisition or at least prefer direct CVC investments over which they have more control. This again corresponds with the views of Walker (1993) who stated that 'shareholders and big business culture combine to make corporate venturing a rarity this side of the Atlantic'. Several venture capitalists believed that the performance of venture capital funds in the UK has not been as good as that of their US counterparts, and that this, together with a more financially-oriented investment philosophy and a lack of dedicated fund opportunities, has left the industry unattractive to corporate investors.

9.   Indirect CVC: possible future levels and scope for development

In the light of the potential advantages and disadvantages of corporate investment in externally managed venture capital funds, and the underdeveloped nature of this activity in the UK at present, the likelihood of, and the scope for, an increase in the levels of indirect CVC are now considered.

9.1   Future involvement of venture capitalist

Many UK venture capitalists will not target the corporate sector for finance in the future. While only 15 (38%) of the 39 venture capitalists in the survey stated that they would consider corporate sources of funding, 20 (51%) said that they would not. The remaining four respondents were indecisive.

9.1.1 Venture capitalists that will target corporates: The venture capital firms that indicated that they would target corporates in the future can be divided into those that had not previously raised finance from corporate sources and those that had. Approximately one-third of the venture capitalists that had not raised finance from corporates previously stated that they would target corporates in the future (Table 7), largely because institutional funds had become less accessible but also because corporates can be particularly good investors and hence are well worth targeting. This not only illustrates the need for alternative sources of venture capital funding in the UK, but also indicates that, for a significant number of venture capitalists that have not raised finance from corporates in the past, the perceived advantages of this source now outweigh the potential disadvantages. Half of the venture capitalists who had raised corporate finance for their funds in the past said that they would continue targeting this source in the future. They justified their decision by highlighting many of the specific advantages of corporate investment outlined in §7.1.

Table 7.   Indirect CVC: future involvement of venture capitalists.

	Venture capitalists who **will** *target corporates in the future*	*Venture capitalists who* **will not** *target corporates in the future*	*Venture capitalists who* **might** *target corporates in the future*	*Total*
Venture capitalists who **have not** raised finance from corporates	7	13	3	23
Venture capitalists who **have** raised finance from corporates	8	7	1	16
Total	15	20	4	39

Most venture capitalists who planned to target corporates in the future stated that their most popular target group would be technology-based companies, which sometimes includes overseas companies looking for windows on UK technology. Others were interested in companies who want to invest for reasons of social responsibility. While 13% of the venture capitalists planning to target corporates expressed a preference for medium-sized companies, a further 13% said that they would target only the largest firms. The venture capitalists believed that their funds would be particularly attractive to corporate investors as they either offered a window on technology, specialized in early stage/high technology investment, or had an impressive investment track record and/or experience of corporare investors. However, few respondents were prepared to tailor their funds specifically for corporate needs.

9.1.2 Venture capitalists that will not target corporates: The venture capital firms that indicated that they would not target corporates in future can also be divided into those that had not previously raised finance from corporate sources and those that had. Just over half of the venture capital firms that had not received corporate finance stated that they would not look to corporates for funding in the future (Table 7). Of these firms many still believed other investment sources to be more accessible or more appropriate. Several others strongly believed that corporates would not invest in their funds if they were approached, and as a result they were not prepared to waste time targeting corporate organizations. A small proportion of the venture capitalists that had received corporate finance before but did not plan to target corporates in future justified this by explaining that their investment strategy had changed and that corporates were therefore no longer suitable for their funds. In general, experiences of indirect CVC have not been entirely favourable as almost half (44%) of the venture capitalists included in this survey, who had previously raised finance from corporates, stated that they would not target them in the future (Table 7). Many had become disillusioned with links with corporates and explained that raising finance from this source, as well as catering for the specific (often strategic) needs of corporate investors, was too time consuming. Thus, exposure to many of the potential disadvantages of indirect CVC has left many venture capitalists unwilling to try again and to accept failure as part of the learning process.

9.2 Expected trends over the next five years

In the opinion of a majority (46%) of survey respondents, there is likely to be no change in the absolute levels of corporate finance committed to UK venture capital funds in the next five years, and just over one-quarter (26%) expected the levels to fall (Table 8). Although several did expect to see an increase in the relative importance of corporate finance as the total contribution from more traditional sources declines, venture capitalists suggested three main reasons why absolute levels of indirect CVC were likely to remain constant or decline. First, the UK venture capital industry will continue to fail to attract corporates in any great numbers because of poor prospects of ROI and strategic benefit, as well as an increasing concentration on MBO deals (rather than early stage, technology-related investments) which are of little interest to corporates. Discussing the future of the UK venture capital industry, Murray (1992a: 85) believed that the industry 'has to be able to demonstrate to institutional and other funders that it can furnish returns on capital that compensate adequately for the additional risks and illiquidity of investment in unquoted small and medium sized firms'. Further, he felt that it was unlikely that 'start-up and early stage deals or the majority of technology-related applicants for risk equity will be seen as attractive core business for other than the most

Table 8.   Possible future levels of indirect CVC in the UK.

*Response to statement**	*Number of respondents*	*Percentage*
Increase	8	21
Decrease	10	26
No change	18	46
No opinion	3	8

*'Absolute increase/decrease in amount of corporate finance invested in venture capital funds in next five years'.

intrepid or specialist venture capitalists' (p. 86). Second, a corporate environment that acts as a constraint to successful venture capital investment is both a cause and effect of the very low levels of indirect CVC in the UK at present as there are few role models for corporates who consequently remain uneducated about the prospects of venture capital investment. Those companies that do get involved will do so through direct investments or via their pension funds. Third, initiatives from policy makers concerning the stimulation of indirect CVC in the UK are non-existent.

In contrast, only 21% of venture capitalists believed that there will be an absolute increase in indirect CVC. First, they felt that UK corporates would begin to recognize the potential benefits of venture capital investment at a time when the pressures on them to innovate are increasing. As Murray (1993: 25) notes, 'the imperative to maintain innovatory impetus by corporates in increasingly global, technology-based industries will encourage large firms to take a long term view on such [CVC] experiments'. Second, a decrease in finance from more traditional sources such as pension funds and insurance companies will make venture capitalists look towards the corporate sector in future.

Of the venture capitalists that stated that they expect to see a decrease in the amount of indirect CVC in the next five years, 80% had received finance from corporates for their funds in the past. Only one-quarter of those respondents expecting an increase in the extent of the strategy had actually been involved with it before. This strongly reinforces the suggestion that venture capitalists' experiences with corporate investors have generally not been favourable in the UK, and as a result it is the venture capitalists who are less experienced in this area that are the more optimistic about the future levels of indirect CVC. Such an outlook may however be unrealistic.

9.3 Scope for development

It would therefore appear that absolute levels of indirect CVC in the UK will either remain constant in the next few years or will decrease. If this is the case the corporate sector will not be able to provide a significant alternative source of funds for the venture capital industry and will not be able to help to combat the predicted 'funds famine' (Murray 1992a: 86). This is particularly distressing since corporate investors appear to favour stages and sectors of investment which, due to their inherent riskiness, are hugely disadvantaged in the venture capital stakes. However, in spite of these seemingly poor prospects, most venture capitalists recognized the potential of corporate investment in venture capital funds. Although some respondents maintained that venture capitalists and corporates cannot be comfortable partners, four of every five supported the encouragement of indirect CVC in the UK. The reasons given to justify this tended to echo many of the advantages for venture capitalists, corporates and small firms outlined earlier.

Venture capitalists identified several forms that encouragement of indirect CVC could take. First, venture capitalists need to provide more innovative and strategically-oriented venture capital investment opportunities for corporates. The establishment of dedicated funds designed specifically for individual corporate needs can provide benefits to all parties. As Honeyman (1992: 51) recognized, for the investing company 'the dedicated fund incorporates the best elements of both direct and indirect [CVC] approaches whilst alleviating most of their inherent disadvantages'. Corporates in turn could attempt to restructure their relationship with the venture capital industry, but must be educated about the venture capital process and the potential benefits. Many of the venture capitalists in this survey saw the role of educator being that of either the Confederation of British Industry (CBI) or the Department of Trade and Industry (DTI). ACOST (1990) recommended that the DTI investigate ways to stimulate CVC through links with the venture capital industry, although the DTI has not acted upon this challenge. The publicizing of role models from the US and elsewhere is an important factor in stimulating corporate venture capital investment. By far the most popular suggestion of the venture capitalists interviewed was some form of tax relief/incentive for participating companies, although four venture capitalists did specifically express their dislike of this potential solution, fearing the creation of market inefficiencies.

10. Conclusions and implications

In the US the extent of indirect CVC has been declining since 1989, while most recent figures suggest that in the UK the significance of corporate sources of finance for venture capital funds is greater than ever. However, despite the number of venture capitalists in this survey that have raised corporate finance in the past and the obvious potential of corporate investment as an important alternative funding source, indirect CVC is still underdeveloped in the UK in comparison with the US. This is due both to an unwilling-ness on the part of corporates to invest, and also a venture capital community that is either unable to attract corporate finance, does not recognize the potential benefits of such investment or has been discouraged by previous experiences.

However, despite the seemingly limited likelihood of an increase in the extent of indirect CVC in the UK a large majority of the venture capitalists included in this survey believed that corporate investment in venture capital funds should be encouraged. Indirect CVC can be advantageous to all parties, and many of the potential disadvantages should be regarded more accurately as pitfalls that can be avoided. Murray (1992a) believed corporates to have an increasing role to play in technology venturing and emphasized the importance of generating reciprocal benefit at acceptable costs to all parties. According to Sykes (1990) corporate venture capital relationships can be improved by organizational and management strategies that focus on communi-cation, balance of needs and objectives and long-term relationships. The views and suggestions of the venture capitalists included in this survey lead to implications for venture capitalists, corporates, small firms and policy makers alike.

10.1 Implications for venture capitalists

Venture capitalists can do much to encourage corporate investment in their funds and hence create an additional, and potentially very beneficial source of finance at a time when contributions from more traditional sources are declining. In order to attract corporate finance they must establish innovative, focused and strategically oriented venture capital funds specifically designed to cater for corporate needs. Funds specializing in early stage investments in high-technology sectors tend to be most attractive to corporate investors. Venture capitalists should recognize the requirements and motivations of the industrial corporation and tailor their funds accordingly. The benefits of dedicated, client-based funds cannot be over-emphasized. Concerns over the potential riskiness of early stage, high-technology financing should be weighed against the possibility of negotiating higher management fees for such investment. When seeking corporate funding the venture capitalist should approach the corporate at the executive committee level, and be prepared to allow the investor to influence investment criteria as well as become involved with both fund and investee company.

10.2   Implications for corporates

Corporates interested in becoming involved with indirect CVC should contact venture capital funds that invest in sectors and investment stages that are of specific interest and discuss their objectives with the venture capital fund managers. They should recognize the long term nature of venture capital and also the importance of patience and flexibility, as well as appreciating the need to consider carefully their own motives before selecting a particular form of venture capital investment that will be suitable for their own needs. Investment in a pooled fund may be most appropriate for financially motivated corporates, while strategic goals may often be better realized via investment in a dedicated fund. Corporates specifically interested in early stage, high-technology investments should be prepared to accept a higher venture capitalist management fee owing to the risky nature of such investments.

10.3   Implications for small firms

Small, early stage, high-technology companies that are seeking to raise venture capital should approach funds in which corporates have invested as such funds typically specialize in early stage, high-technology investments. Although these funds are often difficult to identify, the corporate partners can provide investee companies with industry specific and technical knowledge that venture capitalists alone do not possess, as well as numerous further benefits associated with corporate links. The small firm must decide upon its own motivations and the degree of contact it requires with the corporate investor as the venture capitalist can act as a buffer to the corporate if only limited contact is desired.

10.4   Implications for policy makers

The ACOST report of 1990 stated that 'the contribution of the venture capital industry to overcoming barriers to growth in smaller firms remains limited' (p. 35). This is largely a reflection of the concentration of the venture capital community on MBO deals. True 'Venture' capital is in increasingly short supply with a downward trend in the amount of finance made available by traditional funding sources, particularly for early stage, technology-focused investments. The corporate sector has the potential to provide an alternative and highly beneficial source of funding for venture capital funds which specialize in early stage, high-technology deals in the UK, and policy makers have an important role to play in stimulating corporate interest. Industrial corporations need to be educated about the benefits of venture capital involvement, and venture capitalists need to be made aware of the possibilities of corporate finance. Tax incentives for companies involved in venture capital have an important role to play in encouraging indirect CVC in the UK.

296   KEVIN N. McNALLY

Acknowledgements

This research was funded by an ESRC postgraduate research studentship, and the support of the ESRC is gratefully acknowledged. In addition, the author is indebted to Colin Mason, Gordon Murray, Maurice Anslow, Bill Bygrave, Hollister Sykes and Richard Harrison for their valuable help and advice, and also to the 39 venture capitalists who agreed to participate in this survey.

Notes

1   It will be noted that although the source material, the business literature and/or the press identified 26 of the 49 contacted venture capitalists as having raised finance from corporate sources (Table 2), only 16 of the participating 39 venture capitalists had raised corporate finance. This suggests that either all 10 non-respondents had raised finance from corporates or that these sources were inaccurate.
2   Venture capitalists were not willing to disclose the names of all of the companies that had invested in their funds - only a total of 45 corporate investors were named by respondents.

References

ACOST 1990 *The Enterprise Challenge: Overcoming Barriers to Growth in Small Firms* (London: HMSO).
Ahern, R. 1993 Implications of strategic alliances for small R&D-intensive firms, *Environment and Planning* A, 25: 1511-1256.
Bailey, P. 1985 Venture capital and the corporation, paper presented to the European Chemical Marketing Research Association, Berlin, Germany, 17 October, 1-15.
Block, Z. and MacMillan, I. C. 1993 *Corporate Venturing: Creating New Businesses Within the Firm* (Harvard: Harvard Business School Press).
Burgelman, R. A. 1985 Managing corporate entrepreneurship: new structures for implementing technological innovation, *Technology in Society*, 7: 91-103.
BVCA (British Venture Capital Association) 1992 *The British Venture Capital Association Directory 1992/3* (London: BVCA).
BVCA (British Venture Capital Association) 1993 Report on investment activity (London: BVCA, report for 1992).
BVCA (British Venture Capital Association) 1994 Independent venture capital funds: 1993 Fund raising, Press release 27 January (London: BVCA).
Bygrave, W. D. and Timmons, J. A. 1992, *Venture Capital at the Crossroads* (Harvard: Harvard Business School Press).
Cary, L. 1993 *The Venture Capital Report: Guide to Venture capital in the UK and Europe*, 6th edn (London: Management Today).
Clark, R. 1987 *Venture Capital in Britain, America and Japan* (Beckenham: Croom Helm).
Dickson, M. 1993 Market upswing sparks a revival, *Financial Times* 24 September, VII.
Drummond R. 1993 Venture capital and the early stage deal, *European Venture Capital Journal*, January/February, 13-15.
European Venture Capital Journal 1990 Focus on corporate venturing: corporate venture capital: trends, strategies and programmes in Europe, March/April, 3-12.
European Venture Capital Journal 1993 U.K. venture investing up 15% last year, April/May, 3-4.
Financial Times 1992a Venture capital famine forecast, 21 January, 12.
Financial Times 1992b Sharp decline in venture capital, 23 January, 7.
Hall, G. 1989 Lack of finance as a constraint on the expansion of innovatory small firms, in Barber, J., Metcalfe, J. S. and Porteous, M. (eds), *Barriers to Growth in Small Firms* (London: Routledge), 39-57.
Hardymon, G. F., DeNino, M. J. and Salter, M. S. 1983 When corporate venture capital doesn't work, *Harvard Business Review*, May/June, 114-120.
Honeyman, K. F. 1992 Corporate venturing as a development tool: benefits, pitfalls and strategies for success, undergraduate dissertation, Middlesex Business School.
INC 1993 What the VC crowd wants now, August, 32.
Journal of Applied Corporate Finance 1992 Roundtable on U.S. risk capital and innovation (with a look at Eastern Europe), 4(4): 48-78.
Littler, D. A. and Sweeting, R. C. 1984 Business innovation in the UK, *R&D Management*, 14(1): 1-10.
Littler, D. A. and Sweeting, R. C. 1987 Corporate development - preferred strategies in U.K. companies, *Long Range Planning*, 20(2): 125-131.

MacDonald, M. 1991 Strategic alliances and corporate venturing: a growing role for larger corporations, in *Creating Threshold Technology Companies in Canada: The Role for Venture Capital*, discussion paper, Science Council of Canada, Ottawa, 23–30.

MacMillan, H. 1931 *Report of the Committee on Finance and Industry*, Cmnd. 3897 (London: HMSO).

Mason, C. M. and Harrison, R. 1992 The supply of equity finance in the U.K.: a strategy for closing the equity gap, *Entrepreneurship and Regional Development*, 4: 357–380.

Mast, R. 1991 The changing nature of corporate venture capital programs, *European Venture Capital Journal*, March/April, 16–33.

Murray, G. 1991a The changing nature of competition in the UK venture capital industry, *NatWest Bank Quarterly Review*, November, 65–80.

Murray, G. 1991b Change and maturity in the UK venture capital industry 1991–95, Report for the British Venture Capital Association (Coventry: Warwick Business School).

Murray, G. 1992a A challenging marketplace for venture capital, *Long Range Planning*, 25(6): 79–86.

Murray, G. 1992b 'The second equity gap': exit problems for seed and early stage venture capitalists and their investee companies, paper presented at The European Foundation for Entrepreneurship Research, London, December.

Murray, G. 1993 Third party equity support for new technology based firms in the UK and continental Europe, paper presented at the Institute for Management, Innovation and Technology Seminar: Finance for Small Firms, Brussels, 29 November.

Murray, G. 1994 Third party equity – the role of the UK venture capital industry, in Davis, T. W. and Buckland, R. (eds), *Finance in Growing Firms* (London: Routledge).

Murray, G. and Lott, J. 1992 Have venture capital firms a bias against investment in high technology companies?, paper presented at the Babson Entrepreneurship Research Conference, INSEAD, France, July.

NEDO 1986 *Corporate Venturing: A Strategy for Innovation and Growth*, Report GPB 8008 (London: HMSO).

Oakey, R. P. 1993 Predatory networking: the role of small firms in the development of the British bio-technology industry, *International Small Business Journal*, 11(4): 9–22.

Oakley, P. G. 1987 External corporate venturing: the experience to date, in Rothwell, R. and Bessant, J. (eds), *Innovation: Adaptation and Growth* (Amsterdam: Elsevier), 287–296.

Ormerod, J. and Burns, I. 1988 *Raising Venture Capital in the UK* (London: Butterworths).

Pratt, G. 1990 Venture capital in the United Kingdom, *Bank of England Quarterly Bulletin*, February, 78–83.

Sykes, H. B. 1990 Corporate venture capital: strategies for success, *Journal of Business Venturing*, 5: 37–47.

UK Venture Capital Journal 1987 Current issues facing the UK venture capital industry, *UK Venture Capital Journal*: Special Report, March, 10–17.

Vachon, M. 1993 Venture capital reborn, *Venture Capital Journal*, January, 32–36.

Walker, J. 1993 Specialists in a sea of generalists – the specialised investor in the 1990s, *Venture Capital Report*, Henley-on-Thames, September.

Winters, T. E. and Murfin, D. L. 1988 Venture capital investing for corporate development objectives, *Journal of Business Venturing*, 3: 207–222.

[15]

THE USE OF COVENANTS: AN EMPIRICAL ANALYSIS OF VENTURE PARTNERSHIP AGREEMENTS*

PAUL GOMPERS   and   JOSH LERNER
Harvard University   Harvard University

ABSTRACT

This article examines covenants in 140 partnership agreements establishing venture capital funds. Despite the similar objectives and structures of these funds and the relatively limited number of contracting parties, the agreements are quite heterogenous in their inclusion of covenants. We examine two complementary hypotheses that suggest when covenants will be used. Covenant use may be determined by the extent of potential agency problems: because covenants are costly to negotiate and monitor, they will be employed only when these problems are severe. Alternatively, covenant use may reflect the supply and demand conditions in the venture capital industry. The price of venture capital services may shift if the demand for venture funds changes while the supply of fund managers remains fixed in the short run. The evidence suggests that both factors are important. This is in contrast to previous studies which have either focused exclusively on costly contracting or provided only weak support for the effects of supply and demand on contracts.

I. INTRODUCTION

LONG-TERM contracts govern the relationship between principals and agents when repeated short-term or implicit contracts are too costly or difficult to enforce. In this article, we explore two complementary hypotheses that may help explain the differences in the use of covenants and restrictions in long-term contracts governing venture funds.

First, because negotiating and monitoring specific covenants are costly,

* We thank Michael Eisenson and Scott Sperling of the Aeneas Group, T. Bondurant French and Tim Bliamptis of Brinson Partners, Robert Moreland of Kemper Financial Services, and Jesse Reyes and Kelly McGough of Venture Economics for generously providing us with access to their files. Jay Light, William Sahlman, and Robert Vishny helped us in this process. We would also like to thank George Baker, Susan Chaplinsky, Steven Kaplan, Ralph Lerner, Peter Pashigian, Sam Peltzman, William Sahlman, Howard Stevenson, an anonymous referee, and seminar participants at Boston University, Harvard University, the Massachusetts Institute of Technology, and the University of Chicago for their helpful comments and suggestions. Research assistance was provided by Tim Dodson, Meredith Fitzgerald, and Jay Yang. Financial support was provided by the Division of Research, Harvard Business School.

[*Journal of Law and Economics*, vol. XXXIX (October 1996)]

contracting parties should weigh the potential costs and benefits of relying on particular covenants. The ease of monitoring and the potential to engage in opportunistic behavior may vary among funds, leading to different sets of optimal covenants in different contracts. Because contracting is costly, it is probable that more restrictive contracts will be employed when monitoring is easier and the potential for opportunistic behavior is greater.

A second hypothesis relates the utilization of covenants to variation in supply and demand. In the short run, the supply of venture capital services may be fixed, with a modest number of venture partnerships raising funds of a carefully limited size each year. Demand for venture investing services has shifted sharply over the past 15 years. Increases in demand may lead to higher prices when contracts are written. Not only may the fees paid directly to the venture capitalists rise, but restrictions on activities that enrich the venture capitalists at their investors' expense may be lifted. The influence of both factors determines how monetary and private benefits are allocated along a Pareto-efficient frontier of contracts.

We construct a sample of 140 executed contracts from a major endowment and two investment managers that select venture capital investments for pension funds and other institutional investors. Venture capital limited partnership agreements are a potentially valuable source of information on contractual provisions. Because investors in a limited partnership must avoid direct involvement in the activities of the fund in order to maintain limited liability, the covenants and restrictions in the partnership contract are critical in determining the general partners' behavior. Considerable time and expense are devoted to negotiating the final form of the document. A single limited partnership agreement governs the relationship between the limited and general partners over the fund's life of a decade or more. Unlike other agreements (for example, employment contracts or strategic alliances), these contracts are rarely renegotiated. The heterogeneity of venture organizations allows us to analyze the importance of demand shifts and costly contracting in determining the extent of covenant use in partnership agreements.

We examine which of these 140 agreements includes 14 covenant classes and the factors associated with their inclusion or deletion. The evidence indicates that *both* supply and demand conditions and variations in the cost of contracting are important in determining the number and kind of covenants in the contracts. In univariate comparisons, fewer restrictions are found in funds established during years with greater inflows of new capital, funds in which limited partners do not employ investment managers, and funds where general partners enjoy higher levels of compensation. For instance, funds closed in years when the venture pool was growing at above the median rate had an average of four classes of restrictions; funds closed in other years had more than seven.

We employ regression analyses to analyze the number of covenants, and we find support for both hypotheses. Both hypotheses continue to be supported when we examine first differences, exploring the changes in the number of covenants in successive funds raised by the same venture organization. These results are in contrast to earlier studies of contractual provisions, which have either focused solely on the costly contracting hypothesis or found only limited evidence for the importance of supply and demand conditions.

This article is organized as follows. Section II presents a brief history of the venture capital industry. The theoretical literature on contractual completeness and its empirical implications are presented in Section III. In Section IV, we describe the construction of the sample. The empirical analysis is presented in Section V. Section VI concludes the article.

II. THE VENTURE CAPITAL INDUSTRY

Entrepreneurs often develop ideas that require substantial capital to implement. Most entrepreneurs do not have sufficient funds to finance these projects themselves and must seek outside financing. Start-up companies that lack substantial tangible assets, expect several years of negative earnings, and have uncertain prospects are unlikely to receive bank loans or other debt financing. Venture capitalists finance these high-risk, potentially high-reward projects, purchasing equity stakes while the firms are still privately held. Venture capitalists have backed many high-technology companies, including Microsoft, Intel, Lotus, Apple Computer, and Genentech, as well as a substantial number of service firms.

Whether the firm is in a high- or low-technology industry, venture capitalists are active investors. They monitor the progress of firms, sit on boards of directors, and mete out financing based on the attainment of milestones. Venture capitalists retain the right to appoint key managers and remove members of the entrepreneurial team. In addition, venture capitalists provide entrepreneurs with access to consultants, investment bankers, and lawyers.

The first modern venture capital firm, American Research and Development (ARD), was formed in 1946. A handful of other venture funds were established in the decade after ARD's formation. Most, like ARD, were structured as publicly traded closed-end funds. The first venture capital limited partnership, Draper, Gaither, and Anderson, was formed in 1958. Imitators soon followed, but limited partnerships accounted for a minority of the venture pool during the 1960s and 1970s. The remainder of venture capital organizations were either closed-end funds or small business investment companies (SBICs), federally guaranteed risk-capital pools that proliferated during the 1960s. The annual flow of money into new venture funds during these years never exceeded a few hundred million dollars and usually was much less.

As Figure 1 shows, funds flowing into the venture capital industry and the number of active venture organizations increased dramatically during the late 1970s and early 1980s. The increase in new capital contributions outpaced growth in the number of active organizations, suggesting that the short-run supply of venture organizations may have been fixed.[1] Starting a new venture capital firm is difficult. Raising a limited partnership may take more than a year, especially for funds with no track record. When demand expanded, the supply of venture capital organizations was fixed for some time. We test this claim empirically by examining the relationship between the growth in fund size and the growth in annual inflows to the venture capital industry. The correlation coefficient between annual observations of these two variables (both expressed in constant 1992 dollars) from 1968 to 1992 is 0.48. This is significant at the 2 percent confidence level.

The single most important factor accounting for the increase in money flowing into the venture capital sector was the 1979 amendment to the "prudent man" rule governing pension fund investments. Prior to that date, the Employee Retirement Income Security Act of 1974 prohibited pension funds from investing substantial amounts of money in venture capital or other high-risk asset classes. The Department of Labor's clarification of the rule explicitly allowed pension managers to invest in high-risk assets, including venture capital. The rule change opened the door to pensions' tremendous capital resources. Table 1 shows that, in 1978, when $424 million was invested in new venture capital funds, individuals accounted for the largest share (32 percent). Pension funds supplied just 15 percent. Eight years later, when more than $4 billion was invested, pension funds accounted for more than half of all contributions.

An associated change during the 1980s was the increasing role of investment advisers. During the late 1970s and early 1980s, almost all pension funds invested directly in venture funds. Because venture capital was a small portion of their portfolios, few resources were devoted to monitoring and evaluating these investments. During the mid-1980s, investment advisers (often referred to as "gatekeepers") entered the market to advise insti-

[1] Practitioner accounts emphasize that venture capitalists have highly specialized skills, which are difficult to develop or even identify. For instance, Robert Kunze of Hambrecht & Quist notes: "The life of the associate [in a venture capital organization] is akin to playing house. Since associates never make the actual investment decision . . . it's impossible to tell whether or not they'll be successful venture capitalists if and when they get the chance." Robert J. Kunze, Nothing Ventured: The Perils and Payoffs of the Great American Venture Capital Game (1990).

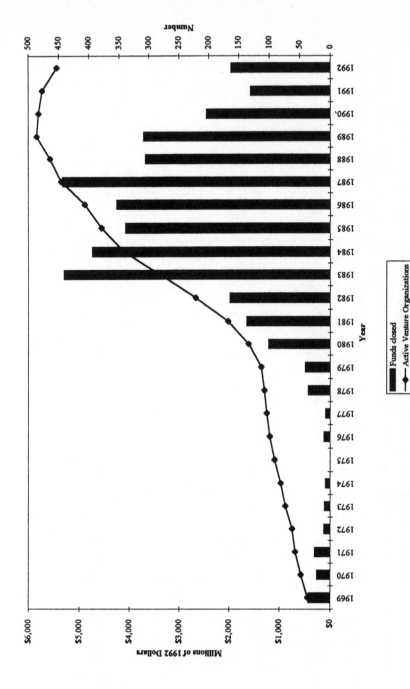

FIGURE 1.—Funds committed to independent venture capital partnerships and the number of active venture organizations. The fund commitments are in constant 1992 dollars. The number of active venture organizations is defined as all those firms that have raised an independent venture capital limited partnership within the last 10 years. The information is from the Venture Economics funds database.

TABLE 1

SUMMARY STATISTICS FOR VENTURE CAPITAL FUND-RAISING BY INDEPENDENT VENTURE PARTNERSHIPS

	1978	1979	1980	1981	1982	1983	1984	1985	1986	1987	1988	1989	1990	1991	1992
First closing of funds:															
Number of funds	25	28	54	81	97	147	150	99	86	115	79	89	51	35	31
Size (millions of 1992 $)	424	482	1,208	1,642	1,976	5,289	4,728	4,065	4,246	5,321	3,664	3,699	2,442	1,563	1,950
Sources of funds (in percent):															
Private pension funds	15	31	30	23	33	26	25	23	39	27	27	22	31	25	22
Public pension funds	*	*	*	*	*	5	9	10	12	12	20	14	22	17	20
Corporations	10	17	19	17	12	12	14	12	11	10	12	20	7	4	3
Individuals	32	23	16	23	21	21	15	13	12	12	8	6	11	12	11
Endowments	9	10	14	12	7	8	6	8	6	10	11	12	13	24	18
Insurance companies	16	4	13	15	14	12	13	11	10	15	9	13	9	6	14
Foreign investors	18	15	8	10	13	16	18	23	11	14	13	13	7	12	11
Independent venture partnerships as a share of the total venture pool (in percent):†			40	44	58	68	72	73	75	78	80	79	80	80	81

NOTE.—The information is from the Venture Economics funds database and various issues of the *Venture Capital Journal*.

* Public pension funds are included with private pension funds in these years.

† This series is defined differently in different years. In some years, the *Venture Capital Journal* states that nonbank small business investment companies and publicly traded venture funds are included with independent venture partnerships. In other years, these funds are counted in other categories.

tutional investors about venture investments. The gatekeepers pooled resources from their clients, monitored the progress of existing investments, and evaluated potential new venture funds. By 1991, one-third of all pension fund commitments were made through an investment adviser. One-fifth of all money raised by new funds came through an investment adviser.

A final change in the venture capital industry during this period was the rise of the limited partnership as the dominant organizational form. In a venture capital limited partnership, the venture capitalists are general partners and control the fund's activities. The investors serve as limited partners. Investors monitor the fund's progress, attend annual meetings, but cannot become involved in the fund's day-to-day management if they are to retain limited liability. Venture partnerships have predetermined, finite lifetimes (usually 10 years, though extensions are often allowed). Most venture organizations raise funds every 2–5 years. Table 1 shows that partnerships have grown from 40 percent of the venture pool in 1980 to 81 percent in 1992.

The steady growth in commitments to the venture capital industry was reversed in the late 1980s. Returns on venture capital funds declined because of overinvestment in various industries and the entry of inexperienced venture capitalists. (Between 1978 and 1988, the number of active venture organizations increased fourfold.) As investors became disappointed with returns, they committed less capital to the industry. The recent activity in the initial public offering market and the exit of many inexperienced venture capitalists have led to an increase in returns. New capital commitments have risen accordingly. These cycles in fund-raising introduce significant variations in the demand for the services of venture capitalists.

III. DETERMINANTS OF COVENANTS

A. *Theoretical Suggestions*

Economists have argued that transactions subject to repeated bargaining problems should be governed by long-term contracts.[2] For example, a coal mine operator may seek to expropriate rents by raising prices once a utility has built a plant near the mine shaft. The terms and conditions that govern the contractual relationship between the two parties are critical to limiting opportunistic behavior and ensuring allocational efficiency. A venture partnership presents many of the same problems: once the funds have been

---

[2] Benjamin Klein, Robert G. Crawford, & Armen A. Alchian, Vertical Integration, Appropriable Rents and the Competitive Contracting Process, 21 J. Law & Econ. 297 (1978); Oliver E. Williamson, Transaction-Cost Economics: The Governance of Contractual Relations, 22 J. Law & Econ. 233 (1979).

raised, the limited partners have very limited recourse to these funds. One of the few remedies is to insist on terms and conditions that will limit the general partner's ability to behave opportunistically.

Two approaches to understanding the determinants of contractual provisions have emerged in the financial and organizational literatures. Both approaches assume that observed contracts are optimal given the contractual environment. The two hypotheses should be viewed as complements. Both effects may be at work simultaneously. Our tests examine the relative importance of each hypothesis in determining contractual outcomes.[3]

The costly contracting theory predicts that because negotiation and enforcement of explicit provisions are costly, covenants are included only when the benefits of restricting activity are greater than the costs. Williamson advances similar arguments about factors that influence contractual completeness.[4] Because the ease of monitoring and incentives to pursue opportunistic behavior vary, the optimal set of restrictions differs across contracts.

Various investigations provide support for the costly contracting hypothesis. Smith and Warner argue that the complexity of debt contracts reflects the cost of contracting.[5] Crocker and Reynolds argue that the degree of specificity in payment terms found in U.S. government jet engine procurement contracts is related to the level of technological and production uncertainties.[6] Malitz shows that three specific classes of bond covenants are more common for issuers with characteristics that may proxy for a greater need for monitoring.[7]

A second hypothesis contends that relative supply and demand conditions in the venture capital market affect the covenants and restrictions in long-

---

[3] An alternative approach to the question of covenant inclusion is suggested by Sanford Grossman & Oliver Hart, The Costs and Benefits of Ownership: A Theory of Vertical and Lateral Integration, 94 J. Pol. Econ. 691 (1986). These authors argue that ownership is the ability to exclude someone from access to a particular asset. Ownership should be assigned to the party who will be least likely to engage in wasteful ex post renegotiating. Contractual covenants can be loosely interpreted as a mechanism that reserves ownership of particular activities for the limited partners. (Under partnership law, the general partner is assumed to have those rights not explicitly reserved by the limited partners.)

[4] Oliver E. Williamson, The Economic Institutions of Capitalism: Firms, Markets, Relational Contracting (1985).

[5] Clifford W. Smith, Jr., & Jerold B. Warner, On Financial Contracting: An Analysis of Bond Covenants, 7 J. Fin. Econ. 117 (1979).

[6] Keith J. Crocker & Kenneth J. Reynolds, The Efficiency of Incomplete Contracts: An Empirical Analysis of Air Force Engine Procurement, 24 RAND J. Econ. 126 (1993).

[7] lleen Malitz, On Financial Contracting: The Determinants of Bond Covenants, Fin. Mgmt., Summer 1986, at 18.

term contracts. If the demand for the services of experienced venture capitalists changes rapidly while the supply of those venture capitalists is fixed in the short run, the price of venture capital services should rise: venture capitalists' expected total compensation should increase.

The price of venture capital services is the compensation that general partners of the fund receive. This compensation has two components. The first component is monetary compensation paid to fund managers. The venture capitalist may also receive private benefits from certain activities. For ease of explication, we focus on private benefits that enhance the venture capitalist's reputation in a certain area. For example, the venture capitalist may seek to invest in leveraged buyouts (LBOs) because, if he succeeds, he can raise a specialized LBO fund. The benefits of these reputation-building activities accrue exclusively to the venture capitalist. Because the expected return to limited partners is likely to be diminished by these activities, they should seek to prohibit them.

The numbers of venture capitalists and investors are small, so the allocation of private benefits will be affected by relative supply and demand conditions. A sudden increase in demand for venture capital investing services should increase their price. Competition among venture capitalists does not lead to allocating all the gains to the investor because venture capital funds are imperfect substitutes for each other. Only a small number of venture capitalists may be raising a fund at any particular time, and these firms are likely to be differentiated by size, industry focus, location, and reputation. Many venture organizations will limit both how often they raise funds and the size of the funds that they raise, in the belief that excessive growth reduces returns. Meanwhile, managers who allocate alternative investments for institutions often operate under limitations about the types of funds in which they can invest (for instance, rules that prohibit investments into first funds raised by venture organizations) and are pressured to meet allocation targets by the end of the fiscal year. Institutional investors have few alternatives to investing in new partnerships: the market for secondary interests in existing venture partnerships is illiquid and very thin.

It might appear puzzling that much of the adjustment takes place through *both* the insertion or deletion of covenants and explicit monetary compensation. Why should the entire adjustment not take place through the adjustment of compensation? One possibility is that these adjustments in the consumption of private benefits are an optimal response. The combination of expected fund returns and reputation-building activity by the venture capitalist define a Pareto frontier of possible contracts. The level of expected returns cannot be increased without curtailing reputation-building activity and vice versa. If venture capitalists optimize the mixture of compensation, then increases in demand are likely to lead to both increased monetary compensation and reduced restrictiveness. In many cases, it may be easier and cheaper to adjust contractual restrictiveness.

A related explanation is suggested by the literature on agency issues among institutional investors.[8] These covenants represent a less visible way to make price adjustments than explicit modifications of the split in capital gains. Deviations from the standard 80 percent/20 percent division of profits are likely to attract widespread attention in the institutional investor community.[9] The inclusion or deletion of covenants, however, is much less likely to attract notice. Investment officers responsible for choosing venture capital investments may find that concessions made in this manner attract less scrutiny from regulators or superiors.

While they are featured prominently in practitioners' accounts of contracting, supply and demand theories of contractual design have received little attention in academic circles. Hubbard and Weiner present a model that derives predictions about the relative importance of transaction costs and "market power" in determining contractual provisions.[10] They test those predictions in a sample of natural gas contracts. While they find some monopsonistic effects on the initial contract prices (by using absolute and relative size of the transacting parties as a proxy for market power), they find little support for market power in other contractual provisions.[11]

B. Empirical Implications of Costly Contracting

The costly contracting theory predicts that contracting parties should balance the benefits of restricting activities with the cost of negotiating the provisions, writing the contractual clauses, and monitoring compliance. Fund- and firm-specific factors increasing the benefits of restrictions or decreasing monitoring costs should lead to a greater number of restrictions.

Monitoring costs may be related to fund size. A large fund should be

---

[8] Josef Lakonishok, Andrei Shleifer, & Robert W. Vishny, The Structure and Performance of the Money Management Industry, Brookings Papers Econ. Activity: Microecon., 1992, at 339.

[9] For a recent example, see Asset Alternatives, Warburg Points the Way toward a Lower Carry, 4 Private Equity Analyst 7 (July 1994).

[10] R. Glenn Hubbard & Robert J. Weiner, Efficient Contracting and Market Power: Evidence from the U.S. Natural Gas Industry, 34 J. Law & Econ. 25 (1991).

[11] The costly contracting and supply and demand hypotheses are not mutually exclusive. In fact, the supply and demand hypothesis assumes that certain activities of the general partner impose costs on limited partners and need to be controlled by restricting those activities. A third possibility is that contractual provisions are benign and persist because there are no costs or benefits to their inclusion. This suggestion appears to run counter to the protracted and costly bargaining over covenants that precedes the signing of venture partnership agreements and many other types of contracts.

easier to monitor because it makes more investments and provides more opportunity to evaluate the policies of the venture capitalists. If that is the case, we would expect that larger funds would have more covenants and restrictions. The benefits of restricting certain activities may also be greater in larger funds. Because larger funds may have greater scope to make investments that do not necessarily benefit the limited partners (for example, substantial investments in leveraged buyouts or other venture funds), restrictions on these types of investments may be important.

Investors may not, however, need to restrict the activities of venture organizations that have reputations as fair and reasonable players. Reputational concerns make opportunistic behavior less attractive and reduce the need for covenants. The likelihood of including covenants that restrict activities of the general partner should be significantly reduced for reputable venture capital organizations.

The sensitivity of compensation to performance may also reduce restrictions. Jensen and Meckling argue that agency costs decline as the financial rewards of managers become more closely tied to the firm's future prospects.[12] Increasing the sensitivity of the venture capitalists' compensation to performance should reduce incentives to make investments that do not maximize limited partners' returns. The perceived need for covenants should thus fall.

The relative benefits of covenants may also increase as the scope for opportunistic behavior rises. Investments in early-stage and high-technology companies may increase the venture capitalist's ability to engage in opportunistic activities. These investment classes potentially involve the greatest asymmetric information and allow venture capitalists more opportunity to exploit their knowledge. Accounting performance may shed little light on the performance of a young firm; assessing the health of a high-technology firm is likely to require a detailed understanding of the technical position of the company and its competitors. Restrictions on activities of the general partners may thus be more likely. Monitoring compliance with the covenants in these types of funds may, however, be more difficult. Consequently, we have an ambiguous prediction about the relationship between the type of fund and the number of covenants.

A final empirical implication of the costly contracting view is that the

---

[12] Michael C. Jensen & William H. Meckling, Theory of the Firm: Managerial Behavior, Agency Costs, and Ownership Structure, 3 J. Fin. Econ. 305 (1976). While the more visible portion of venture capitalists' return, their share of profits, is bunched between 20 percent and 21 percent, other aspects of compensation vary. Consequently, the sensitivity of pay to performance varies considerably. See Paul A. Gompers & Josh Lerner, An Analysis of Compensation in the U.S. Venture Capital Partnership (unpublished manuscript, Harvard Univ. 1995).

number of covenants may change over time if investors learn about the venture capital industry. Because venture limited partnerships have become widespread only during the past 15 years and the market has only gradually learned about the incentives and activities of venture capitalists, early contracts may be significantly different from more recent agreements. In particular, early contracts may have far fewer covenants and restrictions than later contracts. If all potential future outcomes cannot be foreseen, the cost of writing and monitoring specific contracts may be very high. As the process and incentives become better understood, contracts could include more specific restrictions.[13]

C. *Empirical Implications of the Supply and Demand Hypothesis*

The supply and demand hypothesis suggests that, when the demand for venture capital services is high relative to a fixed supply of venture capital providers, the number of restrictions should decline. The bulk of the covenants prevent behavior that enriches venture capitalists at the investors' expense. Thus, the general partner's "compensation" increases with reductions in the number of restrictions. Several factors proxy for shifts in relative demand.

While it is impossible to directly measure the supply of, and demand for, venture capital services, we can measure capital inflows relative to the existing venture pool. If the short-run supply of venture services is fixed, changes in inflows may primarily reflect changes in demand. When the annual influx of funds is a large fraction of the existing venture pool (demand is high), the average number of covenants should fall.

The presence of an investment manager may affect the likelihood of including restrictive covenants in venture agreements. Investment managers not only select the funds in which pension funds invest, but also negotiate the terms and conditions of the partnership agreement. Investment managers typically place the funds of several pensions into a single venture fund. Investment managers believe that this bundling allows them to insert restrictions that otherwise would not be included in the partnership agree-

---

[13] The structure of railroad sidetrack agreements in the late nineteenth and early twentieth centuries is examined in Russell Pittman, Specific Investments, Contracts, and Opportunism: The Evolution of Railroad Sidetrack Agreements, 34 J. Law & Econ. 565 (1991). The author argues that the provisions in these contracts evolved in response to specific opportunistic behavior that took place. Similarly, evidence that few debt contracts prior to the leveraged buyout boom of the mid-1980s included event covenants related to buyouts or recapitalizations is presented in Kenneth Lehn & Annette Poulsen, Contractual Resolution of Bondholder-Stockholder Conflicts in Leveraged Buyouts, 34 J. Law & Econ. 645 (1991). After the risk of expropriation became known, these types of risks were addressed with new types of covenants.

ment.[14] Raising a fund without the participation of these investment managers should indicate that the demand for the experienced venture capitalists' services is high. Therefore, funds without gatekeepers should have fewer covenants.[15] Anecdotal evidence supporting this hypothesis is found in discussions of the fund-raising strategies of venture capital firms. Some established venture organizations, such as Greylock, explicitly refuse to take money from investment managers.

The demand for top-performing venture capital organizations should also be high relative to the supply of their services. While older, better-performing venture organizations do add general partners to their funds, they tend to limit growth in the belief that large organizations lose their ability to operate effectively. While direct measures of past performance are difficult to find, several proxies for performance can be tested. First, older venture organizations are likely to be better on average than new firms because poorly performing organizations will be unable to raise new funds. Older firms therefore should have fewer covenants. Second, funds with higher compensation should have fewer covenants. The level of compensation also proxies for high demand for the venture organization's services.

The supply and demand hypothesis also predicts that pay sensitivity should be negatively related to the number of covenants. If the venture capitalist is taking more compensation in the form of private benefits at the expense of potential returns, limited partners want to tie the venture capitalist's monetary compensation more closely to fund returns.

Two difficulties with these predictions must be discussed. First, age and total compensation may be related to reputation. The greater the venture capitalists' reputational capital is, the less likely they are to engage in opportunistic behavior that might destroy future returns to their reputation. Larger and more highly compensated venture capital firms may have fewer

---

[14] See, for instance, Jason Huemer, Brinson Partners on a Roll, 32 Venture Capital J. 32 (June 1992).

[15] An alternative interpretation is that funds selected by investment managers have a greater potential for agency problems. A particular concern is that the investment manager and general partners may engage in collusive behavior. To address these potential problems, limited partners may demand more covenants. It is very difficult to design a test that can distinguish between these two interpretations, but there are at least two reasons why the agency hypothesis is problematic. First, it is unclear why the investment manager would want to engage in collusive behavior with the venture capitalists. Investment managers receive all their compensation from the limited partners. These fees are typically independent of the returns generated by the venture funds that they have selected and of the value of the funds' assets. Second, investment managers are very sensitive to reputational concerns. Most of their clients are pension funds and endowments, whose trustees are under a considerable amount of regulatory and public scrutiny. If an investment manager is revealed to have behaved in a questionable manner, the repercussions for him are likely to be severe.

restrictions because they have less incentive to exploit investors, not because their funds are in greater demand.

Second, the costly contracting hypothesis may generate a similar time-series pattern. In particular, it may be that the costs of opportunism for the venture capitalists vary over time. During periods when there is a particularly heavy inflow of funds, fewer covenants are needed because the cost of opportunistic behavior (for instance, forgone future fund-raising) is greater.

This interpretation, while seemingly plausible, is problematic for two reasons. First, venture partnerships typically raise funds only every several years. A year of rapid growth in the venture pool tends to be followed by another year of rapid growth, but there is no correlation across several years.[16] Thus, it is unclear why worries about future fund-raising should be particularly intense in high-growth years. Second, this hypothesis assumes that limited partners can rapidly identify opportunistic behavior by venture capitalists. In actuality, venture capital investments are long-term by nature, and it is often difficult for outsiders to assess the status of the private firms in a venture capitalist's portfolio. Consequently, it takes a long time for opportunistic behavior to be identified.[17]

IV. THE SAMPLE

This section describes the construction of the sample of partnership agreements. The initial partnership agreement governs the partnership over its life. This agreement is important because it is the crucial mechanism for limiting the behavior of venture capitalists. Many of the oversight mechanisms found in corporations—for example, powerful boards of directors and the market for corporate control—are not available here. While limited partners can serve on advisory boards that review certain policy issues, if they become involved in the day-to-day management of a venture fund, they risk losing their limited liability.[18] No liquid market for partnership interests exists, and limited partners are frequently restricted from selling

---

[16] The average venture organization that raised a fund between 1968 and 1987 and raised a follow-on fund did so 2.9 years later. Using data from 1968 to 1994, we find that the flow into venture capital funds (expressed as a percentage of the venture pool in the previous year) has a correlation coefficient with its 1-year lag of 0.873 (with a p-value of .000). The correlation coefficient with its 3-year lag is -0.105 (with a p-value of .634).

[17] To cite one example, Hambrecht & Quist raised a fund in 1981 that was plagued by a wide array of organizational problems and had exceedingly poor returns. The venture organization was nonetheless able to raise one dozen funds with nearly half a billion dollars in capital over the remainder of the decade. See Ralph King, Jr., "The Money Corner," 145 Forbes 38 (March 5, 1990).

[18] Jack S. Levin, Structuring Venture Capital, Private Equity, and Entrepreneurial Transactions (1994).

their partnership interests. Consequently, the primary remedy for the limited partners is legal action triggered by a violation of the covenants.[19]

We restrict our analysis to U.S.-based independent private partnerships primarily engaged in venture capital investments: investments in equity or equity-linked securities of private firms with active participation by the fund managers in the management or oversight of the firms. We eliminate funds whose stated mandate is to invest more than 50 percent of their funds in other types of assets, such as the securities of firms undergoing leveraged buyouts or being acquired, "special situations," other venture funds, or publicly traded securities.[20]

A variety of other organizations are also not included, even though they may make venture investments. These include publicly traded venture capital funds, wholly owned subsidiaries of financial and industrial corporations, funds with a single limited partner, and SBICs. The excluded organizations are governed by different regulations which often affect their charters. Finally, we omit organizations headquartered outside the United States. These partnerships are subject to foreign laws, which may have complex effects.

We use the 140 partnership agreements in the files of two gatekeepers and one limited partner. (These data sources are described in detail in the Appendix.) We assess the completeness and representativeness of this sample by comparing these funds with a database of venture capital funds compiled by Venture Economics' Investors Services Group. This database includes over two thousand venture capital funds, SBICs, and related organizations.[21]

Table 2 examines the independent venture partnerships in the Venture Economics database that closed between 1978 and 1992. We compare the

[19] For accounts of recent litigation, see Asset Alternatives, Iowa Suits Test LPs' Authority to Abolish Fund, Private Equity Analyst, May 1994, at 1; and E. S. Ely, Dr. Silver's Tarnished Prescription, Venture, July 1987, at 54. For a more detailed discussion of the latter case, see Lincoln Nat'l Life Ins. Co. v. Silver, 1987 U.S. Dist. LEXIS 240 (N.D. Ill., January 13, 1987), count dismissed, 1990 U.S. Dist. LEXIS 13667 (N.D. Ill., October 4, 1990), 1991 U.S. Dist. LEXIS 13584 (N.D. Ill., September 24, 1991), 1991 U.S. Dist. LEXIS 13857 (N.D. Ill., September 30, 1991), adopted, summ. judgmt. granted, 1991 U.S. Dist. LEXIS 15758 (N.D. Ill., October 30, 1991), 1991 U.S. Dist. LEXIS 15804 (N.D. Ill., October 30, 1991), summ. judgmt. granted, 1992 U.S. Dist. LEXIS 8968 (N.D. Ill., June 23, 1992), mot. granted, mot. denied, 1993 U.S. Dist. LEXIS 11325 (N.D. Ill., August 12, 1993).

[20] Many of the venture capital organizations in the sample raised an LBO fund during the 1980s. We do not include such funds, even if all the other funds associated with the organization are devoted to venture capital. "Funds of funds"—venture funds that invest more than 50 percent of their capital in other venture partnerships—are also excluded. We exclude all these partnerships because their investment opportunities are substantially different and their contractual terms may consequently differ.

[21] The database is described in detail in Gompers & Lerner, *supra* note 12.

TABLE 2

THE CHARACTERISTICS OF THE SAMPLE OF 140 VENTURE PARTNERSHIP AGREEMENTS

	Included in Our Sample	Not Included in Our Sample	p-Value, Test of No Difference
Number of observations	140	1,030	
Size of fund (millions of 1992 dollars)	98.6 [73.4]	43.2 [28.9]	.000 [.000]
Age of venture organization at time of first closing (years)	7.34 [5.75]	3.88 [1.33]	.000 [.000]
Previous funds raised by venture organization	3.58 [2]	1.65 [1]	.000 [.000]
Fund based in California? (in percent)	39.4	28.6	{.010}
Date of fund's first closing	December 1985 [February 1986]	April 1985 [December 1984]	.032 [.027]

NOTE.—The first two columns compare the characteristics of the independent venture partnerships in the Venture Economics funds database whose first closing was between 1978 and 1992 that were and were not included in our sample. We present both the mean and the median (in brackets) of several measures. The third column presents the p-values of t-tests, Wilcoxon signed-rank tests (in brackets), and a Pearson χ^2-test (in braces) of the null hypotheses that these distributions are identical.

characteristics of the funds included in our sample and those not included using t-, Wilcoxon signed-rank, and Pearson χ^2-tests. We find that larger funds by more established partnerships are significantly more likely to be included in our sample.[22] In addition, funds based in California (the center of the U.S. venture industry) are more likely to be included. Finally, the typical fund in the sample closed somewhat more recently than the other funds in the Venture Economics database.

These partnership agreements are complex, often extending for 100 pages or longer. Our procedure for coding the documents was as follows. First, we reviewed the earlier literature and identified the broad areas involved in partnership agreements.[23] A research assistant then culled the con-

[22] We examine whether the mixture of firms may have changed over time. In each of the three periods examined—1978–82, 1983–87, and 1988–92—the funds are significantly larger, and the venture organizations are significantly more established than those not included in the sample.

[23] We employed Joseph W. Bartlett, Venture Capital Law, Business, Strategies, and Investment Planning (1988); Joseph W. Bartlett, Venture Capital Law, Business, Strategies, and Investment Planning: 1994 Supplement (1994); Craig E. Dauchy & Mark T. Harmon, Structuring Venture Capital Limited Partnerships, 3 Computer Law. 1 (November 1986); Michael J. Halloran, Agreement of Limited Partnership, in 1 Venture Capital and Public Offering Negotiation (Michael J. Halloran, Lee F. Benton, Robert V. Gunderson, Jr., Keith L. Kearney, & Jorge del Calvo eds. 1992); William A. Sahlman, The Structure and Governance

tractual provisions in these areas from a subsample of 40 contracts. We then used these 40 descriptions to design a coding form capturing the key features of the agreements. The actual coding of the 140 contracts was done by an MBA candidate who had previously received a law degree and spent several years practicing contract law.

V. EMPIRICAL ANALYSIS

In this section, we examine the determinants of covenant inclusion or omission. We characterize each venture partnership using a series of proxies that measure the probability of opportunistic behavior and supply and demand conditions for venture capital services. We examine whether 14 major classes of covenants are included in each agreement and how the inclusion of covenants varies with these proxies.

The results indicate that both sets of proxies are important in explaining the number of covenants. In univariate comparisons, the most significant differences are associated with measures of relative supply and demand conditions, especially the inflow of venture capital in that year. In regressions—whether cross-sectional analyses of the entire sample or first-difference analyses of those organizations that raised multiple funds—both sets of proxies have significant explanatory power.

Before presenting the analysis, however, we qualitatively discuss the 14 classes of restrictions. Each covenant is related to a particular type of opportunistic activity that the general partners might undertake for their own personal benefit but may impose costs on the limited partners. Our description of the covenants will focus on the potential agency costs that might arise if the covenants were not included. The tests in Sections V B and V C will then examine how the number of covenants varies with potential agency problems in the fund and with the relative supply and demand for venture capital services.

A. Key Covenant Classes

This analysis focuses on 14 covenant classes in partnership agreements. These classes include all those restrictions that are found in (i) at least 5 percent of the agreements in our sample and (ii) no more than 95 percent of agreements (between 7 and 133 out of the 140 contracts). In this way, we enhance the tractability of the analyses by eliminating several classes that are either standardized ''boilerplate'' or else exceedingly rare.

---

of Venture Capital Organizations, 27 J. Fin. Econ. 473 (1990); Venture Economics, Terms and Conditions of Venture Capital Partnerships (1989); and Venture Economics, 1992 Terms and Conditions of Venture Capital Partnerships (1992).

480   THE JOURNAL OF LAW AND ECONOMICS

Because the analysis is focused on the number of covenant classes employed, it does not do full justice to the restrictions' complexity. Many variants of each covenant are found in the partnership agreements. The qualitative descriptions of the 14 classes of restrictions provide a sense of the complexity of these terms. In the descriptions and the analyses, we divide these covenants into three broad families: those relating to the overall management of the fund, the activities of the general partners, and the permissible types of investments.

1. Covenants Relating to Overall Fund Management

The first set of restrictions limits the amount invested in any one firm. These provisions are intended to ensure that the general partners do not attempt to salvage an investment in a poorly performing firm by investing significant resources in follow-on funding. The general partners typically do not receive a share of profits until the limited partners have received the return of their investment. The venture capitalists' share of profits can be thought of as a call option: the general partners may gain disproportionately from increasing risk of the portfolio at the expense of diversification. This limitation is frequently expressed as a maximum percentage of capital invested in the fund (typically called committed capital) that can be invested in any one firm. Alternatively, the limit may be expressed as a percent of the current value of the fund's assets. In a few cases, the aggregate size of the partnership's two or three largest investments is capped.

The second covenant class limits the use of debt. As option holders, general partners may be tempted to increase the variance of their portfolio's returns by leveraging the fund. Increasing the riskiness of the portfolio would increase the value of their call option at the investors' expense. Partnership agreements often limit the ability of venture capitalists to borrow funds themselves or to guarantee the debt of their portfolio companies (which might be seen as equivalent to direct borrowing). Partnership agreements may limit debt to a set percentage of committed capital or assets and in some instances also restrict the maturity of the debt to ensure that all borrowing is short-term.[24]

The third restriction relates to coinvestments with the venture organiza-

---

[24] A related provision—found in virtually all partnership agreements—is that the limited partners will avoid unrelated business taxable income. Tax-exempt institutions must pay taxes on UBTI, which is defined as the gross income from any unrelated business that the institution regularly carries out. If the venture partnership is generating significant income from debt-financed property, the limited partners may have tax liabilities (see Bartlett, *supra* note 23). In the analysis below, we code funds as having a restriction on debt only if there are limitations beyond a clause concerning UBTI.

tion's earlier and/or later funds. Many venture organizations manage multiple funds, formed several years apart. These can lead to opportunistic behavior.[25] Consequently, partnership agreements for second or later funds frequently require that the fund's advisory board review such investments or that a majority (or supermajority) of the limited partners approve these transactions. Contracts also address these problems by requiring that the earlier fund invest simultaneously at the same valuation. Alternatively, the investment may only be allowed if one or more unaffiliated venture organizations simultaneously invest at the same price.

A fourth class of covenant relates to reinvestment of profits. For several reasons, venture capitalists may reinvest capital gains rather than distributing the profits to the limited partners.[26] The reinvestment of profits may require approval of the advisory board or the limited partners. Alternatively, such reinvestment may be prohibited after a certain date, or after a certain percentage of the committed capital is invested.

2. Covenants Relating to Activities of the General Partners

Five frequently encountered classes of restrictions curb the activities of the general partners. The first of these limits the ability of the general partners to invest personal funds in firms. If general partners invest in selected firms, they may devote excessive time to these firms and may not terminate funding if the firms encounter difficulties. To address this problem, the size of the investment that the general partners can make in any of their fund's portfolio firms is often limited. This limit may be expressed as a percentage of the fund's total investment or (less frequently) of the net worth of the venture capitalist. In addition, the venture capitalists may be required to seek permission from the advisory board or limited partners. An alternative

---

[25] Consider, for instance, a venture organization whose first fund has made an investment in a troubled firm. The general partners may find it optimal for their second fund to invest in this firm in the hopes of salvaging the investment. Distortions may also be introduced by the need for the venture capitalists to report an attractive return for their first fund as they seek investors for a third fund. Many venture funds will write up the valuation of firms in their portfolios to the price paid in the last venture round. By having the second fund invest in one of the first fund's firms at an inflated valuation, they can (temporarily) inflate the reported performance of their first fund.

[26] First, many partnerships receive fees on the basis of either the value of assets under management or adjusted committed capital (capital less any distributions). Distributing profits will reduce these fees. Second, reinvested capital gains may yield further profits for the general (as well as the limited) partners. A third reason why venture capitalists may wish to reinvest profits is that such investments are unlikely to be mature at the end of the fund's stated life. The presence of investments that are too immature to liquidate is a frequently invoked reason for extending the partnership's life beyond the typical contractual limit of 10 years. In these cases, the venture capitalists will continue to generate fees from the limited partners (though often on a reduced basis).

approach employed in some agreements is to require the venture capitalists to invest a set dollar amount or percentage in every investment made by the fund.[27]

A second restriction addresses the reverse problem: the sale of partnership interests by general partners. Rather than seeking to increase their personal exposure to selected investments, general partners may sell their share of the fund's profits to other investors. While the general partnership interests are not totally comparable with the limited partners' stakes (for instance, the general partners will typically only receive distributions after the return of the limited partners' capital), these may still be attractive investments. Limited partners may worry that such a sale will reduce the general partners' incentives to monitor their investments. Partnership agreements may prohibit the sale of general partnership interests outright or else require that these sales be approved by a majority (or supermajority) of the limited partners.

A third area for restrictions on the general partners is fund-raising. The raising of a new fund will raise the management fees that venture capitalists receive and may reduce the attention that they pay to existing funds. Partnership agreements may prohibit fund-raising by general partners until a set percentage of the portfolio has been invested or until a given date.[28]

Some partnership agreements restrict general partners' outside activities. Because outside activities are likely to reduce the attention paid to investments, venture capitalists may be required to spend "substantially all" (or some other fraction) of their time managing the investments of the partnership. Alternatively, the general partners' involvement in businesses not in the venture fund's portfolio may be restricted. These limitations are often confined to the first years of the partnership or until a set percent of the fund's capital is invested, when the need for attention by the general partners is presumed to be the largest.

A fifth class of covenant relates to the addition of new general partners. By adding less experienced general partners, venture capitalists may reduce the burden on themselves. The quality of the oversight provided, however, is likely to be lower. As a result, many funds require that the addition of

---

[27] Another issue relating to coinvestment is the timing of the investments by the general partners. In some cases, venture capitalists involved in the establishment of a firm will purchase shares at the same time as the other founders at a very low valuation, then immediately invest their partnership's funds at a much higher valuation. Some partnership agreements address this problem by requiring venture capitalists to invest at the same time and price as their funds.

[28] Alternatively, fund-raising may be restricted to a fund of certain size or focus. For instance, the venture organization may be allowed to raise a buyout fund, which would presumably be managed by other general partners.

new general partners be approved by either the advisory board or a set percentage of the limited partners.

While many issues involving the behavior of the general partners are addressed through partnership agreements, several others typically are not. One area that is almost never discussed in the sample is the vesting schedule of general partnership interests. If a general partner leaves a venture organization early in the life of the fund, he may forfeit all or some of his share of the profits. If venture capitalists do not receive their entire partnership interest immediately, they are less likely to leave soon after the fund is formed. A second issue is the division of profits among the general partners. In some funds, most profits accrue to the senior general partners, even if the younger partners provide the bulk of the day-to-day management. While these issues are addressed in agreements between the general partners, they are rarely discussed in the contract between the general and limited partners.

3. Covenants Restricting the Types of Investment

The third family of covenants limit the types of assets in which the fund can invest. These restrictions are typically structured in similar ways: the venture fund is allowed to invest no more than a set percent of capital or asset value in a given investment class. An exception may be made if the advisory board or a set percentage of the limited partners approve. Occasionally, more complex restrictions will be encountered, such as the requirement that the sum of two asset classes not exceed a certain percent of capital.

Two fears appear to motivate these restrictions on investments. First, compared to other investors in a particular asset class, the general partners may be receiving compensation that is inappropriately large. For instance, the average money manager who specializes in investing in public securities receives an annual fee of about 0.5 percent of assets,[29] while venture capitalists receive 20 percent of profits in addition to an annual fee of about 2.5 percent of capital. Consequently, limited partners seek to limit the ability of venture capitalists to invest in public securities. Similarly, the typical investment manager receives a onetime fee of 1 percent of capital for investing an institution's money in a venture fund.[30] Partnership agreements often also include covenants that restrict the ability of the general partners to invest capital in other venture funds.

[29] Lakonishok, Shleifer, & Vishny, *supra* note 8.
[30] Venture Economics, Investment Managers—a Force in the Venture Capital Industry, 29 Venture Capital J., September 1989, at 10.

484   THE JOURNAL OF LAW AND ECONOMICS

A second concern is that the general partners will opt for classes of investments in which they have little expertise in the hopes of gaining experience. For instance, during the 1980s, many venture funds began investing in leveraged buyouts. Those that developed a successful track record proceeded to raise funds specializing in LBOs; many more, however, lost considerable sums on these investments.[31] Similarly, many firms invested in foreign countries during the 1980s. Only a relative handful proved sufficiently successful to raise funds specializing in these investments.[32]

B. Univariate Comparisons

Table 3 summarizes representation of the 14 primary covenant classes. The top panel indicates the percent of contracts that include each provision in three 5-year periods (1978–82, 1983–87, and 1988–92). The initial impression is one of persistent heterogeneity in the distribution of these covenants. Differences are striking in view of the concentration of capital providers and advisers in this industry: relatively few limited partners provide the bulk of capital, and partnership documents are prepared by a modest number of law firms. The second panel demonstrates the marked increase in the number of covenant classes in agreements executed after 1987. This effect is driven by the pronounced increase in provisions relating to the management of the fund and types of investment. In fact, all nine covenant classes in these two families increase in frequency during the sample period. Weighting observations by fund size makes little difference in this analysis or in those reported below.

This increase contrasts with the decline in four of the five covenants relating to the activities of the general partner. The overall pattern is consistent with the costly contracting hypothesis. During the early period when venture capital limited partnerships were a relatively recent phenomenon, restricting the activities of the general partner was important. Because potential agency problems relating to the management of the fund or investments were difficult to predict, restrictions were general in nature. As investors learned about which agency costs were probable, specific restrictions concerning fund management and investments were written. General restrictions on venture capitalists' activities, which may have limited their flexibility undesirably, were consequently dropped.

We analyze how the number of restrictions varies with eight variables, four of which measure potential agency problems. The first two relate to

---

[31] The poor performance of venture-backed LBOs such as Prime Computer has been much discussed in Liz R. Gallese, Venture Capital Strays Far from Its Roots, 139 N.Y. Times Magazine S24 (April 1, 1990); quantitative support of these claims is found in analyses of the returns of funds with different investment objectives by Venture Economics, Venture Capital Performance—1989 (1989).

[32] For a practitioner discussion, see Kunze, *supra* note 1.

TABLE 3

THE NUMBER OF COVENANTS IN 140 VENTURE PARTERNSHIP AGREEMENTS, BY YEAR

	PERCENTAGE OF CONTRACTS WITH COVENANT IN:		
	1978–82	1983–87	1988–92
Covenants relating to the management of the fund:			
Restrictions on size of investment in any one firm	33.3	47.1	77.8
Restrictions on use of debt by partnership	66.7	72.1	95.6
Restrictions on coinvestment by organization's earlier or later funds	40.7	29.4	62.2
Restrictions on reinvestment of partnership's capital gains	3.7	17.6	35.6
Covenants relating to the activities of the general partners:			
Restrictions on coinvestment by general partners	81.5	66.2	77.8
Restrictions on sale of partnership interests by general partners	74.1	54.4	51.1
Restrictions on fund-raising by general partners	51.9	42.6	84.4
Restrictions on other actions by general partners	22.2	16.2	13.3
Restrictions on addition of general partners	29.6	35.3	26.7
Covenants relating to the types of investment:			
Restrictions on investments in other venture funds	3.7	22.1	62.2
Restrictions on investments in public securities	22.2	17.6	66.7
Restrictions on investments in leveraged buyouts	.0	8.8	60.0
Restrictions on investments in foreign securities	.0	7.4	44.4
Restrictions on investments in other asset classes	11.1	16.2	31.1
Total number of partnership agreements in sample	27	68	45
Average number of covenant classes	4.4	4.5	7.9
Average number of covenant classes (weighted by fund size)	4.4	4.6	8.4

NOTE.—For the 14 classes of covenants, the table indicates the percentage of venture partnership agreements with such a restriction in each 5-year period. The second panel indicates the number of partnership agreements in each period and the mean number of covenant classes (the simple average and the average weighted by fund size).

fund focus. General partners of early-stage and high-technology funds may have more scope to engage in opportunistic behavior. The costly contracting hypothesis predicts that limited partners in these funds demand covenants that restrict potential agency problems. We determine the fund's focus by examining the contracts and offering documents that are used to promote the funds.[33]

A third proxy for potential agency costs is fund size.[34] All else being equal, limited partners should add more restrictions to larger funds. There

[33] In many cases, the information will be in the offering document, but not in the partnership agreement. In the few cases where we do not have the offering document, we use the information about the fund focus recorded in the Venture Economics funds database.

[34] One concern is that fund size is a proxy for the reputational capital of the venture organization, not the individual venture capitalists. Ideally, we would have a measure of the cu-

should be increasing returns to scale in negotiating and monitoring compliance with covenants. Larger funds, however, are raised by more established venture firms who may not wish to risk their reputational capital by engaging in opportunistic behavior. We determine fund size using the Venture Economics funds database.

Our fourth measure is the elasticity of compensation with respect to performance, or pay sensitivity. Both the supply and demand hypothesis and costly contracting hypothesis predict that fund managers who have compensation more closely tied to performance have fewer restrictive covenants. As pay is tied more closely to the fund's monetary returns, the need for restrictive covenants is reduced. We compute compensation measures using the detailed information on the management fees, division of profits, and timing of payments from the partnership agreements. For measures that cannot be computed in advance, we use historical averages. We first calculate the elasticity of compensation to performance.[35] We then compute the net present value of the base and variable compensation, under the assumption that assets under the venture capitalists' management grow by 20 percent annually.

The second set of variables controls for relative supply and demand conditions in the venture capital market. The first measure is the inflow of new capital into venture funds in the year the fund is established. Because the supply of venture capital services is fixed in the short run, a large growth in capital commitments suggests that demand for venture capital services is high relative to supply, causing the number of covenants to decline and total compensation to rise. While fund-raising activity was relatively sluggish before and after, the years 1982–86 were characterized by a dramatic

---

mulative experience of the venture capitalists associated with the fund. Unfortunately, constructing such a measure is problematic. Many venture capitalists have diverse backgrounds: for instance, as founders of entrepreneurial firms, corporate managers, or university researchers. It is unclear how individual experience should be aggregated. Even if such a measure could be designed, only about half of the private placement memoranda provide detailed information on the general partners' backgrounds. Obtaining biographical information on venture capitalists elsewhere is often very difficult. To address this concern, we examine whether the venture capitalists in older, larger venture organizations had more prior experience. We look at 267 venture organizations established between 1978 and 1985 that had a board seat on at least one firm that went public in the 7 years after the fund closed. To assess experience, we look at the boards on which the venture capitalists served prior to the closing of the fund. (We total the inflation-adjusted market capitalization of all initial public offerings on whose boards these venture capitalists served.) Older and larger venture organizations tend to have more experienced venture capitalists. The correlation coefficients, 0.29 and 0.25, respectively, are significant at the 1 percent confidence level.

[35] More specifically, we use the increase in the net present value of compensation associated with an increase in the asset growth rate from 20 percent to 21 percent. This is near the mean of venture performance during the 1980s (Venture Economics, *supra* note 31). The procedure is described in detail in Gompers & Lerner, *supra* note 12.

growth in the venture capital pool. We measure the growth of the venture pool by computing the ratio of total capital committed to venture funds in the year the fund closed to the amount raised in the previous 10 years.[36]

An alternative measure of the relative demand for the general partners' services is the presence or absence of investment managers. The absence of investment managers should be an indication of high demand. To determine whether an investment manager advised a client to invest in the fund, we examine the lists of names and addresses of limited partners that are typically appended to the partnership agreement. When the limited partner is advised by an investment manager, this is usually indicated.[37] In addition, we obtain the names of the venture funds in which five major investment managers have allocated funds.[38]

A third proxy for the venture capital supply and demand conditions is the total compensation that they receive. Venture capitalists may increase both their monetary compensation and their consumption of private benefits in response to increased demand. As described above, we calculate total compensation assuming a 20 percent growth rate and express it as a fraction of the fund's capital.

The final measure that we employ is the age of the venture organization. We anticipate that more experienced venture capitalists will have greater demand for their services. Older firms have been able to raise a series of funds and should have higher ability on average. Using the Venture Economics funds database, we compute the time from the closing of the venture organization's first fund to the closing of this fund.

Table 4 summarizes the univariate comparisons of the number of restrictions. Fund focus and the presence of an investment manager are dummy variables that equal one for firms with each characteristic. In the other cases, funds are divided by whether they are above or below the median of each measure. We compare the mean and median number of restrictions.

---

[36] The calculations are made using the Venture Economics funds database. We use inflation-adjusted dollars throughout. Because we are concerned that the results may be sensitive to the definition of the venture growth rate, we also employ three alternative measures. These are (i) the ratio of total capital committed to venture funds in the year the fund closed to the amount raised in the previous 5 years (to correct for the fact that much of the capital of older funds already has been returned to the limited partners), (ii) the ratio of new capital to the number of active venture organizations (defined as those that had raised a fund in the previous 10 years), and (iii) the absolute growth in venture capital pool in the year the fund closed.

[37] Because the investment manager will typically handle the continuing administrative work concerning the partnership (for example, liquidating stock distributions and responding to any proposed modifications of the partnership agreement), the address of the limited partner will be listed as care of the investment manager.

[38] We thank the director of alternative investments at a major pension fund for providing us with information on the investment decisions of three gatekeepers.

TABLE 4

THE NUMBER OF COVENANT CLASSES IN 140 VENTURE PARTNERSHIP AGREEMENTS FOR VARIOUS SUBGROUPS

	NUMBER OF COVENANTS FOR FUNDS WHERE THIS IS:		*p*-VALUE, TEST OF NO DIFFERENCE
	True	False	
Focus on early-stage investments	5.0	5.3	.567
	[5]	[5]	[.524]
Focus on high-technology investments	5.3	5.2	.790
	[5]	[5]	[.877]
Presence of investment manager	5.8	3.8	.001
	[6]	[3]	[.001]

	NUMBER OF COVENANTS FOR FUNDS THAT ARE:		*p*-VALUE, TEST OF NO DIFFERENCE
	Above Median	Below Median	
Size of venture fund	5.2	5.2	.691
	[5]	[5]	[.752]
Sensitivity of general partner compensation to performance	4.7	5.9	.717
	[5]	[6]	[.534]
Rate of growth of venture pool in year of fund's closing*	4.0	7.2	.000
	[4]	[8]	[.000]
Total compensation of the general partners	4.2	6.4	.017
	[4]	[6]	[.033]
Age of venture organization in year of closing	5.5	5.0	.414
	[5]	[5]	[.464]

NOTE.—The first two columns compare the mean and median (in brackets) number of covenant classes for funds in the sample that fall into various categories. In the first panel, firms are divided by their focus and the presence of an investment manager; in the second panel, by whether they are above or below the median on several measures. The third column presents the *p*-values of *t*-tests and Wilcoxon signed-rank tests (in brackets) of the null hypotheses that these distributions are identical.

* The rate of the growth of venture pool is significant at the 1 percent level using three alternative definitions.

We find significant differences in the number of restrictions when we divide the contracts by three measures suggested by the supply and demand hypothesis: the growth rate of the venture pool in the year of the fund's closing (measured the four different ways), the presence of an investment manager as an adviser to one or more limited partners, and total compensation of the general partners. Funds established at times when the venture pool grew rapidly, where an investment manager was not involved, or in which the venture capitalists were highly compensated have significantly fewer restrictions. The differences are significant whether we compare means or medians. When we divide the funds by indicators that we expect to be associated with a greater need for monitoring—for instance, whether the fund focuses on early-stage and high-technology investments—we find no significant differences in the number of covenants.[39]

C. Regression Analyses

We examine these patterns using regression analyses in Table 5. The dependent variable is the number of covenant classes included in the partnership agreement (out of a total of 14). We employ two econometric specifications: ordinary least squares (OLS) and Poisson. The latter may more accurately reflect the nonnegative, ordinal nature of the dependent variable.[40] Because the dummy variables for funds with an early-stage and high-technology focus are highly correlated, we use only one of these variables at a time. Because we are missing data in some cases, we employ only 124 out of the 140 observations.[41]

The top panel presents the OLS and Poisson regressions. In each, the coefficients of the variables measuring the growth rate of the venture pool and the presence of one or more investment managers are significant. Consistent with the supply and demand hypothesis, funds established at times when the venture capital pool is growing rapidly and in which investment managers do not advise the limited partners have fewer restrictions.

We test whether the independent variables that proxy for agency problems or supply and demand conditions jointly differ from zero. In the second panel, we present the *p*-values from tests of the null hypothesis of no difference. Using both specifications, the null hypothesis is rejected for supply and demand proxies at the one percent level. The variables seeking to

---

[39] Our results are not driven by all-or-nothing covenant inclusion. Most covenant classes are positively correlated with other covenant classes, and many of the correlations are significant. The correlation coefficients are reasonably small, however. For example, the average correlation coefficient among restrictions on the fund's management is 0.169, and 33 percent are significant at the 1 percent confidence level. The highest correlation is among the restrictions on investments. Ninety percent of the correlation coefficients are significant at the 1 percent level; the average correlation coefficient is 0.432. The largest correlation across covenant classes is between restrictions concerning fund management and investment activity. The average correlation coefficient is 0.258. Fifty-five percent are significant at the 1 percent level, with 80 percent significant at the 5 percent level.

[40] The standard errors in the OLS regression are heteroscedastic-consistent, while those in the Poisson regression are not adjusted in this manner. The usefulness of Poisson regressions in these settings is discussed in G. S. Maddala, Limited-Dependent and Qualitative Variables in Econometrics (1983).

[41] In some cases, we do not know the size of the fund. In other cases, we cannot calculate the base compensation since it is set in a budget negotiated annually between the limited and general partners or else is based on the debt taken on by the firms in the venture capitalists' portfolio.

TABLE 5

REGRESSION ANALYSIS OF THE NUMBER OF COVENANT CLASSES IN VENTURE PARTNERSHIP AGREEMENTS, USING ORDINARY LEAST SQUARES (OLS) AND POISSON SPECIFICATIONS

A. REGRESSION ANALYSIS

	INDEPENDENT VARIABLES									ROOT MEAN SQUARE ERROR		
SPECIFICATION	Early-Stage Focus?	Sensitivity of Pay to Profits	Size of Venture Fund	Venture Pool Growth	Investment Manager?	Total Compensation	Age of Venture Organization	Constant	ADJUSTED R^2		χ^2-STATISTIC	p-VALUE
OLS	.19 [.34]	−51.67 [1.63]	.005 [1.45]	−5.06 [5.83]	1.47 [2.23]	−13.19 [1.33]	−.06 [1.11]	12.51 [2.85]	.22	2.658		
Poisson	.01 [.16]	−8.30 [1.60]	.001 [1.42]	−.98 [5.05]	.27 [2.82]	−2.23 [1.74]	−.01 [1.67]	2.89 [4.92]			53.19	.000

B. TESTS OF SIGNIFICANCE OF INDEPENDENT VARIABLES

Specification	p-Value, Test of Whether Agency Proxies Are Zero	p-Value, Test of Whether Market Power Proxies Are Zero
OLS	.231	.000
Poisson	.214	.000

NOTE.—In the first panel, the dependent variable is the number of covenant classes (out of a total of 14) included in the partnership agreement. The first two rows present the coefficients of an ordinary least squares regression (with absolute heteroscedastic-consistent t-statistics in brackets); the second, a Poisson regression (with absolute t-statistics in brackets). The second panel presents the p-values of F- and χ^2-tests that the sets of variables which proxy for agency costs (early-stage focus, sensitivity of pay to performance, and size of the venture fund) and for the venture organization's market power (venture pool growth, presence of an investment manager, total compensation, and age of the venture organization) are equal to zero. The regressions use 124 partnership agreements for which complete data are available.

measure the costly contracting hypothesis, however, cannot be shown to differ from zero. These regressions suggest that the relative demand for venture capital services is a critical determinant of the number of covenants.[42]

We examine the robustness of the analysis to the use of alternative dependent variables. We explore whether results could be driven by one covenant (or one set of restrictions) by considering each of the three covenant families separately. Table 6 presents three regressions which employ as dependent variables the number of restrictions relating to the fund management, the activities of the general partners, and the investment type. We present only the regressions using an OLS specification; results using a Poisson specification are similar.

The results in Table 6 support both the supply and demand and costly contracting hypotheses. The results show that fund size is important in determining the number of covenants relating to the management of the fund and the type of investment. The potential agency problems relating to fund management and investments are likely to increase with the size of the fund, while the potential for agency problems involving general partners may not. (The number of investments is likely to increase linearly with fund size, while the number of general partners typically only increases slowly with size.) In these two regressions, the costly contracting proxies are jointly different from zero. The coefficients of the venture pool growth and investment manager variables have the sign predicted by the supply and demand hypothesis in all three regressions (and are significant at the 5 percent confidence level in two). The measures of supply and demand are jointly significant in all three regressions. Formal tests of the significance of these variables are presented in the second panel of Table 6.

---

[42] We undertake several modifications of these regressions to address concerns about their robustness. First, we add a variable that indicates the date that the fund closed to control for any trend in the number of covenants. While the primary results are robust to the addition of this variable, the trend term is positive and highly significant. This might indicate that the market has been learning about potential agency costs over time and continues to include more specific restrictions. Second, we address the concern that two of the independent variables—the amount and performance sensitivity of the compensation—are determined at the same time as the dependent variable by deleting the two compensation variables. While a venture organization will typically announce a target fund size in advance, the compensation will be negotiated at the same time as the terms and conditions of the partnership. We rerun the regressions omitting these measures. Third, we reestimate the regressions using three alternative measures of the venture pool growth (described in Section VB above) because we are concerned that the results may reflect the particular measure that we employ. Finally, we employ a dummy variable for a fund with a high-technology (rather than an early-stage) focus. In all cases, the independent variables associated with the supply and demand hypothesis remain jointly significant at the 1 percent confidence level. Those addressing the costly contracting hypothesis are in each case insignificant at conventional confidence levels.

TABLE 6

REGRESSION ANALYSIS OF THE NUMBER OF COVENANT CLASSES IN VENTURE PARTNERSHIP AGREEMENTS, DIVIDED INTO THREE FAMILIES

A. REGRESSION ANALYSIS

DEPENDENT VARIABLE	INDEPENDENT VARIABLES								ADJUSTED R^2	ROOT MEAN SQUARE ERROR
	Early-Stage Focus?	Sensitivity of Pay to Profits	Size of Venture Fund	Venture Pool Growth	Investment Manager?	Total Compensation	Age of Venture Organization	Constant		
Number of covenants relating to the management of the fund	.04 [.17]	−17.78 [1.82]	.003 [3.41]	−1.38 [3.06]	.35 [1.48]	−3.74 [1.08]	−.03 [1.11]	4.04 [2.76]	.14	1.024
Number of covenants relating to the activities of the general partners	.10 [.40]	−1.34 [.09]	.001 [.44]	−.56 [1.38]	.59 [2.02]	−3.16 [.93]	−.06 [2.27]	3.60 [2.12]	.10	1.205
Number of covenants relating to the types of investment	.05 [.18]	−32.56 [2.02]	.003 [2.42]	−3.12 [6.92]	.53 [1.99]	−6.28 [1.16]	−.02 [.84]	4.87 [2.11]	.32	1.345

B. TESTS OF SIGNIFICANCE OF INDEPENDENT VARIABLES

Dependent Variable	p-Value, Test If Agency Proxies Are Zero	p-Value, Test of Whether Market Power Proxies Are Zero
Number of covenants relating to the management of the fund	.005	.011
Number of covenants relating to the activities of the general partners	.954	.000
Number of covenants relating to the types of investment	.042	.000

NOTE.—The dependent variable is the number of covenant classes in each family included in the partnership agreement. The table presents the coefficients of an ordinary least squares regression (with absolute heteroscedastic-consistent t-statistics in brackets). The second panel presents the p-values of F-tests that the sets of variables which proxy for agency costs (early-stage focus, sensitivity of pay to performance, and size of the venture fund) and for the venture organization's market power (venture pool growth, presence of an investment manager, total compensation, and age of the venture organization) are equal to zero. The regressions use 124 partnership agreements for which complete data are available.

An alternative empirical approach is to examine first differences to determine if changes in the explanatory variables are related to changes in the number of covenants. Such a first-differences analysis eliminates many unobserved organization-specific characteristics that may be correlated with the explanatory variables. Table 7 shows how the number of covenant classes changes in subsequent funds of the same venture organization. We divide the funds by whether there were changes in the presence of a gatekeeper, the focus of the fund, or the rate of growth of the venture industry in the year of the fund's closing. The effects are in the expected direction. For example, the number of covenants increases by 2.4 when a gatekeeper supplies capital to the current fund but not to the previous fund. Declining growth rates in the venture pool also lead to an increase in the number of covenants. Both results are consistent with the supply and demand hypothesis. In addition, early-stage and high-technology funds have more scope to engage in opportunistic activities, so restricting their activities is more valuable. The second panel tests the significance of these differences. The differences in the number of covenants are significant at the five percent confidence level in the growth rate analysis; those relating to fund focus are of borderline significance.

The first-difference regressions are presented in Table 8. Unlike the earlier regressions, a change in the focus of the fund to either early-stage or high-technology investments increases the number of covenants significantly, by approximately two. This is consistent with the costly contracting hypothesis. Changes in the gatekeeper status do not significantly affect the number of covenants, which may reflect the smaller sample size in these first-difference analyses. Finally, a decline in the growth rate of the venture pool increases the number of covenants in the contracts. These results are generally consistent with both the costly contracting and supply and demand hypotheses.

VI. CONCLUSION

In this article, we examine the use of contractual covenants in venture capital partnership agreements. We examine two complementary explanations for the presence of these restrictions: differences in the need for oversight and in supply and demand conditions for venture capital services. The evidence from a sample of 140 contracts indicates that *both* factors are important determinants of contractual restrictiveness. The proxies for supply and demand conditions are consistently significant in univariate and regression analyses. When the covenants are broken down into families, proxies for potential agency problems are significantly related to covenants that restrict the management of the fund and investment activities, while the sup-

TABLE 7

The Change in the Number of Covenant Classes Included in the Current and Previous Venture Partnership Agreements

	Change in Number of Restrictions		
	Mean	SE	No. of Observations
Gatekeeper status:			
When a gatekeeper invested in this fund but not in previous fund	+2.4	1.1	14
When a gatekeeper invested in this and in previous fund	+1.4	.5	45
When no gatekeeper invested in this fund	+1.5	.9	16
Stage focus:			
When this is an early-stage fund and previous fund is not early-stage	+4.3	2.4	6
When this and previous fund specialize in early-stage investments	+1.4	1.0	10
When this and previous fund do not specialize in early-stage investments	+1.6	.5	49
When previous fund specializes in early-stage investments and this one does not	+.6	1.4	10
Technology focus:			
When this is a high-tech fund and previous fund is not high-tech	+3.6	1.5	11
When this and previous fund specialize in high-tech investments	+2.3	.9	16
When this and previous fund do not specialize in high-tech investments	+1.2	.5	41
When previous fund specializes in high-tech investments and this one does not	-.4	1.7	7
When the growth rate of the venture pool at time of this fund's closing is:			
Greater than at time of last fund's closing	-.9	.7	15
Between 0 percent and 10 percent below last fund's closing	+1.8	.9	21
Between 10 percent and 20 percent below last fund's closing	+2.4	.8	20
More than 20 percent below last fund's closing	+2.7	.8	19

	Test Statistic	p-Value
Do cases where a gatekeeper invested in this fund and not in previous fund differ from others?	.87	.389
Do cases with an early-stage focus in this fund and not in previous fund differ from others?	1.85	.068
Do cases where a high-tech focus in this fund and not in previous fund differ from others?	1.94	.057
Do cases with various venture pool growth rate changes differ?	3.46	.021

NOTE.—The observations are divided by whether there is a change in whether the fund has a gatekeeper among its investors, a change in fund focus (either to or from a focus on early-stage or high-technology investments), and a change in the growth rate of the venture capital pool in the year of the fund's closing. There are a total of 14 covenant classes. The second panel presents the results of t-tests and an F-test of the significance of these differences. The sample consists of 75 second and later venture funds where information is available on an earlier fund of the venture organization.

TABLE 8

Regression Analysis of the Change in the Number of Covenant Classes in Venture Partnership Agreements

| DEPENDENT VARIABLE | INDEPENDENT VARIABLES | | | | Constant | ADJUSTED R^2 | F-STATISTIC | p-VALUE |
	Change in Whether Early-Stage Focus	Change in Whether High-Tech Focus	Change in Gatekeeper Presence	Change in Growth Rate of Venture Pool				
Change in number of restrictions	1.90 [2.07]		-.10 [.13]	-3.77 [2.46]	1.30 [2.85]	.08	3.15	.030
Change in number of restrictions		2.01 [2.33]	-.39 [.52]	-3.28 [2.16]	1.17 [2.58]	.09	3.56	.018

NOTE.—The dependent variable is the difference in the number of covenant classes (out of a total of 14) included in the current and previous partnership agreements. Independent variables are the change in fund focus (either to or from a focus on early-stage or high-technology investments), the change in whether the fund has a gatekeeper among its investors, and the change in the growth rate of the venture capital pool in the year of the fund's closing. The table presents the coefficients of ordinary least squares regressions (with absolute *t*-statistics in brackets). The sample consists of 75 second and later venture funds where information is available on an earlier fund of the venture organization.

495

ply and demand proxies are related to all three groups. The results are robust to a variety of modifications.

This article differs from earlier empirical analyses of contract structure. Earlier analyses have either focused exclusively on the costly contracting hypothesis or found weak support for the claim that supply and demand conditions affect contractual form. Our results suggest that the relative neglect of the supply and demand hypothesis is unwarranted. The paucity of academic work on supply and demand effects contrasts with the weight placed on this factor in practitioner accounts. While our description of the supply and demand hypothesis is informal, we hope that further theoretical and empirical work will examine the role of shifts in supply and/or demand in determining contractual forms.

APPENDIX

A NOTE ON DATA SOURCES

This analysis uses the partnership agreements found in the files of the Aeneas Group, Brinson Partners, and Kemper Financial Services. Each of these organizations has been involved in venture investing for at least 15 years and has extensive files on venture capital organizations.

The Aeneas Group is the affiliate of Harvard Management Company that handles the university endowment's private-market investments. Their files on venture investments date back to the late 1970s. Aeneas's venture investment strategy was shaped by the philosophy of Walter Cabot, who ran Harvard Management between 1974 and 1990. While investing in risky asset classes such as venture capital and oil and gas, he emphasized the importance of conducting business with established and reputable financial intermediaries.[43]

Kemper Financial Services and Brinson Partners are investment managers. Kemper has invested in venture capital on a regular basis since 1978; Brinson (which formerly was a unit of First Chicago), since 1979. Institutions such as pension funds frequently seek to diversify their portfolios to include privately held assets. They may not have the resources to evaluate potential investments or may not wish to grapple with the complications posed by these investments. (For instance, venture capitalists frequently liquidate investments in firms by distributing thinly traded shares to investors.) Investment managers select and manage private investments for institutions.[44] They usually invest in a variety of funds, but new funds by unproven venture capitalists are likely to be underrepresented.[45]

All three organizations began collecting information on a regular basis in the late 1970s. The occasional earlier documents in these files do not appear to have been gathered systematically. We consequently restrict our analysis to funds that closed

---

[43] Karen Grassmuck, The Much-Praised and Often-Criticized ''Architect'' of Harvard's Endowment Growth Steps Down, Chron. Higher Educ., 1990, at A25.

[44] Venture Economics, *supra* note 30.

[45] Edwin A. Goodman, Gatekeepers' ''Reforms'' Reap Negative Consequences, 30 Venture Capital J., 1990, at 25.

in the period from 1978 through 1992. We only employ in the analysis the cases where we have executed partnership agreements: the terms and conditions of contracts may change between the initial draft and the actual contract.

We determine whether a fund meets our selection criteria in two ways. The organizations' files typically contain, in addition to an executed partnership agreement, the private placement memorandum that was used to market the fund. The memoranda typically have a section that describes the purposes of the partnership and provides information on the fund's general partners and the venture capital organization. We also check a database of venture capital funds compiled by Venture Economics (described in the text) to insure that we have not inadvertently included inappropriate cases. If we are unsure whether a fund corresponds to our criteria, we do not include it.

BIBLIOGRPAHY

Asset Alternatives. "Iowa Suits Test LPs' Authority to Abolish Fund." *Private Equity Analyst* 4 (May 1994): 1, 9.

Asset Alternatives. "Warburg Points the Way toward a Lower Carry." *Private Equity Analyst* 4 (July 1994): 7.

Bartlett, Joseph W. *Venture Capital Law, Business, Strategies, and Investment Planning.* New York: Wiley, 1988.

Bartlett, Joseph W. *Venture Capital Law, Business, Strategies, and Investment Planning: 1994 Supplement.* New York: Wiley, 1994.

Crocker, Keith J., and Reynolds, Kenneth J. "The Efficiency of Incomplete Contracts: An Empirical Analysis of Air Force Engine Procurement." *Rand Journal of Economics* 24 (1993): 126–46.

Dauchy, Craig E., and Harmon, Mark T. "Structuring Venture Capital Limited Partnerships." *Computer Lawyer* 3 (November 1986): 1–8.

Ely, E. S. "Dr. Silver's Tarnished Prescription." *Venture* 9 (July 1987): 54–58.

Gallese, Liz R. "Venture Capital Strays Far from Its Roots." *New York Times Magazine* 139 (April 1, 1990): S24–S39.

Gompers, Paul A., and Lerner, Josh. "An Analysis of Compensation in the U.S. Venture Capital Partnership." Unpublished manuscript. Boston: Harvard University, 1995.

Goodman, Edwin A. "Gatekeepers' 'Reforms' Reap Negative Consequences." *Venture Capital Journal* 30 (December 1990): 25–28.

Grassmuck, Karen. "The Much-Praised and Often-Criticized 'Architect' of Harvard's Endowment Growth Steps Down." *Chronicle of Higher Education* 36 (June 6, 1990): A25–A27.

Grossman, Sanford, and Hart, Oliver. "The Costs and Benefits of Ownership: A Theory of Vertical and Lateral Integration." *Journal of Political Economy* 94 (1986): 691–719.

Halloran, Michael J. "Agreement of Limited Partnership." In *Venture Capital and Public Offering Negotiation,* edited by Michael J. Halloran, Lee F. Benton, Robert V. Gunderson, Jr., Keith L. Kearney, and Jorge del Calvo, 1:1–217. Englewood Cliffs, N.J.: Prentice Hall, 1992.

Hubbard, R. Glenn, and Weiner, Robert J. "Efficient Contracting and Market

Power: Evidence from the U.S. Natural Gas Industry." *Journal of Law and Economics* 34 (1991): 25–67.

Huemer, Jason. "Brinson Partners on a Roll." *Venture Capital Journal* 32 (June 1992): 32–36.

Jensen, Michael C., and Meckling, William H. "Theory of the Firm: Managerial Behavior, Agency Costs, and Ownership Structure." *Journal of Financial Economics* 3 (1976): 305–60.

King, Ralph, Jr. " 'The Money Corner.' " *Forbes* 145 (March 5, 1990): 38–40.

Klein, Benjamin; Crawford, Robert G.; and Alchian, Armen A. "Vertical Integration, Appropriable Rents and the Competitive Contracting Process." *Journal of Law and Economics* 21 (1978): 297–326.

Kunze, Robert J. *Nothing Ventured: The Perils and Payoffs of the Great American Venture Capital Game.* New York: HarperBusiness, 1990.

Lakonishok, Josef; Shleifer, Andrei; and Vishny, Robert W. "The Structure and Performance of the Money Management Industry." *Brookings Papers on Economic Activity: Microeconomics,* 1992, pp. 339–91.

Lehn, Kenneth, and Poulsen, Annette. "Contractual Resolution of Bondholder-Stockholder Conflicts in Leveraged Buyouts." *Journal of Law and Economics* 34 (1991): 645–73.

Levin, Jack S. *Structuring Venture Capital, Private Equity, and Entrepreneurial Transactions.* Chicago: Commerce Clearing House, 1994.

Maddala, G. S. *Limited-Dependent and Qualitative Variables in Econometrics.* New York: Cambridge University Press, 1983.

Malitz, Ileen. "On Financial Contracting: The Determinants of Bond Covenants." *Financial Management* 15 (Summer 1986): 18–25.

Pittman, Russell. "Specific Investments, Contracts, and Opportunism: The Evolution of Railroad Sidetrack Agreements." *Journal of Law and Economics* 34 (1991): 565–89.

Sahlman, William A. "The Structure and Governance of Venture Capital Organizations." *Journal of Financial Economics* 27 (1990): 473–521.

Smith, Clifford W., Jr., and Warner, Jerold B. "On Financial Contracting: An Analysis of Bond Covenants." *Journal of Financial Economics* 7 (1979): 117–61.

Venture Economics. "Investment Managers—a Force in the Venture Capital Industry." *Venture Capital Journal* 29 (September 1989): 10–17.

Venture Economics. *Terms and Conditions of Venture Capital Partnerships.* Needham: Venture Economics, 1989.

Venture Economics. *Venture Capital Performance—1989.* Needham: Venture Economics, 1989.

Venture Economics. *1992 Terms and Conditions of Venture Capital Partnerships.* Boston: Venture Economics, 1992.

Williamson, Oliver E. "Transaction-Cost Economics: The Governance of Contractual Relations." *Journal of Law and Economics* 22 (1979): 233–61.

Williamson, Oliver E. *The Economic Institutions of Capitalism: Firms, Markets, Relational Contracting.* New York: Free Press, 1985.

[16]

1042-2587-97-214$1.50
Copyright 1998 by
Baylor University

The Monitoring of Venture Capital Firms

Ken Robbie
Mike Wright
Brian Chiplin

This paper analyzes the monitoring of venture capital firms by their funds providers, which has been hitherto generally neglected by academic researchers. The changing nature of competition in a mature market has introduced increased pressures for the enhanced monitoring of venture capital firms, especially in relation to target returns and reporting requirements. The paper provides evidence on the nature and extent of these monitoring arrangements derived from interviews and a questionnaire survey of leading players in the UK market.

The venture capital process can be characterized as involving two sets of key relationships, those between venture capital firms and the entrepreneurs in whom they invest and those between venture capital firms and their funds providers. There is a substantial literature on the relationship between the venture capital firm and its investees (see e.g. Sapienza & Gupta, 1994). However, the monitoring relationship between venture capital firms and their funds providers has been relatively neglected. This omission raises a number of important issues for both academic researchers and practitioners. For academic researchers questions are raised concerning the extent and nature of the monitoring by funds providers of venture capital firms, the information required, and the implications for the performance of the industry. For practitioners, examination of the operation of funds providers may provide insights into their objectives and information needs.

CONCEPTUAL ISSUES

Previous literature that helps in formulating expectations about the nature of monitoring relationships between venture capitalists and their funds providers is sparse. An agency theory perspective has been used to examine the issues in a pioneering study by Sahlman (1990), which analyzed the nature of the relationship between funds providers and venture capital firms and identified the mechanisms used to help minimize these agency problems. These mechanisms included incentives for mutual gain, the specific prohibition of certain acts on the part of the venture capital firm that would cause conflicts of interest, limited life agreements, mechanisms to ensure gains are distributed to investors, expenditure of resources on monitoring the venture capital firm, and the regular provision of specific information to the funds providers by the venture capital firm. Venture capital firms' [w1]remuneration is typically based on an annual management fee plus some percentage of the realized profits from the fund. Sahlman points out that good venture capital firms, by accepting a finite funding life and performance-dependent compensation, are signalling their quality in relation to weak ones, but that the funds provider has to invest in intensive screening in order to guard against false signalling. Sahlman's study addressed the actions of funds providers very much as 'stylised facts,' without a detailed examination of the nature of targets set and the monitoring process. More recently, an empirical study by Gompers and Lerner (1996) finds evidence that the use of covenants in the contracts between funds providers and venture capital firms is both a means of dealing with agency problems but also a reflection of supply and demand conditions in the industry.

A significant agency problem may also arise in the valuation of investments for the purposes of reporting to providers of funds. It is venture capital firms as agents who are responsible for such valuations and on which their performance will be judged (Fried & Hisrich, 1994). However, since it may take many years for a venture capital investment to come to fruition, considerable subjectivity surrounds the valuation of investments in any particular year before the investment is realized. In the absence of clear and complete rules, management may have the scope and incentive to report biased interim investment values. The adoption of different valuation practices also makes it difficult to compare the performance of individual venture capital firms. In the UK, the British Venture Capital Association (BVCA) has introduced guidelines that recommend four appropriate valuation methods for its members. Evidence from UK venture capital firms shows that almost nine-tenths of BVCA members have adopted these guidelines and that the most popular of the valuation methods available is cost (less provision)(57% of cases), followed by price earnings multiples (25%), third party valuations (14%) and net assets (4%) (Wright & Robbie, 1996a).

Notwithstanding these points, there are reasons for questioning the extent of funds providers monitoring of their investments in venture capital firms. The extent and nature of monitoring by funds providers may be influenced by the effort-cost-return trade-offs. If, as is typically the case, venture capital forms a very small percentage of pension funds' and other institutions' asset portfolios, a de minimis approach to monitoring may be adopted. Possible changes to regulations concerning the ability of institutions to treat venture capital investments as an asset class may to some extent change this position. A second issue concerns the nature of the monitoring of executives in institutions providing funds to venture capitalists. Lax monitoring by pension fund trustees and executive remuneration that is not significantly influenced by the performance of investments in venture capital firms may also mean that the monitoring of such firms is at best passive. Changes in corporate accountability regimes in pension funds, whereby trustees focus greater attention on the use executives make of funds, may be expected to lead to closer monitoring of investments in venture capital firms. This may take the form of more regular meetings, more detailed requirements for information, and tighter contractual arrangements regarding the balance between fund management fees and performance-related returns. It may also be expected to be associated with some increase in the role of intermediaries ('gatekeepers') in identifying appropriate venture capital funds in which pension funds, etc. may invest.

A further monitoring problem facing providers of funds to venture capital firms is access to comparator information resulting from the private nature of venture capital investments and of many venture capital firms themselves. Bygrave (1994), for example, noted that until the late 1980s in the US there was an astonishing paucity of reliable information to support venture capitalists' high expectations. Recent developments that involve the publication of mean and upper quartile returns on various stages of investment by a number of national venture capital associations in Europe (UK, France and Holland) goes some way to alleviating these informational problems, which may be expected to influence the setting of target rates of return by funds providers. However, evidence also suggests that these actual returns are some way below expected returns (Manigart, Wright, Robbie, Desbrieres, & de Waele, 1997). This is particularly a problem for early-stage investments, whereas actual returns for later-stage and buy-out investments are close to expectations. Increasing information availability may be expected to have an impact on the setting of benchmark rates of return by funds providers, perhaps in terms of industry upper quartiles rather than means, and of returns to

Table 1

Investment Activity and Fund Raising

Year	No. of BVCA members (Full)	No. of companies financed	Amount invested (£m)	Amount invested in UK(£m)			Independent funds raised (£m)
				Independent	Captive	Semi-captive	
1984	34	479	190	88	51	N/A	N/A
1985	50	635	433	140	138	N/A	N/A
1986	65	708	584	208	176	N/A	N/A
1987	77	1,298	1,029	685	249	N/A	645
1988	90	1,527	1,394	1,018	280	N/A	492
1989	107	1,569	1,647	1,030	390	N/A	1,964
1990	120	1,559	1,394	717	389	N/A	759
1991	121	1,386	1,153	736	253	N/A	390
1992	115	1,297	1,434	621	361	269	413
1993	113	1,202	1,422	571	319	341	588
1994	117	1,208	2,074	900	349	420	2,551
1995	115	1,163	2,535	1,004	642	494	749

Source: BVCA

venture capitalists being structured such that they are required to earn above these levels for their investors before being able to achieve higher returns themselves (so-called 'hurdle rates of return').

The nature of the monitoring of venture capitalists may also vary between independent and captive types of firm. The former typically involve funding from limited-life funds, whereas the latter may typically be funded on a more open-ended basis. It is well-known that, in general, subsidiaries and divisions of large groups are required to conform to group monitoring systems even though their particular market circumstances may be different (Jones, Rickwood, & Greenfield, 1993). Captive venture capital firms that are subsidiaries of banks and insurance companies, for example, may thus be required to provide at least monthly management accounting information. To the extent that other activities in the institution operate on an open-ended basis, this information may be more likely to be required to be presented in terms of returns on assets rather than internal rates of return, which may be more appropriate for limited-life funds. Where funds providers to venture capitalists also invest in listed securities, where it is more feasible to undertake regular valuations, venture capital firms may also be expected to provide more frequent valuations of their portfolios. This may be expected to be more likely in independent venture capital firms.

THE GROWTH OF VENTURE CAPITAL IN THE UK

Since 1980, the UK venture capital industry has developed rapidly to become the second largest, world-wide, and the largest in Europe. By 1995, the UK market had raised a cumulative total of ECU 21.5 billion for investment in venture capital projects, accounting for 43.3% of the European total (EVCA, 1996). Moreover, after the recessionary period of the early 1990s, the market was characterized by a considerable degree of buoyancy; amounts invested reached peak levels by 1995, record amounts of funds had been raised and were available for investment, exit markets were strong and had been augmented by the introduction of the Alternative Investment Market (AIM), and encouraging performance figures were being published by the BVCA.

After growing rapidly throughout the 1980s the number of venture capital firms in the UK peaked at the height of the last recession (Table 1). In the early 1990s the number of BVCA members fluctuated a little but by 1995 had fallen to 115 and by mid-1996 to 108. The total number of companies financed in any one year peaked in 1989 and has since declined by a quarter. However, the average size of investment has increased substantially over this period. Following an initial peak in 1989, annual total amounts invested fell during the recession, but in the last two years have set successive record levels.

The growth in venture capital activity over the last decade has been achieved with marked increases in amounts invested by both independent and captive firms (Table 1). Greatest growth has occurred among independents, although between 1994 and 1995 the amount invested by captives almost doubled. Recent more-detailed analysis also shows that semi-captives have become a significant part of the industry.

The majority of venture capital investments in the UK have consistently been in the expansion area (BVCA, 1996a). From a peak of 38% seen in 1989, the proportion of investments going into early-stage projects has fallen sharply and accounted for less than a sixth of the total in 1995. In contrast, the proportion of investments involving management buy-out and buy-in transactions is now at its highest ever level at 31%. Similarly, the share of the total value of annual investments involving management buy-outs and buy-ins is also at a record at just below three-quarters of the total, having risen from a little over a half in 1991. Despite this fall in market share, the actual amounts invested in early-stage projects has increased over the most recent period, reaching £85 million in 1995 compared with £69 million in 1993 (BVCA, 1996a).

THE CURRENT COMPETITIVE POSITION

Roure, Keeley, and Vander Heyden. (1990), Ooghe et al. (1991), and Murray (1995) argue that market development is likely to be associated with greater competition. The current competitive position in the UK and its implications can be analyzed utilizing the Porter framework (Porter, 1980; see also Bruno, 1986). Evidence is drawn both from secondary sources and from the authors' interviews with senior venture capitalists (see below).

Power of Customers

Although potential investees have to pass venture capital firms' screening procedures, large amounts of available funds suggests that investees are in a relatively strong position. This may be all the more so for the more attractive deals. The possibility to float a company on a stock market such as AIM at a high valuation both enhances the alternatives available to customers and also raises the potential valuation they can achieve from venture capital firms. A strong takeover market also raises the prospect that both entrepreneurs and corporate vendors, as in the case of buy-outs, may be able to bid up the valuation of their enterprise. Entrepreneurs exiting from existing portfolios and seeking to reinvest in further ventures also have a significant degree of power, having successfully been through the process before and having generated a substantial degree of personal wealth (Wright, Robbie, & Ennew, 1997). First-time entrepreneurs, however, may be less aware of the process and appear to make relatively little use of intermediaries until after they have selected their venture capital firm (Murray, et al, 1996).

New Entrants

The growing evidence of venture capital performance and of continued rationalization in the industry has implications for the raising of funds by potential new entrants both with regard to the size of funds required to achieve a viable market presence and in the need to have a strong track record in order to attract funds. Moreover, they may need to have close existing personal links with funds providers in addition to their track record. At present, there are few new entrants into the UK market. New entrants include executives spinning off from existing firms, including captives that because of other internal organizational pressures, may be reassessing their mode of presence in the venture capital market. This is in addition to a small number of non-domestic entrants, notably from the US. Future entrants may be expected to continue to come from these sources, where in the former case executives are frustrated by lack of upward mobility or remuneration, and in the latter case where domestic markets are over-crowded and teams of investment executives can be recruited, the last offering an alternative option for individuals facing difficulties raising funds as independents. Entrepreneurs exiting from portfolios also offer a potential for the development of new entrants.

Substitutes

Although the activities of business angels has grown in the UK in recent years (Mason & Harrison, 1996) their role in comparison with US experience remains as yet more limited because of the presence of relatively fewer high net worth individuals and the need to further develop matching services. Business angels would appear to have a more complementary role to formal venture capital firms at the smaller earlier-stage end of the market. Similarly, although there has been growing evidence of entrepreneurs exiting from venture capital firms portfolios with significant gains, this has yet to be converted into a major substitute for formal venture capital funding (Wright, Robbie, & Ennew, 1997). Banks that may be both complementary and substitutes in certain segments of the market are developing their relationship services with customers.

Power of Suppliers of Finance

The trend of US funds coming into the UK may over the longer term be expected to continue, perhaps involving pension funds from smaller states in the US not already present in the UK. The extent to which this development occurs may be influenced by the nature of any shift from country-specific to global or regional emphases by funds providers. If developments are towards the latter, then medium-sized UK funds may be below the critical mass required. More positively, were Europe to be targeted as an investment area, then UK venture capital firms' greater expertise may be advantageous.

Other formal sources of finance, especially Venture Capital Trusts and governmental agency funds, may be expected to make some contribution at the margin and for smaller earlier-stage transactions, though the extent of the latter's role depends significantly on the outcome of the next election.

As regards future developments in sources of funds, it may be expected that increasing transparency about the performance of individual venture capital firms in relation to industry averages is likely to increase rationalization but would mean that good performers would have little difficulty in raising funds. The venture capital firms responding to the survey reported in detail in subsequent sections ranked funds providers' emphasis on previous performance as being the most important factor affecting competition for funds in the next five years. This may have the effect that established funds providers increasingly concentrate their investments on fewer key relationships with well-known venture capital firms in whom they had previously invested successfully. Moreover, in cases of good performance, institutional investors may be more likely to commit a larger amount to a particular venture capital fund. There may be some residual inertia whereby funds providers maintain relationships with venture capital firms with acceptable rather than outstanding performance.

Correspondingly, there may become fewer providers of domestic funds as some with poor returns exit the market and as mergers in the corporate and financial services sectors lead to reduced numbers of major UK pension funds and the number of major insurance companies interested in venture capital. This may be offset were venture capital to become an accepted asset class in institutional investors' portfolios, which could lead to increased allocations to venture capital funds, though liquidity requirements could offset such a shift.

Rivalry

The pressures from other market forces is having and may be expected to continue to have a major impact on inter-venture capital firm rivalry. Good performers may be expected not just to obtain funds but to do so on terms that suffer less from erosion by funds providers. Moreover, good performers may be placed in a stronger competitive position through having generated substantial amounts of cash from successful exits in the mid-1990s. Good and large performers may also be in a strong position to avoid or at least reduce the need for syndication, a trend that is already present in the UK. However, rivalry may also be increased through the behavior of venture capital firms seeking to enhance their relationships and reporting to funds providers who are perceived to focus more strongly on returns earned by a group of key firms.

Competition to access good deals is intense, especially at the larger buy-out end of the market, and has already led to venture capital firms being more proactive in seeking out new forms of deals such as investor-led buy-outs. These may pose particular issues about the need for venture capital firms to be able to add value, especially where there is a requirement to enter into an auction to obtain the deal (Wright & Robbie, 1996b). This puts pressure on venture capital firms in the context of potentially greater scrutiny by funds providers of the rates of return being earned. This increased rivalry in accessing deals is also associated with greater pressure on venture capital firms to differentiate themselves from their competitors through the provision of a greater range of services to investee companies and this may be expected to continue into the future. Good-performing early- and innovation-stage venture capital firms may possess difficult-to-acquire skills that reduce the possibility of increased rivalry in this sector from firms squeezed elsewhere.

The Monitoring of Venture Capital Firms

The current and expected competitive position of the UK venture capital industry introduces a number of pressures for increased monitoring of venture capital firms by their funds providers. These pressures can be identified as emanating from both the side of funds providers and venture capital firms themselves. For funds providers the pressures can be identified as follows. First, increasing transparency of returns provides a greater opportunity for benchmarking venture capital firms. Second, the increasing trend towards venture capital investments being recognized as an asset class suggests a growing need for closer scrutiny of performance. Third, increasing pressure on funds providers' trustees in respect of corporate accountability has a clear feed-through effect on the monitoring of venture capital firms in whom investments are being made. Fourth, the increasing trend towards focusing on a smaller number of key relationships involving larger amounts of investment in any one venture capital firm emphasizes the need to monitor more closely because of the potential for problems arising from reduced diversification. Moreover, there may be expected to be scale benefits from monitoring fewer larger investments. Fifth, the need for funds providers to develop their investment strategies has introduced a need for a greater degree of non-standard information. Sixth, the increasing role of gatekeepers also implies a greater pressure for monitoring.

From the point of view of venture capital firms the pressures for increased monitoring may be identified as follows. First, a developing perception by venture capital firms of the need to demonstrate performance in the top quartile for the industry if they are to receive funding brings with it an increased acceptance of the monitoring role of funds providers. Second, the rationalization of funds providers reduces the alternative sources available to venture capital firms. Third, pressure from funds providers on management fees and carried interest produces an increased emphasis for venture capital firms to demonstrate that a high level of service is being provided. Fourth, and following from the previous point, there is an increased need for venture capital firms to differentiate themselves from their competitors to help their fund-raising ability and this is an extra means of doing so.

The changing conditions in the market reviewed above raises the expectation that funds providers will become more proactive in their monitoring of venture capital firms. As part of this change it is also expected that in the light of information availability on performance, venture capital funds providers will increasingly set specific target returns, and these returns will incorporate benchmark comparisons with alternative investment sources.

However, what is not clear is the nature of the reporting mechanisms and monitoring relationships within which information on valuations is provided. If expectations of a more proactive monitoring stance and greater focus on target returns hold, it may also be expected that more regular and systematic reporting requirements will be introduced.

DATA AND METHODOLOGY

The study of the governance of venture capital firms adopted a two-stage approach that involved a series of in-depth face-to-face interviews based on a structured questionnaire checklist, followed by a mailed questionnaire survey to the remaining UK venture capital firms not covered in the first stage. At the first stage a sample of leading venture capital firms and individuals closely involved in the industry was identified with the aid of the BVCA. In total, interviews were conducted with 25 individuals, principally Chief Executives of venture capital firms, but also including three who represented gatekeepers and law firms.

The questionnaire checklist for the in-depth interviews was devised by the researchers on the basis of past studies and recent developments that appeared to be occurring in the industry. The checklist was piloted with members of the BVCA and others, with several new questions being added at this stage. Interviewees agreeing to participate in the survey were sent a copy of the final questionnaire well in advance of the interview date. It was stressed to the interviewees that the study sought their views on market developments as individuals rather than as representatives of their particular firm. These interviews were conducted in June and July of 1996. Interviews lasted between one and two and a quarter hours and were all tape-recorded. In order to enhance the willingness of interviewees to provide full and frank answers, they were assured that the tape-recordings would remain with researchers and would not be given to any other party. In addition, the researchers also gave assurances that material from the interviews would be used to provide a general overview of developments, rather than being individually attributable.

The second stage of the study involved the development of a mail questionnaire, which focused on governance issues. The items included in the questionnaire were derived both in the same way as for the in-depth interviews and from the items identified in the earlier interviews. The questionnaire survey was conducted in August to mid-September 1996, with a reminder letter being sent in early September. Questionnaires were sent to all the member firms of the BVCA not interviewed as part of the first stage. The results from the interview stage were integrated with the mail questionnaire responses to provide an overall perspective. In total, this process produced 77 responses from a total of 108 BVCA members, representing a response rate of 71.3%. As with the detailed interviews, respondents were overwhelmingly senior people in the industry: 59.7% were CEOs or equivalent; 23.4% were directors/partners; and 16.9% were assistant directors/investment managers or equivalent.

The previous section has suggested that the venture capital industry may be in a period of transition where it might be expected that monitoring behavior might undergo substantial change. One of the aims of the research, therefore, was to seek to establish what patterns might be expected to emerge during this transition.

The interviews and questionnaire survey were designed to provide an answer to the following questions :

Monitoring Policies

- What is the current approach of funds providers to the monitoring of venture capital firms?
- Is the general approach likely to change over the next five years?
- Given the agency problems involved is there a difference between the policies of funds providers to independent venture capital firms as compared with captives or semi-captives?

Performance Targets

- What performance targets do funds providers set for the venture capital firms in which they invest?
- Are these targets likely to change over the next five years?
- Is there a difference between independent and other types of venture capital firm?

Monitoring Information

- What type of information is required by funds providers for the monitoring of venture capital firms?
- Is the type of information required likely to change over the next five years?
- Are there any differences between independent and other types of venture capital firm?

Monitoring Actions

- Do funds providers take any actions in respect of the venture capital firms in which they invest?
- Are any changes anticipated over the next five years?
- Is the position different between independent and other types of venture capital firm?

A standard chi-square test of independence is used to analyze the difference between independent and non-independent (captive, semi-captive, and other) venture capital firms. To analyze the changes between now (1996) and 2001 the null hypothesis of inertia (i.e. each firm expects the same in 2001, as occurs now) is tested using the chi-square distribution with the 1996 figures generating the expected values for 2001 which can be compared to the actual responses supplied by the firms for 2001.

RESULTS

Funds Providers' Monitoring Policies

Most venture capital firms (75%) see their funds providers currently having a passive or

Table 2

Funds Providers' Monitoring Policy

	All		Independent		Non-independent	
	1996	2001	1996	2001	1996	2001
Passive	43.2	17.8	47.7	18.6	36.7	16.7
Reactive	32.4	41.1	29.5	41.9	36.7	40.0
Proactive	18.9	32.9	15.9	32.6	23.4	33.3
Highly Proactive	5.4	8.2	6.8	7.0	3.3	10.0

Source: CMBOR/BVCA

reactive monitoring policy (Table 2). Using a chi-square test, the hypothesis that independent and non-independent firms are the same is strongly supported. Although the numbers are small it does seem, however, that captive venture capitalists are a little more likely to view their funds providers, that is, their parent companies, as more proactive than do other types.

Overall, there is an expectation that over the next five years there will be a shift away from passive monitoring policies. The chi-square test shows that these changes are significant at the 1% level (value 21.5). Of the 74 firms in the sample, some 31 see themselves moving into a more active category, with 42 staying the same, and only one firm expecting a decrease. While the single most likely approach is expected to be reactive, almost a third of venture capital firms expect funds providers to become proactive compared to around a fifth currently (Table 2). The changes are not statistically significant at the 10% level.

Performance Targets Set by Funds Providers

While venture capital firms may be set multiple performance targets, it is clear from Table 3 that a single one is the most common (62% of responses). Less than 12% are set two

Table 3

Number of Performance Targets Set by Funds Providers (%)

	All		Independent		Non-independent	
	1996	2001	1996	2001	1996	2001
0	14.5	6.6	20.0	8.9	6.5	3.2
1	61.8	64.5	53.3	60.0	74.2	71.0
2	11.8	15.8	11.1	15.6	12.9	16.1
3	6.6	7.9	6.7	8.9	6.5	6.5
4	3.9	3.9	6.7	4.4		3.2
5	1.3	1.3	2.2	2.2		

Source: CMBOR/BVCA

Table 4

Performance Targets Set by Funds Providers

	1996						2001					
	All		Independent		Non-Independent		All		Independent		Non-Independent	
	A	B	A	B	A	B	A	B	A	B	A	B
Specific raw IRR	21.3	30.3	21.7	33.3	20.5	25.8	16.7	25.0	14.1	22.2	20.9	29.0
IRR > return on other assets by given %	24.1	34.2	21.7	33.3	28.2	35.5	26.3	39.5	26.8	42.2	25.6	35.5
IRR adjusted for life of fund	4.6	6.6	5.8	8.9	2.6	3.2	3.5	5.3	5.6	8.9		
Cash amount generated over given period	14.8	21.1	17.4	26.7	10.3	12.9	14.9	22.4	16.9	26.7	11.6	16.1
IRR + cash	13.9	19.7	15.9	24.4	10.3	12.9	19.3	28.9	21.1	33.3	16.3	22.6
Annual return on capital*	5.6	7.9	1.4	2.2	12.8	16.1	7.9	11.8	4.2	6.7	14.0	19.4
No specific target	10.2	14.5	13.0	20.0	5.1	6.5	5.3	7.9	7.0	11.1	2.3	3.2
Other	5.6	7.9	2.9	4.4	10.3	12.9	6.1	9.2	4.2	6.7	9.3	12.9

A: % responses   B: % companies   *hypothesis of independence rejected at 3% level

Source: CMBOR/BVCA

targets, and 14.5% are given no specific target. Overall, there is no statistically significant difference between the types of venture capital firm. However, it is worth noting that a fifth of independent companies in the sample are given no specific target, while that position applies to only one of the captive or semi-captive firms. For these latter, 70% and 80% respectively, are set a single target.

In five years a much lower percentage (less than 7% — Table 3) are expected to be set no specific target, while there is some increase in the proportions set two or more, the most marked change occurring for the independent companies. However, these changes are not statistically significant at the 10% level.

The most common target currently is an IRR that exceeds the rate of return on other asset classes by a given percentage (24% of responses: 34% of companies — Table 4), closely followed by a specific IRR (21% and 30%, respectively). The difference in responses between independent venture capital companies and others are not statistically significant at the 10% level for all the targets except an annual return on capital. In that case the hypothesis of independence can be rejected at the 3% level: captives, in particular, are more likely to be set such a target.

There is relatively little change in the distribution of these targets in five years' time. For only one of the variables (combination of IRR and cash amount generated) is the difference significant at the 5% level, and even here only 7 of the 76 firms show a change adding 50% to the number of firms using this target. The difference in responses between the two types of firm for 2001 are not statistically significantly different at the 10% level for all targets.

Table 5

Amount of Monitoring Information Required

No.	All		Independent		Non-independent	
	1996	2001	1996	2001	1996	2001
0	1.3	2.7	2.2	2.2		3.3
1	6.7	6.7	4.4	4.4	10.0	10.0
2	10.7	12.0	6.7	6.7	16.7	20.0
3	12.0	6.7	13.3	4.4	10.0	10.0
4	24.0	18.7	22.2	24.4	26.7	10.0
5	16.0	21.3	20.0	20.0	10.0	23.3
6	13.3	8.0	13.3	8.9	13.3	6.7
7	8.0	10.7	11.1	11.1	3.3	10.0
8 +	8.0	13.2	6.6	17.8	10.0	6.66

Source: CMBOR/BVCA

Monitoring Information Required by Funds Providers

As Table 5 reveals, venture capital firms are typically required to provide between four and six pieces of information to allow the funds providers to monitor their performance with the modal figure being four (24% of companies).

As Table 6 shows, the most common information required (10% to 12% of responses in each case) are annual reports, semi-annual reports, quarterly reports, semi-annual portfolio valuations, and an annual presentation/visit. Each of these is required from over half of the companies. Thirty-seven percent of the companies are required to provide detailed information on each deal (8% of the responses), but in only 28% of the cases does the funds provider have a seat on the board of the venture capital company.

The differences in reporting requirements between independent companies and the others are not statistically significantly different for all the measures except semi-annual reports and monthly or more frequent reports, where the hypothesis of independence can be rejected at the 1 percent level. At an individual level, the following are worth noting: independents and semi-captives are more likely to be required to provide semi-annual reports; requirements for captives are more likely to involve quarterly reports with nearly 40% also required to produce monthly reports; there is less emphasis on reporting valuations and on an annual presentation among the providers of funds to captives than is the case for independents and semi-captives; however, captives are more likely to be required to provide detailed information on each deal.

There is quite a variety in the combinations of information required across the companies, and there is no combination that is used by a majority. Forty percent of the sample supply both annual and semi-annual reports, while 30% have an annual presentation or visit as well. The most common combination of four items (20% of the sample) is annual and semi-annual reports, an annual presentation or visit, and semi-annual portfolio valuations.

By the millennium, there is expected to be an overall increase in the amount of information required, with the modal number being five items with 72% of the sample expecting to provide four or more pieces of information. There is expected to be some decline in the

Table 6

Monitoring Information Required by Funds Providers

| | 1996 | | | | | | 2001 | | | | | |
| | All | | Independent | | Non-Independent | | All | | Independent | | Non-Independent | |
	A	B	A	B	A	B	A	B	A	B	A	B
Annual reports	12.1	55.4	12.0	56.8	12.3	53.3	10.7	52.1	10.4	54.5	11.5	46.7
Semi-annual reports*	12.4	56.8	14.9	70.5	8.5	36.7	10.7	52.1	12.6	65.9	7.4	30.0
Quarterly reports	11.2	51.4	9.1	43.2	14.6	63.3	11.5	56.2	10.0	52.3	14.8	60.0
Monthly/more frequent reports	3.6	16.2	1.0	4.5	7.7	33.3	3.4	16.4	1.3	6.8	7.4	30.0
Annual portfolio valuations	8.0	36.5	8.7	40.9	6.9	30.0	6.5	31.5	6.9	36.4	5.7	23.3
Semi-annual portfolio valuations	10.4	47.3	10.1	47.7	10.8	46.7	10.1	49.3	10.0	52.3	10.7	43.3
More frequent portfolio valuations	4.1	18.9	3.8	18.2	4.6	20.0	5.9	28.8	5.2	27.3	7.4	30.0
Annual presentation/visit	10.9	50.0	11.5	54.5	10.0	43.3	8.4	41.1	8.2	43.2	9.0	36.7
Semi-annual presentation/ visit	3.6	16.2	3.8	18.2	3.1	13.3	3.9	19.2	4.3	22.7	3.3	13.3
More frequent presentation/ visit	2.1	9.5	1.4	6.8	3.1	13.3	3.9	19.2	4.3	22.7	3.3	13.3
Detailed information on each deal	8.3	37.8	8.7	40.9	7.7	33.3	8.7	42.5	9.5	50.0	8.2	33.3
Investor has seat on board	6.2	28.4	6.7	31.8	5.4	23.3	6.7	32.9	7.4	38.6	5.7	23.3
Access to investor relations executives as required	4.1	18.9	4.8	22.7	3.1	13.3	5.1	24.7	6.1	31.8	3.3	13.3
Regular access to investee companies	1.2	5.4	1.4	6.8	0.8	3.3	2.2	11.0	2.2	11.4	0.8	3.3
Other	1.8	8.1	1.9	9.1	1.5	6.7	2.2	11.0	1.7	9.1	1.6	6.7

A: % responses   B: % companies   *hypothesis of independence rejected at 1% level

Source: CMBOR/BVCA

emphasis on annual and semi-annual reports and on annual presentations or visits. There is also expected to be something of a shift away from annual and semi-annual portfolio valuations to more frequent ones. There are very slight indications of a shift towards the provision of information on individual deals and funds providers having a seat on the board, and almost a quarter expect there to be a requirement for access to investor relations executives on demand.

The same statistically significant differences between independents and others are observed as is the case for the 1996 data, but the general pattern is that the hypothesis of inde-

Table 7

Monitoring Actions Required by Funds Providers

No.	All		Independent		Non-independent	
	1996	2001	1996	2001	1996	2001
0	66.2	55.2	67.4	54.8	64.3	56.0
1	19.7	25.4	18.6	21.4	21.4	32.0
2	11.3	13.4	11.6	19.0	10.7	4.0
3		3.0		2.4		4.0
4	2.8	3.0	2.3	2.4	3.6	4.0

Source: CMBOR/BVCA

pendence cannot be rejected at the 10% level. Regarding individual types of venture capitalist, there are a number of notable departures from the overall position, and for both captives and independents there is evidence of an expected shift to more frequent reporting, typically towards a quarterly emphasis. Captives are more likely to see a shift towards more frequent valuations than twice a year. Independents, in particular, expect to see a shift away from annual presentations and visits towards more frequent interactions with the providers of their funds: there is also an expectation that they will be more likely to be required to provide detailed information on each deal. Independents also envisage a more noticeable increase in requirements to have investors on their boards and to allow access to investor relations executives as required, but still only in around a third of cases. Some increase is expected in allowing funds providers access to investee companies, but in very few cases. However, the only two variables for which the changes are statistically significant at the 5% level are more frequent portfolio valuation and regular access by funds providers to investee companies.

As regards combinations of information, some 41% are expecting to provide annual and semi-annual reports; 32% are, in addition, expecting an annual presentation or visit; and 24% are expecting to include semi-annual portfolio valuations as well.

Monitoring Actions by Funds Providers

Despite their extensive reporting requirements and even though such requirements are expected to increase, funds providers are unlikely to take monitoring actions (Table 7). In two-thirds of cases funds providers do not currently take any monitoring actions and by the millennium over half still expect that position to remain. In 19% of cases only one monitoring action is currently taken and, thus, two or more actions only applies to 14% of the sample. By the millennium, 25% of cases are expected to involve one monitoring action and 19%, two or more. These changes are not, however, statistically significant at the 10% level.

The most common action currently taken is an increased amount or frequency of reporting, followed by the introduction of board representation (Table 8). In five years' time an increased amount or frequency of reporting remains the most likely, if any, action taken, but it is expected to be closely followed by re-negotiation of fees towards the end of the fund life (Table 8). For all the actions listed it is not possible to reject the hypothesis of independence at the 10% level and hence that there are no significant differences between the responses of independents and other types of venture capital firm. Further, for none of the actions is it pos-

Table 8

Monitoring Actions by Funds Providers

	1996						2001					
	All		Independent		Non-Independent		All		Independent		Non-Independent	
	A	B	A	B	A	B	A	B	A	B	A	B
Increased amount and/or frequency of reporting	12.9	15.5	13.7	16.3	11.8	14.3	12.8	16.4	12.7	16.7	12.9	16.0
Introduction of board representation	8.2	9.9	9.8	11.6	5.9	7.1	9.3	11.9	10.9	14.3	6.5	8.0
Establishment of divestment policy after investee flotation	4.7	5.6	3.9	4.7	5.9	7.1	5.8	7.5	7.3	9.5	3.2	4.0
Suspension of new investment funds	4.7	5.6	3.9	4.7	5.9	7.1	2.3	3.0	1.8	2.4	3.2	4.0
Suspension of payment of management fees	1.2	1.4			2.9	3.6	3.5	4.5	3.6	4.8	3.2	4.0
Pressure to remove executives	3.5	4.2	2.0	2.3	5.9	7.1	4.7	6.0	3.6	4.8	6.5	8.0
Re-negotiation of fees towards end of fund life	8.2	9.9	9.8	11.6	5.9	7.1	11.6	14.9	12.7	16.7	9.7	12.0
Other	1.2	1.4			2.9	3.6	7.0	9.0	5.5	7.1	9.7	12.0
No actions	55.3	66.2	56.9	67.4	52.9	64.3	43.0	55.2	41.8	54.8	45.2	56.0

Source: CMBOR/BVCA

sible to reject the hypothesis that there is no change in response between 1996 and 2001 at this level of significance.

Case Study Evidence

The detailed face-to-face interviews provided further insights into the governance activities of funds providers. In particular, they illustrate that moves to enhance governance are developing both from funds providers and from venture capital firms' awareness of the changing governance needs in an environment of increasing competition for funds noted earlier.

An important observation is that venture capital investments are a relatively insignificant part of most pension fund and insurance companies' investment portfolio. As a result, pressure for change in the governance stance of funds providers was expected to be moderated unless trustees and auditors began to place greater emphasis on increased accountability. In the UK, recent policy debate has placed considerable emphasis on the accountability aspect of corporate governance (Keasey & Wright, 1993). However, by the same token, it was also the view that pension funds and insurance companies were themselves becoming more aware of monitoring issues.

It was also the case that venture capital firms, aware of these developments and in an environment of increasing competition for funds, were themselves changing their stance towards governance. Apart from making efforts to increase the performance of funds as a means of improving their fund-raising ability, venture capital firms saw themselves becoming increasingly proactive in enhancing their service to funds providers, in particular promoting an image of being more aware and more responsive to the needs of institutions. Venture capital firms may place increasing emphasis on enhancing the service they provide to suppliers of funds in order to differentiate themselves in the marketplace. Actions include being proactive in providing greater information on performance and developments in funds and generally being more imaginative in identifying and satisfying the requirements of funds providers. Importantly, it was also recognized that there was a need to maintain personal contacts from the beginning of involvement with funds providers and throughout the life of a fund rather than simply at the time of raising funds. It was seen to be the case that not all funds are likely to have the resources to provide such services, which may mean that smaller funds in particular may be placed at a competitive disadvantage. Difficulties in obtaining finance for smaller funds were expected to increase as larger funds found it easier to obtain increased amounts from a smaller number of investors.

It was also seen to be important by some venture capital firms to be proactive in providing information in order to restrict the scope for the development of the influence of gatekeepers. There was a strong view that the role of gatekeepers in the UK buy-out market in particular would increase over the next five years. If this is the case, gatekeepers may be expected to have an important role in the governance of venture capital firms in that they may have serious consequences for the development of relationships between venture capital firms and ultimate funds providers. The role of gatekeepers was seen as being driven by two factors. First, gatekeepers may be especially useful in the case of funds providers who are new entrants to the UK market, so that their role could decline as investors become more familiar with a market. Second, and especially relevant to gatekeepers acting on behalf of US investors, is the increasing demand for greater accountability to trustees of pension funds. To the extent that the trend of the US presence in the UK identified earlier continues, the role of gatekeepers in governance may be expected to increase. In addition, gatekeepers may have a role in aiding existing small investors who do not have the resources to undertake their own direct monitoring.

The nature of performance targets set by funds providers was expected to change in differing ways. For some venture capital firms, expectations reflected the fact that they were captives, so that targets set in terms of IRRs were not particularly relevant. For the other cases there was a strong view that performance targets would increasingly be set in terms of exceeding the returns from other asset classes (e.g. the FT-All Share Index) by a certain margin. The importance of the performance data provided by the BVCA was also seen in expectations by some interviewees that they would be expected to provide information that compared their performance with other venture capital firms and especially to show that they would be in the top quartile of funds. However, there were concerns that institutional investors may still wish to focus on short-term annual performance of venture capital firms which may be misleading given the nature of the product.

The interviews also shed light on the rationale behind funds providers not setting specific targets. There was a view that institutions would discuss expected achievements prior to making an investment. This approach appeared to be especially relevant to those cases with good track records, and emphasizes the importance of relationships. Few interviewees expected there to be either a shift away from IRR-based performance measurement or a broadening of measures to incorporate the amounts of cash generated over a longer period.

As seen in previous sections, reporting requirements by funds providers are multi-layered. The emphasis on written reports was highlighted by observations that where annual meetings were held these were often poorly attended. It was also pointed out that where half yearly reports were produced as well as quarterly ones, these tended to be more comprehensive, including portfolio valuations and the effects of carried interest. The value of quarterly valuations of unquoted investments was questioned.

Recent developments in corporate accountability, as well as issues concerning levels of performance, were reported in the interviews to have a strong influence on the increase in reporting. Where interviewees were also involved in more personal monitoring links such as having investors on their board, providing the opportunity to meet executives undertaking deals, visits to investee firms, and encouraging regular telephone contact, an important issue was raised concerning the availability of resources to provide such a service.

Although important changes are expected over the next five years, it was also reported in the interviews that to a certain degree major changes had already occurred to get to this level and frequency of reporting. However, there were expectations by some of further changes, including a move to more specific and standardized information in order to reduce what was seen by some as an excessive amount of material now being produced. The observation was also made that the timescale of quarterly reporting may be too short, given expected developments in venture capital firms' portfolios.

Where funds providers had never taken any monitoring actions, this typically involved those venture capital firms who had consistently demonstrated good performance. In one case where significant problems had been experienced, the parental funds provider had instigated very close monitoring. Where actions had been taken, these took a variety of forms. Where venture capital funds had been performing below expectations, actions by funds providers tended to be to find a constructive way of resolving problems. Although there was a view that actions in such circumstances might include removal of management, it was more likely that the approach would be to retain management but require them to stop making investments in a particular fund and suspending fees until performance returned to target levels. There were seen to be advantages in venture capital firms being proactive in drawing the attention of funds providers when problems were developing. Other actions included renegotiations of fees towards the end of a fund's life and the establishment of a policy of divestment of shares once an investee firm had gone public. It was anticipated that funds providers' actions will increasingly focus on persuading venture capital firms to give greater consideration to the management of exits in order to maximize returns to investors rather than to maximize carried interest.

The interviews also identified a further area of action by funds providers. Interviewees recognized that there has already been some reduction in management fees and carried interest rates and that there will continue to be some tightening of terms required by funds providers. Management fees, for example, could be under pressure for managers who have several funds investing in mature industries. However, venture capital firms with good track records were expected to be able to maintain their rates of carried interest, though there was something of a view that there should be a shift to stepped rates, which would provide for super-returns for very good performance rather than simple hurdle rates. The pressure on terms was seen to be especially important at the large buy-out end of the market, with venture capital firms with early-stage investments reporting little pressure in this area, since a key issue for funds providers was being able to access those firms with the necessary specialist skills.

CONCLUSIONS AND IMPLICATIONS

This paper has examined developments in funds providers monitoring of venture capital firms in the context of recent developments in the venture capital market. The main findings can be summarized as follows:

1. There is a clear expectation of a shift away from passive approaches to the monitoring of venture capital firms, although new approaches may be as much reactive as proactive.

2. There are statistically significant differences between the monitoring requirements for independent venture capital companies and all other types.

3. There is some expectation of a shift towards target IRRs set in relation to the returns on other asset classes or returns for the better performers in the venture capital sector, within the context of the use of multiple performance targets. However, this shift is not expected to be strong.

4. Similarly, there is some evidence of an expected increased use of targets set in the form of a combination between IRRs and cash amounts generated.

5. Between now and the next millennium it was expected that the proportion of venture capital firms that do not set specific target rates of return would halve.

6. Reporting requirements are multi-layered, but there was an anticipated shift toward the greater use of quarterly reporting and portfolio valuation as well as more frequent direct contact between venture capital firms and their funds providers.

7. In a significant minority of cases it was anticipated that there would be an increased requirement to provide regular access to investor relations executives as well as seats on boards for funds providers.

8. Funds providers typically engage in few monitoring actions and this was generally expected to continue. The most notable change was expected to be some increased use of renegotiations of management fees towards the end of a fund's life.

9. The relatively minor share of venture capital in institutional investors' portfolios was viewed as an important influence on a more reactive approach to monitoring, raising issues about its cost-effectiveness; these aspects were expected to be exacerbated where there was little pressure on corporate accountability. These aspects were also expected to change over time.

10. Venture capital firms report that they have already made major enhancements to their reporting and communication approaches and that there was growing emphasis on being proactive in providing early warning signals about impending problems.

11. There were concerns about the risk that reporting overload could develop, with there being a growing need to strike an appropriate balance between the provision of specific information to meet funds providers needs and standardized information.

12. Changes to the remuneration structures for venture capital firms are also an important part of the monitoring process, with venture capital firms reporting a shift towards more performance-oriented structures and some downward pressure overall in the more competitive larger buy-out sector. However, good performers were expected to continue to be in a strong position to maintain their remuneration structures.

13. The expected increased role of gatekeepers, driven by new US entrants concerned about

corporate accountability, is expected to affect the development of relationships between venture capital firms and funds providers.

The monitoring of venture capital firms seems set to become an increasingly important issue for both practitioners and academic researchers, and the findings of this study suggest a number of specific observations.

For practitioners, the findings emphasize the importance for venture capital firms of developing relationships with funds providers through more frequent direct personal communication that continues over the life of a fund, and through identifying their information needs. The development of relationships appears to have an important influence on the nature of the return target that may be set.

There also appears to be a continuing need to educate funds providers about the nature and timing of the returns to be earned from venture capital, especially given pressures for more frequent reporting. The development of relationships is one means of addressing this issue. However, such developments raise major cost-benefit trade-off and resource issues

For academic researchers, there would appear to be considerable scope for researching governance issues. In contrast to the vast amount of research concerning venture capital firm-investee relationships, examination of funds providers-venture capital firm relationships has been neglected. This paper has provided some initial insights from the perspective of venture capital firms. In the same way that recent research on investor-investee relationships has focused on the entrepreneurs' side and on dyads involving the two parties (Sapienza & Gupta, 1994), similar possibilities would appear to present themselves in respect of funds providers and venture capital firms. Moreover, the changing nature of funds provider-venture capital firm relationships raises issues about the relative importance of principal-agent versus trust and procedural justice-based conceptual approaches in this area, as it has also arisen in the second-tier relationships between venture capital firms and their investees. Procedural justice is concerned with exchange relationships in which one party does not have control over decisions (Korsgaard, Schweiger, & Sapienza, 1995). The theory has clear parallels to the situation faced by the indirect involvement by funds providers in the operations of venture capital firms. Though funds providers may have made considerable contributions to venture capital funds, it is the venture capital executives who control the way in which funds are disbursed and the strategies adopted to achieve the returns that funds providers are seeking. Procedural justice can also be viewed as an important influence on the development of trust and commitment in relations between providers of funds to venture capital firms and the venture capital firms themselves. This perspective links to agency theory in that the development of relationships may ameliorate the need for costly monitoring as it reduces the need for formal mechanisms in the management of exchange relationships, though of course, contract law and standard-form contracts may also be seen as a means of reducing agency costs.

REFERENCES

Beecroft, A. (1994). 'The role of the venture capital industry in the UK. In N. Dimsdale N & M. Prevezer (Eds.), *Capital markets and corporate governance*. Oxford: Oxford University Press.

Bruno, A. (1986). A structural analysis of the venture capital industry. In D. Sexton & R Smilor (Eds.), *The art and science of entrepreneurship*. Cambridge, MA: Ballinger.

BVCA. (1996a). *Report on investment activity*. London: BVCA.

BVCA. (1996b). *BVCA performance measurement survey*. London: BVCA.

Bygrave, W. (1994). Rates of return from venture capital. In W. Bygrave, M. Hay, & J. Peeters, (Eds.), *Realizing investment value*, ch. 1. London: FT-Pitman.

Bygrave, W., & Timmons, J. (1992). *Venture capital at the crossroads*. Boston: Harvard Business School Press.

EVCA. (1996). EVCA yearbook 1996. Zaventem: European Venture Capital Association.

Gompers, P., & Lerner, J. (1996). The use of covenants: An empirical analysis of venture partnership agreements. *Journal of Law and Economics, 39*(2), 463-498.

Jones, S., Rickwood, C., & Greenfield, S. (1993). *Accounting control and management philosophies*. London: ICAEW Research Board.

Keasey, K., & Wright, M (1993). Issues in corporate accountability and governance. *Accounting and Business Research, 23*(91A), 291-303.

Korsgaard, M., Schweiger, D., & Sapienza, H. (1995). The Role of procedural justice in building commitment, attachment and trust in strategic decision-making teams. *Academy of Management Journal, 38*, 60-84.

Manigart, S., Wright, M., Robbie, K., & Desbrieres, P. (1997). Venture capitalists appraisal of investment projects: An empirical European study. *Entrepreneurship Theory and Practice*, forthcoming.

Mason, C., & Harrison, R (1996). Informal venture capital: A study of the investment process, the post-investment experience and investment performance. *Entrepreneurship and Regional Development, 8*, 105-125.

McNally, K. (1994). Sources of finance for UK venture capital funds: The role of corporate investors. *Entrepreneurship & Regional Development, 6*, 275-297.

Murray, G. (1991). *Change and maturity in the UK venture capital industry 1991-95*. London: BVCA.

Murray, G. (1995). The UK venture capital industry. *Journal of Business Finance and Accounting, 22*(8), 1077-1106.

Ooghe, H., Fassin, Y., & Manigart, S. (1991). Growth patterns in the European venture capital industry. *Journal of Business Venturing, 6*, 381-404.

Porter, M. (1980). *The competitive strategy: Techniques for analyzing industries and competitors*. New York: Free Press.

Roure, J., Keeley, R., & van der Heyden, T. (1990). European venture capital: Strategies and challenges in the 90s. *European Management Journal, 8*(2), 243-252.

Sahlman, W. A. (1990). The structure and governance of venture-capital organizations. *Journal of Financial Economics, 27*, 473-521.

Sapienza, H., & Gupta, A. (1994). Impact of agency risks and task uncertainty on venture capitalist-CEO interaction. *Academy of Management Journal, 37*(6), 1618-1632.

Sterling, M., & Wright, M. (1990). *Management buy-outs and the law*. Oxford: Blackwell Law Publishers.

Wright, M., Robbie, K., & Ennew, C. (1997). Venture capital firms and serial entrepreneurs. *Journal of Business Venturing*, forthcoming.

Wright M., Thompson S., & Robbie K. (1992). Venture capital and management-led leveraged buy-outs: A European perspective. *Journal of Business Venturing, 7*, 47-71.

Wright, M., & Robbie, K. (1996a). Venture capital firms and unquoted equity investment appraisal. *Accounting and Business Research, 26*(2), 153-168.

Wright, M., & Robbie, K. (1996b). The investor-led buy-outs: A new strategic option. *Long Range Planning, 29*(5),691-702.

Zahra, S. (1995). Corporate entrepreneurship and financial performance: The case of management leveraged buy-outs. *Journal of Business Venturing, 10*(3), 225-247.

Ken Robbie is Senior Research Fellow and Deputy Director at the Centre for Management Buy-Out Research, University of Nottingham.

Mike Wright is Professor of Financial Studies and Director of the Centre for Management Buy-Out Research, University of Nottingham.

Brian Chiplin is Professor of Industrial Economics and Director of the Centre for Management Buy-Out Research, University of Nottingham.

Acknowledgements: Financial support for CMBOR from BZW Private Equity and Deloitte & Touche Corporate Finance is gratefully acknowledged. Financial support from the BVCA for part of the research results reported here is also acknowledged. An earlier version of this paper was presented at the 10th Anniversary conference of the Centre for Management Buy-out Research held at the University of Nottingham in September 1996 and at the Babson Entrepreneurship Conference in 1997. The authors are grateful for the comments made by the conference participants.

[17]

SPECIALIZATION

VERSUS DIVERSIFICATION

AS A VENTURE CAPITAL

INVESTMENT STRATEGY

EDGAR NORTON and BERNARD H. TENENBAUM
Fairleigh Dickinson University

EXECUTIVE SUMMARY

Much important work has informed us of rates of return earned by venture capitalists, the importance of venture capitalists to the "going public" process, and the criteria venture capitalists use to evaluate deals. This paper seeks to add to the literature by testing hypotheses, based upon both the finance and strategic management literature, regarding certain venture capitalist investment practices.

Venture capitalists seek to control or manage risk (Driscoll 1974; MacMillan, Siegel, and SubbaNarasimha 1985). Financing structure and investment strategy provide several means for venture capitalists to do this. Tools available to the venture capitalist include portfolio diversification to spread risk across different industries, firms, or hot/cold IPO markets to minimize unsystematic or investment-specific risk. Information sharing, networking, and specialization can also be used to control unsystematic risk.

Several hypotheses are developed from these conflicting perspectives. Data used to test the hypotheses are derived from responses to a survey of venture capitalists. Three hundred surveys were mailed to venture capitalists; 98, or 32.7%, returned usable responses.

Portfolio diversification is a well-known means to control risk exposure by reducing unsystematic or specific risks. However, Bygrave (1987, 1988), as well as financial intermediation theorists, argues that maintaining a high degree of specialization is useful for controlling risk as well as for gaining access to networks, information, and deal flow from other venture investors. The analyses of this paper build upon Bygrave's work. We construct more rigorous tests to resolve the conflict between the diversification and information-sharing hypotheses. Our hypothesis tests were usually resolved in favor of the information-sharing view. For example, venture capitalists in the sample that were heavily involved in seed round financing were diversified across fewer numbers of firms and industries.

Address correspondence to Edgar Norton, Department of Economics and Finance, Fairleigh Dickinson University, 285 Madison Avenue, Madison, NJ 07940

The authors received financial support from an FDU Research Grant-In-Aid. Research assistance from Glenn Cates and the staff of the Rothman Institute of Entrepreneurial Studies is gratefully acknowledged. Helpful comments from two anonymous referees helped to improve the paper; the authors, however, are responsible for all shortcomings.

Journal of Business Venturing 8, 431–442

0883-9026/93/$6.00

Further evidence in favor of information sharing is seen in investment patterns across different financing stages. Diversification would imply maintaining a portfolio of investments across the different investment stages. The information sharing/specialization view would argue that it is best to stay focused on a single stage or several "connected" stages. The empirical evidence from the sample once again favors the specialization perspective.

This research provides information of use to venture capitalists, as they seek information on how best to control risk; to entrepreneurs, as they learn of the factors venture capitalists consider in determining their investment strategy; and to academicians, as such studies provide insight to general industry practice and thus help to form the basis of classroom discussion and future research endeavors.

INTRODUCTION

As reported in Sahlman (1990), over one-third of investments by venture capitalists resulted in total absolute losses during the 1969–1985 time frame. About one of 15 investments results in returns that are ten or more times the venture capitalist's investment; the value of these few winners comprise about 49.4% of the ending value of the investor's portfolio and 61.4% of the investor's profits. The average holding period for a venture capital investment is 4.9 years, with about one-third of the investments held longer than six years. These statistics confirm that a successful outcome of a venture capital investment is highly uncertain and develops over a long time horizon. Ruhnka and Young (1991) have found that both the amount of risk and its composition varies across the stages of financing. In early stage financings, total risk is high and its major component comprises factors that are internal to the firm (e.g., team competence, technology development). In later stage financings, total risk declines and the major risk components are risk factors that are external to the firm (e.g, market response, competition, economic downturns).

This paper proposes and tests several hypotheses that deal with portfolio strategy as a means for venture capitalists to manage risk. The empirical results indicate that venture capitalists apparently use specialization and information-sharing strategies to control risk rather than financial diversification.

The following section reviews some means of risk control available to venture capitalists. Section 2 develops hypotheses regarding portfolio risk control. Section 3 describes the survey instrument used in the study. Section 4 reports the results of statistical tests. Concluding comments follow at the end of the paper.

1. RISK CONTROL

Previous studies have found that venture capitalists seek to manage and control risk (Driscoll 1974; MacMillan, Siegel, and SubbaNarasimha 1985). The screening process—in which only 1–3% of proposals receive funding—is certainly one potential means of controlling risk. Other means to control risk exist on both the "micro" or individual investment level and on the "macro" or portfolio level.

Micro Risk

Sahlman (1990) discusses that deal structure and active involvement by the venture capitalist in the portfolio firm are several "micro" methods of controlling risk. For example, rather than giving the entrepreneur a large lump sum of cash up front, most venture capital investments involve staged commitments of capital over time. Staging commitments allows the venture capitalist to maintain the valuable options to abandon, re-value, or expand their investment in the firm. Injecting small increments of capital into the portfolio firm also helps to discipline the entrepreneurial team and keep them focused on developing a marketable product.

Many other deal structure provisions can seek to control "micro" elements of risk. The entrepreneurial team's compensation contract can be structured so that cash salary is low but awards of stock options are high. Venture capitalists may be able to fire team members and repurchase their stock at less than market value. Venture capitalists may sit on the boards of their portfolio firms and be actively involved in the firm's strategy setting and operations (Sahlman 1990; MacMillan, Kulow, and Khoylian 1989; Timmons 1987). Rachet provisions, use of investment vehicles that are senior to the entrepreneur's equity, put options, and redemption options are other means by which the venture capitalist can financially structure an investment in an attempt to control "micro" risk.

Unfortunately, research into various deal-specific risk control factors presents many problems, not the least of which is access to data. Due to their proprietary nature, contracts and term sheets between venture capitalists and entrepreneurs are not available for review. Information concerning general deal structure influences can be accessed through survey instruments (Norton and Tenenbaum 1992a, 1992b) but no "hard" data bases exist to provide this information to researchers. Additionally, whereas bond covenant provisions have language that has become fairly well standardized (Malitz 1986), this is probably not the case in the more fragmented and private venture capital industry. Thus an empirical study of deal structures that have developed to control "micro" risk is hindered by a lack of data availability and the potential complexity of the terms.

Macro Risk

"Macro" or portfolio level risk can also be controlled by the venture capitalist. Both financial theory and strategic management theory have developed perspectives for risk control in portfolios. Mainline finance theory argues that portfolios should contain a diversified collection of assets to minimize the effects of unsystematic or asset-specific risk (see, e.g., Sharpe 1964). However, strategic management theorists, as well as finance researchers who study financial intermediation, contend that portfolio specialization rather than diversification can be used to control portfolio risk (Bygrave 1987; Chan 1983; Campbell and Kracaw 1980). As with deal structure data availability, it is true that information on venture capitalist portfolio practices is not publicly available. However, a survey instrument can request basic information regarding the characteristics of venture capitalists' portfolios. Statistical tests of survey responses can then determine if the sample data support the portfolio diversification or portfolio specialization theories of "macro" risk control.

2. DEVELOPING HYPOTHESES

Portfolio Diversification

Total risk (the variability in asset returns) has two components: systematic or market risk and unsystematic risk. Systematic risk arises from the effects of market or economy-wide influences on the returns to each asset. Unsystematic risk arises from firm, industry, or other asset-specific effects. By constructing a well-diversified portfolio, all unsystematic risk can be diversified away, leaving an investor exposed only to systematic risk influences. With a diversified portfolio, unfortunate circumstances that hurt returns on some assets are balanced by situations that increase returns on other assets.

434 E. NORTON AND B. H. TENENBAUM

Under the premises of the Capital Asset Pricing Model (CAPM), the financial markets reward only systematic risk with higher expected levels of return; exposure to unsystematic risk is not rewarded (Sharpe 1964). The arbitrage pricing theory (Ross 1976) has attracted a great deal of attention and empirical testing in the finance literature as a potential successor to the CAPM. It is a more general theory than the CAPM, but it still assumes that investors are fully diversified and subject only to systematic risk influences. Thus, finance theory generally assumes diversified investors. The only risk of interest is systematic or market risk; all firm or industry specific risk should be diversified away.

Venture capitalists are subject, *a priori*, to a great amount of unsystematic risk in each of their portfolio firms. Venture capitalists may want to diversify across different industries and companies in order to reduce their risk exposure in any one industry or product. Early stage investments carry great amounts of risk (Plummer 1987; Ruhnka and Young 1991). The desire to diversify may be especially strong for investors with large relative commitments to seed and first stage investments.[1] If venture capitalists seek to control unsystematic risk by way of portfolio diversification, the following hypothesis should be true:

> H_1: Venture capitalists that make early stage investments will be more diversified to compensate for their risky individual investments. Thus, investors with greater relative commitments to early stage investments (i.e., seed or first stage) should be invested in relatively more industries and companies than those venture capitalists with lesser commitments to early financing stages.

Another source of asset-specific risk is liquidity risk. Ultimately venture capitalists wish to exit their investments and return either cash or liquid securities to their investment partners. Liquidity risk exists when the venture capitalist has difficulty exiting from an investment and receiving fair market value in return for the investment stake.

In the context of venture capital, there are two aspects to liquidity risk. The first aspect is deal-specific, i.e., the difficulty in exiting from an investment that is either failing or among the "living dead." This aspect of liquidity risk depends upon a great many factors, both internal and external to the entrepreneurial team. It can best be controlled, according to portfolio diversification theory, by constructing a well-diversified portfolio to reduce the effect of unsystematic risk on overall portfolio return.

The second aspect of liquidity risk deals with the timing of an exit from a successful investment. A venture capitalist would much rather seek to exit when the public equity and the acquisition/merger markets are placing fair values on portfolio firms. Returns to the venture capital investor may be lower if cashout occurs in markets that are "cold," or potentially less liquid. Thus, the portfolio diversification perspective implies that venture capitalists should not only seek to diversify across firms and industries but also across different financing stages. By staggering deals across different financing stages, some investments will be ready for cashout in "cold" initial public offering markets, some in "hot." The key is that the venture capitalist will be diversified in terms of cashout and be less likely to liquidate positions in substantial numbers of portfolio firms during cold exit markets. Thus, we have a second portfolio diversification hypothesis:

---

[1] It is the *relative* commitment to early stage investments that affects the investor's portfolio risk, not the absolute commitment. A venture capitalist with $10 million in capital who is 80% invested in (undiversified) seed stage deals is *a priori* exposed to just as much unsystematic risk as a $100 million pool that is 80% invested in (undiversified) seed deals.

H_2: Concerns about their inability to time "cold" and "hot" IPO markets will lead venture capital firms to diversify across different financing stages.

Specialization and Information Sharing

The CAPM includes such assumptions as homogenous investor expectations, no transactions costs, and equal access to information. These premises will not be true in the risk capital market. Thus the analysis of venture capitalists may be similar to those, such as financial intermediaries, that have information or transactions cost advantages over other investors; e.g., Leland and Pyle (1977), Campbell and Kracaw (1980), Chan (1983), and Bygrave (1987, 1988). Sahlman (1990) argues that valuable learning curve effects arise from the venture capitalist's specialized activity. The venture capitalist benefits from gaining institutional knowledge, sharing it with other investors and gatekeepers, earning a reputation for their experience and expertise, and is then able to "cultivate a deal flow based on networks of contacts and relationships" (Sahlman 1990, p. 500).

Financial theory has also developed models for specialized or concentrated investment activity. Levy (1978, 1991) and Merton (1987) construct models, called Generalized Capital Asset Pricing Models (GCAPM), which assume that segmented capital markets arise due to fixed costs of gaining information. As the reason for the segments disappear (i.e., as the fixed costs approach zero), the GCAPM equilibrium becomes identical to the CAPM as a special case. Levy (1978) argues that one source of fixed costs is the cost of discovering and interpreting the effects of events and information on specific firms in the investor's portfolio (e.g., reading and analyzing quarterly financial statements, keeping current on news and trends). In Levy's (1978) model, the existence of fixed costs limit the number of securities that appear in an investor's portfolio. Thus, complete diversification may not occur. Merton (1987) assumes investors possess specialized information that they then use to purchase stocks in specific areas. For example, a computer programmer should focus his/her investment activity in computer hardware and software firms; a physician will mainly invest in pharmaceutical and health-care firms. Under Merton's model, it is costly for investors to acquire information about companies that do business in areas unrelated to the investor's specialized expertise. Thus, the investor will invest only in those stocks about which they are already well-informed.

The assumption of complete diversification is not appropriate according to models that assume that some investors have cost advantages over others. From this perspective, venture capital firms will use their expertise to specialize in certain technical and product areas. Due to their information advantage in certain technologies or markets, and the high fixed costs of gaining expertise in other technical and product areas, it does not make economic sense for venture capitalists to seek portfolio diversification.

The knowledge base of venture capitalists include technological, market, and product expertise, as well as networks comprising experts and investors with similar interests. Venture capitalists seek to manage operating and technical risks by gaining access, by means of their reputation in their specialization, to information flows and deal flows in networks. According to Bygrave (1987, 1988), venture capitalists will invite other venture capitalists to participate in deals where their specialized knowledge is such that it will likely add value to the investment. We posit that venture capitalists that invest in firms involving the greatest amounts of technical and product risk (presumably early stage financing deals) should be more specialized, should have a more narrow industry focus, and may be less diversified than those who finance later stage deals.

Thus, if information sharing and specialization are a means to control risk, we have the following hypothesis to counter H_1:

H_3: Investors in early stage deals will have a narrow focus or industry specialization. Thus, the number of different industries and companies in which the venture capitalist is invested should be inversely related to the relative amount of seed and first stage investing done by the venture capitalist.

Diversification among the various financing stages will also be less important if specialization and networking theory is a better reflection of venture capitalist risk control practice. Venture capitalists will mainly invest in deals of a specific financing stage. Over time, the investor's financing stage profile may change somewhat as follow-on investments occur; but he/she will still seek to specialize in certain financing stages. Thus, the portfolio specialization and networking perspective leads to the following hypothesis to counter H_2:

H_4: The venture capitalist's strategy to specialize in order to enhance their position in networks and information flows will lead them to concentrate in one financing stage or several financing stages which may be related by virtue of subsequent follow-on investments.

Related Work

Bygrave (1987, 1988) reports on theoretical and empirical work related to the topic of this paper. Bygrave applies Pfeffer and Salancik's (1978) resource exchange model to the venture capital industry. The model predicts that the amount of networking or co-investing among venture capitalists should rise as uncertainty rises. In an analysis of the top 61 venture capital firms, Bygrave (1987) finds that the amount of co-investing is significantly greater among venture capitalists investing in high-tech firms than those investing in low-tech firms. He also discovers that the average investment per firm is significantly less for high-tech investments than for low-tech investments. Bygrave's results show that the amount of co-investing is not related to the size of the venture capitalist; small and large high-tech investors do similar amounts of co-investing, as do small and large low-tech investors. These results lead Bygrave (1987) to conclude:

Thus the principal reason for co-investing was not spreading of financial risk. Rather it was the sharing of expertise (p. 151).

Bygrave's test of the conflicting financial diversification and information sharing hypotheses is somewhat weak. For example, the fact that investors in high-tech firms did more co-investing and invested fewer dollars per portfolio firm than investors in low-tech firms is consistent with both the portfolio diversification and the information sharing viewpoints. The fact that the amount of co-investing was not related to the size of the venture capitalist does not disprove financial risk spreading among venture capitalists. Both large and small venture capitalists may have similar co-investing patterns if they have similar exposures to financial or technical risk.

The analysis to be done in this paper builds upon Bygrave's work. We seek to construct more rigorous tests to resolve the conflict between the diversification and information sharing hypotheses.

3. SURVEY STUDY

Surveys were mailed in February/March 1990 to 300 members of the National Venture Capital Association; a second mailing to non-respondents occurred in May/June 1990. A total of 98 responses were received for a response rate of 32.7%. By comparing mean responses from the first and second mailings, the results suggest that response bias does not exist in the sample. Previous versions of the survey were pretested among eight venture capitalists. Their comments and suggestions were incorporated into the final survey format. No one who was part of the pre-test was included in the mailings. The cover letter promised the responses would be held in confidence. Data from the respondents is contained in Table 1.

The typical responding venture capital firm is a private limited partnership (item I).[2] In our sample, 75.5% of the respondents are limited partnerships; from data presented in Sahlman (1990), about 78–80% of the U.S. venture capital firms are organized as limited partnerships. Most of the respondents are larger funds, with over $50 million of total funds managed (item IV). This is also in close agreement with Sahlman's (1990) industry statistics; he reports the average (median) capital size of an independent, private sector venture capitalist is $65 million ($30 million) in 1988. The portfolios of firms in our sample are fairly diversified; over half of the respondents' portfolios have investments in seven or more industries and nearly half have stakes in over 30 companies (items II and III).

The individual numerical responses on the percentage of financing done at each financing stage (item V) are summarized in the four columns presented in Table 1. The financing stages listed in item V are commonly used in the venture capital literature and are in standard use by practitioners (Sahlman 1990). The reported means are based upon the actual numerical responses given by the firms responding to the survey. Our sample appears to be more actively involved in seed stage investing than the industry averages reported in Sahlman (1990, table 1C). According to Sahlman's data, about 12.5% of venture capital funds are invested in seed stage investments, 67.5% in expansion stages, and 20.0% in leveraged buyouts. Our sample has about 24% of capital invested in seed stage deals, about 59% in expansion stage deals, and 17% in LBOs.

Comparing the size and composition of the venture capital firms in our sample to industry data reported in Sahlman (1990), the firms in our sample appear to be representative of firms in the industry. An exception is that the sample firms have relatively more capital invested in seed stage deals than the industry average. This should not make our sample invalid, as the focus of our analysis is on portfolio risk control. The greater relative amount of high-risk early stage investors in our sample may result in stronger tests of our hypotheses.[3]

4. HYPOTHESIS TESTING

Table 2, Panel A, reports correlation coefficients between the percentage of funds invested in early financing stages and diversification measures. Firms more actively involved in seed financing are diversified across a smaller number of industries and firms. This provides evidence against H_1 (financial risk diversification) and provides evidence in favor of H_3 (information sharing).

Contradictory findings occur when first round investments is examined. The number of industries in the portfolio is negatively related to the percentage of first round financing but the correlation coefficient is not significantly different from zero. The number of portfolio

---

[2] The statistical tests reported in this paper were done twice, once using the entire sample and once with only the responses from private limited partnerships. Qualitatively similar results occurred. This paper reports statistical tests using data from the entire sample.

[3] It may be that the portfolio risk control strategies of "department store" venture capitalists differ from those of venture capital "boutiques." As the survey sample was not classified into one category or the other, the respondents are probably a mixture of both "department store" and "boutique" venture capitalists. Given that a number of our sample's characteristics correspond closely to Sahlman's (1990) "population" description, mixing venture capitalists of different investment philosophies should not adversely bias the results of our hypothesis tests.

438 E. NORTON AND B. H. TENENBAUM

TABLE 1 Aggregate Information Collected from Survey Items I through V

	Frequency
I. Type of venture capital firm:	
i. public	6
private	89
missing	3
ii. a. limited partnership	74
b. SBIC/MESBIC	10
c. corporate subsidiary	10
d. other	7
(some respondents checked more than one category)	
II. Number of different industries represented in the firm's portfolio	
1–3 industries:	10
4–6 industries:	25
7–9 industries:	28
10 or more:	33
missing:	2
III. Number of companies in the firm's portfolio	
1–9:	16
10–19:	20
20–29:	13
30 or more:	48
missing:	1
IV. Total amount of funds managed within the venture capital firm	
less than $10 million:	9
$11–20 million:	8
$21–30 million:	9
$31–40 million:	8
$41–50 million:	3
over $50 million:	59
missing:	2

V. Percentage of financing done at each stage by the respondents

	PERCENTAGES					
STAGE	0–9%	10–20%	21–49%	50% or more	Average	Number of firms
start-up or seed	33	23	22	17	23.8%	95
first	25	27	32	10	22.1%	94
second	29	28	30	7	18.3%	94
third	46	24	18	6	13.1%	94
bridge	72	16	4	2	5.7%	94
other	60	9	11	14	17.1%	94

firms is positively and significantly related, at the 10% level, to the amount of first round financing. This provides weak evidence for H_1, the financial risk diversification hypothesis.

Panel B of Table 2 reports the results of *t*-tests on differences in sample means. Venture capitalists reporting a large percentage of seed stage investing (50% of capital or more) were classified as the high seed group; those firms reporting less than 50% seed financing were placed in the low seed group. The high seed group is diversified across fewer industries and

TABLE 2 Relationship Between Early Stage Financing and Venture Capitalist Diversification

Panel A: Correlation coefficients between the percentage of funds invested in different financing stages and venture capitalist diversification measures. The probability values from a one-tailed test are in parentheses.

	Investor characteristics:	
Early stage round:	Number of industries in the portfolio	Number of companies in the portfolio
Seed	−.1861 (.037)	−.1666 (.054)
First	−.0446 (.336)	.1434 (.085)

Panel B: Results presented are t-ratios and, in parentheses, the probability values from a one-tailed test. The test seeks to determine if there is a relationship between venture capitalists with large early stage capital commitments and the diversification of their portfolio. The comparison in the t-test is between the number of different industries and firms in the portfolios of those venture capital firms with 50% or more of their funds invested in the listed stage against firms that have fewer than 50% of their funds invested in the designated financing stage. A negative t-ratio implies investors with 50% or more of their funds in the listed stage have less-diversified portfolios than those investors that have fewer than 50% of their funds invested in the listed stage.

	Investor characteristics:	
Early stage round:	Number of industries in the portfolio	Number of companies in the portfolio
Seed:	−1.49 (0.07)	−2.21 (.015)
First:	−1.74 (.043)	−1.92 (.030)

has investments in a smaller number of companies than the low seed group. The respondents were similarly grouped according to their percentage of first round investments. The venture capitalists that have a large percentage of first round investments also are less diversified across industries and companies, in support of H_3.

Though some conflicting results occur when correlation coefficients are examined, the results of t-tests that focus on investors with large relative commitments to early stage investments indicate strong evidence in favor of the information sharing hypothesis, H_3. These tests provide some empirical evidence that, among the venture capitalists in the sample, the management of technical, marketing, and other firm-specific risks via specialization is of greater importance than managing financial risk.[4]

Table 3 shows the correlation matrix of the percentage of funds invested in the different financing stages. Diversification and H_2 would be supported if no pattern of significant correlations occurred; e.g., a venture capitalist's involvement in first stage financing should have no impact on the degree of second stage investment.

---

[4] These results are not being driven by smaller venture capitalists. Venture capitalists across all size categories (item IV in Table 1) occur across all diversification measures (number of industries, number of companies in the portfolio) and financing stages.

440   E. NORTON AND B. H. TENENBAUM

TABLE 3   Relationship Between the Percentage of Funds Invested by Venture Capitalists in Each Financing Stage

	First	Second	Third	Bridge	Other
Seed	.0318	−.2904	−.3758	−.1713	−.3857
	(.381)	(.002)	(.000)	(.049)	(.000)
First		.1368	−.3865	−.2521	−.3743
		(.094)	(.000)	(.007)	(.000)
Second			.0347	−.1019	−.4025
			(.370)	(.164)	(.000)
Third				.1862	−.1906
				(.036)	(.033)
Bridge					−.1780
					(.043)

Note: Correlation coefficients between the percentage of venture capitalist funds invested in the various financing stages. Correlations are based upon actual numerical responses given in the survey. Probability values from a one-tailed test are in parentheses.

Evidence of related investment patterns would indicate support for H_4 (information sharing). If venture capitalists specialize, the percentage of financing in a given stage may be positively related to those of nearby stages as a result of follow-on investments. In addition, a negative relationship should exist between financing stages that are not consecutive. For example, whereas seed and first round investing may be positively correlated as a result of follow-on investments, seed and third stage financing should be negatively related.

The latter is what appears in Table 3. For the most part, positive correlations exist between successive financing stages (as seen on the diagonal).[5] This implies some degree of follow-on investment activity occurs in the firms' portfolios. Off-diagonal correlations, which represent non-connected financing stages, are mostly negative and statistically significant. The evidence from Table 3 supports the specialization hypothesis, H_4. No support of the portfolio diversification hypothesis, H_2, is indicated.

5. CONCLUSIONS

This paper reviews responses to a survey completed by 98 venture capitalists. The paper seeks to determine if venture capitalists attempt to control risk through competing portfolio strategies. We examine various sources of risk and how strategies to manage risk can affect portfolio construction.

Portfolio diversification is a method to reduce risk exposure by financial means. Venture capitalist portfolios can reduce unsystematic risk by investing in a diversified set of firms or industries. The portfolios can also be diversified against the risk of liquidation during cold IPO markets by containing investments in different stage deals.

Bygrave's (1987, 1988) work on the role of networks, specialization, and information sharing argues otherwise. To control risk, venture capitalists should seek to specialize in order to exploit their technical and product expertise. The specialization hypothesis implies venture capitalists will have portfolios that are less diversified across companies, industries, and financing stages.

---

[5] "Other" stage financing involves mainly leveraged buyout and management buyout deals in our sample. Thus, they should not be considered as a follow-on investment to a "bridge" deal.

The survey data allow for several statistical tests of conflicting hypotheses from the diversification and networking perspectives. Most of the conflicts were resolved in favor of the specialization and information sharing theory. Evidence favoring the specialization hypothesis includes the finding that investors in seed deals are less diversified across different industries and firms. Another finding is that venture capitalists appear to specialize in certain financing stages rather than stagger their investments over different financing stages.

This paper reports fairly robust empirical evidence in favor of the perspective that venture capitalists control portfolio risk through their efforts to specialize, to build reputation capital, and to become important members of information and deal flow networks.

Additional work is needed to better understand the theory and process of venture capitalist risk control. This paper has examined risk management from the "macro," or overall portfolio perspective. Research is also needed on risk management at the "micro," or individual investment, level, although such studies are hindered by lack of access to data. It is also of interest to examine the interrelationship, if any, between risk management at the macro and micro levels. Also, why aren't venture capitalist "supermarkets" more prevalent? Venture capitalist supermarkets can allow the best of both worlds—an overall portfolio diversified in terms of time and industry, with experts overseeing sub-portfolios that are specialized in terms of industries and financing stage.

REFERENCES

Bygrave, W. Spring 1987. Syndicated investments by venture capital firms: a networking perspective. *Journal of Business Venturing* 2(2):139–154.

Bygrave, W. Spring 1988. The structure of the investment networks of venture capital firms. *Journal of Business Venturing* 3(2):137–157.

Campbell, T., and Kracaw, M. 1980. Information production, market signalling, and the theory of financial intermediation. *Journal of Finance* 35(4):863–882.

Chan, Y. December 1983. On the positive role of financial intermediation in allocation of venture capital in a market with imperfect information. *Journal of Finance* 38(5):1543–1568.

Driscoll, F. March 1974. Venture capital: the risk–reward business. *IEEE International Convention.*

Leland, H., and Pyle, D. May 1977. Information asymmetries, financial structure, and financial intermediation. *Journal of Finance* 32(2):371–387.

Levy, H. 1978. Equilibrium in an imperfect market: a constraint on the number of securities in a portfolio. *American Economic Review* 68:643–658.

Levy, H. 1991. Possible explanation of no-synergy merger and small firm effect by the generalized CAPM. *Review of Quantitative Finance and Accounting* 1(1):101–128.

MacMillan, I., Kulow, D., Khoylian, R. January 1989. Venture capitalists' involvement in their investments: extent and performance. *Journal of Business Venturing* 4(1):27–34.

MacMillan, I., Siegel, R., and SubbaNarasimha, P. Winter 1985. Criteria used by venture capitalists to evaluate new venture proposals. *Journal of Business Venturing* 1(1):119–128.

Malitz, I. Summer 1986. On financial contracting: the determinants of bond covenants. *Financial Management* 15(2):18–25.

Merton, R. July 1987. A simple model of capital market equilibrium with incomplete information. *Journal of Finance* 42(3):483–510.

Norton, E., and Tenenbaum, B. July 1992a. Factors affecting the structure of U.S. venture capital deals. *Journal of Small Business Management*, 30(3):20-29.

Norton, E., and Tenenbaum, B. 1992b. The effects of venture capitalists' characteristics on the structure of the venture capital deal. *Journal of Small Business Management*, forthcoming.

Pfeffer J., and Salancik, G. 1978. *The External Control of Organizations.* New York: Harper and Row.

Plummer, J. 1987. *QED Report on Venture Capital Financial Analysis.* Palo Alto, CA: QED Research, Inc.

442 E. NORTON AND B. H. TENENBAUM

Ross, S. December 1976. The arbitrage theory of capital asset pricing. *Journal of Economic Theory* 13:341–360.

Ruhnka, J., and Young, J. March 1991. Some hypotheses about risk in venture capital investing. *Journal of Business Venturing* 6(2):115–133.

Sahlman, W. October 1990. The structure and governance of venture–capital organizations. *Journal of Financial Economics 27(2):473–521.*

Sharpe, W. June 1964. Capital asset prices: a theory of market equilibrium under conditions of risk. *Journal of Finance* 19(3):425–442.

Timmons, J. 1987. Venture capital: more than money. In Pratt, S. and J. Morris, eds., *Pratt's Guide to Venture Capital Sources.* 12th edition. Wellesley Hill, MA: Venture Economics.

Name Index